Texas Marital
Property Rights

Texas Marital Property Rights

Fifth Edition

J. Thomas Oldham
John H. Freeman
Professor of Law
University of Houston Law Center

Carolina Academic Press
Durham, North Carolina

Library of Congress Cataloging-in-Publication Data

Oldham, J. Thomas, 1948-
  Texas marital property rights / J. Thomas Oldham. -- 5th ed.
      p. cm.
  Includes index.
  ISBN 978-1-59460-831-5 (alk. paper)
  1. Marital property--Texas--Cases. I. Title.

KFT1297.O42 2010
346.76401'664--dc22

                    2010027688

CAROLINA ACADEMIC PRESS
700 Kent Street
Durham, North Carolina 27701
Telephone (919) 489-7486
Fax (919) 493-5668
www.cap-press.com

This book was inspired by Vern L. Oldham, Esq. (1912–1988)
and Pauline D. Oldham (1920–1996)

———————

This book is dedicated to the many law students at University of Houston, University of Colorado, Cambridge University, and George Washington University who have helped me gain whatever insight I have into this subject. I would also like to thank Jennifer Hopgood and Danielle Raffield for their "terrific" editing help.

Contents

Table of Cases

Preface for the Student

These materials constitute a general introduction to Texas marital property rights. More detailed discussions of the matters addressed in these materials can be found in the various Texas family law treatises that are available, such as the Marital Property and Homesteads material included by West as a portion of its Texas Practice series, written by Professor Leopold, and the Texas Practice Guide—Family Law, written by Gagnon, Murphy & Vanden Eykel, also published by West. In addition, there are various course materials that are prepared from time to time by the State Bar of Texas, such as the annual marriage dissolution and advanced family law courses. The University of Houston Law Center also prepares materials in connection with its continuing legal education programs relating to Texas family law. Professor McKnight normally comments upon recent developments in Texas marital property rights in the annual survey of Texas law published by the SMU Law Review. In addition, Principles of Community Property by Vaughn & de Funiak is a useful general comparative community property treatise. The author has also published a comparative treatise regarding property division at divorce entitled Divorce, Separation and the Distribution of Property.

Marital property rights disputes frequently arise in connection with a divorce. Pleadings commonly used in such cases can be found in the Texas Family Law Practice Manual, published by the State Bar of Texas. Professor David Crump's Biography of a Family Case: Smith v. Smith (1977) is a good illustration of how marital property rights issues arise in a divorce case.

Please note that the Texas Family Code recently has been reorganized; references to Texas Family Code sections in cases frequently will be to the old section numbers. Your Texas Family Code should have a cross-reference table to show you what the current section number is that correlates to the old number.

Texas Constitution
Article XVI, Section 15

All property, both real and personal, of a spouse owned or claimed before marriage, and that acquired afterward by gift, devise or descent, shall be the separate property of that spouse; and laws shall be passed more clearly defining the rights of the spouses in relation to separate and community property; provided that persons about to marry and spouses, without the intention to defraud pre-existing creditors, may by written instrument from time to time partition between themselves all or part of their property, then existing or to be acquired, or exchange between themselves the community interest of one spouse or future spouse in any property for the community interest of the other spouse or future spouse in other community property then existing or to be acquired, whereupon the portion or interest set aside to each spouse shall be and constitute a part of the separate property and estate of such spouse or future spouse; spouses also may from time to time, by written instrument, agree between themselves that the income or property from all or part of the separate property then owned or which thereafter might be acquired by only one of them, shall be separate property of that spouse; if one spouse makes a gift of property to the other that gift is presumed to include all the income or property which might arise from that gift of property; spouses may agree in writing that all or part of their community property becomes the property of the surviving spouse on the death of a spouse; and spouses may agree in writing that all or part of the separate property owned by either or both of them shall be the spouses' community property.

Texas Marital Property Rights

Chapter One

An Overview of the Community Property System

A. Marriage as a Partnership

When a couple "marries" in Texas, this significantly changes certain property rights of the parties. For example, the student will discover later in this course that each spouse has a fifty per cent interest in all wages earned by the other spouse during the marriage. This interest vests immediately when the wages are received by the employee spouse. The rationales for these spousal property rights will be explored below.

It is frequently stated that spouses have shared property rights because marriage is a "partnership." What is meant by this term? Is a spouse different from a good friend, a roommate, a child, or a parent? To some, a justification for the shared property rights of spouses can be found in certain differences between the relationship between spouses and the relationship between friends or between other family members.

In many marriages, a couple conceives and raises one or more children. This can dramatically affect the economic situation of the spouses. It is common for one spouse, frequently the female, to assume primary responsibility for satisfying childcare responsibilities. These childcare responsibilities normally force the spouse who assumes the responsibilities to stop working outside the home for a certain period, or at least to work part-time rather than full-time. The other spouse, normally the male, continues to work full-time. In this situation, many have concluded that it would be unfair to allow the spouse who works outside the home to retain sole ownership of all salary earned while the other is fulfilling childcare responsibilities for the family. See Prager, *Sharing Principles and the Future of Marital Property Law*, 25 UCLA L. Rev. 1 (1977). The Texas response generally has been to give the homemaker an interest in the wages earned during marriage by the spouse working outside the home.

Dean Prager has also argued that the "marital partnership" property system encourages spouses to remain married. She contends that this system induces spouses to accommodate and compromise, while the separate property model would "reinforce self-interested choices which can be detrimental to the marriage."

As you might expect, the marital partnership model has not received universal acclaim. One scholar has asked:

> Shall we adopt the rather characteristic tendency of our country and of our time, to think dominantly in terms of money, of wealth, of things and [announce] that justice as between husband and wife consists in the having of equal shares in all "things" acquired during marriage.... Or shall we accept an approach simultaneously less mercenary and more individualistic, and regard marriage as

a sharing of experiences, not primarily concerned with wealth.... The vaunted protection of married women is an intellectual hang-over from the time when woman was a salable chattel and ill consorts with ... modernity and wisdom.

Powell, *Community Property—A Critique of Its Regulation of Intra-Family Relations*, 11 Wash. L. Rev. 12, 15–16, 38 (1936).

Other writers have questioned whether the marital partnership system should be applied to all marriages, including marriages involving spouses who do not have a child. See Oldham, *Is the Concept of Marital Property Outdated?*, 22 J. Fam. L. 263 (1983–84).

All American states have now adopted some variant of the marital partnership system. A compelling reason for the adoption of this system has been the recent increase in the divorce rate, and the great hardship suffered by some divorced women. See Weitzman, *The Economic Consequences of Divorce: Social and Economic Consequences of Property, Alimony and Child Support Awards*, 28 UCLA L. Rev. 1181 (1981). See also, Glendon, *The Transformation of Family Law* (1989).

The marital partnership system has also been justified on the grounds that it fulfills the expectations of the parties. If this is the primary justification for the marital partnership system, the spouses should be free to change their respective property rights by agreement. We shall see in a later chapter that courts have imposed significant limits upon the freedom of parties to contractually modify the community property system. This suggests that significant policy considerations underlie the community property system. Is this true? What policy concerns are involved? Even if there are policy concerns, are they strong enough to limit the ability of spouses to make a different property arrangement? This topic will be considered in detail in a later chapter.

The marital partnership system does not give a spouse an interest in all property of the other spouse. Spouses only share rights in property accumulated during marriage as a result of the efforts of either. Property accumulated during marriage by gift or inheritance, or property accumulated before marriage or after divorce, is not part of the community estate. This "separate" property is excluded from the marital estate because the other spouse cannot be said to have contributed in any way to its accumulation. Since spouses have shared property rights in "community" property, but do not have any rights in the "separate" property of the other, the determination whether property is "separate" or "community" can be quite important in Texas.

Do the cases set forth below correctly apply marital partnership theory?

Zaruba v. Zaruba

Texas Court of Civil Appeals—Corpus Christi, 1973
498 S.W.2d 695, writ dism'd

NYE, Chief Justice.

This is an appeal from a decree of divorce and a judgment dividing the properties of the husband and wife. The trial was to the court without a jury. The husband's appeal complains primarily of the division of the properties and the award of attorneys' fees.

The record shows that the husband and wife were married and separated on the same day and did not live together thereafter. The wife was in her mid-twenties and the husband was about 50 years old at the time of the marriage. Although the court granted the husband the divorce on the grounds of living apart for more than three years, the court found that the wife was not at fault and was not responsible for the separation of the parties.

The husband owned two Chevrolet dealerships and other separate properties at the time of the marriage. The community estate of the parties increased considerably during the nearly 20 years of marriage. In dividing the properties of the parties, the trial court found that it had considered all of the facts and circumstances of the case, including the separate and community character of each asset, and concluded that the division of the property in the judgment was just, right, fair and equitable, having due regard for the rights of each party.

The trial court filed extensive findings of fact and conclusions of law. The findings are all inclusive. They are drawn in chronological order and in very readable form. Generally, we do not include such findings in the opinion, but because they relate to all of the ultimate and controlling issues in the case, we have included them as an appendix to this opinion.

The appellant's third and fourth points of error are to the effect that the court's division of the community and separate property was unjust, unfair, and amounted to an abuse of discretion, and that the judgment entered concerning such property is erroneous because it is against the weight and preponderance of the evidence, or the evidence is insufficient as a matter of law to support the judgment. Under these points of error the appellant complains that the trial court has awarded the wife a disproportionate share of the property of the parties. Various inventories filed show that the community and separate estate was worth up to almost $1,000,000.00. The wife's share awarded by the court at the time of the divorce amounted to approximately $268,790.98. All of the other property, both separate and community, was awarded to the husband, subject to the payment of the property herein awarded to the wife. The husband contends that the trial court erroneously treated as a part of the community estate some or all of his separate property, with the result that the wife has received a disproportionate share of the community and/or separate property of the husband. The trial court found and concluded that:

After considering the facts and circumstances of this case, including the community or separate character of each asset, the cause of the parties' separation, the disparity in earning powers and business opportunities, capacities and abilities, and the relative conditions of the parties, and the size of their separate and community estates, I conclude that the division of the estate, assets and debts of the parties as set forth in the Judgment is just, right, fair and equitable, having due regard for the rights of each party.

The facts and equities of this case support an unequal division of the community estate in favor of Mildred Novak Zaruba.

After reviewing the evidence we hold that the trial court's findings of fact covering the division of the property are supported by sufficient evidence. The findings of the trial court are not against the overwhelming weight and preponderance of the evidence as to be clearly wrong, manifestly unjust, or shocking to the conscience of the court.

APPENDIX

FINDINGS OF FACT

I find as a fact the following:

1. Anthony Zaruba and Mildred Novak Zaruba were married to each other on November 18, 1950.

2. Anthony Zaruba and Mildred Novak Zaruba lived apart without cohabitation for more than three (3) years prior to the filing of this cause of action for divorce.

3. One child was born of the marriage, Paul Anthony Zaruba, who is now over the age of eighteen years, and no other child was born to or adopted by the parties during the marriage.

4. Shortly after the parties were married and prior to the birth of their son, Anthony Zaruba separated himself from Mildred Novak Zaruba.

5. After the birth of Paul Anthony Zaruba, Anthony Zaruba refused to live as husband and father with Mildred Novak Zaruba and Paul Anthony Zaruba, and he has remained separated from them.

6. Mildred Novak Zaruba was not at fault and was not responsible for the continued separation of the parties.

7. Mildred Novak Zaruba reared and maintained a home for Paul Anthony Zaruba, the child of the parties.

8. Although Anthony Zaruba had substantial income and net worth throughout this marriage, he contributed only a small amount per month to support his wife and son before the child reached eighteen years of age.

9. Anthony Zaruba is a competent, astute and experienced businessman well trained in the operation of automobile dealerships and in making investments in securities and real estate, and he is able to generate substantial income from the sources available to him.

10. Mildred Novak Zaruba has no experience or training in any profession or trade and is unable to generate substantial income.

11. The earning powers and business opportunities of Anthony Zaruba are greatly in excess of the earning powers and business opportunities of Mildred Novak Zaruba.

12. The great majority of the inventory acquired after marriage in the two Chevrolet dealerships was purchased with community credit.

13. Substantial items of the separate and community property of the parties have been commingled so as to defy resegregation and identification.

14. Community and separate funds were so mixed and commingled in all bank accounts of the parties as to defy resegregation and identification.

15. Anthony Zaruba did not regularly withdraw the profits arising from the operation of the Chevrolet dealerships, but allowed them to remain in the businesses and they were indiscriminately mixed and commingled with the original separate capital in the businesses.

CONCLUSIONS OF LAW

I conclude as a matter of law as follows:

1. A substantial community estate was accumulated during the marriage of the parties.

2. Substantial items of separate and community property of the parties have been so commingled as to defy resegregation and identification.

3. After considering the facts and circumstances of this case, including the community or separate character of each asset, the cause of the parties' separation, the disparity in earning powers and business opportunities, capacities and abilities, and the relative conditions of the parties, and the size of their separate and

community estates, I conclude that the division of the estate, assets and debts of the parties as set forth in the Judgment is just, right, fair and equitable, having due regard for the rights of each party.

4. The facts and equities of this case support an unequal division of the community estate in favor of Mildred Novak Zaruba.

DISCUSSION

A more recent case similar to *Zaruba* is *Wilson v. Wilson*, 44 S.W.3d 597 (Tex. App.— Fort Worth 2001, no pet).

Later in this chapter it will be mentioned that other community property states have concluded that spouses should stop accumulating community property before the date the divorce decree is entered. Is this a good idea? If so, when should spouses stop accumulating community property?

Shea v. Shea
California Court of Appeals, 1980
169 Cal. Rptr. 490

BROWN, Presiding Justice.

Thomas M. Shea appeals an interlocutory judgment dissolving his marriage to Sandra E. Shea. The appeal concerns only the trial court's finding Thomas' veteran's education benefits received during marriage were community property, and the court's method of computing the community interest in the parties' residence.

Thomas served in the United States Navy from January 1969 to January 1973. In May 1973 he began receiving veteran's education benefits (38 U.S.C. Sec. 1651 *et seq.*) which continued with a few interruptions during the summer months when he was not in school, until December 1978. In June 1974, he bought a house, taking title in his own name. He made a down payment of $3,000, paid almost $1,500 in "points" and closing costs, and obtained a loan for the balance of the purchase price. He then began making monthly payments on the loan. Each installment included interest, taxes and insurance, as well as reduction of the loan principal. Sandra and Thomas were married November 27, 1974, and separated May 17, 1979.

At trial Thomas contended the veteran's benefits were his separate property and he sought to introduce evidence showing he had used these funds for most of the house payments made during the marriage. The trial court found the benefits received during marriage were community property and calculated the community interest in the house accordingly. The court did not permit Thomas to offer evidence showing the source of money used for house payments during the marriage. In computing the community interest in the house, the court used the full amount of the monthly payments made during the marriage, instead of the amount by which these payments reduced the principal.

I. *The Veteran's Education Benefits*

Where one spouse has served in the armed forces before marriage, are veteran's education benefits received during marriage community property?

Congress has enacted a comprehensive program of veteran's education benefits to make service in the armed forces more attractive to prospective recruits and to make educational opportunities available to veterans who otherwise would not be able to afford them, or whose educations have been interrupted by military service (38 U.S.C. Sec. 1651). To receive the benefits, a veteran must meet eligibility requirements, including a minimum of 180 days of service (Sec. 1652); a veteran must have served at least 18 months on active duty to be eligible to receive benefits for the maximum period of 45 months (Sec. 1661(a)). A veteran must apply for the benefits, but the Veterans Administration "shall" approve the application unless the veteran or his planned course of study is ineligible (Sec. 1671). Benefits are payable only while the veteran is enrolled and making satisfactory progress in an approved educational program (Sec. 1674, 1683, 1772). The benefits are "an educational subsistence allowance to meet, in part, the expenses of the veteran's subsistence, tuition, fees, supplies, books, equipment, and other education costs" (Sec. 1681), but the statute does not expressly limit the purposes for which the veteran may use the funds. A veteran with dependents receives an increased allowance, based on the number of dependents (Sec. 1682).

The veteran's educational allowances provided by this statutory scheme are a form of employee benefits, similar in nature to the wide variety of fringe benefits — for example, employer-paid life insurance, tuition reimbursement programs, and pensions — furnished by public and private employers. Like other types of employee benefits, the veteran's education allowance is designed to attract prospective employees, and entitlement to these benefits can be attained only by service with the employer. Consequently, the general principles governing characterization of fringe benefits flowing from the employment relationship determine whether veteran's education benefits are community property.

Under the community property system, each spouse's time, skill, and labor are community assets, and whatever each spouse earns from them during marriage is community property. Fringe benefits are not a gift from the employer but are earned by the employee as part of the compensation for his services. Accordingly, fringe benefits are community property to the extent they are earned by employment during marriage. Conversely, where a fringe benefit is earned by employment before marriage, it is the separate property of the employee even if received after marriage.

Here Thomas' military service occurred entirely before marriage, and his veteran's education benefits are his separate property unless the parties expressly or impliedly agreed these funds would be community property. Since the record contains no evidence of such an agreement, the trial court's finding the benefits community property is not supported by the evidence.

The judgment is reversed.

———————

DISCUSSION

As *Shea* suggests, the time of payment is not critical when characterizing property. The crucial fact is when the right was acquired and how. So, for example, we will learn that pension payments can be partially community property even though not paid until many years after divorce. Similarly, if a winning lottery ticket is bought during marriage with community funds, and the benefits are paid annually after divorce, these payments would be community property. See *Mayes v. Stewart*, 11 S.W.3d 440 (Tex. App. — Houston [14th Dist.] 2000, pet. denied).

B. Alimony

A Texas court can award temporary alimony to a spouse while the divorce action is pending, but post-divorce alimony may only be awarded in limited circumstances. This approach arguably is consistent with the marital partnership concept. If the marriage ends in divorce, each spouse shares the fruits of the marriage. If the partnership was financially successful, there normally will be significant assets to share; if the partnership was not successful, there will be little property remaining at divorce.

Can the Texas view be criticized? All forty-nine other states give courts substantially greater discretion to award post-divorce alimony. What is the justification for this majority view? A number of empirical studies a few decades ago found that many spouses have little property at divorce. See Weitzman, *The Economic Consequences of Divorce: Social and Economic Consequences of Property, Alimony and Child Support Awards*, 28 UCLA L. Rev. 1181 (1981). If this is true, the parties will have to rely upon their respective post-divorce earning capacities at divorce for their post-divorce support. However, if the woman has devoted her energies to homemaking and child care, her earning capacity at divorce frequently is not great. So, many argue that the Texas system discriminates against women, since there can be a significant disparity between the earning capacities of the spouses at divorce, and the Texas system makes no attempt to adjust for this. Studies to date have shown that, even with post-divorce alimony, divorced women do suffer significant hardship after divorce. See Weitzman, *supra*.

C. Dissolution of the Partnership

A marriage can be dissolved by death or divorce. At death, the decedent can devise one-half of the community estate, and the survivor retains the other one-half; each spouse retains all rights to his or her separate estate. At divorce, the court can divide the community estate equitably; each spouse retains his or her separate estate.

Spouses normally continue to accumulate community property until the marriage dissolves. If a marriage is dissolved by death, all wages earned before the date of death by either spouse are community property. No argument could seriously be made that any other date should be adopted for the dissolution date.

If the marriage is dissolved by divorce, the answer is less clear. Parties frequently separate for a significant time before the divorce becomes final. It therefore could be said that the partnership ceases before the date of divorce. If community property exists only because of the marital partnership, community property rights should no longer be created after the marital partnership has ended. If this argument is accepted, what date should be used for the "de facto" dissolution date? Some states look to the date of final separation; others look to the date a separation agreement was signed or the divorce action was filed. See Cal. Fam. Code § 771; Wash. Rev. Code § 26.16.140 (both choosing the date of final separation).

Texas has adopted no specific statute regarding when the marital partnership ends. *Zaruba, supra,* reflects the Texas rule that spouses continue to accumulate community property until they divorce, regardless of the length of separation. What should happen if the parties marry in Texas, permanently separate, and the wife stays in Texas and the husband goes to Washington? Are the wages after separation community property? See *Seizer v. Sessons*, 940 P.2d 261 (Wash. 1997). (These things happen. Honest. I didn't make this up.)

Chapter Two

Common-law Marriage and Putative Marriage

A. Ceremonial Marriage

Most persons in Texas marry ceremonially. The general standards governing ceremonial marriage in Texas are set forth in Chapter 2 of the Family Code. A ceremonial marriage basically is one whereby two adults, after they obtain a marriage license, participate in a marriage ceremony conducted by a person authorized by the statute to conduct such a ceremony.

B. Common-law Marriage

Claveria v. Claveria
Supreme Court of Texas, 1981
615 S.W.2d 164

POPE, Justice.

The question presented is whether there is some evidence, more than a scintilla, of a common-law marriage. This case arose as a probate matter in which Patricio Claveria contested the will of Otha Faye McQuaid Claveria. The probate court dismissed the contest after sustaining a plea to abate which stated that Patricio was not an interested person as defined by the Probate Code. The trial court concluded that Patricio had no interest in the estate property because his ceremonial marriage to Otha Faye was void by reason of a prior undissolved common-law marriage. The court of civil appeals reversed the judgment, holding that there was no evidence of the prior common-law marriage. We hold that there was evidence of the marriage and remand the cause to the court of civil appeals to determine the factual insufficiency points.

Otha Faye died testate on March 4, 1978, leaving all of her property to her two children by a former marriage. Patricio and Otha Faye were ceremonially married in November, 1974, and he claims a community and homestead interest in the property acquired since that time. His only claim in the trial court and on appeal is that he is an interested party by reason of his marriage to Otha Faye. He has not asserted that he has an interest as a putative spouse nor because of any other right of ownership in the property. The inference should not be drawn from this opinion, that a marriage is always essential to proof of an interest in an estate. The points that were presented in the court of civil appeals relate only to the validity of the marriage between Patricio and Otha Faye.

After Patricio's and Otha Faye's ceremonial marriage, they lived together as husband and wife until Otha Faye died on March 4, 1978. We must begin, therefore, with the presumption that their marriage was valid. The presumption that the most recent marriage is a valid one continues until one proves the impediment of a prior marriage and its continuing validity.

After some evidence of a prior and continuing marriage has been introduced, the weight of such evidence must be determined by the finder of fact.

A valid common-law marriage consists of three elements: (1) an agreement presently to be husband and wife; (2) living together as husband and wife; and (3) holding each other out to the public as such.

When two persons not living together occasionally refer to each other as a spouse, these isolated references have been held, in some instances as a matter of law, not to have established a common-law marriage. Further, the act of one of the parties to an alleged common-law marriage in celebrating a ceremonial marriage with another person without having first obtained a divorce, tends to discredit the first relationship and to show that it was not valid. Still, the circumstances of each case must be determined based upon its own facts.

The record discloses several items of direct evidence which establish the fact of a prior undissolved common-law marriage between Patricio Claveria and Carolina Mendoza Claveria. Both Patricio and Carolina testified at the trial; and while they both denied they had ever been married, they both also produced evidence of their common-law marriage. Some of their denials appear from the record to express the belief that the questions concerned a ceremonial marriage. In any event, there was evidence about the elements of a common-law marriage.

Patricio and Carolina both testified that they had lived together in 1967 in San Antonio for some two and a half months. A deposition that Patricio gave in a worker's compensation case in 1972, two years before his ceremonial marriage to Otha Faye, is also in the record. In that earlier court proceeding, he testified that he was married, and that his wife's name was Carolina. He testified that his wife was not employed, that she was a housewife. When asked if she had been a housewife for several years, he answered, "about 16 years married." The evidence was not retracted nor otherwise explained.

Patricio and Carolina lived together in a house and lot in San Antonio that they purchased through the Veterans Administration. The grantees in the deed were Patricio Claveria and wife, Carolina Claveria. They executed a deed of trust to secure the payment of the purchase price in the amount of five thousand three hundred and fifty dollars, and they did so as husband and wife. The acknowledgment to the deed of trust was taken as husband and wife and there was a recital, in the quaint custom of the times, that Carolina was examined "privily and apart from her husband" when the document was explained to her. Carolina admitted that she had signed the document and had done so as a wife. This is direct evidence of the common-law marriage.

Carolina testified that she had lived all her life in San Antonio. Patricio testified that he had lived only in San Antonio and Dallas. Certificates from the district clerks of Bexar and Dallas Counties show that there has been no divorce or annulment decree from either of those counties which involved Patricio or Carolina.

We have in this case direct evidence by Patricio that he and Carolina were husband and wife and that they lived together as such. We have the recorded deed in which both Patricio and Carolina represented to the Veterans Administration that they were married.

We have the notarial acknowledgment by both of them that they were husband and wife. We have Patricio's and Carolina's solemn acknowledgment which was filed in the public records. There is, therefore, some evidence that the two lived together and held themselves out to the public as husband and wife. From the nature of that proof, their agreement to be married may also be inferred.

The law recognizes a common-law marriage, but a common-law divorce is unknown to Texas law. The marriage arises out of the state of facts; but once the common-law status exists, it, like any other marriage, may be terminated only by death or a court decree. Once the marriage exists, the spouses' subsequent denials of the marriage, if disbelieved, do not undo the marriage.

Patricio also urges that the common-law marriage between him and Carolina was impossible, because Carolina was already married in 1967 when the common-law marriage arose, having ceremonially married Luis Ochoa in 1945, some twenty-two years earlier. Carolina so testified, but the trial court, in this instance, determined that there was no existing impediment at the time of Carolina's and Patricio's common-law marriage. An alleged spouse's testimony is not conclusive. The trial court could also rely upon the unrebutted presumption of the validity of the 1967 common-law marriage of Patricio and Carolina. Carolina testified in this case that she and Luis Ochoa lived together two months, separated, and that she had not seen him since 1945. The long absence of Luis Ochoa for twenty-two years before the 1967 common-law marriage, without any proof that he was still alive at that time, gave rise to the presumption of his death.

The court of civil appeals was in error in its holding that there was no evidence of an undissolved common-law marriage between Patricio and Carolina and in rendering judgment that no such marriage arose. We reverse the judgment of the court of civil appeals and remand the cause to that court to pass upon the factual insufficiency and the great weight of the evidence points that were presented to that court but not decided.

DISCUSSION

In 1989, the Texas legislature amended Tex. Fam. Code § 1.91(b). The prior version of 1.91 permitted a court to presume that parties had agreed to be married if they lived together as husband and wife and held themselves out to the community as husband and wife. The new version provided: "A proceeding in which a marriage is to be proved under this section must be commenced not later than one year after the date on which the relationship ended...." The effect of this provision was unclear to this writer. The Texas Supreme Court apparently concluded it was a statute of limitation that applied to parties for all purposes. In effect, it provided for a common-law divorce if an action was not filed within one year. In *White v. State Farm Mut. Auto Ins. Co.*, 907 F. Supp. 1012 (E.D. Tex. 1995) the court held that the statute was unconstitutional. In 1995, the legislature again changed Section 1.91(b). The amendment deleted the one-year statute of limitations and added a new Section 1.91(b). The enacting legislation provides that the current version does not permit any person barred by the former statute to initiate a divorce action based on a common-law marriage. Under the current version of 1.91(b) (2.401 (b)), it once again appears clear that there is no such thing as a Texas common-law divorce. If an action is filed more than two years after the parties separated, the proponent of the marriage must rebut the statutory presumption that the parties did not agree to marry. See *Joplin v. Borusheski*, 244 S.W.3d 607 (Tex. App.—Dallas 2008, no pet.).

Remember that Tex. Fam. Code § 2.401 (a) (2) requires parties to live together **in Texas** and to hold themselves out as husband and wife **in Texas**. So, evidence of such behavior in other states cannot establish a Texas common-law marriage. See *Winfield v. Renfro*, 821 S.W.2d 640 (Tex. App.—Houston [1st Dist.] 1991, writ denied). The *Winfield* case also held that extremely minimal holding out in Texas (i.e., residing in a hotel for a few nights registered as husband and wife) is not sufficient to establish a common-law marriage. In *Smith v. Deneve*, 285 S.W.3d 904 (Tex. App.—Dallas 2009, no pet.) the court similarly held that if a couple introduced themselves on four occasions that they were married, this was not sufficient to create a marriage. Is this sensible?

Generally **both** parties must hold themselves out to the community as a married couple. If only one person does this, it's not sufficient. See *Lee v. Lee*, 981 S.W.2d 903 (Tex. App.—Houston [1st Dist.] 1998, no pet.).

As *Claveria* shows, declarations of marital status in official documents, such as a real estate purchase, can be significant. In *Eris v. Phares*, 39 S.W.3d 708 (Tex. App.—Houston [1st Dist.] 2001, pet. denied), the appellate court found it important that the woman had purchased realty from the man, and the deed stated she was a "single person."

Tex. Fam. Code § 1.91 once provided that a court could assume that the parties had agreed to be married if it was established that the parties lived together and held themselves out as husband and wife. In 1989 this provision was deleted. When this provision was deleted, this raised the question of whether the new Section 1.91 required proof of an agreement to be married and how such an agreement would be proved. In *Russell v. Russell*, 865 S.W.2d 929 (Tex. 1993) the Texas Supreme Court concluded that such an agreement could be established via circumstantial evidence.

Consolidated Underwriters v. Kelly

Commission of Appeals of Texas, Section B, 1929
15 S.W.2d 229

SPEER, Justice.

Louisa Kelly seeks to recover compensation under our Workmen's Compensation Law as the surviving wife of Joe Kelly, the employee, who died from an injury received in the course of his employment. The whole case turns upon the question of whether or not Louisa was the surviving wife of the deceased. Her claim was based upon an alleged common-law marriage to Joe Kelly, and the validity of the claim depends upon the effect of the existence of a prior marriage of Louisa as an impediment to the consummation of the asserted common-law marriage between her and Joe. The trial court instructed a verdict setting aside the award of the Industrial Accident Board and denying the plaintiff's petition for compensation, on the theory that the undisputed evidence showed that she was not the wife of Joe Kelly at the time of his death. The Court of Civil Appeals first reversed and rendered the judgment in favor of the common-law wife, but afterward on rehearing remanded the cause to the trial court with instructions. 300 S.W. 981.

The Court of Civil Appeals found as follows:

> In 1920, Joe Kelly had some trouble with appellant's sister, while he was living at Amelia, La. Thereupon he deserted appellant and left Louisiana, and appellant did not hear from him until 1925. At the time Joe Kelly deserted appellant, they were not husband and wife, and as neither of them had previously married, they were single persons in the eyes of the law. A few months after Joe Kelly

deserted appellant, she heard that he was dead, and in March, 1920, contracted a ceremonial marriage with one George Brown, under authority of a marriage license duly issued and duly executed, thereby becoming his lawful wife. Recognizing the validity of this marriage, she lived with George Brown at her home in Amelia, La., until 1925, when, learning that Joe Kelly was living in Beaumont, Tex., she deserted her husband and joined Joe Kelly at Beaumont in October, 1925, and lived with him continuously from that date as his wife until his death on the 19th of January, 1926. They resumed their relations with the intention of living together as husband and wife until their death. Joe Kelly introduced her to his Beaumont friends as his wife, and she acknowledged him openly as her husband. They lived and cohabited as husband and wife, and received their friends in their home as such, and their friends recognized them as husband and wife. The relations between Joe and appellant were such that, except for the fact that Louisa had a living husband, the law would have declared their status to be that of a common-law marriage. There is no evidence against that conclusion. But for the fact that George Brown, Louisa's husband, was living when she rejoined Joe Kelly in Beaumont, the conditions under which they resumed their relations would have made them husband and wife. George Brown died about Thanksgiving, 1925; but neither appellant nor Joe Kelly knew of that fact, and appellant had no knowledge of it until after Joe's death. The death of George Brown made no change in their relations. They made no new contract in relation thereto, but from October, 1925, when they reunited their lives in the city of Beaumont, Tex., there was no change in their relations until Joe's death in January, 1926.

These findings are amply supported by the evidence and are in keeping with the implied findings of the trial court, and are therefore binding upon us. The Court of Civil Appeals held that these facts as matter of law constituted Louisa the wife of Joe on January 19, 1926, the day he received the fatal injury, saying:

> Because of the sanctity of the marriage relation, a sound public policy impels the law to infer consent to have been given at the first moment when the parties were able to enter into the contract.... As they desired marriage, and intended their relations to be that of husband and wife, this continuing intent must be recognized during all the time they cohabited as such, and therefore the agreement upon which they renewed their relations made them husband and wife from the moment the bar to their lawful marriage was removed.

We approve the conclusion of the Court of Civil Appeals that Joe and Louisa were husband and wife at the date of the former's death. We do not approve the statement that "a sound public policy impels the law to infer consent" under the circumstances found, but we do agree that the facts as found authorized an inference of fact as to matrimonial intent at a time when no legal impediment existed. It is undoubtedly true that the agreement for marriage, whatever be the evidences of an attempt to execute it, so long as the legal impediment existed, was of no effect. The consummation of the marriage, however, cannot be denied for the want of agreement, but must be denied because of the legal impediment which prevented its consummation. The same matrimonial agreement, however, made at a time when no legal impediment existed to have this dissolving effect, would, upon every consideration, be lawful. It frequently happens, especially in common-law marriages, that the marriage which, of course, includes the agreement to marry, is proved by circumstances, technically known as cohabitation. Proof that a couple lived together under the same name, introducing each other as husband and wife, respectively, recognizing their children, and the many other respects tending to show their marital status, is sufficient to prove a marriage. It is not necessary in addition to offer evidence of the statutory celebration, or of the actual agreement of the parties to be husband and wife. These essential facts are embraced in the marriage which is thus proved by circumstances. So here the facts showing that, after Brown's death, the parties continued their relations deporting themselves as husband and wife and considering themselves such, are sufficient to prove as a matter of fact that they intended their relations to be marital, and since there then existed no legal impediment, their agreement and relations were valid and lawful. Their continued living together as husband and wife after the removal of the impediment bespeaks a continued intention and agreement, day by day, to be husband and wife, and this being true, the Court of Civil Appeals was right in reversing the judgment of the trial court.

We therefore recommend that the judgment of the Court of Appeals be affirmed.

———————

DISCUSSION

It is possible in Texas to marry ceremonially or by common law. In either case, both spouses must have the capacity to marry. For example, each spouse must be sane, of sufficient age, and not under the influence of drugs or alcohol at the time of the marriage. In addition, neither spouse may be married to another. If one spouse is married to another at the time of a purported marriage, the marriage is void.

Review Tex. Fam. Code § 2.401. What is "living together … as husband and wife"? See *Allen v. Allen*, 966 S.W. 2d 658, 661 (Tex. App.—San Antonio 1998, pet. denied) ("we do not believe 'cohabitation' would encompass … situations involving a frequent overnight guest or someone who stores personal property at someone else's home."). What period of cohabitation is required to establish a common-law marriage?

Ballesteros v. Jones, 985 S.W.2d 485 (Tex. App.—San Antonio 1998, pet. denied) involved a dispute relating to an allegation that a common law marriage existed. The couple each had a separate residence; for many years, the man spent three or four nights a week at the woman's house and kept clothes there. They never filed joint tax returns but introduced themselves socially as a married couple. Should this be considered a common law marriage?

Why is common-law marriage still accepted in Texas? In the past, one explanation was that it was difficult for citizens to travel to the government office and obtain the appropriate license, and that few ministers were available. Is this still true? If not, is there any other justification for common-law marriage? See Caudill, *Legal Recognition of Unmarried Cohabitation: A Proposal to Update and Reconsider Common-Law Marriage*, 49 Tenn. L. Rev. 537 (1982).

In *Claveria*, would it have made any difference if Carolina had died before Otha?

C. The Putative Spouse

What happens if a person marries another without knowing that the other person is already married? We have already discovered that the marriage is void. Where does this leave the person who married in good faith?

Lazzarevich v. Lazzarevich
California Court of Appeals, 1948
200 P.2d 49

VALLEE, Justice.

The Settled Statement reveals the following facts: The parties were married in Los Angeles on March 18, 1921. One child, a daughter, was born, the issue of this marriage. Subsequently defendant (as plaintiff) filed an action for divorce in Los Angeles County. An interlocutory decree was granted the husband and entered on March 18, 1932. On September 6, 1933, without the husband's knowledge or request, his attorney had a final decree of divorce entered. Subsequent to the entry of the interlocutory decree and several months prior to the entering of the final decree, and thereafter, defendant continually sought a reconciliation with his wife. They became reconciled in July of 1935. Both parties testified that before the reconciliation occurred defendant informed plaintiff that no final decree had been entered. Defendant testified that he so believed and so informed plaintiff. The parties then took a trip to Reno, Nevada, the Pacific Northwest, and on their return stopped at Merced, California. While there, defendant made inquiry of the county clerk concerning the remarriage of the parties. He was informed that since no final decree had been entered in the divorce action no remarriage was necessary. This information defendant imparted to plaintiff. Thereafter, on April 23, 1936, a son was born to the parties. As an aftermath of domestic difficulties which arose between them, plaintiff, on August 1, 1945, consulted her attorneys about a divorce. On August 10, 1945, she was informed by them that the court records disclosed the entry of a final decree of divorce on September 6, 1933. Plaintiff testified that she would not have lived with defendant if she had not believed that she was his wife. The parties remained separated from August 1, 1945, until October 1, 1945, when the plaintiff, upon the promise of defendant that he would remarry her if she would return to him, again became reconciled. They again separated on April 1, 1946.

The rights and remedies afforded a woman who cohabits with a man, believing in good faith that they are validly married, may be epitomized generally as follows:

(1) In some jurisdictions she has an action in damages for deceit against her putative husband in those cases where by fraud or misrepresentation he has induced her to enter into the supposed marriage relation.

(2) In those jurisdictions in which the community property doctrine prevails, it is generally recognized that a de facto spouse is entitled to the rights accorded a lawful spouse in the property acquired during the de facto marriage.

(3) In some jurisdictions, including California, the deluded woman is permitted to recover the reasonable value of her services over and above the value of the support and maintenance furnished her by her supposed husband.

In *Sanguinetti v. Sanguinetti*, 9 Cal. 2d 95, the court said:

> Where an invalid marriage has been procured by fraud of the de facto husband, who is aware of the invalidity of the marriage, the right of the wife who has acted in good faith to recover the reasonable value of her services over and above the value of the support and maintenance furnished her by her supposed husband, has been sustained in a number of jurisdictions, including this state.

There is no valid distinction between the case at bar and cases dealing with a situation where the parties engaged in a marriage ceremony. In the latter class of cases, the putative wife believes in the existence of a valid marriage in good faith, believes that she is a lawful wife, her services are rendered solely because of that belief, and upon those grounds recovery is permitted. In the case at bar plaintiff had been the lawful wife of defendant. She, in good faith, believed that a second marriage ceremony was unnecessary because the original marriage had never been dissolved, that she was still his lawful wife, and the services were rendered solely because of that belief. In each case the putative husband has been unjustly enriched by the amount by which the reasonable value of the services rendered to him by his de facto wife exceed the amount devoted by him to her support and maintenance.

The evidence supports the finding that plaintiff rendered services to defendant over and above the support and maintenance furnished her by her supposed husband and the conclusion that she was entitled to compensation therefor.

There is no evidence which would have warranted the trial court in finding that the services rendered by plaintiff prior to August 10, 1945, were voluntarily rendered without any agreement or understanding that she would be compensated therefor, or that she had been fully compensated therefor, or that she has received one-half of all the property acquired by the parties after their reconciliation in July, 1935. The trial court did not err in rendering judgment in favor of plaintiff for services rendered and for contributions advanced by her prior to August 10, 1945.

A different result must obtain as to services performed by plaintiff after August 10, 1945. As we have noted, the parties separated on August 1, 1945. On August 10, 1945, plaintiff discovered that the final decree of divorce had been entered on September 6, 1933. On October 1, 1945, she went to live with defendant and continued to do so until April 1, 1946. The essence of the right of a putative wife to recover for services rendered the putative husband is her belief in the validity of a marriage between them. After August 10, 1945, plaintiff was no longer an innocent, deluded, putative wife. She no longer believed that she was defendant's wife. She knew that she was not. The relationship between the parties was meretricious after October 1, 1945. Plaintiff was fully aware of the nature of the relationship. The fact that she returned to defendant upon his promise to remarry her is of no importance.

In the absence of an express agreement that plaintiff would be compensated for services performed after that date she has no right to compensation therefor. Here there was no express agreement that she should be compensated.

The court found that plaintiff during a period of 126 months, from July 31, 1935, until April 1, 1946, performed work and services for defendant. The court also found that the reasonable value of the services performed during the period of 126 months was $50 a month for ninety-seven months and $25 a month for twenty-nine months. Plaintiff performed the services for which she is entitled to recover for 120 months prior to August 10, 1945, the date she discovered that the final decree of divorce had been entered September 6, 1933. As we hold that plaintiff is not entitled to recover for six months after August 10, 1945, for which the court found that the reasonable value of the services was $50 a month, the number of months that she performed services of the reasonable value of $50 a month is ninety-one months. Under the findings, plaintiff is entitled to recover the sum of $10,277.50 from defendant, as follows: For services rendered, $5,275.00, being ninety-one months at $50.00 a month and twenty-nine months at $25.00 a month; for contributions, $5,002.50, being twenty-nine months at $172.50.

DISCUSSION

A person who marries in good faith is regarded as a "putative spouse," even if one of the spouses who participated in the marriage ceremony already was married to another.

Although the later attempted "marriage" is therefore void, in Texas the person unaware of the prior marriage is generally treated as a lawful spouse as long as the person in good faith believed the marriage was valid. Putative spouse status ends when the innocent spouse becomes aware of the invalidity of the marriage; as *Lazzarevich* suggests, after that time the putative spouse is treated as a cohabitant. Is this always a reasonable rule? What is expected of the innocent spouse? In an age of no-fault divorce, presumably the "guilty" spouse could be induced to divorce the prior spouse and marry the putative spouse. What if the guilty spouse will not divorce the prior spouse? Does it matter if the couple has had children?

What constitutes "good faith" for purposes of the putative spouse doctrine? Is Patricio Claveria a putative spouse? Does it matter if he believed that there was common-law divorce in Texas, or was not aware that Texas accepted common-law marriage? How about Otha Claveria? Are there any policy reasons for distinguishing between Otha and Patricio?

In theory, a putative spouse should be treated in the same manner as a lawfully married spouse. See *Dean v. Goldwire*, 480 S.W.2d 494 (Tex. Civ. App.—Waco 1972, writ ref'd n.r.e.); *Lee v. Lee*, 112 Tex. 392, 247 S.W. 828 (Tex. 1923). Also, the alimony statute applies to putative spouses. Tex. Fam. Code Sec. 8.060. Texas cases have not always given a putative spouse all the rights given spouses. See *Tex. Employers Ins. Ass'n v. Grimes*, 269 S.W.2d 332 (Tex. 1954).

One person simultaneously can have a lawful spouse and a putative spouse. What happens then?

Estate of Vargas

California Court of Appeals, 1974
36 Cal. App. 3d 714

FLEMING, Justice.

For 24 years Juan Vargas lived a double life as husband and father to two separate families, neither of which knew of the other's existence. This terrestrial paradise came to an end in 1969 when Juan died intestate in an automobile accident. In subsequent heirship proceedings the probate court divided his estate equally between the two wives. Juan's first wife Mildred appeals, contending that the evidence did not establish Juan's second wife Josephine as a putative spouse, and that even if Josephine were considered a putative spouse an equal division of the estate was erroneous.

Mildred presented evidence that she and Juan married in 1929, raised three children, and lived together continuously in Los Angeles until Juan's death in 1969. From 1945 until his death Juan never spent more than a week or 10 days away from home. They acquired no substantial assets until after 1945. Josephine countered with evidence that she met Juan in 1942 while employed in his exporting business. They married in Las Vegas in February 1945. Josephine knew Juan had been previously married, but Juan assured her he had acquired a divorce. In July 1945 they moved into a home in West Los Angeles and there raised a family of four children. After 1949 Juan no longer spent his nights at home, explaining to Josephine that he spent the nights in Long Beach in order to be close to his business, but he and Josephine continued to engage in sexual relations until his death in 1969. He visited Josephine and their children every weekday for dinner, spent time with them weekends, supported the family, and exercised control over its affairs as husband and father. Throughout the years Josephine continued to perform secretarial work for Juan's business at home without pay.

The foregoing evidence amply supports the court's finding that Josephine was a putative spouse. An innocent participant who has duly solemnized a matrimonial union which is void because of some legal infirmity acquires the status of putative spouse. Although Josephine's marriage was void because Juan was still married to Mildred, Josephine, according to her testimony, married Juan in the good-faith belief he was divorced from his first wife. Her testimony was not inherently improbable; her credibility was a question for determination by the trial court.

The more difficult question involves the equal division of Juan's estate between Mildred and Josephine. California courts have relied on at least two legal theories to justify the award of an interest in a decedent's estate to a putative spouse. The theory of "quasi-marital property" equates property rights acquired during a putative marriage with community property rights acquired during a legal marriage. Subsequent to the time of Juan's death this theory was codified in Civil Code Section 4452:

> Whenever a determination is made that a marriage is void or voidable and the court finds that either party or both parties believed in good faith that the marriage was valid, the court shall declare such party or parties to have the status of a putative spouse, and, if the division of property is in issue, shall divide, in accordance with Section 4800, that property acquired during the union which would have been community property or quasi-community property if the union had not been void or voidable. Such property shall be termed "quasi-marital property."

A second legal theory treats the putative marriage as a partnership:

> In effect, the innocent putative spouse was in partnership or a joint enterprise with her spouse, contributing her services—and in this case, her earnings—to the common enterprise. Thus, their accumulated property was held in effect in tenancy-in-common in equal shares. Upon death of the husband, only his half interest is considered as community property, to which the rights of the lawful spouse attach.

Sousa v. Freitas, 10 Cal. App. 3d 660.

In practice, these sometimes-conflicting theories have proved no more than convenient explanations to justify reasonable results, for when the theories do not fit the facts, courts have customarily resorted to general principles of equity to effect a just disposition of property rights. For example, in *Brown v. Brown*, 274 Cal. App. 2d 178, 82 Cal. Rptr. 238, the court found that a legal wife's acquiescence in a putative wife's 28-year marriage equitably estopped the legal wife from claiming any interest in the community property.

The present case is complicated by the fact that the laws regulating succession and the disposition of marital property are not designed to cope with the extraordinary circumstance of purposeful bigamy at the expense of two innocent parties.

In the present case, depending on which statute or legal theory is applied, both Mildred, as legal spouse, and Josephine, as putative spouse, have valid or plausible claims to at least half, perhaps three-quarters, possibly all, of Juan's estate. The court found that both wives contributed in indeterminable amounts and proportions to the accumulations of the community. Since statutes and judicial decisions provide no sure guidance for the resolution of the controversy, the probate court cut the Gordian knot of competing claims and divided the estate equally between the two wives, presumably on the theory that innocent wives of practicing bigamists are entitled to equal shares of property accumulated during the active phase of the bigamy. No injury has been visited upon third parties, and the wisdom of Solomon is not required to perceive the justice of the result.

The judgment is affirmed.

DISCUSSION

If the husband had been alive when the property rights of the parties were at issue, would the *Vargas* solution be appropriate? This was done in *Waterhouse v. Star Land Co.,* 71 So. 358 (La. 1916). One Texas case suggests that the putative spouse should get 50% of all property accumulated by the husband, and the husband and the lawful wife should share the other 50%. See *Routh v. Routh,* 57 Tex. 589, 602 (1882) (Bonner, J., concurring).

Vryonis v. Vryonis
California Court of Appeals, 1988
248 Cal. Rptr. 807

Appellant Speros Vryonis, Jr. (Speros) purports to appeal a judgment on bifurcated issues wherein the trial court held respondent Fereshteh R. Vryonis (Fereshteh) had the status of a putative spouse.

Because Fereshteh reasonably could not believe she was validly married under California law, we order the issuance of a peremptory writ.

FACTUAL & PROCEDURAL BACKGROUND

Speros was the director of and a teacher at the Center for Near Eastern Studies at UCLA. Fereshteh was a visiting professor at the Center, and the parties met there in the fall of 1979. She was an Iranian citizen, a member of the Shiah Moslem Twelve Imams religious sect, and involved in the local Islamic community. Speros was a nonpracticing member of the Greek Orthodox Church.

Prior to arriving in the United States in 1979, Fereshteh spent six years in England, where she earned a Ph.D. at Cambridge University. She had been married before and was the mother of two children.

The parties saw each other occasionally during 1980 and 1981 in connection with Center activities. They dated in February and March of 1982, but Fereshteh repeatedly stated she could not date Speros without marriage or a commitment because of her strict religious upbringing. Speros responded he could not marry as he did not know her and that he was a "free man."

Nonetheless, on March 17, 1982, at her Los Angeles apartment, Fereshteh performed a private marriage ceremony. According to Fereshteh, the marriage conformed to the requirements of a time specified, "Muta" marriage, authorized by the Moslem sect of which she was an adherent. Fereshteh was unfamiliar with the requirements of American or California marriage law. However, she believed the ceremony created a valid and binding marriage, and Speros so assured her.

The parties kept the marriage secret and did not hold themselves out as husband and wife. All indicia of marriage were lacking. The parties did not cohabit, but rather, maintained separate residences. They did not inform relatives or friends of the marriage. Speros did not have a key to Fereshteh's apartment, and Fereshteh only had a key to Speros' house for three months. Speros continued to date other women. Fereshteh did not use Speros' surname. The parties did not commingle their finances, nor did they assume any support obligations for one another. They did not take title to any property jointly. During the period of time in question, Speros and Fereshteh filed separate tax returns, each claiming single status. They spent 22 nights together in 1982, only a few in 1983, and none in 1984.

On frequent occasions, Fereshteh requested Speros to solemnize their marriage in a mosque or other religious setting, which Speros refused.

In July 1984 Speros informed Fereshteh he was going to marry another woman, after which time Fereshteh began informing people of the purported marriage. In September 1984, about two and one-half years after the date of the private marriage ceremony, Speros married the other woman.

Fereshteh thereafter petitioned for dissolution on October 15, 1984, seeking attorney's fees, spousal support and a determination of property rights. Speros moved to quash the summons based on lack of jurisdiction in that a marriage did not exist. The motion was denied. The trial court held a bifurcated hearing in March 1985 to determine first the validity of the marriage and putative spouse status.

In the statement of decision and judgment on bifurcated issues, the trial court held Fereshteh had a good faith belief a valid marriage existed between her and Speros, and specifically found:

> 3. On March 14, 1982, in Los Angeles, California, the Petitioner performed a private religious marriage ceremony between herself and the Respondent which conformed to the requirements of a Muslim Mota [sic] marriage.

> 4. No marriage license was obtained. And only the Petitioner and Respondent were present during the ceremony. No written documents were made to declare or record or otherwise authenticate the existence of a marriage between the parties, either at the time of the ceremony or thereafter. 5. The Respondent required the Petitioner to keep the marriage secret and to live in a separate residence. 6. The Petitioner believed in good faith that a valid marriage existed as a result of the ceremony, the consent expressed by Respondent, Respondent's subsequent actions, and statements of the Respondent. 7. The Petitioner had no knowledge of the marriage laws of California and was ignorant as to any impediment to the validity of the marriage and justifiably relied on Respondent's assertions that the Petitioner and Respondent were husband and wife. 8. On March 14, 1982, when the marriage ceremony was performed, the Respondent stated his consent to the marriage but did not intend such statements and participation in the ceremony to constitute a valid California marriage. 9. The ceremony performed between the parties on March 14, 1982, did not constitute a valid California marriage due to the Respondent's lack of intention that such ceremony constituted a valid marriage and due to the subsequent lack of recordation or authentication of such marriage ceremony. 10. The Petitioner has the status of a putative spouse....

The finding of putative marriage would allow Fereshteh in subsequent proceedings to assert claims for spousal support and property division. The trial court ordered Speros to pay $10,000 as a partial contributory share of Fereshteh's attorney's fees.

Speros filed the purported appeal.

CONTENTIONS

Speros contends: (1) the trial court erred as a matter of law in finding putative spouse status because (a) there was no evidence of a void or voidable marriage in that neither party made any attempt to comply with the statutory requirements of solemnization and recordation, and (b) there was no objective evidence to sustain the finding of Fereshteh's good faith belief in the existence of a valid marriage without the existence of the usual indicia of a marriage; (2) the ruling in effect resurrects common law marriage, contravening public policy; and (3) it was error to allow Fereshteh to testify as an expert regarding Islamic custom and practice and the Muta marriage.

DISCUSSION

1. General principles of putative marriage doctrine.

Civil Code section 4100 defines the marriage relationship as "a personal relation arising out of a civil contract between a man and a woman, to which the consent of the parties capable of making that contract is necessary. Consent alone will not constitute marriage; it must be followed by the issuance of a license and solemnization as authorized by this Code...."

Section 4200 sets forth the procedural requirements for a valid California marriage as one which "must be licensed, solemnized, authenticated, and the certificate of registry of marriage filed as provided in this article; but noncompliance with its provisions by others than a party to a marriage does not invalidate it."

Where the marriage is invalid due to some legal infirmity, an innocent party nevertheless may be entitled to relief under the long recognized protections of the putative marriage doctrine. Said doctrine was codified in section 4452, enacted in 1969.

Section 4452 sets forth the rights of a putative spouse as follows: "Whenever a determination is made that a marriage is void or voidable and the court finds that either party or both parties believed in good faith that the marriage was valid, the court shall declare the party or parties to have the status of a putative spouse, and, if the division of property is in issue, shall divide, in accordance with Section 4800, that property acquired during the union which would have been community property or quasi-community property if the union had not been void or voidable. The property shall be termed 'quasi-marital property.'"

In addition to enjoying property rights in the nature of those afforded marital partners (Secs. 4452, 4800), a putative spouse may also obtain spousal support. (Sec. 4455.)

2. Requirements of a void/voidable marriage construed to mean invalid marriage.

As set forth ante, section 4452 requires a threshold determination of a void or voidable marriage.

A void marriage is an incestuous (Sec. 4400), bigamous or polygamous one (Sec. 4401). A voidable marriage is defined as one where there was (a) no capacity by one party to consent due to youth or unsoundness of mind, (b) fraudulently or forcibly obtained consent, (c) physical incapacity of entering into a marriage, or (d) a living spouse of either party who has been absent five years or more and believed dead. (Sec. 4452.)

The circumstances here do not give rise to either a void or a voidable marriage. However, that in and of itself does not preclude relief under the putative marriage doctrine. A fact situation may involve neither a void nor a voidable marriage, and yet relief is afforded, based upon the reasonable expectations of the parties to an alleged marriage entered into in good faith.

3. Inquiry into good faith belief in a valid marriage.

Fereshteh seeks affirmation of the trial court's finding she had a good faith belief she was validly married to Speros, urging the only necessary finding to establish a putative marriage is that one spouse believed in good faith a valid marriage existed.

Speros urges more than a "good faith belief, however wild" is required. He posits the requisite state of mind must be a good faith belief in a valid California marriage, and that there must also be some objective indicia of valid marriage by which to measure such belief.

It is unclear from the statement of decision whether the trial court found Fereshteh believed she had celebrated a valid Muta marriage and held thereby a belief sufficient to confer putative spouse status, or whether the trial court determined Fereshteh had a good faith belief she was validly married under California law.

If the trial court based its putative marriage finding on Fereshteh's belief she had celebrated a valid Muta marriage, the ruling was error because the required good faith belief is in the existence of a lawful California marriage. If the trial court found Fereshteh had a good faith belief she was validly married under California law, the ruling was error because the requisite good faith belief must have a reasonable basis.

a. Good faith belief must be objectively reasonable.

While a trial court may be tempted to base a finding of putative spousal status merely on the subjective good faith in a valid marriage held by a credible and sympathetic party, more is required. "Good faith belief" is a legal term of art, and in both the civil and criminal law a determination of good faith is tested by an objective standard.

A proper assertion of putative spouse status must rest on facts that would cause a reasonable person to harbor a good faith belief in the existence of a valid marriage. Where there has been no attempted compliance with the procedural requirements of a valid marriage, and where the usual indicia of marriage and conduct consistent with a valid marriage are absent, a belief in the existence of a valid marriage, although sincerely held, would be unreasonable and therefore lacking in good faith.

While solemnization is not an absolute prerequisite to establishing a putative marriage, it is a major factor to be considered in the calculus of good faith. Lacking some diligent attempt to meet the requisites of a valid marriage, a claim of good faith belief in a valid marriage would lack any reasonable basis.

Consideration of such factors provides a framework for determining whether a petitioner had reason to believe a valid marriage existed. Without a reasonable basis for an alleged good faith belief, even an honestly held belief in the existence of a valid marriage will not be in good faith and therefore insufficient to come within section 4452.

(i). Application here.

Fereshteh testified her belief in the validity of the purported marriage rested on her having performed the Muta ceremony, combined with Speros' assurance the marriage was valid.

As indicated, Fereshteh performed a private marriage ceremony at her apartment, with only the two of them present. The ceremony was not solemnized by a third party. No license was obtained and there was no authentication or recordation. In short, there was no attempt to meet the statutory requirements of section 4200 with respect to the formation of a valid California marriage.

Because the parties made no colorable attempt at compliance, Fereshteh could not believe reasonably a valid California marriage came into being. Fereshteh's ignorance of the law does not compel a contrary conclusion. Further, her reliance on Speros' assurances is unavailing. Unlike *Monti*, wherein Shirley relied on Clifford's statement that the divorce dissolving their indisputably valid marriage was never finalized (*In re Marriage of*

Monti, supra, 135 Cal. App. 3d at p. 53, 185 Cal. Rptr. 72), there was no endeavor here to comply with legal formalities.

Subsequent events are not germane to whether there was a proper effort to create a valid marriage in the first instance. However, later conduct sheds further light on whether Fereshteh had reason to believe she was married to Speros. We observe the parties did not reside together, but continued to maintain separate households. They did not assume any support obligations for one another. They spent no more than five or six nights together in any given month during the marriage. Speros continued to date other women, of which fact Fereshteh was aware. Fereshteh did not use Speros' name. There was no merging of finances, nor was there any joint accumulation of real or personal property. Fereshteh and Speros filed separate tax returns, each claiming single status. For the two and one-half year period following the purported marriage, the parties did not hold themselves out as husband and wife. It was only when Speros told Fereshteh he was to be married that Fereshteh published the fact of their purported marriage.

In sum, the alleged private marriage went unsolemnized, unlicensed and unrecorded. Thereafter, the parties did not cohabit, or hold themselves out as husband and wife, and in no way approximated the conduct of a married couple. Because the facts were at odds with the formation and existence of a valid marriage pursuant to California law, Fereshteh could not rely on Speros' statements reasonably to believe she was married. Notwithstanding Fereshteh's sincerity, her belief was unreasonable and therefore not in good faith.

> b. Required belief in valid marriage construed to mean lawful marriage.

As noted, the trial court may have based its finding of putative spouse status on Fereshteh's belief she had conducted a valid Muta marriage. However, case law reflects the requisite belief is in a lawful marriage, that is to say, a marriage which complies with statutory requirements.

Although in many situations, there is little practical difference between lawful and valid, the use of the latter term in this context may engender confusion. The putative marriage doctrine protects the expectations of innocent parties who believe they are lawfully married. When the basis of the doctrine is stated as a good faith belief in a valid marriage, Fereshteh's belief she had celebrated a valid Muta marriage initially might seem sufficient to come within the doctrine. However, our overview discloses the doctrine requires a belief a marriage is lawful within the meaning of the Civil Code.

Assuming the trial court based its finding of putative marriage on Fereshteh's belief she had conducted a valid Muta marriage, the ruling was error.[1]

CONCLUSION

The fact that the purported marriage was neither void nor voidable is without import, as section 4452 merely requires a threshold determination a marriage is legally infirm.

Under the putative marriage doctrine, the requisite good faith belief must have a reasonable basis, as a sincere but objectively unreasonable belief is not in good faith. Further, the belief must be in a lawful marriage. A belief one's marriage conforms to the precepts of one's faith is insufficient to come within the doctrine.

---

1. Moreover, the putative marriage doctrine operates to protect expectations in property acquired through joint efforts. (*Schneider v. Schneider,* 183 Cal. at pp. 339–340, 191 P. 533.) Where, as here, there is neither cohabitation, pooling of earnings, acquisition of jointly owned property, nor any economic interdependence, the rationale of section 4452 would not be served.

Fereshteh's belief she conducted a valid Muta marriage ceremony is not what is contemplated by section 4452. Even assuming Fereshteh believed she was validly married under California law, because her belief is objectively unreasonable, the requisite good faith is lacking.

DISPOSITION

Let a peremptory writ of mandate issue, directing the trial court to vacate its judgment on bifurcated issues and to make a different order consistent with this opinion. Speros to recover costs on appeal.

DISCUSSION

In *Cardwell v. Cardwell*, 195 S.W.3d 856 (Tex. App.—Dallas 2006, no pet.) the wife separated from her husband. Many years later, she ceremonially married another. A few years after that she learned she had never been divorced from the previous husband. Her claim that she was a putative spouse during the time before she learned of the impediment was rejected on the basis that she made no reasonable inquiry into her marital status before she remarried.

Garduno v. Garduno, 760 S.W.2d 735 (Tex. App.—Corpus Christi 1988, no writ) discusses the relationship between common-law marriage and putative marriage, where a spouse initially believes the other spouse has been divorced from a previous spouse and then learns otherwise. The spouse who in good faith believes that her marriage is valid can be a putative spouse. However, once the spouse learns that her "husband" did not divorce his first wife, the second "wife" no longer can accrue putative spouse benefits. If the "husband" does divorce the first wife, the man and the second "wife" can then establish a common-law marriage.

Chapter Three

Disputes Between Unmarried People

A. Engagement Disputes

1. Breach of Promise of Marriage

The breach of promise action is a relic of another era. Centuries ago, the appropriate age for a bride was quite limited and long engagements were common. If the man broke the engagement, the woman might not be able to find a marriage partner. So, an engagement historically was treated like a contract. If a party "breached" the contract, the innocent party could sue the other for damages. In addition to out-of-pocket damages, the innocent party could recover damages for humiliation and loss of the future economic benefit that would have resulted from the marriage. *See* H. Clark, *Law of Domestic Relations* (1968), Sec. 1.1 *et seq.*; *Funderburgh v. Skinner*, 209 S.W. 452 (Tex. Civ. App.—Texarkana 1919, no writ). Many commentators, including Gilbert and Sullivan in "Trial By Jury," have argued that the breach of promise action should be abolished.

Stanard v. Bolin

Supreme Court of Washington, 1977
565 P.2d 94

HAMILTON, Justice.

This appeal presents the question of whether the common-law action for breach of promise to marry should be abolished. The trial court concluded that the action was contrary to public policy and dismissed the plaintiff's (appellant's) complaint with prejudice under CR Sec. 12(b)(6) for failure to state a claim upon which relief can be granted. We accepted review and conclude that the action is not contrary to public policy.

In October, 1974, plaintiff and defendant (respondent) were introduced to each other by mutual friends, and their courtship developed soon thereafter. During the course of their courtship, defendant assured plaintiff that he was worth in excess of $2 million, was planning to retire in 2 years, and that the two of them would then travel. Defendant also promised plaintiff that she would never have to work again and that he would see to the support of her two teen-age boys. He also promised to see that the plaintiff's mother would never be in need.

27

On September 22, 1975, plaintiff accepted defendant's proposal of marriage. There-after, defendant took her to a jewelry store and purchased an engagement ring and match-ing wedding rings. The parties found a suitable home for their residence and signed the purchase agreement as husband and wife. At the insistence of defendant, plaintiff placed her home on the market for sale and sold most of her furniture at a public auction. The parties set December 13, 1975, as their wedding date, reserved a church, and engaged a minister to perform the service. Dresses for plaintiff, her mother, and the matron of honor were ordered, and a reception was arranged at a local establishment. The parties began informally announcing their plans to a wide circle of friends. After the wedding date was set, plaintiff's employer hired another person and requested plaintiff to assist in teach-ing the new employee the duties of her job.

On November 13, 1975, defendant informed plaintiff that he would not marry her. This came as a great shock to plaintiff and caused her to become ill and lose sleep and weight. Plaintiff sought medical advice and was treated by her physician. Plaintiff also had to take her home off the market and repurchase furniture at a cost in excess of that which she received for her older furniture. In addition, plaintiff was forced to can-cel all wedding plans and reservations, and to explain to her matron of honor, her mother, and her children, that she was not marrying. Plaintiff was also obliged to re-turn wedding gifts and to face her friends and neighbors, each of whom felt entitled to an explanation.

In her first claim for relief, plaintiff sought damages to compensate her for her pain, impairment to health, humiliation, and embarrassment. Plaintiff's second claim sought damages to compensate her for her loss of expected financial security.

The breach-of-marriage-promise action has its origins in the common-law. Professor Clark, a well-known authority on family law, has posited that 17th Century English con-ceptions of marriage as largely a property transaction caused the English common-law courts to intervene in a subject matter which, up until the 17th Century, had been almost ex-clusively under the jurisdiction of the ecclesiastical courts. See H. Clark, *The Law of Do-mestic Relations in the United States 2* (1968) (hereafter cited as Clark). In any event, the action was carried forward into the common-law of Washington (see RCW Sec. 4.04.010) and was recognized by this court as early as 1905. See *Heasley v. Nichols*, 38 Wash. 485, 80 P. 769 (1905). Because the action has its origins in the common-law and has not been acted upon by the legislature, it is proper for us to reexamine it and determine its con-tinued viability in light of present-day society.

The breach-of-promise-to-marry action is one not easy to classify. Although the action is treated as arising from the breach of a contract (the contract being the mutual promises to marry), the damages allowable more closely resemble a tort action. Thus, the plaintiff may recover for loss to reputation, mental anguish, and injury to health, in addition to re-covering for expenditures made in preparation for the marriage and loss of the pecuniary and social advantages which the promised marriage offered. In addition, some states allow aggravated damages for seduction under promise to marry and for attacks by the defen-dant on the plaintiff's character. Furthermore, some states allow punitive damages when the defendant's acts were malicious or fraudulent. For a comprehensive discussion of the damages allowable under a breach-of-promise-to-marry action and a collection of cases, see Annot., *Measure and Elements of Damages for Breach of Contract to Marry*, 73 A.L.R.2d 553 (1960), and C. McCormick, *Handbook on the Law of Damages* 397–406 (1935).

The action in its present form is subject to almost uniform criticism by the commen-tators, although our research has not disclosed any cases in which a court has abolished the action.[1] In essence, these criticisms are: (1) the action is used as an instrument of oppression and blackmail; (2) engaged persons should be allowed to correct their mistakes without fear of publicity and legal compulsion; (3) the action is subject to great abuse at the hands of gullible and sympathetic juries; (4) it is wrong to allow under the guise of contract an action that is essentially tortious and penal in nature; and (5) the measure of damages is unjust because damages are allowed for loss of social and economic position, whereas most persons marry for reasons of mutual love and affection. See *e.g.*, 1 C. Vernier, *American Family Laws* 26–27 (1931); Brown, *Breach of Promise Suits*, 77 U. Pa. L. Rev. 474 (1929); Wright, *The Action for Breach of the Marriage Promise*, 10 Va. L. Rev. 361 (1924); White, *Breach of Promise of Marriage*, 10 L. Quar. Rev. 135 (1894). Although some of these criticisms are not without merit, we do not believe they justify an outright abolishment of the action.

When two persons agree to marry, they should realize that certain actions will be taken during the engagement period in reliance on the mutual promises to marry. Rings will be purchased, wedding dresses and other formal attire will be ordered or reserved, and honeymoon plans with their attendant expenses will be made. Wedding plans such as the rental of a church, the engagement of a minister, the printing of wedding invitations, and so on, will commence. It is also likely that the parties will make plans for their future residence, such as purchasing a house, buying furniture, and the like. Further, at the time the parties decide to marry, they should realize that their plans and visions of future happiness will be communicated to friends and relatives, and that wedding gifts soon will be arriving. When the plans to marry are abruptly ended, it is certainly foreseeable that the party who was unaware that the future marriage would not take place will have expended some sums of money and will suffer some forms of mental anguish, loss to reputation, and injury to health. We do not feel these injuries should go unanswered merely because the breach-of-promise-to-marry action may be subject to abuses; rather, an attempt should be made to eradicate the abuses from the action.

One major abuse of the action is allowing the plaintiff to bring in evidence of the defendant's wealth and social position. This evidence is admissible under the theory that the plaintiff should be compensated for what she or he has lost by not marrying the defendant.

Although damages for loss of expected financial and social position more closely resemble the contract theory of recovery than the other elements of damages for breach of promise to marry, we do not believe these damages are justified in light of modern society's concept of marriage. Although it may have been that marriages were contracted for material reasons in 17th Century England, marriages today generally are not considered property transactions, but are, in the words of Professor Clark, "the result of that complex experience called being in love." Clark, *supra* at 2. A person generally does not choose a marriage partner on the basis of financial and social gain; hence, the plaintiff should not be compensated for losing an expectation which he or she did not have in the first place. Further, the breach-of-promise-to-marry action is based on injuries to the plaintiff, and

---

1. The action has been abolished or modified by statute in some states. See Ala. Code tit. 7, Sec. 114; Cal. Civ. Code Ann. Sec. 43.5 (West); Colo. Rev. Stat. Sec. 13-20-202; Conn. Gen. Stat. Ann. Sec. 52-572b (West Supp.1977); Fla. Stat. Ann. Sec. 771.01 (West); Ind. Code Ann. Sec. 34-4-4-1 (Burns Supp.1976); Me. Rev. Stat. Ann. tit. 14, Sec. 854 (West); Md. Cts. & Jud. Proc. Code Ann. Sec. 5-301 (1974); Mass. Gen. Laws Ann. ch. 207, Sec. 47A (West); Mich. Stat. Ann. Sec. 25.191; Nev. Rev. Stat. Sec. 41.380; N.H. Rev. Stat. Ann. Sec. 508:11; N.J. Stat. Ann. Sec.2A:23-1 (West); N.Y. Civ. Rights Law Sec. 80-a *et seq.* (McKinney); Pa. Stat. Ann. tit. 48, Sec. 171 (Purdon); W.Va. Code Sec. 56-3-2a (Supp.1976); Wis. Stat. Ann. Sec. 248.01 (West Supp.1976); Wyo. Stat. Sec. 1-728.

evidence of the defendant's wealth tends to misdirect the jury's attention when assessing the plaintiff's damages towards an examination of the defendant's wealth rather than the plaintiff's injuries.

Professor McCormick has concluded that evidence of the defendant's wealth has a more potent effect upon the size of the verdict than any instruction on damages. See C. McCormick, *Handbook on the Law of Damages* 399, n. 36 (1935). If this is so, then it presents a very strong reason for disallowing any evidence of the defendant's wealth and social position. We conclude that damages for loss of expected financial and social position should no longer be recoverable under the breach-of-promise-to-marry actions. This means that evidence of the defendant's wealth and social position becomes immaterial in assessing the plaintiff's damages.

Other damages subject to criticism are those damages given for mental anguish, loss to reputation, and injury to health. It is argued that these injuries are "so vague and so little capable of measurement in dollars that they give free rein to the jury's passions, prejudices and sympathies." See Clark, *supra* at 12. This argument has little merit, for it places no faith in the jury's ability to evaluate objectively the evidence regarding plaintiff's injuries and render a just verdict. If a jury's verdict is tainted by passion or prejudice, or is otherwise excessive, the trial court and the appellate court have the power to reduce the award or order a new trial.

Lack of ability to quantify damages in exact dollar amounts does not justify abolishing the breach-of-promise-to-marry action. In her complaint plaintiff alleged that she had suffered pain, impairment to health, humiliation, and embarrassment as a result of defendant's breach of his promise to marry. If this is true, and we must assume it is for purposes of review, then she is entitled to compensation for these injuries.

As for retaining aggravated damages for seduction under a promise to marry, and the like, since plaintiff here was not seeking aggravated damages, we leave a decision on aggravated damages for a future case in which the issue for these damages arises. Also, we note that although other states allow punitive damages, these damages are not allowed in this state because they are not authorized by statute. See *Steele v. Johnson*, 76 Wash. 2d 750, 458 P.2d 889 (1969).

We also do not believe the action should be abolished so that engaged persons are free from compulsion to choose whether to end an engagement. Although the policy of the state should not be to encourage a person to marry when he or she has begun to have second thoughts about a prospective mate, it is also the policy of the state to afford an avenue of redress for injuries suffered due to the actions of another. Allowing recovery for injuries, which are foreseeable at the time of entering into the relationship, should not be denied on the presumption the defendant would rather enter into the marriage than pay damages for the injuries caused. Furthermore, it is hard to conceive of a plaintiff suing a defendant in order to coerce the defendant into a marriage which would be unstable at best. It is possible that there may be such a plaintiff, but that is no reason for abolishing the action for all plaintiffs, for that would cause most plaintiffs to go uncompensated for their injuries at the expense of a few unworthy plaintiffs.

In conclusion, we have decided that the breach-of-promise-to-marry action should be retained as a quasi-contract, quasi-tort action for the recovery of the foreseeable special and general damages which are caused by a defendant's breach of promise to marry. However, the action is modified to the extent that a plaintiff cannot recover for loss of expected financial and social position, because marriage is no longer considered to be a property transaction.

The judgment of the trial court is reversed on plaintiff's first claim for relief, and remanded for further proceedings consistent with this opinion. The judgment is affirmed on plaintiff's second claim for relief, which sought damages for loss of prospective economical and social advantage.

WRIGHT, Chief Justice, and ROSELLINI, STAFFORD, HOROWITZ, BRACHTEN-BACH and HICKS, Justices, concur.

UTTER, Justice (dissenting).

The majority, in a well-written opinion, has set forth the historical background of the action for breach of promise to marry. It states the policy reasons for abolishing the action, but chooses to retain its major underpinnings. The sole change is to modify the doctrine to the extent that a plaintiff can no longer recover for loss of expected financial and social position, but may still recover foreseeable special and general damages caused by breach of a defendant's promise to marry.

I believe the change advocated does not go far enough. Motive of the defendant may still, apparently, be considered in assessing damages. *Warner v. Benham*, 126 Wash. 393, 218 P. 260 (1923). Where the breach of promise to marry is wanton or deliberate, the effect is to allow exemplary damages, contrary to the public policy of our state. *Wyman v. Wallace*, 15 Wash.App. 395, 549 P.2d 71 (1976). In *Wyman*, at page 395, 549 P.2d at page 73, the Court of Appeals abolished the action for alienation of affections of a spouse by an unrelated third person on the ground, among others, that "the element of punishment is so inextricably interwoven into any award of damages for alienation of the affections of a spouse that the true nature of the award is punitive." This is no less true in this case than it was in *Wyman*. In addition, in 1973 our state adopted a new dissolution of marriage act. RCW Sec. 26.09. The establishment of the fact that a marriage is "irretrievably broken" is now a sufficient ground for dissolution, with no finding of fault necessary. The trial judge observed in his memorandum decision on motion to dismiss:

> The current public policy expressed in the 1973 Dissolution Act is to disregard fault in the judicial determination of property rights at the dissolution of a marriage. Fault is not to be considered in determining which party shall have the decree. There are no damages as such in a dissolution. Is it not obvious, however, that one of the parties to a dissolution suffers at least as much humiliation, embarrassment, mental suffering and loss of financial expectation and security as does a party to the breakup of an engagement?

It is significant that there was no divorce by judicial decree at common-law when the breach of promise action came into being. *Tupper v. Tupper*, 63 Wash. 2d 585 [388 P.2d 225]. Should not the public policy declared in the divorce statutes be applicable to engagements? I believe it is.

The majority lists the almost uniform criticisms of the action by commentators:

> (1) the action is used as an instrument of oppression and blackmail; (2) engaged persons should be allowed to correct their mistakes without fear of publicity and legal compulsion; (3) the action is subject to great abuse at the hands of gullible and sympathetic juries; (4) it is wrong to allow under the guise of contract an action that is essentially tortious and penal in nature.

I believe these criticisms are sufficient grounds, given the recently enunciated policy of the state in the dissolution of marriage act, to justify our abolition of this now obsolete, judicially created, cause of action.

DOLLIVER, Justice, concurs.

———————

Scanlon v. Crim
Texas Court of Appeals — Dallas, 1973
500 S.W.2d 554, writ ref'd n.r.e.

BATEMAN, Justice.

This is a breach of promise case. The appellant was plaintiff in the trial court and appeals from an adverse summary judgment. Appellant alleged that she and appellee became engaged to marry each other in 1965, that this agreement was confirmed by appellee numerous times until in April, 1970, when he breached it by informing appellant he would not marry her. He married another woman the next month. We need not recite in greater detail the allegations in support of her claim for substantial damages.

Appellee alleged *inter alia* that by the adoption on November 7, 1972, of an amendment to the Constitution of Texas the public policy of the state was changed to the extent that the common-law cause of action for breach of promise was abolished. The amendment, which became Section 3a of article I, is as follows: "Equality under the law shall not be denied or abridged because of sex, race, color, creed, or national origin. This amendment is self-operative."

The trial court rendered summary judgment that appellant take nothing on the sole ground that "as a matter of law, no cause of action exists because same would discriminate against sex of a party as prohibited by" said amendment. Appellee argues, in support of the trial court's ruling, that under "the present state of mores in American life" a man has no right to sue a woman for breach of promise and that this closing of the courthouse door to him while leaving it open to women was a discrimination which the amendment removed by closing the courthouse door also to women.

Appellant attacks this ruling on several grounds but we find it necessary to discuss only one; *i.e.*, that the trial court has misinterpreted the amendment and has given it an effect never contemplated by the legislators who proposed it or by the voters who adopted it. We agree with this contention.

Our determination of the parties' legal rights cannot be controlled by the practical difficulty a male plaintiff may have in persuading a jury to award damages to him for this kind of wrong. Although we know of no such case in which a male plaintiff has prevailed, we cannot assume that a jury would be disposed to violate its oath and disregard the evidence in rendering its verdict. Nor can we say as a matter of law that a recovery by a man for breach of promise of marriage would now be forbidden by public mores in view of current sentiment against discrimination based on sex, which has recently led to numerous changes in the law, including the equal rights amendment.

We know of nothing in Texas law to prohibit a suit by a man for damages for breach of promise of marriage. *Wells v. Hardy*, 51 S.W. 503 (Tex. Civ. App. — Austin 1899, no writ), was a case in which a male sued a female for damages for her breach of promise to marry him. His petition described her as being only 18 years of age, and the trial court sustained a special exception on the ground that because of her minority she was not bound by her contract. This was affirmed and the Supreme Court refused writ of error. None of the three courts said that the man had no cause of action because of his sex. We, therefore, do not agree with appellee that a male plaintiff has no right to maintain such a suit. Neither do we agree that the said constitutional amendment destroyed the right of a woman to do so. It is just as reasonable to say that it removed discrimination by recognizing the right of both men and women to bring such suits.

In *Felsenthal v. McMillan*, 493 S.W.2d 729 (Tex. 1973), the question was whether Texas should continue to recognize a husband's right of action for criminal conversation and, speaking through Chief Justice Greenhill, the court said: "At common-law, only the husband could bring the action. Because of equal protection, the wife also has been held to be able to maintain the action in all states where the matter has arisen.... [W]e could not live with the action on any other basis."

As we also pointed out in that opinion, the legislatures of a number of other states have specifically abolished causes of action for alienation of affections, criminal conversation and breach of promise to marry, or one or more of them, but the Texas Legislature has not seen fit to do so. Such suits have been severely criticized by numerous law writers.

While the Supreme Court did not see fit in *Felsenthal* to abolish the cause of action for criminal conversation, the four dissenting members of the court were in favor of doing so. The court, in *Kelsey-Seybold Clinic v. Maclay*, 466 S.W.2d 716 (Tex. 1971), recognized the validity of a cause of action for alienation of affections, although this decision was also by a divided court. In the present state of the law in Texas, therefore, we are compelled to hold that appellant has alleged a valid cause of action as against the contention that the right of action was abolished by the adoption of the said constitutional amendment.

DISCUSSION

Scanlon proclaims that the breach of promise action remains possible under Texas law. Is this a sensible result? In a divorce, can a spouse sue the other for the "humiliation" and "loss of future benefits" that will be incurred as a result of the divorce? If such damages would still be permitted in a breach of promise action, how would the "loss of future benefits" be computed? Many courts and commentators have concluded that, in a world of no-fault divorce, the breach of promise action makes little sense.

The *Scanlon* opinion concluded that the breach of promise action should be retained because, at the time, Texas law authorized actions for criminal conversation and alienation of affection. These are tort actions that could be brought by a spouse against a third party if that third party had sexual relations with the other spouse or induced that spouse to divorce, respectively. Does the breach of promise action present the same policy concerns as those presented by criminal conversation and alienation of affections? The criminal conversation and alienation of affections actions were later abolished. *See* Tex. Fam. Code §§ 1.106, 1.107. Does Tex. Fam. Code § 1.108 affect this claim? Does the enactment of Tex. Fam. Code Sections 1.106 and 1.107 affect the *Scanlon* analysis?

What is an "engagement"? Is it different from a commercial contract? Are any social policies relevant to such commitments that are not involved in a commercial contract? If one prospective spouse decides he or she does not want to marry, should this person be encouraged by the system to marry?

Should the breach of promise action be abolished? If so, are there any damages incurred in such a situation that should still be recoverable?

2. Engagement Gifts

Prospective spouses frequently transfer property from one person to the other before the marriage. If the marriage does not occur, the question arises whether the premarital "gifts" must be returned to the donor.

Curtis v. Anderson

Texas Court of Appeals — Austin, 2003
106 S.W.3d 251, pet. denied

YEAKEL, Justice.

This is an appeal from a summary judgment in a suit brought by appellant Michael Curtis to recover a diamond ring from appellee Michele Anderson after Curtis terminated the couple's engagement. Curtis sued for breach of an oral agreement and conversion, and the trial court granted Anderson a summary judgment. Curtis appeals arguing that Anderson was not entitled to summary judgment because the ring was a conditional gift, and Anderson's possession of the ring became an unlawful conversion when Anderson refused to return the ring. We will affirm the judgment of the trial court.

FACTUAL BACKGROUND

In the summer of 2000, Curtis and Anderson became engaged to be married. Curtis gave Anderson a ring. Approximately six or eight weeks later, the engagement ended. Anderson refused to return the ring to Curtis. Curtis alleges that at the time that he gave her the ring, Anderson agreed that if the wedding was called off she would return the ring.

The only summary judgment evidence before the trial court were excerpts from Curtis's deposition. Concerning the agreement to return the ring, Curtis testified that "we had a mutual understanding that I clearly stated and she accepted that if I did not-if we did not become married that I would retain-retain the stone." He admitted that the "mutual understanding" was not reduced to writing. When asked who "broke off the engagement," he testified, "I did.... I did it for several reasons. One is that I felt like she had some sexual hang-ups. I felt that she had some previous general issues with men, and she also had a very volatile temper." Based on this record, the trial court granted summary judgment in favor of Anderson.

DISCUSSION

Anderson's sole ground for seeking summary judgment was that Curtis could not prevail because the statute of frauds prohibits the enforcement of any alleged oral agreement concerning return of the ring. *See* TEX. FAM. CODE ANN. § 1.108 (West 1998). Curtis argues by his first issue that the statute of frauds is not applicable; he claims the case is governed instead by the conditional-gift rule. According to Curtis, the ring was a conditional gift, and because the contingent condition of marriage was not met, the gift was not completed and the ring should be returned to him. In his second issue, he contends that he presented sufficient evidence to establish the elements of a tort claim for conversion....

Statute of Frauds

The application of the conditional-gift rule assumes that there is no binding agreement between the parties about ownership of the engagement ring should the marriage not occur. If a binding agreement between the parties exists, then application of the conditional-gift rule is not appropriate. Curtis contends that when he and Anderson became engaged, Anderson agreed that she would return the ring if they did not marry. He testified that their "mutual understanding" was an express agreement, but their "mutual understanding" was not reduced to writing.

In response, Anderson asserted in her motion for summary judgment that Curtis's contract and conversion claims could not prevail because of the statute of frauds found in section 1.108 of the family code, which prohibits enforcement of oral agreements in consideration of marriage. TEX. FAM. CODE ANN. § 1.108 (West 1998). According to Anderson, even if she agreed to return the ring, her promise is unenforceable because it is not in writing.

In 1997, the legislature added section 1.108 to the Family Code. (footnote omitted) It states:

> A promise or agreement on consideration of marriage or nonmarital conjugal cohabitation is not enforceable unless the promise or agreement or a memorandum of the promise or agreement is in writing and signed by the person obliged by the promise or agreement.

Id. This statutory provision has yet to be interpreted by any court. We must decide whether section 1.108 encompasses agreements between engaged parties regarding the disposition of engagement gifts should the engagement fail. The court's objective in interpreting statutes is to determine legislative intent. (citation omitted) In determining legislative intent, first we look to the plain and common meaning of the words used by the legislature. (citation omitted) Unless a statute is ambiguous, courts abide by the clear language of the statute and enforce it as written. (citation omitted)

Although section 1.108 was obviously intended to apply to prenuptial agreements, its plain language is broad enough to include Anderson's alleged promise to return Curtis's ring. An engagement ring is a special symbol in our culture. It is traditionally given by a man to a woman upon the woman's acceptance of the man's proposal of marriage—it is a symbol of the couple's engagement and their mutual agreement to marry. Clearly, engagement rings are traditionally given in contemplation of marriage or "on consideration of marriage." *See* TEX. FAM. CODE ANN. § 1.108. We hold that Curtis's allegation that he and Anderson had expressed their "mutual understanding" that the ring would be returned if the marriage did not occur comes within the scope of this statute as written. Therefore, to be enforceable any such agreement must be in writing.

Conditional-Gift Rule

In the absence of an enforceable agreement, we turn to the conditional-gift rule. Although we agree that the conditional-gift rule applies in this case, it does not operate in Curtis's favor. As applied by Texas courts, the rule contains an element of fault. Texas courts have held that the rule operates to require that the ring be returned to the donor if the donee is at fault in terminating the engagement. *See McLain v. Gilliam*, 389 S.W.2d 131 (Tex. Civ. App.—Eastland 1965, writ ref'd n.r.e.); *Shaw v. Christie*, 160 S.W.2d 989 (Tex. Civ. App.—Beaumont 1942, no writ). (footnote omitted) The court in *McLain* expressed the rule as follows:

> A gift to a person to whom the donor is engaged to be married, made in contemplation of marriage, although absolute in form, is conditional; and on breach of the marriage engagement by the donee the property may be recovered by the donor. 389 S.W.2d at 132.

In this case, Curtis as donor judicially admitted to terminating the engagement. He does not contend that Anderson was at fault in ending the engagement. His only complaint about Anderson was her refusal to return the ring after he terminated their relationship. When asked in his deposition why he terminated the engagement, he vaguely complained about Anderson's "hang ups" and her temper. He made no attempt to justify his action and unequivocally admitted the decision to end the engagement was his. Thus, this case involves the opposite situation than that involved in *McLain* and *Shaw;* here, the *donor* was responsible for breaching the promise to marry.

This is a case of first impression in Texas. We have found no Texas case in which the *donor* was responsible for terminating the engagement. We have examined cases in other jurisdictions, and it appears that most courts apply a conditional-gift rule in adjudicating ownership of engagement gifts when the marriage fails to occur.[2] However, there is a split of authority over injecting the issue fault into the rule.

Some jurisdictions that have considered similar situations have allowed the donee to keep the engagement gift if the donor terminates the engagement.[3] One court articulated its reasoning as follows:

> On principle, an engagement ring is given, not alone as a symbol of the status of the two persons engaged, the one to the other, but as a symbol or token of their pledge and agreement to marry. As such pledge or gift, the condition is implied that if both parties abandon the projected marriage, the sole cause of the gift, it should be returned. Similarly, if the woman, who has received the ring in token of her promise, unjustifiably breaks her promise, it should be returned. When the converse situation occurs, and the giver of the ring, betokening his promise, violates his word, it would seem that a similar result should follow, i.e., he should lose, not gain, rights to the ring. In addition, had he not broken his promise, the marriage would follow, and the ring would become the wife's absolutely. The man could not then recover the ring. The only difference between that situation and the facts at bar, is that the man has broken his promise.

Spinnell v. Quigley, 56 Wash. App. 799, 785 P.2d 1149, 1150 (1990) (citing *Mate v. Abrahams,* 62 A.2d 754, 754–55 (N.J. County Ct.1948)).

Others apply the conditional-gift rule without considering fault. Courts adopting this no-fault approach reason that (1) it is practically impossible for courts to determine "fault" in the break-up of an engagement or whether a particular break-up was justified; (2) engagements are meant to be a period of evaluation, and a party should not be penalized for ending a doomed relationship; and (3) the underlying public policy favoring no-fault divorces should also apply to engagements. *See, e.g., Fierro v. Hoel,* 465 N.W.2d 669 (Iowa Ct. App.1990); *Heiman v. Parrish,* 262 Kan. 926, 942 P.2d 631 (1997); *Benassi v. Back & Neck Pain Clinic, Inc.,* 629 N.W.2d 475 (Minn. Ct. App.2001); *Albinger v. Har-*

---

2. *See generally* Barbara Frazier, Comment, *"But I Can't Marry You": Who is Entitled to the Engagement Ring When the Conditional Performance Falls Short of the Altar,* 17 J. Am. Acad. Matrimonial Law 419 (2001); Brian L. Kruckenberg, Comment, *"I Don't": Determining Ownership of the Engagement Ring When the Engagement Terminates,* 37 Washburn L.J. 425 (1998); Elaine Marie Tomko, Annotation, *Rights in Respect of Engagement and Courtship Presents When Marriage Does Not Ensue,* 44 A.L.R. 5th 1 (1996).

3. *Hahn v. United States,* 535 F.Supp. 132 (D.S.D.1982); *Simonian v. Donoian,* 96 Cal. App. 2d 259, 215 P.2d 119 (1950); *White v. Finch,* 3 Conn. Cir. Ct. 138, 209 A.2d 199 (1964); *Schultz v. Duitz,* 253 Ky. 135, 69 S.W.2d 27 (1934); *Spinnell v. Quigley,* 56 Wash. App. 799, 785 P.2d 1149 (1990); *see also Hooven v. Quintana,* 44 Colo. App. 395, 618 P.2d 702 (1980); *Beberman v. Segal,* 6 N.J. Super. 472, 69 A.2d 587 (1949).

ris, 310 Mont. 27, 48 P.3d 711 (2002); *Aronow v. Silver,* 223 N.J. Super. 344, 538 A.2d 851, 853 (1987) ("The fault rule is sexist and archaic, a too-long enduring reminder of the times when even the law discriminated against women."); *Vigil v. Haber,* 119 N.M. 9, 888 P.2d 455 (N.M. 1994); *Gagliardo v. Clemente,* 180 A.D.2d 551, 580 N.Y.S.2d 278 (1992); *McIntire v. Raukhorst,* 65 Ohio App. 3d 728, 585 N.E.2d 456 (1984); *Brown v. Thomas,* 127 Wis. 2d 318, 379 N.W.2d 868 (1985).

Texas courts, including this Court,[4] have applied the fault-based conditional-gift rule when a donee breaks the engagement. We believe that the same rule should apply when the donor defaults. We hold that absent a written agreement a donor is not entitled to the return of an engagement ring if he terminates the engagement....

CONCLUSION

We hold that when an agreement between an engaged couple as to the disposition of engagement gifts is not in writing, any dispute arising over ownership when the engagement is broken is subject to the fault-based conditional-gift rule. We affirm the summary judgment granted by the trial court.

DISCUSSION

This rule creates some grey areas in application. What if both parties agree not to marry? What if one person decides not to marry after the other party assaults her or has an affair? Who should be said to have "broken" the engagement?

Can an engagement gift be recovered, under the majority rule, if a prospective spouse dies before the wedding? *See Hahn v. United States,* 535 F. Supp. 132 (D.S.D. 1982).

B. Disputes between Cohabitants

1. In General

If two people know they are not validly married to each other, live together, share a sexual relationship, and neither believes that a valid marriage exists, the people are "cohabitants." Another term sometimes used is "meretricious relationship."

In the past, unmarried cohabitants were considered morally quite offensive. Because of this, claims related to the relationship were considered barred, pursuant to the doctrine of illegality. So, even if a couple executed a written agreement regarding property rights, this agreement was considered unenforceable. *See* Oldham & Caudill, *A Reconnaissance of Public Policy Restrictions upon Enforcement of Contracts Between Cohabitants,* 18 Fam. L. Q. 93 (1984). In Texas, however, equitable remedies were sometimes permitted. *See Cluck v. Sheets,* 141 Tex. 219, 171 S.W.2d 860 (1943).

The illegality rule frequently left a dependant cohabitant in a precarious financial situation when the relationship ended. The "severability" exception evolved as a means to

---

4. *See Dyess v. Fagerberg,* No. 03-93-00148-CV (Tex. App.—Austin Sept. 28, 1994, no writ) (not designated for publication); *McLain v. Gilliam,* 389 S.W.2d 131 (Tex. Civ. App.—Eastland 1965, writ ref'd n.r.e.); *Shaw v. Christie,* 160 S.W.2d 989 (Tex. Civ. App.—Beaumont 1942, no writ).

enforce some types of agreements between cohabitants. Under the traditional severability exception, the illegality doctrine only barred enforcement of a contract between cohabitants if the contract was directly related to the immoral relationship. So, if the cohabitants made an agreement about something not directly related to their relationship, such as an investment or a business venture, that contract could be severed from their immoral relationship and enforced. *See McCall v. Frampton*, 438 N.Y.S.2d 11 (N.Y. App. Div. 1981).

Although the severability exception was helpful in some cases, in most instances the cohabitants did not make agreements regarding matters that were severable from the relationship. So, as long as the illegality rule was enforced, dependent cohabitants suffered great financial hardship when the relationship ended.

Marvin v. Marvin
Supreme Court of California, 1976
18 Cal. 3d 660

TOBRINER, Justice.

Plaintiff [Michele Triola] avers that in October of 1964 she and defendant [Lee Marvin] "entered into an oral agreement" that while "the parties lived together they would combine their efforts and earnings and would share equally any and all property accumulated as a result of their efforts whether individual or combined." Furthermore, they agreed to "hold themselves out to the general public as husband and wife" and that "plaintiff would further render her services as a companion, homemaker, housekeeper and cook to defendant."

Shortly thereafter plaintiff agreed to "give up her lucrative career as an entertainer [and] singer" in order to "devote her full time to defendant as a companion, homemaker and cook"; in return defendant agreed to "provide for all of plaintiff's financial support and needs for the rest of her life."

Plaintiff alleges that she lived with defendant from October of 1964 through May of 1970 and fulfilled her obligations under the agreement. During this period the parties as a result of their efforts and earnings acquired in defendant's name substantial real and personal property, including motion picture rights worth over $1 million. In May of 1970, however, defendant compelled plaintiff to leave his household. He continued to support plaintiff until November of 1971, but thereafter refused to provide further support.

On the basis of these allegations plaintiff asserts two causes of action. The first, for declaratory relief, asks the court to determine her contract and property rights; the second seeks to impose a constructive trust upon one half of the property acquired during the course of the relationship.

After hearing argument the court granted defendant's motion [for judgment on the pleadings] and entered judgment for defendant. Plaintiff moved to set aside the judgment and asked leave to amend her complaint to allege that she and defendant reaffirmed their agreement after defendant's divorce was final. The trial court denied plaintiff's motion, and she appealed from the judgment.

In the case before us plaintiff, basing her cause of action in contract, maintains that the trial court erred in denying her a trial on the merits of her contention. Although the court did not specify the ground for its conclusion that plaintiff's contractual allegations stated no cause of action, defendant offers some four theories to sustain the ruling; we proceed to examine them.

Defendant first and principally relies on the contention that the alleged contract is so closely related to the supposed "immoral" character of the relationship between plaintiff and himself that the enforcement of the contract would violate public policy. He points to cases asserting that a contract between nonmarital partners is unenforceable if it is "involved in" an illicit relationship.

A review of the numerous California decisions concerning contracts between nonmarital partners, however, reveals that the courts have not employed such broad and uncertain standards to strike down contracts. The decisions instead disclose a narrower and more precise standard: a contract between nonmarital partners is unenforceable only to the extent that it explicitly rests upon the immoral and illicit consideration of meretricious sexual services.

Although the past decisions hover over the issue in the somewhat wispy form of the figures of a Chagall painting, we can abstract from those decisions a clear and simple rule. The fact that a man and woman lived together without marriage, and engaged in a sexual relationship, does not in itself invalidate agreements between them relating to their earnings, property, or expenses. Neither is such an agreement invalid merely because the parties may have contemplated the creation or continuation of a nonmarital relationship when they entered into it. Agreements between nonmarital partners fail only to the extent that they rest upon a consideration of meretricious sexual services. Thus the rule asserted by defendant, that a contract fails if it is "involved in" or made "in contemplation" of a nonmarital relationship, cannot be reconciled with the decisions.

The three cases cited by defendant which have declined to enforce contracts between nonmarital partners involved consideration that was expressly founded upon illicit sexual services. In *Hill v. Estate of Westbrook* [1950] 95 Cal. App. 2d 599, the woman promised to keep house for the man, to live with him as man and wife, and to bear his children; the man promised to provide for her in his will, but died without doing so. Reversing a judgment for the woman based on the reasonable value of her services, the Court of Appeal stated that "the action is predicated upon a claim which seeks, among other things, the reasonable value of living with decedent in a meretricious relationship and bearing him two children. The law does not award compensation for living with a man as a concubine and bearing him children. As the judgment is, at least in part, for the value of the claimed services for which recovery cannot be had, it must be reversed." Upon retrial, the trial court found that it should not sever the contract and place an independent value upon the legitimate services performed by claimant. We therefore affirmed a judgment for the estate. [*Hill v. Estate of Westbrook* (1952) 39 Cal. 2d 458].

In the only other cited decision refusing to enforce a contract, *Updeck v. Samuel* (1964), 123 Cal. App. 2d 264, the contract "was based on the consideration that the parties live together as husband and wife." Viewing the contract as calling for adultery, the court held it illegal.

The decisions in the *Hill* and *Updeck* cases thus demonstrate that a contract between nonmarital partners, even if expressly made in contemplation of a common living arrangement, is invalid only if sexual acts form an inseparable part of the consideration for the agreement. In sum, a court will not enforce a contract for the pooling of property and earnings if it is explicitly and inseparably based upon services as a paramour. The Court of Appeal opinion in *Hill*, however, indicates that even if sexual services are part of the contractual consideration, any severable portion of the contract supported by independent consideration will still be enforced.

[Defendant's proposed] standard which inquires whether an agreement is "involved" in or "contemplates" a nonmarital relationship is vague and unworkable. Virtually all agreements between nonmarital partners can be said to be "involved" in some sense in the fact of their mutual sexual relationship, or to "contemplate" the existence of that relationship. Thus defendant's proposed standards, if taken literally, might invalidate all agreements between nonmarital partners, a result no one favors. Moreover, those standards offer no basis to distinguish between valid and invalid agreements. By looking not to such uncertain tests, but only to the consideration underlying the agreement, we provide the parties and the courts with a practical guide to determine when an agreement between nonmarital partners should be enforced.

[W]e base our opinion on the principle that adults who voluntarily live together and engage in sexual relations are nonetheless as competent as any other persons to contract respecting their earnings and property rights. Of course, they cannot lawfully contract to pay for the performance of sexual services, for such a contract is, in essence, an agreement for prostitution and unlawful for that reason. But they may agree to pool their earnings and to hold all property acquired during the relationship in accord with the law governing community property; conversely they may agree that each partner's earnings and the property acquired from those earnings remains the separate property of the earning partner. So long as the agreement does not rest upon illicit meretricious consideration, the parties may order their economic affairs as they choose, and no policy precludes the courts from enforcing such agreements.

In the present instance, plaintiff alleges that the parties agreed to pool their earnings, that they contracted to share equally in all property acquired, and that defendant agreed to support plaintiff. The terms of the contract as alleged do not rest upon any unlawful consideration. We therefore conclude that the complaint furnishes a suitable basis upon which the trial court can render declaratory relief. The trial court consequently erred in granting defendant's motion for judgment on the pleadings.

As we have noted, both causes of action in plaintiff's complaint allege an express contract; neither assert any basis for relief independent from the contract. *In re Marriage of Cary*, [1973], 34 Cal. App. 3d 345, however, the Court of Appeals held that, in view of the policy of the Family Law Act, property accumulated by nonmarital partners in an actual family relationship should be divided equally. Upon examining the *Cary* opinion, the parties to the present case realized that plaintiff's alleged relationship with defendant might arguably support a cause of action independent of any express contract between the parties. The parties have therefore briefed and discussed the issue of the property rights of a nonmarital partner in the absence of an express contract. Although our conclusion that plaintiff's complaint states a cause of action based on an express contract alone compels us to reverse the judgment for defendant, resolution of the *Cary* issue will serve both to guide the parties upon retrial and to resolve a conflict presently manifest in published Court of Appeals decisions. If *Cary* is interpreted as holding that the Family Law Act requires an equal division of property accumulated in nonmarital "actual family relationships," then we conclude that *Cary* distends the act. No language in the Family Law Act addresses the property rights of nonmarital partners, and nothing in the legislative history of the act suggests that the Legislature considered that subject. The delineation of the rights of nonmarital partners before 1970 had been fixed entirely by judicial decision; we see no reason to believe that the Legislature, by enacting the Family Law Act, intended to change that state of affairs. But, although parties to a nonmarital relationship obviously cannot have based any expectations upon the belief that they were married, other expectations and equitable considerations remain. The parties may well expect that property will be divided in accord with the parties' own tacit understanding and that in the absence of such understanding the courts will fairly apportion property accumulated through mutual effort. We need not treat nonmarital partners as putatively married persons in order to apply principles of implied contract, or extend equitable remedies; we need to treat them only as we do any other unmarried persons.

The remaining arguments advanced from time to time to deny remedies to the nonmarital partners are of less moment. There is no more reason to presume that services are contributed as a gift than to presume that funds are contributed as a gift; in any event the better approach is to presume, as Justice Peters suggested, "that the parties intend to deal fairly with each other." (*Keene v. Keene* [1962] 57 Cal. 2d 657, 674).

The argument that granting remedies to the nonmarital partners would discourage marriage must fail; as *Cary* pointed out, "with equal or greater force the point might be made that the pre-1970 rule was calculated to cause the income producing partner to avoid marriage and thus retain the benefit of all of his or her accumulated earnings." (34 Cal. App. 3d at p. 353).

In summary, we believe that the prevalence of nonmarital relationships in modern society and the social acceptance of them, marks this as a time when our courts should by no means apply the doctrine of the unlawfulness of the so-called meretricious relationship to the instant case. As we have explained, the nonenforceability of agreements expressly providing for meretricious conduct rested upon the fact that such conduct, as the word suggests, pertained to and encompassed prostitution. To equate the nonmarital relationship of today to such a subject matter is to do violence to an accepted and wholly different practice. We are aware that many young couples live together without the solemnization of marriage, in order to make sure that they can successfully later undertake marriage. This trial period, preliminary to marriage, serves as some assurance that the marriage will not subsequently end in dissolution to the harm of both parties. We are aware, as we have stated, of the pervasiveness of nonmarital relationships in other situations.

The mores of the society have indeed changed so radically in regard to cohabitation that we cannot impose a standard based on alleged moral considerations that have apparently been so widely abandoned by so many. We conclude that the judicial barriers that may stand in the way of a policy based upon the fulfillment of the reasonable expectations of the parties to a nonmarital relationship should be removed. As we have explained, the courts now hold that express agreements will be enforced unless they rest on an unlawful meretricious consideration. We add that in the absence of an express agreement, the courts may look to a variety of other remedies in order to protect the parties' lawful expectations.

The courts may inquire into the conduct of the parties to determine whether that conduct demonstrates an implied contract or implied agreement of partnership or joint venture or some other tacit understanding between the parties. The courts may, when appropriate, employ principles of constructive trust or resulting trust (see *Hyman v. Hyman*, Tex. Civ. App., 1954, 275 S.W.2d 149). Finally, a nonmarital partner may recover in *quantum meruit* for the reasonable value of household services rendered less the reasonable value of support received if he can show that he rendered services with the expectation of monetary reward. (See *Hill v. Estate of Westbrook, supra*, 39 Cal. 2d 458, 462).[5]

---

5. Our opinion does not preclude the evolution of additional equitable remedies to protect the expectations of the parties to a nonmarital relationship in cases in which existing remedies prove inadequate; the suitability of such remedies may be determined in later cases in light of the factual setting in which they arise.

Since we have determined that plaintiff's complaint states a cause of action for breach of an express contract, and, as we have explained, can be amended to state a cause of action independent of allegations of express contract,[6] we must conclude that the trial court erred in granting defendant a judgment on the pleadings.

The judgment is reversed and the cause remanded for further proceedings consistent with the views expressed herein.

CLARK, Justice. (concurring and dissenting)

Conceivably, under the majority opinion a party may recover half of the property acquired during the relationship on the basis of general equitable principles, recover a bonus based on specific equitable considerations, and recover a second bonus in *quantum meruit*. The general sweep of the majority opinion raises but fails to answer several questions. First, because the Legislature specifically excluded some parties to a meretricious relationship from the equal division rule of Civil Code Section 4452, is this court now free to create an equal division rule? Second, upon termination of the relationship, is it equitable to impose the economic obligations of lawful spouses on meretricious parties when the latter may have rejected matrimony to avoid such obligations? Third, does not application of equitable principles—necessitating examination of the conduct of the parties—violate the spirit of the Family Law Act of 1969, designed to eliminate the bitterness and acrimony resulting from the former fault system in divorce? Fourth, will not application of equitable principles reimpose upon trial courts the unmanageable burden of arbitrating domestic disputes? Fifth, will not a *quantum meruit* system of compensation for services—discounted by benefits received—place meretricious spouses in a better position than lawful spouses? Sixth, if a *quantum meruit* system is to be allowed, does fairness not require inclusion of all services and all benefits regardless of how difficult the evaluation?

When the parties to a meretricious relationship show by express or implied in fact agreement they intend to create mutual obligations, the courts should enforce the agreement. However, in the absence of agreement, we should stop and consider the ramifications before creating economic obligations which may violate legislative intent, contravene the intention of the parties, and surely generate undue burdens on our trial courts.

DISCUSSION

Marvin approves *quantum meruit* recovery for cohabitants. A basic element of such a recovery is an expectation of compensation when the services were rendered. Is this true in a cohabitation situation? In making such a determination, should it matter whether the services were rendered in the home or at an outside business? See *Kitchen v. Frusher*, 181 S.W.3d 467 (Tex. App.—Fort Worth 2005, no pet.).

What is the holding of the California Supreme Court in *Marvin*? Is the illegality rule abolished?

If the illegality rule does not apply, a court can now award a recovery in California if the parties' conduct demonstrates an implied contract or implied agreement of partnership, or some other tacit understanding of the parties. What evidence will be relevant to

---

6. We do not pass upon the question whether, in the absence of an express or implied contractual obligation, a party to a nonmarital relationship is entitled to support payments from the other party after the relationship terminates.

such a determination? Is this a useful standard? Should there be a presumption that the parties have an agreement to share?

Are Justice Clark's concerns warranted?

On remand, the trial judge rendered a verdict in favor of Michelle Triola Marvin for $104,000. This judgment was appealed.

Marvin v. Marvin

California Court of Appeals, 1981
176 Cal. Rptr. 555

COBEY, Associate Justice.

Defendant, Lee Marvin, appeals from that portion of a judgment ordering him to pay to plaintiff, Michelle Marvin, the sum of $104,000, to be used by her primarily for her economic rehabilitation.

Defendant contends, among other things, that the challenged award is outside the issues of the case as framed by the pleadings of the parties and furthermore lacks any basis in equity or in law. We agree and will therefore modify the judgment by deleting therefrom the challenged award.

FACTS

This statement of facts is taken wholly from the findings of the trial court, which tried the case without a jury. The parties met in June 1964 and started living together occasionally in October of that year. They lived together almost continuously (except for business absences of his) from the spring of 1965 to May or June of 1970, when their cohabitation was ended at his insistence. This cohabitation was the result of an initial agreement between them to live together as unmarried persons so long as they both enjoyed their mutual companionship and affection.

More specifically, the parties to this lawsuit never agreed during their cohabitation that they would combine their efforts and earnings or would share equally in any property accumulated as a result of their efforts, whether individual or combined. They also never agreed during this period that plaintiff would relinquish her professional career as an entertainer and singer in order to devote her efforts full time to defendant as his companion and homemaker generally. Defendant did not agree during this period of cohabitation that he would provide all of plaintiff's financial needs and support for the rest of her life.

Furthermore, the trial court specifically found that: (1) defendant has never had any obligation to pay plaintiff a reasonable sum as and for her maintenance; (2) plaintiff suffered no damage resulting from her relationship with defendant, including its termination and thus defendant did not become monetarily liable to plaintiff at all; (3) plaintiff actually benefited economically and socially from the cohabitation of the parties, including payment by defendant for goods and services for plaintiff's sole benefit in the approximate amount of $72,900.00, payment by defendant of the living expenses of the two of them of approximately $221,400.00, and other substantial specified gifts;[7] (4) a confidential and fiduciary relationship never existed between the parties with respect to

---

7. The trial court also found that "defendant made a substantial financial effort to launch plaintiff's career as a recording singer and to continue her career as a nightclub singer."

property; (5) defendant was never unjustly enriched as a result of the relationship of the parties or of the services performed by plaintiff for him or for them; (6) defendant never acquired any property or money from plaintiff by any wrongful act.

The trial court specifically found in support of its challenged rehabilitation award that the market value of defendant's property at the time the parties separated exceeded $1 million, that plaintiff at the time of the trial of this case had been recently receiving unemployment insurance benefits, that it was doubtful that plaintiff could return to the career that she had enjoyed before the relationship of the parties commenced, namely, that of singer, that plaintiff was in need of rehabilitation—*i.e.*, to learn new employable skills, that she should be able to accomplish such rehabilitation in two years and that the sum of $104,000 was not only necessary primarily for such rehabilitation, but also for her living expenses (including her debts) during this period of rehabilitation, and that defendant had the ability to pay this sum forthwith.

Moreover, the trial court concluded as a matter of law that inasmuch as defendant had terminated the relationship of the parties and plaintiff had no visible means of support, "in equity," she had a right to assistance by defendant until she could become self-supporting. The trial court explained that it fixed the award at the highest salary that the plaintiff had ever earned, namely, $1,000 a week for two years, although plaintiff's salary had been at that level for only two weeks and she ordinarily had earned less than one-half that amount weekly.

DISCUSSION

The trial court apparently based its rehabilitative award upon two footnotes in the opinion of our Supreme Court in this case. (*Marvin v. Marvin* (1976) 18 Cal. 3d 660, 134 Cal. Rptr. 815, 557 P.2d 106). These are footnotes 25 and 26, which respectively read as follows:

> Our opinion does not preclude the evolution of additional equitable remedies to protect the expectations of the parties to a nonmarital relationship in cases in which existing remedies prove inadequate; the suitability of such remedies may be determined in later cases in light of the factual setting in which they arise.

> We do not pass upon the question whether, in the absence of an express or implied contractual obligation, a party to a nonmarital relationship is entitled to support payments from the other party after the relationship terminates.

Id. at 684–85, 134 Cal. Rptr. 815, 557 P.2d 106.

There is no doubt that Footnote 26 opens the door to a support award in appropriate circumstances. Likewise, under Footnote 25, equitable remedies should be devised "to protect the expectations of the parties to a nonmarital relationship." The difficulty in applying either of these footnotes in the manner in which the trial court has done in this case is that, as already pointed out, the challenged limited rehabilitative award of the trial court is not within the issues of the case as framed by the pleadings, and there is nothing in the trial court's findings to suggest that such an award is warranted to protect the expectations of both parties.

Quite to the contrary, as already noted, the trial court expressly found that plaintiff benefited economically and socially from her relationship with defendant and suffered no damage therefrom, even with respect to its termination. Furthermore, the trial court also expressly found that defendant never had any obligation to pay plaintiff a reasonable sum as and for her maintenance and that defendant had not been unjustly enriched by reason of the relationship or its termination and that defendant had never acquired anything of value from plaintiff by any wrongful act.

Furthermore, the special findings in support of the challenged rehabilitative award merely established plaintiff's need therefor and defendant's ability to respond to that need. This is not enough. The award, being nonconsensual in nature, must be supported by some recognized underlying obligation in law or in equity. A court of equity admittedly has broad powers, but it may not create totally new substantive rights under the guise of doing equity.

The trial court in its special conclusions of law addressed to this point attempted to state an underlying obligation by saying that plaintiff had a right to assistance from defendant until she became self-supporting. But this special conclusion obviously conflicts with the earlier, more general, finding of the court that defendant has never had and did not then have any obligation to provide plaintiff with a reasonable sum for her support and maintenance and, in view of the already-mentioned findings of no damage (but benefit instead), no unjust enrichment and no wrongful act on the part of defendant with respect to either the relationship or its termination, it is clear that no basis whatsoever, either in equity or in law, exists for the challenged rehabilitative award. It therefore must be deleted from the judgment.

DISPOSITION

The judgment under appeal is modified by deleting therefrom the portion thereof under appeal, namely, the rehabilitative award of $104,000 to plaintiff, Michelle Marvin. As modified it is affirmed. Costs on appeal are awarded to defendant, Lee Marvin.

---

2. The Implied Contract to Share

The *Marvin* trial court found that the cohabitants did not have an implied contract to share property accumulated during the relationship. How would a court make this determination?

In the following case, the court found that the couple had entered into an implied contract to share. Why? Did the relationship or the behavior of the parties differ from that involved in *Marvin*?

How is an implied contract to share different from common-law marriage?

Alderson v. Alderson
California Court of Appeals, 1986
225 Cal. Rptr. 610

MERRILL, Justice.

In the instant case, the trial court ruled in favor of Jonne and held that she was entitled to an undivided half interest in the parties' properties. In so ruling, the court impliedly found that the parties' conduct over the twelve-year period they were together, evidenced an implied contract between them to share equally any and all property acquired during the course of their relationship, as alleged in the complaint. The court also impliedly found this contract to be legal and enforceable under *Marvin* and not resting on "a consideration of meretricious sexual services." Our review of these findings, nec-essarily begins and ends with the question of whether or not they are supported by sub-stantial evidence. After fully examining the record before us, we have determined that they are.

Evidence that the parties impliedly agreed to share equally in their acquisitions in-cludes the following: Jonne's testimony to this effect; the fact that the parties held them-selves out socially, as well as otherwise, as husband and wife; the fact that Jonne and the couple's three children, in fact, took Steve's surname; the fact that the pair pooled their financial resources and then drew upon the same to purchase the subject properties; the fact that the decision to purchase said properties was, in most cases, made jointly; the fact of Jonne's participation in the properties other than financial (she kept the books on the properties, helped repair and fix up the properties, paid the bills and collected the rents); and finally, the fact that title to ten of the properties was taken by Jonne and Steve jointly and in the case of seven of these purchases, was taken as husband and wife.

Evidence that consideration for the implied agreement between the parties did not rest on meretricious sexual services includes the absence of any evidence to the contrary and Jonne's own testimony.[8] Said testimony establishes that the implied agreement between

---

8. [Defense Counsel]:

Q. Mrs. Alderson, in your complaint, you described that you had a contract with Mr. Alder-son by which you would share the ownership of all of the property you acquired during the time you lived together, is that a fair statement of what you are saying in the case?
A. Yes.
Q. According to the terms of your contract you were going to do something for the prop-erty you were to acquire, is that correct?
A. I was going to do something?
Q. Yes. You each were going to do things for each other, is that correct?
A. You mean both to work and—
Q. Yes.
A. Uh huh.
Q. For instance, you were going to cook for you and Mr. Alderson, is that right?
A. I was. I was his wife. I mean, whatever a wife does.
Q. Okay. Well, let me list the things that a wife does and ask you if that's what you under-stood you were going to do as part of this contract, all right. Did you understand that as part of your contract you were going to cook?
A. I—as far as a contract, written, saying I did this and he did this, we just were living to-gether as we were married. We did anything that any other married couple did and we pooled together resources, we saved money, we didn't buy things so we had money to buy houses.
Q. Let me ask this: Was it your understanding that you were going to stay home and cook for the time that you lived together as long as you didn't work, and Mr. Alderson was going to go out and earn the money?
A. There was no such understanding. If I had a job, I worked and we—it was our money. If I didn't have a job, I had children to take care of.
Q. Let me explain what I am driving at. In every contract the parties have some under-standing as to what each are going to do. If I hire someone to paint my house, my under-standing is that he is going to paint the house and his understanding is that I pay him, say, a thousand dollars. And I am asking you whether you had an understanding that you were supposed to do certain things, or were expected to do certain things and if you don't do those things, then this would be an extreme disappointment by Mr. Alderson. That's what I am trying—driving at. If you had not cooked and refused to cook at all times, would your living arrangement have continued?
A. Yes. I mean it would—if I had a broken arm and couldn't cook, I wouldn't expect him to leave me.
Q. Would you expect him to give you half of everything?

Jonne and Steve was very general and nonspecific. The parties never bothered to actually spell out the terms of their agreement or the consideration therefor. Jonne testified that her part of the consideration was to be Steve's wife and to do "whatever a wife does." However, she also said, "if you took one specific thing away, there [were] so many other things that we both did, one wouldn't make any difference, or two or three."

Such an agreement can hardly be deemed the type disapproved in *Marvin*. A contract based on "many things," no one of which is in itself crucial, is not the same as one based upon a consideration of meretricious sexual services. Before a nonmarital contract is to be deemed unenforceable under *Marvin*, it must be found to explicitly rest upon a consideration of meretricious sexual services and even then the contract will fail "only to the extent" that it does so. Here, there is no evidence that the agreement between Jonne and Steve, or any part thereof, explicitly rests upon such a consideration.

Nor does the fact that the couple engaged in sexual relations and that Jonne perceived this as part of her "role" alter this conclusion. As the *Marvin* court pointed out, the fact that a man and woman live together without marriage, and engage in a sexual relationship, does not in itself invalidate agreements between them relating to their earnings, property or expenses. (*Marvin v. Marvin, supra*, 18 Cal. 3d at pp. 670–671, 134 Cal. Rptr. 815, 557 P.2d 106). In today's society when so many couples are living together without the benefit of marriage vows, it would be illogical to deny them the ability to enter into enforceable agreements in respect to their property rights.

Appellant's reliance on *Jones v. Daly* (1981) 122 Cal. App. 3d 500, 176 Cal. Rptr. 130, is misplaced. In *Jones*, the surviving partner to a "cohabitors agreement" between two males filed an action for declaratory relief against the executor of the deceased partner's estate. According to the complaint, the agreement had been made orally and had provided that the partners would live and cohabit together and would combine their efforts and earnings and share equally all property accumulated as the result of their efforts. Part of plaintiff's consideration for the agreement, was that he would "render his services as a lover, companion, homemaker, traveling companion, housekeeper and cook." (*Id.* at p. 505, 176 Cal. Rptr. 130.)

A. Yes, there were many things, if you took one specific thing away, there was so many other things that we both did, one wouldn't make any difference, or two or three.
Q. All right. You told me that you had a contract with Mr. Alderson, is that correct, or did you have a contract?
A. I don't know what you mean by contract, an agreement written on paper?
Q. No.
A. Verbal contract?
Q. Yes.
A. We were living together. We were living—I mean, we were married and anything any other married couples do, we were just the same. We had higher expectations than some because we wanted property; we wanted investments; we wanted things for the future for the kids.
Q. Let me ask this: As far as your understanding went you were going to be getting half of everything Mr. Alderson earned, is that correct?
A. It was ours. There was no—I mean, if I left the house there was no talk of my leaving as far as me getting half and him getting half, was both of ours. If something happened to him it was all mine, if something happened to me, it was all his....
Q. Let me ask about the—about the role of a wife. As you performed your duty in the house, did that include being the cook for the family, the housekeeper, the companion of Mr. Alderson, the lover of Mr. Alderson and mother of the children?
A. Yes.
Q. Were all of those essential parts of being a wife, as you understood them?
A. Yes.

The trial court sustained a demurrer without leave to amend and dismissed the case. The Court of Appeal affirmed. Relying on *Marvin*, the appellate court held that a contract for the pooling of property and earnings is unenforceable if it is explicitly and inseparably based on services as a paramour, and in this case the complaint showed the surviving partner's rendition of sexual services was an inseparable part of the consideration for the cohabitation agreement.

The instant case is readily distinguishable from *Jones*. As indicated ... (in footnote 1), nowhere in Jonne's complaint or in the testimony adduced at trial, was there evidence that the implied contract between the parties, either in its entirety or in part, explicitly rested upon a consideration of meretricious sexual services.

————————

3. Other Views

Not all courts have accepted the *Marvin* approach to disputes between cohabitants. For example, the New York Court of Appeals has approved an action between cohabitants regarding an express contract, but has not approved recovery based upon an implied contract or the additional equitable remedies sanctioned by the California Supreme Court. *See Morone v. Morone*, 413 N.E.2d 1154 (N.Y. 1980).

Washington has adopted a very different approach, giving parties to stable, unmarried cohabitant relationships shared property regardless of the existence of any agreement. *See Connell v. Francisco*, 898 P.2d 831 (Wash. 1995).

A new Texas statute provides that a promise or an agreement "on consideration of nonmarital conjugal cohabitation" is not enforceable unless it is written. *See* Tex. Fam. Code § 1.108. What are the advantages and disadvantages of such a policy? What effect will this statute have on cohabitant disputes in Texas? Does this mean that no claim can now be made by a cohabitant in Texas if there is no written agreement? *See Comment*, 25 Hous. L. Rev. 979 (1988). *Zaremba v. Cliburn*, 949 S.W.2d 822 (Tex. App. — Fort Worth 1997, writ denied) held all claims are barred if there is no written agreement.

In a more recent case, *Smith v. Deneve*, 285 S.W.3d 904 (Tex. App. — Dallas 2009, no pet.) the court outlines the elements of various grounds for recovery in disputes between unmarried partners, and does not suggest that all such claims would be barred if there is no written agreement. In *Sahagun v. Ibarra*, 90 S.W.3d 860 (Tex. App. — San Antonio 2002, no pet.) the court granted a resulting trust remedy.

O'Farrill Avila v. González
Texas Court of Appeals — San Antonio, 1998
974 S.W.2d 237, pet. denied

HARDBERGER, Chief Justice.

INTRODUCTION

... This is an appeal from a breach of contract case. The trial judge found that appellant, Jos Antonio O'Farrill Avila (O'Farrill), had breached two contracts with appellee,

Louisa González-Chacon (González). The court awarded González $200,000 on the contract claims, plus attorneys' fees and fees for appeal to this court and to the supreme court. We affirm the judgment as modified.

FACTS

This lawsuit arises from a three-year domestic relationship between the parties, a relationship that has produced a daughter, a corporation, and a tangle of litigation, including a paternity suit, tort claims, contract claims, alter ego claims, and child support claims. Many of the issues have been resolved; some are still pending.

In the case before us, the trial judge was asked to consider the validity and effect of two agreements between the parties: a promise, written and signed by O'Farrill on July 5, 1994, to pay González $5,000 per month, and an agreement between the two regarding the purchase of the home they shared in San Antonio. The trial court determined that both agreements reflected enforceable contracts.

The July 5 document, written and signed by O'Farrill in Mexico City, is a bare promise to make monthly payments to González. The document makes no mention of duration of these payments or of any return promise made by González. The trial court allowed extrinsic evidence on both issues. González testified that, in exchange for the money, she had promised to live with the child in San Antonio and to remain home with her rather than seek employment. As for the duration of the agreement, González admitted that the agreement was silent on the matter, but she testified that her understanding was that O'Farrill did not want his child raised by strangers, and the money therefore was a guarantee that González would remain with the child throughout the formative years, until the child was settled in school. O'Farrill did not appear at trial to controvert this testimony.

The second agreement between the parties was to purchase a home in San Antonio. According to González, she agreed to contribute $60,000 up front for the home, and O'Farrill agreed to make monthly payments on the remaining debt. As proof of this agreement, González offered her own testimony and the loan documents for the home. These papers reflected only the agreement between the purchasers and the loan company. González testified that she performed her part of the agreement fully, but that O'-Farrill ceased making mortgage payments after less than two years, when González initiated legal action against him. The bank holding the mortgage on the home has foreclosed on the property. Again, O'Farrill was not present at trial to present controverting testimony.

In [three] points of error, O'Farrill appeals the judgment against him, claiming that (1) there is legally or factually insufficient evidence to support the existence of the two contracts; (2) there is legally or factually insufficient evidence to support the finding that O'-Farrill breached the agreements; (3) the trial court erred in admitting parol evidence to prove the contracts and their terms ...

POINT ... OF ERROR ... : THE CONTRACT CLAIMS

O'Farrill's first ... [point] of error address the existence and breach of the agreements between the parties. Points of error one and two allege that the evidence is legally or factually insufficient to support a finding that the contracts existed or that they were breached. Point ... of error three ... address[es] the admission of parol evidence to show consideration for and the duration of O'Farrill's promise to pay González $5,000 per month....

Consideration

O'Farrill claims that the promise to pay González $5,000 per month cannot be enforced because it has not been proven as a contract. A contract, O'Farrill correctly asserts, must be supported by consideration, and this agreement recites no consideration. González testified at trial that she gave consideration for O'Farrill's promise: her promise to remain in San Antonio and to stay at home with the couple's daughter. González's testimony, coupled with the fact that she did remain in San Antonio with the child, provides some evidence to support this claim. O'Farrill did not offer any contrary evidence. We do not find González's evidence so weak as to render the result wrong or manifestly unjust result.

O'Farrill counters that this evidence is legally insufficient, because González is barred by the parol evidence rule from introducing extrinsic evidence regarding consideration.

When parties have entered a valid agreement that embodies all the terms of that agreement, parol evidence may not be used to show inconsistent prior or contemporaneous agreements. (citation omitted) This rule does not preclude enforcement of prior or contemporaneous agreements that are not inconsistent with or do not vary or contradict the express or implied terms of the agreement. (citation omitted)

The document presented to the trial court is, on its face, no more than a unilateral promise to pay, which is not an enforceable contract. (citation omitted) González argues that extrinsic evidence is allowed to prove that mutual promises were exchanged. We agree. "The rule is that it may in fact be shown [with extrinsic evidence] that consideration exists even if the consideration takes the form of a promise." CALAMARI & PERILLO, CONTRACTS § 3-7(f) (3rd ed.1987). The rationale for this rule is that, without consideration on both sides, the agreement is at best a partial integration, and a showing of consideration would not contradict any of its terms. *Id.*

Even if the promises were not mutual at the time of contracting, the parties' performance on the agreement renders the contracts enforceable. The Texas Supreme Court stated in *Hutchings v. Slemons,* 141 Tex. 448, 174 S.W.2d 487 (1943):

> Though a contract be void for lack of mutuality at the time it is made, and while it remains wholly executory, yet, when there has been even a part performance by the party seeking to enforce the same, and in such part performance such party has rendered services or incurred expense contemplated by the parties at the time such contract was made, which confers even a remote benefit on the other party thereto, such benefit will constitute an equitable consideration, and render the entire contract valid and enforceable.

Hutchings, 174 S.W.2d at 489.

O'Farrill next argues that González's promise is illusory, because she can remain in the United States only at the mercy of the U.S. government. An illusory promise is a promise that fails to bind the promisor, who retains the option of discontinuing performance. (citation omitted) González's promise to O'Farrill does not fall within this definition. While it may be true that the United States government might deport González, this is not relevant to *her* duties under the alleged agreement. She is bound to perform unless performance is rendered impossible.

González's promise to O'Farrill was twofold: she promised to remain in the States *and* she promised to forego pursuing her career to stay home with the couple's daughter. Even if the first promise were illusory, the second is not. She has, so far, performed her part of the agreement, arguably to her detriment.

Duration

O'Farrill argues that the agreement between himself and González is too uncertain to be enforceable. Specifically, O'Farrill complains that the agreement itself contains no specific term of duration for the monthly payments and that González's testimony on this issue was inconsistent: her pleadings suggested that the payments were to be for life; at trial she claimed they were to be for ten or fifteen years, or until the child was not so dependent on a parent being at home. O'Farrill asserts that a contract cannot be enforced when one of the parties is unclear on its duration.

The law on certainty of contract terms is anything but certain. It is difficult to derive clear guidelines from the case law. Courts at least pay lip service to the notion that a contract must be reasonably certain to be enforceable. *See Bendalin v. Delgado*, 406 S.W.2d 897, 899 (Tex. 1966); *University Nat'l Bank v. Ernst & Whinney*, 773 S.W.2d 707, 710 (Tex. App.—San Antonio 1989, no writ). A fatal lack of definiteness may concern the time for performance, the price to be paid, the work to be done, the service to be rendered, or the property to be transferred. *University Nat'l Bank*, 773 S.W.2d at 710.

Courts have also been willing to supply missing terms when necessary to effectuate the purposes of the parties under the agreement. *Lake LBJ Mun. Utility Dist. v. Coulson*, 692 S.W.2d 897, 906 (Tex. App.—Austin 1985), *rev'd on other grounds*, 734 S.W.2d 649 (Tex. 1987). The absence of a duration term does not necessarily suggest that the parties did not enter into an enforceable agreement; such incomplete agreements are often enforced. *See id.* (courts "routinely" supply reasonable time for performance when duration term is omitted). When the duration of a contract is not expressly dictated by the agreement, courts will frequently presume that the parties intended the agreement to last for a reasonable time. *Marshall v. Marshall*, 735 S.W.2d 587, 592 (Tex. App.—Dallas 1987, writ ref'd n.r.e.). This is especially true in cases where the agreement contemplates that one party will make substantial expenditures or other investments in accordance with performance. *Clear Lake City Water Auth. v. Clear Lake Utilities Co.*, 549 S.W.2d 385, 391 (Tex. 1977).

The reasonableness of the implied duration term is determined by "the circumstances in evidence surrounding the situation of the parties and the subject matter under which the contract was executed." *Cheek v. Metzer*, 116 Tex. 356, 291 S.W. 860, 863 (Tex. Comm. App. 1927, opinion adopted). When assuming that the parties meant for a contract to last a reasonable time, courts rely upon what would be reasonable in light of the circumstances available to the parties at the time the contract was made. *Hall v. Hall*, 158 Tex. 95, 308 S.W.2d 12, 16 (1957).

Here, the trial court had sufficient evidence that an agreement had been made, especially in light of the parties' performance, full or partial, of that agreement. This agreement is sufficiently certain to be enforced, and the parties' duties are sufficiently detailed, as described by González's testimony. (footnote omitted) The question, then, is whether the trial judge had sufficient evidence on which to arrive at a reasonable duration of performance, or whether, as O'Farrill suggests, the contract was necessarily terminable at will.

We find that the trial court had evidence of the circumstances at the time this agreement was made. The couple had a baby. González testified that O'Farrill was concerned that the child have a full-time mother. González had a career, and staying home with the child would entail sacrificing that career, at least for awhile. González also testified that the concern about having a full-time mother would naturally lessen when the child entered school. We find that, based on this uncontroverted testimony, the trial court could have arrived at a reasonable duration term....

Statute of Frauds

O'Farrill next contends that both agreements fall within the Statute of Frauds because both, by necessity, could not be performed within one year.[9] TEX. BUS. & COM.CODE Ann. §26.01(b)(6) (Vernon 1987). O'Farrill's argument fails for several reasons.

Similarly, O'Farrill's argument that the contract falls within the statute because it is a promise by one person to answer for the debt of another, their corporation, is a misreading of the cited provision. *See id.* at §26.10(b)(2). This is not a surety agreement between the two; the oral agreement simply reflects the ex-partner's differing duties in their joint purchase of a home. There was sufficient evidence at trial that the Statute of Frauds did not apply or that an exception to the Statute applied. As González points out, partial performance removes the contract from the Statute of Frauds. *See Central Power & Light Co. v. Del Mar Conservation Dist.,* 594 S.W.2d 782, 790 (Tex. Civ. App.—San Antonio 1980, writ ref'd n.r.e.). When there is strong evidence of a contract and application of the Statute of Frauds would injure the person relying on the contract and allow the other party unearned benefit, partial performance will allow a remedy. *Carmack v. Beltway Dev. Co.,* 701 S.W.2d 37, 40 (Tex. App.—Dallas 1985, no writ). Further, where one party has fully performed under a contract, the Statute of Frauds may be unavailable to the other party if he knowingly accepts the benefits and partly performs. *Id.*

González testified that she had fully performed her end of the agreements. She put $60,000 of her own money down on the house. In addition, she remained in San Antonio and did not pursue her career, as agreed in the Mexico City agreement. O'Farrill partly performed on both agreements. First, he made the $5,000 monthly payments for several months. Second, according to González's uncontroverted testimony, O'Farrill paid the monthly mortgage on the Inwood home for almost two years, ceasing to make payments only when González filed suit against him....

We affirm the judgment as reformed. (concurrence and dissent omitted)

---

4. Cohabitants' Disputes and General Contract Doctrine

Many cohabitation cases to date have addressed whether it is possible for a cohabitant to advance a claim relating to the cohabitation. Most states now permit an action based upon an express contract. Even in those states, however, normal contract rules will apply. For example, an action must be brought within the applicable limitations period for a breach of contract. *See Estate of Fincher,* 119 Cal. App. 3d 343, 174 Cal. Rptr. 18 (1981).

Trimmer v. Van Bomel, 434 N.Y.S.2d 82 (N.Y. Sup. Ct. 1980) involved a claim by a male that his former cohabitant had promised, if he gave up his business and travelled with her, she would, among other things, pay all his costs and expenses for sumptuous living for the rest of his life. The court concluded that this did not establish an enforceable claim, since the terms of the alleged contract were too vague. Most courts agree with this

---

9. O'Farrill also claims the agreement to purchase the Inwood house must have been in writing because it was an agreement to purchase real estate. *See* TEX. BUS. & COM. CODE ANN. §26.01(b)(4) (Vernon 1987). Because the doctrine of partial performance applies to both agreements, we need not reach this issue. However, this provision of the Statute of Frauds applies to agreements to buy and sell land between owners and purchasers. The agreement before us was simply an agreement between two buyers as to how they would delegate the duties between them when they purchased a home.

analysis. See, e.g., *Friedman v. Friedman*, 24 Cal. Rptr.2d 892 (Cal. App. 1993). But see *Sopko v. Estate of Roccomonte*, 787 A.2d 198 (N.J. App. Div. 2001).

5. Conflicts of Law

We have seen that U.S. state rules regarding the rights of unmarried partners are not uniform. What should happen if an unmarried couple lives for a while in state #1, moves to state #2, and breaks up? For example, assume the partners made an oral agreement in California (state #1) and then moved to Texas (state #2). Is the agreement enforceable? See Reppy, *Choice of Law Problems Arising When Unmarried Cohabitants Change Domicile*, 55 S.M.U.L. Rev. 273 (2002).

6. Relevance of Partnership Doctrine

Harrington v. Harrington
Texas Court of Appeals—Houston [1st Dist.], 1987
742 S.W.2d 722, no writ

DUGGAN, Justice.

In this appeal from a divorce judgment, the appellant attacks the court-ordered division of certain real property that he claims as his separate property. The divorce decree recites: "The Court further finds that the property situated at 2639 Talbot, Houston, Harris County, Texas, was purchased for the mutual benefit, use and ownership of both parties and accordingly, it is ORDERED that BRIAN K. HARRINGTON and M. GAY FOWLER HARRINGTON be awarded and each party is hereby awarded as tenants in common an undivided one-half interest in said property...."

In two points of error, the appellant contends that the court abused its discretion in concluding that the parties owned the Talbot property as tenants in common, because (1) that finding unconstitutionally divested him of his separate property, resulting in an unjust division, and (2) there was no evidence to support a finding of oral partnership/joint venture, and the evidence establishes that the appellant owned the property as separate property for two years before the marriage.

The appellant asserts that he acquired the property two years before the marriage, that no common law marriage existed at that time, and that the credit application and title to the property were solely in his name. He argues that there is no evidence to support a finding by the trial judge that this was community property, and he has rebutted any presumption that the property was community property. Thus, he argues, the trial court unconstitutionally divested him of his separate property when it awarded a one-half interest of the Talbot property to the appellee as community property. He quotes the language of the trial judge at the end of the hearing, "The Court finds the Talbot Street property to be part of the community, and the parties will own it as tenants-in-common." The docket sheet shows a similar entry.

The appellee does not dispute the appellant's discussion of authorities that define the difference between separate and community property. But she asserts that these principles do not apply to this case, because the trial court did not, as the appellant contends, erroneously designate the Talbot property as community property and divide it as such.

Rather, the court found that the property was purchased by the parties as tenants in common, pursuant to an oral partnership. Thus, the court merely recognized that the parties owned the property as partners before their marriage, and upon divorce, the court correctly granted the appellant his undivided one-half interest as his separate property.

At the appellant's request, the trial court made findings of fact and conclusions of law. The court found that the parties began to live together in December 1971; that they were ceremonially married on December 18, 1977; and that they stopped living together as husband and wife on May 30, 1985. The court found that they lived in leased residences in their joint names from 1972 until the purchase of the Talbot Street residence; that in the spring of 1975, the parties agreed to look for a home to purchase in West University Place; that they looked for prospective homes together for a period of approximately three months; that both parties agreed on the choice of the home to purchase, i.e., the Talbot Street property; and that both parties attended the closing of the sale of the Talbot Street house. The court further found that at the time of purchase, the appellee had a bachelor's degree in journalism; that the appellant had a master of business degree in finance and had taken courses in business law; and that at that time of the purchase, the appellee was terminating her employment to attend law school full time.

The court further found that at the time of the purchase of the home, the parties agreed that title to the property would be taken in the appellant's name, at appellant's suggestion, for credit purposes and convenience only, but intended the residence to be owned, used, and enjoyed jointly. The parties expended labor and money in improvements to the home and planned to use the appellee's separate property funds to remodel the home. Finally, the court found that the reason for the marriage was to have children and that the appellee became pregnant immediately after the parties married.

The trial court concluded that the parties entered into an oral partnership/joint venture to own and occupy the home located on Talbot Street jointly; that they took title to the home in appellant's name for convenience and credit purposes only; and that the parties owned the home as tenants in common.

The judgment of the court and its findings of fact and conclusions of law do not characterize the Talbot Street property as community property. We thus disagree with the appellant's basic premise in point of error one that the court erroneously divided that property as community property, and improperly divested him of his separate property. Because of this holding, the appellant's argument and authorities are inapplicable to the present case, and we overrule point of error one.

In point of error two, the appellant contends that the court erred in concluding that the parties owned the Talbot Street home as tenants in common, because there is no evidence to support a finding of oral partnership/joint venture. The appellant contends that the record establishes as a matter of law that he owned the home as his separate property for three years before the marriage.

A partnership is generally defined as an association among two or more persons to carry on as co-owners a business for profit. *See, e.g.,* Tex. Rev. Civ. Stat. Ann. art. 6132b, sec. 6 (Vernon 1970). A joint venture is similar, but is generally limited to a single transaction. *C.C. Roddy, Inc. v. Carlisle,* 391 S.W.2d 765 (Tex. Civ. App.—Fort Worth 1965, writ ref'd n.r.e.). In determining whether a partnership exists between spouses or cohabitants in the purchase or ownership of property, the parties' intent is an important factor. *Negrini v. Plus Two Advertising, Inc.,* 695 S.W.2d 624, 631 (Tex. App.—Houston [1st Dist.] 1985, no writ); see also *Cluck v. Sheets,* 141 Tex. 219, 171 S.W.2d 860 (1943); *Small v. Harper,* 638 S.W.2d 24 (Tex. App.—Houston [1st Dist.] 1982, writ ref'd n.r.e.).

The appellee pled that an oral partnership existed in the parties' purchase and ownership of the property, entitling her to an undivided one-half interest in the property. After making the findings of fact described above, the trial judge also reached that conclusion and entered judgment for the appellee on this question. After reviewing the record, we find that there is some evidence of probative force to support the court's findings and conclusion.

There was testimony that the parties lived together for about three years in residences leased in both their names; that they eventually decided that they wanted to live in a house together and went house-hunting together; and that they found the house that they liked after about three months. The appellee testified that she had no legal background at the time the Talbot house was purchased, and that she did not then understand the nature of separate versus community property. She testified that the appellant told her that because she was earning so little money at the time, he would apply for the loan himself and put his name on it. She agreed and had no concern that he would ever assert that the property was his alone. She testified that they always referred to the property as "our home," and that the appellant never claimed the property was his alone before the separation. They both contributed to improving the house, including painting, wall papering, remodeling, and repairs. At no time did the appellant ever indicate to her that he intended her to have no ownership interest in the house. The appellee also testified that she spent much of her separate property income on the house and on living expenses for the children, and that although she and her husband had separate bank accounts, she did not carefully segregate out her separate property income until after the separation.

Viewing only the evidence that tends to support the verdict and drawing the inferences favorable to the verdict, we find that there is some evidence to support the trial court's findings and conclusion that the parties intended to purchase and own the Talbot Street property as partners. We thus find no abuse of discretion in the trial court's judgment that that property is owned by the parties as tenants in common, with each having an undivided one-half interest as separate property.

The judgment of the trial court is affirmed.

DISCUSSION

Has anything changed in Texas law since 1987 that might undermine this case as valid Texas authority?

7. Less Conventional Relationships

Most reported "cohabitation" cases have involved two heterosexual adults who cohabited and were unmarried during the relationship. Most cases suggest that the illegality rule no longer applies to claims arising from such relationships.

The scope of the new *Marvin* principles is somewhat unclear. In *Marvin*, Lee was married to another during the initial period of cohabitation, but the parties had separated and a divorce action had been filed. This presented no public policy concern, at least to the California Supreme Court. Do you agree? In addition, in *Marvin* evidence was introduced that the relationship between Lee and Michelle was not monogamous. Does this matter?

In *Marriage of Bauder*, 605 P.2d 1374 (Or. App. 1980), a male cohabited with a married couple and established some sort of sexual relationship with them. When the arrangement was dissolved, the male brought a *Marvin* action against the couple. The court assumed that *Marvin* applied. Is this clear? What is the rationale of the *Marvin* line of cases? Does *Marvin* apply to all cohabitants?

This issue has arisen in cases involving disputes between homosexual cohabitants.

Jones v. Daly

California Court of Appeals, 1981
122 Cal. App. 3d 500

LILLIE, Associate Justice.

Plaintiff appeals from judgment dismissing his action for declaratory and other relief entered after the trial court sustained defendants' demurrer to the complaint without leave to amend.

Defendants are the executors of the estate of James Daly, who died in July 1978. The complaint contains seven causes of action. The first cause of action (for declaratory relief) alleges: Plaintiff, Randal Jones, first met James Daly in December 1975. Between that time and March 1976, they "met on frequent occasions, dated, engaged in sexual activities and, in general, acted towards one another as two people do who have discovered a love, one for the other." In March 1976 plaintiff and Daly orally agreed that plaintiff would move into Daly's condominium with Daly, quit his job, go travelling with Daly and "cohabit with him [Daly] as if [they] were, in fact, married." They also entered into an oral agreement (referred to hereinafter, in the language of the complaint, as "cohabitors agreement") whereby each agreed: during the time "they lived and cohabited together," they would combine their efforts and earnings and would share equally any and all property accumulated as a result of their efforts, whether individual or combined, except that Daly would give plaintiff a monthly allowance for his personal use, and they "would hold themselves out to the public at large as cohabiting mates, and [plaintiff] would render his services as a lover, companion, homemaker, traveling companion, housekeeper and cook to Daly"; and "in order that [plaintiff] would be able to devote a substantial portion of his time to Daly's benefit as his lover, companion, homemaker, traveling companion, housekeeper and cook," plaintiff would abandon "a material portion" of his potential career as a model, and in return Daly would furnish financial support to plaintiff for the rest of his life. Pursuant to and in reliance on the "cohabitors agreement," plaintiff and Daly "cohabited and lived together continuously" from March 1976 until Daly's death, and plaintiff allowed himself to be known to the general public "as the lover and cohabitation mate of Daly." Plaintiff performed all of the terms and conditions required to be performed by him under the "cohabitors agreement." During the time that plaintiff and Daly "lived and cohabited together" they acquired as a result of their efforts and earnings, substantial real and personal property (hereinafter, in the language of the complaint, "cohabitors' equitable property"). Plaintiff does not know the exact nature and extent of such property, but he believes it has a value in excess of $2 million and will amend the complaint to reflect the true value when it is ascertained. Under the "cohabitors agreement," all of the "cohabitors' equitable property" was to be shared and divided equally between plaintiff and Daly. All of such property is in the possession of defendant executors and under their control. Plaintiff has demanded that defendants recognize his interest in the "cohabitors' equitable property," but defendants refuse to do so.

The fourth cause of action seeks half of the "cohabitors' equitable property" on the theory of a constructive trust. The fifth cause of action alleges an implied in fact agreement between plaintiff and Daly for the equal division of all assets standing in Daly's name. The sixth and seventh causes of action are common counts which seek $300,000 as the reasonable value of plaintiff's services to Daly.

Defendants demurred generally to all causes of action. The trial court sustained the demurrer to each cause of action without leave to amend "per moving points and authorities." One of the arguments advanced by defendants in support of their demurrer was that under *Marvin v. Marvin* (1976) 18 Cal. 3d 660, 134 Cal. Rptr. 815, 557 P.2d 106, the "cohabitors agreement" is unenforceable because the complaint shows on its face that plaintiff's rendition of sexual services to Daly was an express and inseparable part of the consideration for the agreement.

In determining whether the "cohabitors agreement" rests upon illicit meretricious consideration, we are guided by the following principles: "[A] contract between nonmarital partners, even if expressly made in contemplation of a common living arrangement, is invalid only if sexual acts form an inseparable part of the consideration for the agreement. In sum, a court will not enforce a contract for the pooling of property and earnings if it is explicitly and inseparably based upon services as a paramour." (*Marvin v. Marvin, supra*, 18 Cal. 3d 660, 672, 134 Cal. Rptr. 815, 557 P.2d 106). The complaint herein alleges: Following their initial meeting, plaintiff and Daly "dated, engaged in sexual activities and, in general, acted towards one another as two people do who have discovered a love, one for the other"; plaintiff orally agreed "to cohabit with [Daly] as if [they] were, in fact, married"; at the same time they entered into the "cohabitors agreement" whereby they agreed that during the time "they lived and cohabited together" they would hold themselves out to the public at large as "cohabiting mates" and plaintiff would render his services to Daly as "a lover, companion, homemaker, traveling companion, housekeeper and cook"; in order that plaintiff would be able to devote his time to Daly's benefit "as his lover, companion, homemaker, traveling companion, housekeeper and cook," he would abandon his career; plaintiff and Daly "cohabited and lived together" and pursuant to and in reliance on the "cohabitors agreement," plaintiff allowed himself to be known to the general public as the "lover and cohabitation mate" of Daly. These allegations clearly show that plaintiff's rendition of sexual services to Daly was an inseparable part of the consideration for the "cohabitors' agreement," and indeed was the predominant consideration.

Plaintiff argues that the complaint is not subject to the foregoing interpretation because the "accepted California concept of cohabitation is the mutual assumption of those marital rights, duties and obligations which are usually manifested by married people, including but not necessarily dependent upon sexual relations" [*Boyd v. Boyd* (1964) 228 Cal. App. 2d 374, 381, 39 Cal. Rptr. 400]; and while one meaning of the word "lover" is paramour, it also may mean a person in love or an affectionate or benevolent friend. [Webster's Third New Internat. Dict. (1966) p. 1340]. Pleadings must be reasonably interpreted; they must be read as a whole and each part must be given the meaning that it derives from the context wherein it appears. [*Speegle v. Board of Fire Underwriters* (1946) 29 Cal. 2d 34, 42, 172 P.2d 867; *National Automobile & Cas. Ins. Co. v. Payne* (1968) 261 Cal. App. 2d 403, 408, 67 Cal. Rptr. 784]. The complaint alleges that plaintiff and Daly engaged in sexual activities, agreed to cohabit and to hold themselves out to the public as cohabiting mates, and entered into the "cohabitors agreement" whereby plaintiff was to render services to Daly as a lover. Viewed in the context of the complaint as a whole, the words "cohabiting" and "lover" do not have the innocuous meanings which plaintiff ascribes to them. These terms can pertain only to plaintiff's rendition of sexual services to Daly.

Marvin states that "even if sexual services are part of the contractual consideration, any severable portion of the contract supported by independent consideration will still be enforced." That principle is inapplicable in the present case. There is no severable portion of the "cohabitors' agreement" supported by independent consideration. According to the allegations of the complaint, the agreement provided that the parties would share equally the earnings and property accumulated as a result of their efforts while they lived together and that Daly would support plaintiff for the rest of his life. Neither the property sharing nor the support provision of the agreement rests upon plaintiff's acting as Daly's traveling companion, housekeeper or cook as distinguished from acting as his lover. The latter service forms an inseparable part of the consideration for the agreement and renders it unenforceable in its entirety.

DISCUSSION

How is the plaintiff's claim in *Jones* barred by illegality, while the claims in *Marvin* and *Alderson* were not? What is the holding of *Jones*?

A case somewhat similar to *Jones* arose the next year in Texas.

Small v. Harper
Texas Court of Appeals — Houston [1st Dist.], 1982
638 S.W.2d 24, writ ref'd n.r.e.

DYESS, Justice.

This is an appeal from a summary judgment. The appellant, Jo Ann Small, brought this suit against Aldean Harper, to recover her claimed portions of lands and other property acquired over a period of at least 12, and possibly 15 years. The main theory of recovery is an alleged breach of an oral partnership, whereby the appellant claims that she and the appellee agreed to commingle their resources and assets, to invest in real estate and other property, and to share the profits between themselves.

Alternatively, the appellant characterizes the transactions as joint ventures, claiming, in a manner similar to her assertions under the breach of partnership theory, that she is entitled to her share of the benefits from the joint ventures and, in that connection, to an accounting and partition. A second alternative theory of recovery requests that a resulting trust or constructive trust be imposed to protect the appellant's interests in the investments.

After the initial round of pleadings was filed and depositions of the parties had been taken, the appellee moved for summary judgment, which the court granted and entered on May 28, 1981.

[W]e examine the appellee's (movant's) summary judgment proof to determine its legal sufficiency. Has the appellee established her entitlement to a summary judgment on the issues expressly presented to the trial court by conclusively proving all the essential elements of her defense as a matter of law?

The appellee offered as summary judgment evidence certain portions of the appellant's sworn deposition testimony as follows:

> Jo Ann Small: And in a matter of a few months we became homosexual lovers and we continued as such until I separated from my husband in July of 1965.
>
> I refer to it as a *marriage*-type relationship. (Emphasis supplied).

In our relationship the division of labor was housework, cooking, yard keeping, et cetera. Her job was to manage our money. She did all of the bill paying, the bookkeeping, the investing, and so on. When I, for example, would receive a paycheck, I would endorse it and hand it over to her. And thus my ignorance about income other than my own.

We were considering it a mate relationship.

I played the role of her lover and her mate.

Q. Well, you have already characterized your relationship with Miss Harper. You have said it was a homosexual relationship. You have said in your pleadings that the two of you formed a partnership for profit. When did that take place?

Jo Ann Small: A partnership for profit I presume would refer to the fact that we agreed that we would live together, and that we would accumulate together; and always the goal at the end was a comfortable retirement, and we were always talking about details of that. We had even discussed—in view of her earlier retirement, for example, one thing that we talked about was delicacies and kind of restaurant on Highway 290, because that was a market need in that area. We talked about the home we would build to live in as a retirement home.

Q. My question is: When did this partnership for profit commence? What were those circumstances?

Jo Ann Small: Well, I felt that I was describing that to you just now.

Q. I meant when.

Jo Ann Small: From the beginning of our personal relationship.

Q. And what was the agreement between you and Miss Harper as to the contribution of assets to this personal partnership for profit?

Jo Ann Small: We had no agreement about that. We were all—we were both working under the assumption that all that either of us earned or could make from investments together or from whatever source would go into a common fund from which we operate.

Q. Did that include real estate?

Jo Ann Small: Surely.

Leaving any possible legal consequences of the homosexual and/or lesbian portion of the relationship aside for the moment, the controlling question is whether the offered portions of the appellant's deposition raise any fact issue or issues supportive of any one of the appellant's alternative theories of recovery as pleaded. In our opinion, the deposition testimony raised a number of issues regarding the women's business affairs. It raised the issue of whether they combined funds to invest in stocks with the expectation of sharing the proceeds jointly; it raised the issue of whether they pooled their assets to purchase other items, such as property and personalty; and finally, it raised the issue of whether they commingled their incomes to achieve monetary gains. Summary judgment should have been denied unless the public policy of Texas requires a different result under the particular facts of this case.

While the lesbian relationship of the parties, if such it be as described by the appellant, could present this court with a novel question—*i.e.*, the property rights of heterosexuals *vis-a-vis* the property rights of homosexuals—it is our opinion that such question is not controlling in the instant case because of the way contributions of work and capital were made and because of the way properties were jointly acquired, generally, but not always, in the names of both of the parties. We come now as squarely to grips with the homosexual and/or lesbian aspects of this case as our judicial needs require.

Fortunately, for our guidance, the Supreme Court of Texas, in the early case of *Hayworth v. Williams*, 102 Tex. 308, 116 S.W. 43 (1909) addressed this issue, deciding whether Margreth Williams, notwithstanding the invalidity of her marriage, would be entitled to an interest in the property involved in the case because she contributed to its acquisition.

In order for the significance of this question to be appreciated, and in order that the Supreme Court's answer be understood, the factual background of the case should be summarized.

In 1859, Margreth Williams "entered into a marriage, in form," with a man named Thomas Jefferson, whom she knew was married to another woman. The two moved from Pennsylvania to New Orleans, and then, a few years later, to the property in question, deeded to Jefferson for cash consideration. Margreth and their children remained on the land, "cultivating the same and improving it by building fences, etc.," but Jefferson returned to New Orleans after only a few months, returning to the land only periodically. In fact, sometimes he would be gone for a "number of years" before showing up for a brief visit. During this time, Margreth claimed the land as her own, and claimed also to be the wife of Jefferson. The suit before the court was brought in 1905 by Jefferson for the purpose of recovering the land. *Id.*, 116 S.W. at 44–45.

With the above factual background before it, the court decided that Margreth Williams' right in the property was a question of fact to be submitted to the jury. If she could show that the money used to buy the land was acquired in whole or in part by her labor with Jefferson before the land was purchased, she would be entitled to a share of the land in the same proportion that her labor contributed to the purchase money.

The court pointed out that Margreth Williams need not "prove that she produced by her labor a part of the very money that was used in purchasing the land."

If she and Jefferson were working together to a common purpose, and the proceeds of labor performed by them became the joint property of the two, then she would occupy the position that a man would have occupied in relation to Jefferson under the same circumstances; each would own the property acquired in proportion to the value of his labor contributed to the acquisition of it.

We note also that in *Cluck v. Sheets*, 141 Tex. 219, 171 S.W.2d 860 (1943), the Supreme Court recognized a like rule, investing title to property in a woman who lived with a man and accumulated real property in conjunction with him without the parties ever entering into either a ceremonial, common-law or putative marriage. See also *Lovell v. Lovell*, 202 S.W.2d 291 (Tex. Civ. App.—1947, no writ); ___ Texas Law Review 725 [*sic*].

Based on the above explanation, we hold that there are no public policy considerations of the State of Texas that would prevent the appellant from recovering on the claims she has made.

We have decided thus far that the appellee did not prove all the elements of her defense as a matter of law, that fact issues were raised in the appellee's summary judgment evidence, and that public policy considerations are not a bar to recovery by the appellant.

We hold that summary judgment should have been denied to the appellee, not only because the grounds expressly presented to the trial court by movant's motion were insufficient as a matter of law to support summary judgment, but also because the nonmovant's motion demonstrated that there were genuine issues, as to material facts, requiring resolution upon a trial of the case.

We reverse the judgment of the trial court and remand the case for a new trial.

DISCUSSION

After *Small*, are all cohabitation contracts between homosexuals enforceable in Texas (subject to the statute of frauds requirement)?

C. Disputes at Divorce Regarding Premarital Expenditures

Nelson v. Nelson

Texas Court of Appeals—Eastland, 2006
193 S.W.3d 624, no pet.

STRANGE, Justice.

This is an appeal from a division of property incident to divorce. In seven issues, Kenneth Russell Nelson, appellant, challenges the trial court's division of the community estate and its economic reimbursement and economic contribution awards. We affirm in part and reverse and remand in part.

Background Facts

The parties were married on April 9, 1995. Prior to their marriage, appellant purchased five acres of land from his parents. He still owed them $8,000 on the purchase price when he married appellee, Bessie Mae Nelson. Appellee owned a home in Stephenville. She sold her house prior to the marriage and realized approximately $17,500. She deposited this money into appellant's checking account.

The parties built a home on appellant's five-acre tract. Construction started several months before the marriage. The parties did most of the work themselves and, prior to their marriage, spent $16,616.51 from appellee's house sale on construction costs. The house was substantially complete at the time of the marriage, needing only interior finishing work. The parties spent approximately $5,600 in community funds to complete the house....

Reimbursement of Funds Spent by Appellee Prior to Marriage

Appellant contends ... that, if the trial court correctly characterized the $16,616.51 spent by appellee on the marital home as her separate property, it nonetheless erred by finding she was entitled to reimbursement because those funds were spent prior to the date of marriage. (footnote omitted) Appellant relies on TEX. FAM. CODE ANN. § 3.408 (Vernon Supp. 2005) which defines a reimbursement claim to include a "payment by one marital estate of the unsecured liabilities of another marital estate." Appellant urges that this precludes reimbursement for any payments made prior to marriage because by definition a "marital estate" cannot exist prior to marriage.

Appellee concedes that she does not have a claim for economic contribution for prenuptial expenditures but contends that the court had the authority under TEX. FAM. CODE ANN.

§ 7.007 (Vernon Supp.2005) to award reimbursement. This statute instructs courts to apply equitable principles to:

(1) determine whether to recognize the claim after taking into account all the relative circumstances of the spouses; and

(2) order a division of the claim for reimbursement, if appropriate, in a manner that the court considers just and right, having due regard for the rights of each party and any children of the marriage.

Tex. Fam. Code Ann. § 7.007(b) (Vernon Supp.2005).

We believe appellant reads Section 3.408 too narrowly. Unlike Tex. Fam. Code Ann.§ 3.403 (Vernon Supp.2005) which defines economic contribution claims in mandatory terms, the definition of economic reimbursement in Section 3.408 is simply a non-exhaustive list of two potential reimbursement claims. Neither example is defined by the timing of the event. Section 3.408(b). (footnote omitted) The legislature also provided five instances in which a reimbursement claim may not be awarded. See Tex. Fam. Code Ann. § 3.409 (Vernon Supp.2005). These instances are specific categories of expenditure, such as child support and student loan payments. None turn on the timing of the expenditure. Consequently, we do not believe the legislature intended that a reimbursement claim could never exist for prenuptial expenditures.

Reimbursement is an equitable remedy. *Vallone v. Vallone*, 644 S.W.2d 455, 458 (Tex. 1982). The Family Code specifically provides that courts are to "resolve a claim for reimbursement by using equitable principles." Section 3.408(c). Because reimbursement is an equitable doctrine, a court of equity is bound to look at all the facts and circumstances to determine what is fair, just, and equitable. *Penick v. Penick*, 783 S.W.2d 194, 197 (Tex. 1988).

Great latitude must be accorded to the trial court in applying equitable principles to determine reimbursement claims because this does not involve simply balancing the ledgers between competing marital estates. The discretion to be exercised in evaluating a claim for reimbursement is equally as broad as the discretion exercised by a trial court in making a just and proper division of the community estate. (citation omitted)

The trial court found, and we have previously affirmed, that the $16,616.51 spent by the parties on prenuptial construction costs was appellee's separate property. That money helped fund a house on appellant's separate property. The trial court did not abuse its discretion when it found that appellee was entitled to reimbursement. Appellant's ... issue is overruled....

Conclusion

The judgment of the trial court is affirmed in part and reversed and remanded in part. The portion of the judgment that characterizes the $16,616.51 spent on house construction as Bessie Mae Nelson's separate property and imposes a lien on Kenneth Russell Nelson's separate property is affirmed.

DISCUSSION

Premarital financial transactions can create a number of marital property issues. In *Marriage of Murray*, 15 S.W.3d 202 (Tex. App.—Texarkana 2000, pet. denied) the parties jointly bought a house before marriage. The female paid the down payment; both parties signed the note. The deed was in both their names. Payments were made by both during marriage. At divorce, who owns the house?

D. Disputes between People Who Date but Do Not Cohabit

Soap operas and tabloids suggest that a married person sometimes has an affair with a third person. If an agreement is made between the married person and the third party, is this enforceable? Are any equitable remedies available? What if two unmarried people date but do not live together? Can a *Marvin* claim be brought when they break up?

Cochran v. Cochran
California Court of Appeals, 2001
106 Cal.Rptr.2d 899

WILLHITE, J.

I. INTRODUCTION

Plaintiff and cross-complainant Patricia A. Cochran appeals from the judgment of dismissal entered after the trial court sustained without leave to amend the demurrers which defendant and cross-defendant Johnnie L. Cochran, Jr., brought to her cross-complaint for rescission of their 1983 property settlement agreement. She also appeals from the summary judgment entered for the defendant on her complaint for breach of an alleged agreement for lifetime support. For the reasons set forth below, we reverse both judgments.

II. PROCEDURAL HISTORY

This is the third appeal arising from two separate, but related, actions between appellant Patricia A. Cochran (appellant) and respondent Johnnie L. Cochran, Jr. (respondent) arising out of their long-term, nonmarital relationship.

The first action (Super. Ct. L.A. County, 1995, No. BC124156) was filed in March 1995, The operative, first amended complaint of April 1995 was primarily concerned with respondent's alleged breach of a supposed *Marvin* agreement to provide appellant with lifetime support. In *Cochran v. Cochran* (1997), 66 Cal.Rptr.2d 337 (*Cochran* I), we held that the statute of limitations for breach of a *Marvin* agreement did not begin to run until the defendant failed to perform as the agreement required. As a result of our decision, all that remained of the complaint in *Cochran I* were causes of action based on the alleged *Marvin* agreement.

The second action (Super. Ct. L.A. County, 1996, No. EC021315) was filed in November 1996 while the appeal in *Cochran* I was still pending. The original complaint in the second action included a cause of action seeking to rescind a 1983 property settlement agreement because the agreement was induced by fraud. The operative first amended complaint omitted the rescission claim, but sought damages for intentional infliction of emotional distress based on a message left on a telephone answering machine which appellant construed as a death threat. In *Cochran v. Cochran* (1998), 76 Cal.Rptr.2d 540 (*Cochran II*), we held that the message was not actionable as a death threat.

After our decision in *Cochran I* became final, that action was remanded to the trial court. On January 26, 1998, respondent cross-complained against appellant, contending she had breached the confidentiality provisions of their 1983 property settlement agreement by appearing on television to discuss their relationship. Appellant answered the cross-complaint on February 11, 1998, and filed a cross-complaint of her own ("the fraud cross-complaint"), seeking to rescind the 1983 settlement agreement because it allegedly had been induced by respondent's fraud. Respondent dismissed his cross-complaint without prejudice on March 13, 1998. He then demurred to the fraud cross-complaint, contending among other things that it was barred by the statute of limitations and was contrary to certain verified allegations in the *Cochran I* complaint concerning the validity of the settlement agreement. By minute order dated April 2, 1999, the trial court sustained the demurrers without leave to amend on two grounds: (1) the fraud cross-complaint was barred by appellant's earlier allegations; and (2) the action was also barred under the law of the case doctrine by our decision in *Cochran I.*

In November 1999 respondent moved for summary judgment on the Cochran I complaint, contending appellant could not prevail on her remaining *Marvin* claims because: (1) the parties were not cohabiting when the agreement was made; (2) the alleged promise of support was made under circumstances which made it unreasonable to believe the statements were a contractual offer; (3) the alleged promise to support was too uncertain to be enforced; and (4) in any event, the claim was barred by the statute of limitations. The motion was granted and judgment for respondent was entered December 21, 1999. This appeal followed.

IV. SUMMARY JUDGMENT STANDARD OF REVIEW

A defendant moving for summary judgment meets his burden of proof showing that there is no merit to a cause of action if that party has shown that one or more elements of the cause of action cannot be established or that there is a complete defense to that cause of action. Once the defendant does so, the burden shifts back to the plaintiff to show that a triable issue of one or more material facts exists as to that cause of action or to a defense to the cause of action.

Appellant and respondent began their relationship in 1966, at a time when respondent was still married to his first wife. Appellant later changed her surname to match respondent's. In 1973, the parties' son was born. In 1974, appellant and respondent bought a house in North Hollywood. Title was eventually placed in both their names as Joint tenants. Respondent also owned a home on Hobart Street. He and appellant split their living time between the two homes. Respondent stayed with appellant and then-son at the North Hollywood home from two to four nights a week. He kept clothes there and took meals at the house. Respondent held himself out to the world as appellant's husband. In 1978, respondent divorced his first wife.

In 1983, they experienced relationship troubles after appellant learned respondent was unfaithful. On October 21, 1983, they signed the property settlement agreement. Pursuant to the settlement agreement, respondent quitclaimed to appellant all his interest in their North Hollywood house. He agreed, among other things, to pay child support of $350 each month, to buy appellant a new car, to pay for construction of a swimming pool at the North Hollywood house, and to provide medical and dental insurance for their son. The agreement was expressly limited to claims then existing and included assurances of all disclosure as to all assets then owned by the parties. It did not include a waiver or release of future or unknown claims.

Within one to three weeks of signing the settlement agreement, respondent told appellant he wanted to keep things as they had been before. He also promised to care for her "financially, emotionally and legally" for the rest of her life. In return, she agreed to maintain their home and care for respondent and their son.[5] After that time, he continued to live with appellant and her son "as he had before." Appellant said respondent "wanted me to continue providing a home and continue our lifestyle and he was going to continue supporting me." The support agreement was formed as part of discussions about the future of their relationship, their continued love for each other, and then-desire to eventually marry. Appellant said she wanted proof of respondent's fidelity before marriage, "so we were working on that."

Appellant said in her declaration that after the support agreement was formed, respondent "continued to live with me and our son at the [North Hollywood] house as he had done before.... He continued to support me as he had promised until February 1995." Much of respondent's summary judgment motion centered on the form of that support, and whether it was sufficient to make the agreement enforceable or was so sporadic that it constituted a breach of the agreement which set the statute of limitations running by 1985.

In 1985, respondent married his second wife. Between 1984 and late 1992 or January 1993, appellant worked for a company named Ipson. During those years, respondent helped pay for various of appellant's expenses. He gave her cash and paid her bills as needed, including utilities and medical insurance. He twice provided her with new cars and sometimes paid for car repairs. Respondent also gave appellant credit cards issued in either her name or respondent's, with respondent paying the charges she incurred. During those years, respondent "paid child support for [their son] ... and gave me money whenever I needed it. [Respondent] paid amounts over the $350.00 required in the [1983] Settlement Agreement because he and I understood that more was required to maintain the standard of living to which me [sic] and our son were accustomed. Throughout this period of time, [respondent] and I spoke on a regular basis and [respondent] knew what my financial needs were. When I needed funds he always provided funds as he promised." Cancelled checks produced by respondent showed child support payments of $1,000 were made at least as of 1991 through January 1995. A notice from appellant's bank showed that respondent wrote her a check for $4,500 in or about May 1991. However, appellant admitted that the support she received was not regular, either in amount or time of payment.

Respondent produced copies of more than 200 cancelled checks in connection with payments made to appellant or their son between September 1990 and December 1998. Many were made payable to appellant, but bore notations indicating they were for child support or other expenses related to the parties' son. Several were payable to appellant herself: a July 1993 deposit of $1,500 to appellant's bank account; an August 1993 check for $375; a September 1993 check for $1,500 bearing the notation "Expenses"; and many others between January 1994 and February 1995 in amounts ranging from $1,800 to $3,557. Respondent admitted that he was unsure whether the checks he produced were all those relating to the support of either appellant or their son. He admitted that there might be other checks written on different accounts.

Respondent also contends that the support agreement is unenforceable because he and appellant did not cohabitate, or live together. Viewing the evidence in appellant's

5. Respondent's summary judgment motion did not dispute appellant's assertion that respondent made such a promise. For ease of reference, we will refer to the agreement which appellant contends she entered as "the support agreement."

favor, it appears that before entering the 1983 settlement and support agreements, respondent stayed at the North Hollywood house two to four nights a week. Appellant and the parties' son sometimes stayed at respondent's house on Hobart Street. Appellant stated in her declaration that after respondent made his support promises, he continued to live with her as he had before. However, from her deposition testimony it is apparent that after respondent remarried in 1985, he stayed at the house less often. Appellant testified she was not sure whether respondent ever spent the night after his remarriage, although he did come for frequent visits, wife appellant continuing to prepare his meals.

The *Marvin* court held "that adults who voluntarily *live together* and engage in sexual relations are nonetheless as competent as any other persons to contract respecting their earnings and property rights." So long as the agreement does not depend upon meretricious sexual relations for its consideration, or so long as that portion of the consideration may be severed from other proper forms of consideration, such agreements are enforceable.

In *Taylor v. Fields* (1986), 224 Cal.Rptr. 186 (*Taylor*), the court seized upon the italicized "live together" reference in *Marvin* to hold that a dead man's mistress, who never lived with the decedent, was not entitled to enforce their purported *Marvin* agreement. Examining *Marvin* and other related decisions, the *Taylor* court held that cohabitation was a prerequisite to recovery under *Marvin*. Because the appellant's agreement in *Taylor* rested upon an illicit sexual relationship for its consideration, it was not enforceable. *Taylor* was followed by *Bergen v. Wood* (1993), 18 Cal.Rptr.2d 75 (*Bergen*). The plaintiff in *Bergen* had a long-term sexual relationship with the decedent, acting as his hostess and social companion. Though he had supposedly promised to support the plaintiff, they never lived together. In reversing a judgment for the plaintiff, the *Bergen* court noted that cohabitation was required under *Marvin* "not in and of itself, but rather, because from cohabitation flows the rendition of domestic services, which services amount to lawful consideration for a contract between the parties. We make the additional observation that if cohabitation were not a prerequisite to recovery, every dating relationship would have the potential for giving rise to such claims, a result no one favors." Citing both *Marvin* and *Taylor*, the *Bergen* court noted that recovery under *Marvin* "requires a showing of a stable and significant relationship arising out of cohabitation." Because the plaintiff never lived with her decedent, it was impossible to sever the sexual component of the relationship from other appropriate consideration.

Citing *Taylor* and *Bergen*, respondent contends that his relationship with appellant did not involve cohabitation, since the evidence showed that he spent as little as one night a week at appellant's house after their property settlement agreement was reached in 1983. As a result, he characterizes their relationship as no more than "dating." On the other hand, appellant relies on *Bergen's* statement that cohabitation was required not in and of itself, but in order to establish lawful consideration through the performance of domestic services. Since appellant provided such services, she contends there was lawful consideration even absent cohabitation. Alternatively, she contends that there was sufficient evidence to raise a triable issue of fact as to the issue of cohabitation.

We save for another day the issue whether consenting adults need cohabit *at all* in order to enter an enforceable agreement regarding their earnings and property. Assuming for discussion's sake that cohabitation is required, we conclude that the rationale of *Marvin* is satisfied in appropriate cases by a cohabitation arrangement that is less than full-time. Here, as so construed, there was sufficient evidence to raise a triable issue of fact on the cohabitation element.

Both *Taylor* and *Bergen* considered claims by parties who served, in effect, as the mistress or girlfriend of their respective decedents. Neither plaintiff had ever cohabited with their" respective decedents. Moreover, neither decision considered whether anything less than a full-time living arrangement was necessary to show cohabitation. By contrast, in the present case, when respondent supposedly entered the support agreement, in late October or early November of 1983, he and appellant had shared a relationship for approximately 17 years. That relationship produced a son, whom they were raising together. They held themselves out to the world as husband and wife. Appellant legally changed her surname to respondent's. They had jointly owned their home until respondent quitclaimed his interest as part of their settlement agreement. Appellant performed a variety of domestic chores for respondent, including raising their son and maintaining the house. Respondent kept clothes at the house, "spent family time there" and "slept there on a regular basis."

Here, the parties had shared a long-term, stable and significant relationship. In this context, evidence that they lived together two to four days a week both before and at the time they entered their *Marvin* agreement is sufficient to raise a triable issue of fact that they cohabitated under *Marvin*.

VI. DISPOSITION

For the reasons set forth above, we direct the trial court to enter nunc pro tune a judgment dismissing the fraud cross-complaint based upon its orders sustaining respondent's demurrers to that pleading. To the extent appellant appeals from the order sustaining those demurrers, we deem the appeal to be taken from that judgment. The judgment of dismissal on the fraud cross-complaint and the summary judgment on the complaint are reversed. Appellant to recover her costs on appeal.

TURNER, P.J., and ARMSTRONG, J., concurred.

———————

Adams v. Jensen-Thomas
Washington Court of Appeals, 1977
571 P.2d 958

McINTURFF, Justice.

Both parties appeal from a verdict settling a dispute between them as to property involved in a four-year affair outside the marriage of one of the parties. We reverse.

In the summer of 1970 the plaintiff, Mernis M. "Buster" Adams, a married man, began seeing the defendant, Frances C. Jensen, a divorced woman. From then until the spring of 1974 he regularly transferred property to her and paid sums of money to her for various expenses. In all, more than $30,000 was involved. During the term of their relationship the couple did not live together, although they did spend many evenings and weekends with one another, at either the Jensen home or at Sacheen Lake. Nor did they hold themselves out to be husband and wife. In fact, both parties were well aware of the Adams marriage, which continued until May of 1974.

An eventual marriage was discussed by the parties, and Mr. Adams maintains that all of the property transferred to Ms. Jensen was in the contemplation of their marriage and to establish a "nest egg." His failure to earlier dissolve his marriage, however, caused at least one cleavage in their relationship, and, finally, the sometimes stormy *affaire de coeur* ended in April 1974.

In June 1975 Mr. Adams brought the instant action against Ms. Jensen, seeking a return of the property he had transferred to her and asking damages for the breach of her promise to marry him. He asked that a trust in his favor be declared over the transferred property. A jury trial resulted in a verdict of $4,298.00 for the plaintiff. He appeals on the grounds that the amount is grossly inadequate and asks this court to impose a trust on the property for him. She cross appeals from the awarding of any judgment.

Mr. Adams complains of the trial court's failure to impose a trust over the transferred property or, in the alternative, of its failure to order the return of all the property under the theory that it was transferred as a conditional gift.

Ms. Jensen appeals from the denial of her motion to dismiss and for a directed verdict, made at the close of plaintiff's case and at the end of trial, and the court's refusal to instruct the jury on the applicable statute of limitations.

Because we believe that the issues raised by Ms. Jensen are dispositive, we first consider the refusal of the trial court to grant her motion to dismiss or for a directed verdict.

Because under the facts presented by plaintiff there was no theory upon which he could recover, the trial court erred in denying the defendant's motion for a directed verdict or dismissal.

Plaintiff sought to recover the property he transferred to Ms. Jensen under the theory of conditional gift. As a matter of public policy, gifts made between engaged persons cannot be reclaimed upon the dissolution of the betrothal where, at the time the gift was made, either the donor or the donee was then married to another, at least where the parties were aware of the existing marriage. Thus his claim under this theory was not supportable.

Nor is the breach of promise theory available to the plaintiff here.

A promise of marriage made by or to a person who, to the knowledge of the parties concerned, then has a spouse living is absolutely void in its inception and cannot give rise to an action for its breach, even though such promise is not to be performed until after the death of, or divorce from, such spouse. Such contracts are in violation of the marital duty and are contrary to morality and public policy.

Hence, neither of the legal theories pursued by Mr. Adams is applicable here because of his marital status during the time of his relationship with Ms. Jensen.

Nonetheless, Mr. Adams contends that the cases which have carved out exceptions to the rule of *Creasman v. Boyle*, 31 Wash. 2d 345, 353, 196 P.2d 835 (1948) (*i.e.*, accumulated properties belong to one in whose name legal title stands), will allow him to recover. He suggests the facts are such to require a tracing of the property and its return to him under the theory of *West v. Knowles*, 50 Wash. 2d 311, 311 P.2d 689 (1957). Alternatively, a resulting trust in his favor should be found by applying *Walberg v. Mattson*, 38 Wash. 2d 808, 232 P.2d 827 (1951). Finally, he maintains that a constructive trust is applicable on the strength of *Omer v. Omer*, 11 Wash.App. 386, 523 P.2d 957 (1974), and *Proctor v. Forsythe*, 4 Wash.App. 238, 480 P.2d 511 (1971).

In this case, these contentions are without merit. General equity principles do not support his request for trust relief nor do the rules which have emerged from the other meretricious relationship cases. The facts here differ markedly from them in that the parties did not live together in a stable, long-term relationship nor did they hold themselves out to be husband and wife.

Finally, we reject Mr. Adams' request to trace the assets involved and award them to either of the parties as was done in *West v. Knowles, supra.* That case is inapposite. There the couple lived together for 10 years, holding themselves out to the world as husband and wife. Again, the stability of the relationship is distinguishable from the surreptitious situation presented here. So, too, are the expectations of the parties. In this clandestine relationship, which is necessarily unstable because of the existing marriage of one of the parties, the trial court's remarks are apropos: "Neither can have participated in this type of an experience and not expect to take the risks or pay the price involved."

DISCUSSION

In *Adams*, the court emphasized that the parties did not live together. Does it make sense to distinguish between promises made by people who are living together and those who are living separately?

Adams, Bergen, Cochran, and *Taylor* suggest that *Marvin* should be limited to those cohabitation cases involving "stable and significant" relationships. What are these? Would this be a good idea? Why are the courts reluctant to extend *Marvin* to all adults who have a sexual relationship?

Isn't there a better justification for not granting Buster the equitable relief he requests? Can you think of any other justification for the *Adams* holding? Would the result have been the same if Buster's ex-wife had sued Ms. Jensen-Thomas?

E. Tort Claims

In this chapter, potential claims between unmarried people based upon contract and equitable doctrines have been discussed. Some recent cases have considered whether a tort claim can be advanced between two unmarried people who share a sexual relationship.

Stephen K. v. Roni L.

California Court of Appeals, 1980
105 Cal. App. 3d 640

BEACH, Associate Justice.

Cross-plaintiff Stephen K. appeals from a judgment of dismissal entered upon an order sustaining, without leave to amend, cross-defendant Roni L.'s demurrer to Stephen's cross-complaint in which he sought to recover general and punitive damages from Roni for the alleged "wrongful birth" of his child. We affirm the judgment.

BACKGROUND

The minor child, its guardian *ad litem*, and its mother brought a paternity suit against Stephen K. (Stephen). After admitting paternity, Stephen filed a cross-complaint "for fraud, negligent misrepresentation and negligence." The cross-complaint alleged that Roni L. (Roni), the child's mother, had falsely represented that she was taking birth control pills and that in reliance upon such representation Stephen engaged in sexual intercourse with Roni which eventually resulted in the birth of a baby girl unwanted by Stephen. Stephen further alleged that as a "proximate result" of Roni's conduct he had become obligated to support the child financially, and had suffered "mental agony and distress" all to his general damage in the amount of $100,000. Stephen also sought punitive damages of $100,000 against Roni for having acted "with oppression, fraud, and malice" towards him.

Roni moved for a judgment on the pleadings claiming that (1) to allow Stephen to recover damages would be against public policy, and (2) Stephen had failed to establish damages. The trial court treated Roni's motion as a general demurrer to the cross-complaint and ordered the action dismissed. Stephen appeals.

ISSUE ON APPEAL

The sole issue in this case is: As between two consenting sexual partners, may one partner hold the other liable in tort for the birth of a child conceived in an act of intercourse where the one partner relied on the other partner's false representation that contraceptive measures had been taken? We conclude that in this case Roni's conduct complained of by Stephen did not give rise to liability.

DISCUSSION

The critical question before us is whether Roni's conduct towards Stephen is actionable at all. Stephen claims it is actionable as a tort. Neither statutory nor judicial recognition of such a claim in California or elsewhere in the United States has been brought to the attention of this court. Though the presentation of the matter as a legal issue is somewhat novel, the social conditions underlying it have existed since the advent of mankind.

Broadly speaking, the word "tort" means a civil wrong, other than a breach of contract, for which the law will provide a remedy in the form of an action for damages. It does not lie within the power of any judicial system, however, to remedy all human wrongs. There are many wrongs which in themselves are flagrant. For instance, such wrongs as betrayal, brutal words, and heartless disregard of the feelings of others are beyond any effective legal remedy and any practical administration of law. The present case falls within that category.

We are in effect asked to attach tortious liability to the natural results of consensual sexual intercourse. Stephen's claim is one of an alleged wrong to him personally and alone. Procedurally and technically it is separate and apart from any issue of either parent's obligation to raise and support the child. Although actually requiring the mother to pay Stephen monetary damages may have the effect of reducing her financial ability to support the child, we need not get into this area of discussion or resolve such problems as may exist in that area. In the posture of the case as presented to us, the state has minimal if any interest in this otherwise entirely private matter. Claims such as those presented by plaintiff Stephen in this case arise from conduct so intensely private that the courts should not be asked to nor attempt to resolve such claims. Consequently, we need not and do not reach the question of whether Stephen has established or pleaded tort liability on the part of Roni under recognized principles of tort law. In summary, although Roni may have lied and betrayed the personal confidence reposed in her by Stephen, the circumstances and the highly intimate nature of the relationship wherein the false representations may have occurred, are such that a court should not define any standard of conduct therefor.

We are aware of decisions in this and other jurisdictions which have, under certain circumstances, attached tortious liability to the birth of a child. Even though some of the cases involve the recognition of changed social and moral attitudes, all of them are distinguishable from the present case. First, in none of those cases did the plaintiffs seek so radical a change in the socially accepted ideas and views of sexual conduct, family relationship, parental obligations, and legal and moral responsibility for one's own conduct as does Stephen. In *Zepeda v. Zepeda* (1963) 41 Ill.App.2d 240, 190 N.E.2d 849, an illegitimate child sued its father for "wrongful life." In *Zepeda*, the defendant had induced the child's mother to have sexual intercourse with him by promising to marry her. However, unknown to the mother, the defendant was already married. The birth of the plaintiff as an illegitimate child resulted. The child sued to recover damages against its father, claiming that his illegitimate birth as the result of the fraud perpetrated by his father upon his mother deprived him of his right to have a normal home and stigmatized him as a bastard. The court concluded that while a tort had been committed by the father against the plaintiff child, it would affirm the dismissal of the complaint because to do otherwise would have wide-ranging social consequences. A similar result was reached in *Williams v. State* (1966) 18 N.Y.2d 481, 276 N.Y.S.2d 885, 223 N.E.2d 343. There the illegitimate child, born to a mentally deficient mother as a consequence of a rape by another patient during the mother's confinement as a patient at the state hospital, sued the state hospital for its negligence in failing to safeguard her mother. The plaintiff claimed that as a result, she was forced to bear the stigma of illegitimacy and to suffer the deprivations of normal childhood and familial property rights. Though acknowledging that the allegations of the complaint, if true, indicated grievous neglect by the state, the court denied recovery because of "policy and social reasons."[10]

The claim of Stephen is phrased in the language of the tort of misrepresentation. Despite its legalism, it is nothing more than asking the court to supervise the promises made between two consenting adults as to the circumstances of their private sexual conduct. To do so would encourage unwarranted governmental intrusion into matters affecting the individual's right to privacy.

We reject Stephen's contention that tortious liability should be imposed against Roni, and conclude that as a matter of public policy the practice of birth control, if any, engaged in by two partners in a consensual sexual relationship is best left to the individuals involved, free from any governmental interferences. As to Stephen's claim that he was tricked into fathering a child he did not want, no good reason appears why he himself could not have taken any precautionary measures. Even if Roni had regularly been taking birth control pills, that method, though considered to be the most reliable means of birth control, is not 100 percent effective. Although slight, there is some statistical probability of conception.

The judgment is affirmed.

Kathleen K. v. Robert B.
California Court of Appeals, 1984
198 Cal. Rptr. 273

HASTINGS, Associate Justice.

In this action, plaintiff and appellant Kathleen K. seeks damages because she contracted genital herpes, allegedly by way of sexual intercourse with defendant and re-

-----

10. The *Zepeda* and *Williams* cases have been discussed in a number of law reviews. See *e.g.*, Toplinson, *Torts—Wrongful Birth and Wrongful Life* (1979) 44 Missouri L. Rev. 157; Wolff, *Wrongful Life: A Modern Claim Which Conforms to the Traditional Tort Framework* (1978) 20 William & Mary L. Rev. 125; Comment (1963–64) 49 Iowa L. Rev. 1005; Ploscowe, *An Action For "Wrongful Life"* (1963) 38 New York U. L. Rev. 1078).

spondent Robert B. The trial court granted respondent's motion for judgment on the pleadings based upon failure to state a cause of action. We reverse the judgment.

The complaint sets forth four causes of action: (1) negligence (alleging that respondent inflicted injury upon appellant by having sexual intercourse with her at a time when he knew, or in the exercise of reasonable care should have known, that he was a carrier of venereal disease); (2) battery; (3) intentional infliction of emotional distress; and (4) fraud (alleging that respondent deliberately misrepresented to appellant that he was free from venereal disease, and that appellant, relying on such representations, had sexual intercourse with respondent, which she would not have done had she known the true state of affairs).

In granting respondent's motion for judgment on the pleadings, the trial court relied upon the case of *Stephen K. v. Roni L.*, 105 Cal. App. 3d 640, 164 Cal. Rptr. 618. In *Stephen K.*, the father of a child filed a cross-complaint against the child's mother who had brought a paternity action, claiming that the mother had falsely represented to him that she was taking birth control pills. The father alleged that in reliance upon that misrepresentation, he engaged in sexual intercourse with the mother, resulting in the birth of a child which he did not want. He further alleged that as a proximate result of the misrepresentation, he had become obligated to support the child financially and had suffered emotional distress.

In affirming dismissal of the cross-complaint, the court held that the misrepresentation was not actionable:

> The claim of Stephen is phrased in the language of the tort of misrepresentation. Despite its legalism, it is nothing more than asking the court to supervise the promises made between two consenting adults as to the circumstances of their private sexual conduct. To do so would encourage unwarranted governmental intrusion into matters affecting the individual's right to privacy. We reject Stephen's contention that tortious liability should be imposed against Roni, and conclude that as a matter of public policy the practice of birth control, if any, engaged in by two partners in a consensual sexual relationship is best left to the individuals involved, free from any governmental interference.

(*Stephen K. v. Roni L., supra,* 105 Cal. App. 3d 640, 644–645, 164 Cal. Rptr. 618).

After the trial court entered its judgment, the First District Court of Appeal decided the case of *Barbara A. v. John G.*, 145 Cal. App. 3d 369, 193 Cal. Rptr. 422 (hrg. den. September 29, 1983). In *Barbara A.*, a woman who suffered an ectopic pregnancy and was forced to undergo surgery to save her life, which rendered her sterile, brought an action against the man who impregnated her (her former attorney), alleging that she consented to sexual intercourse in reliance on the man's knowingly false representation that he was sterile. The court reversed a judgment on the pleadings in favor of the defendant and held that the complaint stated causes of action for battery and for deceit.

The court distinguished *Stephen K.*, noting that: "In essence, Stephen was seeking damages for the 'wrongful birth' of his child resulting in support obligations and alleged damages for mental suffering. Here, no child is involved; appellant is seeking damages for severe injury to her own body." (145 Cal. App. 3d at pp. 378–79, 193 Cal. Rptr. 422). We conclude that these same factors distinguish this case from *Stephen K.*, and accordingly hold that *Barbara A.* is controlling here.

Respondent, urging us to follow *Stephen K.*, criticizes *Barbara A.* in several respects. First, he argues that the viability of appellant's cause of action should not depend upon whether the injury alleged is mental or physical. However, the *Barbara A.* court did not focus solely on the type of injury involved in *Stephen K.*, but upon the fact that Stephen was alleging an injury which had significant public policy overtones:

> To assess damages against the mother for false representations about birth control would have the practical effect of reducing or eliminating support from the father by way of offset. Erasing much or all of the father's financial support, to the detriment of the child, is clearly against public policy and the statutory mandate.

> Further, we think it is not sound social policy to allow one parent to sue the other over the wrongful birth of their child. Using the child as the damage element in a tortious claim of one parent against the other could seldom, if ever, result in benefit to a child.

145 Cal. App. 3d at p. 379, 193 Cal. Rptr. 422.

In the present case, as in *Barbara A.*, there is no child involved, and the public policy considerations with respect to parental obligations are absent.

Respondent also argues that it is not the business of courts to "supervise the promises made between two consenting adults as to the circumstances of their private sexual conduct." (*Stephen K. v. Roni L., supra*, l05 Cal. App. 3d at pp. 644–45, 164 Cal. Rptr. 618).

Respondent correctly focuses on the constitutional right of privacy as the crux of this case. Courts have long recognized the right of privacy in matters relating to marriage, family and sex and accordingly have frowned upon unwarranted governmental intrusion into matters affecting the individual's right of privacy. The key word here, however, is *unwarranted*. The right of privacy is not absolute, and in some cases is subordinate to the state's fundamental right to enact laws which promote public health, welfare and safety, even though such laws may invade the offender's right of privacy. Examples cited by the *Barbara A.* court were the penal statutes acts, registration of convicted sex offenders, the recently enacted criminal statute prohibiting spousal rape (Pen. Code, Sec. 262), and the various laws relating to the paternity of children. In each of these cases, the right of privacy is outweighed by the right of the state to protect the health, welfare and safety of its citizens. The *Barbara A.* court concluded that the right of privacy "does not insulate a person from all judicial inquiry into his or her sexual relations," and expanded the exceptions to the right of privacy to impose liability upon "one sexual partner who by intentionally tortious conduct causes physical injury to the other." (145 Cal. App. 3d at p. 381, 193 Cal. Rptr. 422).

This is precisely the type of conduct alleged in appellant's complaint. Appellant has alleged that she sustained physical injury due to respondent's tortious conduct in either negligently or deliberately failing to inform her that he was infected with venereal disease. The disease which appellant contracted is serious and (thus far) incurable. The tortious nature of respondent's conduct, coupled with the interest of this state in the prevention and control of contagious and dangerous diseases[11] brings appellant's injury within the

---

11. Respondent's argument that genital herpes is not a venereal disease is unpersuasive. Although herpes is not listed among the "venereal diseases" covered by the Health & Safety Code (specifically Section 3001), that section was enacted in 1957, long before herpes achieved its present notoriety. We are not inclined to bar appellant's cause of action on the basis that genital herpes is not a venereal disease. It is a disease that can be propagated by sexual contact. Like AIDS it is now known by the public to be a contagious and dreadful disease. At the core of this action is the misrepresentation of defendant that he did not have a contagious disease that could be passed to his partner. If a person knowingly has genital herpes, AIDS or some other contagious and serious disease, a limited representation that he or she does not have a venereal disease is no defense to this type of action.

type of physical injury contemplated by the court in *Barbara A*. The constitutional right of privacy does not protect respondent here.

It should be noted that several out-of-state cases, cited by the court in *Barbara A.*, have held that a woman's consent to sexual intercourse was vitiated by the man's fraudulent concealment of the risk of infection with venereal disease. [*DeVall v. Strunk* (Tex. Civ. App.— 1936) 96 S.W.2d 245; *Crowell v. Crowell* (1920) 180 N.C. 516, 105 S.E. 206; *State v. Lankford* (1917) 29 Del. 594, 102 A. 63]. Respondent contends that these cases are old and, if decided today, would be dismissed under the public policy considerations outlined in *Stephen K., supra*. He distinguishes *Crowell* and *Lankford* (involving suits by a wife against her husband for damages resulting from contraction of venereal disease) on the basis that a husband and wife occupy a confidential relationship of trust and confidence in one another which does not exist between non-married persons. However, a certain amount of trust and confidence exists in any intimate relationship, at least to the extent that one sexual partner represents to the other that he or she is free from venereal or other dangerous contagious disease. The basic premise underlying these old cases—consent to sexual intercourse vitiated by one partner's fraudulent concealment of the risk of infection with venereal disease—is equally applicable today, whether or not the partners involved are married to each other.

We are also unpersuaded by respondent's argument that this is really an action for seduction (which he calls "the use of deception to effect intercourse"), and is therefore barred by Civil Code Section 43.5. "Seduction imports the idea of illicit intercourse accomplished by the use of arts, persuasions, or wiles to overcome the resistance of a female who is not disposed of her own volition to step aside from the paths of virtue." Appellant is not complaining that respondent induced her to "step aside from the paths of virtue," and in fact she willingly engaged in sexual intercourse with him. This is an action for damages based upon severe injury to appellant's body, which allegedly occurred because of respondent's misrepresentation that he was disease-free. Such an action is not barred by Civil Code Section 43.5.

In summary, we conclude that *Stephen K. v. Roni L.*, on which the trial court relied, is inapplicable here, and that the reasoning of *Barbara A. v. John G.*, in which a hearing was denied by our Supreme Court, is controlling.

The judgment is reversed.

DISCUSSION

Is *Stephen K.* fair to the allegedly misled father? What if the female has substantial assets? In other words, is the issue privacy or child support?

Can *Stephen K.* and *Barbara A.* be resolved? Is the rule in California: "the female wins"?

What damages are appropriate in *Barbara A.*, if the action is permitted? What if she had not aborted the pregnancy?

Should the defendant in *Kathleen K.* be liable if he was not aware he had herpes? What if he knew he had herpes, but was not aware he was contagious at the time? Does the carrier have a duty to disclose the infection, or is misrepresentation required? What damages are appropriate? Does *Kathleen K.* have any relevance to AIDS? Disputes like *Kathleen K.* have arisen between spouses, where one allegedly transmits herpes to the other. Tort claims between spouses are discussed in Chapter 7.

Does the illegality doctrine have any place here? In all three cases, the parties apparently did not have a stable and significant relationship. Does this matter? What if one of the parties was married to another? Should it matter if the behavior of the parties violated the state's criminal law?

In the movie, *The Big Chill*, a married man impregnated an unmarried friend after she requested this service. Does the man have an obligation to support the child in this situation? What if the female promised to be solely responsible for the child support? See *Fournier v. Lopez*, 5 Fam. L. Rep. (BNA) 2204–05 (Cal. App. 1978).

Perry v. Atkinson
California Court of Appeals, 1987
240 Cal. Rptr. 402

HUFFMAN, Associate Justice.

Plaintiff Lee Perry appeals a judgment favoring defendant Richard Atkinson after the court granted summary adjudication of issues and sustained Atkinson's demurrer to Perry's second amended complaint for fraud and deceit.

FACTUAL[12] AND PROCEDURAL BACKGROUND

Perry and Atkinson met in July 1976. Although Atkinson was married, he and Perry began having an intimate relationship which continued for more than a year. During that year, Perry and Atkinson developed a relationship of trust and confidence. In August 1977 Perry learned she was pregnant with Atkinson's child. When Perry told Atkinson, he became upset and urged her to have an abortion. Perry did not want to have an abortion, but Atkinson persisted. He told Perry that although he would like her to have this child, he wanted to postpone doing so for a year. He promised Perry that even if they were not together in a year, he would conceive a child with her by artificial insemination.

Based on Atkinson's promise, Perry terminated her pregnancy by an abortion, causing her physical and mental pain. After the abortion, Perry discovered Atkinson had never intended to keep his promise of another baby. As a result, Perry became depressed, requiring psychiatric treatment, incurring extensive medical bills and losing six months of earnings.

Perry sued Atkinson for fraud and deceit and intentional infliction of emotional distress. In essence, Perry alleged she terminated her pregnancy by an abortion based on Atkinson's promise he would impregnate her the following year either through sexual intercourse or artificial insemination. Perry alleged Atkinson's representation was false; he had no intention of impregnating her again; and he made these statements to deceive her in order to have her abort the pregnancy. As to Perry's first amended complaint, Atkinson moved for summary judgment or alternatively summary adjudication of issues. Before the hearing on Atkinson's motions, Perry filed a second amended complaint, adding allegations of physical harm and further facts regarding her confidential relationship with Atkinson. Atkinson demurred to Perry's second amended complaint.

After hearing, the court rendered its written decision, denying Atkinson's motion for summary judgment as to Perry's cause of action for intentional infliction of emotional distress, and granting Atkinson's motion for summary adjudication as to the

---

12. This appeal properly arises from the court's sustaining a demurrer without leave to amend. (See Discussion I, infra.) Thus, in stating the facts, we must treat every material, issuable fact properly pleaded as true. (*Commercial Standard Ins. Co. v. Bank of America* (1976) 57 Cal. App. 3d 241, 129 Cal. Rptr. 91.)

fraud and deceit cause of action. The court reasoned public policy prohibits a cause of action for fraud and deceit concerning intimate matters involving procreation. The court concluded that to control the promises of the parties by legal action would constitute an unwarranted governmental intrusion into matters affecting the individual's right to privacy. The court also sustained without leave to amend Atkinson's demurrer to Perry's fraud and deceit cause of action in her second amended complaint, reasoning such cause of action would violate public policy and constitute an unwarranted governmental intrusion into matters affecting an individual's right to privacy. The court entered judgment in favor of Atkinson on the cause of action for fraud and deceit.[13] We conclude on the facts here no cause of action exists for fraud and deceit and accordingly affirm the judgment.

DISCUSSION

I

Perry contends the court erred in granting summary adjudication of issues as to her first amended complaint because her second amended complaint superseded the first. She asserts once the court sustained the demurrer without leave to amend, it had nothing to summarily adjudicate as to that cause of action.

Perry filed her first amended complaint on September 22, 1982, and her second amended complaint, with the court's permission, on July 24, 1985. The court heard Atkinson's summary judgment motion to Perry's first amended complaint on September 27, 1985, and took the matter under submission. The court issued its memorandum decision on October 3, granting summary adjudication as to Perry's cause of action for fraud and deceit on her first amended complaint. On October 4, the court heard Atkinson's demurrer to the fraud and deceit cause of action in her second amended complaint, but ruled that issue was moot in light of its memorandum decision granting summary adjudication.

On October 15, Perry filed a motion for reconsideration, arguing, in part, the summary adjudication was improper because the first amended complaint had been superseded by the second. On October 28, the court issued two orders: one granting summary adjudication of the fraud and deceit cause of action in Perry's first and second amended complaints and another sustaining without leave to amend Atkinson's demurrer to the fraud and deceit cause of action in Perry's second amended complaint. On November 1, the court denied Perry's reconsideration motion.

We agree with Perry the court improperly granted summary adjudication as to the fraud and deceit cause of action in her first amended complaint. The record reflects the court granted Perry leave to file her second amended complaint with respect to her causes of action for fraud and deceit and intentional infliction of emotional distress. Once Perry did so, that complaint superseded her first amended complaint. (*Foreman & Clark Corp. v. Fallon* (1971) 3 Cal. 3d 875, 884, 92 Cal. Rptr. 162, 479 P.2d 362; *Avalon Painting Co. v. Alert Lbr. Co.* (1965) 234 Cal. App.2d 178, 182, 44 Cal. Rptr. 90.) Thus, we treat the

---

13. Perry proceeded to trial on her causes of action for intentional infliction of emotional distress. During trial, Atkinson, through his attorneys, offered to settle the emotional distress claims for $250,000 if Perry agreed to release Atkinson from liability for any other claims antedating the proposed settlement. Perry agreed, reserving her right to appeal the court's dismissal of her fraud and deceit cause of action. The parties also agreed that if Perry were successful on appeal, she would accept an additional $25,000 as her damages for the fraud and deceit cause of action and not take the case back through trial.

summary adjudication order as void and consider the appeal as properly from the sustaining of a demurrer without leave to amend.

II

Perry contends her second amended complaint states a cause of action for fraud and deceit which is factually and legally sufficient to withstand Atkinson's demurrer. The gravamen of Perry's complaint is that Atkinson defrauded her by promising to impregnate her if she had an abortion—a promise he did not intend to keep—on which he intended her to rely and on which she did rely to her detriment. Such misrepresentation, she asserts, is actionable as a tort.

In deciding whether Perry can state a cause of action for fraud and deceit, our inquiry must be directed to the specific conduct giving rise to such a claim. Although Perry's cause of action is couched in terms of a tort, the behavior of which she complains is Atkinson's breach of a promise to impregnate her after she had an "unwanted" abortion. Thus, the issue before us is whether Perry has a cause of action for fraudulent breach of a promise to impregnate.

In *Stephen K. v. Roni L.* (1980) 105 Cal. App. 3d 640, 164 Cal Rptr. 618, the defendant father (Stephen) in a paternity action cross-complained against his child's mother (Roni), alleging Roni had falsely represented she was taking birth control pills and in reliance on that representation, Stephen had sexual relations with her resulting in the birth of a child he did not want. The court held Roni's conduct towards Stephen was not actionable, reasoning "although Roni may have lied and betrayed the personal confidence reposed in her by Stephen, the circumstances and the highly intimate nature of the relationship wherein the false representations may have occurred are such that a court should not define any standard of conduct therefor." (*Id.* at p. 643, 164 Cal. Rptr. 618.) The court further stated that Stephen's claim of tortious misrepresentation was "nothing more than asking the court to supervise the promises made between two consenting adults as to the circumstances of their private sexual conduct. To do so would encourage unwarranted governmental intrusion into matters affecting the individual's right to privacy." (*Id.* at p. 644–645, 164 Cal. Rptr. 618.)

We find the court's reasoning in *Stephen K.* persuasive as applied to the facts here. Although Atkinson may have deliberately misrepresented his intentions to Perry in order to persuade her to have the abortion, their procreative decisions were so intensely private that we decline to intervene. Tort liability cannot apply to the choice, however motivated, of whether to conceive or bear a child.

Further, the California Legislature recognizes that certain sexual conduct and interpersonal decisions are, on public policy grounds, outside the realm of tort liability. For example, Civil Code section 43.5 provides in part that no cause of action exists for alienation of affection, seduction of a person over the age of legal consent, or breach of promise of marriage. Also, Civil Code section 43.4 precludes a cause of action for a fraudulent promise to marry or cohabit after marriage, entailing not only the marriage ritual but fulfillment of all "matrimonial obligations and expectations." (*Boyd v. Boyd* (1964) 228 Cal. App.2d 374, 377, 39 Cal. Rptr. 400.) If no cause of action can exist in tort for a fraudulent promise to fulfill the rights, duties and obligations of a marriage relationship, then logically no cause of action can exist for a fraudulent promise by a married man to impregnate a woman not his wife. (See *Langley v. Schumacker* (1956) 46 Cal. 2d 601, 604–607, 297 P.2d 977 (Spence, J., dissenting) [superseded by Civ. Code, Sec. 43.4 as stated in *Boyd v. Boyd, supra,* 228 Cal. App.2d at p. 376, 39 Cal. Rptr. 400]).

Perry contends Atkinson's right to privacy in fraudulently inducing her to have an abortion must give way to Perry's right to protection from and compensation for physical harm and to the government's interest in protecting the health and welfare of its citizens. In support of her argument, Perry cites *Barbara A. v. John G.* (1983) 145 Cal. App. 3d 369, 193 Cal. Rptr. 422 and *Kathleen K. v. Robert B.* (1984) 150 Cal. App. 3d 992, 198 Cal. Rptr. 273.

In *Barbara A.*, the court was confronted with the issue of whether a woman who had suffered injuries from an ectopic pregnancy has a cause of action in tort against the responsible man for his misrepresentations of infertility. The court held the plaintiff could state a cause of action for battery and deceit because the right to privacy does not insulate sexual relations form judicial scrutiny when that right is used as a shield from liability at the expense of the other party. (*Barbara A. v. John G., supra,* 145 Cal. App. 3d at p. 381, 193 Cal. Rptr. 422.) The court attempted to distinguish *Stephen K.* on both factual and public policy grounds:

> In essence, Stephen was seeking damages for the "wrongful birth" of his child [footnote omitted] resulting in support obligations and alleged damages for mental suffering. Here, no child is involved; appellant is seeking damages for severe injury to her own body. Although the *Stephen K.* court alluded to Stephen's claim as separate and apart from the issue of either parent's obligation to raise and support the child, it reached its decision without attempting to resolve the problem of the mother's reduced financial ability to support the child if she were required to pay damages to the father. We think this concern over the child, and not governmental intrusion into private sexual matters, ... is the central issue in *Stephen K.* and compels different public policy considerations. (*Id.* at pp. 378–379, 193 Cal. Rptr. 422.)

We see no significant distinction between *Stephen K.* and *Barbara A.* In both the complaining parties alleged they engaged in sexual relations induced by a false representation regarding their partners' procreative ability. Both cases fall squarely within Civil Code section 43.5, subdivision (c) precluding a cause of action for seduction. (See *Barbara A. v. John G., supra,* 145 Cal. App. 3d at p. 386, 193 Cal. Rptr. 422 (Scott, J., dissenting).)

The *Barbara A.* court attempts to distinguish its holding from that of *Stephen K.* on the ground that no child is involved and the public policy considerations regarding parental obligations are absent in *Barbara A.* However, the court in *Stephen K.* specifically refused to address the issues of child support and parental obligations. (*Stephen K. v. Roni L., supra,* 105 Cal. App. 3d at p. 643, 164 Cal. Rptr. 618.) Instead, it based its holding on the public policy consideration that "the practice of birth control, if any, engaged in by two partners in a consensual sexual relationship is best left to the individuals involved, free from any governmental interference." (*Id.* at p. 645, 164 Cal. Rptr. 618.) Because *Stephen K.* and *Barbara A.* cannot readily be reconciled, we choose here to follow the sound reasoning of *Stephen K.*

Moreover, Perry's reliance on *Kathleen K.* is misplaced. In that case, a woman brought an action against a man because she had contracted genital herpes through sexual intercourse with him. Citing *Barbara A.*, the court held the constitutional right of privacy did not protect the defendant from his tortious conduct in failing to inform the plaintiff he was infected with venereal disease. "The right of privacy is not absolute, and in some cases is subordinate to the state's fundamental right to enact laws which promote public health, welfare and safety, even though such laws may invade the offender's right of privacy." (*Barbara A. v. John G., supra,* 145 Cal. App. 3d at p. 380 [193 Cal. Rptr. 422]. *Kath-*

leen K. v. Robert B., supra, 150 Cal. App. 3d at pp. 996–997, 198 Cal. Rptr. 273.) The court further reasoned that "as in Barbara A., there is no child involved, and the public policy considerations with respect to parental obligations are absent." (Id. at p. 996, 198 Cal. Rptr. 273.)

Kathleen K. is distinguishable from the present case. The tortious transmission of a contagious disease implicates policy considerations beyond the sexual conduct and procreative decisions of two consenting adults. The state's interest "in the prevention and control of contagious and dangerous diseases" (*Id.* at p. 996, 198 Cal. Rptr. 273), is sufficient to allow a cause of action for fraudulent concealment of the risk of infection with venereal disease. The absence of such policy considerations here compels a different result.

In essence, Perry seeks judicial enforcement, by way of damages, of a promise to impregnate. The courts should not undertake the adjudication of promises and representations made by consenting adults regarding their sexual relationships. Once we attempt to determine in court, by means of tort law, the bona fides of promises such as are alleged here, we will of necessity be required to set standards for the making and performing of such promises. The court in *Stephen K.* and the Legislature by its actions in passing statutes such as Civil Code sections 43.4 and 43.5 have given wise counsel against such folly.

Public policy compels our holding no cause of action exists for Atkinson's fraud and deceit in misrepresenting his intentions to provide Perry with the means to have a child.

Judgment affirmed.

Chapter Four

Pensions and Other Fringe Benefits of Employment

At divorce, the court is directed to divide the "estate" of the parties. Tex. Fam. Code §7.001. This has been interpreted to mean the community property of the parties. In order to determine the extent of the parties' community property, courts must construe the scope of the term "property."

Until the 1970s, courts took a fairly conservative view toward what constituted divisible "property." Only "vested" rights constituted property; contingent rights frequently were considered "mere expectancies," even if the rights were acquired during marriage from a community source. During the past few decades, in some circumstances Texas courts have reconsidered the scope of divisible "property." Cases involving pension rights and other fringe benefits of employment obtained during marriage present this issue.

A. Pensions

1. In General

Johnson v. Johnson
Supreme Court of Arizona, 1981
131 Ariz. 38

HOLOHAN, Vice Chief Justice.

Appellant, Julia Johnson, filed an appeal from the judgment of the superior court in a dissolution proceeding. The court of appeals modified the judgment. *Johnson v. Johnson*, 131 Ariz. 47, 638 P.2d 714 (1980). Both appellant and appellee, Emery Johnson, filed petitions for review. We granted review. The opinion of the court of appeals is vacated.

The principal issue in this case is the proper method to be used in determining the wife's interest in the husband's retirement plan. During the 15-year marriage of the parties, the husband accumulated vested rights in both a profit sharing plan and a pension plan through his employment with a Tucson law firm. At the time of trial, there was $17,047.14 in the profit sharing plan and $55,380.77 in the pension trust, for a total of $72,427.91. The distribution of the funds under both plans lies within the discretion of an administrative committee. Although the committee has discretion to order early distribution of these funds, in the normal course of events the funds would not become available to the husband until he reaches retirement age, at least fifteen years from now.[1] Because the husband had no right to immediate payment, the trial court discounted the value of the funds at 6% interest for 22 years (the amount of time between the date of the divorce decree and the date when the husband would reach age 65).

VALUATION OF THE WIFE'S COMMUNITY INTEREST IN THE RETIREMENT PLANS

The pension and profit sharing accounts in this case constitute an appreciable portion of the marital estate. Indeed, it is now commonly recognized that pension rights are one of the most valuable of marital assets upon divorce. These pension rights are generally viewed as a form of deferred compensation for services rendered by employees. As such, it is well settled in Arizona and elsewhere that pension rights, whether vested[2] or nonvested,[3] are community property insofar as the rights were acquired during marriage, and are subject to equitable division upon divorce. The difficulty in the present case arises in attempting to determine the exact dollar amount of the wife's community interest in the husband's pension.

A non-employee spouse may be awarded his or her community interest in the employee spouse's pension benefits under either of two methods. The first has been called the "present cash value method," in which the court determines the community interest in the pension,[4] figures the present cash value of that interest, and awards half of that amount to the non-employee spouse in a lump sum, usually in the form of equivalent property; the employee thus receives the entire pension right free of community ties. Under the "reserved jurisdiction method," the court determines the formula for division at the time of the decree but delays the actual division until payments are received,[5] retaining jurisdiction to award the appropriate percentage of each pension payment if, as, and when, it is paid out.

The present cash value method provides a number of advantages over the reserved jurisdiction method,[6] especially when the anticipated date of retirement is far in the future.

---

1. The terms of the plan provide that participating employees shall retire at age 65 and may retire early after reaching age 60. According to the record, the husband was 42 years old when the petition for dissolution was filed in October, 1978, which now makes him 45. He will reach age 60 in 1996 15 years from now.

2. A "vested" pension right is one in which the right to be paid is not subject to forfeiture if the employment relationship terminates before the employee retires. *Brown, supra,* 15 Cal. 3d at 842, 544 P.2d at 563, 126 Cal. Rptr. at 635, 94 A.L.R.3d at 166–67. Vested rights must be distinguished from "matured" rights, which are unconditional rights to immediate payment. Often an employee's right vests after a certain term of employment but will not mature until the employee reaches retirement age and elects to retire. Id.

3. A "non-vested" pension right is one which is forfeited if the employment relationship terminates before retirement, e.g., because the employee quits, is discharged, or dies. *Brown, supra,* 15 Cal. 3d at 842, 544 P.2d at 563, 126 Cal. Rptr. at 635, 94 A.L.R.3d at 166–67.

4. The community share of the pension is determined by dividing the length of time worked during the marriage by the total length of time worked toward earning the pension. *In re Marriage of Judd,* 68 Cal. App. 3d 515, 522, 137 Cal. Rptr. 318, 321 (1977).

5. The court determines the community share of the pension as in footnote 4, *supra,* multiplies each future pension payment by that figure to determine what part of the payment is community property, then divides that part between the spouses.

6. The major disadvantage of the present cash method is that the employee spouse bears the risk of paying the community for rights which may never mature. *In re Marriage of Skaden,* 19 Cal. 3d 679, 688, 566 P.2d 249, 253, 139 Cal. Rptr. 615, 619 (1977). Additionally, the employee may feel cheated because he or she receives only an "expectancy" of receiving money in the future, while the non-employee spouse receives "real" assets such as home equity or stocks.

The former spouses are spared further entanglement because the litigation is completed, and the problems of continued court supervision and enforcement of the employee's duty to pay the ex-spouse's share are avoided. It is our view that the present cash value method is preferred if the pension rights can be valued accurately and if the marital estate includes sufficient equivalent property to satisfy the claim of the non-employee spouse without undue hardship to the employee spouse.

In this case, the present cash value method is clearly preferable in that the reserved jurisdiction method would require continued court supervision for at least 15 years. Moreover, the Johnsons' marital estate has sufficient other property available to make a current equitable division of all community property including the wife's interest in the pension fund.

The accuracy of any attempt to value a retirement plan is heavily dependent upon the type of plan which confronts the court. The two major kinds of pension plans are "defined contribution" and "defined benefit" plans. Under a defined contribution plan, a specified amount of money is periodically contributed to a fund by the employer, the employee, or both. This fund is invested and the earnings are divided proportionally among all plan participants. At any moment in time, there is a specific amount of money assigned to the account of each participant. These plans are thus analogous to a savings account. The total amount of benefits receivable under such a plan depends upon the success of fund investments. By contrast, under a defined benefit plan, the benefits are specified in advance, usually as a percentage of salary and related to years of service, and no account is kept for the employee. Both the pension and profit sharing programs in the present case are in the nature of defined contribution plans, as shown by the specific amounts that are credited to the husband's account.

With either type of plan, its present cash value must be determined before a present lump-sum satisfaction of the parties' interests can be made. Various actuarial calculations are used to discount the present value of the retirement plan to reflect contingencies affecting the eventual payout, including discounts for mortality,[7] interest,[8] probability of vesting,[9] and probability of continued employment.[10] However, not all of these calculations are applicable to every retirement plan.

Valuation depends in part on the type of plan involved. In a defined contribution plan, employing individual accounts to which contributions are credited, the best estimate of present value is the amount currently credited to the employee's account. An adjustment, however, must be made if the account figure is not vested or if it is not payable when the employee dies prior to reaching retirement age. If those factors are present, then the account balance must be discounted for the probability of vesting and for the probability of survival to retirement.

---

7. If the right to be paid under the plan is contingent upon the employee's surviving to a certain age, the calculation of present value must take into account the probability that the employee will attain that age, based on standard mortality tables and on the employee's physical condition.

8. This involves discounting the value of the sum to be obtained in the future to take account of the interest that could be earned if the money were available for investment today.

9. If the employee's rights under the plan have not yet vested or are subject to divestment, the present value should be discounted to reflect the possibility that the rights will not vest or may be divested.

10. Most pension plans provide increased benefits for longer term employment. In defined contribution plans, the longer employment period results in more total contributions to the fund. Under defined benefit plans, the benefits are usually set at a percentage of the average salary during the employee's last three or five years of employment. The longer the employee continues to work, the higher the ending salary is likely to be, and the higher the eventual benefits will be.

In the present case the employee's rights in the plans are vested and are not subject to forfeiture if death occurs prior to retirement. Therefore, the discounts for mortality and probability of vesting are inapplicable here. Under a defined contribution plan, the probability of continued employment discount does not significantly alter the present cash value of the plan. The interest discount is also inapplicable because a defined contribution plan is presently earning interest for the employee. The trial court incorrectly discounted the value of the fund because no consideration was given to the fact that the fund was earning interest and would continue to earn interest. There was no need to discount the value of the account because the value of a defined contribution plan, such as that of appellee, is the present amount credited to the account.

DISCUSSION

The two most common types of pension plans are defined benefit plans and defined contribution plans. Under a defined benefit plan, the employer agrees to pay an employee who has satisfied the minimum requirements (*e.g.*, length of employment, age, etc.) a monthly retirement payment pursuant to a certain formula set forth in the employer's pension plan. For example, a possible formula could be:

Monthly payment = .03 × last monthly salary × number of years of service with the employer.

Under this formula, after retirement the retiree would receive 90% of his last monthly salary if he had worked for the employer for 30 years. An important point to notice is that, prior to retirement, funds are not contributed to the employee's account; the employer makes deposits to a general retirement fund in an amount estimated to satisfy all retirement obligations. Defined benefit plans normally are funded by the employer.

Defined benefit plan rights are always initially "unvested." This means that if the employee dies, quits, or is fired before the "vesting date" the employee has no interest in the plan. So, an employee with unvested retirement rights possesses a contingent interest in the benefits; it is uncertain whether the employee will ever receive any benefits.

At some point, as specified in the particular pension plan, the benefits "vest." After benefits vest, the employee will receive benefits, if he survives until retirement age, even if he is fired or quits. (In *Cearley*, the next case in these materials, the court sometimes uses the term "accrued" and "unaccrued" instead of vested and unvested.) The employee does not necessarily have the right to retire at this point, however. Also, it is not certain the employee will enjoy the benefits, even after vesting. If the employee dies before retirement, under some plans the employee receives nothing.

When the employee has the right to retire, the benefits "mature." Most employees do not accept this early retirement option; they frequently work for a significant period after the maturity date. When the employee retires, the benefits are "in pay status," because the employee is receiving benefits.

The other type of pension plan (other than a "defined benefit" plan) is a "defined contribution" plan. Under these plans, separate accounts are kept for each employee. Contributions are periodically made to each employee's account based on some formula, such as a percentage of the profits of the employer or a percentage of the employee's salary. This type of plan can be funded by the employer or by both the employer and the employee (via payroll deductions). Employee contributions must be immediately vested; employer contributions vest according to the specified vesting schedule. When an employee with a defined contribution plan interest retires, his retirement benefit is the annuity that can be purchased with the balance in his account at retirement. *Johnson, supra,* involved defined contribution plans.

A good general reference for pension issues is Troyan, "Pension Evaluation for Marriage Dissolutions Actions: A Pension Evaluator's Perspective," 3 *Valuation & Distribution of Marital Property*, at ch. 45 (1986).

Until 1976, Texas courts did not consider unvested pension plan rights divisible property.

Cearley v. Cearley
Supreme Court of Texas, 1976
544 S.W.2d 661

DANIEL, Justice.

This is a divorce case in which the only remaining question concerns the propriety of the trial court granting the wife a fractional interest in future military retirement benefits if and when received by the husband.

Prior to the divorce on June 3, 1975, Robert L. Cearley had served for 19 years as an enlisted man in the Air Force, during which period he and Shirley had been married for 18 years. Robert was to have completed the 20 years necessary for receipt of retirement benefits on May 7, 1976, and his enlistment at the time of the divorce extended to August 31, 1976.

The trial court ordered that "If and when Robert L. Cearley ... retires and receives a retirement benefit ... then, and in such an event, the Petitioner [Shirley Cearley] is to receive one-half (½) of 18 of the fraction of the number of years of active service until retirement...." The Court of Civil Appeals reversed and rendered only that portion of the judgment awarding the wife a share of the contingent retirement benefits. Tex. Civ. App., 536 S.W.2d 96. We reverse the judgment of the Court of Civil Appeals and affirm the judgment of the trial court.

The Court of Civil Appeals held that the trial court was without authority to order division of the husband's prospective military retirement benefits because no vested interest had been acquired therein at the time of the judgment. We have jurisdiction under Section 2 of article 1728 because the above decision is in conflict with the decision of the Court of Civil Appeals in *Miser v. Miser*, 475 S.W.2d 597 (Tex. Civ. App. 1971, writ dism'd), on a question of law material to a decision of this case.

Military Retirement Pensions Earned During Coverture are Community Property

Section 5.01 of the Family Code provides that community property consists of the property, other than separate property, acquired by either spouse during marriage. A spouse's separate property consists of the property acquired by the spouse by gift, devise or descent. Despite an earlier view that retirement and pension plans were gifts bestowed by benevolent employers on retiring employees, they are now regarded as a mode of employee compensation earned during a given period of employment. The earlier view was rejected in *Lee v. Lee*, 112 Tex. 392, 247 S.W. 828 (1923), in the following language construing a corporate employee's benefit:

> It was in no sense a donation to the employee for individual merit, but was manifestly additional compensation for faithful and continuous service. It was as

much a fruit of his labors as his regular wages or salary. It was in the strictest sense a 'grain' added to the common acquests of the marital partnership, and the direct result and fruit of his labor and services.

It is now well established that matured private retirement, annuity, and pension benefits earned by either spouse during the marital relationship are part of the community estate and thus subject to division upon dissolution of the marriage. *Herring v. Blakeley*, 385 S.W.2d 843 (Tex. 1965).

The same characterization of community property was first given to military retirement benefits by this Court in *Busby v. Busby*, 457 S.W.2d 551 (Tex. 1970), which approved a holding in *Kirkham v. Kirkham*, 335 S.W.2d 393 (Tex. Civ. App. — [sic] 1960, no writ), that "the military retirement pay account was not a gift or gratuity but an earned property right which accrued to him by reason of his years in military service; the military retirement pay account was earnings of the husband during marriage, and as such, community property."

Future Pension Benefits As Contingent Community Property Rights

While the status of military pension benefits earned during marriage is now firmly established as community property, the decisions in this and other community property states have differed as to whether the pension payments must have vested or matured before they are subject to apportionment by a divorce court, or whether future contingent payments may be apportioned "if, as, and when" they mature and are received by the retired spouse. The argument of the husband, and the holding of the Court of Civil Appeals in the instant case, is that the power of the divorce courts to "order a division of the estate of the parties" does not apply to future military retirement benefits because they have not been "acquired" or vested during the marriage. Sections 3.63 and 5.01, Texas Family Code (1975).

For such contingent or inchoate rights to reach the status of assets of the estate of the parties, the Court of Civil Appeals held that "all events [must] have occurred which fix the liability of the government" to pay retirement benefits, adding: "The conditions must be such as would entitle the claimant [husband] to institute an action, if necessary, for a money judgment." This is a more rigid *requirement* than has been found in any other case or writing on the subject. It comes nearer to the rule of *French v. French*, 17 Cal. 2d 775, 112 P.2d 235 (1941), which plagued the California courts until the Supreme Court of California reversed itself in *Brown v. Brown*, 15 Cal. 3d 838, 126 Cal. Rptr. 633, 544 P.2d 561 (1976). The *French* case, *supra*, involved the wife's claim to a community interest in a portion of the prospective retirement pay of her husband an enlisted man in the Fleet Reserve, payable if and when he completed additional years of service. The California Supreme Court held that this "non-vested" pension right was a mere "expectancy" and thus not a community asset subject to division upon dissolution of a marriage. Reliance on the date of collectibility as the inception of contingent pension rights earned during coverture was soon recognized to be inconsistent with basic community property principles. The *French* decision led to much criticism and attempts by lower California courts to find reasons for distinguishing the case and extending community property protection to unmatured retirement benefits.

We shall quote at length from *Brown v. Brown, supra*, because of the California Supreme Court's long and careful study of the community property aspects of the question which now faces this Court:

> Upon reconsideration of this issue, we have concluded that *French v. French* should be overruled and that the subsequent decisions which rely on that prece-

dent should be disapproved. As we shall explain, the *French* rule cannot stand because nonvested pension rights are not an expectancy but a contingent interest in property; furthermore, the *French* rule compels an inequitable division of rights acquired through community effort. Pension rights, whether or not vested, represent a property interest; to the extent that such rights derive from employment during coverture, they comprise a community asset subject to division in a dissolution proceeding. [15 Cal. 3d at 843, 126 Cal. Rptr. at 634, 544 P.2d at 562].

We conclude that *French v. French*, and subsequent cases erred in characterizing nonvested pension rights as expectancies and in denying the trial courts the authority to divide such rights as community property. This mischaracterization of pension rights has, and unless overturned, will continue to result in inequitable division of community assets. Over the past decades, pension benefits have become an increasingly significant part of the consideration earned by the employee for his services. As the date of vesting and retirement approaches, the value of the pension right grows until it often represents the most important asset of the marital community.

The present case illustrates the point. Robert's pension rights, a valuable asset built up by 24 years of community effort, under the *French* rule would escape division by the court as a community asset solely because dissolution occurred two years before the vesting date. [15 Cal. 3d at 847, 126 Cal. Rptr. at 638, 544 P.2d at 566].

In dividing nonvested pension rights as community property the court must take account of the possibility that death or termination of employment may destroy those rights before they mature. In some cases the trial court may be able to evaluate this risk in determining the present value of those rights. (See *DeRevere v. DeRevere, supra* 5 Wash. App. 741, 491 P.2d 249: *Thiede, op. cit., supra*, 9 U.S.F. L. Rev. 635, 654.) But if the court concludes that because of uncertainties affecting the vesting or maturation of the pension that it should not attempt to divide the present value of pension rights, it can instead award each spouse an appropriate portion of each pension payment as it is paid. This method of dividing the community interest in the pension renders it unnecessary for the court to compute the present value of the pension rights, and divide equally the risk that the pension will fail to vest. [15 Cal. 3d 848, 126 Cal. Rptr. at 639, 544 P.2d at 567].

This method of apportioning prospective unmatured military retirement benefits as part of the community estate had been approved by Texas and New Mexico courts several years earlier. *Mora v. Mora*, 429 S.W.2d 660 (Tex. Civ. App. 1968, writ dism'd); *Webster v. Webster*, 442 S.W.2d 786 (Tex. Civ. App. 1969, no writ); *Miser v. Miser*, 475 S.W.2d 597 (Tex. Civ. App. 1971, writ dism'd); *LeClert v. LeClert*, 80 N.M. 235, 453 P.2d 755 (1969). In those cases the pension benefits had not matured at the time of divorce because the husbands had not retired. Although all but *Miser* had served the number of years required for their pension benefits to have accrued, all were still on active duty when their marriages were dissolved; they had not received the required honorable discharges; neither had they met other contingencies enumerated by the Court of Civil Appeals in the instant case as being necessary for such contingent benefits to be apportioned as part of the community estate. Yet, in each of those cases apportionment of the unmatured retirement benefits was ordered or approved if, as, and when received in the future by the prospective retiring spouse, just as the trial court ordered in the instant case.

The *Mora*, *Webster* and *LeClert* decisions were cited with approval by this Court in *Busby v. Busby*, 457 S.W.2d 551 (Tex. 1970), which affirmed a partition of matured military benefits, with the wife's portion to be paid "if, when, and as" the benefits were paid to the husband.

Apportionment As Contingent Property Interest

While the status of unaccrued and unmatured military retirement benefits earned wholly or partially during marriage is a question of first impression for this Court, we believe that most of the objections to their treatment as a contingent property interest were anticipated and answered by this Court in *Busby v. Busby, supra.* For instance, the husband there argued that he never possessed a "property right" in his disability retirement benefits during the marriage; that they were a mere expectancy, because he had not retired prior to the divorce, and the rights were subject to forfeiture by death or dishonorable discharge prior to his retirement. These arguments were overruled. The Court held that the benefits were community property at the time of the divorce even though they had not matured and were not at that time subject to possession and enjoyment. As heretofore indicated, the Court cited with approval the decisions in *Mora*, *Webster*, and *LeClert, supra*, which held that the contingencies merely made such benefits subject to non-maturity or divestment. It was held that the fact that the benefits were subject to divestment under certain conditions did not reduce the benefits to a "mere expectancy." See also *Nail v. Nail*, 486 S.W.2d 761, 762 (Tex. 1972). Even the dissent in *Busby*, which objected to the recognition of matured retirement benefits as vested property rights, stated that the court granting the divorce "[can] and should take it [retirement benefits] into consideration" in exercising its broad powers under article 4638 [now Section 7.001 of the Family Code], to the end that an order might be entered "that is just and equitable under the circumstances" citing *Mora v. Mora, supra*, and *Kirkham v. Kirkham, supra*.

In *Herring v. Blakeley*, 385 S.W.2d 843 (Tex. 1965), this Court held that profit sharing and retirement plans may be classed as community property even though none of the funds were available or subject to possession at the time of the divorce. The Court said: "Community rights may exist in interests that cannot be reduced to possession, such as remainder or reversion rights." A similar analogy was made in *Brown v. Brown, supra*, with respect to the community interest in a contingent fee earned during the marriage but which had not matured at the time of the divorce. See *Waters v. Waters*, 75 Cal. App. 2d 265, 170 P.2d 494 (1946). Although a serviceman's military pension is not payable before the date of its maturity, it is not "earned" on that day. Rather it is a form of deferred compensation which is earned during each month of his military service. *LeClert v. LeClert, supra.* The portion that he earned during the months of coverture became contingent earnings of the community which may or may not bloom into full maturity at some future date. We hold that such rights, prior to accrual and maturity, constitute a contingent interest in property and a community asset subject to consideration along with other property in the division of the estate of the parties under Section 3.63 of the Family Code.

Any other decision would result in an unnecessary multiplicity of suits. The present case is a good example. The trial court has properly settled the matter in the divorce judgment if, as, and when the retirement benefits mature. It was shown at the trial that the husband was to have completed the 20 years necessary for accrual of his retirement benefits on May 7, 1976, with the possibility of maturity at the end of his current enlistment on August 31, 1976. It is possible that either or both of these events have occurred. If the trial court were reversed on the basis set forth by the Court of Civil Appeals, then Shirley Cearley, in order to obtain her share of the benefits which were earned during the marriage, would have to file a second lawsuit against Robert Cearley for partition thereof after the date that the retirement benefits mature.

The bench and the bar were cautioned by this Court in *Busby v. Busby, supra,* to inquire as to the existence of insurance or retirement programs in all divorce suits "to the end that the final judgment fully disposes of all property valuables of the community." Pension and retirement benefits have become an increasingly significant part of the consideration earned for military, governmental, and private services, sometimes being of the principal asset accumulated by the community. *Brown v. Brown, supra; Kirkham v. Kirkham, supra.* The administration of justice will best be served if contingent interests in retirement benefits are settled at the time of the divorce, even though it may be necessary in many instances for the judgment to make the apportionment to the nonretiring spouse effective if, as, and when the benefits are received by the retiring spouse. We approve this method of apportionment and award of contingent interests in military retirement benefits because of the uncertainties affecting the accrual and maturity of such benefits. This method will forego the difficulty of computing a present value and will fairly divide the risk that the pension may fail to mature.

The judgment of the Court of Civil Appeals in this case is reversed and the judgment of the trial court is affirmed.

Taggart v. Taggart
Supreme Court of Texas, 1977
552 S.W.2d 422

POPE, Justice.

Ann Taggart instituted this suit against George Taggart for the partition of military retirement benefits that were not divided when the parties were divorced. The trial court, upon a finding that the parties were married during the time that eight-ninths of the retirement benefits accumulated, rendered judgment that plaintiff was entitled to four-ninths of all retirement pay received by her former husband. The court ordered defendant George Taggart to receive plaintiff's share in trust for the plaintiff and make monthly disbursement to her of her share. The court of civil appeals reversed that judgment and rendered judgment that plaintiff take nothing. 540 S.W.2d 823. We reverse the judgment of the court of civil appeals and reform that of the trial court.

On June 5, 1943, George Taggart entered the United States Navy. Ann and George Taggart were married on October 7, 1947, and they were divorced on January 5, 1968. The divorce proceedings made no mention of retirement benefits.

On July 1, 1964, three and one-half years before the divorce, George completed the equivalent of twenty years of active duty. George did not retire but elected to be placed in the Fleet Reserve. As an enlisted man in the regular Navy, he had to complete thirty years of active duty before he was eligible for retirement based on years of service. Mr. Taggart was retired from the Navy on April 1, 1974. Ann Taggart instituted this suit for the recovery of her share of the retirement benefits since April 1, 1974. She did not seek any part of the retainer pay that George Taggart earned for his service in the Fleet Reserve, nor was there any plea of limitations urged in this case.

The court of civil appeals decided this case in August, 1976, at which time the supreme court had granted a writ of error but had not written its opinion in *Cearley v. Cearley,* 544

S.W.2d 661 (Tex. 1976). We decided in *Cearley* that retirement benefits are subject to division as vested contingent community property rights even though the present right has not fully matured. We refused to follow the California case of *French v. French*, 17 Cal. 2d 775, 112 P.2d 235 (1941), which treated an unmatured pension right as a nonvested expectancy instead of a vested right. In *Cearley*, we held that military retirement benefits were community property even though the benefits at the time of the divorce "had not matured and were not at the time subject to possession and enjoyment." There is no necessity to again analyze the relevant Texas decisions or the opinion of the California court in *Brown v. Brown*, 15 Cal. 3d 838, 126 Cal. Rptr. 633, 544 P.2d 561 (1976), which rejected the rule of *French v. French, supra,* and recognized a present contingent right subject to divestment.

Since *Cearley* controls this case, we hold that Ann Taggart owned as her part of the community estate a share in the contingent right to military benefits even though that right had not matured at the time of the divorce. It appears, however, that the trial court did not make the correct computation of her fractional interest.

The trial court computed Ann Taggart's one-half interest in George Taggart's retirement benefits upon the basis of his twenty years of service as a member of the regular Navy. At the end of the twenty years, he was not entitled to receive any retirement benefits based upon his term of service because he had to serve in the Fleet Reserve for an additional ten years. It was, therefore, his three hundred and sixty months of service that entitled him to the retirement benefits. According to the undisputed evidence Ann and George Taggart's marriage coincided with his service in the Navy for a period of two hundred and forty-six months. The correct computation of Ann Taggart's vested interest is that she was entitled only to one-half of 246/360th's of the retirement pay.

The judgment of the court of civil appeals is reversed; the judgment of the trial court is reformed to adjudge the correct fractional interest to Ann Taggart and as reformed is affirmed.

YARBROUGH, Justice, dissenting.

I respectfully dissent.

I find no fault in the position of the majority insofar as they seek to include military retirement benefits, which have accrued during the term of the marriage, in the corpus of the community estate to be divided by the trial court at the time of the divorce. I do feel, however, that good reasons exist for applying this rule prospectively *in futuro* to those divorce actions filed after the date of this court's opinion, and I oppose the view and principle of the majority opinion only to the extent that it operates retroactively, and serves to resurrect the problems of a divorce, and its attendant property settlement agreements of many years standing.

In the case at bar, the property of the parties was divided pursuant to court decree in 1968. At the time of their divorce in 1968, military retirement, benefits payable in the future were assumed to be of a contingent, non-vested character, and therefore outside the jurisdictional power of the court, and accordingly not subject to division by inclusion in court approved and/or drafted property settlements.[1] Notwithstanding that assumption,

---

1. This view prevailed until this court's opinion in 1976 in *Cearley v. Cearley*, 544 S.W.2d 661 (Tex. 1976) when lawyers and trial courts were first authoritatively advised that unmatured retirement benefits were subject to division. The issue regarding division of matured retirement benefits was first addressed in 1970 by this court in *Busby v. Busby*, 457 S.W.2d 551 (Tex. 1970). The instant case had been decided by the court of civil appeals before this court's decision in *Cearley, supra,* and

which we now recognize to have been erroneous, courts were then free to make virtually any distribution of the remaining community and separate property as seemed just and appropriate, in order to do equity among the partners. We cannot know to what extent, if any, the expectation of retirement benefits influenced the various courts in dividing properties among divorcing partners. The bounds of judicial discretion in divorce property settlements have known little appellate limitation or review, and what courts could not do officially, they have often done unofficially. It is more than a "reasonable assumption" that such benefits have been, in many if not most instances, of major consideration to the court in effecting a property settlement between partners. We now modify those carefully drafted settlements en masse, and invite all formerly divorced partners to assert new claims to a part of their former spouse's military retirement benefits under circumstances which preclude any review or adjustment of either the original property settlement, or of the equities that were developed as a part of that earlier division.

It is probable that many of the men and women, who are now post-divorce military retirees, have adjusted their life style to the income provided by the benefits. Presumably, many have new families, new ties, new obligations and responsibilities, including "second families." In an effort to provide and plan for such responsibilities, many retirees have made irrevocable elections with respect to dependent, and survivorship benefits, the disruption of which will, in many instances, create hardship if not havoc.

Additionally, and perhaps most regrettably, the majority opinion now authorizes the resurrection of past disputes and personal disappointments long since laid to rest as the parties again come to the bar of justice for yet another round of bitter controversy over the question of who is entitled to how much of the retirement benefit, a question which most parties, their lawyers, and all courts, believed to have been answered and finally resolved pursuant to earlier court decrees now many years old.

By the majority's holding today, we encourage all formerly divorced couples with military benefits to relive the pain of their divorce with attendant social disruptions to the life and life style of both the former partners and their new families. Certainly, a better result would have been achieved by applying this rule prospectively to divorce actions filed in the future.

DISCUSSION

Cearley announced that the community has an interest in all retirement rights, to the extent that the benefits were earned by services rendered during marriage. *Taggart* gives *Cearley* retroactive effect.

Taggart provides an important lesson for fledgling family lawyers. It is important to list *all* property of the parties in the divorce decree, even if you are certain that the property is now considered your client's separate property. Otherwise, if Texas law later changes and the property in question is considered community property, the former spouses will hold the property as tenants in common. If this occurs, the other spouse may bring an action to partition the property in question, regardless whether the divorce court considered this property when the divorce property division was fashioned. (Under current Texas law, the partition can be equitable, and does not have to be equal. See Tex. Fam. Code § 9.203.) In contrast, if the decree awarded the property to your client, no post-divorce

---

understandably, that court followed the long recognized rule that such benefits were not subject to division.

partition action would be possible. The decree does not have to expressly mention the property for the post-divorce action to be barred. For example, in *Marriage of Moore*, 890 S.W.2d 821 (Tex. App.—Amarillo 1994, no writ) the decree stated that "all community property ... not otherwise awarded by this decree shall continue to be owned by the parties in equal undivided interests." The appellate court concluded that this divided all the spouses' community property, even property not mentioned in the decree, so no post-divorce partition action was possible.

After *Taggart*, many non-employee spouses involved in pre-*Cearley* divorces brought partition actions to recover an interest in the retirement benefits of the former spouse. In these partition actions, Texas courts were reluctant to conclude that the decree awarded the pension rights to the employee spouse. (In many cases the pension benefits were by far the most valuable part of the community estate.) Laches was rarely invoked. *See Yeo v. Yeo*, 581 S.W.2d 734 (Tex. Civ. App.—San Antonio, 1979, writ ref'd n.r.e.).

Taggart accepts the pro rata deferred payment approach (sometimes called the "time rule") to determine the community interest in pension benefits. Under this approach, the fractional community interest in the pension received is (years worked while married) / (total years worked at the time of retirement). In *Taggart*, the husband worked for 360 months, and was married 246 of these months. So, under the basic pro rata approach the community share of each pension payment actually received was 246/360. This share is sometimes referred to as the "coverture fraction."

Under the traditional pro rata deferred payment approach, the community shares in the pension rights only if benefits are actually received. The non-employee spouse begins to share only when the employee retires.

The pro rata approach is only sensible when each year of employment is of approximately the same value for purposes of the pension benefits.

In re Marriage of Poppe

California Court of Appeals, 1979
97 Cal. App. 3d 1

KAUFMAN, Justice.

Daniel G. Poppe (hereinafter former husband) appeals from an order of the court dated September 18, 1978, ... granting the application of Josephine A. Poppe (former wife) fixing her interest in the Naval Reserve pension being received by former husband.

Former husband entered the Navy on July 1, 1937. He served on active duty from that date until July 13, 1946, at which time he became a member of the Naval Reserve. On February 23, 1946, the parties were married. The parties separated on June 16, 1973, and their marriage was subsequently dissolved as previously indicated. After the separation of the parties, former husband continued serving in the Naval Reserve until he retired on October 31, 1977.

Retirement benefits paid to Navy personnel retiring from active duty are based on the number of years served and the amount of the retiree's salary during active service. Contrastingly, the amount of the pension paid to Naval Reserve retirees is a percentage of the base pay for the rank achieved arrived at on the basis of the number of points accumulated by the retiree during his service in the Naval Reserve. Essentially one point is earned for each drill attended. For example, 14 or 15 points would be earned during the annual two weeks' training duty. For periods of active duty, one point is credited for each day.

To be eligible for retirement a Naval Reservist must have been credited with a minimum number of "qualifying" years of service, that is, years in which 50 or more points were earned. However, if the minimum "qualifying" years requirement is met, all points earned are counted in the calculation of the pension notwithstanding that in some years less than 50 points were earned.

Former husband retired with a total of 5,002 points of which more than 3,000 were earned during the period he was in active duty prior to the marriage. The number of points accumulated during the marriage was 1,632. The balance of former husband's points were earned by him for his participation in the Naval Reserve after the separation of the parties. It was former husband's contention in the trial court that former wife's interest in the pension should be computed by multiplying one-half times the fraction 1632/5002 times the amount of the pension, $592 per month. Apportioning the pension in that fashion, former wife's share would amount to approximately $95.50 per month, and former husband had been paying that sum to former wife. However, the trial court determined that former husband's "qualifying" years totaled 31.50 and apportioned the pension on the basis of the "time rule" by dividing the 27.50 years between marriage and separation by the 31.5 "qualifying" years so that former wife's share amounts to $253.60 per month.

Former wife asserts that the "time rule" is the normal basis for apportioning retirement benefits earned in part during coverture and was appropriately employed by the court in the case at bench. Although the "time rule" is not the only acceptable method for apportioning retirement benefits between the community and separate estates, it is apparently the method most frequently employed.

However, apportionment on the basis of the "time rule" is appropriate only where the amount of the retirement benefits is substantially related to the number of years of service. The rule and its rationale were aptly stated in *Marriage of Judd*, 68 Cal. App. 3d 515, 522–23, 137 Cal. Rptr. 318, 321:

> Where the total number of years served by an employee-spouse is a substantial factor in computing the amount of retirement benefits to be received by that spouse, the community is entitled to have its share based upon the length of service performed on behalf of the community in proportion to the total length of service necessary to earn those benefits. The relation between years of community service to total years of service provides a fair gauge of that portion of retirement benefits attributable to community effort.

Thus it is that in each and all of the cited cases the amount to be received in retirement benefits depended upon or was substantially related to the number of years of service rendered.

In the case at bench the amount of former husband's pension is not substantially related to the number of years he served in the Naval Reserve. The only relationship between the number of years of service and the pension is that to be eligible for the pension former husband must have served a minimum number of "qualifying" years, years in which he earned 50 or more points. That condition having been satisfied, all points earned, whether in a "qualifying" year or not, counted in fixing the amount of his pension. The number of points that can be earned in a year may be as high as 364 or as low as 1, depending on the nature and frequency of the service rendered, not the number of years served. Thus the amount of the pension is not a function of the number of years of service; the number of years of service during the marriage is not a fair gauge of the community contribution; and the court's apportionment of the pension on the basis of the number of "qualifying" years served as compared to the number of years of service during the marriage must be said to be unreasonable, arbitrary and an abuse of discretion.

DISCUSSION

Poppe involves a case where an advocate successfully argued that it would be unfair to apportion the community interest in the pension based upon time. This argument is also possible for defined contribution plans. For such plans, it is fairly easy to determine what the balance was at the time of marriage and what it is at the time of divorce. The community interest might then be computed by simply subtracting the former from the latter, rather than by using the "time rule" allocation approach. *See, e.g., Maslen v. Maslen*, 822 P2d 982 (Idaho 1991). *See also Baw v. Baw*, 949 S.W.2d 764 (Tex. App.—Dallas 1997, no writ); *Smith v. Smith*, 22 S.W.3d 140 (Tex. App.—Houston [14th Dist] 2000, no pet.).

Of course, this "subtraction approach" is not the only possible approach to use if a spouse had a defined contribution pension right when the spouses marry. Tex. Fam. Code § 3.007(c) authorizes the employee to trace any capital gains during marriage arising from premarital contributions.

It is quite important to understand how the employee's rights accrue under the pension plan involved. For example, in *In re Marriage of Joiner*, 766 S.W.2d 263 (Tex. App.— Amarillo), *overruled by* 755 S.W.2d 496 (Tex. App.—Amarillo 1988, no writ), the husband had worked for his employer for approximately twenty years as of the time of divorce. He had accrued rights in the employer's profit-sharing plan. The husband married after he began working for the employer. Under the terms of the plan, employees began accruing rights after five years of service. Should the first five years of employment be counted when determining the husband's separate property interest in the plan?

In *Bloomer v. Bloomer* 927 S.W.2d 118 (Tex. App.—Houston [1st Dist.] 1996, writ denied), the court noted that the *Poppe* approach was "more appropriate" than the time rule for dividing military benefits, but was not required.

In re Marriage of Henkle
California Court of Appeals, 1987
234 Cal. Rptr. 351

KING, Associate Justice.

In this case we hold that once maximum retirement benefits have been earned, further employment thereafter during marriage, does not count as service during marriage for the purpose of applying the time rule to determine the community interest in an employee spouse's retirement pay.

The Henkles married in 1969 and separated six years later in 1975. At the time of marriage Robert was an Air Force colonel with 26 years service. He retired in 1975 with 32 years of service.

After 20 years of service a member of the military may retire with 50 percent of his/her base pay. Thereafter 2.5% per year is added until, after 30 years of service, the maximum of 75 percent is reached.

"Benefits like pensions are part of the compensation an employee receives for his services and they are community property to the extent they are earned by employment during marriage." "Although the 'time rule' is not the only acceptable method for apportioning retirement benefits between the community and separate estates [citations], it is apparently the method most frequently employed. However, apportionment on the basis of 'time rule' is appropriate only where the amount of the retirement benefits is substantially related to the number of years of service." (*In re Marriage of Poppe* (1979), 97 Cal. App. 3d 1, 8, 158 Cal. Rptr. 500.)

The Poppe court rejected the time rule where retirement benefits were based on a point system "depending on the nature and frequency of the service rendered, not the number of years served." But Poppe does not govern this case, since Robert's retirement benefits were substantially related to the number of years served. In these circumstances, "the community is entitled to have its share based upon the length of service performed on behalf of the community in proportion to the total length of service necessary to earn those benefits."

Delsa argues the community interest in Robert's retirement pay is 6/32 because she was married to him for six of his thirty-two years of service. However, only the first 30 of those years were necessary to earn the benefits; Robert acquired no increase in percentage thereafter. Under Delsa's theory, if Robert had already served 30 years when the parties married, and served 10 more years during marriage, the community would have a 10/40 or 25 percent interest in a separate property asset fully earned and owned by Robert prior to marriage. Such a result flies in the face of the rule that "the community owns all pension rights *attributable to employment during the marriage*."

Unlike a vesting period during which no benefits are acquired, but which is a prerequisite to receiving later-acquired benefits, Robert's service during the last two years of marriage was not necessary to earn any benefits nor did it earn any additional benefits.

His situation is also distinguishable from that in which courts have held "the first few years of service (during the marriage) must be given just as much weight in computing total service as the last few years (after separation)." (*In re Marriage of Anderson* (1976) 64 Cal. App. 3d 36, 39, 134 Cal. Rptr. 252.) In those cases the pension's post-separation increase in value by reason of continued employment is not entirely separate property "because the amount of the pension is dependent upon the total number of years in service." By contrast, the last two years of Robert's military service did not contribute to the total number of years of service — 30 — on which the amount of retirement pay depends.

The community interest is 4/30 of Robert's military retirement pay; thus Delsa's community share is 2/30 of the benefit.

The order is reversed and the cause remanded with directions to recompute Delsa's interest in Robert's retirement pay in accordance with the formula established herein.

DISCUSSION

Under the pro rata deferred payment apportionment approach for defined benefit plans, the community shares in the pension rights if and when the benefits are received. This result has certain undesirable consequences. For example, the non-employee spouse may need money at the time of divorce, and it could cause great hardship to defer payment of the pension interest. Also, the traditional deferred payment approach required spouses to continue to deal with one another, and this can cause problems.

For these reasons, some courts attempt to compute the present value of the community interest in the pension. To do this, for defined benefit plan rights, the aggregate amount which will be received must be computed. This is done by looking to life expectancy tables. For example, assume that the employee has retired at the time of divorce.

If the employee has a life expectancy at divorce of ten years, and the pension will stop when the employee dies, for valuation purposes it would be assumed that the employee will receive benefits for ten more years. However, the aggregate value of these benefits must be "reduced to present value," because the right to receive money in the future is worth less than the right to receive money immediately. If money is not received until the future, the recipient loses the right to invest the money for a certain period. Also, if the amount to be received is a fixed amount not adjusted for inflation, inflation will also reduce the real value of the amount to be received.

If the employee has not retired at the time of divorce, the present value computation becomes even more complicated. For example, an assumption must be made about when the employee will retire. Also, the value of the pension must be discounted for the possibility that the employee will die before retirement, and thereby receive no pension. If the benefits have not vested, the value must also be discounted for the possibility that the employee will quit or be fired. In light of these complexities, it is fairly easy to see why many family lawyers have close relationships with accountants and actuaries to obtain assistance regarding these valuation issues.

If the spouses were not married throughout the employee's career, the community would not have an interest in all the present value of the pension. The community interest would only be the percentage of time the employee had worked while married.

For a discussion of the present value calculation approach, see generally Troyan, Poll, Cantwell & Weston, Vol. 3, *Valuation & Distribution of Marital Property* (1986), at Sec. 45.23 *et seq.*

The present value method is complex. Also, it is only based on probabilities; the spouse could actually receive much more or less than the estimated amount. These concerns have caused courts to favor the pro rata deferred payment approach.

A recent Missouri case sets forth a "simple" present value calculation for a defined benefit plan. This case is set forth below.

In re Marriage of Cox
Missouri Court of Appeals, 1987
724 S.W.2d 279

[Here the husband had been in the military for approximately 22 years. About 2.7 years of service were rendered before marriage, and the husband was married for the remainder of the period. Under a pro rata approach, the separate property portion would be 12.3%, and the community property portion 87.7%. He had retired before the parties divorced, and was receiving a monthly pension payment of $942.03. At the time of the trial, the husband was 47 years old, in good health, and had a life expectancy of 27.7 years.]

[The husband] complains that the trial court erred in finding the nondisability retirement pension had a present cash value of $114,409.39. At trial, Louis contended that the present cash value of the non-disability military retirement pay was $942.03, the amount he received each month. Patsy presented evidence that Louis' life expectancy at the time of trial was 27.7 years, and the present value of a dollar receivable at the end of each month for 27.7 years was $121.45. The amount of dollars received each month ($942.03) multiplied by the present value of a dollar receivable at the end of each month for 27.7 years ($121.45) equals $114,409.39, the amount found by the trial court to be the present value of the total ... pension. Louis' contention that the present cash value is $942.03 is absurd. This court finds no error in the trial court's finding....

DISCUSSION

Remember that a present value calculation for a defined contribution plan might be much easier. See *Johnson, supra.*

Some courts are reluctant to accept *Cearley.* In *In re Marriage of Joiner,* 766 S.W.2d 263 (Tex. App.—Amarillo), *overruled by* 755 S.W.2d 496 (Tex. App.—Amarillo 1988, no writ), the court considered a complicated issue regarding the husband's profit-sharing plan. The husband began working in 1967, the marriage was in 1973, and the parties divorced in 1987. Under the husband's plan, employees began participating in the plan after five years of service. Vesting was gradual, not immediate; an employee became 20% vested after the sixth year of service, and then the vested percentage increased 20% every year for the next four. After ten years of service, the employee was 100% vested. The husband had participated in the plan for about one year, and had a 20% vested interest in the plan, when the parties married. He was still working at the time of the divorce.

The court begins its downhill slide by announcing that the court would apply the inception of title characterization approach, not a version of the pro rata approach. (The inception of title approach will be discussed in detail in chapter 8.) To be fair, the Texas Supreme Court has never explained why it has normally deviated in the pension area from the normal Texas characterization approach (inception of title) for acquisitions over time. Still, the court does apply the inception of title approach in a weird way. The court determined that, because the husband only had a 20% vested interest at the time of marriage, 20% of the plan was his separate property. The remaining 80% was community. This emphasis on vesting, rather than on the value of the rights derived from the time of service, must be wrong. For example, imagine that the spouses had married in 1977. Under the court's analysis, the plan would thereby be 100% separate property, even though the husband would have worked for ten years during marriage. [In the opinion written on rehearing, the court does suggest that a reimbursement award of some sort could be possible in such an event. 766 S.W.2d at 264.]

The correct resolution of this problem is not as easy to set forth. First, the court must decide how to treat the first five years of service. The *Joiner* appellate court was willing to ignore them. 755 S.W.2d at 498. (The trial court didn't.) After this is determined, three approaches could be used to apportion the community and separate interests. A time allocation could be used; if the first five years of service are to be ignored, the community property percentage (coverture fraction) of the value of the plan at the time of divorce would be 14/15. On the other hand, because this is a defined contribution account, relative contributions during and prior to marriage could be compared. A third alternative would be to calculate a present value of the profit-sharing plan as of the time of marriage; the difference between this and the value at the time of divorce would be community property.

Berry v. Berry

Supreme Court of Texas, 1983
647 S.W.2d 945

KILGARLIN, Justice.

The sole question presented for consideration is the value of Elna Berry's interest in the retirement benefits of her ex-husband, Giles Berry. The judgment of the trial court awarded Mrs. Berry one-half of such benefits as would have existed at the time of divorce. The court of appeals reversed and held that she was entitled to receive 34.21% of the retirement benefits actually received. 636 S.W.2d 865. We reverse the judgment of the court of appeals and affirm the trial court's judgment.

The parties were married on November 11, 1939. On May 22, 1940, Mr. Berry was employed by Southwestern Bell Telephone Company. The couple was divorced on September 13, 1966. The decree of divorce was silent as to the distribution of retirement benefits. Mr. Berry continued working for Southwestern Bell until his retirement on July 8, 1978. After his retirement, Mrs. Berry brought this suit to collect her share of the retirement benefits.

Trial was to the court. Evidence adduced at trial, principally from Marshall Kemp, District Staff Manager, Employee Benefits, Southwestern Bell, revealed that had Mr. Berry terminated his employment at the time of divorce, he would not have been entitled to any retirement benefits because he was not yet sixty years of age, which was a prerequisite under the noncontributory retirement plan. Further, the evidence showed that total length of service under the plan is used as a multiplier in order to reach the amount of benefits payable. An additional factor in computation of benefits is the highest salary paid an employee over a consecutive sixty-month period. Mr. Berry's highest sixty months were his last five years of employment, and his average annual pay during that time was $21,184.67. Kemp testified that as of the date of trial, Giles Berry was being paid retirement benefits in the amount of $946.34 per month. He further testified that assuming Mr. Berry had been eligible to retire as of September 13, 1966, retirement benefits would have amounted to $221.21 per month. Based upon this limited financial data, the trial court rendered judgment that Mrs. Berry was entitled to receive $110.60 per month from Mr. Berry, after the date of judgment, and $3,207.40, representing $110.60 per month from the date of Mr. Berry's retirement until the date of judgment, December 30, 1980.

The court of appeals reversed, reasoning that because Elna Hettie Berry had been married to Giles Berry twenty-six out of his thirty-eight years of employment with Southwestern Bell, she was thereby entitled to be awarded 34.21% (1/2 × 26/38) of Giles Berry's retirement benefits. Accordingly, the court of appeals rendered judgment for Mrs. Berry in the amount of $6,702.20 for her share of accrued benefits through April 1980[1] and further rendered judgment that after that date Mrs. Berry was to receive 34.21% of all retirement benefits received by Mr. Berry.

The court of appeals reached its judgment by *following Bankston v. Taft*, 612 S.W.2d 216 (Tex. Civ. App.—Beaumont 1981, writ dism'd). *Bankston* and *Disbrow v. Thibodeaux*, 596 S.W.2d 174 (Tex. Civ. App.—Houston [14th Dist.] 1980, no writ), both follow the formula for distribution of retirement benefits as set out in *Taggart v. Taggart*, 552 S.W.2d 422 (Tex. 1977). Both courts of appeals cases hold that the divorced wife's community interest in retirement benefits is based upon the amount of retirement benefits actually received subsequent to the date of their former spouse's retirement even though the parties were divorced prior to retirement. These courts, however, have read into *Taggart* issues which were not before this Court in that case. *Taggart* only held that the divorced wife "owned as her part of the community estate a share in the contingent right to military benefits even though that right had not matured at the time of the divorce." *Id*. at 423. It is true that this Court did apply a formula based on the num-

---

1. The record fails to reveal the significance of April 1980, for calculation purposes, but it is probably related to the trial date of May 16, 1980.

ber of months in which marriage coincided with employment, divided by the number of months Taggart was in the Navy. We did not, however, determine whether the community's interest in retirement benefits should be valued as of the date of divorce, as opposed to the time the benefits were actually received. Thus, the courts of appeals' reliance on *Taggart* was misplaced.

In truth, this Court has already resolved the issue presented in this case. In *Herring v. Blakeley*, 385 S.W.2d 843 (Tex. 1965), our Court stated: "We have concluded that the employee's interest in both plans was community property, and that as of the date of the divorce, Ellen Davis Herring is entitled to one-half of the value of these plans." Id. at 845. The foregoing was not mere obiter dicta as evidenced by the following language:

> We come now to the judgment to be entered in this case. Since there is no evidence of the value of James Herring's interest in the two plans on the date of the divorce, the cause is remanded to the trial court with instructions to ascertain such value and to award to Ellen Davis Herring one-half the value of James Herring's interest in both plans as of August 2, 1960, the date of the divorce.

Id. at 848. See *In re Marriage of Rister*, 512 S.W.2d 72 (Tex. Civ. App.—Amarillo 1974, no writ). *In Rister*, the issue of the value of retirement benefits was squarely before the court, and the opinion states:

> However, to the extent that the benefits do increase as a result of future increased earnings, the formula used by the trial court has the effect of awarding benefits accruing to appellant after the divorce from appellee.

> We hold that pension benefits accruing as compensation for services rendered after a divorce are not a part of the estate of the parties subject to division on divorce.

Id. at 74.

Retirement and pension benefits are a mode of employee compensation. *Lee v. Lee*, 112 Tex. 392, 403–04, 247 S.W. 828, 833 (1923). It is clear from the record in this case that twelve additional years of work following divorce, which included some twelve to fourteen pay raises, plus union contract negotiations for an improved benefits plan, brought about the increase in retirement benefits paid to Mr. Berry. These post-divorce increases cannot be awarded to Mrs. Berry, for to do so would invade Mr. Berry's separate property, which cannot be done. *Cameron v. Cameron*, 641 S.W.2d 210 (Tex. 1982).

Mrs. Berry argues, however, that it was not Mr. Berry's additional twelve years of employment that caused an increase in the retirement benefits, but rather the retirement benefit plan was merely keeping pace with inflationary trends. She offers no evidence to support this contention other than Mr. Berry's admission on cross-examination that he was aware that inflation has been high in the years following the parties' divorce. Mrs. Berry argues that it was not her burden to produce testimony on inflationary effects because under the holding of *Dessommes v. Dessommes*, 505 S.W.2d 673 (Tex. Civ. App.—Dallas 1974, writ ref'd n.r.e.) (hereinafter *Dessommes II*), the burden of producing evidence was on the ex-husband. In any event Mr. Berry met his burden through the testimony of Mr. Kemp. Further, we reject the concept of inflation as a factor for our consideration as it relates to the current value of retirement benefits.

We do not perceive *Dessommes II* as being in conflict with this opinion, for in that case a remand was ordered so that the former husband might prove what portion of the commingled retirement funds were attributable to contributions made since the divorce. If anything, the Dallas court opinion in *Dessommes II* is a precursor to our holding here. Unlike

Mr. Berry, however, Mr. Dessommes, in the third trial, failed to make that proof required of him. The Texarkana court, therefore, awarded Mrs. Dessommes one-half of the retirement benefits as paid.[2]

We are not to be understood as overruling *Taggart v. Taggart, supra,* or disapproving of its progeny, *e.g., Bankston v. Taft, supra; Disbrow v. Thibodeaux, supra; In the Matter of the Marriage of Gongwer,* 554 S.W.2d 49 (Tex. Civ. App.—Amarillo 1977, no writ), insofar as those opinions approve an apportionment formula for determining the extent of the community interest in retirement benefits. When the value of such benefits is in issue, however, the benefits are to be apportioned to the spouses based upon the value of the community's interest at the time of divorce. Accordingly, insofar as *Bankston v. Taft, supra,* and *Disbrow v. Thibodeaux, supra,* are in conflict with this opinion, they are disapproved.

There remains our disposition of this cause. As we are convinced that the opinion of the court of appeals in this case invades the separate property of Mr. Berry, the judgment of that court is reversed and the judgment of the trial court is affirmed.

DISCUSSION

Berry challenges the assumption that every month of employment contributes equally to pension rights. The court concluded that, for the defined benefit plan involved the last years of employment were worth more than earlier years, since during the last years of employment the employee's salary increased due to promotions and raises, and the defined benefit formula was improved.

In *Berry* the employee was married when he began working, and was still working at divorce. In the court's view, in this situation the application of the *Cearley/Taggart* pro rata deferred payment approach to determine the community share of the benefits divided the employee's separate property, since the last years were much more valuable than the earlier years. The benefit due if the employee would have retired at the time of divorce is the appropriate measure for the community claim, in the court's view. This is to some degree doubletalk, since the employee's rights were not matured at the time of divorce. The court must be saying that the *hypothetical* retirement benefit due under the defined benefit plan formula in existence at the time of divorce should be computed. Even though the community benefit is valued as of the date of divorce, in *Berry* the community did not begin to receive any retirement benefits until the employee actually retired, and no inflation adjustment was permitted.

Is the legacy of *Berry* clear? *Berry* was a partition action. What relevance does it have to a divorce property division? Is the pro rata deferred payment approach now forbidden in a Texas divorce?

In *Berry,* the employee was promoted after divorce and the pension plan formula was improved. While it is conceivable that these facts could limit the scope of *Berry,* the case has been applied to most cases when the employee is working at divorce and the employee participated in a defined benefit pension plan. *See also Albrecht v. Albrecht,* 974 S.W.2d 262 (Tex. App.—San Antonio 1998, no pet.).

---

2. 543 S.W.2d 165 (Tex. Civ. App.—Texarkana 1976, writ ref'd n.r.e.).

After *Berry*, what is the best way to deal with pension rights if you are representing the non-employee spouse, if the employee spouse is still working at the time of divorce? Would you try to do it differently if you are representing the employee spouse?

In *Berry*, the spouse had retired when the partition action was brought. What would have occurred if the employee was still working?

Berry presents an important retroactivity issue. What is the effect of *Berry* upon prior final decrees that compute the community share of the pension in a way inconsistent with *Berry*? As a general rule, if a decree divides separate property, but the decree is not appealed and becomes final, the decree is res judicata. See chapter 15 *infra*. The Supreme Court has applied this rule to *Berry* problems in *Baxter v. Ruddle*, 794 S.W.2d 761 (Tex. 1990).

Berry obviously is a significant opinion. It is discussed in detail in a very thoughtful student comment at 37 Baylor L. Rev. 106 (1985).

After *Berry*, it was somewhat unclear whether the time rule could be used to determine the amount of the separate property claim to defined benefit retirement benefits at divorce, if that separate property claim stems from pre-marriage work. This idea was challenged in *Humble v. Humble*, 805 S.W.2d 558 (Tex. App. — Beaumont 1991, writ denied). The employee spouse had begun work thirty years before he married. The couple then divorced twelve years later, apparently while the spouse was still working. *Berry* obviously requires the computation of a hypothetical retirement benefit at the time of divorce. The *Cearley/Taggart* approach to pre-marriage employment would apply the time rule to this hypothetical benefit to determine the separate property claim. (Under the *Humble* facts, this led to the conclusion that the separate property claim was 73% of the hypothetical benefit.) The non-employee spouse argued in *Humble* that *Berry* totally supplants the time rule, and that the amount of the community claim should be computed by subtracting the hypothetical benefit earned at the time of *marriage* from the hypothetical benefit earned at the time of *divorce*. When an employee marries late in his or her career, this extension of *Berry* would result in a much larger community claim. The court did not accept this extension of *Berry*, however; the appellate court affirmed the trial court's application of the time rule to determine the fraction of the hypothetical benefit at divorce that would be community. Under this construction of *Berry*, *Berry* can only limit the community claim that otherwise would have resulted under *Cearley/Taggart*; it can never increase it. The court's analysis in *Humble* was followed in *Parliament v. Parliament*, 860 S.W.2d 144 (Tex. App. — San Antonio 1993, writ denied). See also *Hudson*, *infra*. The effects of *Berry* are also discussed in *May v. May*.

May v. May
Texas Court of Appeals — Corpus Christi, 1986
716 S.W.2d 705, no writ

NYE, Chief Justice.

This is an appeal from a division of retirement benefits in a divorce action. In anticipation of their divorce, the parties entered into an agreement which disposed of many of the matters in controversy. The matters that were submitted to the trial court concerned the characterization and division of appellant's three retirement plans. This appeal concerns only the trial court's disposition of two of the plans.

Appellant's first two points of error and appellee's cross-point complain of the division of appellant's San Antonio Fire Department pension benefits. The third point of error concerns appellant's Air National Guard benefits.

The trial court divided appellant's accrued, non-vested, and unmatured civilian retirement benefits earned from the San Antonio Fire Department.[1] The trial court made the following findings of fact:

1. Parties were married on April 8, 1967.

12. Respondent began his employment with the City of San Antonio in June, 1969, and accumulated retirement credit continuously from that date through the date of trial.

13. Respondent [had] worked 15 years out of the 20 which are required for the retirement to vest.

14. The number of months Respondent was married while accumulating credit towards City of San Antonio retirement, through trial, [equaled] 184 months.

15. That a certified actuary determining the present value of Respondent's Fireman Retirement was stipulated to and admitted into evidence without objection. If Respondent retired [at] the date of divorce his present monthly Accrued Pension Benefit would be $667.79.

16. The present value of Petitioner's community interest in Respondent's City of San Antonio Retirement plan is $25,000. Said amount reflects the value of Petitioner's interest in Respondent's Fire Department Retirement plan projected upon contingencies and anticipated future value based upon historical inflation trends.

The trial court awarded appellee (the non-employee spouse) the following portion of appellant's benefits:

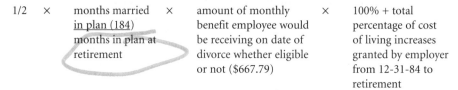

| 1/2 | × | months married in plan (184) months in plan at retirement | × | amount of monthly benefit employee would be receiving on date of divorce whether eligible or not ($667.79) | × | 100% + total percentage of cost of living increases granted by employer from 12-31-84 to retirement |

An employee spouse's accrued benefits in a retirement plan which have been earned during marriage, but which have not vested and matured at the time of divorce, constitute a contingent interest in property and a community asset subject to division upon divorce. *Cearley v. Cearley*, 544 S.W.2d 661, 666 (Tex. 1976); *Miser v. Miser*, 475 S.W.2d 597, 600 (Tex. Civ. App. — Dallas 1971, writ dism'd). Although this is a well-settled point in Texas law, uncertainty still exists as to the proper method of dividing future interests in retirement benefits.

Upon divorce, the non-employee spouse is entitled to a certain percentage (in this case, the trial court awarded one-half) of the community interest in the pension benefits. Unless the marriage spans the entire term of employment under the plan through to retirement, so that all benefits were earned during the marriage and are community prop-

---

1. We use the term "accrued" benefits in the actuarial sense, meaning the specific dollar amount allotted to an employee at any given time under the pension plan. By "vested" benefits, we mean that the employee has an unconditional ownership interest in certain pension benefits. By "matured" benefits, we mean that the employee qualifies for immediate possession and enjoyment of the benefits. *Comment, An Interdisciplinary Analysis of the Division of Pension Benefits in Divorce and Post-Judgment Partition Actions: Cures for the Inequities in* Berry v. Berry, 37 Baylor L. Rev. 106, 121–22 (1985).

erty, an apportionment must be made between those benefits earned during marriage and those earned while not married, which are separate property. Once the community's fractional interest has been determined, the value of the benefits is multiplied by that fraction which yields the specific amount of the non-employee spouse's interest in the benefits. This method of division is reflected in the following formula:

$$\frac{1}{2} \quad \times \quad \frac{\text{no. months married under plan}}{\text{no. months employed under plan}} \quad \times \quad \text{value}$$

(Community Share)   (Community Interest)   (Value)

$$= \text{amount of non-employee spouse's share}$$
(Amount of Share)

See Comment, 37 Baylor L. Rev. at 136.

This relatively straight-forward equation is still the source of much confusion. The uncertainty has arisen in part because the denominator of the community interest fraction and the valuation element have not been consistently defined in case law. The "number of months employed under the plan" has been calculated at both the time of divorce and the time of retirement. The valuation variable has also been calculated for both the date of divorce and the date of retirement. The dates at which these two variables should be calculated is the central question to be determined in this case.

The leading cases in this area are *Taggart v. Taggart*, 552 S.W.2d 422 (Tex. 1977), which spoke to the apportionment element of the equation, and *Berry v. Berry*, 647 S.W.2d 945 (Tex. 1983), which primarily considered the valuation element. Each of these elements has been considered by the Supreme Court in relative isolation from one another. However, these two elements operate jointly in any division of retirement benefits. The interplay between these two variables is reflected in the instant case where the trial court apparently used a mixed formula for division by calculating the apportionment denominator from the date of retirement (*Taggart*) and the valuation element from the date of divorce (*Berry*).

Both parties agree that the trial court erred in this regard. Appellant argues in his first point of error that the trial court abused its discretion, as a matter of law, by calculating the denominator in the apportionment fraction as of the date of retirement instead of the date of divorce, thereby divesting appellant of some of his separate property. By cross-point, appellee agrees that the trial court abused its discretion in calculating the apportionment fraction from the date of retirement instead of divorce. However, appellee contends that this miscalculation divests her of separate property by multiplying a continually reducing apportionment fraction by a value which already has been discounted back to the value of the benefits at the time of divorce. The trial court improperly calculated these two variables of the formula, and we find that this formula used by the trial court was incorrect. It worked to the detriment of the non-employee spouse.

Taggart v. Taggart involved the partition of military retirement benefits. The employee spouse began employment under the plan in 1943, married in 1947, completed twenty years of service and was eligible for retirement in 1964, divorced in 1968, and actually retired in 1974. The trial court had awarded the non-employee spouse "four-ninths of *all retirement pay*," which the employee spouse had and would receive after retirement. (Emphasis added). Four-ninths represents one-half of the fractional amount of time the parties had been married and accumulating benefits over the employee spouse's years of service as of 1964, the date he was eligible to retire (three and one-half years before divorce). The trial court then applied this fraction to the value of the benefits as of the date of retirement.

The Supreme Court ruled the trial court had incorrectly computed the apportionment formula. 552 S.W.2d at 424. The Court reasoned that it was the employee spouse's thirty years of service (360 months) which entitled him to the benefits he received at retirement. The Court held that the correct calculation was "one-half of 246/360th's of the retirement pay." Although the Court makes no specific mention of the value of the benefits, we can infer that it used the trial court's valuation date, retirement. See *Heisterberg v. Standridge*, 656 S.W.2d 138, 147 n. 4 (Tex. App.—Austin 1983, no writ). The *Taggart* formula can be expressed as:

1/2   ×   no. months married under plan no.   ×   value of benefits as
              months employed under plan as of   of date of retirement
              the date of retirement

                                            = non-employee spouse's share

Ten years after *Taggart*, the Supreme Court decided *Berry v. Berry*. That case involved the partition of civilian retirement benefits. The parties were married in 1939, before Mr. Berry became employed under the plan in 1940. The couple was divorced in 1966, while the benefits were still unmatured. Mr. Berry retired in 1978, after thirty-eight years of service, and began receiving retirement benefits.

The trial court awarded Mrs. Berry one-half of the benefits "as would have existed at the time of divorce." There was evidence that Mr. Berry actually received $946.34 per month in retirement benefits, but that had he been eligible to retire at the time of his divorce his monthly benefits would have amounted to $221.21. To reach the result it did, the trial court must have calculated the apportionment fraction as of the date of divorce. Thus, the equation would be:

1/2   ×   no. months married under plan   ×   value as   =   Mrs. Berry's share
              no. years employed under plan   of date
              as of date of divorce   of divorce

1/2   ×   26   × $221.21   = $110.60/mo.
              26

The Court of Appeals reversed and applied the *Taggart* division formula. It ruled that, since Mr. Berry had been employed thirty-eight years under the plan, the community's interest was 26/38 or 34.21% "of all benefits received by Mr. Berry." The Court obviously valued the benefits as of date of retirement. Under the Court of Appeals' *Taggart* formula, Mrs. Berry would have been entitled to:

1/2   ×   26   × $946.34   = $323.74/mo.
              38

In its opinion, the Supreme Court, for the first time, recognized that other factors affect the division of retirement benefits. The Court noted that, under this retirement plan, the "total length of service under the plan is used as a multiplier in order to reach the amount of benefits payable." Additionally, it noted that "the highest salary paid an employee over a consecutive sixty-month period" was another factor used in computing benefits under this plan. Mr. Berry's highest paid sixty months were in his last five post-divorce years. He had received twelve to fourteen pay raises after his divorce, and had benefited from an improved retirement plan due to union negotiations. To value the benefits as of the date of retirement would allow Mrs. Berry to share in the increases in benefits due to Mr. Berry's post-divorce earnings and efforts.

The Court pointed out that it had already held that retirement benefits should be valued as of the date of divorce. *Herring v. Blakeley*, 385 S.W.2d 843, 848 (Tex. 1965). Then the Court quoted *In re Marriage of Rister*, 512 S.W.2d 72, 74 (Tex. Civ. App.—Amarillo 1974, no writ), in which that court recognized that valuing benefits at the date of retirement would allow the non-employee spouse to receive benefits accruing to the employee spouse as a result of increased future earnings after the divorce.

This recognition points out a limitation of the *Taggart* formula. Valuing retirement benefits as of the date of retirement and then multiplying by half of the community's proportional share assumes that the community's interest in the benefits is equally earned during each month of employment, so that the non-employee spouse is entitled to a straight percentage of the whole benefit. *Heisterberg v. Standridge*, 656 S.W.2d at 145. Such was not the case in *Berry*, and is not the case in most, if not all, retirement plans.

The Supreme Court, in *Berry*, expressly declined to overrule *Taggart*. The Court cautioned that, while it "did apply a formula based on the number of months in which marriage coincided with employment, divided by the number of months Taggart was in the Navy," *Taggart* should not be read as ruling on the date at which benefits should be valued.[2]

In *Berry*, the Court held that when the value of benefits is in issue, the benefits are to be apportioned based on their value at the date of divorce. Although the Supreme Court did not overrule *Taggart*, neither did it follow *Taggart*, on the facts of the case, and apply an apportionment formula dated at retirement to the value of the benefits as of the date of divorce. The *Berry* Court affirmed the trial court and awarded Mrs. Berry $110.60 of Mr. Berry's $946.34 monthly retirement payments. Had the Court applied a *Taggart* fraction to the *Berry* value, as did the trial court in the case at bar, Mrs. Berry only would have been entitled to:

$$1/2 \quad \times \quad \frac{26}{38} \quad \times \quad \$221.21 \quad = \quad \$75.67/\text{mo.}$$

We view the present body of law to mean that the *Taggart* formula is applicable in cases where apportionment is the only issue. We perceive such cases to be those where the parties are divorced after the employee spouse has retired or terminated employment under the plan. See *Anderson v. Anderson*, 707 S.W.2d 166 (Tex. App.—Corpus Christi 1986, writ ref'd n.r.e.); *Harrell v. Harrell*, 700 S.W.2d 645 (Tex. App.—Corpus Christi 1986, no writ); *Workings v. Workings*, 700 S.W.2d 251 (Tex. App.—Dallas 1985, no writ); *Neese v. Neese*, 669 S.W.2d 388 (Tex. App.—Eastland 1984, writ ref'd n.r.e.). In these instances, the concern is to shield the accrued benefits attributable to the employee spouse's premarriage earnings, if any, from the non-employee spouse. This is the function of the apportionment fraction. There is no danger that the non-employee spouse might reap some benefit from the employee spouse's post-divorce earnings because there are none.[3]

---

2. One commentator has suggested that, in not overruling *Taggart*, the Court merely intended to "renew prior supreme court approval of apportionment as the preferred 'method' of dividing pension benefits ... [and] to reassure the continued viability of apportionment and the 'if, as, and when' method of distribution...." *Comment*, 37 Baylor L. Rev. at 144–45.

3. If one assumes that retirement benefits are not equally earned in each year of employment under a plan, one could logically argue that, in instances where the employee spouse was employed and accruing benefits under a plan for a significant period of time before marriage, a straight *Taggart* formula division might divest the employee spouse of separate property even if retirement occurs before divorce, unless the value of the benefits attributable to pre-marriage earnings is factored out of the division formula.

In any case where divorce occurs prior to the employee spouse's retirement or termination of employment (i.e., where the amount of retirement benefits could still be increased by future earnings), valuation necessarily becomes an issue in the division, and *Berry*, by its own terms, controls. When the employee spouse continues to accrue additional benefits under the plan because of continued employment, there is a danger that the non-employee spouse's share might comprise some of the value of the accrued benefits earned after divorce. *Berry* prohibits such a result. It requires the benefits be valued as of the date of divorce, not retirement.

Because the case at bar is one in which divorce occurred before retirement, *Berry* dictates that the benefits be valued as of the date of divorce. We hold that equity and the rule against divestiture of separate personal property dictate that the denominator of the apportionment fraction must be calculated from the date of divorce also. The trial court in this case ordered a division of benefits according to a formula which divides the benefits as valued at the date of divorce by an apportionment fraction calculated from the date of retirement. This mixture of the two formulas was error, because it divested the non-employee spouse of a portion of her separate property. But see *Dunn v. Dunn*, 703 S.W.2d 317 (Tex. App.—San Antonio 1985, writ ref'd n.r.e.); *Rankin v. Bateman*, 686 S.W.2d 707 (Tex. App.—San Antonio 1985, writ ref'd n.r.e.).

The *Taggart* apportionment fraction is a reducing fraction in that the non-employee spouse's share reduces as the employee spouse continues employment under the plan after divorce. In *Taggart*, the non-employee spouse's share was determined by comparing the time married to the entire period of employment under the plan; yet, that ratio was applied against the value of the plan benefits which accumulated over the same period. In *Berry*, the value of the benefits was frozen at the date of divorce, as was the non-employee's pro rata share. Accordingly, we hold that in cases such as this, where the *Berry* valuation is mandated, the denominator of the apportionment fraction must also be calculated as of the date of divorce.

In the instant case, the parties were married before appellant began employment under the plan. As of the date of divorce, appellant had worked 184 months under the plan while married; therefore, the apportionment fraction would be 184/184. Appellant argues that, under the *Berry* formula, appellee's share of his retirement benefits should be:

$$1/2 \quad \times \quad \frac{184}{184} \quad \times \quad \$667.79 \quad = \quad \$333.89 \text{ (as, if, and when received)}$$

The value in this equation is based on Finding of Fact Number Fifteen in which the trial court found that, if appellant had retired at the date of divorce, the amount of his monthly benefits payment would be $667.79. At trial, the actuary testified as follows:

MR. RESENDEZ: So typically what I am saying, Your Honor, is that if this person on a hypothetical basis continues to work and retires at 20 years and then is retired until death, he would receive $667.79 per month, which has a present value of $68,446.63. Her share would be equal to $251.76. This amount is roughly 37.7 percent of the $667.79.

In his second point of error, appellant complains of the fourth variable in the trial court's division formula which awarded appellee a portion of the total percentage of the cost of living increases granted by appellant's employer from the date of divorce to the date of retirement. Appellant argues the trial court abused its discretion in making this award, as it unlawfully divests him of separate property. We agree.

We find that this issue is again controlled by *Berry*. The Supreme Court stated, "we reject the concept of inflation as a factor for our consideration as it relates to the current value of retirement benefits." *Berry*, 647 S.W.2d at 947. Thus, *Berry* prohibits non-employee spouses from sharing in post-divorce increases in retirement benefits, as that would be a divestiture of separate property under *Cameron v. Cameron*, 641 S.W.2d 210 (Tex. 1982). See also *Heisterberg v. Standridge*, 656 S.W.2d at 146.

The case at bar is clearly distinguishable from *Neese v. Neese*, 669 S.W.2d 388, cited by appellee. In that case, the employee spouse was retired and receiving benefits when the parties divorced. The court in that case found that *Berry* was not controlling because all of the benefit increases were community property as there had been no post-divorce employment or accrual of benefits. Thus, both spouses were entitled to share in the increases and decreases in retirement benefits. This Court also reached the same holding based upon a similar fact situation in *Harrell v. Harrell*, 700 S.W.2d at 647–48.

The employee spouse in the instant case did not retire before divorce; therefore, *Berry* prohibits the non-employee spouse, appellee, from sharing in any post-divorce increases in the value of appellant's retirement benefits.[4] The trial court erred in awarding appellee any portion of appellant's post-divorce cost of living increases.

By his third point of error, appellant complains the trial court abused its discretion in mischaracterizing his separate property interest in his Air National Guard retirement benefits as community property, thereby divesting him of separate property.

The trial awarded appellant the Air National Guard retirement plan in its entirety. The trial court also modified the parties' property settlement agreement by ordering appellant to pay appellee $5,164.00 from community property funds set aside to him in the agreement. Appellant claims the court awarded him his retirement benefits provided that he pay appellee this lump sum in return for exclusive rights in the plan.

Appellant complains that the trial court should have divided these benefits according to the *Berry* formula, instead of awarding appellee a lump sum. We find nothing in the record to reflect the present value of the total benefits under the plan.

Tex. Fam. Code Ann. Sec. 3.63(a) (Vernon Supp. 1986) authorizes a trial court to divide the estate of the parties in a manner the trial court deems just and right. This trial court was well within its discretion to award appellant all of these benefits instead of dividing them. See *In re Marriage of Butler*, 543 S.W.2d 147, 150 (Tex. Civ. App. — Texarkana 1975, writ dism'd). It would also be in the trial court's discretion to order appellant to pay a lump sum to appellee in lieu of any interest she has in the benefits. The trial court has broad discretion in the division of property upon divorce, and this discretion will not be disturbed on appeal unless there is an abuse of discretion. Appellant's third point of error is overruled.

The judgment of the trial court is affirmed insofar as it awards appellant all the benefits from his Air National Guard plan and awards appellee the sum of $5,164.00.

The portion of the judgment which awards appellee an interest in post-divorce cost-of-living increases in appellant's San Antonio Fire Department retirement benefits is reversed. We here render judgment that appellee take none of these increases.

The portion of the judgment which awards appellee an interest in appellant's San Antonio Fire Department retirement benefits is also reversed. We sever and remand to the trial court with instructions to divide the benefits according to the *Berry* formula, with

---

4. We are mindful that this rigid prohibition may deprive the non-employee spouse of increases he/she may fairly be entitled to, see Comment, 37 Baylor L. Rev. at 152–64; however, *Berry* governs in this regard.

the denominator of the apportionment calculated as of the date of divorce and then multiplied by the value of the benefits as of the same date, whatever amount the trial court determines that value to be.

AFFIRMED in part; REVERSED and RENDERED in part; and REVERSED and REMANDED in part.

DISCUSSION

Note that *Berry/May* does not bar giving a non-employee a share of post-divorce COLAs if the employee has already retired before divorce. *See Sutherland v. Cobern*, 843 S.W.2d 127 (Tex. App.—Texarkana 1992, writ denied).

Hudson v. Hudson
Court of Appeals of Texas—Houston [14th Dist.], 1989
763 S.W.2d 603, no writ

PAUL PRESSLER, J.

Upon divorce appellant was awarded $188,800.72 as a portion of one of the appellee's retirement annuities. We affirm.

Mr. Hudson, at the time of his retirement on September 1, 1986, had thirty-five years of service with Exxon Company, U.S.A. Mr. and Mrs. Hudson were married on November 18, 1975. They were separated in February 1986 and divorced on October 9, 1987. Mr. Hudson worked for Exxon during the entire period of their marriage. Two annuities were part of Mr. Hudson's retirement benefits plan. One of the annuities was based upon the length of his employment. The award of the other is not appealed by the appellant, but rather by the appellee.

At his retirement, Mr. Hudson had 422 months of credited service under the first annuity plan. The Hudsons were married for 130 of Mr. Hudson's 422 months of employment with Exxon. On September 1, 1986 the annuity had a present value of $1,114,323.90. The trial court computed the community property portion of this annuity by multiplying the present value of the annuity times a fraction with the number of months of the marriage (130) as the numerator and the total months of credited service (422) as the denominator.

$(1,114,323.90 \times 130/422 = 343,274.04)$

The separate property portion of the annuity was determined by multiplying the present value of the annuity times a fraction with the number of months he was in the program prior to the marriage (292) as the numerator and the total months of credited service (422) as the denominator.

$(1,114,323.90 \times 292/422 = 771,049.86)$

Based on this, Mrs. Hudson was awarded 55% of the community property portion of this annuity or ($188,800.72).

In her first three points of error, appellant claims that the trial court erred in its calculation of the community and separate property portions of the first annuity plan. Appellant attempts to differentiate this case, from the military retirement benefits cases decided by the Texas Supreme Court, *Grier v. Grier*, 731 S.W.2d 931 (Tex. 1987); *Cameron v. Cameron*, 641 S.W.2d 210 (Tex. 1982); *Taggart v. Taggart*, 552 S.W.2d 422 (Tex. 1977); *Cearley v. Cearley*, 544 S.W.2d 661 (Tex. 1976). Those military benefits were constant once retirement had been reached. Here the annuity increases proportionately with each year of additional service. In this respect, the benefits are similar to the benefits divided *in Berry v. Berry*, 647 S.W.2d 945 (Tex. 1983). Mr. Berry's benefits were based on his last five years of service. There, however, the parties were already divorced at the time of Mr. Berry's retirement, but he had already served enough time to vest his retirement at the time of the divorce. Here, Mr. Hudson had not vested his retirement at the time of the marriage, and they were still married at the time of his retirement. The annuity benefits here are based upon total length of service, not the party's salary in his last years of service. Some facts, therefore, make this a case of first impression. The only recent retirement benefits case where the parties were still married at the time of retirement is *Cameron v. Cameron, supra*. In *Cameron*, the Texas Supreme Court upheld the fractional apportionment of the husband's military retirement benefits upon divorce. In doing so, they followed the division set out in *Taggart v. Taggart, supra*; *Cearley v. Cearley, supra*; *Busby v. Busby*, 457 S.W.2d 551 (Tex. 1970); *Herring v. Blakely*, 385 S.W.2d 843 (Tex. 1965). This is the same apportionment method used in this case. Appellant argues that because the proportionate increase in the benefits under the annuity were greater during the marriage, she is entitled to 55% of the proportionate increase. At the time of the marriage, the annuity value was $1,702.00 per month. At retirement, it had a value of $9,448.00 per month. The increase in the lump sum value during the marriage was $947,531.41. Therefore, appellant claims to be entitled to 55% of the $947,531.41. In *Berry* the Supreme Court held:

> It is clear from the record in this case that twelve additional years of work following divorce which included some twelve to fourteen pay raises, plus union contract negotiations for an improved benefit plan, brought about an increase in retirement benefits paid to Mr. Berry. These post-divorce increases cannot be awarded to Ms. Berry, for to do so would [be] to invade Mr. Berry's separate property, which cannot be done.

Berry, 647 S.W.2d at 947; citing *Cameron, supra*. Following this rationale, Mrs. Hudson could be entitled to 55% of the increase in the lump sum value of the annuity. Retirement and pension benefits are a method of employee compensation, and thus community property. *Lee v. Lee*, 112 Tex. 392, 247 S.W. 828 (1923).

However, the retirement benefits divided in *Berry*, are different in several aspects. They were based upon the average salary during his last five years of employment during which the parties were not married. Had the benefits in this case been based on the same criteria, appellant's analysis could apply. However here, the retirement benefits were based on years of service. The proportionate increase in the lump sum value would have been quite different without Mr. Hudson's service prior to the marriage. Since these annuity benefits are determined by the number of years of service, the fractional apportionment method is proper. The plan before us resembles a military benefits plan. The fractional apportionment method of *Grier, supra; Cameron, supra; Taggart, supra; Cearley, supra; May v. May*, 716 S.W.2d 705 (Tex. App.—Corpus Christi 1986, no writ), should be used when the plan is based on years of service. The increase in the lump sum value was partially a result of his service, before marriage. The service by Mr. Berry after divorce, in the Berry case, is analogous to Mr. Hudson's service prior to the marriage. Awarding Mrs. Hudson with 55% of the proportionate increase would be crediting her for Mr. Hudson's service before marriage. This would be invading Mr. Hudson's separate property. A division based upon any formula other than the fractional apportionment method used would have not only produced an inequity, but also divested Mr. Hudson's separate property interest in the annuity. The trial court was correct in its analysis and application of the fractional apportionment method. Points of error one through three are overruled.

In six cross-points, the appellee complains that the trial court erred in its division of the other annuity. This annuity, hereinafter referred to as HARC2, is awarded only to executives of Exxon. Section 5.02 of the Texas Family Code states: "Property possessed by either spouse during or on dissolution of the marriage is presumed to be community property. The degree of proof necessary to establish that property is separate is clear and convincing evidence." Tex. Fam. Code Sec. 5.02 (Vernon Supp. 1988). The burden of proving the property is separate is on the party asserting that it is separate. It is not clear from the record when Mr. Hudson obtained the HARC2 annuity. It is, therefore, presumed that it is community property.

The trial court awarded 50% of the HARC2 annuity to each party. It is apparent it was considered community property. It appears that the plan was acquired when Mr. Hudson became president of Esso China during the marriage. However, this is not clear. The presumption that it is community property, therefore, controls. Although this annuity was also based upon years of service and the average of the last three years salary, Mr. Hudson was not eligible for it until he obtained an executive position. Had this plan been available, or started accruing from the beginning of his service, the fractional apportionment method, as used with the first annuity, would have been proper. Regardless, the appellee has failed to meet the burden under section 5.02 of the Texas Family Code. The trial court was correct in its division. Appellee's cross-points are overruled.

Judgment is affirmed.

DISCUSSION

Are you persuaded that *Berry* does not govern the first annuity? Is it clear that the second annuity is 100% community property?

A statute was enacted in 2005 to modify how to calculate the community property claim to a defined benefit pension right. The statute was somewhat unclear, but appeared to intend to implement the approach advocated by Mrs. Hudson (and rejected) in this case. This statute was repealed in 2009.

Harvey v. Harvey

Court of Appeals of Texas — Austin, 1995
905 S.W.2d 760, no writ

JONES, Justice.

More than two years after the signing of a decree granting a divorce to Gary Dennis Harvey, appellant, and Patricia Felter Harvey, appellee, Patricia moved for enforcement and clarification of the decree. The trial court signed an order purporting to clarify a portion of the original decree relating to Gary's retirement benefits. On appeal, Gary asserts that the clarification order makes an impermissible substantive change in the original division of property and is therefore invalid and unenforceable. We will affirm.

FACTUAL AND PROCEDURAL BACKGROUND

Gary and Patricia were granted a divorce by a decree dated May 16, 1990. At the time of the divorce, Gary was employed by the Minnesota Mining and Manufacturing Company ("3-M") and was a participant in 3-M's "tax qualified" retirement plan. The original divorce decree divided the accrued benefits of this retirement plan as follows: Petitioner

[Gary Harvey] is awarded the following as Petitioner's sole and separate property, and Respondent [Patricia Harvey] is divested of all right, title, interest, and claim in and to such property:

* * *

5. All benefits payable under the 3-M Pension plan other than those benefits specifically awarded to PATRICIA FELTER HARVEY herein.

* * *

Respondent [Patricia] is awarded the following as Respondent's sole and separate property, and Petitioner [Gary] is divested of all right, title, interest, and claim in and to such property:

* * *

12. A portion of retirement benefits pursuant to the following provisions: This Decree of Divorce shall be a "qualified domestic relations order" pursuant to Section 414(p) of the Internal Revenue Code. In compliance with that provision, the following is ORDERED and specified: This qualified domestic relations order assigns a portion of the benefits payable in the 3-M Pension Plan ("the Plan") at 3-M to PATRICIA FELTER HARVEY in recognition of the existence of her marital rights in GARY DENNIS HARVEY's retirement benefits as defined by Texas law in *Berry v. Berry,* 647 S.W.2d 945 (Tex.1983). Participant in the Plan is GARY DENNIS HARVEY.... Alternate Payee is PATRICIA FELTER HARVEY.... On the date of this divorce, Participant's present accrued benefit for retirement at normal retirement age under the Plan is $1,387.00 per month. As part of a just and right division of the estate of the parties, the Court awards, assigns, and grants to Alternate Payee 45 per cent of the present value of Participant's accrued benefits as of October 21, 1988. Alternate Payee may elect any form of payment of her portion of the available benefits, being 45% of Participant's accrued benefits as of October 21, 1988, and shall have the right to elect to receive said benefit payments on or after the earliest date on which benefits are available, so long as the election is not contrary to the terms of the Plan.... In the event Participant elects to retire from the Plan prior to normal retirement age and by reason of such early retirement the Plan provides an early retirement subsidy, the Alternate Payee is entitled to 45% of any early retirement subsidy paid to Participant.

* * *

All benefits payable under the 3-M Pension Plan other than those payable to PATRICIA FELTER HARVEY shall be payable to GARY DENNIS HARVEY in such manner and form as GARY DENNIS HARVEY may elect in his sole and undivided discretion, subject only to Plan requirements.

The decree made no mention of survivor benefits, nor did it designate Patricia as Gary's "surviving spouse."

Upon submission of the original decree to 3-M, a 3-M representative concluded that the decree failed to meet the statutory requirements to be a qualified domestic relations order ("QDRO"). In a November 14, 1990 letter to both parties, the 3-M representative pointed out certain technical problems with the decree as drafted and what remedies should be taken to comply with ERISA standards.[1] The letter also mentioned that:

---

1. These technical problems consisted of: (1) not specifying the number of payments that will be made to Patricia; (2) not detailing when such payments will begin and how long they are to continue; (3) not specifying the form in which the payments are to be made; and (4) not correctly designating

You should also be aware that, as the Decree is presently drafted, the Plan would not make any payments to Ms. Harvey in the event that Mr. Harvey died before the date on which it was required to begin making payments to Ms. Harvey. This situation may be avoided by including in the Decree language naming Ms. Harvey as Mr. Harvey's surviving spouse for purposes of section 205 of ERISA, to the extent of the benefits assigned by the Decree.

The 3-M representative attached to his letter a draft of an acceptable order, which incorporated the terms of the original decree, made the necessary technical changes to satisfy the requirements for a QDRO, and contained a provision designating Patricia as Gary's "surviving spouse" for purposes of receiving survivor benefits under the 3-M retirement plan.

About two years after receiving this correspondence from 3-M, Patricia moved for clarification of the original decree and offered the 3-M draft to the trial court. Gary objected, arguing that the "surviving spouse" language was a substantive modification of the original decree in violation of section 3.71 of the Family Code. Following a non-evidentiary hearing, the court granted Patricia's motion. On August 4, 1994, the court signed an order reciting that "[t]he Court finds that the prior order should be clarified as ordered below … [and] that this clarifying order does not substantively modify the prior order of this Court." The order also added the following language:

> In the event that the Participant dies before payments to the Alternate Payee begin, the Alternate Payee shall be considered the "surviving spouse" of the Participant for purposes of Section 205 of the Employee Retirement Income Security Act of 1974, as amended (but only to the extent of the accrued benefit assigned by this Order).

DISCUSSION

Gary's brief presents four points of error. In point of error one, he asserts that the trial court's order "was not a clarification of the original decree … but was actually a modification of the original decree … in that it granted to wife a new benefit and thus a substantially greater share of the husband's benefits than the wife was originally awarded." In point of error two, he asserts that the trial court's change in the terms of the original decree was barred by the doctrine of res judicata. In point of error three, he asserts that the change in terms "was not legally or factually supported by any evidence." In point of error four, he asserts that Patricia's motion was time-barred under section 3.70(c) of the Family Code.

Aside from the mere recitation of point of error two, Gary's brief makes no argument whatsoever concerning the doctrine of res judicata. Accordingly, point of error two is waived. Tex. R. App. P. 74(f); *Johnson v. Garza,* 884 S.W.2d 831, 836 (Tex. App.—Austin 1994, writ denied).

Aside from the mere recitation of point of error three, Gary's brief makes no argument whatsoever concerning either the legal or factual sufficiency of the evidence to support the trial court's order. Accordingly, point of error three is waived. *Id.*

With respect to point of error four, the only relevant argument in Gary's brief is contained in a footnote in which he quotes section 3.70(c) of the Family Code: After rendition of a decree of divorce or annulment, the court retains the power to enforce the

---

"3-M" as "Minnesota Mining & Manufacturing Company." *See* 26 U.S.C.A. §414(p)(2) (West Supp. 1995); 29 U.S.C.A. §1056(d)(3)(C) (West Supp. 1995).

property division made under Section 3.63 of this code. A motion to enforce the division of tangible personal property in existence at the time of the decree must be filed within a period of two years after the decree was signed or becomes final after appeal, whichever is the later, or the suit is barred. A motion to enforce the division of future property not in existence at the time of the original decree must be filed within a period of two years after the right to the property matures or accrues or after the decree becomes final, whichever is the later, or the suit is barred. Tex. Fam. Code Ann. §3.70(c) (West 1993). Even assuming that this footnote, which contains no citation of authority, is enough to preserve error, we conclude that no error exists. The retirement benefits that are the subject of this dispute did not constitute "tangible personal property in existence at the time of the decree." Rather, it is clear that such benefits were in the nature of future property, and Gary presented no evidence showing that Patricia's right to such property had matured. We overrule point of error four. Thus, except for the footnote referred to above, Gary's brief is devoted entirely to the issue raised in point of error one. As mentioned earlier, Gary argues in point of error one that the trial court's order was not a true clarification, but was actually a substantive modification which conferred a new benefit on Patricia. Since neither party attempted to present any evidence, this point of error essentially argues that as a matter of law the trial court's order represented a substantive modification of the original decree. We disagree.

The supreme court has made clear that trial courts lack the authority to change the property division in a final divorce decree. *McGehee v. Epley,* 661 S.W.2d 924, 926 (Tex. 1983); *Schwartz v. Jefferson,* 520 S.W.2d 881, 888 (Tex. 1975). In appropriate circumstances, however, a clarifying order may be issued. The Family Code contains at least two relevant provisions: Except as provided by this subchapter and by the Texas Rules of Civil Procedure, a court may not amend, modify, alter, or change the division of property made or approved in the decree of divorce or annulment. Further orders may be entered to enforce the division, but these orders shall be limited to orders in aid of or in clarification of the prior order. The court may specify more precisely the manner of effecting the property division previously made if the substantive division of property is not altered or changed. Fam. Code §3.71(a). "On a finding by the court that the original form of the division of property is not specific enough to be enforceable by contempt, the court may issue a clarifying order setting forth specific terms to enforce compliance with the original division of property." *Id.* §3.72(b). A proper clarification order is consistent with the prior judgment and "merely enforces by appropriate order the controlling settlement agreement." *Young v. Young,* 810 S.W.2d 850, 851 (Tex. App.—Dallas 1991, writ denied); *see* Fam. Code §§3.71(a), 3.72(b).

We construe Gary's first point of error to assert that as a matter of law the parties' intent reflected in the original decree was *not* to grant Patricia survivor benefits. We disagree with this assertion. Although the original decree did not specifically mention "survivor benefits," it did expressly recognize Patricia's marital rights in the 3-M pension plan, awarded Patricia "45 per cent of the present value of [Gary's] accrued benefits," and stated that Patricia "may elect any form of payment of her portion of the available benefits."[2] In

---

2. We recognize that a QDRO must expressly designate the former spouse as the participant's "surviving spouse" in order to entitle the non-employee spouse to survivor benefits. *See* 29 U.S.C.A. §1056(d)(3)(F). In the present case, however, the original decree was not a proper QDRO, so the question here is not resolved by strict ERISA law, but by Texas law relating to the authority of a trial court to clarify an ambiguous divorce decree to fulfill the intentions of the parties. We express no opinion as to whether a decree that *is* a proper QDRO may be clarified in a way that changes the technical disposition of property.

the absence of evidence that the 3-M plan treated survivor benefits as being separate and distinct from "retirement benefits," and in the absence of any evidence of the parties' intentions in that regard, we conclude that Gary has not demonstrated as a matter of law that the parties intended for the decree granting Patricia forty-five per cent of Gary's "retirement benefits" to exclude survivor benefits from that grant. Point of error one is overruled.

We affirm the trial court's order.

DISCUSSION

Harvey makes a few interesting points. One is that a property division decree may later be clarified, but modification is not possible in most instances. *Harvey* outlines the requirements of a "qualified domestic relations order," a requirement that needs to be satisfied when dividing most private pensions at divorce.

Grier v. Grier

Supreme Court of Texas, 1987
731 S.W.2d 931

ON MOTION FOR REHEARING

WALLACE, Justice.

This post-divorce declaratory judgment action presents a question as to the proper characterization and division of military retirement benefits. The Griers were divorced in 1975. At the time of the divorce Edward was a major in the United States Army. The divorce decree did not dispose of Edward's military retirement benefits, as these benefits were not divisible community property at the time of the decree. Eight months after the divorce, Edward was promoted to the rank of lieutenant colonel.

In 1983 Elsie Grier filed suit in a California court seeking partition of Edward's retirement benefits. Edward brought this action for a declaratory judgment that his retirement benefits had been declared non-community property under the divorce decree of 1975. The trial court rendered judgment that Edward's military retirement benefits were subject to partition as community property and awarded Elsie Grier a 37.45% interest in Edward's future gross retirement benefits based upon the rank of lieutenant colonel. The court of appeals reversed and rendered judgment awarding Elsie 37.45% of Edward's "disposable retired pay" payable to a major who would have retired on the date of the Grier's divorce. 713 S.W.2d 213. We affirm the judgment of the court of appeals as modified herein.

Elsie Grier contends that the court of appeals erred in reversing the trial court and in awarding a portion of Edward's retirement benefits based on the rank of major, rather than on the rank of lieutenant colonel. We disagree with this contention. At the time of the Grier's divorce in 1975, Edward held the rank of major, but had been placed on a promotion list by the 1975 AUS Lieutenant Colonel's Promotion Board. Edward was not actually promoted to the rank of lieutenant colonel until May 2, 1976, some eight months after the divorce. It is undisputed that Edward did not become entitled to any of the increased pay or retirement benefits accompanying his elevation in rank until after his divorce from Elsie Grier.

In *Berry v. Berry*, 647 S.W.2d 945 (Tex. 1983), we settled the question of the valuation and apportionment of the community's interest in retirement benefits. Such benefits are to be apportioned to the spouses bases on the value of the community's interest at the time of divorce. Since Edward did not become entitled to the increase in his military retirement pay resulting from his promotion until after his divorce, an order awarding Elsie a share of Edward's retirement benefits upon the dissolution of a marriage, the valuation of the community's interest in such benefits is to be based on the retirement pay which corresponds to the rank actually held bye the services spouse on the date of the divorce.

The judgment of the court of appeals is modified to the extent that Elsie Grier is awarded 37.45% of Edward Grier's gross retired or retainer pay based on the rank of major which is currently payable to such officer who would have retired with 20 years of service in September 1975 together with increases which may occur other than increases attributable to elevation in rank or service rendered by the military spouse after the date of divorce. As modified, the judgment of the court of appeals is affirmed.

· DISCUSSION

Is there anything significant about the penultimate sentence of the opinion? How does this change *Berry*?

Phillips v. Parrish, 814 S.W.2d 501 (Tex. App.—Houston [1st Dist.] 1991, writ denied) involved a situation almost identical to *Berry*. The spouses married before the employee-spouse began working, and the decree did not mention the pension rights. The non-employee spouse sued for a post-divorce partition of these benefits while the husband was still working. The trial court found that the benefits were worth $449.51/month at the time of divorce and $1340.35/month at the time of trial. The appellate court first rejected the employee-spouse's claim that the wife's interest was limited to 50% of $449.51. The court construed *Grier* as permitting post-divorce adjustments, as long as the increases did not result from the employee's post-divorce services. The court also approved the trial court's award to the wife of a percentage of the pension benefits (30%), rather than a fixed amount. How can this be appropriate, when the employee spouse is still working at divorce? If *Phillips* is correct, what is left of *Berry*?

This excerpt seems to reflect the way most Texas courts have applied *Berry* and *Grier*:

> Post-divorce increases in retirement benefits—such as raises, promotions for services rendered, and contributions-attributable to the employee spouse's continued employment are his separate property. Those that are not-such as cost-of-living increases accruing on the non-employee spouse's community portion of the benefits—are subject to community property division.

Reiss v. Reiss, 40 S.W.3d 605, 611 n.5 (Tex. App.—Houston [14th Dist.] 2001, no pet.).

Regarding the division of a defined contribution plan, the court in *Boyd v. Boyd*, 67 S.W.3d 398 (Tex. App.—Fort Worth 2002, no pet.) stated:

> Randall's complaint is about the award to Ginger of a one-half interest in any post-divorce increases in the value of his 401(k) plan, not about the 50–50 division of the plan value at divorce. Ginger agrees that she is not entitled to an interest in the future increases in the value of Randall's 401(k) plan to the extent that the increases result from post-divorce contributions of his separate property.

> Our research has not revealed any cases in which a court has addressed whether a nonemployee spouse is entitled to post-divorce increases in the value of a defined contribution plan that are not attributable to the employee spouse's continued employment. Randall's 401 (k) plan was valued at $166,777 at the date of

divorce and the divorce decree awards Ginger 50% of that amount, or $83,388. Post-divorce increases in the value of the $83,388 will not be attributable to Randall's post-divorce employment or to his contributions of the separate property to the plan. Thus, the future increases in Ginger's share will not be Randall's separate property, and they were subject to the trial court's just and right division.

Gillmore v. Gillmore
Supreme Court of California, 1981
629 P.2d 1

BIRD, Chief Justice.

I.

Vera and Earl Gillmore separated in 1978 after a marriage of 14 years. The trial court issued an interlocutory decree dissolving their marriage on November 27, 1978, and entered a final judgment of dissolution on January 19, 1979. The decree awarded Vera physical custody of their minor child as well as $225 per month child support and $100 per month spousal support.

The community property was divided evenly, with the exception of Earl's interest in a retirement plan managed by his employer, Pacific Telephone Company. The court found that Earl would become eligible to retire on April 11, 1979, at which time he would be entitled to a monthly benefit of $717.18. Vera's interest in that benefit was found to be approximately $177.14 per month. The court specifically reserved jurisdiction over the retirement plan.

Earl continued to work after he became eligible to retire in April 1979. He represented that he was a "healthy, active man" in his early 50s, and he intended to work for some time to come. He was not required to retire until he reached the age of 70.

In July 1979, Vera requested an order directing Earl to pay to Vera her share of the pension benefits immediately, retroactive to the date he became eligible to collect them. Earl responded with a request to modify child and spousal support. The trial court denied both requests, retained jurisdiction over the retirement benefits, and held that it had discretion to delay distribution of the benefits until Earl actually retired.

II.

Under California law, retirement benefits earned by a spouse during a marriage are community property, subject to equal division upon the dissolution of that marriage. This is true whether the benefits are vested or nonvested, matured or immature. Vera and Earl agree that Earl's retirement benefits are community property to the extent they were earned during their marriage. The sole disagreement concerns the timing of the distribution of those benefits. Vera contends that the trial court abused its discretion when it refused to order Earl to begin immediate payments to her of her share. Earl claims that the trial court had discretion to postpone distribution of the benefits until he actually retired and began to receive payments from the pension plan.

Under the cases and statutory law, Earl cannot time his retirement to deprive Vera of an equal share of the community's interest in his pension. It is a "settled principle that one spouse cannot, by invoking a condition wholly within his control, defeat the community interest of the other spouse."

Earl's retirement benefits are both vested and matured. He will not forfeit his benefits if he leaves his employment voluntarily, is terminated or retires, the only condition precedent to payment of the benefits is his retirement, a condition totally within his control. A unilateral choice to postpone retirement cannot be manipulated so as to impair a spouse's interest in those retirement benefits.

In re Marriage of Stenquist, supra, 21 Cal. 3d 779, 148 Cal. Rptr. 9, 582 P.2d 96, involved a husband's election to receive disability benefits (usually separate property), rather than retirement pay (usually community property). This court held that the husband could not use this election to deprive his wife of her interest in his retirement benefits. "[T]o permit the husband, by unilateral election of a 'disability' pension, to transmute community property into his own separate property (*In re Marriage of Fithian, supra,* 10 Cal. 3d 592, 602, 111 Cal. Rptr. 369, 517 P.2d 449), is to negate the protective philosophy of the community property law as set out in previous decisions of this court." (*Stenquist, supra,* 21 Cal. 3d at p. 782, 148 Cal. Rptr. 9, 582 P.2d 96.)

The result of the husband's unilateral decision in *Stenquist* would have been to deprive the wife of any interest in his retirement benefits. In the present case, Vera is no less entitled to protection. The fact that the deprivation she faces is less than total is not decisive. Earl would deprive Vera of the immediate enjoyment of an asset earned by the community during the marriage. In so doing, he would subject Vera to the risk of losing the asset completely if Earl were to die while he was still employed. Although Earl has every right to choose to postpone the receipt of his pension and to run that risk, he should not be able to force Vera to do so as well.[1]

Similar results were reached in two earlier cases. In *In re Marriage of Martin, supra,* 50 Cal. App. 3d 581, 123 Cal. Rptr. 634, the appellate court held that where the only condition to receipt of the benefits by one spouse was the employee spouse's decision to retire and apply for them, the benefits should be divided as community property. The language of the court is instructive. "The only condition to the payment of the pension benefits is a condition entirely within [the husband's] control, and that is not an uncertainty precluding division of the asset upon dissolution of marriage." (*Martin, supra,* 50 Cal. App. 3d at p. 584, 123 Cal. Rptr. 634). Similarly a trial court decision to order the immediate payment of a share of a husband's vested, matured pension benefits to his wife, where the husband was eligible to retire but had not yet done so, was upheld in *Bensing v. Bensing, supra,* 25 Cal. App. 3d at pages 892–93, 102 Cal. Rptr. 255.

---

1. Earl claims that the trial court's decision resulted in an equal division of the retirement benefits since he and Vera will receive their shares of the benefits at the same time—the time that he chooses to retire. However, he overlooks the fact that both the timing of receipt and the control of an asset are important aspects of its value." Postponement, especially late in life, is often the equivalent of complete defeat. Not only are the employee spouse's chances of dying on the job increasing with each passing year (in which case the pension rights would vanish under most plans), the present value of money is much more valuable as a person enters the last years of his life." (Note, *In re Marriage of Stenquist: Tracing the Community interest in Pension Rights Altered by Spousal Election* (1979) 67 Cal. L. Rev. 856, 879, fn. 76). A benefit which may be received at some unknown time in the future is of less value than one received immediately. [*In re Marriage of Tammen* (1976) 63 Cal. App. 3d 927, 931, 134 Cal. Rptr. 161; see Projector, *Valuation of Retirement Benefits in Marriage Dissolutions* (1975) 50 L.A. Bar Bull. 229]. Further, a benefit over which an individual has no control is of less value than a benefit that can be managed personally. Thus, Earl's decision to wait to receive his pension when it will be most profitable and most convenient for him deprives Vera of both the immediate enjoyment of her benefits and the power to manage them to her own advantage. Her financial situation may involve factors significantly different from his. Both the husband and the wife should be able to make their independent decisions about how to handle their shares of the community property.

These cases, however, do not preclude the employee spouse from choosing among alternative retirement plans. The employee spouse retains the right (1) to change or terminate employment; (2) to agree to a modification of the retirement benefits; or (3) to elect between alternative benefits. (*In re Marriage of Brown, supra*, 15 Cal. 3d at p. 849, 126 Cal. Rptr. 633, 544 P.2d 561). "[T]he employee spouse retains the right to determine the nature of the benefits to be received." (*In re Marriage of Stenquist, supra*, 21 Cal. 3d at p. 786, 148 Cal. Rptr. 9, 582 P.2d 96, fn. omitted.)

The right of the employee spouse is nonetheless limited by the fact that the nonemployee spouse owns an interest in the retirement benefits. Thus, *Brown* notes that the employee spouse has a right to agree to "a reasonable ... *nondetrimental* modification of the pension system" (*In re Marriage of Brown, supra*, 15 Cal.3d at p. 849 fn. 11, 126 Cal. Rptr. 633, 544 P.2d 561, emphasis added), and *Stenquist* finds that the employee spouse retains the right to elect "higher than ordinary retirement benefits." (*In re Marriage of Stenquist, supra*, 21 Cal. 3d at p. 786, fn. 6, 148 Cal. Rptr. 9, 582 P.2d 96). If the right to choose among alternative retirement plans is exercised in a way which impairs the nonemployee's interest in the benefits, the nonemployee spouse must be compensated.[2]

Thus, although the husband in *Stenquist* had every right to choose a disability pension rather than retirement pay, his choice did not prevent the court from ordering him to pay to the wife an amount equivalent to what her interest would have been had he chosen retirement pay. Similarly, Earl retains the right to determine what retirement benefits he will receive. He can retire now or at some time in the future. He also retains the option of choosing between the alternative pension plans offered by his employer. However, if he opts for an alternative that deprives Vera of her full share of the retirement benefits, he must compensate her for the interest she loses as a result of his decision.

Compensation is possible here because the value of Vera's interest is known to the court. Also, the only condition to the payment of the benefits, Earl's retirement, is entirely within his control. However, "if the court concludes that because of uncertainties affecting the vesting or maturation of the pension that it should not attempt to divide the present value of pension rights, it can instead award each spouse an appropriate portion of each pension payment as it is paid." (*In re Marriage of Brown*, supra, 15 Cal. 3d at p. 848, 126 Cal. Rptr. 633, 544 P.2d 561, fn. omitted). In this case, the pension benefits have already vested and matured. There are no "uncertainties affecting ... vesting or maturation" that could lead the trial court to conclude that distribution of the pension must be delayed. Therefore, the trial court abused its discretion when it refused to order the immediate distribution of this vested and mature retirement benefit.

Earl's claim that he is being forced to retire misses the point. He is free to continue working. However, if he does so, he must reimburse Vera for the share of the community property that she loses as a result of that decision. His claim that the court lacks jurisdiction to order him to make payments to Vera because it lacks jurisdiction over his separate

---

2. Trial courts can limit the employee spouse's freedom to choose to the extent necessary to protect the interests of the nonemployee spouse. For instance, *In re Marriage of Lionberger* (1979) 97 Cal. App. 3d 56, 67–70, 158 Cal. Rptr. 535, affirmed a trial court order precluding the husband from choosing a pension plan option that would have decreased the size of his wife's interest. In *Phyllipson v. Board of Administration, supra*, 3 Cal. 3d 32, 48, 89 Cal. Rptr. 61, 473 P.2d 765, the court ordered the husband to choose a particular retirement benefit because such an order was the only way to protect the wife's interest. See *also Ball v. McDonnell Douglas Corp.* (1973) 30 Cal. App. 3d 624, 630–631, 106 Cal. Rptr. 662, in which the appellate court noted that the trial court could have made an order limiting the employee's freedom to choose among alternative plans if the nonemployee spouse had requested it.

property also lacks merit. Earl alone will make the decision to use separate property to reimburse Vera, when and if he decides not to retire. His situation is not unlike that faced by a couple ordered to divide a house that they own as community property. If one of the spouses chooses to keep the house, he or she is free to use separate property to purchase the other's interest. Here, Earl must divide his retirement benefits with Vera. If he does not wish to retire, he must pay her an amount equivalent to her interest.[3]

In the past, this court has encouraged trial courts, if feasible, to award all pension rights to an employee spouse, compensating the nonemployee spouse with other community property of equal value. This type of a division was not possible here since the trial court severed the issue of retirement benefits from the division of the remainder of the community property. At the time the retirement benefits were to be divided, the community property had already been distributed. As a result, there was no longer any community property which could be offset against the retirement benefits.

Frequently, parties are able to arrive at a reasonable settlement of these issues. For example, the nonemployee spouse may choose to wait, preferring to receive the retirement benefits when the employee spouse actually retires. The nonemployee may thereby ensure some protection for the future and may be able to share in the increased value of the pension plan. (See *In re Marriage of Adams, supra,* 64 Cal. App. 3d at p. 186, 134 Cal. Rptr. 298).[4] However, if the nonemployee spouse chooses to receive immediate payments, as Vera does, he or she has a right to do so.

There are various ways in which Earl could compensate Vera. He could "buy out" her share of the retirement benefits, paying her the present value of her share of the pension plan. (See Projector, supra, 50 L.A. Bar Bull. 229; Hardie, *Pay Now or Later: Alternatives in the Disposition of Retirement Benefits on Divorce* (1978) 53 State Bar J. 106). Or, he could begin to pay her a share of the retirement payments on a monthly basis. (E.g., *In re Marriage of Martin, supra,* 50 Cal. App. 3d at p. 585, 123 Cal. Rptr. 634; *Bensing v. Bensing, supra,* 25 Cal. App. 3d at pp. 893–894, 102 Cal. Rptr. 255). Both of these methods of payment constitute an equal distribution of the benefits. However, the parties may have preferences based on numerous factors not presently before this court, including

---

3. One commentator argues that when an employee who is eligible to retire chooses to continue working, part of his or her salary is actually attributable to community effort:

[F]rom an economist's perspective, the employee spouse's compensation for continued employment is not the full amount of his paycheck. Rather, his compensation is only that amount above the pension benefits that he will not receive while he continues working. For example, in the matured pension situation, if the employee can receive retirement pay in the amount of X dollars without working, then his actual compensation for services rendered is not the amount of his paycheck, Y dollars, but Y minus X dollars. This is nothing more than a reapplication of the benefits foregone' formula of *Stenquist* [2] Cal. 3d 779, 148 Cal. Rptr. 9, 582 P.2d 96]. [Fn. omitted]. Therefore, rather than penalizing the spouse for not retiring, the contrary is true—the community is being penalized because it is forced to subsidize the employee spouse's salary, which becomes his separate property.

Note, In re Marriage of Stenquist: Tracing the Community Interest in Pension Rights Altered by Spousal Election, supra, 67 Cal. L. Rev. 856, 879.

Since this court does not find any taking of separate property, it is not necessary to discuss Earl's constitutional claim.

4. The nonemployee spouse, of course, cannot have it both ways. The decision to ask for distribution of the retirement benefits before the employee spouse actually retires "constitutes an irrevocable election to give up increased payment in the future which might accrue due to increased age, longer service and a higher salary." (*In re Marriage of Luciano, supra,* 104 Cal. App. 3d at p. 961, 164 Cal. Rptr. 93, citation omitted). Thus, if Vera chooses to receive her share of the retirement benefits immediately, she will forfeit her right to share in the increased value of those benefits in the future.

the tax consequences of the alternative plans. Therefore, the exact method of distribution must be left to the discretion of the trial court on remand.

III.

That portion of the trial court's order denying Vera's request for the immediate distribution of her share of Earl's retirement benefits is reversed. The cause is remanded to the trial court for further proceedings consistent with the views expressed in this opinion.

DISCUSSION

Gillmore gives the non-employee spouse the right to sell her interest in the pension plan to the employee spouse when the pension rights mature and the employee spouse chooses to continue working. Why does the California court choose to establish this right?

Is the *Gillmore* rationale applicable in Texas?

The Retirement Equity Act of 1984 (Public Law 98-397) permits (but does not require) a divorce court to award a non-employee spouse a pension benefit from the employee's pension plan that begins when the employee's interest matures, even if the employee retires later. See Retirement Equity Act Sec. 104(a). For example, *see Harvey v. Harvey*, 905 S.W.2d 760 (Tex. App.—Austin 1995, no writ).

An order to divide an interest in a private plan must be a "qualified domestic relations order," frequently called a QDRO. For a discussion of some problems encountered drafting such orders, see Schulman & Kelley, *Complex QDRO Issues Every Family Law Attorney Must Consider*, 9 Am.J.Fam.L. 57 (1995).

The rules discussed in this chapter only apply to pension rights. Sometimes the scope of the employee's pension rights is not clear.

Whorrall v. Whorrall

Texas Court of Appeals—Austin, 1985
691 S.W.2d 32, writ dism'd

SHANNON, Chief Justice.

Richard commenced employment with IBM on January 30, 1956, and as of the date of his marriage to Ilene on February 11, 1977, he had accrued twenty-one years (252 months) of service with the company. He retired in July of 1982, and, therefore, his period of service during his marriage to Ilene was sixty-five months. His total service with IBM was 317 months, of which 252 months, or seventy nine and one-half percent was before his marriage to Ilene.

Upon his retirement in July 1982, Richard received, in addition to his ordinary retirement, a "Special Payment" in the amount of $75,000.00 which was to be paid semi-monthly over a three-year-period.

The district court determined that the "Special Payment" was entirely community property, and divided it into two portions: that sum in the husband's possession at date of trial ($5,300.00), and that amount receivable over the remainder of the three year period ($43,751.40).

The district court awarded one-half of each portion to Richard and Ilene, therefore each party received:

Payment in possession at date of trial $2,650.00

Future payments $21,875.70

Richard insists that the district court erred in finding the payment was entirely community property because such was "a supplementary retirement benefit," as a matter of law, since it allegedly was "based upon Husband's prior service with, and contributions to the company." Accordingly, he urges that only that part of the benefit earned or accrued during the marriage, or 65/317 (twenty and one-half percent) is community. *Cearley v. Cearley*, 544 S.W.2d 661 (Tex. 1976); *Taggart v. Taggart*, 552 S.W.2d 422 (Tex. 1977). It follows, the argument continues, that the other seventy-nine and one-half percent interest is Richard's separate property. Richard argues alternatively that there is "insufficient evidence" to support the district court's finding that the payment was entirely community property.

Richard suggests that the primary basis for the "Special Payment" was to specially compensate him for his prior service to the company. As a result, he would characterize the payment as but a form of a retirement benefit which was earned during the tenure of his employment with IBM. To qualify as a "retirement benefit" capable of being apportioned between his separate and the community estate, the payment must be an "earned property right which accrued by reason of years of service," *Busby v. Busby*, 457 S.W.2d 551 (Tex. 1970); or must be a "form of deferred compensation which is earned during each month of service," *Cearley v. Cearley*, 544 S.W.2d 661, 665 (Tex. 1976).

In his first point of error, Richard argues that there was "insufficient evidence" to support the court's finding that the payment is entirely community. To the contrary, this Court has concluded that the record, as a whole, reveals that there is sufficient evidence for the determination that the payment was not to compensate appellant for past services. As such, this defeats both Richard's insufficient evidence argument and also his "separate property as a matter of law" argument.

Paul Turner, personnel administration manager for the Austin IBM plant, testified that Richard had made significant contributions to the company in the past, but more recently he had not been so productive. In fact, he had been graded down from Facilities Manager to Senior Engineer. His most recent responsibilities had not supported his level, but based upon his past contributions, the company management did not think it appropriate to reduce his level further. His position would not be filled after his retirement. Had Richard refused to retire, he would not have received the "Special Payment." Richard had expressed a strong interest in a special package and it appeared to management that he would retire upon receiving an attractive offer. It is a fair conclusion from the evidence that Richard and IBM were bargaining for an incentive to permit him to retire early so that the company could terminate his unproductive position.

Turner testified further about the nature of the Special Payment. No such payments were made on an employee-wide scale. Such payments were "unique" and "strictly discretionary" and rarely given. A condition of the payments, although not the primary purpose, was that the employee not compete with IBM.

In discussing the Special Payment program at other IBM plant sites in the country, Turner stated: "All of them have been associated with our desire to offer employees an opportunity to leave the company, if they choose, voluntarily, to help rebalance our manpower throughout the company."

The Special Payment program appears primarily to be an incentive to coax an employee into an early retirement. The fact that such payment is purely discretionary with the company negates the notion that it is earned or accrued over the employee's tenure. It should be noted, as well, that the company did not report this payment on the W-4P form which is the proper retirement withholding form. Although there is some evidence which bore upon appellant's past service, much more evidence supported the nature of the payment to be an incentive to obtain retirement of high ranked, unproductive employees.

DISCUSSION

Do you agree with the court? Is there any other argument that could result in the "Special Payment" not being considered 100% community? A case similar to *Whorrall* is *Henry v. Henry*, 48 S.W.3d 468 (Tex.App — Houston [14th Dist.] 2001, no pet.).

Regarding the husband's basic defined benefit pension plan, because the husband was retired at divorce, the community claim to that pension is calculated based on *Taggart* and the portion of the employee's career he was married. *Marriage of Jordan*, 264 S.W.3d 850 (Tex. App. — Waco 2008, no pet.).

Marriage of Wade, 923 S.W.2d 735 (Tex. App. — Texarkana 1996, writ denied) involved a spouse who worked as an insurance agent. He signed a contract during marriage that gave him the right to receive, when he died or retired, certain payments based upon the premiums generated during the last year of work. He was working at the time of divorce. The court treated this right to receive the future payment as a retirement benefit. The court valued this right as of the date of divorce by computing what the spouse would receive if he had retired as of the date of divorce. He then was obligated to pay his former wife 50% of this amount when he died or retired.

2. Pension Rights and the Death of a Spouse

If a spouse dies while married, the spouse normally can devise one-half of each item of community property. If the person has divorced before the date of death, all property awarded the decedent in the divorce normally goes in the decedent's estate. Some states have established a pension rights exception to these general rules.

In re Estate of Allen
California Court of Appeals, 1980
166 Cal. Rptr. 653

DEARMAN, Justice.

In this case, following the death of a retired airline employee's spouse, the controller sought to impose an inheritance tax on one-half of the pension that the surviving employee spouse was receiving, despite the fact that receipt of the pension preceded and was unaffected by the decedent's passing. We concur in the superior court's conclusion that such a tax would be improper by virtue of the fact that the community property interest of the non-employee spouse did not pass to her husband at her death but simply terminated at that time. In reaching this conclusion we reject the controller's two preliminary contentions and hold that the prong of the "terminable interest" rule articulated in *Waite v. Waite* (1972) 6 Cal. 3d 461, 99 Cal. Rptr. 325, 492 P.2d 13, is still viable and that the rationale of *Waite*, which involved a public pension plan, is equally applicable to the private pension plan involved here.

Orpha and Herbert Allen had been married for 36 years when Orpha Allen died in 1977. By then Mr. Allen had retired from Pan American World Airways, his employer throughout the marriage, and was receiving retirement income from Pan American.

The terms of the retirement plan were simple. Mr. Allen would receive $515.46 per month until he died. If he predeceased his wife she would receive $344.48 per month until her death. The couple had chosen this plan, with its survivor annuity, over one that would have conferred higher monthly benefits while Mr. Allen lived but no benefits after his death.

Orpha Allen died testate and made her husband her sole devisee and legatee. Mr. Allen petitioned the superior court to set aside and confirm the community property so that inheritance taxes could be assessed under Revenue and Taxation Code Sec. 13551. The latter statute allowed taxation of the passage of a deceased spouse's interest in community property to his or her surviving spouse. Mr. Allen did not list his pension as a community asset. The inheritance tax referee, however, ruled that Mrs. Allen's community property interest in the pension her husband would receive for the rest of his life (he was 64) had "passed" to Mr. Allen within the meaning of Sec. 13551 and computed its value to be $52,864.70. A total of $3,992.30 was assessed in taxes.

Mr. Allen filed his objections in the superior court contending that various decisions of the California Supreme Court had established that his wife's community property interest in the pension had terminated at her death and that she had no power to devise it. He argued that he continued to receive $515.46 per month pursuant only to his prior contractual arrangement with Pan American and that no transfer had occurred within the meaning of the California Inheritance Tax Act. The superior court agreed and struck the interest in the pension from the list of taxable assets. The controller appeals.

Distinguished by what is called in this litigation the "terminable interest" rule, comprised of two California Supreme Court holdings, pension rights must be perceived as a unique species of community property. In *Waite v. Waite* (1972) 6 Cal. 3d 461, 99 Cal. Rptr. 325, 492 P.2d 13, the decision bearing directly on the instant case, the trial court, upon the divorce of a judge and his wife, ordered the controller to pay directly to Mrs. Waite "or her devisee or heirs" one-half of all benefits payable to her husband under the Judge's Retirement Act. This order followed as a matter of course the usual community property rule, embodied in Probate Code Sec. 201: "Upon the death of either husband or wife, one-half of the community property belongs to the surviving spouse; the other half is subject to the testamentary disposition of the decedent, and in the absence thereof goes to the surviving spouse, subject to the provisions of Sections 202 and 203 of this code." However, the Supreme Court sustained Judge Waite's objection to that part of the order regarding payment to Mrs. Waite's heirs. The court held that the state's concern lay in providing subsistence only for the judge and his dependents and not the objects of the non-employee spouse's bounty. Despite some ambiguity in the opinion, *Waite* has consistently been interpreted as having limited Mrs. Waite's community property interest in the pension to an interest that survived only as long as she did.

Relying heavily on Reppy, *Community and Separate Interests in Pensions and Social Security Benefits After Marriage of Brown and ERISA* (1978) 25 U.C.L.A. L. Rev. 417, 443–482, the controller argues that Waite should not be extended to private pension plans. The gist of the argument is that the terminable interest rule is unfair to non-employee spouses and conflicts with the principle of spousal equality embodied in decisions such as *In re Marriage of Brown* (1976) 15 Cal. 3d 838, 126 Cal. Rptr. 633, 544 P.2d 561.

First, the controller has failed to identify a single unfairness attributable to *Waite's* contribution to the terminable interest rule. By extension of *Waite*, Mrs. Allen's share in the pension could not be passed on to third persons of her choice but automatically went to her husband; likewise, under the plan at issue here the pension payments cease at Mr. Allen's death and thus he, just like his wife, owns no pension rights that can be devised to third persons. While the retirement plan pays Mr. Allen more after Mrs. Allen's death than it would have paid Mrs. Allen had she outlived her husband, the *Waite* holding is in no way responsible for that inequality; community property law does not yet dictate the economic terms of a pension package.

Moreover, the result in *Waite* not only created little inequality; it was clearly powered by its own consideration of fairness. The court in *Waite* focused on the special purpose of the pension at issue there:

> The purpose of the pension was to provide provision for the subsistence of the employee and his spouse. Once the spouse dies, of course, her need for subsistence ends, and the state's interest in her sustenance reaches a coincident completion. When this termination occurs, the state's concern narrows to the sustenance of the retired employee; its pension payments must necessarily be directed to that sole objective.

6 Cal. 3d at 473, 99 Cal. Rptr. 333, 492 P.2d 21.

The court thus highlighted the unique place of such a pension in community property law: it is property that is meant to be shared by the spouses and only the spouses, and one whose purpose would be wholly defeated by allowing the deceased spouse to bequeath his or her share to third persons. It seems perfectly appropriate to the function of pension benefits that they automatically pass to the surviving spouse.

The judgment is affirmed.

DISCUSSION

What is the rationale of the "terminable interest rule" discussed in *Allen*? Is this persuasive? California no longer accepts the terminable interest rule. See Cal. Fam. Code. § 2610.

Valdez v. Ramirez

Supreme Court of Texas, 1978
574 S.W.2d 748

DANIEL, Justice.

The issue presented by this case is whether a husband's community interest in his surviving wife's civil service retirement benefits is inheritable upon his death by adult children of his former wife. We hold that it is not.

Lillie Valdez had worked as a United States Civil Service employee for 352 months prior to her retirement in 1971. For 340 months of her employment she was married to Tomas Valdez, Sr. Based on her 352 months of service she began receiving retirement benefits in 1971 under the Federal Civil Service Retirement Act. 5 U.S.C.A. Sec. 8331, *et seq.* In 1973, Tomas, Sr., died intestate, leaving Olga Ramirez and Tomas Valdez, Jr., his adult children by a previous marriage, as the heirs to his half of the community estate.

Olga and Tomas, Jr., brought this suit to recover a portion of Lillie's retirement benefits based on Tomas, Sr.'s, community interest in the benefits. After a non-jury trial, the trial court rendered judgment for Olga and Tomas, Jr., awarding them one-half of 340/352 of the retirement benefits that Lillie has received since Tomas, Sr.'s, death and that she will receive in the future. The Court of Civil Appeals affirmed. 558 S.W.2d 88. We reverse the judgments of the courts below and render judgment that plaintiffs take nothing against Lillie Valdez.

A settled marital property rule in Texas is that a spouse has a community property interest in that portion of the retirement benefits of the opposite spouse earned during their marriage. *Taggart v. Taggart*, 552 S.W.2d 422 (Tex. 1977); *Cearley v. Cearley*, 544 S.W.2d 661 (Tex. 1976); *Busby v. Busby*, 457 S.W.2d 551 (Tex. 1970). In each of the above cases, the non-employed spouse was alive, and we dealt with the question only as it concerned fixed or contingent rights in a division of the community asset upon divorce. We found no conflict between our application of Texas' community property law and federal laws which provided such benefits.

The question in this case is different and is one of first impression in this State. It calls for a decision of whether the interest of a spouse who died prior to any division or divorce should pass to his heirs under the Texas Probate Code Sec. 45, or should be paid to the living and earning spouse in accordance with a joint survivorship option which she had exercised under the Federal Civil Service Retirement Act. 5 U.S.C.A. Sec. 8339.

At the outset, it is recognized that under ordinary circumstances, where there is no contract or provision of law to the contrary, Section 45 of the Texas Probate Code would govern the distribution of a deceased spouse's interest in the community property as the Court of Civil Appeals has ruled.[1]

On the other hand, however, there are at least four categories of assets known as nonprobate assets, not subject to disposition by will and not subject to the rules of intestate distribution. Examples are: (1) property settled in an inter vivos trust, where title remains in the trustee notwithstanding the settlor's death; (2) property passing by right of joint survivorship, as in a valid joint bank account; (3) property passing at death pursuant to terms of a contract, such as provided in life insurance policies, and under contributory retirement plans; and (4) property passing by insurance or annuity contracts created, funded and distributed as directed by federal statutes. In the context of the Texas community property system, this disposition of such nonprobate assets is governed by lifetime transfer rules, not by death-time transfer rules of the Probate Code. See Johanson, *Revocable Trusts and Community Property: The Substantive Problem*, 47 Texas L. Rev. 537 (1969).

Lillie Valdez's retirement benefits were provided for by her contract of employment as a civil service employee of the United States Government. The terms and considerations of her employment and compensation are set out in Part III of the Civil Service Act, 5 U.S.C.A.

---

1. Section 45 of the Texas Probate Code Annotated, states:
Upon the dissolution of the marriage relation by death, all property belonging to the community estate of the husband and wife shall go to the survivor, if there be no child or children of the deceased or their descendants; but if there be a child or children of the deceased, or descendants of such child or children, then the survivor shall be entitled to one-half of said property, and the other half shall pass to such child or children, or their descendants. But such descendants shall inherit only such portion of said property as the parent through whom they inherit would be entitled to if alive. In every case, the community estate passes charged with the debts against it.

Secs. 2101–8913. Included in that portion of the Act is a comprehensive program providing retirement benefits for civil service employees. 5 U.S.C.A. Secs. 8331–8348. Upon retirement, employees are paid benefits under the Act based on their contributions to the retirement program and length of government service.

The Civil Service Act specifies which persons are entitled to receive retirement benefits. Provisions are made only for payment to the employee, or, in the case of the employee's death, to the surviving spouse and the employee's children under 18 years of age (with age exceptions for incapacitated children and students). 5 U.S.C.A. Sec. 8341. The Act provides for no payment to persons outside of the employee's immediate family.[2] It would be contrary to the whole contract, policy, and plan of the Retirement Act for nearly one-half of Mrs. Valdez's monthly payments to be taken from her and awarded to her deceased husband's adult children. This would subvert the underlying purpose of the Act, which is to provide financial support and security to aged employees and their immediate families. It is also contrary to the election made by Mrs. Valdez under Sec. 8339(j) for a joint survivor annuity for the benefit of herself and her husband.

While Lillie Valdez was employed by the federal government and earning future rights to a retirement annuity, those contingent rights were community property, but such inchoate rights are characterized by the Family Code as "special community" under the wife's sole management and control.

Thus, while being earned, the right to a future Civil Service retirement annuity was the special community of Lillie Valdez, subject to her sole management, control and disposition. As manager of this "special community" asset, she had the contract right to select a mode of payment. As indicated, she selected the joint and survivor option in accordance with 5 U.S.C.A. Sec. 8339. Although this option provided a lower monthly payment to her and her husband while both were living, and a lower payment to her if she survived him, it also created in the husband a right to an annuity if he survived her. 5 U.S.C.A. Sec. 8341. At the time of the exercise of this option, the inchoate and contingent rights of the community to future retirement annuity payments was fixed by federal statute. By virtue of Lillie Valdez's election to take a joint and survivor annuity, this annuity constituted community income during their joint lives. Mr. Valdez along with Mrs. Valdez had full enjoyment of this matured community asset during their joint lives. Had Mr. Valdez survived his wife, he would have succeeded to full enjoyment of the survivor portion of the annuity payments; no interest therein would have been included in Mrs. Valdez's probate estate to pass under her will or by intestacy. Since Mr. Valdez predeceased Mrs. Valdez, we hold that she succeeded to the survivor portion of the annuity benefit as set forth in the terms of the contract with her employer, the United States Government. These annuity benefits should continue to be paid to her in accordance with the terms of the Civil Service Retirement Act.

---

2. The Act's policy of retaining the benefits in the hands of the intended recipients is exhibited in the protections of 5 U.S.C.A. Sec. 8346(a), which provides:

The money mentioned by this subchapter [the Civil Service Retirement Act] is not assignable, either in law or equity, except under the provisions of Section 8345(g) of this title [which gives the Civil Service Commission the power to approve assignments], or subject to execution, levy, attachment, garnishment, or other legal process, except as otherwise may be provided by Federal laws.

Prior to 1975 the assignment prohibition of Sec. 8346(a) was absolute.

Accordingly, the judgments of the courts below are reversed and judgment is here rendered that plaintiffs take nothing from Lillie Valdez.

ON MOTION FOR REHEARING

In their motion for rehearing Respondents Ramirez and Valdez, Jr. make two attacks on our treatment of the Civil Service Retirement benefits in this case as a joint survivorship annuity payable solely to Petitioner Lillie Valdez after the death of her husband.

By electing to give up her maximum higher single life annuity which (even though community property) would absolutely terminate at her death, Mrs. Valdez received for herself and her husband a matured right to receive future income from the joint and survivor annuity under the terms of the Civil Service Retirement Act. Since he predeceased her, the Act provides that she shall continue to receive the payments during her lifetime.[3]

Respondents' second point urges that Mrs. Valdez could not elect to create a valid joint survivorship in this instance because community property cannot be the subject of a joint survivorship agreement under Texas law. *William v. McKnight*, 402 S.W.2d 505 (Tex. 1966); *Hilley v. Hilley*, 161 Tex. 569, 342 S.W.2d 565 (1961). As indicated in our original opinion, we are dealing here with a type of joint and survivorship annuity which was created by federal law. The Civil Service Retirement Act has a clearly declared federal purpose of providing a definite amount of financial support and security for retired federal employees, their spouses, and certain children of retired employees. A joint survivorship annuity clearly authorized by federal law to serve a federal purpose may preempt conflicting state laws in the absence of its use to perpetuate a fraud by one spouse on the other. *Free* v. Bland, 369 U.S. 663, 82 S.Ct. 1089, 8 L.Ed.2d 180 (1962). In the instant case there has been no suggestion that Mrs. Valdez made the election authorized by the Civil Service Retirement Act for any purpose other than to provide for herself and her husband the broadest possible joint and survivorship benefits payable under the federal Act.

The motion for rehearing is overruled.

Allard v. Frech

Supreme Court of Texas, 1988
754 S.W.2d 111

MAUZY, J.

This case involves the proper characterization of retirement benefits and joint savings account proceeds in a probate action. The trial court rendered judgment characterizing the husband's retirement benefits and joint savings account proceeds as community prop-

---

3. Mrs. Valdez's payments continued after her husband's death on the same reduced basis which she elected upon retirement until Congress amended the Act in 1974 to provide that such payments to widowed retirees shall be recomputed and paid as if the annuity had not been reduced for each month that the retired employee remains unmarried. P.L. 93-474, 88 Stat. 1438, 5 U.S.C.A. Sec. 8339(j).

erty and awarded the wife's estate one-half of the husband's retirement benefits and one-half of the proceeds in the joint savings account. The court of appeals affirmed these findings of the trial court holding that the proceeds from the husband's retirement plan were properly characterized as community property and that the funds held in the joint savings account were not held in joint tenancy with right of survivorship. 754 S.W.2d 111. We affirm.

Billie J. Allard and Billy L. Allard were married from 1945 until Mrs. Allard's death on April 11, 1983. Shortly after the marriage, Mr. Allard began working for General Dynamics Corporation and retired from his position in May 1982. As a result of his employment, Mr. Allard subscribed and contributed community funds to a qualified private retirement plan. Under the terms of the options available to him at the time of his retirement, Mr. Allard selected an option providing for lifetime benefits with a guaranteed ten-year minimum, but such election was not signed by Mrs. Allard. Mr. Allard began receiving retirement benefits of $1,008.00 per month beginning June 1982 and has received monthly benefits since that time.

On April 25, 1983, Martha Parten Frech, Mrs. Allard's sister, offered a will dated January 12, 1983, into probate. Mr. Allard contested the will and offered a later will dated March 22, 1983, which was rejected by the court. After the will offered by Mrs. Frech was admitted to probate, as independent executrix, she filed an "Inventory, Appraisement, and List of Claims" to which Mr. Allard objected. The issues presented during trial were limited by agreement of the parties to those concerning the value and characterization of certain property. After a trial on the merits, the trial court approved the inventory and signed the approval order awarding the decedent's estate one-half of the husband's retirement benefits, as well as one-half of the sums on deposit in a joint savings account containing a survivorship provision. The trial court made additional findings which are not challenged by the parties and thus not before this court.

The court of appeals affirmed the judgment of the trial court regarding the husband's retirement benefits and the proceeds in the joint savings account. The court of appeals held that the benefits from the husband's retirement plan were properly characterized by the trial court as community property, thus, Mrs. Allard's half-interest in the retirement benefits properly passed under her will to the Allards' daughter and grandchildren. The court of appeals further held that a partition of community funds in Texas is not implicit in the mere execution of a joint tenancy with right to survivorship agreement, and that actual partition of community funds must be accomplished in an active not passive manner. Therefore, in light of the absence of a partition agreement or spousal gift, the court of appeals concluded that the funds in the joint savings account were community property, with no right of survivorship in Mr. Allard. 735 S.W.2d at 317.

The initial question presented for this court's consideration involves the proper method to be utilized in dealing with retirement benefits in instances where the marriage is terminated by the death of the non-employee spouse. In this case, Mr. Allard possessed a retirement plan with General Dynamics in the amount of $102,080.00 which vested in 1982 prior to the death of his wife. Mr. Allard contends that his wife's one-half interest in his retirement benefits should not be allowed to continue after her death and pass under her will to the Allard's adult child and grandchildren. Focusing his argument in part on the inequities involved in allowing "able-bodied young adults capable of supporting themselves" to share in his retirement benefits, Mr. Allard urges this court to apply the result of *Valdez* v. *Ramirez*, 574 S.W.2d 748 (Tex. 1978) to this case, or alternatively, to adopt the terminable interest rule. We decline to extend the holding in Valdez to the facts of this case.

Likewise, we reject Mr. Allard's contention that the terminable interest rule should be adopted and applied in this case.

In *Valdez*, a United States Civil Service employee had been receiving retirement benefits under the Federal Civil Service Retirement Act for two years when her husband died intestate. In response to the issue of whether the deceased husband's interest in his wife's civil service retirement benefits was inheritable by his adult children of a former wife, we concluded that the wife's retirement benefits remaining after her husband's death were her separate property; consequently, the benefits could not pass by the intestacy of her husband. *Valdez*, 574 S.W.2d at 751. This decision was primarily based on the preemption of Texas community property law by the requirements of the Federal Civil Service Act which provided for the payment of retirement benefits only to the employee, or in the case of the employee's death, to the surviving spouse and the employee's minor, incapacitated or student children. We held that it would be contrary to the entire contract, policy, and plan of the Federal Retirement Act for nearly one-half of Mrs. Valdez's monthly payments to be taken from her and awarded to her deceased husband's adult children. *Valdez*, 574 S.W.2d at 750. Mr. Allard argues that the same equitable result should be reached in this case.

We hold that the court of appeals correctly distinguished *Valdez* from the instant case. *Valdez* involved a federal retirement plan pursuant to a federal statutory scheme in which the employee-spouse exercised the joint and survivorship option provided by her retirement plan. Contrastingly, the instant case is distinguishable in that it involves a private retirement plan in which Mr. Allard selected an option, which was not signed by the deceased, guaranteeing him retirement benefits for ten years. The retirement plan in this case contained a joint and survivorship option which Mr. Allard declined to exercise. Consequently, the holding and result in *Valdez* is distinguishable here.

In further support of his position, Mr. Allard argues that according to *Valdez*, retirement benefits are non-probate assets, thus not subject to disposition by will and not subject to the rules of intestate distribution. *Valdez*, 574 S.W.2d at 750. However, it is important to note that while Texas law recognizes provisions in pension plans as being nontestamentary in nature, section 450(a)(1) and (3) of the Texas Probate Code permit benefits under pension plans to "pass to a person designated by the decedent." Therefore, since there is no indication that the decedent, Mrs. Allard, agreed to the disposition of the retirement benefits, there appears to be no valid reason to deny Mrs. Allard the opportunity to dispose of her community interest in the retirement plan. Thus, we hold that in light of the settled marital property rule in Texas that a spouse has a community property interest in that portion of the retirement benefits of the opposite spouse earned during their marriage, the retirement benefits in this case were properly characterized as community property, and thus, one-half of such benefits was properly included in the wife's estate. See *Taggart v. Taggart*, 552 S.W.2d 422 (Tex. 1977); *Cearley v. Cearley*, 544 S.W.2d 661 (Tex. 1976); *Busby v. Busby*, 457 S.W.2d 551 (Tex. 1970). Additionally, Mr. Allard urges this court to adopt the terminable interest rule which provides that the non-employee spouse's pension interest terminates at the death of either spouse. See *Matter of Estate of Allen*, 108 Cal. App. 3d 614, 166 Cal. Rptr. 653 (Court of Appeals [1st Dist.] 1980); *Waite v. Waite*, 6 Cal. 3d 461, 99 Cal. Rptr. 325, 492 P.2d 13 (1972); *Benson v. City of Los Angeles*, 60 Cal. 2d 355, 33 Cal. Rptr. 257, 384 P.2d 649 (1963). In spite of the application of the rule by the California courts in these three cases, it has been widely viewed in California as creating an unfair deprivation and misallocation of the non-employee spouse's full share of pension benefits representing community property accrued and accumulated during the marriage to the employee spouse. See *Taylor v. Taylor*, 189 Cal.

App. 3d 435, 234 Cal. Rptr. 486 (Cal. Ct. App. 1987). California's struggle with the terminable interest rule culminated in 1986 with an amendment to the California Family Law Act specifically requiring the court to assure that each party receives a full community property share of the retirement plan. Cal. Civ. Code Ann. Sec. 4800.8 (West Supp. 1987). This legislation was intended to abolish the terminable interest rule and has since been held to be retroactive. *Taylor*, 234 Cal. Rptr. at 491. We find no reason in this case to set aside the basic principles of community property law, which when applied in this case, entitled the non-employee spouse to her share of the retirement benefits. In regard to Mr. Allard's request that this court adopt the terminable interest rule, we decline to do so and conclude that such matter is better left to the legislature.

DISCUSSION

Was it important in *Allard* that the employee spouse had not chosen a joint and survivor opinion? If spouses desire that the survivor receive 100% of continuing pension payments, how should their wills be drafted? Would a marital agreement be helpful? See Chapter 20, *infra*.

Allard is discussed in Casenote, 20 St. Mary's L. J. 373 (1989).

The federal preemption issue apparently was not fully briefed in *Allard*. Based upon the Supremacy Clause, federal law can alter the results that otherwise would occur under Texas law (see chapter 13 *infra*). In *Ablamis v. Roper*, 937 F.2d 1450 (9th Cir. 1991), the Ninth Circuit determined that the result dictated in *Allard* violated the provisions of ERISA (a federal statute); therefore, the non-employee spouse could not devise a portion of the pension benefit. The same result was reached in *Meek v. Tullis*, 791 F.Supp. 154 (W.D.La. 1992). This issue is discussed in greater detail in Chapter 13.

If the benefit is a federal benefit, the result could be governed by *Valdez, supra*, not *Allard. See Hoppe v. Godeke*, 774 S.W.2d 368 (Tex. App. — Austin 1989, writ denied).

Note that the Texas Supreme Court in *Allard* states that the legislature could adopt the terminable interest rule if it chooses to. Tex. Govt. Code § 804.101 does adopt a terminable interest rule for government pensions. In *Kunin v. Feofanov*, 69 F.3d 59 (5th Cir. 1995) the Fifth Circuit upheld the constitutionality of this statute.

B. The Community Interest in Other Fringe Benefits

1. Severance Pay

Wright v. Wright
California Court of Appeals, 1983
189 Cal. Rptr. 336

ANDREEN, Associate Justice.

The primary question raised by this appeal is whether termination pay received by a spouse after separation is community or separate property. Other issues raised in husband's laborious brief need not be addressed because of our treatment of this contention.

The parties separated on June 23, 1976, after 12 years of marriage. On July 13, 1976, husband received $24,208.64 (net) from his employer, San Joaquin Community Hospital Corporation. Husband testified it was not a bonus for past work, but equaled approximately one year's pay and was given because of his termination due to harassment caused by wife and her father.

By stipulation, the deposition testimony of Joe B. Hurst, the hospital administrator, was received into evidence. It establishes that husband was employed at the hospital from 1972 until July 13, 1976, and had attained the position of assistant administrator. Wife's father was the hospital chaplain.

Hurst related that husband was paid his normal rate of pay for the first six months of 1976, and was then given a lump sum payment of $24,208.64 in July. He was paid that amount because he was leaving the hospital and in recognition that he would experience difficulty securing further employment. Hurst's testimony shows the lump sum payment was voluntary on the hospital's part and was not part of the employment contract. Hurst stated that part of the difficulties which he expected husband to encounter would be due to some actions he anticipated wife and her father, the chaplain, would take. They had threatened to ruin him financially, professionally, and personally. It was the chaplain's behavior in response to the divorce which caused Hurst, on July 13, 1976, to recommend, and husband accept, termination of husband's employment at the hospital.[1]

Wife contends the termination payment was based on services rendered during marriage and therefore is community property. Husband contends it is separate property since the payment was made after separation. (Civ. Code, Sec. 5118).[2]

Neither party has cited relevant case law. Independent research, however, has found persuasive precedent.

This case is analogous to *In re Marriage of Flockhart* (1981) 119 Cal. App. 3d 240, 173 Cal. Rptr. 818. The employee there was compensated by the United States government for loss of future earnings because his employment was affected by the expansion of Redwood National Park. He lost his job after his separation from his wife. The payment of replacement income was held to be the employee's separate property. He received the payments not because of any contractual agreement with his prior employer but because of his loss of employment in the timber industry.

---

1. We quote from Hurst's testimony:

[T]here was approximately one year's compensation paid at the time Mr. Wright ended his employment, not inconsideration of work for that year or his past performance—I think this is important to remember—but in consideration of the fact that he was leaving our employment in a responsible position with a number of difficulties that I was aware of that he would be facing, particularly in the securing of other positions. And as it still remains, field positions in hospital administration are difficult, at best, for a person with Mr. Wright's previous background and experience.

A. No, [counsel]. It was not considered a merit increase. I think that Mr. Wright was involved in some situations that I was acquainted with, and that I realized were going to affect his future ability to secure employment; that were going to give him an opportunity to experience a great deal of problems. And as a result of this, it is customary in administrative circles to grant termination pay, if you want to call it this—or not termination. Excuse me—pay for an employee when they leave a responsible position where there may be the expectation they're going to have trouble securing another position.

Mrs. Wright indicated to me a number of situations in Mr. Wright's and her personal relationship, her attitude about this particular situation; what she anticipated doing about it. I received the same kind of profession from her father with certain indications as to the types of difficulty that would be raised in order that Mr. Wright would be sure to pay for whatever his experience was going to be.

2. Civil Code Section 5118 provides: "The earnings and accumulations of a spouse and the minor children living with, or in the custody of, the spouse, while living separate and apart from the other spouse, are the separate property of the spouse."

Similarly, the instant case is analogous to cases involving disability benefits. Such payments serve the principal purpose of compensating the disabled employee for his/her injury, including prospective loss of earnings and diminished earning capacity. Disability payments paid after separation consistently have been held to be the separate property of the spouse who receives them, except for that portion of the payment which is payable as a pension. Likewise, workers' compensation awards paid after separation are the separate property of the injured spouse. The purpose underlying the separate property treatment of both is compensation for future loss of earnings, not payment for services previously performed. The rulings are not based on the fact that the right to the payments accrued after separation.

In the case at bench the termination payment was made in recognition that husband would encounter difficulty in securing future employment which would entail prospective loss of earnings. Since it was paid after separation it is clear it was separate property.

In re Marriage of Skaden (1977) 19 Cal. 3d 679, 139 Cal. Rptr. 615, 566 P.2d 249 is distinguishable. Skaden was employed as an insurance agent. His contract provided that if he was terminated two or more years after the effective date, he would receive termination benefits consisting of specific percentages of net premiums, collected within a five-year period of termination, on policies he had sold prior to termination. It was held that since the right derived from the terms of the agent's agreement, it was a property right which was community in character. The court noted that, "[n]othing in the agreement suggests that such benefits are consideration for termination." (At p. 687, 139 Cal. Rptr. 615, 566 P.2d 249.) The court further stated:

> We think it clear from the foregoing that the termination benefits contemplated by the subject contract were, like pension benefits, "a form of deferred compensation for services rendered." The right to these benefits" derived from the terms of the employment contract" and under those terms became vested upon the expiration of two years after the date of execution. Manifestly, then, under the cases we have cited, that right is property subject to division, to the extent of its community character, upon dissolution of the marriage. (Civ. Code, Sec. 4800.)

At pp. 687–688, 139 Cal. Rptr. 615, 566 P.2d 249 (fn. omitted).

Skaden is inapposite, since the right to a percentage of the insurance premiums earned on policies issued during coverture was a contract right payable irrespective of continued employment. Even though in the disability cases the payments were pursuant to a contract right, they were made because the employment was no longer available. The instant case is like the disability cases: the payment was made because the employee faced diminished earnings in the immediate future.

The judgment is reversed. The trial court is directed to vacate its judgment awarding wife one-half of the termination benefit and to enter a new judgment declaring the sum to be the separate property of husband.

***

DISCUSSION

In *Wright* the husband received a lump-sum severance payment after the parties separated. (Remember that, in California, spouses stop accumulating community property after separation.) The wife argued that this payment was really a bonus for past services rendered during marriage, so the community had an interest. The court concluded that the payment was to compensate the husband for post-separation lost wages, so the community should not have an interest.

As a general rule, a severance payment received during marriage (in California, before separation) normally would be community property. If the spouse is required to waive tort claims against the employer to receive the benefit, should this change the result? See *Reiss v. Reiss*, 40 S.W.3d 605 (Tex. App.—Houston [1st Dist.] 2001), *rev'd on other grounds*, 118 S.W.3d 439 (Tex. 2003).

In re Marriage of DeShurley
California Court of Appeals, 1989
255 Cal. Rptr. 150

TODD, Associate Justice.

Margaret J. DeShurley appeals a judgment confirming the separate property nature of severance pay received by John R. DeShurley from Continental Airlines pursuant to a bankruptcy court order.

FACTS

Margaret and John married on December 31, 1950, and separated on October 15, 1984. John was employed as a pilot with Continental Airlines from August 13, 1951, until about October 1, 1983, when he joined a strike called by the Air Line Pilots Association, International (ALPA).

On October 31, 1985, in the United States Bankruptcy Court, Southern District of Texas, Houston Division, Case number 83-04019-H2-5, Continental Airlines and the ALPA submitted their pending claims, controversies and related litigation to the court for resolution. The bankruptcy court, in essence, ordered (1) the strike terminated, (2) no recrimination or retaliation be taken against striking pilots, (3) the parties to dismiss all litigation between them pending in federal courts, (4) striking pilots be given the option of being recalled and reinstated or severance pay.

The severance pay option provided that active pilots on Continental's seniority list as of September 24, 1983, could elect severance pay in exchange for waiving the right to recall and waiving the right to claims against the company connected with the strike. The amount of severance pay was to be computed by multiplying $4,000 times the number of years of active service with Continental as of September 24, 1983.

John opted for the severance pay option and his severance pay was calculated at $126,800. According to the set schedule, John receives 10 percent before December 15, 1985, 15 percent before June 30, 1986, and the remainder in 20 quarterly payments, with 10 percent interest to be paid on amounts due after eight quarters from September 30, 1986.

John and Margaret worked out a division of their marital estate with the exception of the severance pay, which John claimed was his separate property. The trial court agreed.

DISCUSSION

Margaret contends the severance pay is community property, and she is entitled to one-half of it. We disagree.

In *In re Marriage of Skaden* (1977) 19 Cal. 3d 679, 139 Cal. Rptr. 615, 566 P.2d 249, the California Supreme Court found termination benefits paid to an insurance agent under an employment agreement to be community property. The benefits consisted of a percentage of insurance premiums collected on insurance policies sold by the agent. The Skaden court held the benefits were community property because they were deferred compensation for the agent's previous endeavors. (Id. at pp. 687–688, 139 Cal. Rptr. 615, 566 P.2d 249.)

Following *Skaden*, the issue of whether termination or severance benefits were community or separate property was raised in four published cases: *In re Marriage of Flockhart* (1981) 119 Cal. App. 3d 240, 173 Cal. Rptr. 818; *In re Marriage of Wright* (1983) 140 Cal. App. 3d 342, 189 Cal. Rptr. 336; *In re Marriage of Kuzmiak* (1986) 176 Cal. App. 3d 1152, 222 Cal. Rptr. 644; and most recently *In re Marriage of Horn* (1986) 181 Cal. App. 3d 540, 226 Cal. Rptr. 666.

In *Horn*, this court reviewed and analyzed the previous four cases and concluded the chief characteristics in cataloging termination or severance benefits is whether the benefits constitute (a) deferred compensation for past services or (b) present compensation for loss of earnings. If the benefits are deferred compensation for past earnings, the benefits are community property; if they are present compensation for loss of earnings, they are separate property.

Horn further said the character of the benefits is to be determined by considering all relevant circumstances.

At issue in *Horn* was the severance pay received by the husband from the National Football League (NFL) on his retirement from football. During the husband's playing days, the management of the NFL and the National Football League Players Association added a severance pay provision to the collective bargaining agreement, which provided any player with two or more seasons with the NFL is entitled to a lump sum of severance pay, the amount to be based on the player's number of NFL seasons. In finding the severance pay to be community property, the *Horn* court noted the characteristics:

> "... (a) it is derived from a contract right; (b) it is based on the number of seasons worked; (c) it must be paid back to the NFL if the player returns to professional football within one year of receipt; (d) it will be paid back to him when he again leaves football, but no additional amount will have accrued for the seasons worked after his return; (e) it is given to the player's stated beneficiary or estate if he dies; (f) it is received in a lump sum after a certain period of time has passed following the player's notification to the club of his intent to permanently retire from professional football."

The *Horn* court characterized the severance pay as community property because the husband had an absolute right to it based on his eight seasons with the NFL and the contractual agreement. The court noted that in *In re Marriage of Flockhart, supra, In re Marriage of Wright, supra,* and *In re Marriage of Kuzmiak, supra,* (in all three cases it was held the severance pay was separate property) there were no absolute rights to receive severance pay, with the husbands in those three cases receiving severance pay only because a loss of work was forced upon them. The *Horn* court also noted the three cases did not involve a contractual right to a payment.

Here, the severance pay contains the following characteristics: (1) it is not derived from a contract but rather stems from a court order; (2) it represents an option between returning to work and foregoing the right to return to work in exchange for a payment; and (3) its amount is based on the number of years John worked for Continental.

The trial court was correct in characterizing John's severance pay as "compensation for [John] electing to forego future employment with Continental Airlines." It was not intended as a form of deferred compensation for services previously rendered, but rather represented present compensation for loss of his future earnings. Further, we note any salary John would have earned had he opted to go back to work at Continental Airlines would have been his separate property. (Civ. Code, Sec. 5118, "The earnings and accumulations of a spouse and the minor children living with, or in the custody of, the spouse, while separate and apart from the other spouse, are the separate property of the spouse.")

Margaret raises the following arguments: (1) John had an absolute right to the severance pay; (2) the severance pay was not designed to ease John's transition back into the work place or to replace lost income; and (3) the amount of severance pay was tied to his number of years of employment, which coincided with the years of the marriage.

We reject the characterization of John's severance pay as an absolute right; had John opted to return to work he would not have received the severance pay. Margaret bootstraps to this argument the observation that in *In re Marriage of Skaden, supra* and *Horn, supra* (community property cases), the severance pay would have been paid regardless of whether the employee was terminated voluntarily or involuntarily, while in *In re Marriage of Flockhart, supra, In re Marriage of Wright, supra*, and *In re Marriage of Kuzmiak, supra* (separate property cases), the termination was involuntary. We fail to see how this argument helps Margaret. John's termination was voluntary; he had the option to be recalled and reinstated, but chose instead severance pay. The voluntariness of John's termination alone, however, does not aid Margaret's argument. There is nothing in the record to indicate whether the severance pay was designed to ease John's transition back into the work force, a need arising from the circumstances of the involuntary termination, as was the case in *In re Marriage of Wright, supra, and In re Marriage of Kuzmiak, supra*. Further, the record does reflect the severance pay was intended to compensate John for foregoing the right to return to work and presumably earn income. In a similar vein is *In re Marriage of Flockhart, supra*, where a federal employee whose job was adversely affected by expansion of Redwood National Park received "weekly lay-off" benefits. The Flockhart court held the benefits were separate property, saying they were intended to presently compensate the employee for loss of earnings.

Finally, with respect to Margaret's point that John's severance pay was tied to the number of years he worked for Continental Airlines, in Horn, supra, we said such a factor is not determinative of whether the severance pay is "for services previously rendered." (See also *In re Marriage of Kuzmiak, supra*, where the military separation pay was based on the number of years served and it was held to be separate property.)

We conclude, based on all relevant circumstances, John's severance pay represents present compensation for loss of earnings and is therefore his separate property.

JUDGMENT AFFIRMED.

---

2. Disability Benefits

Andrle v. Andrle

Texas Court of Appeals — Eastland, 1988
751 S.W.2d 955, writ denied

ARNOT, J.

This is an appeal from a divorce decree. The sole issue, on appeal, is whether the trial court abused its discretion by divesting appellant of one-half interest in future benefits under a private policy of disability insurance. Because we find the policy is community property, we affirm the judgment of the trial court.

Appellant, Stephen G. Andrle, and appellee, Deanna Lou Andrle, were married on January 15, 1959, and divorced on August 6, 1987. During the marriage, appellant obtained a policy of disability insurance through Western Life Insurance Company. This disability insurance policy was not related to appellant's employment. The premiums for the disability policy were paid with community funds of the parties.

During the marriage, because appellant had suffered disabilities and Western Life had denied coverage, a lawsuit was filed. As a result of the lawsuit, Western Life tendered a lump sum settlement of $38,992.32 and commenced making disability payments to appellant of $1,200.00 per month. From each monthly payment, $400.00 is paid to the attorneys who represented appellant in the lawsuit against Western Life.

Appellant agrees that the lump sum settlement proceeds and the net monthly payments received prior to the divorce were assets of the community estate with each party being entitled to one-half. However, appellant argues that the trial court abused its discretion in awarding appellee one-half interest in the monthly disability insurance proceeds received after the date of divorce, urging these proceeds are his separate property. We disagree.

The disability insurance policy was purchased during the marriage of the parties with community funds. The disability insurance carried by appellant at the time of divorce was a property right that belonged to the community estate. The benefits from a vested property right are community property even though paid after divorce. See *Busby v. Busby*, 457 S.W.2d 551 (Tex. 1970); *Simmons v. Simmons*, 568 S.W.2d 169 (Tex. Civ. App.—Dallas 1978, writ dism'd); *Mathews v. Mathews*, 414 S.W.2d 703 (Tex. Civ. App.—Austin 1967, no writ).

Appellant first argues that future payments are mere expectancies and, therefore, not subject to division, citing as authority *Cunningham v. Cunningham*, 183 S.W.2d 985 (Tex. Civ. App.—Dallas 1944, no writ). Unlike the case before us, *Cunningham* was concerned with the division of commissions earned on life insurance policies which may or may not be renewed "irrespective of the wish or will of either party." The court held that the right to renewals was not a vested property right but merely an expectancy.

Addressing the argument of whether or not rights to disability proceeds were an expectancy, the court in Mathews found:

> There are no onerous acts or duties imposed upon appellant by the policies in order to keep the policies in force and the disability payments continuing. Of course, appellant must not make a miraculous recovery or his payments will cease.

The rights to disability compensation are a property right not a mere expectancy.

Alternatively, appellant argues that the payments are his separate property because the proceeds acquire the character of the thing they replace: namely, his ability to earn money by personal labor. Appellant cites as authority *Rolater v. Rolater*, 198 S.W. 391 (Tex. Civ. App.—Dallas 1917, no writ). In *Rolater*, the wife purchased casualty insurance with her separate funds insuring the house which was her husband's separate property and the contents which were hers. After a loss, a part of the proceeds was used to rebuild her husband's house. When awarded only the amount of the premium she had paid as a charge against her husband's estate, the wife complained that the proceeds of the insurance policy were community property to which she was entitled to half. The court held that, when the house upon the land is destroyed by fire and there exists an insurance policy covering the loss, the proceeds occupy the same status which the house did, the separate estate of the husband. The court reasoned that to hold otherwise would allow one spouse the authority to convert the separate estate of another into the joint property of both for a wholly inadequate consideration without the other's consent.

This reasoning does not apply to the case before us. Appellee did not convert appellant's separate estate into community property. The policy was purchased during the marriage with community funds. The status of property so far as being separate or community property is fixed by facts which existed at inception of the title. *Cade v. Dudney*, 379 S.W.2d 370 (Tex. Civ. App.—Eastland 1964, writ ref'd n.r.e.). Based upon the doctrine of inception of title, it was a vested right of the community.

The judgment of the trial court is affirmed.

DISCUSSION

Should disability benefits be characterized based upon the consideration used to purchase the policy, or upon what the proceeds replace? In contrast to Texas, California cases focus on the latter. *See In re Marriage of Saslow*, 710 P.2d 346 (Cal. 1985). So, unless the disability benefits replace retirement benefits, the benefits received after divorce would be the injured spouse's separate property. As you can see, *Andrle* focuses on the character of the premium. Does *Andrle* or *Saslow* reflect a more sensible policy?

Tex. Fam. Code § 3.008 reverses *Andre* and adopts California's "replacement" approach for disability benefits and workman's compensation awards. *See Sooy v. Sooy*, No. 04-06-00509-CV, 2007 WL 516259 (Tex. App.—San Antonio Feb. 21, 2007, no pet.) (mem. op., not designated for publication).

3. Stock Options

Senior employees frequently receive stock options as incentive compensation. The terms of such options vary. In general, however, the employee is given an option to purchase, from the company, a certain specified number of shares of the company's stock for a price that approximates the market price of the stock as of the date of grant. The option normally is not exercisable for a certain period, and then the option remains exercisable for a specified period. The option normally remains exercisable only as long as the employee remains employed by the company. The option becomes valuable when the market price of the stock rises above the exercise price. If this occurs, the manager can buy the stock from the company for the specified price and either keep the stock or resell the stock at the market price for a profit.

In re Marriage of Nelson
California Court of Appeals, 1986
222 Cal. Rptr. 790

ANDERSON, Presiding Justice.

Appellant and cross-respondent, Harold F. Nelson, Jr. (hereafter Harold), appeals from portions of the interlocutory judgment dissolving his marriage to cross-appellant and respondent, Mary K. Nelson (hereafter Mary).

Both parties raise issues regarding property distributed in the judgment.

A large portion of the trial court's decree involved the characterization and apportionment of stock options issued to Harold by his employer, the Ampex Corporation. These fell into three separate categories: those that were granted and became exercisable before the parties separated; those that were granted before the parties separated but were not exercisable until after they separated (hereafter the intermediate options); and those that were granted after the parties separated (hereafter the post-separation options). The first group was characterized by the trial court as wholly community property, the second partly community property and partly Harold's separate property (using a time rule) and the third wholly Harold's separate property.

Other property owned by the parties was characterized as follows: A one-half interest in a parcel of real property located in Maui, Hawaii (hereafter the Hawaiian property), was declared a community asset. The couple's house in Half Moon Bay, California, was also found to be community property. A year-end bonus paid to Harold six months after the parties separated was determined to be his separate property.

III. Intermediate Options Partly Community Property

The trial court's statement of decision contains the following discussion: "The stock options owned but not exercisable as of the date of separation were in part community property for the same reason that a pension plan which is subject to divestment by termination of employment had a community property aspect. They were granted for services rendered and to be rendered...."

Harold disputes the trial court's finding. He does not attack the court's apportionment of the value of these options between community and separate property, but rather argues that they had no community aspect at all. In making this argument he relies primarily on the following assertions: that the options are not analogous to non-vested pension benefits, thus making reference to cases like Brown and Judd inapropos; that the options had no value before their date of exercisability, so that upon becoming exercisable they were post-separation earnings within the meaning of section 5118; and in similar vein, that the price of the Ampex Company stock must increase in value after the date of exercisability for the employee to realize a gain so the options reward only future rather than past efforts on the employee's part.

In re Marriage of Hug (1984) 154 Cal. App. 3d 780, 201 Cal. Rptr. 676, refutes Harold's arguments: "we hold that in marital dissolution actions the trial court has broad discretion to select an equitable method of allocating community and separate property interests in stock options granted prior to the date of separation of the parties, which became exercisable after the date of separation." Implicit in this statement is a recognition of employee stock option grants as "not an expectancy but a chose in action, a form of property ..." susceptible of division in spite of being contingent or not having vested.

IV. Intermediate Options Properly Apportioned

Mary argues that not only the above-cited holding of Hug should apply to this case, but also the formula for apportionment of the intermediate stock options as between community and separate property which it approved. There the number of options determined to be community was the product of a fraction in which the numerator was the period in months from the commencement of the spouse's tenure with his employer to the date of the couple's separation, and the denominator was the period in months between commencement of employment and the date when each group of options first became exercisable. This fraction was then multiplied by the number of shares of stock which could be purchased with each block of options, yielding the community figure.

In contrast, the trial court here utilized a formula in which the numerator was the number of months from the date of grant of each block of options to the date of the couple's separation, while the denominator was the period from the time of each grant to its date of exercisability.

Our reading of *In re Marriage of Hug* convinces us that no modification of the trial court's formula for apportionment is necessary. Hug specifically states, "we stress that no single rule or formula is applicable to every dissolution case involving employee stock options. Trial courts should be vested with broad discretion to fashion approaches which will achieve the most equitable results under the facts of each case." (*In re Marriage of Hug, supra*, 154 Cal. App. 3d at p. 792, 201 Cal. Rptr. 676.) We find nothing inequitable in the formula adopted by the trial court; in fact, under the circumstances of this case it was probably a better method of division.[4]

V. Anticipated Taxation of Options Properly Credited

It is clear from the face of the option grants that any gain realized upon their exercise is taxable as ordinary income. In recognition of this fact, the trial court ordered that the portion of the options valued as community property be reduced to reflect an assumed tax rate of 20 percent, and correspondingly credited Harold directly with one-half this amount. The court ordered, in addition, that should Harold actually realize a tax consequence in excess of 20 percent upon exercising any of the "community options," he would be credited for the further reduction in their value as community assets.

Credit for the increased tax rate would be limited to its effect on the community property value of the options as set forth in the interlocutory judgment. The court further ordered, "[i]n the event that the actual tax attributable to the exercise of the Ampex/Signal stock options is less than the twenty percent (20%) offset provided for above [$9,243.76], Respondent [Harold] shall reimburse to petitioner [Mary] one-half (1/2) of the difference between the actual tax attributable to exercise of the options and the amount of the offset provided for herein [$9,243.76]."

Harold argues that the trial court should have offset the community property value of the options by 55 percent, his "more likely income tax rate," and eliminated the adjustment mechanisms cited above. In support of this he points out that the court, in assigning to him a tax loss carry forward as an asset, recognized his 55 percent incremental bracket. He states, "[i]f the court assumes realization of value [of the options], as it has done, it must also assume income taxation."

The case law does not support Harold's argument. In distributing community assets, a trial court is obliged to consider tax consequences only where it is proven that an *immediate and specific* liability will arise upon the ordered division. In the situation at hand, the time at which a tax liability may arise and the extent of that tax liability are exclusively within Harold's control. He is under no obligation as a result of the interlocutory

---

4. The major difference we discern between the Ampex options and those before the court in Hug is that while both reward future productivity, the Hug options appear to have been designed to attract new employees and/ormore generously reward past services. (*Id.*, at pp. 783, 789, 201. Cal. Rptr. 676.) As previously discussed, only prospective increases in the value of Ampex stock could result in a profit to the Ampex option holders. It was therefore appropriate to place more emphasis on the period following each grant to the date of separation, as the trial court did here, than on the employee's entire tenure with the company up to the time of separation as the Hug court did.

judgment to immediately exercise the options. "The trial court need not ... consider tax consequences that may or may not arise after the division of the community property."

This is not to say that the trial court erred in ordering that Harold be issued a credit against possible tax liability and establishing a mechanism for possible future credits. Section 4800 directs the trial court to divide community assets equally upon dissolution of a marriage, and where economic circumstances warrant to "award any asset to one party on such conditions as it deems proper to effect a substantially equal division of the property." The specific economic circumstance present in this case is the fact that the options are nonassignable and therefore had to all be given to Harold. The court's tax reimbursement formula was therefore a substitute for what, as it declared, would have been a more equitable distribution: "to divide them [the options] in kind and let each party be at the mercy of his/her own tax circumstance."[5]

VI. Post-Separation Stock Options and Bonus Both Separate Property

Mary maintains that in line with the principles of *In re Marriage of Brown, supra,* and *In re Marriage of Judd, supra,* a portion of both Harold's grant of 1,750 Ampex stock options, received 25 days after the couple's legal date of separation, and his year-end bonus, received some 8 months after separation, is community property. The trial court ruled in regard to these assets, "[t]hose [options] which had not been granted as of separation are confirmed to husband as his separate property," and "[t]he Court is not persuaded ..." by Mary's claim "that all or some portion of a $9,000 bonus received post-separation by Mr. Nelson [Harold] is community property because it was paid either in consideration for or in recognition of services rendered during marriage."

We recall for purposes of this discussion the trial court's explanation of why it characterized the intermediate options as partly a community asset. In its wording it expressly recognized the holdings of Brown and Judd that contractual rights earned wholly or in part during marriage, even if not vested at the time of separation, are partially community assets. We therefore conclude that in characterizing the post-separation bonus and stock options as Harold's separate property, it made the *factual* determination that these assets had not, even in part, accrued to Harold before his separation from Mary. That being the case, our mandate on appeal is solely to determine whether or not there is support in the record for the trial court's findings under the previously set forth "substantial evidence rule."

Harold testified that he was granted the 1,750 post-separation options concurrent with his promotion to treasurer of Ampex, as approved by its Board of Directors on October 28, 1980 (25 days after separation). Like the previous option grants, the purchase price of each option was the fair market value of Ampex stock on the date of the grant; thus, as Harold testified, the value of Ampex stock had to rise after the date of grant in order for the grantee to realize a profit. Though Harold admitted that he knew of his impending promotion before separating from Mary, there is no indication that the board's ratification was a foregone conclusion. Also, Harold testified that there was no mention of the option grant before the board acted. From this it was reasonable for the trial court to

---

5. Harold also argues that the trial court's program of reimbursement is flawed because the value of the options could plunge, he could then exercise them, his tax liability would be very low because he would realize very little income, and yet he would be compelled to reimburse Mary the difference between his 20 percent allowance and the tax he was actually required to pay. We find this contention overly speculative and contradictory of the basic thrust of his argument, that the value of the options should have been further discounted.

conclude that Harold had no expectation of being granted this block of options and enjoyed no financial gain from them until after his separation from Mary.

In the case of the bonus, the strongest evidence that it was a guaranteed yearly form of compensation was the fact that Harold received one both in 1980 and 1981. He testified at one point, however, "[t]here is no contract associated with the bonuses. It's a decision is [sic] made yearly at the end of the year and I know only what I'm told." He also testified that some employees who had received bonuses in 1980 received lesser ones or none at all in 1981. The trial court had the option of believing this testimony and concluding that Ampex employees had only an expectancy of a year-end bonus rather than a right to one contingent solely upon continued employment.

We therefore affirm the trial court's characterization of the 1,750 stock options granted October 29, 1980, and the $9,000 bonus paid in May 1981 as Harold's separate property.

We therefore remand this case to the trial court solely for the purpose of determining the property of awarding attorney's fees and costs on appeal. In all other respects the interlocutory judgment is affirmed.

DISCUSSION

Do you agree with the court's discussion of the character of the bonus? Do you understand the difference between *Hug* and *Nelson* regarding how the community claim to the stock options was calculated?

Texas courts have, since the *Cearley* case, fairly easily concluded that options can be community property even though not yet exercisable. *See, e.g., Bodin v. Bodin*, 955 S.W.2d 380 (Tex. App.—San Antonio 1997, no writ) ("unvested options constitute a contingent interest in property").

Tex. Fam. Code Section 3.007 now clarifies that the Texas rule is like *Nelson*.

4. Other Benefits

Lorenz v. Lorenz
California Court of Appeals, 1983
146 Cal. App. 3d 464

SCHNEIDER, Associate Justice.

Helma Lorenz (hereinafter wife) appeals from a judgment of dissolution of her marriage to James B. Lorenz (hereinafter husband). The issues raised by appellant do not necessitate an elaborate recitation of the facts. Suffice it to say that the marriage of the parties was dissolved on November 25, 1981. Petition for dissolution had been filed by wife in March 1980 and issues of property and support rights were resolved by the lower court following a trial.

Wife raises the following issues on appeal:

1. The court should have determined that term life insurance policies, on the life of husband, were a community asset, subject to division.

    ....

3. The court erred in not evaluating and dividing husband's vacation benefits.

Appellant's first and third contentions both concern the power of the trial court to divide assets which have no economic value. Those issues will both be discussed under this first rubric. As to the first asset, husband is the named insured under two policies of life insurance, one issued through the Veterans Administration and one through his employment. They have a face value of $10,000 each, and both are term policies. The court found: "Any life insurance policies on respondent's life are found to have no cash value."

As to the second asset, wife contends that the trial court should have determined that husband's accrued vacation pay was an asset subject to division. The record does not reflect that appellant was entitled to any accrued vacation pay. Rather, he testified that he had accumulated 120 hours of vacation time, but that if it was not used, he would not be paid for it.

"It is well established that the word 'property', as used in the statutes relating to community property, does not encompass every property right acquired by either husband or wife during marriage...." (*In re Marriage of Aufmuth* (1979) 89 Cal. App. 3d 446, 461, 152 Cal. Rptr. 668). Rather, it is implicit in the scheme of community property laws that property have certain attributes—that it be susceptible of ownership in common, of transfer, and of survival.

We recognize that certain intangible assets are property under community property statutes. However, each of those assets, although intangible, was acknowledged to have economical monetary value. In order to qualify as property, within the meaning of our community property laws, an asset must be "of such a character that a monetary value for division with the other spouse can ... be placed upon it." (*Todd v. Todd* (1969) 272 Cal. App. 2d 786, 791, 78 Cal. Rptr. 131.)

No such monetary value can be placed upon the assets claimed here by wife. The mere fact that these assets are of benefit to husband does not compel the conclusion that that benefit must, or can, be divided. We imagine that there are many "assets" held by a spouse at the time of marriage, particularly those arising out of employment, which are not subject to division. For example, an employee may be entitled to use the facilities of a health club owned by his employer, to purchase meals at an employer-owned cafeteria at reduced prices, or to receive a discount for purchases made at an employer-owned retail establishment. An employee may be given the privilege of choosing to work four ten-hour days per week rather than five eight-hour days per week, thus entitling him or her to a three-day weekend. All of these benefits, although of value to the employee spouse, are not convertible into cash. They are, therefore, not divisible on dissolution of the marriage.

In many California cases, courts have recognized the value of whole life insurance as its cash surrender value, and have divided that value when the policy was determined to be community property. However, unlike whole life insurance, term life insurance is generally accepted as having no value, since once its term has expired it is worthless.

Appellant relies on a series of cases which have found a community interest in life insurance, even term insurance, on the death of the insured. In those cases, the courts have held that the proceeds of insurance, whether term or otherwise, then payable, were community property, to the extent that premiums thereon were paid from community funds. Those cases do not support the proposition asserted by wife here: that the term policy itself, at the time of dissolution of a marriage, has a value which can then be divided. The proceeds or benefits of the policy, of course, have a value. However, until those benefits are payable, the policy itself is worthless.

The parties cite no California cases addressing the divisibility of term life insurance, and our research has discovered none. Nonetheless, we are persuaded that the trial court properly ruled that the policies of term life insurance were not property subject to division on dissolution of the marriage.

Likewise, the trial court properly concluded that appellant's accumulated vacation time was not an item of community property subject to division.

DISCUSSION

Should accrued vacation time be deemed property if the spouse has the option of receiving cash for it if the vacation time is not taken? For a case that disagrees with the *Lorenz* view regarding vacation benefits, *see Marriage of Hurd*, 848 P.2d 185 (Wash. App. 1993).

Various valuable rights have been considered divisible property at divorce. For example, in *Marriage of Alford*, 40 S.W.3d 187 (Tex. App.—Texarkana 2001, no pet.), a spouse's frequent flyer points were divided.

Smith v. Smith, 733 S.W.2d 915 (Tex. App.—Houston [1st Dist.] 1987 writ ref'd n.r.e.) suggests that vacation and sick pay benefits can be community property.

Chapter Five

Goodwill and Professional Degrees

A. Goodwill

Goodwill has generally been defined as "the advantage or benefit, which is acquired by an establishment, beyond the mere [aggregate] value of the capital stock, funds [and] property [on hand], in consequence of general public patronage ... which it receives from constant or habitual customers, on account of its local position, or common celebrity, or reputation for skill...." Story, *Commentaries of the Law of Partnerships* (1868), Section 99, at 170. This value sometimes is referred to as the expectation of continued public patronage. In other words, a beginning business has no goodwill and is merely worth the value of its tangible assets; the value of an established business is not as easy to determine.

It does seem intuitively correct that an established business has a value in excess of its tangible assets, and that this additional value should be considered divisible property. However, it must be remembered that the respective earning capacities of each spouse at divorce remain that spouse's separate property. This is a basic concept of the community property system.

Normal commercial goodwill does not present a significant characterization issue. Goodwill that attaches to a business, not the individual owner, is saleable property, and it is not the earning capacity of the spouse. It is the probable future return on a certain investment. So, if a business is started by a spouse during marriage with community property, the value of that business, including its commercial goodwill, is community property.

Characterization becomes more complicated when it is alleged that the business established during marriage has goodwill due to the skill and reputation of the spouse. It could be said that such a personal service business can have "goodwill," since it has an expectation of continued public patronage.

Nail v. Nail

Supreme Court of Texas, 1972
486 S.W.2d 761

STEAKLEY, Justice.

Section 3.63 of the Texas Family Code requires the Court in a decree of divorce to "order a division of the estate of the parties in a manner that the court deems just and right." The controlling question here is whether in this divorce proceeding the accrued goodwill of the medical practice of the husband, a doctor of medicine specializing in ophthalmology, based as it is on his personal skill, experience and reputation, as well as upon his continuing in the practice, constitutes property that is subject to division as part of the estate of the parties. The trial court and a divided court of civil appeals considered that it was. We hold that it was not.

The problem is posed in this manner. Petitioner, Dr. James B. Nail, Jr., and his wife, Alice J. Nail, Respondent, were married in 1945. He was subsequently licensed to practice medicine and has practiced in Wichita Falls, Texas, since 1956. His wife sued him for divorce which was granted by judgment dated August 12, 1971.

[The trial court awarded the wife $40,000 as her share of the husband's practice, and he appealed. The Supreme Court reiterated these trial court findings]:

> That during their marriage, James Barry Nail, Jr., completed his pre-medical education, graduated from medical school, completed his internship and his residency in ophthalmology.

> That the value of the assets of the medical practice of James Barry Nail, Jr., is $131,759.64, including all fixtures, furniture, equipment, and the value of the good will that has accrued thereto during the marriage of Alice Jane Nail and James Barry Nail, Jr.

> That the approximate value of Defendant's office equipment and office furniture is $735.47. That James Barry Nail, Jr., has an earning capacity of approximately $52,000.00 per year. That the earning capacity of James Barry Nail, Jr., will increase in subsequent years.

> That Alice Jane Nail is not trained for any employment.

As noted, the trial court found the value of the husband's medical practice to be $131,759.64, inclusive of fixtures, furniture, equipment and accrued goodwill; but the court further found the value of the furniture and equipment to be only approximately $735.47, thus leaving a valuation of accrued goodwill in the sum of $131,024.17. The further finding that the wife's community interest therein was $40,000 was derived, at least in part, from the testimony of a witness offered by the wife as an expert that the valuation of the goodwill of a professional practice would have "a starting point" of "multiplying one full year's billings by one or one and a half." This seems so in light of the trial court finding that the husband had an annual earning capacity of approximately $52,000, one and one-half of which would be $78,000. In any event it is apparent that the award to the wife of $40,000, payable in future monthly installments if, and so long as, the husband practiced his profession, rested upon the conclusion that the accrued goodwill of the husband's practice constituted property which was subject to division by the court.

Alice J. Nail asserts that the problem is solved by precedents in our State which recognize that a professional man can acquire and voluntarily sell good will. Cited are *Randolph v. Graham*, 254 S.W. 402 (Tex. Civ. App.—San Antonio 1923, writ ref'd), where it was stated that "[t]he goodwill of a professional man may be as much an asset and a thing to be sold as that of a merchant." So it is said, the husband's medical practice with its goodwill was owned by the marital partners; and as such, it was property in existence at the time of the divorce that was subject to valuation and partition in a manner within the discretion of the trial court.

We have found no case in point and solution of the problem is not easy. The division of authority on the question of whether goodwill may exist in a profession dependent on personal qualities of the owner has been stated in this manner:

It has frequently been held that goodwill does not adhere to a business or profession dependent solely on the personal ability, skill, integrity, or other personal characteristics of the owner. According to other decisions, however, goodwill may exist in a professional as well as a commercial business, and may be sold together with the estate, and irrespective of whether there is technically a goodwill adherent to a business or profession dependent on personal qualities of the owner, contracts disposing thereof coupled with an agreement that the seller would not compete, if otherwise valid, are enforced. In any case, an involuntary sale cannot be made of a goodwill based on professional reputation.

38 C.J.S. Goodwill, Section 3, pp. 952–53.

It cannot be said that the accrued goodwill in the medical practice of Dr. Nail was an earned or vested property right at the time of the divorce or that it qualifies as property subject to division by decree of the court. It did not possess value or constitute an asset separate and apart from his person, or from his individual ability to practice his profession. It would be extinguished in the event of his death, or retirement, or disablement, as well as in event of the sale of his practice or the loss of his patients, whatever the cause. Cf., *Busby v. Busby*, 457 S.W.2d 551 (Tex. 1970), and the cases there referred to with approval, where the husband's existing entitlement to future military retirement benefits was held to constitute a vested property right. The crucial consideration was the vesting of a right when the husband reached the requisite qualifications for retirement benefits; the fact that the benefits were subject to divestment under certain conditions did not reduce the right to a mere expectancy. The goodwill of the husband's medical practice here, on the other hand, may not be characterized as an earned or vested right or one which fixes any benefit in any sum at any future time. That it would have value in the future is no more than an expectancy wholly dependent upon the continuation of existing circumstances. Accordingly, we hold that the goodwill of petitioner's medical practice that may have accrued at the time of the divorce was not property in the estate of the parties; and that for this reason the award under attack was not within the authority and discretion vested in the trial court by Section 3.63 of the Texas Family Code.

It is to be understood that in resolving the question at hand we are not concerned with goodwill as an asset incident to the sale of a professional partnership or corporation apart from the person of an individual member.

The judgments below are reversed and the cause is remanded to the trial court for further proceedings consistent with opinion.

DISCUSSION

What is the court concerned about in *Nail*? The court appears to accept that Dr. Nail's practice had goodwill. Still, the court held that the community had no claim to any part of the goodwill, at least in part because the goodwill was not an earned or vested property right. Is this the issue?

In many professions, it is considered unethical to sell a practice; it is considered selling clients. In any event, personal goodwill is difficult to transfer, since the client's allegiance is to the individual, not to the business. In contrast, commercial goodwill can easily be sold. Does this matter?

Why does the *Nail* court conclude that a vested pension right is property, but personal goodwill is merely an expectancy?

Can you think of any other more persuasive arguments that could be made to support the *Nail* result?

What is the holding in *Nail*?

Does *Nail* apply to all personal service businesses?

The pension cases decided after *Nail* have stirred the personal goodwill waters somewhat. These cases seem to drive a stake through the heart of the "mere expectancy/vested right" school. See chapter 4, *supra*. Has *Nail* been impliedly overruled?

For a court of appeals case quite critical of *Nail, see Guzman v. Guzman*, 827 S.W.2d 445, 448 n.3 (Tex. App.—Corpus Christi), *writ denied,* 843 S.W.2d 486 (Tex. 1992).

Geesbreght v. Geesbreght
Texas Court of Appeals—Fort Worth, 1978
570 S.W.2d 427, writ dism'd

MASSEY, Chief Justice.

[The husband and another medical doctor started during marriage a corporation that provided doctors for emergency rooms at various hospitals. The husband rendered most of the medical services at Harris Hospital, one hospital that contracted with the corporation; the other shareholder and other employees rendered medical services at other hospitals. The pivotal issue was whether the divorce court could consider the goodwill of the corporation.]

"Goodwill" is sometimes difficult to define. In a personal service enterprise such as that of a professional person or firm, there is a difference in what it means as applied to "John Doe" and as applied to "The Doe Corporation" or "The Doe Company." If "John Doe" builds up a reputation for service it is personal to him. If "The Doe Company" builds up a reputation for service there may be a change in personnel performing the service upon a sale of its business but the sale of such business naturally involves the right to continue in business as "The Doe Company." The "goodwill" built up by the company would continue for a time and would last while the new management, performing the same personal services, would at least have the opportunity to justify confidence in such management while it attempted to retain the "goodwill" of the customer clients of the former operators.

At least the opportunity to have time to try to preserve the "goodwill" already existent and to use it as an entrance into the identical field of operations in a personal service type of business would be present where the name of the business is a company name as distinguished from the name of an individual. Therein does it have value, plus the value of the opportunity to justify confidence in the new management by the customer/clients of the predecessor owner(s).

It is as applied to the foregoing that we consider Emergency Medicine to possess what we treat as "goodwill" as part of its worth and value under the circumstances of this case, and therefore an asset which would have value to some extent apart from John's person as a professional practitioner.

It is clear that in the event John sold his stock to another physician then—save perhaps at Harris Hospital—there would be an opportunity to retain the contracts of Emergency Medicine if the services of its employed physicians in the various emergency rooms continued to be satisfactory.

On this it was shown that the Emergency Medicine contracts generally had either a 30 or 60 day cancellation provision "without cause," and a 24 hour cancellation provision "with cause." Also shown was that Dr. Riggs had a contract with John relative to sale or transfer of John's stock. In the event of John's death, Dr. Riggs is by this contract entitled to all of John's stock at the price of $50,000.00, and in the event John desires to sell his stock before that time, Dr. Riggs has the privilege of purchasing it at a price of $50,000.00.

We think it obvious that to take the figure of $16,000.00, which was proved to have been the "book value" of John's 500 shares of stock in Emergency Medicine Consultants, and use it as the "actual value" of the stock as its worth to be taken into consideration by the court in the division of the estate upon divorce was, under the circumstances of the case, reversible error. We hold that it resulted in gross inadequacy in the award on property division as applied to Mary Lee; that it also resulted in an award to her which was so contrary to the greater weight and preponderance of the whole of the evidence on trial as to be clearly erroneous. The value of the stock in Emergency Medicine Consultants was enhanced by some "goodwill" which was existent as applied to that professional corporation apart from the person of John Geesbreght.

DISCUSSION

Does *Geesbreght* correctly apply *Nail*? Does it make sense to distinguish between goodwill generated by the personal services of a spouse, and goodwill generated by the personal services of others?

Do the cases below make the same distinction?

In *Hirsch v. Hirsch*, 770 S.W.2d 924 (Tex. App.—El Paso 1989, no writ) the court held there could be no divisible goodwill in a one-person professional corporation.

Assume that, shortly before divorce, a professional spouse sells her sole proprietorship community property practice for cash. Assume she has to sign a covenant not to compete with the buyer for a certain period, most of which is after the date of the divorce. Are the proceeds community property? *See Austin v. Austin*, 619 S.W.2d 290 (Tex. App.—Austin 1981, no writ); *Dillan v. Anderson*, 358 S.W.2d 694 (Tex. Civ. App.—Dallas 1962, writ ref'd n.r.e.).

Simpson v. Simpson
Texas Court of Appeals—Dallas, 1984
679 S.W.2d 39, no writ

GUITTARD, Chief Justice.

The controversy concerns the valuation of the community estate, which includes shares in a professional corporation and interests in pension and profit sharing plans. Mrs. Simpson asserts that a proper valuation of these assets would show that the division was grossly disproportionate.

Goodwill of Corporation

Dr. Simpson, a pathologist, was employed by Simpson and Steele, a professional corporation of which he and Dr. Steele were equal owners. The two doctors provided pathology services for two hospitals. The contracts for the services were between the two doctors and the hospitals and made no mention of the corporation. The executive director of one of the hospitals testified that the contracts were with the doctors as individuals and that he was unaware of the existence of the corporation until the day of the trial. Moreover, the contracts provide that the hospitals may terminate them at any time on sixty days' notice.

Mrs. Simpson asserts that the nature of the practice of pathology is such that the corporation has goodwill apart from the individual goodwill of the doctors, as did the corporation in *Geesbreght v. Geesbreght*, 570 S.W.2d 427, 434–36 (Tex. Civ. App.—Fort Worth 1978, writ dism'd). On this theory her expert witness testified that the corporation had a value of over $900,000. Dr. Simpson contends that the goodwill of the corporation is indistinguishable from the individual goodwill of himself and Dr. Steele, and does not constitute an asset of the community estate, as held in *Nail v. Nail*, 486 S.W.2d 761, 763–64 (Tex. 1972).

We conclude that the issue is one of fact under the present record. In the absence of formal findings of fact, we must presume that every disputed factual issue was found in support of the judgment if there is sufficient evidence to support the finding. Accordingly, we hold that the trial court could properly find that the corporation had no substantial goodwill and thus disregard the testimony of Mrs. Simpson's expert on this issue.

Finn v. Finn

Texas Court of Appeals—Dallas, 1983
658 S.W.2d 735, writ ref'd n.r.e.

VANCE, Justice.

The questions presented in this appeal concern the trial court's division of property upon the divorce of Frank and Joellen Finn. The wife asserts fourteen points contending that various errors committed by the trial court resulted in an unfair and unjust property division. For the reasons stated below, we hold that the wife was improperly denied discovery of documents essential to prove the value of the community interest in the husband's law practice. We therefore reverse and remand the property division for a new trial.

The Finns were married for more than twenty years. During the entire time the couple was married the husband worked for a large Dallas law firm. The law practice is structured as a partnership in which the husband has been a senior partner for over ten years. Although the wife also has a law degree, she did not practice law during the marriage, but instead devoted her time to maintaining the home and raising their four children. The parties agreed on the value of most of the community property, but the value of the husband's law practice was hotly contested.

1. Goodwill of Law Firm

The wife contends that the trial court erred by instructing the jury to exclude the goodwill of the law firm and its future earning capacity from the valuation of the community interest in the husband's law practice. Relying on the Fort Worth Court of Civil Appeals decision in *Geesbreght v. Geesbreght*, 570 S.W.2d 427 (Tex. Civ. App.—Fort Worth 1978, writ dism'd), the wife argues that the husband's law firm has goodwill which is separate and apart from the husband's professional ability. Therefore, the wife argues that the husband's professional partnership is analogous to the professional corporation addressed by the court in *Geesbreght* and the goodwill attached to the law firm is property subject to division upon divorce.

The husband, relying on the supreme court opinion in *Nail v. Nail*, 486 S.W.2d 761 (Tex. 1972) contends that the goodwill is not a vested property right which fixes a benefit in any sum at a future time. In support of his contention, the husband notes that the partnership agreement under which the law firm operates makes no provision for compensating a senior partner for the goodwill of the firm in the event of his death or withdrawal. The husband argues that the goodwill of the professional partnership is analogous to the individual professional practice addressed by the court in *Nail*, in that under the terms of the operating agreement any benefit conferred on the husband due to the goodwill of the firm is a mere expectancy contingent on his continued participation in the firm. Thus, he argues, the goodwill is not property in the community estate subject to division on divorce.

In *Nail* the supreme court noted that "goodwill has no existence as property in and of itself, as a separate and distinct entity, but only as an incident of a continuing business having locality or name." *Nail*, 486 S.W.2d at 763. The court went on to state that professional goodwill attaches to the person of the professional as a result of confidence in his skill and ability. In the case of a solo practitioner the court held that goodwill did not possess value or constitute an asset separate and apart from the professional's ability. *Nail*, 486 S.W.2d at 764. Accordingly, the court held that the goodwill of the professional's practice that may have accrued during the marriage was not property in the community estate. The *Nail* court was particularly concerned with the fact that should a solo practitioner die or cease to practice the goodwill would cease to exist without its value having been realized in any manner other than by enhancing the practitioner's earning capacity. *Nail*, 486 S.W.2d at 764. The *Nail* court specifically reserved the question of goodwill that exists apart from the person of an individual member in a professional partnership or corporation.

In *Geesbreght* the Fort Worth Court of Civil Appeals considered the question of whether goodwill was property subject to division upon divorce in the context of a professional corporation. Dr. Geesbreght and his partner incorporated their professional practice with each partner holding one-half of the corporate stock. The corporation did not do business under the names of the two stockholders and employed many professionals, in addition to the two stockholders, to provide services on behalf of the corporation under its many contracts. The court noted that the corporation had a reputation for providing services in its own name that was built in large part upon the abilities of the professional employees. To that extent, goodwill existed in the corporation separate and apart from the personal ability and reputation of Dr. Geesbreght. *Geesbreght*, 570 S.W.2d at 435. The court went on to hold that this corporate goodwill had a commercial value and to the extent that it enhanced the value of Dr. Geesbreght's stock in the corporation, the goodwill was property subject to division upon divorce. *Geesbreght*, 570 S.W.2d at 436. The issue of whether the community estate was entitled to share in the goodwill of the corporation was not before the *Geesbreght* court. It was undisputed that Dr. Geesbreght's stock in his professional corporation was community property and to the extent that the goodwill enhanced the value of the stock, it was community property subject to division upon divorce.

Read together, *Nail* and *Geesbreght* indicate a two-pronged test to determine whether the goodwill attached to a professional practice is subject to division upon divorce. First, goodwill must be determined to exist independently of the personal ability of the professional spouse. Second, if such goodwill is found to exist, then it must be determined whether that goodwill has a commercial value in which the community estate is entitled to share.

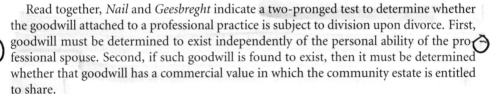

Evidence in the present case indicates that the husband's law firm has goodwill independent of his professional ability. Like the professional corporation in *Geesbreght*, the firm does not conduct business under the names of the senior partners, but rather operates under the names of two founding partners no longer practicing with the firm. The record reflects that at the time of trial the law firm consisted of twenty senior partners, twenty-two junior partners and forty-three associates. The husband has been practicing law with the firm for over twenty-five years; however, the firm has been providing legal services to the public for more than ninety years. A large part of the firm's reputation for providing services was built upon the professional abilities of the husband's predecessors in the firm as well as the abilities of his present partners and professional employees. Under these circumstances we recognize that the firm has goodwill independent and apart from the professional ability of the husband.

The inquiry does not stop here, as the wife contends, but must continue to determine whether his goodwill has commercial value to which the community estate is entitled. Without question the goodwill of a long established firm has commercial value. The question which confronts us is whether the community estate is entitled to share in the value of the law firm's goodwill.

The community estate is not entitled to a greater interest than that to which the husband is entitled in the firm's goodwill. The extent of the husband's interest is governed by the partnership agreement.[1] Under the terms of the partnership agreement, should the husband die or withdraw, he is entitled only to 1) the amount contained in his capital account, 2) any earned income which had not been distributed, and 3) his interest in the firm's reserve account less ten percent of his proportionate share in the accounts receivable for clients' disbursement.[2] By a vote of three fourths of the senior partners,

---

1. The wife urges us to follow a line of California cases which have held the accrued goodwill of a professional practice to be community property subject to division upon divorce. *Slater v. Slater*, 100 Cal. App. 3d 241, 160 Cal. Reptr. 686 (1980); *Webb v. Webb*, 94 Cal. App. 3d 335, 156 Cal. Rptr. 334 (1979); *Foster v. Foster*, 42 Cal. App. 3d 577, 117 Cal. Reptr. 49 (1974); *Lopez v. Lopez*, 38 Cal. App. 3d 93, 113 Cal. Rptr. 58 (1974); *Golden v. Golden*, 270 Cal. App. 2d 401, 75 Cal. Rptr. 735 (1969); *Mueller v. Mueller*, 144 Cal. App.2d 245, 301 P.2d 90 (1956). She places particular emphasis upon the *Slater* case which held the wife was not bound by the provisions of the partnership agreement as to the extent of the husband's interest should he withdraw from the partnership to determine the present value of the husband's continued participation in the partnership. Following the rationale of the California courts, the wife urges us to disregard the provisions of the partnership agreement and find accrued goodwill to be community property subject to division. This we decline to do.

The California community property statute mandates an equal division of the community property upon divorce. Cal. Civ. Code Sec. 4800 (a) (Deering Supp. 1983). This has been interpreted to mean a mathematically equal division in the ideal situation. *In re Juick*, 21 Cal. App. 3d 421, 98 Cal. Rptr. 324, 329 (1971). The court in California is not at liberty to make an unequal division of the community property due to disparate earning capacity between the spouses, business opportunities, education, relative physical conditions, relative financial condition and obligations, disparity of ages and size of separate estates. Thus the California court must consider the factor of accrued goodwill under the guise of community property if it is to be considered at all. Such is not the case in Texas. The Texas court is at liberty to make an unequal division of the community property which, when all factors are considered, is a just and right division. Tex. Fam. Code Ann. Sec. 3.63 (Vernon Supp. 19821983); *Murff v. Murff*, 615 S.W.2d 696, 699 (Tex. 1981). Thus, in Texas we are not placed in the position of being compelled to consider the accrued goodwill of a professional partnership as community property or omit it from consideration entirely as are the California courts. Under Texas community property law, we find the accrued goodwill of a professional partnership to be more properly considered as a factor enhancing earning capacity of the professional spouse rather than as community property to be valued and divided for the reasons set forth in the text of this opinion.

2. The agreement also contains extensive provisions regarding retirement benefits which we find unnecessary to detail here.

the husband may be required to withdraw, and in that event he is entitled to the same compensation for his interest as provided for voluntary withdrawal should he continue to practice law elsewhere. Additional compensation is provided should the husband voluntarily withdraw from the firm and cease to practice law. The agreement does not provide any compensation for accrued goodwill to a partner who ceases to practice law with the firm, nor does it provide any mechanism to realize the value of the firm's goodwill.

The lack of any legal right of the husband to realize the value of the firm's goodwill is a decisive factor. It distinguishes the present case from *Geesbreght* wherein the corporate structure provided a mechanism which enabled Dr. Geesbreght to realize the value of accrued goodwill by enhancing the value of his stock. In the present case the only mechanism through which the husband may possibly realize the value of the accrued goodwill is through continuing to practice law as a member of the firm, a circumstance depending not only on his own individual capacity, but also on the uncontrolled discretion of his partners. Thus his position is no better than that of the physician in *Nail*, in which the supreme court found the value of accrued goodwill in an individual professional practice to be realized only through enhanced future earning capacity. Such realization in the future is no more than an expectancy entirely dependent on the husband's continued participation in the firm, and, therefore, is not property in the community estate. *Nail*, 486 S.W.2d at 764. Consequently, we hold that the trial court properly instructed the jury not to consider the law firm's accrued goodwill or future earning capacity[3] when placing a value on the community interest in the husband's law practice.

By this holding we do not mean that the husband's earning capacity as a member of the firm has no relevance to the division of the community estate. Under Section 3.63 of the Family Code disparity in earning capacity of the spouses is a factor which may be considered when making a just and right division of the community property. *Murff v. Murff*, 615 S.W.2d 696, 698 (Tex. 1981). Although goodwill cannot properly be considered in determining the value of the community's interest in the law firm, to the extent that the husband's earning capacity is enhanced by his continued participation in the law firm, the court may consider this factor when assessing any disparity in earning capacity of the spouses.

DISCUSSION

Is there a difference between ignoring goodwill attributable to the personal services of the spouse and ignoring goodwill attributable to personal services rendered by anyone? Which would be the better approach?

---

3. Goodwill has been defined as "the advantage or benefit which is acquired by an establishment beyond the mere value of the capital stock, funds, or property employed therein, in consequence of the general public patronage and encouragement which it receives from constant or habitual customers on account of its local position, or common celebrity, or reputation for skill, or influence, or punctuality, or from other accidental circumstances or necessities, or even from ancient partialities or prejudices." *Estate of Masquelette v. Commissioner of Internal Revenue*, 239 F.2d 322, 325 (5th Cir. 1956) (quoting Story, *Partnerships*, Sec. 99). To the extent that the law firm's future earning capacity is attributable to goodwill, the propriety of its consideration in the valuation of the community estate's interest in the law firm is disposed of by our holding in regard to goodwill. To the extent that the law firm's future earning capacity is attributable to factors other than goodwill, it is not property in the community estate based on the same rationale applied to accrued goodwill.

Finn is concerned about whether the employee spouse has the right to receive the benefits of the goodwill of the practice in any manner other than by continuing to work after divorce. Should this matter? Should the result in *Nail* be different if it could have been established that Dr. Nail could have sold his practice?

Other states have established significantly different rules to govern divorce property division involving personal service businesses. For example, many states have concluded that "personal" goodwill is just as valuable as commercial goodwill and should be divided at divorce, if the business is community property. *See, e.g., In re Marriage of Lopez*, 113 Cal. Rptr. 58 (Cal. App. 1974); *In re Marriage of Lukens*, 558 P.2d 279 (Wash. App. 1976). Even in these states, the goodwill is not valued in terms of the earning capacity of the professional; the goodwill is only the extent to which the earning capacity of the spouse exceeds the earning capacity of a professional with identical skill and experience, but with no established clientele.

Is the issue whether the personal goodwill is valuable? How does the *Lopez/Lukens* view fit with the general view that a spouse's earning capacity at divorce is separate property? States that accept the *Lopez/Lukens* view would answer that *all* of the professional's earning capacity is not community property; only the *excess* earnings attributable to clientele established during marriage create a community claim. Is this persuasive?

Under the California view, did Picasso's "art business" have goodwill? What about Meryl Streep's "acting business"?

If the professional spouse marries a third party shortly after the professional's divorce (which is quite likely), all earnings received during the second marriage will be considered community property of the second marriage. If some portion of the professional's increased future earning capacity would also be considered a part of the community estate of the first marriage, would this be a problem?

When a business appraiser values a business or professional practice to determine a reasonable sales price, when arriving at such a value the appraiser assumes the owner will sign a covenant not to compete with the buyer for a certain period. The argument has been made that, when this valuation methodology is used at divorce, the part of the value due to the assumed covenant should be separate property, because it represents the owner's waiver of a right to compete after divorce. *See* Richard Orsinger, "Blue Sky or Book Value? Complex Issues in Business Valuation," chapter 28, pages 14–15, 2001 Advanced Family Law Materials, State Bar of Texas. This view has been criticized by appraisers and is no longer a part of the Texas Pattern Jury Charge.

Rathmell v. Morrison

Texas Court of Appeals — Houston [14th Dist.], 1987
732 S.W.2d 6, no writ

In points of error ten through fourteen appellant makes several challenges to the trial court's evaluation of the Rathmell companies. These points of error involve the second portion of bifurcated trial, the part tried before the court. The court made a fact finding that the market value of the Rathmell companies on October 1, 1975, the date of the divorce, was $4,857,000. The first contention made under point of error ten is that the trial court erred in valuing the companies without excluding personal good will and by assuming John would continue to work for the companies. The record before this court shows the trial court's finding of market value, but the record does not show whether the trial court included or excluded the personal good will of John or whether the trial court did or did not assume that John would continue to work for the companies. The second contention under point ten is that the court erred in failing to find what portion, if any, of the value of the companies, as found by the court, was attributable to the personal good will of John, and/or the time, toil and talent of John to be expended following the divorce, and/or John's willingness not to compete with the companies.

In considering appellant's point ten and the various contentions made thereunder, it is helpful to review a number of Texas court decisions.

The supreme court has held that the accrued good will in a private medical practice of a sole practitioner is not property in the estate of the parties and therefore not subject to division upon divorce. *Nail v. Nail*, 486 S.W.2d 761, 764 (Tex. 1972). In coming to its conclusion, the supreme court recognized the distinction between good will that may attach to a trade or business and professional good will. From the court's opinion we conclude that professional good will has the following attributes: It attaches to the person of the professional man or woman as a result of confidence in his or her skill and ability. It does not possess value or constitute an asset separate and apart from the professional's person, or from his individual ability to practice his profession. It would be extinguished in the event of the professional's death, retirement, or disablement.

Two courts of appeals have recognized that a professional person practicing with others under a corporate structure or as a partnership may have accrued personal professional good will and that there might exist at the same time good will attributable to the business or partnership. Good will that exists separate and apart from a professional's personal skills, ability, and reputation is divisible upon divorce, *Geesbreght v. Geesbreght*, 570 S.W.2d 427 (Tex. Civ. App.—Fort Worth 1978, writ dism'd), provided the community is entitled to share in the commercial value of that good will. *Finn v. Finn*, 658 S.W.2d 735, 741 (Tex. App.—Dallas 1983, writ ref'd n.r.e.).

Appellant is not a lawyer or a doctor, as were the professionals in *Nail*, *Geesbreght*, and *Finn*. Nevertheless, it is clear that appellant did develop professional good will as the term is used in *Nail*. The Rathmell companies specialized in providing insurance to large businesses and associations. Several witnesses testified that the key to the financial success of the Rathmell companies was John's personality, social contacts, and specialized knowledge of the problems and solutions peculiar to insuring businesses and associations. Personality and social contacts are important in the business because they help "get a foot in the door." Specialized knowledge is needed to get customers the right kind of insurance for a good price. It is undisputed that John was the major "producer" in the companies, meaning he brought in most of the customers. The good will that arose because of these attributes in John attached as a result of confidence in his skill and ability, and did not possess value or constitute an asset separate and apart from John's person or his individual ability to practice his profession, and would be extinguished if he died, or retired, or was disabled. *See Nail*, 486 S.W.2d at 764.

Appellant contends not only that he had accumulated personal professional good will, but that *all* good will associated with the Rathmell companies was his personal good will. We do not agree with appellant's contention that all good will of the companies was his personal professional good will.

There is evidence in the record that the Rathmell companies had good will attributable to the company apart from John Rathmell's personal professional good will. Witnesses testified that the company had several competent key employees who handled the day-to-day needs of clients. The chairman of a company that was the largest client of the Rathmell companies, representing over twenty-seven percent of its total revenues, testified that the Rathmell companies were not a "one-man show," that they had very competent people handling the day-to-day business and that the only reason his company would stay with the Rathmell companies was that they offered competitive prices and services.

In connection with the second contention under point ten appellant complains of the court's refusal to make additional findings of fact requested by appellant. Appellant's request was as follows:

> Respondent requests that the Court find what portion, if any, of the value of the companies … was attributable to (a) the personal good will of the Respondent and/or (b) the time, toil and talent of the Respondent to be expended following the divorce and/or (c) his willingness not to compete with the companies.

We hold that in finding the value of the Rathmell companies the trial court should have excluded value attributable to the factors listed. If the value found by the court did exclude such factors, the court should have so stated in additional findings of fact. Without such additional findings it is impossible to determine whether the trial court included or excluded them. In making this ruling we are not saying that the trial court should find a value including the above-listed factors and then make separate findings of what portion of such value is attributable to each factor. It is only necessary that the trial court's findings show clearly that the value found by the court excluded such factors. Had the second portion of this bill of review been tried to a jury, appellant would have been entitled to an instruction to the jury that in determining the value of the Rathmell companies the jury should exclude value attributable to such listed factors. With such instruction a jury verdict on value would clearly exclude the listed factors. Appellant was entitled to as much from the court in findings of fact in a non-jury trial. Point of error number ten is sustained.

In point of error number eleven appellant urges that the trial court erred in failing to find or conclude whether appellant had a legal right to terminate his employment with the Rathmell companies and to establish a competing business at the time the alleged misrepresentations were made. Appellant specifically requested such a finding in his Request for Additional and Amended Findings and Conclusions.

We think the evidence is undisputed that John Rathmell had no employment contracts with the Rathmell companies that committed him to stay or prohibited him from establishing a competing business. The court did not err in refusing to make findings of fact on an issue that is undisputed.

————————

DISCUSSION

Rathmell confirms that *Nail* extends to all businesses. See also *Smith v. Smith*, 836 S.W.2d 688 (Tex. App. — Houston [1st Dist.] 1992, no writ).

Should the divorce court's determination of the value of the partner's goodwill be affected by the value set forth in the partnership agreement that the spouse will receive upon withdrawal or death? *Keith v. Keith*, 763 S.W.2d 950 (Tex. App. — Fort Worth 1989, no writ) held that a divorce court was not bound by the agreement.

If a state accepts the California/Washington view of the community claim to personal goodwill, other changes could evolve in community property doctrine. See *Golub*, below.

Golub v. Golub

Supreme Court of New York, 1988
527 N.Y.S.2d 946

SILBERMANN, Justice.

This matrimonial action was commenced by service of a summons in June, 1986. After a timely appearance by defendant, a verified complaint was served on or about August 29, 1986. Issue was thereafter joined on November 4, 1986. A sufficient showing having been made at trial that the marriage which had been dying in 1984 was moribund as of 1985, a dual divorce on the grounds of constructive abandonment and abandonment was granted and the trial proceeded as to the ancillary relief.

After listening to the many days of testimony, observing the witnesses' demeanor and manner of testifying and studying the many exhibits offered in evidence, the court makes the following findings.

Statements of Facts

The parties were married amidst a great deal of fanfare including television coverage on February 14, 1982. Although there are no children of this marriage, plaintiff has a daughter, Starlite, by a former marriage.

Plaintiff, Marisa Berenson, is a renowned and celebrated film and television actress and model. At the time of the marriage she apparently enjoyed enormous entree to the world of arts and fashion both in her own right and as the granddaughter of Elsa Schiaparelli, the celebrated couturiere.

At the time of the marriage, defendant, A. Richard Golub, was a successful attorney who had been in private practice for many years and who attracted media and celebrity attention. Indeed, at the time immediately preceding their marriage, defendant was engaged in the trial of a matter involving Brooke Shields which was getting a substantial amount of media coverage.

It is clear that both parties coveted and gained the attention of the press and the company of the "Rich and Famous."

After living at several different locations during the first few months of their marriage, in the fall of 1982, the parties purchased a four story townhouse at 209 East 83rd Street. This house was found by defendant and purchased for $575,000. The purchase was accomplished by the parties' assumption of a then existing small mortgage, and a contribution by plaintiff of $58,000 and defendant of $75,065.61.

On February 1, 1984, the 83rd Street property was sold for $950,000. Defendant had acquired the contract to purchase the townhouse at 42 East 64th Street for $50,000 and paid an additional $55,787.65 for a total cash payment of $105,787.65. Because the purchase of East 64th Street preceded the sale of 83rd Street property by six days, the remainder of the purchase price was covered by a purchase money mortgage of $675,000 and a bridge loan of $250,000.

An examination of the various checks introduced into evidence as well as the testimony of the parties reveals the fact that the parties in effect pooled their income and defrayed their expenses using a flexible and/or pragmatic approach.

Plaintiff's funds, including income from films, television, modeling and a book, were placed mainly in two accounts. (Plaintiff had a separate Paris account as well.) One was called "A. Richard Golub Special Account No. 2" and the second "Echoes of Eternity." Defendant had signatory powers on both these accounts. Throughout the marriage it is evident that defendant made many of the decisions concerning the management of plaintiff's financial matters and how their monies would be spent. Thus, their monies were used interchangeably to pay their various expenses including expenses for the East 83rd Street house, the East 64th Street house, taxes and general living costs.

Beginning at the start of the marriage and continuing thereafter, plaintiff spent almost half of every year in Europe. In September 1985, plaintiff found an apartment in Paris which she leased in her name. Defendant contributed $32,500 toward obtaining the Paris apartment. Plaintiff has had exclusive use of the Paris apartment.

Throughout the marriage plaintiff appeared to have been engaged in pursuing her career both in the United States and abroad, concededly successfully. While in New York, the parties ate frequently in restaurants and seemingly entertained little at home. Housekeeping and child care were tended to by hired help. These homemaking services were solely supervised by the defendant for approximately half of every year while plaintiff was in Europe. Likewise, defendant supervised the renovations made to the marital real estate as well as the negotiations and litigation necessary to vacate the rental apartments that were contained therein.

Increase in Value of Acting and Modeling Career

Defendant contends that the increase in value of plaintiff's acting and modeling career is marital property and he seeks equitable distribution thereof as a result of his contributions thereto. The law of this state is clear that any increase in the value of separate property of a spouse occurring during the marriage which is due in part to the direct or indirect contributions of the other spouse may be considered property. Further, the law is clear that professional licenses are included in the definition of property (*O'Brien v. O'Brien*, 66 N.Y.2d 576, 498 N.Y.S.2d 743, 489 N.E.2d 712) and that this definition has been extended to include academic degrees as well as professional licenses (*McGowan v. McGowan*, 519 N.Y.S.2d 346 [Sup.Ct., Suffolk Co., 1987]).

Plaintiff contends that her celebrity status is neither "professional" nor a "license" and hence not an "investment in human capital subject to equitable distribution." Moreover, plaintiff argues that because a career in show business is subject to substantial fluctuation, it should not be considered.

In *O'Brien*, the fact that the professional license itself had no market value was irrelevant. It is the enhanced earning capacity that the license affords the holder that is of value. In this respect, all sources of enhanced earning capacity become indistinguishable.

> Could it rationally be concluded that, for purposes of equitable distribution upon divorce, the Court of Appeals intended to limit as marital property, licenses enumerated in the Education Law? Hardly, given the definition of a license's value as enunciated in *O'Brien* as being enhanced earning capacity.

(*McGowan, supra.*)

McGowan gives "enhanced earning capacity" an expansive meaning. The same logic used in *McGowan* to extend marital property to include degrees can be applied to include as marital property a spouse's unique ability to commercially exploit his or her fame. In *O'Brien*, it was the privileges conferred by the license that was critical to the Court's decision, not the piece of paper itself. In *McGowan*, it was not the spouse's degree that was divisible; it was the income generated by exercising the privileges associated with the degree that the non-degreed spouse was seeking to share.

In *O'Brien*, the court appears to be speaking of an intangible asset, i.e., "enhanced earning capacity" and not a tangible asset or "res."

In fairness, just as *McGowan* was a logical extension of *O'Brien*, the right of a spouse to share in other valuable assets must be the next step forward.

There is tremendous potential for financial gain from the commercial exploitation of famous personalities, 25 UCLA Law Review 1095. There is a proprietary interest in the product of a celebrity's labors. The right to exploit a celebrity's fame has been held to descend to his heirs, *Price v. Hal Roach Studios, Inc.*, 400 F. Supp. 836. This exemplifies the property nature of a celebrity's fame. A Commercial Endorsement is essentially a "license" to use a person's fame.

> Recognition of the community's interest in certain of these intangible interests indicates a disposition on the part of the judiciary to re-evaluate old notions of property. In light of this, consideration of the community property issues posed by the right of publicity seems overdue.

(25 UCLA Law Review 1095, 1113).

There is an analogy to be made between the right of publicity and professional goodwill. In both rights, there is a secondary meaning generated by a name and benefits derived therefrom. In either case, the right becomes an income producing source.

The courts should treat all matrimonial litigants equally and should not prejudice nor penalize a spouse who is married to a non-professional who may nevertheless become an exceptional wage earner. The O'Brien remedy should be applied evenhandedly to all spouses. Otherwise, what will result is an economic windfall to some and an unfair deprivation to others. Clearly, there are certain fields in which the earning capacity exceeds that of other fields which require licensure. When a person's expertise in a field has allowed him or her to be an exceptional wage earner, this generates a value similar to that of the goodwill of a business.

In *Morimando, supra*, the spouse of a physician's assistant sought to have that spouse's license declared marital property for equitable distribution purposes upon divorce. The Court distinguished this case from *O'Brien* because a physician's assistant does not share the same level of opportunity as does an M.D. A physician's assistant was said to always rely on an employer. The court also referred to the statute applicable to physician's assistants and noted that it "clearly imposes limitations upon the exercise of their functions." The physician's assistant is "destined to remain an employee." Unlike a physician's assistant, an actress/model often functions independently, on a freelance basis and is not at the mercy of his or her employer.

O'Brien is the law. If it is to remain as good law, the rule should be uniformly applied. There seems to be no rational basis upon which to distinguish between a degree, a license, or any other special skill that generates substantial income. In determining the value of marital property, all such income generating assets should be considered if they accumulated while the marriage endured. If one spouse has sacrificed and assisted the other in an effort to increase that other spouse's earning capacity, it should make no difference what shape or form that asset takes so long as it in fact results in an increased earning capacity. The rationale in both *O'Brien* and *McGowan* for awarding the spouse an economic interest in the intangible asset seems to have been based on a view of the asset as "investments in the economic partnership of the marriage and the product of the parties' joint efforts." (*McGowan, supra*).

The noncelebrity spouse should be entitled to a share of the celebrity spouse's fame, limited, of course, by the degree to which that fame is attributable to the noncelebrity spouse (25 UCLA Law Review 1095). The source of the fame must still be traced to the marital efforts.

Thus, as in *O'Brien*, if a spouse devotes himself or herself to the family throughout the marriage, giving up career opportunities, and no liquid assets exist, the court should compensate this spouse for his or her contribution enabling him or her to pursue his or her career and not just a terminable maintenance award. For example, if instead of medical school the spouse went to music school and became a celebrated pianist, in equity both accomplishments must be treated equally.

The question, therefore, presented is should *O'Brien* be extended so as not to prejudice a spouse who is married to a nonprofessional?

This court answers the question in the affirmative and holds that the skills of an artisan, actor, professional athlete or any person whose expertise in his or her career has enabled him or her to become an exceptional wage earner should be valued as marital property subject to equitable distribution. Thus, although plaintiff's celebrity status is neither "professional" nor a "license" (*Morimando, supra*) its increase in value is marital property; despite the difficulties presented in valuing such property.

B. Professional Education

The prior section discusses the potential community claim to a professional practice established by a spouse during marriage. In some instances, a professional will divorce approximately when he graduates, before a significant practice has been developed. In such circumstances, the non-educated spouse has argued that the educated spouse has received a significant benefit due to the professional education, and that the value of this benefit should be included in the community estate.

Frausto v. Frausto
Texas Court of Appeals — San Antonio, 1980
611 S.W.2d 656, writ dism'd

KLINGEMAN, Justice.

This is a divorce action but the appeal herein pertains to the trial court's division of the properties between the parties. Appellant, Manuel Jesus Frausto, complains only of an order in the divorce decree which requires him to pay to appellee, Maria Lourdes Frausto, the sum of $20,000, payable in the amount of $200 per month, "as a part of the division of the estate of the parties and as reimbursement for petitioner's share of the community expense for respondent's education."[1]

---

1. The Decree of Divorce states:

The court further finds that during the marriage the parties have invested approximately $40,000.00 in Respondent's medical education and that Respondent is now a medical doctor, licensed to practice medicine in the State of Texas. It is therefore, DECREED that Respondent, Manuel Jesus Frausto, shall pay to Petitioner, Maria Lourdes N. Frausto, as a part of the division of the estate of the parties and as reimbursement [sic] for Petitioner's share of the community expense for Respondent's education, the amount of $20,000.00 payable in the amount of $200.00 per month, plus interest at 9% per annum on the unpaid balance, with the first payment being due and payable on or before the 10th

By a number of points of error appellant asserts that the trial court erred in holding that (1) the husband's education preparing him for the practice of medicine was community property and a property right divisible on divorce; and (2) appellee was entitled to such sum as reimbursement for her share of the community expense for appellant's education. We agree.

During the early part of the marriage, appellant and appellee were both school teachers. It was agreed by both that the husband would enter medical school. The wife continued to work while the husband was obtaining his medical education, and it is clear that during such period a considerable portion of all expenses of such marriage came from the wife's earnings. After the husband obtained his doctor's license to practice medicine, his earnings at times were substantial, but his work record is spotty, at times he was unemployed, and at other times his earnings were not large by medical standards. The husband testified that he had sustained injuries to both of his legs and that this made it difficult for him to work at times, and that he had quit some jobs because of this problem.

There is evidence that at times the husband was a heavy spender. Despite whatever earnings the husband and wife had, no large community estate was accumulated. Both the husband and wife had college degrees, and the wife had taught school for many years and has continued to work as a school teacher. Two children were born of such marriage, one born in 1973 and the other in 1975. This case is somewhat typical of what sometimes happens when one spouse continues to work while the other spouse is obtaining a degree resulting in high potential earnings for the degreed spouse, and a divorce thereafter ensues.

From the plain language of the decree it is apparent that the award of $20,000 to the wife was an attempt by the trial judge to divide the medical education of appellant as a part of the community estate, or to reimburse appellee for expenditures made by the community for appellant's medical education.

There are no Texas cases directly in point. Two community property states, California and Colorado, have passed on the questions here involved. In *Todd v. Todd*, 78 Cal. Rptr. 131, 272 Cal. App. 2d 786 (1969), the California court held that a spouse's education preparing him for the practice of law is not of such a character that a monetary value for division can be placed on it for a division between the spouses in a divorce proceeding.[2]

This rule was reaffirmed in *In re Marriage of Aufmuth*, 152 Cal. Rptr. 668, 89 Cal. App. 3d 446 (1979), wherein it was held that a determination that a legal education is community property would require a division of post-dissolution earnings, even though such earnings are the separate property of the acquiring spouses. A Colorado court in *In re Marriage of Graham*, 38 Colo. App. 130, 555 P.2d 527 (1976), found that education is not a property item capable of division.[3]

---

day of June, 1979 and a like payment being due and payable on the same day of each month thereafter until said amount of $20,000.00, plus interest at 9% per annum on the unpaid balance, be paid in full. The interest at the rate of 9% per annum of the unpaid balance shall commence as of the date that the first payment id [sic] due, June 10, 1979.

2. "If a spouse's education preparing him for the practice of the law can be said to be 'community property,' a proposition which is extremely doubtful even though the education is acquired with community moneys, it manifestly is of such a character that a monetary value for division with the other spouse cannot be placed upon it." 78 Cal. Rptr. at 134, 272 Cal. App. 2d 786.

3. "We hold, therefore, that although a litigant's education is a factor to be considered, among many others, in arriving at an equitable property division and in determining matters of maintenance and child support, it is not property subject to division under Sec. 14-10-113 C.R.S. 1973." *Id.* at 529. *Graham* cites *Stern v. Stern*, 66 N.J. 340, 331 A.2d 257 (1975), where the court said: "Potential earning capacity is doubtless a factor to be considered by a trial judge in determining what distribution

We agree with the jurisdictions that have held a professional educational degree is not divisible upon divorce.

In *Nail v. Nail*, 486 S.W.2d 761 (Tex. 1972), it was contended that professional good will was an asset capable of being divided upon dissolution of the marriage. The supreme court rejected this contention and stated that the professional goodwill of a doctor does not "possess value or constitute an asset separate and apart from his person or from his individual ability to practice his profession. It would be extinguished in the event of his death, or retirement, or disablement, as well as in the event of the sale of his practice or the loss of his patients, whatever the cause." Although *Nail* does not involve a spouse's education, we regard it as comparable and persuasive.

The trial court, upon divorce, is authorized to divide the "estate of the parties" which has been interpreted to refer to community property alone. *Eggemeyer v. Eggemeyer*, 554 S.W.2d 137 (Tex. 1977). Further, the trial court cannot divest spouses of rights to separate property whether real or personal, *Eggemeyer, supra*. If the trial court awards monthly payments to be made in the future by one spouse to the other, such payments must be referable to property in existence at the time of marriage.

An award of future monthly payments which is specifically referable to an education received by spouses during marriage, as we have in the case before us, violates the rules and authorities hereinbefore set forth, and an award of monthly payments to be made in the future that is based on future earnings is in violation of *Eggemeyer, supra*, because it is an award of separate property, property not acquired during the marriage relationship.

We recognize there are inequities which may result from the failure to compensate the spouse who supports the other spouse through college or professional school. See Castleberry, *Constitutional Limitations on the Division of Property Upon Divorce*, 10 St. Mary's L.J. 37, 56 (1978). However, in an attempt to overcome such difficulties the trial court has wide discretion in dividing the estate of the parties in a divorce decree and may consider many factors including the difference in earning capacity, education and ability of the parties; probable future need for support; fault in breaking up the marriage; and the benefits an innocent spouse may have received from a continuation of the marriage.

We hold that a professional education acquired during marriage is not a property right and is not divisible upon divorce.

We must now consider whether the award of $20,000 can be justified on the basis of reimbursement. It is clear from the language of the decree that to whatever extent it is reimbursement, it is reimbursement for appellee's share of community expenses for appellant's education. This is not a typical reimbursement which ordinarily pertains to payments or contributions made by one spouse out of separate property to the community or by the community to one of the spouse's separate property. Reimbursement is ordinarily allowed where money is spent by one estate, or where improvements are made from one estate to the other estate. See *Dakan v. Dakan*, 125 Tex. 305, 83 S.W. 620 (1935). The rule is sometimes stated that on dissolution of the marriage, if one party has contributed separate property, or if community funds have been applied to the enhancement of the property of the other, reimbursement is allowed. We do not have this here. Any reimbursement here is referable only to the education of one of the spouses, which we have held is not a property right, and which was admittedly paid for from community funds. Moreover, there are no pleadings seeking reimbursement. Ordinarily, an award for re-

---

will be 'equitable' and it is even more obviously relevant upon the issue of alimony. But it should not be deemed property as such within the meaning of the statute."

imbursement is not allowable in the absence of an allegation of liability of such a nature or anything in the pleading to support such a judgment. Under the pleadings and the record we find no justification for such award on the theory of reimbursement.

The trial court's award of $20,000 to appellee as a part of the division of the estate of the parties and as a reimbursement for appellee's share of community expenses for appellant's education constitutes error and is an abuse of the trial court's discretion.

Where an appellate court finds that the trial court abused its discretion in a divorce suit, ordinarily, the proper order is a reversal and remand. As hereinbefore pointed out, it is not possible for us to determine exactly what portion of the community estate was awarded to the husband, and what portion to the wife. Consequently, it is not possible for us to tell to what extent the trial court considered the professional education and degree and substantially higher earning capacity of the husband, in making a division of the community estate between the parties. The interests of justice will best be served by a remand as to that portion of the divorce decree making a division of the property between the parties.

That portion of the divorce decree pertaining to a division of the property between the parties is reversed and remanded to a trial court for a new trial in a manner not inconsistent with this opinion. The divorce decree in all other things is affirmed.

DISCUSSION

Is the result in *Frausto* dictated by *Nail*? Can *Nail* be distinguished?

The Texas Supreme Court has held that a person has a constitutionally protected liberty interest in a graduate education. *UT Medical School v. Than*, 901 S.W.2d 926 (Tex. 1995). Is this consistent with *Frausto*?

A spouse's post-divorce earning capacity is her separate property. So, if a court awards a spouse a percentage of the other spouse's post-divorce earnings, this would constitute automatic reversible error. *See Butler v. Butler*, 975 S.W.2d 765 (Tex. App. — Corpus Christi 1998, no pet.).

Notice the manner in which the reimbursement argument is handled. According to reimbursement theory, the community estate is only entitled to reimbursement if community assets have been expended to improve a spouse's separate property. Once a spouse's earning capacity is deemed not to be property, reimbursement is not possible.

A different issue would arise if the spouses marry after a spouse goes to school, and community funds would be used to pay school loans. The community would have a potential reimbursement claim here for using community funds to pay a separate debt. *See Henry v. Henry*, 48 S.W.3d 468 (Tex. App. — Houston [14th Dist.] 2001, no pet.). However, Tex. Fam. Code § 3.409 now apparently provides that reimbursement may not be granted for this.

Cal. Fam. Code § 2641 permits reimbursement to the community for "community contributions to education or training," which include, at a minimum, tuition, books, fees, supplies and transportation. *Marriage of Watts*, 262 Cal. Rptr. 783 (Cal. App. 1989). Would this be a better approach than *Frausto*?

There is little agreement regarding what is a fair result when spouses divorce shortly after one has completed professional training. Some believe the non-educated spouse supported the other without an expectation of compensation. A related view is that, even if the supporting spouse *hoped* to share in the increased earning capacity of the educated spouse, this should not be compensated at divorce. For example, a New Jersey court made these statements:

> The termination of a marriage represents, if nothing else, the disappointment of expectations, financial and nonfinancial, which were hoped to be achieved by and during the continuation of the relationship. It does not, in our view, represent a commercial loss.

> If the plan fails by reason of the termination of the marriage, we do not regard the supporting spouse's consequent loss of expectation by itself as any more compensable or demanding of solicitude than the loss of expectations of any other spouse who, with the hope and anticipation of the endurance of the relationship ... has invested a portion of his or her life, youth, energy and labor in a failed marriage.

Mahoney v. Mahoney, 442 A.2d 1062 (N. J. App. Div. 1982).

The opposite view is that the supporting spouse should be compensated if one spouse significantly increases his earning capacity during marriage and both spouses have not significantly reaped the benefits of that increased earning capacity.

A spouse's earning capacity normally increases as he or she gains more experience. Are the professional degree cases different? If a professional degree is divisible property, would the earning capacity at divorce of all spouses be divisible property? Should a special remedy be created for the situation where a spouse's earning capacity increases during marriage due to education?

If a special remedy should be created when a spouse goes to graduate school, should it apply to all instances? Should it matter whether the spouse goes to day school or works and goes to night school? Should it make any difference if the living expenses and school expenses of the spouse going to school are paid by that spouse's parents or by the other spouse? Should an art history degree be treated differently from a law degree? What about a college degree?

Chapter Six

Presumptions, Tracing and Commingling

A. Presumptions

1. The General Community Presumption

Read Tex. Fam. Code § 3.003(a). Due to this rebuttable presumption, all property possessed by the spouses at divorce will be deemed community property unless some evidence is offered to rebut the presumption. (It does not have to be established that the property was acquired during marriage for the presumption to apply.) If a spouse can prove an item of property possessed at divorce was acquired before marriage, or acquired after marriage by gift or inheritance, the presumption is rebutted. Also, property acquired from a separate property source can be exchanged during marriage for another thing and not lose its status of separate property, as long as the property possessed at divorce can still be traced to the separate property source.

The tracing theory is aptly described in W. Brockelbank, *The Community Property Law of Idaho* 134 (1962):

> The doctrine may be explained or stated in a variety of ways. Where property is exchanged for other property or is sold and the proceeds of the sale are used to buy other property, the property bought is of the same character as that given in exchange or sold. Property acquired in an exchange partakes of the nature of the property given in exchange. These transactions may be thought of as merely changing the form of property and a change in form has no effect on the character, as community or separate, of the property. There may be many exchanges or sales and the proceeds used to buy other property, but the character of the property, as community or separate, will remain the same as the character of any title to which it can be traced. All along the line, property exchanged is classified in the same category as the property given in exchange and property bought is classified in the same category as the consideration given for it.

In order to rebut the presumption that all property possessed at divorce is community property, it must be established that property was acquired before marriage, or acquired after marriage by gift or inheritance. Note that it sometimes is not simple making the determination whether the mode of acquisition falls in one of these categories. For example, in *Shea*, Chapter 1, *supra*, the husband received education benefit payments during marriage, but the court determined that the benefits actually were earned prior to

165

marriage, so they really constituted property acquired prior to marriage. Similarly, it is not always clear whether property was really acquired by "inheritance" or "gift."

2. Rebutting the Community Presumption by Tracing

Andrews v. Andrews

Supreme Court of Washington, 1921
199 P. 981

BRIDGES, Justice.

A. D. Andrews brought this suit for the purpose of establishing and enforcing an alleged oral contract with his father, Joshua Andrews, to the effect that the latter would, by will or otherwise, at the time of his death, give to the plaintiff all property then owned by him. Upon a trial on the merits the lower court dismissed the action and the plaintiff has appealed.

The appellant alleges that it was orally agreed between Joshua Andrews and the appellant that the former should continue to live with the latter, and receive his care and attention for such length of time as Joshua should desire to live with him, in consideration of which Joshua orally agreed that at the time of his death he would will all his property to his son.

The first question we must discuss is whether the original contract was made. It is a well-settled principle of law that contracts of this character must be established by clear and convincing evidence. The appellant undertook to establish the existence of this contract by the testimony of his wife. At the trial the respondent [the second wife and widow of Joshua Andrews] objected to her testifying concerning any conversations on this subject had between Joshua Andrews and the appellant, for the reason that the appellant's wife was a party in interest.

The court has expressly held that if a like oral contract with the husband was concerning community property, or if the property sought to be acquired by the suit would be community property when acquired, then the wife is an interested party, and is forbidden by the statute to testify concerning the contract.

The whole question here, then, resolves itself into the proposition whether the property which the appellant sought to recover would have been, had he succeeded on recovering it, community property or his separate property. If it would have been community property, then the wife was a party in interest and could not testify, and the objection of the respondent should have been sustained.

We are convinced that the property sought to be acquired by this action would have been community property had it been acquired.

The main question is: Was the property sought to be obtained by this suit acquired by "gift, bequest, devise or descent" within the spirit of the statute?

We are satisfied that it would not have been so acquired. It would have been acquired by contract. There is no element of gift, bequest or devise involved in this case. Joshua Andrews, according to the alleged agreement, was to will his property to his son for a consideration, and that consideration was that the latter was to maintain and support him during the remainder of his life, or such portion thereof as he might elect to accept such maintenance and support. The testimony was that the services to be performed in payment of the property to be acquired were performed by the appellant and his wife. It was their community property which housed and sheltered Joshua Andrews; it was the community money of the appellant and his wife which furnished, and was to furnish, the table from which Mr. Andrews, Sr., was to eat. The testimony shows that the appellant's wife did the housework and cooked the food, and did the other usual duties in the maintenance of the home, and in the care and attention given to Mr. Andrews, Sr. Everything that went into his maintenance was the joint effort of the appellant and his wife. In no true sense was the appellant to acquire this property by gift. He was to acquire it by virtue of a contract which was to be performed on the one side by himself and his wife. Bouvier's Law Dictionary defines "gift" as: "A voluntary conveyance or transfer of property; that is, one not founded on the consideration of money or love. A voluntary, immediate, absolute transfer of property without consideration."

The "gift, bequest, devise or descent" contemplated by the statute as constituting separate property is not based upon contract or consideration, and property willed by one to another in compliance with a contract between the parties is not a gift or bequest in contemplation of the statute.

If the alleged contract had been made by the appellant with a stranger and not with his blood relation, then it would seem to us that every one must say that the property to be acquired under it would be community property, because we have always held that property acquired by the joint efforts of the husband and wife is presumed to be community property. The mere fact that it is alleged that the contract here was made with the appellant's father could not change the legal situation, and the legal effect must be the same as if the contract had been made with entire strangers.

Without the testimony of the appellant's wife, there is not sufficient evidence upon which to base any contract. While the self-sacrifice made by the appellant, and particularly by his wife, are to be highly commended, the rules of law forbid them any compensation.

The judgment must be affirmed.

_____

Estate of Clark

California Court of Appeals, 1928
271 P. 542

GRAIL, Justice.

[Two weeks before H, Major Clark, married W, his son by a prior marriage died. H was son's sole intestate heir, but son had executed a will leaving all his property to others. Son's devisee filed the will for probate in Oklahoma and California. In each case H filed a will contest. The lower court in Oklahoma held son's will void, but the California court held it valid. Pending appeals in both cases, H and son's devisee settled the dispute. H would dismiss his will contests and son's executor would convey to H a half interest in the properties son owned at death, including valuable Oklahoma oil rights. The Oklahoma probate court approved the settlement, finding that H's will contest was bona fide. That court then admitted son's will to probate, and later the executor conveyed the half interest in the oil rights to H while he was married to W. After H died, W claimed a half interest in the oil rights received by H on the theory they were community property. She appeals a denial of this claim.]

All property owned by the husband before marriage, and that acquired afterwards by gift, bequest, devise, or descent, with the rents, issues, and profits thereof, is his separate property.

The Supreme Court has construed the definitions of separate property to include "property taken in exchange for, or in the investment, or as the price of the property so originally owned or acquired."

In case the will was held to be invalid, Major Clark was the sole heir of his son, and his right to contest the will was cast upon him immediately upon the death of his son. He claimed that his son's will was not a valid will. In this contention he had been sustained by the county court of Noble County, Oklahoma. By way of compromise, however, he consented to the dismissal of his contest and to the admission of the will to probate. The terms of the compromise contemplated, however, that in consideration of withdrawing his contest, Major Clark should receive the half of his son's estate. It is this property and the profits thereof which are involved in his litigation. Had the will been rejected, he would have received all of his son's estate, and beyond doubt it would have been his separate property. The question is whether what he did receive is any the less his separate property because it came to him through the compromise that was effected. It would not be questioned that if, instead of acquiring a clear title to half of his son's estate by withdrawing his contest to the will, Major Clark had adopted the method of having the appeal dismissed and the will denied probate and then transferring to the legatees and devisees one-half of the property, this property would be his separate property.

The right of an heir to transfer his inheritance, even though there is a will or purported will in existence, is recognized by our courts. At the instant of his son's death Major Clark had a property right which he could assign or transfer or surrender for a consideration acceptable to him, and also the statutory right, which of itself is a property right, to contest his son's will. This right was a right vested in him prior to his marriage, and therefore was his separate property. The property involved in his litigation came to Major Clark in exchange or in payment for such property, and was likewise his separate property.

It is true that the property in litigation was acquired by Major Clark during the time he was married to appellant, but it was acquired by way of the compromise of a statutory right which was in itself property and which he owned prior to his marriage. Property acquired by compromise is separate property if the right compromised is separate. The right compromised is the consideration for property obtained by the compromise, and the principle is the same as where property is purchased with separate funds.

Judgment affirmed.

Hamilton v. Hamilton
Louisiana Court of Appeals, 1979
381 So. 2d 517

ELLIS, Justice.

This is a suit for partition of certain property held in common by Willard Hamilton and Suzanne Hamilton, who were married in 1973, legally separated in 1977, and subsequently divorced. At issue is the status of certain items which were shower gifts, received prior to the marriage.

Mrs. Hamilton claims them to be her separate property, because they were given to her at a miscellaneous shower given for her prior to the marriage. Mr. Hamilton claims that the gifts were made to both of the parties in contemplation of the marriage. There is no evidence in the record as to whether the donors intended the gifts to be for Mr. Hamilton, Mrs. Hamilton or both of them.

The items in question include eight dinner plates, one salad plate, one bread and butter plate, three cups and saucers and a vegetable bowl; two ice tea glasses and two water glasses; some monogrammed glasses; two silver trays; a ceramic soap dish; a cake and pie saver; a candle holder; wooden salt and pepper shakers; a coffee percolator; and some towels. The trial judge was of the opinion that these items were "obviously for the use of plaintiff and defendant jointly," and concluded that the parties owned them in common.

The validity of the manual donation is dependent on the intention of the donor to give and the delivery of the thing to the donee. The intention of the donor controls the identity of the donee or donees. The delivery may be made to the donee, or to one of them, if there be more than one, or even through a third party.

Although the gifts in this case were made at a shower given for the bride, Mrs. Hamilton, before the wedding, we find that the intent of the donors is the fact controlling the present ownership of the gifts. We agree with the trial judge that, absent any proof as to the intent of the donors, it must be presumed that gifts of the nature here involved, which would appear to be for use by both parties, are therefore jointly owned by them.

The judgment appealed from is therefore affirmed at the cost of defendant, Mrs. Hamilton.

Affirmed.

DISCUSSION

As *Hamilton* suggests, ownership of wedding gifts depends upon the intent of the donor. In Texas, if it is determined that the donor intended a gift to both parties, the gift is 50% separate property of each spouse, not community property. *See Roosth v. Roosth*, 889 S.W.2d 445 (Tex. App. — Houston [14th Dist.] 1994, writ denied). At divorce, unless the parties agreed to a division of the gifts, all would have to be sold and the proceeds equally divided.

Holby v. Holby
Arizona Court of Appeals, 1981
638 P.2d 1359

BIRDSALL, Justice.

The twenty-one year marriage of appellant husband and appellee wife was dissolved in the trial court. For the most part they agreed on the division of their community property.

On appeal the husband contends that the court committed error in [f]inding that certain stock was a gift to the wife and therefore her separate property.

Each Christmas for several years the wife's employer gave her shares of Proctor and Gamble stock. There were thirty-three shares in her name at the time of dissolution of the marriage. The stock certificates came with a cover letter stating they were gifts. Each year the appellee was given a choice of either cash or the stock and chose the stock. The trial court considered the stock to be gifts and therefore appellee's separate property. We disagree. The stock was clearly a remuneratory gift. The "gift" from employer to employee, even though made at Christmas and labeled a gift, was in consideration of services rendered.

The decree is modified to provide that the stock be divided equally between the parties. As so modified, it is affirmed.

_____

DISCUSSION

The above cases suggest that it is not always clear whether an acquisition is a "gift" or an "inheritance" for community property purposes. The inquiry must go beyond whether the transfer is referred to as a gift or whether the property was received as an inheritance.

In some instances it is unclear whether transfers within families were gifts. In *Williams v. Williams*, No. 2-08-033-CV, 2008 WL 5194227 (Tex. App.—Fort Worth Dec. 11, 2008, no pet.) (mem. op., not designated for publication), the court found it significant that a gift tax return was filed with the IRS before the marriage broke down.

3. Spousal Gift Presumption

The character of property normally is determined solely by tracing. However, acts of the spouses after acquisition of the property can change the character of the property. For example, one spouse may give the other spouse an interest in some or all of the one spouse's separate estate. If a spouse acquires property using separate funds, and yet record title includes the name of the other spouse, some courts have concluded that a presumption arises that the spouse intended to thereby make a gift to the other spouse. This presumption is rebuttable.

Johnson v. Johnson
Texas Court of Appeals—Texarkana, 1979
584 S.W.2d 307, no writ

RAY, Justice.

This is a divorce case. Stanley Joseph Johnson, appellee, and Adele Louise Johnson, appellant, both petitioned the court for a divorce and a division of the estate of the parties. The residence of the parties was declared to be the separate property of the husband and it is from that portion of the judgment that the wife has perfected her appeal.

Appellant-wife submits two points of error for our consideration and asserts that the trial court erred in failing to find that she owned an undivided one-half interest in the residence as her separate property. The trial court found that the residence was the separate property of the husband.

The pertinent facts in this case are that appellee-husband proposed marriage in May of 1973; that he came from Florida to Longview in search of a dwelling; that on July 7, 1973, he signed a contract to purchase a house in which he alone was named as the purchaser; that the parties were married on August 14, 1973; that on August 24, 1973, a deed was executed naming both husband and wife as grantees; that the husband paid the entire purchase price out of his separate funds; and, that suit for divorce was filed on May 16, 1978.

Appellant contends that a presumption of gift of an undivided one-half interest in the house and land arose when the husband paid for the property out of his separate funds but had her named along with himself as the grantees in the deed. Ordinarily, property acquired during marriage is characterized as community property. Tex. Family Code Ann. Sec. 5.01. There was a presumption that the property here involved was community, but that presumption was overcome when the parties stipulated that the house and land were paid for out of separate funds of the husband and that the contract to purchase the property was entered into prior to the marriage. However, because the deed named husband and wife as grantees, a second presumption arose, a presumption that the husband intended to give his wife an undivided one-half interest in the residence.

The question before the trial court was whether or not the evidence adduced at the trial was sufficient to overcome the presumption of a gift to the wife of an undivided one-half interest in the property. The question before this Court is whether there was sufficient evidence of probative value presented to the trial court on which it could resolve the fact question of gift *vel non*. The favorable facts supporting the trial court's judgment are that:

The inventory and appraisement filed by the wife pursuant to the order of the court shows that the wife did not claim an undivided one-half interest in the property as her separate property, but on the contrary, showed that she claimed no interest in real estate as her separate property; that the only interest claimed in the property in question was a community interest; that the wife testified in substance that the husband had never told her that he was making a gift to her of any interest in the property; that the wife assumed it was community property; that the husband had entered into a contract to purchase the property in which he alone was named as purchaser; that the husband had paid for the property solely out of his separate funds; that he was unfamiliar with Texas community property laws; that he did not instruct anyone to insert the name of his wife in the deed; that he did not see the deed or examine it before it was recorded; that the inventory filed by the husband listed the residence as his separate property; that the husband's testimony was that he never talked to his wife about giving her the property and she never talked to him about his having given her any interest in the property; that he purchased the property for himself; and, there was nothing else in writing other than the deed to indicate a gift. We have concluded that the totality of the evidence in this case together with the inferences to be drawn therefrom sustain the trial court's judgment. The evidence was sufficient to overcome the presumption of a gift, thus leaving a fact issue to be determined by the trial court, the trier of the facts in this case. The issue of whether or not there was a gift was highly disputed. We cannot say that the trial court was without sufficient evidence to conclude that the husband did not intend to make a gift to the wife of an undivided one-half interest in the real property. The trial court was in a better position to determine the credibility of the witnesses and the weight to be given their testimony and we see no reason to substitute our judgment for that of the trial court.

The judgment of the trial court is affirmed.

DISCUSSION

How much evidence should be required to rebut the presumption of gift that arises from title? What if a realtor or title company placed the name of both parties on the title documents and the spouse contributing separate property did not object? Is this sufficient to show no donative intent?

Some courts do not accept that a presumption of gift arises if a deed from a third party is made out to both spouses. *See Von Hutchins v. Pope*, 351 S.W.2d 642 (Tex. Civ. App. — Houston [14th Dist.] 1961, writ ref'd n.r.e.). The presumption of gift also arises if the conveyance is from one spouse to the other. *See Babb v. McGee*, 507 S.W.2d 821 (Tex. Civ. App. — Dallas 1974, writ ref'd n.r.e.).

One court has held that, due to Tex. Prob. Code § 438, a deposit of separate funds into a joint bank account remains the separate property of the spouse who contributed the funds. *Marriage of Case*, 28 S.W.3d 154 (Tex. App. — Texarkana 2000, no writ).

4. Presumptions That Cannot Be Rebutted

The presumptions mentioned above are rebuttable presumptions. There is one important presumption for marital property rights purposes that is not rebuttable. When there is a "significant recital," the presumption arising from title is not rebuttable. A significant recital is used to clarify the status of property as separate property. If the title document states that the property is the separate property of one spouse, and the other spouse "participated" in the transaction, this title creates a presumption that cannot be rebutted that the property is the separate property of the record owner. Many cases have discussed what constitutes participation for purposes of this presumption, and no firm rule has resulted. The basic requirement, however, is that the other spouse has seen the title designation and not objected. Indeed, a careful lawyer representing a spouse purchasing property during marriage with separate property should ask the other spouse to sign a document that expressly approves the recital contained in the title document that the property is the purchaser's separate property.

B. Commingling

1. In General

At dissolution of the marriage, separate property can be established only if the acquiring spouse can trace the property to a separate property source. This becomes quite complicated if community and separate property are mixed. This commonly occurs in bank accounts.

It is important to keep in mind that commingling separate and community funds does not itself transmute separate funds to community. As stated in *Stahl v. Stahl*, 97 Idaho 794, 430 P.2d 685 (1967):

> It appears to be plaintiff's contention that if a dollar which is separate property is deposited in a bank account in which there is a dollar which is community property, the dollar which was separate property becomes community property; and if a dollar which is community property is deposited in a bank account in which there is a dollar which is separate property, the latter dollar becomes community property; and that, in either case, all property purchased with the deposited funds is community property. That is not the law. Where separate and community funds are so commingled that it is impossible to trace the source of the funds, the whole will be treated as community property. The presumption that

property acquired during marriage is community is controlling only when it is impossible to trace the source of the specific property.

As *Stahl* suggests, a separate property bank account does not become community property merely because community property is deposited. This result is consistent with common sense. For example, imagine that a person has $100 in a bank account when he marries. If $10 of community property is added to the account, and the balance is now $110, what is in the account? It is clear that the account contains $100 separate property, and $10 community. The game becomes less simple, however, if the spouse makes a withdrawal. Assume that the spouse withdraws $10, and the balance is $100. What was withdrawn?

There are two basic types of bank account disputes. One type involves a dispute regarding the character of a withdrawal. In such disputes, money was withdrawn from a commingled account during marriage and invested; at dissolution, the character of the investment is at issue. The other type of dispute involves the amount remaining in the account at divorce; withdrawals during marriage presumably were dissipated. The cases below involve both types of disputes.

See v. See

Supreme Court of California, 1966
415 P.2d 776

TRAYNOR, Chief Justice.

Plaintiff Laurance A. See and cross-complainant Elizabeth Lee See appeal from an interlocutory judgment that grants each a divorce. Elizabeth attacks the finding that there was no community property at the time of the divorce.

The parties were married on October 17, 1941, and they separated about May 10, 1962. Throughout the marriage they were residents of California, and Laurance was employed by a family-controlled corporation, See's Candies, Inc. For most of that period he also served as president of its wholly-owned subsidiary, See's Candy Shops, Inc. In the twenty-one years of the marriage he received more than $1,000,000 in salaries from the two corporations.

Laurance had a personal account on the books of See's Candies, Inc., denominated Account 13. Throughout the marriage his annual salary from See's Candies, Inc., which was $60,000 at the time of the divorce, was credited to this account and many family expenses were paid by checks drawn on it. To maintain a credit balance in Account 13, Laurance from time to time transferred funds to it from an account at the Security First National Bank, hereafter called the Security Account.

The funds deposited in the Security Account came primarily from Laurance's separate property. On occasion he deposited his annual $15,000 salary from See's Candy Shops, Inc. in that account as a "reserve against taxes" on that salary. Thus there was a commingling of community property and separate property in both the Security Account and Account 13. Funds from the Security Account were sometimes used to pay community expenses and also to purchase some of the assets held in Laurance's name at the time of the divorce proceedings.

Over Elizabeth's objection, the trial court followed a theory advanced by Laurance that a proven excess of community expenses over community income during the marriage establishes that there has been no acquisition of property with community funds.

Such a theory, without support in either statutory or case law in this state, would disrupt the California community property system. It would transform a wife's interest in the community property from a "present, existing and equal interest" into an inchoate expectancy to be realized only if upon termination of the marriage the community income fortuitously exceeded community expenditures. It would engender uncertainties as to testamentary and *inter vivos* dispositions, income, estate and gift taxation, and claims against property.

Property acquired by purchase during a marriage is presumed to be community property, and the burden is on the spouse asserting its separate character to overcome the presumption. The presumption applies when a husband purchases property during the marriage with funds from an undisclosed or disputed source, such as an account or fund in which he has commingled his separate funds with community funds. He may trace the source of the property to his separate funds and overcome the presumption with evidence that community expenses exceeded community income at the time of acquisition. If he proves that at that time all community income was exhausted by family expenses, he establishes that the property was purchased with separate funds. Only when, through no fault of the husband, it is not possible to ascertain the balance of income and expenditures at the time property was acquired, can recapitulation for the total community expenses and income throughout the marriage be used to establish the character of the property.

A husband who commingles the property of the community with his separate property, but fails to keep adequate records cannot invoke the burden of record keeping as a justification for a recapitulation of income and expenses at the termination of the marriage that disregards any acquisition that may have been made during the marriage with community funds. If funds used for acquisitions during marriage cannot otherwise be traced to their source and the husband who has commingled property is unable to establish that there was a deficit in the community accounts when the assets were purchased, the presumption controls that property acquired by purchase during marriage is community property. The husband may protect his separate property by not commingling community and separate assets and income. Once he commingles, he assumes the burden of keeping records adequate to establish the balance of community income and expenditures at the time an asset is acquired with commingled property.

The trial court also followed the theory that a husband who expends his separate property for community expenses is entitled to reimbursement from community assets. This theory likewise lacks support in the statutory or case law of this state. A husband is required to support his wife and family. Indeed, husband and wife assume mutual obligations of support upon marriage. These obligations are not conditioned on the existence of community property or income. The duty to support requires the use of separate property of the parties when there is no community property. There is no right to reimbursement under the statutes.

Plaintiff has not met his burden of proving an excess of community expenses over community income at the times the other assets purchased during the marriage were acquired. The part of the judgment finding them to be his separate property is therefore reversed. Since the property issues were tried on the theory that the nature of the property could be determined by proving total community income and expenditures and since the parties may have additional evidence that would otherwise have been presented, plaintiff's failure to overcome the presumption that the assets are community property is not conclusive. We therefore remand the case for retrial of the property issues.

DISCUSSION

See sets forth the basic rule that if separate and community funds are mixed in a bank account, many withdrawals are made, and the character of the withdrawals cannot be determined, the account will be deemed all community property. This is sometimes referred to as the "strict tracing" approach.

In *See*, the court refers to the family expense doctrine. This doctrine creates a presumption that "family living expenses" will be deemed paid with community funds. This doctrine stems from the reasonable view that the community estate should be held responsible for family expenses incurred during marriage. The California court concluded that this did not mean that the spouse merely had to establish that the family living expenses throughout the marriage exceeded community income; the court required the spouse to establish *at the time each item was purchased* that family expenses during the marriage exceeded the aggregate amount of community income up to that time.

The husband's argument rejected in *See* has been referred to as the "total recapitulation approach." Is it reasonable? Would it matter if it could also be shown that family living expenses exceeded family income every month the parties were married? See *Coggin v. Coggin*, 204 S.W.2d 47 (Tex. Civ. App. — Amarillo 1947, no writ)(yes).

Assume the spouses' living expenses during year #1 of marriage exceed their income by $5,000. In year #2, assume the income exceeds expenses by $5,000. Should there by any community property after year #2?

McKinley v. McKinley
Supreme Court of Texas, 1973
496 S.W.2d 540

DENTON, Justice.

Flora and Royal McKinley were married on January 15, 1965. Prior to the marriage Royal opened two savings accounts which were the source of funds used to purchase the certificates which are the subject of this suit. Immediately prior to the marriage one account was in the amount of $9,570.27 in the Dallas Federal Savings and Loan. Between January 15, 1965, and Royal's death on October 15, 1970, numerous deposits and withdrawals were made in both accounts, and on January 2, 1968, withdrawals from both accounts were used to purchase the savings certificates which are the property in contention in this appeal.

The trial court made findings of fact, that, *inter alia*, the sources of the money to purchase said savings certificates were the joint checking account and/or joint savings accounts; that no evidence of probative value was offered as to the nature of any of the transactions in regard to the two joint savings accounts; and that the deceased commingled all funds held by him in joint savings and checking accounts. The court then concluded that the said certificates heretofore mentioned in the total sum of $26,400 were the community property of the parties to the marriage and not the separate property of Royal C. McKinley.

The court of civil appeals held that the separate funds of Royal McKinley lost their identity because of the many transactions which commingled the funds in the name of both of them and the certificates became community property.

Petitioner contends that there is no evidence to support the trial court's finding that the total amount of the two savings certificates was community property, and that the court of civil appeals erred in holding that the trial court's conclusion of law was correct.

There are two savings certificates involved here: One in the amount of $10,400, and the other in the amount of $16,000. The $10,400 certificate was purchased from the First Federal Savings & Loan Association with funds which were in a savings account in that same institution. Similarly, the $16,000 certificate was purchased from the Dallas Federal Savings & Loan Association with funds which came primarily from monies in a savings account with Dallas Federal Savings & Loan. For ease of discussion the certificates will be discussed separately and will be referred to by the name of the respective savings and loan association, or by the value of the certificate.

In late 1964, Royal McKinley had $9,500 on deposit in a First Federal Savings & Loan savings account. It is uncontroverted that this $9,500 was Royal's separate property. By December 31, 1965, the interest earned by this account was $472.03, and on January 5, 1966, $472.03 was withdrawn. The $9,500 originally deposited remained in the account and continued to earn interest until, on December 31, 1967, the account balance was $10,453.81. From January 5, 1966, to December 31, 1967, no withdrawals were made from this account, and all deposits are shown on the account statement to have been "dividends." On January 2, 1968, $10,400 was withdrawn from the savings account and, on the same date, was used to purchase First Federal Savings & Loan savings certificate No. 101046 in the amount of $10,400. The First Federal certificate remained on account and untouched until Royal's death on October 15, 1970.

In *Tarver v. Tarver*, 394 S.W.2d 780 (Tex. 1965), this Court reiterated the basic presumption that all property possessed by a husband and wife when their marriage is dissolved is their community property. At the time *Tarver* was decided the presumption was created by article 4619, Sec. 1, Vernon's Texas Civil Statutes, and the presumption remains by the clear language of Section 5.02 of the Family Code, V.T.C.A.: "Property possessed by either spouse during or on dissolution of marriage is presumed to be community property." It is the general rule that to discharge the burden imposed by the statute a spouse, or one claiming through a spouse, must trace and clearly identify property claimed as separate property. It is further well settled that when the evidence shows that separate and community property have been so commingled as to defy resegregation and identification, the burden is not discharged and the statutory presumption prevails. *Tarver v. Tarver, supra.*

In applying these principles to the $10,400 savings certificate, it seems clear that the $9,500 originally on deposit with the First Federal Savings & Loan was traced in its entirety into savings certificate No. 101046, and that $9,500 of that certificate was clearly identified as separate property. We therefore hold that $9,500 of savings certificate No. 101046 in the face amount of $10,400 is separate property.

With respect to the $16,000 savings certificate purchased from the Dallas Federal Savings & Loan Association, the tracing problem is a bit more difficult. It might be helpful to mention at the outset that the $16,000 certificate came into existence with the consolidation of three smaller certificates in the amounts of $10,000, $4,000 and $2,000. The sources of the funds used to purchase the $4,000 and the $2,000 certificates are known. The $4,000 came from a savings account opened in 1969 by Flora and Royal McKinley as joint tenants with right of survivorship; and the $2,000 came from a joint checking account. There can be no dispute that these monies were community funds. Our concern then is with the $10,000 which ultimately found its way into the $16,000 certificate.

In November 1964, savings account No. 61152, was opened by Royal McKinley with the Dallas Federal Savings & Loan Association, and on December 31, 1964, this account had a balance of $9,570.27. It is undisputed that this sum was Royal's separate property.

Between January 15, 1965, the date of Royal and Flora's marriage, and January 2, 1968, the date the $10,000 in question was withdrawn to purchase savings certificate No. 106146, numerous deposits and withdrawals were made. Of $7,740.34 deposited during this period, $1,140.34 came from dividends earned by the account. The source of the remaining $6,600 deposited in this account is not known. Two withdrawals were made during this period: The first on January 5, 1966 was in an amount equal to the total of the dividends earned to that date ($437.99), and the second, on March 30, 1966, in the amount of $4,985.91. The January 2, 1968 withdrawal of $10,000, used to purchase the certificate, left a balance of $1,886.71 in the account.

With respect to the $16,000 savings certificate, petitioner made no attempt to trace any of the separate funds in the Dallas Federal Savings account, or to identify any amount claimed to be the separate property of Royal McKinley. The only evidence with regard to these monies is the account sheet from Dallas Federal Savings & Loan and it is wholly inconclusive as to the nature of funds deposited or withdrawn. To come to any conclusion about the property status of the $16,000 certificate would require surmise and speculation. The burden to overcome the statutory presumption was on Keith McKinley, and we cannot say that he has sustained that burden. We therefore hold that the Dallas Federal Savings & Loan certificate is community property.

The judgments below are reversed; the cause is remanded to the trial court for entry of judgment in accordance with this opinion.

DISCUSSION

Interest earned during marriage in a separate property account is community property. How did the *McKinley* court determine that a portion of one certificate was traced, but a portion of the other was not? Does the court make any assumptions about withdrawals made during marriage from the two commingled accounts? Are these assumptions consistent?

McKinley accepts the "identical sum inference." The court infers from the withdrawal of an unusual amount from a commingled account that it was a withdrawal of community property interest, when the withdrawal was made soon after the interest was posted, and the withdrawal was in an amount exactly equal to the interest. Courts have also applied this concept when the withdrawal and deposit amounts do not exactly correspond. For example, in *Estate of Hanau*, 730 S.W.2d 663 (Tex. 1987) the husband sold separate property stock (City Investing) for $6,021, and the proceeds were deposited in his brokerage account. This account apparently was commingled. (The parties stipulated that "transactions in the husband's account were from his income.") On the same day the City Investing stock was sold, the husband purchased, through his brokerage account, Trans World stock for $6,170. The Supreme Court concluded that, because the purchase of the Trans World stock occurred on the same day as the sale of the City Investing stock, and no other transactions occurred on that day, this showed that the Trans World stock was separate property.

Snider v. Snider
Texas Court of Appeals—Dallas, 1981
613 S.W.2d 8, no writ

CARVER, Justice.

[In a probate dispute, the trial court found that the decedent's bank account at the Mercantile Bank was all community property. The executors appealed.]

The executors also urge that the trial court erred in holding that the deceased husband's savings account in the Mercantile Bank (which pre-existed the marriage) was found by the trial court to belong to the community estate because of subsequent deposits and withdrawals by the community. On the date of the marriage, the balance in the account was $27,642.45. Upon dissolution of the community by the husband's death, the balance was $35,809.80. The account grew by interest from time to time, as well as by new deposits, and was reduced by withdrawals from time to time. The witness Wofford testified that an additional deposit of $10,000.00 of separate funds of the husband was made after the marriage and that the remaining deposits, as well as withdrawals, were made by the community. The passbook for this account was introduced into evidence and supports the separate character and balance of the account on the date of marriage. Between the marriage on October 3, 1972, and October 20, 1972, no interest was earned and no deposits were made, but withdrawals reduced the balance to $19,642.45. Between October 20, 1972, and April 23, 1973, there were entries of earned interest, deposits of unknown character, and withdrawals, but the balance was never below $19,642.45. On April 23, 1973, a separate property deposit of $10,000.00 was made and the identifiable separate property interest in the account became $19,642.45 plus $10,000.00 or $29,642.45. Subsequent interest earned, deposits, and withdrawals to the date of the husband's death never reduced the account balance to or below $29,642.45. We hold that this record traces and identifies the husband's separate interest in the Mercantile savings account to the extent of $29,642.45 with the remainder of the account being deemed community for want of tracing or identity. *See McKinley v. McKinley*, 496 S.W.2d 540 (Tex. 1973); *Schmidt v. Huppmann*, 73 Tex. 112, 11 S.W. 175 (1889); *Peterson v. Peterson*, 595 S.W.2d 889 (Tex. Civ. App.—Austin 1980, no writ); *Harris v. Ventura*, 582 S.W.2d 853 (Tex. Civ. App.—Beaumont 1979, no writ); *Sibley v. Sibley*, 286 S.W.2d 657 (Tex. Civ. App.—Dallas 1955, writ dism'd).

DISCUSSION

Why is it important, where there were many deposits and withdrawals, that the balance never was lower than $29,642.45? How does this establish that the separate funds are still there? Do you see why the community out first tracing method is sometimes called the lowest intermediate balance approach?

The "community out first rule" is sometimes used when the dispute pertains to the character of funds remaining in a commingled account. Under this view, if separate and community funds have been mixed in an account, any withdrawals during marriage are deemed community property until all community deposits have been offset. *See Welder v. Welder*, 794 S.W.2d 420 (Tex. App.—Corpus Christi 1990, no writ). In other words, this view assumes that all withdrawals during marriage are used to pay for family living expenses. This is generally quite sensible, unless either spouse has separate property investments for which payments are being made.

A few courts have applied community out first to a situation to determine the character of property bought with a withdrawal from a commingled account. *See Scott v. Scott*, 973 S.W.2d 694 (Tex. App.—El Paso 1998, no pet.).

The "strict tracing" line of cases do not apply the community out first rule. In order to establish that withdrawals during marriage were community property, the spouse must establish that each withdrawal was used to pay a family living expense. If this cannot be done, the withdrawal normally is presumed to have been separate property when the dispute pertains to funds remaining in the account.

What approach yields the most sensible result?

The commingling issue most commonly is presented in connection with a dispute over funds remaining in an account. Withdrawals made during marriage have been dissipated and are untraceable. However, in *McKinley* the dispute pertained to the character of the funds withdrawn from the commingled account to purchase the certificates of deposit. The remaining amount in the account presumably was dissipated. What presumption should apply to the character of the withdrawal in this situation?

Issues pertaining to commingling are discussed by Stewart Gagnon and others in Chapter M of the 1988 Advanced Family Law Materials, prepared by the Texas Bar.

All courts are not enthusiastic about the community out first rule. For example, in *Smith v. Smith*, 22 S.W.3d 140 (Tex. App.—Houston [14th Dist.] 2000, no pet.) the court said this in note 5:

> "We also note that a blind application of the community-out-first presumption does not uphold the policy reason for the presumption's original application. In *Sibley v. Sibley*, 286 S.W.2d 657, 659 (Tex. Civ. App.—Dallas 1955, writ dism'd w.o.j.), the court said that the spouse expending funds was in relationship to the funds as a trustee in relationship to a trust. In *Sibley*, the question involved the husband's spending funds from an account in which community funds had been commingled with the wife's separate funds. The application of the community-out-first presumption thus preserved the wife's separate estate. Here, however, application of the community out first rule leads to the husband's preserving his separate estate at the expense of the community. Were we to view the husband as a trustee acting in the best interest of the beneficiary, we would apply not the community-out-first presumption, but a separate-out-first presumption. We would presume the husband spent his own funds before spending the community funds thus leaving community funds in the account for possible disbursement to the beneficiary—the wife—upon dissolution of the marriage. The husband would have the burden of rebutting the separate-out-first presumption. We apply the community-out-first presumption because it seems to be established law."

2. Equitable Limits to Commingling

As a general rule, if community and separate funds are mixed, and the separate funds cannot be traced, the whole fund is considered community property. In some instances, however, this result is so contrary to common sense that courts apply some limits to the commingling rule.

Horlock v. Horlock

Texas Court of Appeals—Houston [14th Dist.], 1975
533 S.W.2d 52, writ dism'd

COULSON, Justice.

THE RIGHT OF THE HUSBAND'S SEPARATE ESTATE TO
REIMBURSEMENT FROM THE COMMUNITY ESTATE

As a part of the findings of fact, the trial court found that at the time of the marriage the appellee owned properties having a net value of approximately $1,000,000. Subsequent to the marriage the appellee sold separate property real estate for approximately $700,000. The appellee also received payments in excess of $200,000 under certain contracts which had been entered into prior to the marriage and which the appellee had already performed. The total value of the separate property sold and collected subsequent to the marriage was $921,000. The appellee, in his role as manager of his separate estate and the parties' community estate, placed the proceeds of these sales into an investment account at the First City National Bank of Houston. The account existed prior to marriage and had been in use by the appellee, who was engaged in the real estate business. He had become established as a successful businessman in various phases of the building and apartment businesses, including construction, ownership and management.

The appellee commingled the proceeds of the sale of his separate property with the community property of the parties. The appellee admitted at trial and admits in his brief that the proceeds of the sale of his separate property have become completely commingled with the community estate. Appellee made no attempt at trial to trace the use of the proceeds of the sale of his separate property into any other transactions. The trial court determined in its conclusions of law that the appellee was entitled to reimbursement by reason of using his separate funds to enhance, improve and increase the value of the community estate. The trial court did not determine the amount of such reimbursement; however, the court did find as a fact that during the marriage specific properties owned by the appellee prior to the marriage were sold for a total sum in excess of $900,000, which was placed in the investment account at First City National Bank of Houston and thereafter used for the enhancement of the community estate.

It is the appellant's position that the appellee is not entitled to reimbursement to his separate estate. The appellant further contends that, although the appellee may have utilized the proceeds of the sale of his separate property for the benefit of the community estate, the appellee allowed his separate property to become completely commingled with the community estate to a point at which segregation of the two estates is impossible. Appellant argues that the application of the doctrine of reimbursement is precluded by Texas Family Code Annotated Sec. 5.02, which states: "Property possessed by either spouse during or on dissolution of marriage is presumed to be community property."

The appellant contends that neither of the two recognized methods of escaping the effect of the presumption of community property, tracing or reimbursement, is applicable in this case. Here, tracing is impossible. Appellant contends that the appellee is also unable to rely upon reimbursement because the appellee cannot show that the specific use to which the proceeds of the sales of his separate property were put benefited the community. Appellant argues that the appellee cannot rely on the gross assumption that the $921,000 was used to benefit the community, in the absence of some direct evidence of how those funds were spent. It is the appellant's position that at the dissolution of a marriage, a spouse must trace and clearly identify separate property in order to discharge the burden of satisfactorily proving that such property is not community property.

Since the latter 1940s, courts in Texas have acted favorable toward allowing reimbursement and in allowing the tracing of separate funds. For example, in *Hartman v. Hartman*, 253 S.W.2d 480 (Tex. Civ. App.—Austin 1952, no writ), the husband was awarded reimbursement of $30,000 as compensation for the investment of his separate estate in the community business. The husband had entered into the marriage owning separate property valued at $37,794. He was engaged in the construction business and operated out of a single investment banking account. The evidence in *Hartman* showed that during the course of the marriage more than $200,000 passed through the bank account. The facts did not lend themselves to tracing, but the trial court did award reimbursement. See also *Schmidt v. Huppman*, 73 Tex. 112, 11 S.W. 175 (1889); *Farrow v. Farrow*, 238 S.W.2d 255 (Tex. Civ. App.—Austin 1951, no writ). For examples of a more liberal treatment of the tracing doctrine, see *Blumer v. Kallison*, 297 S.W.2d 898 (Tex. Civ. App.—San Antonio 1956, writ ref'd n.r.e.); *Barrington v. Barrington*, 290 S.W.2d 297 (Tex. Civ. App.—Texarkana 1956, no writ). Another development in this area is exemplified by the case of *Sibley v. Sibley*, 286 S.W.2d 657 (Tex. Civ. App.—Dallas 1955, writ dism'd). *Sibley* stands for the proposition that where a bank account contains both community and separate monies, it is presumed that community monies are drawn out first.

Under these cases, the trial court was justified in awarding the husband a separate estate reimbursement. The husband's separate estate served as a strong foundation upon which the community's wealth was built. Throughout the marriage the husband utilized that foundation to provide for the appellant and to establish the $3,000,000 to $4,000,000 estate. Equity is well served by reimbursing him for that initial investment. In this case there is no question of fraud against the wife's estate, against the community, or against any third party creditor. One of these factors could shift the equities involved and preclude the appellee's recovery of reimbursement.

DISCUSSION

Why was the commingled fund not deemed all community property? What is the holding of *Horlock*? Does it apply to all divorces? Does it essentially abandon the commingling rule?

No case since *Horlock* has granted a similar remedy when substantial amounts have been commingled. This suggests *Horlock* is outside the mainstream of Texas family law.

Duncan v. United States

United States Court of Appeals
Fifth Circuit, 1957
247 F.2d 845

BROWN, Justice.

The problem here is whether the following items in the Estate of Dr. Duncan:

Item I.	16 stocks purchased principally through the Hutton & Co. account	$73,268.54
Item II.	Credit Balance Hutton & Co. account	1,783.97
Item III.	State National Bank, El Paso, balance account in name of E.A. Duncan	6,636.33
		$81,688.84

should be treated as the separate property of the decedent or as community property of decedent and his surviving widow. The Commissioner determined that each was separate property. In the Estate's suit for refund, 28 U.S.C.A. Section 1346(a)(1), the Court without a jury on formal findings and conclusions, upheld the Government's contention of separate property.

As the nature of the property interest of the decedent, separate or community, under Texas law determines the impact of the federal estate tax, the controversy rages around the immemorial statutes and considerable body of Texas law which, without a doubt, favors the community and puts on one asserting a contention of separate property in husband or wife a heavy burden.

The Estate's case was simply made. And, with a candid forthrightness, it insists that to the extent the record does not, or cannot, indicate the facts as to the origin of the money which produced Items I, II and III, the presumption operates to make it all community even though, without contradiction and established as an absolute fact, community income during the three years (1947, 1948, 1949) of this short three-year marriage available for investment was only $16,737.19.[1] The result would be that, with neither showing nor purpose of showing circumstances from which gifts of the husband's separate property to the community could be inferred, the application of the presumption not only turns the sow's ear into a silk purse, but by alchemist's wizardry, fills it with gold by making the maximum of all community funds $16,737.19 turn into $81,688.84.

The situation, of course, does call for the initial application of the presumption at least insofar as the stocks in Item I, the balance in Item II is due wholly or partly to payments made through the bank account (Item III). Dr. Duncan had several bank accounts, but it is undisputed that the Item III account was used for the deposit of all professional and personal income and earnings received by him whether of or from his separate estate or the community. It is equally admitted that expenditures for living and household expense were paid out of this account by periodic checks drawn on it and deposited to Mrs. Duncan's checking account in another bank. And, of great importance here, all deposits of cash in the Hutton account were made by checks drawn on this account, Item III.

The act of mixing or commingling separate and community property may have a substantial effect upon the resulting property. For, "It is a well established rule ... that where the husband or wife permits his or her separate property to become so commingled with community property that it cannot be identified, the separate property so commingled becomes community property...." This is particularly true for commingled bank accounts since, "Generally speaking, it is the law that a bank account consisting of separate and

---

1. For the short year 1946, disregarding altogether gains from the sale of his premarriage property, the net income for dividends, interest, professional income was $3,588.62. After deducting contributions, state and federal income taxes actually paid totaling $2,349.88, only $1,193.74 was available. The presumption would neither permit nor require a holding that *all* was earned in the last two months during marriage. The Government's estimate of 1/6 ($598.10) for this purpose is conservative, although later on, for apportionment, we include the whole ($1,193.74).

The maximum total available was:

1946	$598.10
1947	4,137.32
1948	6,024.26
1949	5,977.51
	$16,737.19

This assumes that all of the income available for spending was used to accumulate Items I, II and III since the amount of living and household expenses disbursed by the wife from funds drawn out of the State National Bank account (Item III) were not established in amount.

community funds commingled in such a manner that neither can be distinguished from the other must be regarded as a community account."

The presumption, while strong, is yet a disputable one and subject to being rebutted if adequate proof is made. This recognized in reverse fashion for unless there is satisfactory proof "as to how much separate and how much community funds were used in the purchase of a stock ... it cannot be determined [there is] ... any separate interest in them whatever...." *Smith v. Bailey*, 66 Tex. 553, 554, 1 S.W. 627, 628 (1886); *Hardee v. Vincent*, 136 Tex. 99, 147 S.W.2d 1072, 1074 (1941). "Applying these principles to the present case, we think the plaintiffs below should have shown, with greater certainty, how much of the proceeds of her original stock was used in the purchase of the goods levied on. She should further have more clearly shown how much of these proceeds were her separate property, and how much were profits, or community estate of herself and her husband." *Epperson v. Jones*, 65 Tex. 425, 429.

Where, as in *Phillips v. Vitemb*, 235 F.2d 11 (5th Cir. 1956), there was no showing of a maximum community fund beyond which, in fact, no community estate could exist, the acts of deposits and partial withdrawals were treated as a commingling and the withdrawals as presumptively community. But it was not there held or stated that the presumptive community character of withdrawals would continue when on satisfactory proof, it was demonstrated positively that there were absolutely no community funds, or proceeds, or income from which the so-called presumptive community interest could come.

And that is what was done here in several ways. First, the income tax returns of decedent, and for the years during marriage, his wife, as well, showed all of his and their earnings and receipts. And in the analysis which we make all of this is treated as belonging to the community. And this, even though a part of it was demonstrated on the face of the returns and other papers to be gains from proceeds of the sale of his premarital stocks, and there was no deduction for admittedly living expenses paid out of this fund and account and which are presumptively community disbursements. There was thus no other source whatever from which the "presumed" community contributions could come. The total of these could not possibly have exceeded $16,737.19.

And with the proof establishing to a positive certainty the maximum community funds, there was equally overwhelming proof leaving nothing to surmise or speculation that the husband had substantial separate means which had been, were, and had to be used in these stock acquisitions.

[The court here describes over $130,000 in separate assets, including inheritances from H's first wife and mother, which, the court felt, had to have been the source of most of the assets H possessed at death.]

When facts demonstrate positively and conclusively that on the assumption that every cent of community funds was invested, it was but a fraction of the cost of the property thus acquired, the presumption no longer has any basis in fact, and indeed, flying in the face of the facts, it is overcome. This is far different from the uncertain situations where the mere circumstance of the marriage of a wealthy husband and an impecunious wife followed by a general declining fortune after marriage has been held insufficient, in that form, to overcome the presumption. For here, naught is left to speculation. If the very last penny of all possible community funds is accounted for and falls woefully short of being sufficient to pay for the property of the same kind in which the husband has been trading extensively prior to marriage and which is actually used as the substantial part of the purchase price of the newly acquired property, the presumption, in the face of that absolute showing, must fall. When it is demonstrated that it could not possibly (apart from contemporaneous gifts) have come from the community and, on the other hand, it is equally established that ample separate means were available and specifically employed, the "how much" requirement has been adequately met.

But we do not think that this conclusion supports the full action which the District Court took in holding in effect that since all could not be presumed community, all must be considered to be the opposite— *i.e.*, separate. Consequently, to the maximum extent that community property was available for purchase, or the accumulation of property in question, it will take on that character, *i.e.*, community, unless it can be shown with the positiveness indicated that it was the separate means of a spouse which was used.

When this is applied, we do not find evidence which demonstrates this with the certainty demanded under Texas law. The effect of this may be illustrated by several transactions and deposits of cash in the Hutton account. In February, 1947, a deposit from the State National Bank account was made for $500. On familiar principles, this $500 was presumably community. Part of that went into the purchase of a stock which was treated by the Estate as separate, but at least $234.32 remained. This $234.32 went into the purchase price ($3,584.68) for the first of the Item I stock for 200 shares of Adams Express. As to this stock, the minimum community ownership would be 234/3584.

More graphic is the purchase October 21, 1947, of Groups Security Investment stock for $5,000.38. Just before this purchase, the credit balance from trading in decedent's premarriage separate property stocks (and the one deposit of $500 in cash) was $1,449.91. A deposit from the commingled bank account was made for $5,000. It was never shown what the bank balance was at the time of marriage or any other time except at the time of death (Item III $6,636.33, *supra*). But without more and positive facts, it is impossible as to this deposit or the stocks substantially purchased with it, to say that neither it nor any part of it was community.[2]

Again with a credit balance of zero as of January 1, 1948, which continued down to the time of the first purchases made May 28, 1948, for part of Adams Express and General American Investors totaling $8,105.59, a contemporaneous deposit for $8,106.94 was made. At least to the extent of that year's maximum community funds ($6,024.26, note 1, *supra*), the deposit from the commingled account was community unless, as cannot be done without the detail as to the gyrations of that bank account, the separate character of all or specific parts of that was established. Consequently, to that extent, at least, it is impossible to say that these stocks paid for by presumably community funds were not community.

In 1949, apparently because the credit balance on several of Hutton's monthly statements showed conflicting balances (*e.g.*, $12,813.12 and $4,739.06; $12,456.87 and $3,969.95; $11,714.46 and $3,969.95), a deposit of $5,000 was made March 14, 1949. There was an actual credit balance then of $12,813.12 produced almost wholly by the sale in February of specific premarriage separate stocks. With the deposit, the total credit balance was then $17, 813.12 which was used in March and April to purchase Keystone Selected Industries, and part of Television Fund at a total cost of $7,241.58. Since there is

---

2. Assuming all of 1947 community funds were then available, one would be:
1945 maximum community funds $4,137.32
Less presumed used on first purchase   234.32
Available for deposit Oct. 21, 1947   3,903.00
Community fraction would be: 3903/5000 of $5,000.38

no evidence except these figures, it is impossible to say that the presumptive community deposit of $5,000 was not used in the purchase of these stocks at least to the proportionate extent of the deposit (5000/17813 of $7,241.58) if not to the full extent of the deposit (5000/7241). The next deposit in 1949 was for $6,000 August 2, which then made the actual credit balance approximately $17,714.46 which was to purchase General Motors for $6,221.09. At least to the extent of any remaining balance of "unused" community funds (maximum $5,977.51, note 1 *supra*), there is no way of demonstrating that such community funds did not go into the stock to give it, partially anyway, a community character.

As in these illustrations it is impossible to tell that the presumptive community deposits were not used, partially at least, for the payment of the purchase price of specific stocks, by the same token, it is impossible to state that, to the maximum extent of community funds, they did not go ratably into the purchase of all of these stocks. As this neither is nor can now be demonstrated, it does not overcome the presumption which the law affords to the community that, to this full extent, all was proportionately community property.

With this approach, it is proper then for us to determine the community interest by applying the maximum community means to the whole of decedent's assets. The proportionate interest will then be the ratio that the maximum, $17,332.83,[3] bears to the sum of the cost of stocks in Item I plus Items II and III.

DISCUSSION

The total amount of community property income during the marriage was less than $17,000. Why did that not establish the maximum community claim?

3. Tracing Livestock and Inventory

Texas cases have applied different approaches to tracing livestock and inventory. When a spouse has had a proprietorship business throughout the marriage, courts have treated inventory in existence at dissolution as a mutation of inventory that existed at the time of the marriage. *Schecter v. Schecter*, 579 S.W.2d 502 (Tex. Civ. App.—Dallas 1978, no writ). In contrast, all livestock in existence at the time of dissolution is presumptively community property, unless it can be shown that the livestock was born before the marriage. *Gutierrez v. Gutierrez*, 791 S.W.2d 659 (Tex. App.—San Antonio 1990, no writ). (The offspring born during marriage to animals alive at the time of the wedding are community property—see Chapter 9.)

-----

3. This figure of $17,332.83 is the total for 1947, 1948 and 1949, note 1 *supra*, plus all ($1,193.74) of the net income from all sources for the whole of 1946 as though it were all community, rather than the apportionment of $598.10 on a two-months' basis as used by the Commissioner which made the total $16,737.19.

Chapter Seven

Torts and Damage to Property

A. Damage to Property

Trahan v. Trahan

Louisiana Court of Appeals, 1980
387 So. 2d 35

CUTRER, Justice.

[In this action, the trial court characterized proceeds paid under a homeowner's insurance policy as H's separate property. W appeals.]

The residence in which [H and W] lived was owned by John Trahan before his marriage to Betty Trahan. It was clearly his separate property. While living on the premises certain improvements were made to the residence. Although the extent of the improvements during the marriage is in dispute, it is agreed that a new roof was installed after the marriage.

During the marriage a homeowner's insurance policy covering the residence was purchased in the name of John Trahan. Three or four months later, the home burned and John Trahan received $46,560.00 in insurance proceeds. We conclude that the proceeds from the fire insurance policy were the separate property of John Trahan. The object of the insurance policy was the residence belonging to the separate estate of John Trahan. When that residence burned, the estate, consisting of the residence, was transformed into the insurance proceeds.

We base our conclusion on the case of *Thigpen v. Thigpen*, 91 So. 2d 12 (La. 1956), in which our Supreme Court faced a similar situation. In that case, the parties, Mr. and Mrs. Thigpen, had a number of disputes regarding their community property settlement which was being settled as a result of a divorce proceeding.

During the existence of a previous marriage, Mr. Thigpen and his wife purchased several buildings. Sometime later, the first wife died and the property then became jointly owned by the deceased wife's heirs and Mr. Thigpen. Later, Mr. Thigpen remarried. Clearly the interest in the property purchased during the existence of his first marriage was separate property of the husband as to the second marriage. During the existence of the second marriage, Thigpen purchased a fire insurance policy to cover the buildings. Shortly thereafter the buildings burned and the loss was replaced with funds from the insurance proceeds. The Supreme Court held that these insurance proceeds did not become community property. The court noted that since the premiums were paid out of the community funds, there may have been a justifiable claim for reimbursement for the wife's contributions to the premiums, but this did not make the proceeds themselves community property.

DISCUSSION

How did the court decide that the proceeds of the casualty insurance policy were separate property? The only remedy given the community estate is a reimbursement right. Are any benefits to the community provided by the property to be offset against any such award? If casualty insurance premiums had been paid for years from community funds, how much reimbursement should the community estate receive? If the house had not been damaged, would the community have been entitled to reimbursement for the premiums?

Personal property owned by spouses normally is insured via the spouses' homeowners' insurance policy. If spouses live in one spouse's separate property house, and certain community property and some of the other spouse's separate property is stolen from the house, how would you characterize the insurance proceeds? *Rolater v. Rolater*, 198 S.W. 391 (Tex. Civ. App.—Dallas 1917, no writ) and *Belmont v. Belmont*, 10 Cal.Rptr. 227 (Cal. App. 1961) reach the same result as *Trahan*. See also *McIntire v. McIntire*, 702 S.W.2d 284 (Tex. App.—Houston [1st Dist.] 1985, writ ref'd n.r.e.) (characterizing an insurance recovery for stolen silver).

Tex. Fam. Code §3.008 now confirms that the result in *Trahan* is the Texas rule.

B. Personal Injury

Jurek v. Jurek

Supreme Court of Arizona, 1980
606 P.2d 812

HOLOHAN, Chief Justice.

James T. Jurek filed an appeal challenging the disposition of property made by the superior court in its decree of dissolution of the marriage of the parties. The sole question raised on appeal is whether the superior court erred in awarding the wife one-half of any recovery which the husband might receive for a personal injury he received two days after he filed for dissolution.

The parties had been living separately for approximately four months and on January 28, 1977, the appellant husband filed a petition for dissolution of the marriage. Two days later he sustained an injury which resulted in the loss of his right hand and half of his right forearm. The trial court ruled that the personal injury claim arising out of the husband's injury was a community asset; therefore the wife was entitled to one-half of any proceeds received in satisfaction of the claim.

Initially we reject the husband's assertion that the filing of the dissolution action should alter the scheme of distribution of community assets acquired after the filing of the action but before the granting of the dissolution. This assertion is not supported by the applicable statutes or case law. The appellate courts of this state have consistently held that the community continues to exist, together with its rights and obligations, even when the parties may be living separate and apart.

The long-standing rule in Arizona has been that a cause of action for injury to the person of either spouse during marriage and the damages recovered therefor are community property.

In *Flowers v. Flowers*, 578 P.2d 1006 (Ariz. App. 1978) in a specially concurring opinion Judge Jacobson of the Court of Appeals suggested that the long-standing rule on the community nature of personal injury recoveries was incorrect in light of later developments in the law. Appellant urges that we abandon the rule.

There was no analysis in our early cases of the various component parts which make up a recovery for personal injuries. In other jurisdictions the general rule fell into disfavor. See annotation in 35 A.L.R.2d 1199 (1954); de Funiak and Vaughn, *Principles of Community Property*, Section 82 (2d ed. 1971).

The Arizona statutes applicable to the issue defines the property interests as:

All property acquired by either husband or wife during the marriage, except that which is acquired by gift, devise or descent, is the community property of the husband and wife. A.R.S. Section 25-211.

All property, real and personal, of each spouse, owned by such spouse before marriage, and that acquired afterward by gift, devise or descent, and also the increase, rents, issues and profits thereof, is the separate property of such spouse. A.R.S. Section 25-213.

The proper interpretation of these statutes is the essence of the problem. As stated in de Funiak and Vaughn:

Community property only consists of that which is acquired by onerous title, that is, by labor or industry of the spouses, or which is acquired in exchange for community property (which, of course, was acquired itself by onerous title, again with the exception as to the gift). It must be plainly evident that a right of action for injuries to person, reputation, property, or the like, or the compensation received therefor, is not property acquired by onerous title. The labor and industry of the spouses did not bring it into being. For that matter, it is not property acquired by lucrative title either. What, then, is it? Since the right of action for injury to the person, or for that matter, to the reputation, is intended to bring about compensation for the injury, and the compensation is intended to repair or make whole the injury, so far as is possible in such a case, the compensation partakes of the same character as that which has been injured or suffered loss.

Id. Section 82 at 201 and 202.

Following the decision of the Nevada Supreme Court in the *Boyd* case, the New Mexico Supreme Court in *Soto v. Vandeventer*, 56 N.M. 483, 245 P.2d 826 (1952) held that a cause of action for personal injuries to a wife and for the resultant pain and suffering belonged to her as her separate property. The New Mexico Supreme Court reasoned that the wife brought her body to the marriage and on its dissolution is entitled to take it away, so she should be similarly entitled to compensation from one who has wrongfully violated her right to personal security. To emphasize the point the New Mexico court pointed out:

Under the majority doctrine, if the wife were riding a horse she had brought to the marriage and some driver of a motor vehicle negligently struck her and the horse, throwing both into a wire fence, breaking the leg of each and also disfiguring them, the cause of action for the damage to the horse would belong to the wife, but that for the injury to her would belong to the community and the husband would receive one half of the proceeds of a judgment.

Id., 245 P.2d at 832.

If the personal injury to a spouse results in loss of wages and expenses for hospital and medical care, what is the result? Such losses and expenses are injuries to the community, and the recovery for such items belongs to the community. *Soto v. Vandeventer*, *supra*; de Funiak and Vaughn, Section 82, pages 202 and 203.

In the case at issue the serious injuries to the appellant are personal to him. In the same fashion as pointed out in *Soto*, the body which he brought to the marriage is certainly his separate property. The compensation for injuries to his personal well-being should belong to him as his separate property. Any expenses incurred by the community for medical care and treatment and any loss of wages resulting from the personal injury should be considered community in nature, and the community is entitled to recover for such losses.

The judgment of the superior court awarding to the appellee wife one-half of any recovery received by appellant for his personal injuries is reversed, and the cause is remanded to the trial court for further proceedings. The superior court should determine the actual loss to the community for loss of wages and medical expenses and make an equitable division of any recovery for such items. The remainder of any recovery, after deduction for the community expenses and loss, shall be awarded to the appellant as his sole and separate property.

DISCUSSION

Jurek is an interesting example of a court reaching a conceptually sound characterization result without a specific statute. Texas has a specific statute that is consistent with *Jurek*. Tex. Fam. Code § 3.001(3). The Texas statute is discussed in *Graham v. Franco*, 488 S.W.2d 390 (Tex. 1972).

Tort actions frequently are settled for a lump sum. The settlement could include claims for pain and suffering, medical expenses, lost wages during marriage and lost wages after divorce. What arguments could be made regarding how to characterize such a recovery? See *Kyles v. Kyles*, 832 S.W.2d 194 (Tex. App.—Beaumont 1992, no writ). What would be a sensible result? Is there a way to draft a personal injury settlement to avoid a commingling problem?

This commingling problem can be solved if the amount of the community recovery is clear. This may be possible in some situations. For example, in *Slaton v. Slaton*, 987 S.W.2d 180 (Tex. App.—Houston [14th Dist.] 1999, pet. denied), the wife was injured during marriage due to medical negligence. The wife sued for malpractice, and the husband sued for loss of consortium. The parties settled the claim; after attorney's fees were deducted, they received $450,000. They stipulated that her lost wages were $7800 and medical expenses amounted to $26,260. The court found that this showed that the remainder of the $450,000 ($415,940) was the wife's separate property. Do you agree? What did the court assume?

A spouse was also successful in dealing with a commingling issue in *Smith v. Smith*, 22 S.W.3d 140 (Tex. App.—Houston [14th Dist.] 2000, no pet.). The husband had filed suit before marriage regarding a misrepresentation that had been made to him regarding a townhome be bought before marriage. He recovered $256,248.91. Of this, $81,940.41 constituted prejudgment and post-judgment interest that accrued during marriage. This latter amount was community property. The husband incurred attorneys' fees and expenses of $94,935.74 in the suit, 37.05% of the gross award. The court allocated these charges between the separate and community estates. So, the net community recovery was $51, 581.49 ($81,940.41 × 37.05%), and the remainder of the net recovery ($109,731.68) was separate.

When one spouse is injured by a third party, and the injury suffered by the spouse negatively affects the quality of the marital relationship, the injured spouse may bring a personal injury action, and the other spouse may sue for loss of consortium. This loss of consortium recovery is separate property. *See Whittlesey v. Miller*, 572 S.W.2d 665 (Tex. 1978). A parent's wrongful death claim for the death of a child is separate property. *Williams v. Steves Industries, Inc.*, 678 S.W.2d 205 (Tex. App.—Austin 1984), *aff'd*, 699 S.W.2d 570 (Tex. 1985).

The Texas statute was intended to deal only with tort actions initiated by a spouse against a third party. After the Family Code was adopted, the Texas Supreme Court abolished interspousal tort immunity for intentional torts. *See Bounds v. Caudle*, 560 S.W.2d 925 (Tex. 1977). If one spouse sues the other due to an intentional tort, this could cause characterization complications in Texas. For example, if one spouse injures the other via an intentional tort, and the injured spouse loses wages, the lost wages component of the recovery normally would be community property. Courts have not wanted to let the wrongdoer share in this portion of the recovery, so some exceptions to the normal characterization rules have been created when this issue has arisen in other community property states. *See Freehe v. Freehe*, 81 Wash.2d 183 (1972). No Texas case to date deals with this issue. After *Price v. Price*, discussed in *Twyman, infra*, it appears one spouse may also sue the other for damages resulting from negligence.

Russell v. Russell

New Mexico Court of Appeals, 1987
740 P.2d 127

MINZNER, Judge.

Husband appeals a post-divorce order crediting him with $714.58 against child support and alimony arrearages. Husband contends that the amount of the credit, which represents his community share of a settlement wife received for medical expenses, should be larger. The final decree of divorce entered by the court ordered that any recovery obtained by wife resulting from her claim for toxic shock syndrome would be her separate property, except that portion which was directly attributable to past medical expenses, loss of services to the community and loss of earnings, up to the time of the divorce, which amounts were deemed community property and should be divided equally between husband and wife. On appeal, both parties have assumed that the evidence necessary to support their respective claims is evidence as to the total amount of medical expenses incurred by the community. The appellate issue, however, is not what the total medical expenses were, but what portion of the wife's settlement was directly attributable to medical expenses. We reverse the trial court and remand for further proceedings.

BACKGROUND

Petitioner-appellant (husband) and respondent-appellee (wife) were married in 1965 and divorced in 1983. They had one child, who was 16 at the time of the divorce. When the divorce was granted wife had a potential personal injury claim against Proctor and Gamble for toxic shock syndrome. The findings of fact and conclusions of law entered at that time awarded alimony and child support, and included the following paragraph:

14. Respondent has a potential claim or cause of action against the manufacturers and/or distributors of Rely Tampons and/or others by reason of an illness she contracted in 1980 which required her hospitalization and other substantial medical care since that time. In the event Respondent brings an action or presents a claim against any responsible parties for her said injuries and illness, and in the event Respondent is successful in her claim or action, then that portion of Respondent's claim or cause of action which is directly attributable to past medical expenses, loss of service to the community, and loss of earnings, if any, to the community, up to the time of the dissolution of the parties' marriage, is the community property of the parties and should be divided equally between Petitioner and Respondent. The remaining portion of Respondent's claim or cause of action, including damages for Respondent's physical injury, pain and suffering, is Respondent's separate property.

The final decree adopted the findings of fact and conclusion of law as the court's ruling.

Subsequent to the divorce of the parties, wife filed a motion seeking to have husband held in contempt for failure to pay child support and alimony, and for judgment on the delinquencies. Husband stipulated that he was indebted to wife in the amount of $8,190 for past alimony and child support and in the amount of $2,000, plus interest, for an unauthorized loan obtained on a life insurance policy owned by wife. Husband agreed to make specific payments on these delinquencies. On February 28, 1985, wife filed a motion to enforce stipulation and judgment, asking for arrearages and attorney fees that had been awarded previously. The motion stated that wife's suit against Proctor and Gamble was apparently close to settlement and acknowledged that husband was awarded an interest in that settlement. Wife asked that a receiver be appointed to receive any portion of the settlement due husband, to hold that amount, and to pay future alimony payments from it as they accrue.

After husband was ordered to pay arrearages and make regular payments, a hearing was held with respect to paragraph 14. At the hearing, wife contended that the amount due husband under paragraph 14 was one-half of wife's medical expenses which had not been paid by insurance. She presented a portion of the couple's joint tax return for 1981, showing unreimbursed medical expenses of $1,421.16. Counsel for husband admitted that they had conducted no discovery. Thus, husband did not know the amount of the settlement had received or how much of the settlement was attributable to attorney fees, medical expenses, or loss of future earnings. On cross-examination, wife stated that all of her medical expenses in excess of the $1,421.16 had been paid by Blue Cross and Champus. The entitlement to Champus was due to husband's military service, and the Blue Cross premiums were deducted from his Air Force paycheck.

Wife further testified that she had settled with Proctor and Gamble in April 1985, but that under the terms of the settlement the amount could not be disclosed. She did not know how the settlement figure was determined. She did admit that her total medical expenses were in the area of $80,000 and that the settlement was in excess of that amount.

Following the hearing, husband requested a finding that he was entitled to one-half of $80,000. Findings entered by the trial judge include the following, which are challenged by husband:

14. That no loss of services resulted to the community and no loss of earnings.

15. That the intention of paragraph 14 was to reimburse the community, and in particular the Petitioner, for his one-half of any medical expenses the community incurred [sic] as a result of the Respondents [sic] illness.

....

17. That the only evidence introduced as to medical expenses of the community are shown on Exhibit 1 to the December 16, 1985, hearing and the uncontradicted testimony of the Respondent, which shows the total sum of medical expenses to the community resulting from the illness and during that period to be $1429.15, one-half of which or $714.58, the Petitioner is entitled to recover.

We discuss (1) what portion of wife's settlement, if any, represents community property; and (2) evidence of the amount of medical expenses.

WHAT PORTION OF THE SETTLEMENT REPRESENTS COMMUNITY PROPERTY?

The trial judge found that only an amount equal to medical expenses not paid by insurance was community property. No issue is raised on appeal concerning any right of the community with respect to loss of earnings or loss of services due to wife's illness. Under finding 17, the amount due the community for medical expenses was $1,429.15. It follows from finding 15 that the trial court believed the decree intended to reimburse the community for only those medical expenses the community paid for in cash. That construction of the decree is not supported by the record on appeal.

Paragraph 14 states that any portion of the settlement "directly attributable to medical expenses" is community property and should be divided equally. The language in the decree is clear and therefore must be enforced as written. "Where the decree is clear and unambiguous, neither pleadings, findings, nor matters dehors the record may be used to change its meaning or even to construe it. It must stand and be enforced as it speaks." *Parks v. Parks*, 91 N.M. 369, 372, 574 P.2d 588, 591 (1978). In interpreting the decree to refer to nonreimbursable expenses, the trial court is adding limiting language to the decree. The only way an unmodifiable judgment of property settlement may be modified or set aside is by appeal or pursuant to a motion for relief from judgment. *Parks v. Parks*. Neither procedure was followed in this case. *See Russell v. Russell*, 101 N.M. 648, 687 P.2d 83 (1984) (wherein husband appealed only the alimony award, which was affirmed).

Where the meaning is obscure or ambiguous, the entire record may be resorted to for the purpose of construing the judgment. *Westbrook v. Lea General Hospital*, 85 N.M. 191, 510 P.2d 515 (Ct. App. 1973). However, even if the language in paragraph 14 were not clear, nothing in the record supports the assumption that "medical expenses" refers to only non-reimbursable expenses.

A plain reading of paragraph 14 is also consistent with New Mexico law. This reinforces our conclusion that the decree requires division of any portion of the settlement attributable to medical expenses. While in a personal injury case an award for pain and suffering is separate property, *see Luxton v. Luxton*, 98 N.M. 276, 648 P.2d 315 (1982), a claim for damages to the community for medical expenses and loss of earnings belongs to the community. *Soto v. Vandeventer*, 56 N.M. 483, 245 P.2d 826 (1952); *Rodgers v. Ferguson*, 89 N.M. 688, 556 P.2d 844 (Ct. App. 1976).

The Texas Supreme Court explained the rationale for this rule in *Graham v. Franco*, 488 S.W.2d 390 (Texas 1972), where a wife sued for personal injuries sustained in an automobile accident. The court held that "[t]o the extent that the marital partnership has incurred medical or other expenses and has lost wages, both spouses have been damaged by the injury to the spouse; and both spouses have a claim against the wrongdoer. The recovery, therefore, is community in character." Id. at 396. See W. de Funiak and M. Vaughn, *Principles of Community Property*, Sec. 82 (2d ed. 1971).

The above authorities characterize recovery for medical expenses as a community asset because it represents reimbursement for debts incurred by the community. Under our statutory characterization, all of the medical expenses incurred in this case were community debts. See NMSA 1978, Sec. 40-3-9 (Repl. 1986). We conclude that whether or not they were paid by insurance is irrelevant as far as the characterization of the debt is concerned.

Further, the insurance which paid the expenses was a community asset because the policy was purchased with community funds. See NMSA 1978, Secs. 40-3-8 and -12 (Repl. 1986); *Stroshine v. Stroshine*, 98 N.M. 742, 652 P.2d 1193 (1982) (property acquired during marriage is presumptively community). The right to payment of the community debts was acquired by purchasing insurance with community funds. The community has an interest in the proceeds of the policy. See *Douglas v. Douglas*, 101 N.M. 570, 686 P.2d 260 (Ct. App. 1984) (holding that the marital community, by reason of payment of premiums on a disability insurance policy, acquired an interest in amounts subsequently paid to the injured spouse because of personal injury and disability). See also *Palama v. Palama*, 323 So.2d 823 (La. App. 1975) (fire insurance policy a community asset and proceeds therefrom were due the community).

Since the medical expenses were community debts and the insurance proceeds were community assets, any part of wife's settlement intended to reimburse the community for medical expenses is also community property. The fact that a community debt was paid with community assets is determinative of the issue on appeal. It makes no difference whether the debt was paid with cash or with insurance proceeds; in any event, it was paid by the community. See *Guy v. Guy*, 98 Idaho 205, 560 P.2d 876 (1977) (clearly community labor was the source of the benefit).

If the insurance company has been reimbursed by wife from the proceeds of her settlement, then the community portion of the settlement has been used to pay the community debt, and husband is not entitled to any further portion of the settlement. On the record, however, it does not appear that this has happened. If there is a double recovery of medical expenses, both spouses should share in it equally. The community should not be penalized because the parties protected themselves by purchasing insurance.

CONCLUSION

The case is remanded for a hearing and entry of findings as to the amount of wife's settlement that is directly attributable to medical expenses. The trial court should also determine whether the insurance company has sought recovery from wife for benefits it paid. If the company has been reimbursed by wife for all of its payments, there may be no portion of the settlement left for the community to divide. If it is determined that a substantial amount of the settlement is due husband, it would be appropriate for the trial judge to consider wife's motion for appointment of a receiver, since husband has been less than diligent in meeting his support obligations. Obviously, any amount due husband should first be offset by amounts owed wife for arrearages.

The order is reversed and the case is remanded for further action consistent with this opinion. No costs or attorney fees are awarded.

Twyman v. Twyman

Supreme Court of Texas, 1993
855 S.W.2d 619

CORNYN, Justice.

In this case we decide whether a claim for infliction of emotional distress can be brought in a divorce proceeding. Because the judgment of the court of appeals is based on negligent infliction of emotional distress, and cannot be affirmed on that or any other basis, we reverse the judgment of the court and remand this cause for a new trial in the interest of justice. We deem a new trial appropriate because of our recent decision that no cause of action for negligent infliction of emotional distress exists in Texas. Today, however, we expressly adopt the tort of intentional infliction of emotional distress, and hold that such a claim can be brought in a divorce proceeding.

Sheila and William Twyman married in 1969. Sheila filed for divorce in 1985. She later amended her divorce petition to add a general claim for emotional harm without specifying whether the claim was based on negligent or intentional infliction of emotional distress. In her amended petition, Sheila alleged that William "intentionally and cruelly" attempted to engage her in "deviate sexual acts."[1] Following a bench trial, the court rendered judgment dissolving the marriage, dividing the marital estate, awarding conservatorship of the children to Sheila, ordering William to pay child support, and awarding Sheila $15,000 plus interest for her claim for emotional distress. William appealed that portion of the judgment based on emotional distress, contending that interspousal tort immunity precluded Sheila's recovery for negligent infliction of emotional distress. The court of appeals affirmed the judgment, holding that Sheila could recover for William's negligent infliction of emotional distress.

While this case has been pending, we have refused to adopt the tort of negligent infliction of emotional distress. *See Boyles v. Kerr*, 855 S.W.2d 593 (Tex. 1993). Thus the judgment of the court of appeals cannot be affirmed. We consider, therefore, whether the court of appeals' judgment may be affirmed on alternative grounds. Because Sheila's pleadings alleging a general claim for emotional harm are broad enough to encompass a claim for intentional infliction of emotional distress, we consider whether the trial court's judgment may be sustained on that legal theory.

While this court has never expressly recognized the tort of intentional infliction of emotional distress, we found no reversible error in the court of appeals' opinion in *Tidelands Automobile Club v. Walters*, which did so. 699 S.W.2d 939 (Tex. App.—Beaumont 1985, writ ref'd n.r.e.). There, the court of appeals adopted the elements of the tort as expressed in the RESTATEMENT (SECOND) OF TORTS § 46 (1965) The Restatement elements of intentional infliction of emotional distress are: 1) the defendant acted intentionally or recklessly, 2) the conduct was extreme and outrageous, 3) the actions of the defendant caused the plaintiff emotional distress, and 4) the emotional distress suffered by the plaintiff was severe. *Id.* According to the Restatement, liability for outrageous conduct should be found "only where the conduct has been so outrageous in character, and so

---

1. At trial, Sheila testified that William pursued sadomasochistic bondage activities with her, even though he knew that she feared such activities because she had been raped at knife-point before their marriage. The trial court found that William "attempted to emotionally coerce [Sheila] in 'bondage' on an ongoing basis ..." and "engaged in a continuing course of conduct of attempting to coerce her to join in his practices of 'bondage' by continually asserting that their marriage could be saved only by [Sheila] participating with him in his practices of 'bondage.'"

extreme in degree, as to go beyond all possible bounds of decency, and to be regarded as atrocious, and utterly intolerable in a civilized community." *Id.* cmt. d. Of the forty-six states that have recognized this tort, forty-three have adopted this Restatement formulation. The other three states, although not adopting the Restatement definition, require the equivalent of "outrageous" conduct. Today we become the forty-seventh state to adopt the tort of intentional infliction of emotional distress as set out in § 46(1) of the RESTATEMENT (SECOND) OF TORTS.

We do not, however, adopt this tort only because of its broad acceptance in jurisdictions throughout the United States. As distinguished from the tort of negligent infliction of emotional distress, we believe the rigorous legal standards of the Restatement formulation of intentional infliction of emotional distress help to assure a meaningful delineation between inadvertence and intentionally or recklessly outrageous misconduct. The requirements of intent, extreme and outrageous conduct, and severe emotional distress before liability can be established will, we think, strike a proper balance between diverse interests in a free society. That balance, at minimum, must allow freedom of individual action while providing reasonable opportunity for redress for victims of conduct that is determined to be utterly intolerable in a civilized community.

This holding represents a middle ground between the polar positions adopted by various members of the court.[2] JUSTICE HECHT, joined by JUSTICE ENOCH, in arguing against our express adoption of the tort of intentional infliction of emotional distress, maintains that judges and juries are guided by insufficient standards, that liability may be imposed arbitrarily, that reported cases either supporting or refusing to support an award of damages disclose no uniform patterns, and that the sensitivities of aggrieved people are entirely too subjective and unpredictable. We disagree, and believe that such objections could just as easily be made to well-established causes of action in Texas. For example, one might also contend that the legal standards for ordinary negligence are vague, and that juries must necessarily rely on their own notions of fault. Because jurors' ideas about what is "ordinary" and "reasonable" may vary, the same arguments about lack of uniformity, unpredictability, and personal sensitivities could be made. Yet just as we trust juries to decide questions of negligence, proximate cause, and damages, when guided by appropriate legal standards we think them equally capable of resolving factual disputes giving rise to the tort of intentional infliction of emotional distress.

JUSTICE SPECTOR, joined by JUSTICE DOGGETT, on the other hand, agrees with us that this tort should be adopted, but uses this case as another opportunity to question the wisdom of our decision in *Boyles*, in which we refused to adopt the tort of negligent infliction of emotional distress. They join some amici curiae in implying that the court has disregarded the tort's unique role in addressing women's psychic injuries. One need only identify those who have brought claims for negligent infliction of emotional distress, however, to dispel the suggestion that women will be disproportionately affected. Of the thirty-four Texas appellate cases in which a claim for negligent infliction of emotional distress was alleged, thirteen were brought by women, twelve were brought by men, seven by husbands and wives jointly, one by an executrix on behalf of an estate, and one by a corporation. These cases demonstrate that the tort has been alleged by litigants in a

---

2. At trial, Sheila testified that William pursued sadomasochistic bondage activities with her, even though he knew that she feared such activities because she had been raped at knife-point before their marriage. The trial court found that William "attempted to emotionally coerce [Sheila] in 'bondage' on an ongoing basis ..." and "engaged in a continuing course of conduct of attempting to coerce her to join in his practices of 'bondage' by continually asserting that their marriage could be saved only by [Sheila] participating with him in his practices of 'bondage.'"

wide variety of circumstances. There is simply no factual or legal basis for the suggestion that by choosing not to recognize this particular tort, the court demonstrates insensitivity to female claimants.

JUSTICE SPECTOR also argues that because of our refusal to recognize the tort of negligent infliction of emotional distress some wrongs will go uncompensated because of the difficulty in proving the actor's intent when the actor intends nothing more than to satisfy his own desires. *Infra*, 855 S.W.2d at 644. But in Sheila Twyman's case, and in countless other cases involving both men and women, we believe that our adoption of the Restatement formulation of the tort of intentional infliction of emotional distress provides a reasonable opportunity for redress for outrageous conduct.

Of course, rarely will a defendant admit knowing of a substantial certainty that emotional harm would befall the victim. Juries, however, are free to discredit the defendant's protestations that no harm was intended and to draw necessary inferences to establish intent.

Moreover, Section 46 of the Restatement definition of the tort expressly includes situations in which the actor recklessly inflicts emotional distress. An actor is recklessly when he "knows or has reason to know ... of facts which create a high degree of risk of ... harm to another, and deliberately proceeds to act, or fails to act, in conscious disregard of, or indifference to that risk." Restatement (Second) § 500, cmt. a. Again, on retrial, the jury may consider whether William acted recklessly toward Sheila.

We now consider whether the cause of action for intentional infliction of emotional distress may be brought in a divorce proceeding.[3] In *Bounds v. Caudle*, this court unanimously abolished the doctrine of interspousal immunity for intentional torts. 560 S.W.2d 925 (Tex. 1977). Ten years later, we abrogated interspousal immunity "completely as to any cause of action,"[4] including negligence actions for personal injuries. *Price v. Price*, 732 S.W.2d 316, 319 (Tex. 1987). Under the rules established in *Caudle* and *Price*, there appears to be no legal impediment to bringing a tort claim in a divorce action based on either negligence or an intentional act such as assault or battery.[5]

The more difficult issue is when the tort claim must be brought and how the tort award should be considered when making a "just and right" division of the marital estate. *See* TEX.FAM.CODE § 3.63(b). Of the states that have answered this question, several have held that the tort case and the divorce case must be litigated separately. *See, e.g., Walther* v. Walther, 709 P.2d 387, 388 (Utah 1985); *Windauer v. O'Connor*, 107 Ariz. 267, 485 P.2d 1157 (1971); *Simmons v. Simmons*, 773 P.2d 602, 605 (Colo.Ct.App. 1988). Other states require joinder of the two actions. See, e.g. Tevis v. Tevis, 79 N.J. 422, 400 A.2d 1189, 1196 (1979); *Weil v. Lammon*, 503 So.2d 830, 832 (Ala. 1987).

---

3. CHIEF JUSTICE PHILLIPS, and JUSTICES HECHT and ENOCH rue the court's decision to permit the tort of intentional infliction of emotional distress to be brought in a divorce proceedings. But it appears that much of what they disapprove of is related to the consequences of recognizing *any* tort action between divorcing spouses. Their criticisms would seem to be better directed at the court's earlier decisions to abrogate the doctrine of interspousal tort immunity in *Bounds v. Caudle*, 560 S.W.2d 925 (Tex. 1977), and *Price v. Price*, 732 S.W. 316 (Tex. 1987).

4. CHIEF JUSTICE PHILLIPS' statement that "all conduct actionable between strangers is [not] automatically actionable between spouses" cannot be reconciled with this language. *See* 855 S.W.2d at 627 (Phillips, C.J. dissenting).

5. We necessarily disapprove of the contrary holding in *Chiles v. Chiles*, 779 S.W.2d 127 (Tex. App.—Houston [14thDist.] 1989, writ denied) (declining to recognize intentional infliction of emotional distress as a separate cause of action in a divorce suit).

We believe that the best approach lies between these two extremes. As in other civil actions, joinder of the tort cause of action should be permitted, but subject to the principles of res judicata.[6] Of course, how such claims are ultimately tried is within the sound discretion of the trial court. But joinder of tort claims with the divorce, when feasible, is encouraged. Resolving both the tort and divorce actions in the same proceeding avoids two trials based at least in part on the same facts, and settles in one suit "all matters existing between the parties."[7]

When a tort action is tried with the divorce, however, it is imperative that the court avoid awarding a double recovery.[8] When dividing the marital estate, the court may take into account several factors, including the fault of the parties if pleaded. *See Murff v. Murff*, 615 S.W.2d 696, 699 (Tex. 1981). The trial court may also consider "such factors as the spouses' capacities and abilities, benefits which the party not at fault would have derived from continuation of the marriage, business opportunities, education, relative physical conditions, relative financial condition and obligations, disparity of ages, size of separate estates, and the nature to the property." *Id. See also Young v. Young*, 609 S.W.2d 758, 761 (Tex. 1980). However, a spouse should not be allowed to recover tort damages and a disproportionate division of the community estate based on the same conduct. Therefore, when a factfinder awards tort damages to a divorcing spouse, the court may not consider the same tortious acts when dividing the marital estate. Contrary to CHIEF JUSTICE PHILLIPS' contention, an award for tortious conduct does not replace an analysis of the remaining factors to be considered when the trial court divides the marital estate. 855 S.W.2d at 626 (Phillips, C.J., dissenting). The court may still award a disproportionate division of property for reasons other than the tortious conduct. To avoid the potential problem of double recovery, the factfinder should consider the damages awarded in the tort action when dividing the parties' property. If a jury is used to render an advisory division of the parties' estate, the judge should limit, by appropriate instruction, the jury's consideration of the alleged tortious acts and later consider the award of damages in determining a just and right division of the marital estate.[9]

Sheila Twyman cannot recover based on the findings of fact made by the trial court in this case.[10] It is likely, however, that this case proceeded on a theory of negligent inflic-

---

6. We anticipate that most tort cases between spouses will be joined with the divorce proceeding, however, situations may exist in which the facts supporting the tort action will be different from those supporting a petition for divorce.

7. By holding that these actions may be brought in a single lawsuit we are not authorizing the use of contingent fee arrangements in family law matters. *See* TEX. DISCIPLINARY R. PROF. CONDUCT 1.04 & cmt. 9 (1989), *reprinted in* TEX.GOV'T CODE ANN. tit. 2, subtit. G app. (Vernon Supp. 1993) (STATE BAR RULES art. 10, §9). Rather, attorneys should enter two separate fee arrangements, one for the divorce and the other for the tort claim. *See* Andrew Schepard, *Divorce, Interspousal Torts, and Res Judicata*, 24 FAM.L.Q. 127, 151–52 (1990).

8. For a discussion of the possibility of double recovery in this type of case, *see* Schepard, *supra* at 146–47.

9. In Texas, recovery for personal injuries of a spouse, including pain and suffering, is the separate property of that spouse. TEX.FAM.CODE § 5.01(a)(3); *Graham v. Franco*, 488 S.W.2d 390, 396 (Tex. 1972). Therefore, an award to one spouse from the other does not add to the marital estate, and raises no possibility that the tort award becomes "self-offsetting." *See* Barbara H. Young, *Interspousal Torts and Divorce: Problems, Policies, Procedures*, 27 J.FAM.L. 489, 511 (1989).

10. The Restatement calls for the court to first determine whether the conduct may be reasonably regarded as so extreme and outrageous as to allow recovery and whether severe emotional distress can be found. RESTATEMENT (SECOND) OF TORTS §46 (1965) cmt. h. The trial court made no findings of outrageous behavior or severe emotional distress, and the judgment was based specifically and exclusively on negligent infliction of emotional distress. The divorce decree recites:

After considering the pleadings, the evidence, and the arguments of the attorneys, the Court finds

tion of emotional distress in reliance on this court's holding in *St. Elizabeth Hospital v. Garrard*, 730 S.W.2d 649 (Tex. 1987), which we recently overruled. *See Boyles v. Kerr*, 855 S.W.2d 593 (Tex. 1992). As we noted in *Boyles*, this court has broad discretion to remand for a new trial in the interest of justice when it appears that a case proceeded under the wrong legal theory, and when it appears that the facts when developed on retrial may support recovery on an alternative theory. *Id.* at 603. When, as here, a party presents her case in reliance on precedent that has been recently overruled, remand is appropriate. Therefore, in the interest of justice, we reverse the judgment of the court of appeals and remand this cause to the trial court for a new trial.

DISCUSSION

Twyman clarifies that spousal tort immunity no longer limits tort actions between spouses. If you learn that your client has a potential tort claim against his or her spouse, what would be the best time to assert it? What are the advantages and disadvantages of joining the tort suit with the divorce?

In Texas divorces, the court may consider the "fault" of a spouse in connection with the property division. Does *Twyman* adequately deal with any potential double-counting problems?

After *Twyman*, it is unclear what will constitute intentional infliction of emotional distress. In *Truitt v. Carnley*, 836 S.W.2d 786 (Tex. App. — Fort Worth 1992, writ denied) the appellate court concluded that an intentional infliction of emotional distress claim by a spouse against a third party who allegedly had an affair with the plaintiff's husband was essentially a claim for alienation of affection and criminal conversation, causes of action that have been abolished in Texas.

How will *Twyman* affect divorce negotiations? Are you persuaded by the majority's argument that it is good policy to permit such spousal claims?

Emotional distress damages can be large. In *Massey v. Massey*, 807 S.W.2d 391 (Tex. App. — Houston [1st Dist.] 1991), *aff'd*, 867 S.W.2d 766 (Tex. 1993) the jury awarded the wife emotional distress damages of $362,000. *Massey* suggests that it may not be difficult to convince a jury that a spouse's actions were outrageous.

What is the standard for determining what is "extreme and outrageous"? Should there be one uniform standard, or should the standard be adapted to reflect a person's education or cultural background?

The court in *Toles v. Toles*, 45 S.W.3d 252, 262 (Tex. App. — Dallas 2001, pet. denied) suggests this approach:

> "While occasional malicious and abusive incidents should not be condoned, they must ... be tolerated.... When abusive conduct such as being assaulted, intimidated, and threatened becomes a regular pattern of behavior, it should not be accepted in a civilized society."

---

the facts and law support judgment for Petition [sic] in her tort for negligent infliction of emotional distress upon Petitioner.

Additionally, the trial court made a disproportionate property division based on William's cruel treatment and adultery. It appears that such an award may allow Sheila a double recovery based on the same conduct. A new trial conducted in accordance with the principles announced in this decision should rectify this problem.

Is this a useful approach?

Toles, among other cases, have stated: "In determining whether certain conduct is extreme and outrageous, courts consider the context and the relationship between the parties. Conduct considered extreme and outrageous in some relationships may not be so in other relationships." 45 S.W.3d at 261. How would this standard be applied?

Res judicata concerns can arise when a tort action is filed after divorce. For example, in *Brinkman v. Brinkman*, 966 S.W.2d 780 (Tex. App.—San Antonio 1998, pet. denied), the wife's post-divorce tort claim was barred because evidence pertaining to the tort was admitted in the divorce action.

In *Askew v. Askew*, 28 Cal.Rptr.2d 284 (Cal. App. 1994), the husband claimed at divorce that his wife had lied to him before they married about being sexually attracted to him. If this could be established, could this be the basis of a tort claim?

In *Helena Laboratories Corp. v. Snyder*, 886 S.W.2d 767 (Tex. 1994), a party argued that when his spouse had an affair with a co-worker the employer could be liable for negligent interference with the family relationship. The Texas Supreme Court held that there is no independent cause of action for negligent interference with the family relationship.

Schlueter v. Schlueter

Supreme Court of Texas, 1998
975 S.W.2d 584

OPINION BY: RAUL A. GONZALEZ

This divorce case answers the question of what remedies are available to a spouse alleging fraud on the community committed by the other spouse. The husband transferred various community assets to his father shortly before he filed for divorce. The wife counterclaimed for divorce and brought independent tort claims against her husband and father-in-law, seeking damages for fraud, breach of fiduciary duty, and conspiracy. Based on favorable jury findings, the trial court ordered a disproportionate division of the community estate favoring the wife, and rendered judgment for the wife against the husband and his father for actual and exemplary damages. Holding that a tort cause of action for fraud on the community exists independent of a divorce proceeding, the court of appeals affirmed. We granted writ to resolve a conflict among courts of appeals. Because a wronged spouse has an adequate remedy for fraud on the community through the "just and right" property division upon divorce, we hold that there is no independent tort cause of action between spouses for damages to the community estate. Accordingly, we reverse the judgment against the husband and remand for a new division of the marital estate.

We affirm the remainder of the court of appeals judgment.

Richard and Karen Schlueter married in 1969. In December 1992, Mr. Schlueter began investing in emus. He contributed $3250 of community funds toward two pairs of the birds, but eventually sold his interest to his father, Hudson Schlueter, for $1,000. The emu business was worth at least $10,000 when the sale occurred. Mrs. Schlueter did not know the details of the business and did not find out that her husband had sold his interest to her father-in-law until after Mr. Schlueter filed for divorce.

Shortly before he filed for divorce, Mr. Schlueter accepted a $30,360.41 check from his employer as an incentive for early retirement. Mr. Schlueter turned the check over to his father for deposit in his father's account. His father then wrote himself a check for

$12,565, allegedly to reimburse past loans to Mr. Schlueter. About a week later, Mr. Schlueter filed for divorce.

Mrs. Schlueter counterclaimed for divorce and added independent tort claims against her husband and father-in-law for fraud, breach of fiduciary duty, and conspiracy. All of Mrs. Schlueters' claims against her husband and father-in-law involve their depriving the Schlueters' community estate of assets. Mrs. Schlueter makes no claim that she was deprived of her separate property.

The jury heard the fraud and conspiracy claims in a bifurcated trial. The jury found that Mr. Schlueter committed actual and constructive fraud in dealing with the community assets, that he and his father had fraudulently transferred assets between them, and that they had engaged in a civil conspiracy to injure Mrs. Schlueter. The jury found that $12,850 would compensate the community for Mr. Schlueter's and his father's actions. It found that $35,000 would compensate the community for damage caused by the conspiracy. Finally, the jury found that Mr. Schlueter should pay $50,000 and his father $15,000 in exemplary damages.

At a later date, the trial court heard the divorce action without a jury, divided the marital assets, and rendered judgment on the jury verdict against Mr. Schlueter and his father jointly and severally for $12,850. In its Findings of Fact, the trial court determined that the joint and several judgment was part of the community estate. The court also awarded Mrs. Schlueter $30,000 in, exemplary damages against her husband and $15,000 in exemplary damages against her father-in-law, and awarded Mrs. Schlueter $18,500 from her husband for attorney's fees on appeal.

The court of appeals affirmed. The court held that a spouse may bring an independent tort claim against the other spouse for fraud for which exemplary damages may be awarded, even when the fraud resulted only in a depletion of community assets and not the wronged spouse's separate estate. The court of appeals based its holding on this Court's abrogation of the doctrine of interspousal immunity in the *Bounds*, *Price*, and *Twyman* decisions, and concluded that a person may bring any cause of action against his or her spouse. 929 S. W.2d at 99–100 (construing *Twyman v. Twyman.* 855 S.W.2d 619, 624 (Tex. 1993); *Price v. Price.* 732 S.W.2d 316, 319 (Tex. 1987); and *Bounds v. Caudle*, 560 S.W.2d 925, 927 (Tex.1977)). The court of appeals also affirmed the judgment against the father-in-law, holding that the trial court had not abused its discretion in admitting into evidence a copy of a divorce decree involving Mr. Schlueters' brother.

Relying on *Belz v. Belz*, 667 S.W.2d 240, 247 (Tex. App.—Dallas 1984, writ ref'd n.r.e.), and *In re Marriage of Moore*, 890 S.W.2d 821, 829 (Tex. App.—Amarillo 1994, no writ), Mr. Schlueter alleges that the court of appeals committed reversible error in recognizing a separate cause of action for fraud on the community. Mr. Schlueter and his father, in the father's only point of error, also assert that the court of appeals erred in holding that the trial court did not abuse its discretion in admitting into evidence a copy of the decree from Mr. Schlueters' brother's divorce.

The court of appeals reads the *Twyman*, *Price*, and *Bounds* decisions too broadly: these decisions do not control this case. In *Bounds*, we dealt with whether the interspousal immunity doctrine prevented a deceased woman's children from suing their stepfather for their mother's wrongful death. The stepfather had allegedly shot and killed his wife. We concluded that interspousal immunity should be abolished for willful or intentional torts. From a policy perspective, we stated that suits for willful and intentional torts such as the physical attack in that case would not disrupt domestic tranquility "a home which has already been strained to the point where an intentional physical attack could take place."

We re-examined the doctrine in *Price v. Price,* 732 S.W.2d 316 (Tex. 1987). A wife sued her husband for negligence in causing her injuries in a motorcycle accident. Again this Court considered and rejected the argument that "peace and harmony" in the home would be damaged by suits between spouses, commenting that "it is difficult to fathom how denying a forum for the redress of any wrong could be said to encourage domestic tranquility." We followed up on our holding in *Bounds* by stating, "We now abolish [the interspousal immunity doctrine] completely as to any cause of action. We do not limit our holding to suits involving vehicular accidents only."

Finally, in *Twyman,* we expressly adopted the tort of intentional infliction of emotional distress, and a plurality held that such a claim could be brought in a divorce proceeding. *Twyman,* 855 S.W.2d at 622, 624–26. The plurality noted that under *Bounds* and *Price,* there was no legal impediment to bringing a tort claim in a divorce action "based on either negligence or an intentional act such as assault or battery." Of course, by its facts, *Twyman* expanded that statement by allowing an intentional tort claim for emotional distress, which does not necessarily involve the physical aspects of assault or battery.

The salient characteristic distinguishing *Bounds, Price,* and *Twyman* from the case before us is that all three involved personal injury tort claims. *Twyman,* 855 S. W2d at 621 (intentional infliction of emotional distress); *Price,* 732 S.W2d at 316 (negligence claim for personal injuries); *Bounds,* 560 S. W2d at 926 (wrongful death). Cf. *Cleaver v. George Staton Co. Inc.,* 908 S.W2d 468, 471 n.2 (Ten. App.—Tyler 1995, writ denied) (distinguishing *Twyman,* which involved outrageous spousal conduct, and noting that the trial court could sort out the husband's claims against wife for breach of fiduciary duty and fraud on community estate in the property division, not by a separate cause of action). In discussing the potential for double recovery in *Twyman,* the Court pointed out that recovery for personal injuries of a spouse, including pain and suffering, is the separate property of the injured spouse, and therefore does not add to the marital estate. *Twyman,* 855 S.W.2d at 625 n.20 (citing TEX. FAM. CODE § 5.0l(a)(3) (current version at TEX. FAM. CODE ANN. § 3.001(3))).

Likewise, in response to the concern that interspousal suits would result in fraud and collusion between the participants, the *Price* court stated, "we are unable to distinguish interspousal suits from other actions for personal injury." *Price,* 732 S.W.2d at 318. Therefore, despite its broad language stating that the Court was abolishing the interspousal immunity doctrine "completely as to any cause of action," *id.* at 319, the action in *Price* was one for personal injury, for which any recovery would be separate property of the injured spouse.

Moreover, a factor in *Price* that weighed heavily toward abolishing interspousal immunity "as to any cause of action" was the need to remedy the problem of denying a litigant a forum for the redress of a wrong. *Id.* at 318–19. The Court summed up the holding by saying that the result in the case was "compelled by the fundamental proposition of public policy that the courts should afford [such] redress" *Id.* at 320. However, redress is available in the present case without the creation of a separate tort cause of action between spouses.

Mrs. Schlueter sued her husband for improperly depleting community assets. This state's community properly system provides that upon divorce, the trial court must enter a division of a married couple's estate "in a manner that the court deems just and right," considering the sights of the parties and any children of the marriage. TEX. FAM. CODE ANN. § 7.001. Such a standard may at times lead to a disproportionate division of assets and liabilities of the parties, depending on the circumstances that courts may consider in refusing to divide the marital estate equally.

As this Court stated in *Cameron* v. *Cameron,* 641 S.W.2d 210, 223 (Tex. 1982), "Community property owes its existence to the legal fact of marriage, and when the parties to that compact determine their relationship should end, property acquired during marriage is and should be divided among them in a just and right manner." This is distinguishable from recovery of separate property through an independent tort, which we allowed in *Twyman*, because "separate property ... owes its existence to wholly extramarital factors, things unrelated to the marriage. In relation to that property, the parties are, in essence, strangers; they are separate." *Cameron,* 641 S.W.2d at 223. With these differences in mind, we hold that the well-developed "just and right" standard should continue to be the sole method used to account for and divide community property upon divorce.

Of course, there are also aspects of this state's community property system that provide additional remedies against a spouse for improper conduct involving the community estate. Texas recognizes the concept of fraud on the community, which is a wrong by one spouse that the court may consider in its division of the estate of the parties and that may justify an unequal division of the property. See *Belz* v. *Belz,* 667 S.W.2d 240, 247 (Tex. App.—Dallas 1984, writ ref'd n.r.e.). As the court in *Belz* aptly described it:

> [A] claim of fraud on the community is a means to an end, either to recover specific property wrongfully conveyed, ... or ... to obtain a greater share of the community estate upon divorce, in order to compensate the wronged spouse for his or her lost interest in the community estate.

Id. at 246–47. Just as in the present case, *Belz* involved alleged intentional deprivation of the wife's share of community assets. Nevertheless, despite the intentional nature of the claim, because the fraud was perpetrated on the community, the court correctly distinguished it from cases involving personal injuries for which recovery belongs to the separate estate.

Additionally, it is well settled that a trial court may award a money judgment to one spouse against the other in order to achieve an equitable division of the community estate. See *Murff* v. *Murff,* 615 S.W.2d 696, 699 (Tex. 1981) (allowing money judgment against husband in division of community property where he had substantial sums in savings before separation that had disappeared by the time of trial). Of course, the money judgment can only be used as a means for the wronged spouse to recoup the value of his or her share of the community estate lost through the wrongdoer spouses actions. See *Mazique* v. *Mazique.* 742 S.W.2d 805, 808 (Tex. App.—Houston [1st Dist.] 1987, no writ). Because the amount of the judgment is directly referable to a specific value of lost community property, it will never exceed the total value of the community estate. Still, a sound policy in favor of the wronged spouse is advanced: he or she should not suffer just because when it is time to divide the community, the other spouse has depleted the estate such that there is not enough money or property left to effect a just and right division.

The case of *In re Marriage of Moore.* 890 S. W.2d 821 (Tex. App.—Amarillo 1994, no writ), illustrates this aspect of marital property law. Mr. Moore filed for divorce, and Mrs. Moore counterclaimed for divorce and sought actual and exemplary damages for breach of fiduciary duty to the community estate. Among other things, she alleged that Mr. Moore had conveyed community property to third parties in breach of his fiduciary duty not to commit fraud on the community. The trial court found that Mr. Moore had breached his fiduciary duty, and assessed damages against him separate from the division of the marital estate. Absent a voluntary remittitur by Mrs. Moore of the damages for breach of fiduciary duty, the court of appeals held that it would remand to the trial court for a new property division.

The court correctly said:

> [A] trial court may award a money judgment to one spouse, even as damages for the other spouse's fraud on the community. However, that type of personal judgment is merely a means for recouping the defrauded spouse's share of the community property lost as a result of the wrongdoing spouse's breach of the trust relationship. Such a recovery is not awarded as 'separate damages' for an independent cause of action.

Id. at 828 (citations omitted). The court concluded that the only recourse available to Mrs. Moore for Mr. Moore's breach of fiduciary duty to the community estate was an action for fraud on the community. The court of appeals correctly determined that no independent cause of action exists in Texas to recover separate damages when the wrongful act defrauded the community estate.

Trial courts also have wide discretion and are allowed to take many factors into consideration in making a just and right division, see *Murff,* 615 S.W.2d at 698–99, including wasting of community assets. See Barbara Anne Kazen, *Division of Property at the Time of Divorce,* 49 BAYLOR L. REV. 417, 424–28 (1997) (discussing factors that may be considered by a trial court in effecting a just and right property division). This too allows injured spouses like Mrs. Schlueter to recover her appropriate share of not only that property existing in the community at the time of divorce, but also that which was improperly depleted from the community estate. Waste of community assets is similar to the allegations against the husband here: that without the wife's knowledge or consent, he wrongfully depleted the community of assets of which Mrs. Schlueter was entitled a share. Such behavior is properly considered when dividing a community estate.

Mrs. Schlueter argues that allowing a separate tort cause of action for actual fraud is necessary so that exemplary damages may be awarded for the intentional acts of the wrongdoer spouse. However, heightened culpability does not change the essential character of the wrong: a deprivation of community assets as opposed to a tort committed against a person or his or her separate property. As discussed, the "just and right" standard with accompanying consideration of a wrongdoer spouse's fraud on community assets provides wronged spouses such as Mrs. Schlueter with redress. Moreover, as we have previously held, "recovery of punitive damages requires a finding of an independent tort with accompanying actual damages." *Twin City Fire Ins. Co. v. Davis,* 904 S.W.2d 663, 665 (Tex. 1995); *Federal Express Corp. v. Dutschmann,* 846 S.W.2d 282, 284 (Tex. 1993): cf. *Amoco Prod. Co. v. Alexander,* 622 S.W.2d 563, 571 (Tex. 1981) (explaining in breach of contract action that even if breach is malicious, intentional, or capricious, punitive damages not recoverable without a tort). Because of our holding in the present case that there is no independent tort cause of action for wrongful disposition by a spouse of community assets, the wronged spouse may not recover punitive damages from the other spouse.

However, despite the inappropriateness of punitive damages, it is a logical extension of a standard that calls for a "just and right" division to allow the court to consider that a spouse not only deprived the community of assets to the detriment of the other spouse, but may have done so with dishonesty of purpose or intent to deceive. See *Land v. Marshall,* 426 S.W.2d 841, 846 n. 3 (Tex. 1968). This is the culpability needed for actual fraud on the community, which is one of the allegations by Mrs. Schlueter against Mr. Schlueter. Therefore, while we hold that a separate and independent tort action for actual fraud and accompanying exemplary damages against one's spouse do not exist in the context of a deprivation of community assets, if the wronged spouse can prove the heightened culpability of actual fraud, the trial court may consider it in the property division.

With regard to the causes of action against Mr. Schlucter's father, he has not argued that these separate and independent tort claims against him as a third-party defendant should also be abolished. Therefore, we do not reach that issue. We note that the trial court's $12,850 judgment of actual damages against Mrs. Schlueter's father-in-law was awarded to the community estate. That judgment represents an asset returned to the community estate, making it monetarily whole. Therefore, the trial court, in its just and right division, may not effect a disproportionate property division solely to make up for that formerly lost asset. However, as we have already discussed, the trial court may take into account Mr. Schlueter's conduct that resulted in a defrauding of the community estate.

For all the foregoing reasons, we reverse the court of appeals' judgment against Richard Schlueter for actual and exemplary damages, and attorney's fees on appeal, and remand this cause to the trial court for a new property division. We affirm the remainder of the court of appeals' judgment.

DISSENT: JUSTICE HEGHT, joined by CHIEF JUSTICE PHILLIPS, dissenting.

I respectfully dissent. If one spouse assaults the other, the wronged spouse can obtain not only a disproportionate share of the estate in a divorce proceeding but, if necessary to compensate fully for the wrong done, a judgment for actual damages and, on the requisite showing, punitive damages against the wrongdoer. The same rule applies if one spouse intentionally inflicts emotional distress on the other or negligently injures the other. But if one spouse defrauds the other of an interest in community property, the wronged spouse's sole redress is a disproportionate share of the estate in a divorce proceeding. That is the Court's holding in this case. The Court's only rationale for treating fraud on a spouse differently from other intentional torts is that fraud does not involve personal injuries. Why recovery should depend on whether damages are personal or economic the Court does not explain, except to say at one point that "redress is available in the present case without the creation of a separate tort cause of action between spouses." But the redress of a disproportionate division of the community is equally available for torts causing personal injuries, yet that has not kept the Court from providing for recovery of actual and punitive damages if necessary to fully compensate the wronged spouse. The Court does not, indeed cannot, explain why an uneven division of the community estate is inadequate relief for personal injuries but adequate for fraud.

JUSTICE SPECTOR, dissenting.

The Court today holds that fraud on the community is not an independent tort for which a defrauded spouse can recover actual and punitive damages. Although a disproportionate share of the community estate may serve as an appropriate remedy, I believe that Karen Schlueter should be able to recover from Richard Schlueter the punitive damages found by the jury as well. Accordingly, I dissent.

The Court's decision today signifies a retreat from its abrogation of the interspousal immunity doctrine in *Price* v. *Price*, 732 S. W2d 316 (Tex. 1987). Six years after *Price*, in *Twyman* v. *Twyman*, 855 S.W.2d 619, 624 (Tex. 1993), we stated that "there appears to be no legal impediment to bringing a tort claim in a divorce action based on either negligence or an intentional act such as assault or battery." However, while the Court today affirms the fraud judgment against her father-in-law, the Court nevertheless prohibits Karen Schlueter from recovering from her husband on the same fraud cause of action.

Adopting the Courts approach, the trial judge will simply take the tortfeasorspouse's conduct into account in dividing the community estate. The fraudulently transferred, converted, or wasted community property is rightly returned to the community through a resulting trust, a money judgment against the tortfeasor-spouse, or, as here, a judgment against a third party. These reimbursed funds are community property, in which the tortfeasor-spouse retains a property interest.

While the trial court may consider the tortfeasor-spouse's actions in making a just and right property division, his or her separate property will not be affected. I believe that the wronged spouse should be able to reach the defrauding spouse's separate property to recover punitive damages, in addition to a share of the community, for actual fraud on the community. *See, e.g., Mazique v. Mazique*, 742 S. W.2d 805, 807–08 (Tex. App.—Houston [1st Dist.] 1987, no writ) (awarding a money judgment for actual and punitive damages against husband who had defrauded wife's interest in community estate); see also Thomas M. Featherston, Jr., Marital Property Law—A Trusts & Estates Perspective, STATE BAR OF TEX., ADVANCED FAMILY LAW COURSE 13, 14 (1997) (citing *Mazique*).

Punitive damages punish wrongdoers and serve as an example to others. *Transportation Ins. Co. v. Moriel*, 879 S.W.2d 10, 17 (Tex. 1994); *Hofer v. Lavender*, 679 S.W.2d 470, 474 (Tex. 1984). "Our duty in civil cases, then, ... is to ensure that defendants who deserve to be punished in fact receive an appropriate level of punishment...." *Moriel*, 879 S.W.2d at 17. The imposition of punitive damages here would serve the very purposes for which they were designed: to punish the wrongdoer and deter others from similar conduct.

* * *

This Court is able to fashion remedies to right wrongs. *See Yamini v. Gentle*, 488 S.W.2d 839, 843 (Tex. Civ. App.—Dallas 1972, writ ref d n.r.c.) ("Equity leaves the way open to punish frauds and to redress wrongs perpetrated by means of fraud in whatever form it may appear"). Presented with this opportunity, the Court today fails to do so.

DISCUSSION

Texas has now adopted limits on punitive damages. As a general rule, punitive damages may not exceed the greater of (i) $200,000 or (ii) the sum of the plaintiff's noneconomic damages (up to $750,000) and twice the plaintiff's economic damages. Tex.Civ.Prac. & Rem. Code § 41.008. This limit does not apply if the defendant's conduct would constitute certain felonies, such as aggravated assault, sexual assault, or misapplication of fiduciary property.

An invasion of privacy claim could arise in connection with divorce. *See Clayton v. Richards*, 47 S.W.3d 149 (Tex. App.—Texarkana 2001, pet. denied) (allegations that wife arranged to videotape husband's activities in the bedroom while the wife was away on a trip). A tort claim based on federal wiretapping statutes may also be possible. *See Collins v. Collins*, 904 S.W.2d 792 (Tex. App.—Houston [1st Dist.] 1995), writ denied, 923 S.W.2d 569 (Tex. 1996).

If spouses were owners of a closely-held community property corporation during marriage, and one spouse misappropriates confidential information from the business, a breach of fiduciary duty claim is possible. *Norwood v. Norwood*, No. 2-07-244-CV, 2008 WL 4926008 (Tex. App.—Fort Worth Nov. 13, 2008, no pet.) (mem. op., not designated for publication).

Vickery v. Vickery

Supreme Court of Texas, 1999
999 S.W.2d 342

Justice HECHT, dissenting from the denial of the petition for review

The lower courts in this case awarded mental anguish damages and punitive damages to one spouse for the other's fraud in the division of their marital estate, and awarded mental anguish damages against an attorney for breach of her fiduciary duty to her client. These awards are not permitted under two of this Court's opinions that have issued while this petition for review has been pending. In *Schlueter v. Schlueter*, the Court held that "a separate and independent tort action for actual fraud and accompanying exemplary damages against one's spouse do not exist in the context of a deprivation of community assets".[11] In *Douglas v. Delp*, we held that mental anguish damages cannot be recovered for legal malpractice if plaintiff's loss is entirely economic.[12] If the holdings of *Schlueter* and *Douglas* were applied to the same issues in this case, the petition for review would have to be granted, the court of appeals' judgment reversed, and the case remanded to the district court for further proceedings. But the Court simply refuses to follow *Schlueter* and *Douglas* in this case that has been pending while those cases were being decided. The Court would not tolerate a lower court's refusal to follow our decisions, nor should it,[13] yet the Court will not follow its own decisions in contemporaneous appeals involving the same issues. It is awfully hard to insist on others' adherence to the rule of law when one's own commitment to the rule is, shall we say, intermittent. I would grant the petition for review in this case because I cannot see that *Schlueter* and *Douglas* leave any principled alternative. Accordingly, I respectfully dissent.

The petition for review in the present case was filed almost four months before *Schlueter* was decided, and the Court was well aware of the similarity of the issues in the two cases.[14] I specifically mentioned this case in my dissent to show that *Schlueter* was "not an isolated case."[15] The circumstances of this case, as depicted in the evidence supporting the jury's verdict, present an even stronger argument for recovery that those in *Schlueter*. Mr. Vickery, an attorney, misrepresented to his wife that they needed to divorce to protect their community estate from liability to a former client suing him for malpractice. When Mrs. Vickery balked, her husband enlisted a friend from law school days, Dianne Richards, to initiate divorce proceedings on behalf of Mrs. Vickery but without her consent. Richards also filed an answer and cross-petition for Mr. Vickery. A few weeks later the plaintiff in the malpractice case offered to settle with Mr. Vickery within the limits of his insurance coverage, but he did not disclose that offer to his wife. Instead, he insisted on proceeding with the divorce on the pretext of protecting the community estate and preserving his relationship with Mrs. Vickery and their nine-year-old daughter. Reluctantly acquiescing, Mrs. Vickery agreed to a divorce decree that gave her $1.1 million (about 7.5%) of the $14.6 million community estate. The balance of the estate was either given to Mr. Vickery or left undivided (the decree is vague). The couple's principal residence, a ranch where Mrs. Vickery and her daughter were living, was Mr. Vickery's separate property, although the community had a reimbursement claim that was not addressed in the decree.

---

11. 975 S.W.2d 584, 589 (Tex. 1998).

12. 975 S.W.2d 584, 589 (Tex. 1999).

13. See In re Smith Barney, Inc., 975 S.W.2d 593, 598 (Tex. 1998) (quoting Rodriguez de Quijas v. Shearson/American Express, Inc., 490 U.S. 477, 484 (1989)).

14. *See id.* at 591–592 (Hecht, J., dissenting).

15. *Id.* at 591.

The decree thus did little to accomplish Mr. Vickery's stated purpose in the divorce, to remove community property from the reach of a potential judgment creditor, although Mrs. Vickery may not have realized this at the time. Within six months, Mr. Vickery demanded that Mrs. Vickery agree to a nunc pro tunc decree that included a metes and bounds property description for the residence omitted from the original decree. Mrs. Vickery acceded. The next day Mr. Vickery retained a lawyer to have his former wife evicted from the residence. Shortly after Mrs. Vickery was served with process, Mr. Vickery married one of her best friends.

Realizing at last the depth of her former husband's deception, Mrs. Vickery attempted to negotiate a redivision of their community estate, but without success. Mrs. Vickery then filed the present action for a bill of review setting aside the divorce decree, a different division of the community estate, and actual and punitive damages from Mr. Vickery and attorney Richards. The jury found Mr. Vickery liable for fraud and breach of fiduciary duty and assessed Mrs. Vickery's damages at $6.7 million for loss of marital property and $1.3 million mental anguish, plus $1 million punitive damages. The jury also found that Richards' breach of fiduciary duty caused Mrs. Vickery a $100,000 loss of marital property and $350,000 in mental anguish damages. The district court rendered judgment: setting aside the prior divorce decree as having been obtained through fraud extrinsic to the proceeding; dividing the $14.6 million community estate $8.5 million (58%) to Mrs. Vickery and $6.1 million (42%) to Mr. Vickery; awarding Mrs. Vickery $1.3 million mental anguish damages, $1.5 million prejudgment interest, and $1 million punitive damages against Mr. Vickery; and awarding Mrs. Vickery $350,000 in unspecified damages against Richards. Mrs. Vickery elected to receive the larger share of the estate awarded by the court rather than the $6.7 million for loss of marital property found by the jury.

The court of appeals affirmed in an unpublished opinion, a copy of which is attached as Appendix I. Justice Andell dissented from the denial of rehearing en banc, explaining that he would have held that while Mr. Vickery's conduct should have been considered in dividing the community estate, Mrs. Vickery had no independent tort action against her former husband and thus was not entitled to actual or punitive damages or prejudgment interest. Justice Andell would have remanded the case to the district court to reconsider the community division.

After this Court's decision in *Schlueter* issued, Mrs. Vickery attempted to distinguish that case from hers, arguing that *Schlueter* involved "mere 'fraud on the community'" while the present case involves "actual and intentional fraud." The argument cannot survive even a cursory reading of *Schlueter*. Mrs. Schlueter vigorously contended that "allowing a separate tort cause of action for actual fraud is necessary so that exemplary damages may be awarded for the intentional acts of the wrongdoer spouse."[16] The Court expressly rejected this contention. Mrs. Vickery argues that her former husband's fraud is "particularly repugnant" because he "not only defrauded his spouse but he also tried to hoodwink the courts." The evidence favorable to the verdict indicates that Mrs. Vickery is correct, but Mr. Schlueter's fraud also involved both his spouse and the divorce court. Mrs. Vickery argues that her former husband did not merely deplete community assets, as Mr. Schlueter did by the transfers to his father, but directed his deception at her personally. I cannot see how Mr. Schlueter's deception was any less personal or actionable because he involved his father than was Mr. Vickery's.

Having dissented in *Schlueter*, I am not anxious to see its holding extended, but Mrs. Vickery has not distinguished *Schlueter*, and I think she cannot do so. In my dissent in

---

16. *Schlueter*, 975 S.W.2d at 589.

Schlueter I argued that the present case, then pending, presented compelling reasons to allow one spouse to recover against another for fraud.[17] The Court was unmoved. While I remain in doubt that *Schlueter* was correctly decided, there is no doubt that it is the law. The Court cannot simply pick and choose the cases in which the rule it has announced will apply.

Applying *Schlueter* would require that the actual and punitive damages awarded Mrs. Vickery against her former husband be reversed and the case remanded to the district court to reconsider what division of the community is just and right. The district court may consider Mr. Vickery's "dishonesty of purpose or intent to deceive" and "the heightened culpability of actual fraud"[18] as found by the jury. As I understand *Schlueter*, the court may not simply divide the community estate to award Mrs. Vickery damages she cannot otherwise recover, but it also need not measure her share by the damages she has suffered. The court must consider all relevant factors in dividing the community.

DISCUSSION

For an attempt to distinguish *Vickery* and *Schlueter*, see Christa Brown, "Marital Fraud," Tex. B.J. (July 2000) at 630.

The Texas Supreme Court generally reaffirmed *Schlueter* in *Chu v. Hong*, 249 S.W.3d 441 (Tex. 2008).

---

17. 975 S.W.2d at 589–590.
18. *Douglas*, 975 S.W.2d at 589–590.

Chapter Eight

Reimbursement and Acquisitions Over Time

A. Comparing the Pro Rata Approach to the Inception of Title Approach

1. In General

McCurdy v. McCurdy

Texas Court of Appeals—Waco, 1963
372 S.W.2d 381, writ ref'd

WILSON, Justice.

The problem we are required to solve is whether proceeds of life insurance policies issued to the insured husband before marriage naming his estate as beneficiary (a) belong to the separate estate of the husband after his death, only in proportion to the amount of premiums paid by him before marriage; or (b) belong entirely to his separate estate, with right of reimbursement to the community based on the amount of the premiums paid from community funds during marriage. Appellant urges the first solution; appellee the second, adopted by the trial court, and by us.

The facts are stipulated. Insured and his wife were married August 5, 1960, and their marriage continued until his death, March 16, 1962. Both policies of life insurance were issued to the insured husband before marriage, naming his estate beneficiary. One policy was issued May 22, 1956; the other, February 13, 1959. The 1959 policy was "converted" February 12, 1962, as authorized by the original policy. The nature of the conversion is not shown. Of the total premiums on the two policies, $1,094.66 was paid by the husband before marriage; $657.60 was paid during coverture from community funds. The executor named in the husband's will listed the proceeds as a part of the husband's separate estate. The widow's action against the executor sought determination of the status of the proceeds. The trial court concluded the proceeds constituted a part of the husband's separate estate and decreed that the community estate of husband and wife should be reimbursed on the basis of the payments made out of community funds for premiums.

The problem is directly presented for the first time in this State under these facts. In all other cases we have examined which reached the question, and where the beneficiary was insured's estate, the policies were issued during marriage. Our decision is restricted to the stated facts.

211

In approaching solution to this problem we must look somewhat beyond the immediate consequences of decision in this case. A dominant factor in our conclusion is an effort, within the broad principles of dissonant precedent, to fit life insurance proceeds under the present facts to the pattern of Texas community property law as applied to other types of property. This the Legislature has apparently sought to do by amending art. 23, Sec. 1.

That pattern, as to realty, title to which is acquired before marriage, and a portion of the consideration for which is thereafter paid from community, fixes the character of title at the time of its inception or acquisition.

Why do we not adopt the California solution formula of proportionate premium payments? California has done what we think should here be done; it has made its solution as to life insurance proceeds consonant with its other community property law.

Two reasons for applying the tracing principle to give proportionate ownership of proceeds are suggested: (a) simplicity; (b) just results. These are good reasons, and we have carefully considered others. It does not appear that the inception of title rule is less simple: each method requires computation of the amount of premiums paid out of community funds. Many incidental problems resulting from attempted application of the proportionate ownership rule are avoided. If simplicity be a virtue, we think the inception of title rule is simpler. It facilitates application of general principles of community property law. The inception of title rule is not less equitable in results. While in this case the proceeds which would be proportionately attributable to the community under the tracing theory happened to exceed the community premium payments, in another case the gross premiums so paid out might well exceed the total proceeds. To permit the nature of the property to be determined by the monetary result is not necessarily equitable; and apparent inequity may result under either method, depending on the facts in each case.

In our opinion the proceeds of the policies constitute the separate estate of the deceased insured, and the community estate is entitled to reimbursement on the basis of premiums paid with community funds.

DISCUSSION

Spouses frequently acquire property over time. For example, most people make significant purchases pursuant to a credit transaction; the purchase price is paid over time. Spouses frequently make such payments with some separate property and some community property.

There are two basic ways to characterize property that has been acquired over time. One common method is called the pro rata approach. Under this approach, separate property payments are totalled and compared to the aggregate amount of all payments made. The portion of the separate property contribution would constitute the fractional interest held by the separate estate. The community would own the remainder of the item. All payments are considered when the respective separate and community interests are being computed.

In contrast, under the inception of title approach the determinative time is the time when either spouse first acquires an interest in the property. The character of the property is determined by the consideration transferred at that time. Any later payments do not affect ownership.

For example, in *McCurdy* the court determined that the insurance policy was the decedent's separate property, because the first premium was paid with separate funds. The later premiums paid with community funds would merely create a potential right of reimbursement. In contrast, under the pro rata approach, the community would have a fractional interest in the proceeds, based upon the relative amount of contributions made.

What is the character of the policy if one is purchased before marriage, but the coverage amount or the carrier is changed during marriage? The Texas Supreme Court has held that the policy should not be treated as separate property. *See Barnett v. Barnett*, 985 S.W.2d 520 (Tex. App.—Houston [1st Dist.] 1998), review granted, affirmed in part, reversed in part, 67 S.W.3d 107 (Tex. 2001).

If during a marriage a spouse buys a life insurance policy with community funds on the life a third person and the person dies, the benefits would be community property. *See Dent v. Dent*, 689 S.W. 2d 521 (Tex. App.—Fort Worth 1985, no writ).

Texas courts normally have applied the inception of title approach to characterize acquisitions over time. However, in the pension cases the pro rata approach has been used.

If something is characterized as community property, it then must be valued.

In re Estate of Logan

California Court of Appeals, 1987
236 Cal. Rptr. 368

KING, Associate Justice.

In this case we hold that a term life insurance policy upon the life of one spouse is not divisible as community property under the Family Law Act, even though premiums for the policy before separation were paid with community property funds. An exception will arise if the insured spouse becomes uninsurable during the term paid with community funds, since the right to continued coverage upon payment of future premiums is a valuable community property asset for one who is uninsurable. If the insured dies during the term paid with community funds, the proceeds of the policy are community property. When premiums for a new term have been paid from post-separation separate property earnings and the insured remains insurable, the policy must be confirmed to the insured as separate property.

Frances Jeanne Logan (now Pritchard, hereinafter "Jeanne") appeals from orders denying her any community property interest in the proceeds of her former husband's employment-related term life insurance policy.

Jeanne and William Logan married in 1947 and separated in 1966. William worked for American Airlines which deducted premiums for a company sponsored group term life insurance plan from his salary. Their 1968 interlocutory judgment of divorce ordered William to maintain this life insurance with the couple's minor children as beneficiaries until they reached the age of majority.

When William died in 1984, the children of his marriage to Jeanne were adults. Jeanne brought this action seeking a portion of the proceeds from William's term life insurance. She appeals the trial court's determination that she had no community property interest in these proceeds.

The trial court denied Jeanne's request for a 39.583 percent share[1] in the proceeds of William's American Airlines term life insurance proceeds because "I don't believe term

---

1. In a 1975 proceeding the trial court had amended the interlocutory judgment to provide that Jeanne's community property interest in William's pension was 39.583 percent. Jeanne claimed the same interest in his term life insurance proceeds in these proceedings.

policies are community property," explicitly rejecting contrary authority in *Bowman v. Bowman* (1985) 171 Cal. App. 3d 148, 217 Cal. Rptr. 174 and *In re Marriage of Gonzalez* (1985) 168 Cal. App. 3d 1021, 214 Cal. Rptr. 634, and following the holding in *In re Marriage of Lorenz* (1983) 146 Cal. App. 3d 464, 194 Cal. Rptr. 237. The two appellate court decisions actually in conflict over the issue of whether term life insurance is a community property asset are *Lorenz* and *Gonzalez*, since *Bowman*, without detailed analysis, was decided by the same Division which had decided *Gonzalez* a few months earlier.

The first case to consider a closely related issue was *Biltoft v. Wooten* (1979) 96 Cal. App. 3d 58, 157 Cal. Rptr. 581, which involved a contributory group term life insurance policy available through the insured's employment and paid with bi-weekly deductions from his pay. After separation, but before dissolution, decedent had changed the beneficiary under the policy from his spouse to his children. On appeal the issue was whether the proceeds were community or separate property. The court held the proceeds were part community and part separate according to the proportion that the amount of premiums paid with community property bore to the total amount of premiums paid. The reasoning underlying the decision was that each premium payment did not purchase a new contract of insurance because, if the decedent had tried to purchase the policy after separation, "it is unlikely that he would have been able to obtain the same coverage for the same premium on the same terms of eligibility" and "The decedent's community efforts for the 20 years prior to the separation maintained the policy in force." The court's opinion does not indicate what evidence, if any, was presented to support the conclusion that it was "unlikely" decedent could have purchased the identical policy after separation.

Lorenz distinguished *Biltoft* as a case dealing with the right to proceeds from term insurance upon the death of the insured spouse prior to dissolution. The *Lorenz* analysis was that many fringe benefits of employment such as use of an employer's health club facilities, reduced prices at the company cafeteria or discounts on purchases of an employer's products were of value to an employee, but did not constitute community property divisible upon dissolution. *Lorenz* held that although the benefits of term life insurance have a value, until those benefits become payable, the policy itself is worthless and is not divisible as community property.

The *Gonzalez* court concluded, "*Lorenz* is simply incorrect in the assertion that assets such as term life insurance and accrued vacation time have no economic value...." *Gonzalez* reasoned that the spouses had acquired rights because the policy had been obtained during marriage with community funds. The court concluded, with no indication what evidence existed in the record to support its conclusion, "Undoubtedly the premium rate was very favorable and pursuant to federal statute, husband was not required to establish medical eligibility for coverage. We are confident the same policy acquired today, assuming husband is still insurable, would cost considerably more." (*Id.* at p. 1026, 214 Cal. Rptr. 634.)

To say that "[t]he *Gonzalez* decision has been subject to criticism by members of the Bar" is putting it mildly. In addition to placing another roadblock in the way of simplified dissolution of marriage, the requirements of this decision would also significantly increase the cost of dissolution by requiring each side to employ expert witnesses to testify to the value of term life insurance policies. We suspect that in most cases the cost to the parties of expert witnesses would be greater than the value of the term life insurance policy. We believe the *Gonzalez* and *Bowman* decisions result from an erroneous analysis of the nature of term life insurance policies.

Simply stated, term insurance is life insurance written for a fixed or specified term. To reflect the increasing risk of death as the insured increases in age, term insurance policies either have increasing premiums from year to year or provide decreasing death benefits paid on the insured's death. At the expiration of the term of years, the policy expires without retaining cash value. One advantage of term insurance is its cost. Since it does not retain cash value, the premium cost for comparable coverage is less than it is with whole life insurance. Some forms of term insurance may be converted into permanent or whole life policies or may be automatically renewable at regular intervals at a higher premium. Term life insurance policies typically contain two elements, dollar coverage payable in the event of death and a right to renewal for future terms without proof of current medical eligibility.

As to the element of dollar coverage, term life insurance simply provides for protection against the contingency of the death of the insured during the term of the policy. If the premium for the next term is not paid, the policy is not renewed. In this respect, it is the same as automobile or health insurance. Thus when the premium is paid with community funds, the policy is community property for the period covered by that premium. This is true whether the premium is paid as a fringe benefit by the insured's employer, paid for by the insured, or a combination of both. The policy provides dollar coverage only for the specific term for which the premium was paid. Thus, as to dollar coverage, term life insurance upon which premiums were paid from community funds has no value after the term has ended without the insured having become deceased.

With respect to the element of the right to renew coverage for additional terms, term life insurance has either a significant value or no value at all. The right to renewal upon payment of the premium for the next term is significant because the insured possesses the right even if he or she has become uninsurable in the meantime. Usually, policies require increasing premiums and/or decreasing amounts of coverage as the insured gets older. If, as is usually the case, the insured is insurable at the end of the term purchased with community funds, the renewed policy, that is, the term policy purchased by the payment of the premium with post-separation earnings which are separate property pursuant to Civil Code section 5118, or by the employer as a post-separation fringe benefit, changes character from community to separate property.

At this time, if the insured is insurable, the community has fully received everything it bargained for, dollar protection against the contingency of death during the term paid for with community funds and the right to renew without proof of insurability for an additional term. If the insured remains insurable, the right to renew the policy has no value since the insured could obtain comparable term insurance for a comparable price in the open market. The community having received everything it bargained for, there is no longer any community property interest in the policy and no community asset left to divide.

We believe the courts in *Biltoft*, *Gonzalez* and *Bowman* came to incorrect conclusions because they made unsupported and erroneous assumptions about the nature of term life insurance and the availability to the insured of other comparable insurance. In *Biltoft*, the court assumed "it is unlikely that [decedent] would have been able to obtain the same coverage for the same premium on the same terms of eligibility." In *Gonzalez* the court assumed "[u]ndoubtedly the premium rate was very favorable" and "husband was not required to establish medical eligibility for coverage," and concluded, "We are confident the same policy today, assuming the husband is still insurable, would cost considerably more." To this we ask, where was the evidence to support these assumptions? For all we know, by the time of the appeal, Mr. Gonzalez or Mr. Bowman might well have changed jobs and gotten new employment in the private sector which provided greater term life insurance coverage paid for by the employer. Such coverage is usually available even if the employed might be otherwise uninsurable, since new employees are usually covered under the employer's group life insurance plans without evidence of insurability. The group insurance with the former employers would have ceased when the insured changed employment.

We believe the correct rule to be that term life insurance covering a spouse who remains insurable is community property only for the period beyond the date of separation for which community funds were used to pay the premium. If the insured dies during that period the proceeds of the policy are fully community. Otherwise, the insured remaining insurable, a term policy does not constitute a divisible community asset since the policy is of no value and the community has fully received what it bargained for. If the insured becomes uninsurable during the term paid with community funds, then the right to future insurance coverage which cannot otherwise be purchased is a community asset to be divided upon dissolution. We need not discuss how this right might be valued because we determine Jeanne has no community interest in William's term life insurance policy since he was insurable when he commenced paying the premiums with his post-separation property earnings.

DISCUSSION

As a part of the property settlement, an insured spouse sometimes agrees to retain the former spouse or the children as beneficiaries of the policy. Courts have enforced such commitments if the insured changed the beneficiary after divorce. *Seaman v. Seaman*, 756 S.W.2d 56 (Tex. App.—Texarkana 1988, no writ).

Most courts agree with *Logan* that term insurance is valueless at divorce. Whole life policies, in contrast, do have cash value. *See Grost v. Grost*, 561 S.W.2d 223 (Tex. Civ. App.—Tyler 1977, writ dism'd). In *In re Marriage of Taylor*, No. 07-02-0051-CV, 2002 WL 31001298 (Tex. App.—Amarillo Sept. 4, 2002, no pet.) (not designated for publication), a spouse had a whole life policy at the time of the marriage, and its cash value had increased by the time of divorce. The court treated the increased value as community property.

Tex. Fam. Code § 7.005 addresses a problem that arises when a spouse dies after divorce without changing the beneficiary designation on a life insurance policy. Before the adoption of § 7.005, in some instances, even where the decree awarded the policy to the spouse who died, the former spouse was considered entitled to the life insurance proceeds if the decedent never changed the beneficiary designation after divorce. Section 7.005 generally overrules these cases. *See also Brandon v. Travelers Ins. Co.*, 18 F.3d 1321 (5th Cir. 1994). ERISA may preempt this statute in some instances. See chapter 13.

2. Designating a Life Insurance Beneficiary

Under Texas law, when the first spouse dies, that spouse has the right to devise one-half of each item of community property. However, each spouse during the marriage may make reasonable gifts of community property. These principles interact when community property life insurance proceeds are at issue, because Texas courts treat a life insurance beneficiary designation as an *inter vivos* gift.

Jackson v. Smith

Texas Court of Appeals—Dallas, 1985
703 S.W.2d 791, no writ

ALLEN, Justice.

Betty Jackson ("Betty") appeals from the judgment on an interpleader action brought by Massachusetts Indemnity and Life Insurance Company ("MILICO") to determine who was entitled to the proceeds from a life insurance policy issued to Sylvester Jackson. Betty, the sister of Sylvester Jackson and the designated beneficiary of the policy, claimed that she was entitled to the $70,000 proceeds. Eliza Smith ("Eliza") claimed that, as the alleged common-law wife of Sylvester Jackson, she was entitled to all, or alternatively, one-half of the proceeds because Sylvester Jackson perpetrated a fraud on the community by designating his sister, rather than Eliza, as beneficiary of the life insurance policy which was purchased with community funds. The trial court rendered judgment awarding $34,250 to Eliza, $34,250 to the estate of Sylvester Jackson, and $1,500 to MILICO for attorneys' fees on its interpleader action. Betty brings one cross-point contesting the trial court's judgment. We hold that the trial court erred in awarding $34,250 to Sylvester Jackson's estate. Therefore, we affirm that part of the judgment awarding $34,250 to Eliza Smith and $1,500 to MILICO, and render judgment awarding $34,250 to Betty Jackson.

The case was tried to the court without a jury. The record shows that Eliza and Sylvester Jackson lived together for approximately five years, during which time Sylvester Jackson took out the policy in issue. Sylvester Jackson obtained the policy from Ahmed Kadry and his trainee, Carl Wynn, all of whom worked together for the city of Dallas. Kadry testified that Sylvester Jackson instructed him to designate Betty as the beneficiary of the policy on the insurance application form.

In her fifth point of error, Betty asserts that the trial court erred in finding that Sylvester Jackson and Eliza were husband and wife because no evidence of their common-law marriage was presented at trial. We disagree.

We hold that there was some evidence presented at trial to support the trial court's finding that a common-law marriage existed between Sylvester Jackson and Eliza Smith. Betty's fifth point of error is overruled.

In her third point of error, Betty contests the trial court's finding that fraud on the community existed because the finding was against the weight of the evidence. Betty argues that she, as Sylvester Jackson's sister, was "the natural object of Sylvester Jackson's bounty"; that Sylvester Jackson designated Betty as beneficiary in order to provide for his children; and that Eliza was adequately provided for by Sylvester Jackson's estate distribution.

We may set aside the trial court's finding only if it is so contrary to the great weight of the evidence as to be manifestly unjust. *In re King's Estate,* 150 Tex. at 665, 244 S.W.2d at 661; *Fortner,* 687 S.W.2d at 12. We have reviewed all of the evidence presented at trial, and we conclude that the trial court's finding of fraud on the community is not manifestly unjust.

The "fraud on the community" or "fraud on the spouse" doctrine is a judicially created concept based on the theory of constructive fraud. *Givens v. Girard Life Insurance Company of America,* 480 S.W.2d 421, 425 (Tex. Civ. App.—Dallas 1972, writ ref'd n.r.e.). Constructive fraud is the breach of a legal or equitable duty which violates a fiduciary relationship, as exists between spouses. A presumption of constructive fraud arises where one spouse disposes of the other spouse's one-half interest in community property without the other's knowledge or consent. The burden of proof is then on the disposing spouse or his donee to prove the fairness of the disposition of the other spouse's one-half community ownership. Where the donee or beneficiary is related to the disposing spouse or decedent, the courts look to three factors in determining the fairness of the disposition: (1) the relationship of the beneficiary to the decedent; (2) whether special circumstances tend to justify the gift; and (3) whether the community funds used were reasonable in proportion to the remaining community assets. We hold that the disposing spouse or his donee has the burden to prove these three factors in order to rebut the presumption of constructive fraud.

The record shows that Betty proved that she was the sister of Sylvester Jackson, and that she was caring for Sylvester Jackson's minor children by a previous marriage. The record also reflects, however, that Betty did not carry her burden of proof on whether the community funds life insurance proceeds were a reasonable gift, considering the size of the total community estate. The evidence shows that, in the declaration of heirship proceeding, Eliza was awarded a 1979 Ford pick-up truck, a one-half interest in Sylvester Jackson's home and household possessions, and a one-half interest in two parcels of real estate in East Texas. The record does not establish whether these items were obtained during the common-law marriage of Eliza and Sylvester Jackson; if so, Eliza would be entitled to her one-half community interest as a matter of law upon dissolution of the community estate.

The record also shows that Betty was the designated beneficiary on two other policies insuring the life of Sylvester Jackson. One policy, which was purchased during the marriage of Eliza and Sylvester Jackson, had already paid off the $60,000 proceeds to Betty. The record does not show the time of purchase or the amount of the other policy.

On this state of the record, we cannot say that the trial court erred in finding fraud on the community. Betty failed to introduce evidence as to the total value of the community estate and the proportionate value of the proceeds at issue. She thus failed to carry her burden to prove that Eliza was adequately provided for by the remainder of the community assets. *See Redfearn v. Ford*, 579 S.W.2d 195 (Tex. Civ. App.—Dallas 1979, writ ref'd n.r.e.) (affirming finding of no fraud where wife provided for by insurance proceeds amounting to one-quarter of community estate); *Horlock v. Horlock*, 533 S.W.2d 52, 55–56 (Tex. Civ. App.—Houston [14th Dist.] 1975, writ dism'd) (affirming finding of no fraud where gifts to daughters constituted only 13.1517% of the total estate); *Davis v. Prudential Insurance Company of America*, 331 F.2d 346, 352 (5th Cir. 1964) (reversing judgment awarding proceeds to mother-beneficiary, where proceeds constituted 98% of community estate).

We hold that the trial court's implied finding, that the size of the gift in relation to the total size of the community was a fraud on Eliza Smith's rights, is not manifestly unjust. Betty's third point of error is overruled.

Betty next contends that the trial court erred in awarding one-half of the insurance proceeds to Eliza and one-half to Sylvester Jackson's estate. We agree.

It is axiomatic that Eliza's community property interest in the life insurance proceeds extends to only one-half of those proceeds. *Givens*, 480 S.W.2d at 427. The insured may dispose of his one-half interest, or one-half the amount of the proceeds, as he pleases. *Id.* Thus, where the surviving spouse establishes fraud on the community, that spouse may recover the one half of the proceeds which represents that spouse's one-half interest in the community property. The other half of the proceeds, representing the disposing spouse's community interest, is a gift to the designated beneficiary and is unaffected by constructive fraud.

The trial court's finding of fraud on the community affected only Eliza's half of the proceeds. The other half goes to the designated beneficiary. Accordingly, we modify the trial court's judgment to award $34,250 to Eliza Smith and $34,250 to Betty Jackson. The estate of Sylvester Jackson takes nothing.

DISCUSSION

How does *Jackson* suggest the reasonableness of the beneficiary designation be determined? What fraction of the community estate would be a reasonable fraction to give to a third party? Would this depend upon the relationship between the decedent and the beneficiary and the beneficiary's need?

If a gift of community property is unreasonable and both spouses are alive and still married, the non-donor spouse can recover the total gift for the community estate. If the donor spouse has died, the other spouse can only recover one-half of the gift as the survivor's separate property. This is what occurred in *Jackson*.

If the policy had been first purchased before marriage, the policy is the insured's separate property. The insured could name anyone the beneficiary, subject to community reimbursement claim for premiums paid. *See Camp v. Camp*, 972 S.W.2d 906 (Tex. App.—Corpus Christi 1998, pet. denied).

B. Inception of Title and Credit Purchases

1. In General

Bell v. Bell

Texas Court of Appeals—Houston [14th Dist.], 1980
593 S.W.2d 424, no writ

MILLER, Justice.

The parties were married on January 5, 1975, and separated on November 18, 1977, and are the parents of one child. The wife has admitted that appellant used $15,000.00 of his separate funds as a down payment on the home the couple purchased after their marriage at a total cost of $62,000.00. The home was stipulated to have a value of $85,500.00 at the time of trial, and was then subject to a $46,500.00 mortgage. The balance of the community estate consisted of several shares of International Business Machines Company stock, three automobiles of which two were of small value, and various items of personal property. Answering the second issue, the jury recommended that the couple's community property be divided 60% to the wife and 40% to the husband.

The court decreed an item by item division of the couple's personal property, awarded the homestead to the wife, and appointed her managing conservator.

Tex. Fam. Code Ann. Sec. 3.63 gives to the trial court wide discretion in making division of the property of the parties. There is no requirement that such division be equal, and, unless there is a clear abuse of discretion, appellate courts will not overrule the trial court's allocation. We cannot say that in this case there has been an abuse of discretion in the total value of the distribution to each party, in light of their respective earning powers, capacities and abilities.

Having said that, we must still hold that there is error in the distribution. It is settled law in Texas that the character of marital property is determined by those conditions which exist at the inception of title. Where property is purchased partly with separate cash and partly with community credit, there comes into existence a tenancy in common between the separate and community estates in the proportion that each bears to the total purchase price. *Gleich v. Bongio*, 128 Tex. 606, 99 S.W.2d 881 (Tex. Comm'n. App. 1937, opinion adopted). Further, the trial court has no discretion to take the fee to separate real property of one party and give it to the other party. *Eggemeyer v. Eggemeyer*, 554 S.W.2d 137 (Tex. Sup. 1977). It follows that the trial court erred by allocating the entire fee to the homestead to the wife, when the husband's separate estate was entitled to 15/62nds thereof.

The judgment of the court below with regard to the division of the property is reversed and remanded for further proceedings in light of this opinion. All other parts of that judgment are affirmed.

DISCUSSION

Many acquisitions over time are financed. In other words, when an item is purchased, the seller receives a down payment, and the remainder of the purchase price is paid in the form of a promissory note from the buyer to the seller. Alternatively, the buyer can go to a bank for a loan, sign a note in favor of the bank, and give the seller all cash. Under the inception of title approach, the character of the down payment is not the only consideration relevant. The credit contribution also affects the character of the property.

Under Texas law, credit received during marriage normally is deemed a community contribution. It does not matter whether one or both spouses receive the credit. So, in *Bell* the credit contribution at closing made the house partially community property. Credit obtained before marriage is a separate property contribution. So, the duplex in *Hawkins*, *infra*, was 100% separate property.

As you can see from *Bell*, under the inception of title approach property can be partially community and partially separate, if both types of property were contributed at the time of purchase. The house was purchased during marriage for $62,000, and was worth $85,500 at the time of divorce. How should this appreciation be shared? At divorce, there was a loan balance of $46,500. What estate pays this debt?

Credit obtained during marriage is not always a community contribution. If the lender agrees with the borrower that the lender will only look to the borrower's separate estate to recover the funds borrowed, the loan is a separate property loan. Otherwise, according to the majority Texas rule, any credit received during marriage is a community contribution. *See Jones v. Jones*, 890 S.W.2d 471 (Tex. App.—Corpus Christi 1994, no writ), where the court characterized the proceeds of a loan obtained by the husband during marriage as a community loan, even though the loan was secured by a separate property certificate of deposit. The court noted that the lender did not agree to look solely to the certificate of deposit for repayment. Because community property potentially could have been attached to collect the loan, the court concluded that this was a community contribution. Conversely, if the lender agreed to a non-recourse note secured by separate property (in other words, the lender could only look to the security for repayment), this should make the loan a separate property contribution. A few cases have applied a less stringent test to determine whether a loan is a separate property loan. For example, if the spouses agreed between themselves at the time the loan was obtained that the loan was a separate property loan to one spouse, and the loan was repaid from the separate estate of that spouse, some courts have characterized the loan as a separate property contribution.

Wierzchula v. Wierzchula

Texas Court of Appeals—Houston [14th Dist.], 1981
623 S.W.2d 730, no writ

SMITH, Justice.

This is a divorce suit in which the primary issue is whether certain real property is community property or separate property. Appellant, Margarita Wierzchula, appeals from the trial court judgment awarding the property to Georg Wierzchula, appellee, as his separate property.

On August 2, 1975, Georg Wierzchula, a single man, entered into an earnest money contract to purchase a home located at 3103 Point Clear Drive, Missouri City, Texas. On September 30, 1975, he applied as a single man for a home loan guaranty with the Veteran's Administration and on October 8, 1975, the Veteran's Administration issued a certificate of loan commitment to him as a single man. On November 25, 1975, the parties to this litigation were married. Thereafter, on January 21, 1976, Georg Wierzchula received a deed conveying the property to him as a single man and at the same time he executed a deed of trust and a promissory note in his individual capacity.

By her second point of error, the appellant asserts the trial court erred in holding that the property was the separate property of appellee.

The character of property as separate or community is determined at the time of inception of title. Inception of title occurs when a party first has a right of claim to the property by virtue of which title is finally vested.

Property possessed by either spouse upon dissolution of the marriage is presumptively community property. However, this presumption may be rebutted by proof that the property was the separate property of either spouse. To overcome this presumption the appellee offered proof that he had entered into an earnest money contract while he was still a single man and that the down payment on such contract was made with his separate funds.

The question then arises at what step in the purchase of real property is there claim to the property?

It is well established that a claim to real property can arise before the legal title or evidence of title has been attained. *Welder v. Lambert*, 91 Tex. 510, 44 S.W.281 (1898). In *Welder*, a contract right giving the husband the right to acquire lands was obtained before marriage, but the conditions of the contract were not met until during marriage, at which time title vested. The court held that the property was the husband's separate property because his claim to the property was acquired before marriage.

In our case, the appellee acquired a claim to the property at the time the purchase money contract was entered into. The earnest money date being prior to the marriage of the parties, the appellee's right of claim to the property preceded the marriage, and the character of the property as separate property was established and the community property presumption was rebutted.

A second presumption arises that the property was community property as a result of the note being signed after the marriage. A debt acquired by either spouse during marriage is presumptively a community debt. *Gleich v. Bongio*, 128 Tex. 606, 99 S.W.2d 882 (1937). This presumption is also rebuttable. Proof that the lender agreed to look only to the separate property of one spouse for the security for the debt will rebut this presumption. The agreement between the borrower and the creditor is one of the primary indicators of the character of the loan to be made.

In our case, prior to marriage, the appellee alone made application for a loan as a single man. The loan commitment was made by the Veteran's Administration to the appellee as a single man. The deed was made to the appellee as a single man and the appellee alone signed the note to secure the vendor's lien and deed of trust. The lender's intention appears to be clear that it was looking only to the appellee to meet the obligations contained in the note.

We hold that the trial court did not err in finding the property was the appellee's separate property. The appellant's second point of error is overruled.

DISCUSSION

When real estate is purchased, the buyer normally first signs an earnest money purchase contract. Such a contract sets forth the purchase terms if the buyer approves the condition of the property, obtains appropriate financing, and all other conditions set forth in the contract are satisfied. When the purchase contract is signed, the buyer normally gives a "deposit" to the seller or the seller's broker. This deposit normally is returned to the buyer if the sale is not completed, and is applied to the purchase price if the sale occurs. Title is transferred from the seller to the buyer, and all consideration as delivered to the seller, on the closing date. The closing date normally occurs a few months after the earnest money contract is signed.

The *Wierzchula* court applies the inception of title approach in a technically correct manner. As you can see, however, the result is not too sensible. Some characterization fudging is required to justify the conclusion that the house is 100% separate property. The court concludes that the note was a separate property contribution by the husband. Is this correct, under the majority rule the court says it is applying? If it is a separate property loan, does the community have any claim regarding the house?

Most courts realize that it is unreasonable to look only to the character of the consideration given by a spouse when the earnest money contract is signed for the characterization of real estate purchases. Most courts look to the consideration contributed on the closing date to characterize property. At the closing date, the seller will receive all consideration set forth in the purchase contract. This date gives a clearer reflection of the contributions being made by both estates toward the purchase.

Courts continue to struggle to characterize purchases where a contract is signed before marriage and the deed is received after the wedding. *See Carter v. Carter*, 736 S.W.2d 775 (Tex. App.—Houston [14th Dist.] 1987, no writ), where the court reached a result roughly consistent with *Wierzchula*, except that the community was granted reimbursement. Reimbursement will be discussed in the next section. Cf. *Duke v. Duke*, 605 S.W.2d 408 (Tex. App.—El Paso 1980, writ dism'd).

Option contracts present similar issues. In such situations it could be argued that the character of the option payment should determine the character of the property, since the value of the option derives from the option payment. For example, in *Roach v. Roach*, 672 S.W.2d 524 (Tex. App.—Amarillo 1984, no writ) the husband obtained before marriage the right to purchase certain realty for $2,500. During marriage, the husband used $2,500 of community funds to buy the realty, when it was worth at least $27,000. In this situation, it would not be unreasonable to treat the property as the husband's separate property, subject to a possible reimbursement claim for community funds expended.

2. Reimbursement

Hawkins v. Hawkins

Texas Court of Appeals — El Paso, 1981
612 S.W.2d 683, no writ

OSBORN, Justice.

This is a divorce case in which the Appellant's principal complaint is with regard to an award of $6,500.00 to Appellee for her part of the community estate's right to reimbursement for expenditures benefiting Appellant's separate estate. We reverse and remand.

These parties were married on September 29, 1978, and divorced on July 30, 1980. Up until their separation in February, 1980, they lived in a duplex which Appellant purchased prior to the marriage and therefore was his separate property. The Appellee's nineteen-year-old daughter also lived with them. During this period, they deposited into their one bank checking account the husband's military retirement check of about $700.00 each month plus his real estate commissions earned during the period of about $11,000.00. They also deposited in the same account the daughter's social security check of $305.00 per month, the wife's rental check from her separate property of $190.00 per month and a check for rent on the other part of the duplex for $300.00 a month. From these funds, a payment of $496.00 was made each month to the loan company for payment on the purchase money note given when the duplex was purchased.

The evidence established that the duplex had a market value of $71,000.00 when the parties married and a value of approximately $82,000.00 when they were divorced, although it was then being offered for sale at $87,950.00. The trial court concluded the duplex actually appreciated $13,800.00 during the period of the marriage, one-half of which is $6,900.00. After a deduction of $400.00 as an allowance for expense of the teen-age daughter, the court awarded the wife a reimbursement of $6,500.00 for community funds used to make payments on the duplex.

We conclude that the trial court applied the wrong standard to arrive at the amount of reimbursement and this resulted in an abuse of discretion which requires that the case be reversed and remanded. In *Colden v. Alexander*, 141 Tex. 134, 171 S.W.2d 328 (1943), the Court announced the rule which controls the disposition of this case, as follows:

> Of course, where the husband purchases land on credit before marriage, and pays the purchase-money debt after marriage out of community funds, equity requires that the community estate be reimbursed. Under our law, the income during marriage from the estate of either the husband or the wife is community. The rule of reimbursement, as above announced, is purely an equitable one. *Dakan v. Dakan*, 125 Tex. 305, 83 S.W.2d 620 (1935). Such being the case, we think it would follow that interest paid during coverture out of community funds on the prenuptial debts of either the husband or the wife on land, and taxes, would not even create an equitable claim for reimbursement, unless it is shown that the expenditures by the community are greater than the benefits received.

The basic general rule is set forth in Speer, *Texas Family Law* (5th ed. 1976), where the author in Section 22.38 says:

Under equitable principles, the community is entitled to reimbursement for payments on the purchase price of separately owned property, or in discharging encumbrances thereon. In these instances, the recovery is the spouse's share of the community funds spent.

Payment out of community funds of taxes, interest, and insurance on separate property may or may not afford a basis for reimbursement, according to whether or not there was a benefit to the community.

Expenditures for interest on the prenuptial debts of either spouse, or for taxes on separate property, create no equitable claim for reimbursement, unless the expenditures by the community are greater than the benefits resulting to it. [Footnotes omitted.]

We must sustain the Appellant's first point of error and hold that the trial court erred in awarding reimbursement based upon an increase in equity of Appellant's separate property. Although there is proof that the payments toward debt retirement were $46.00 per month, there has been no showing as to whether the amount paid for taxes, insurance and interest was greater than the benefit received by the community estate through the use and occupancy of the separate property duplex, and, if so, the amount of the excess for which the Appellee would be entitled to reimbursement. In the interest of justice, we remand so that these matters may be developed upon another hearing.

DISCUSSION

Hawkins presents a characterization issue frequently encountered at divorce. Here one spouse had purchased the realty before marriage. The spouses lived in the duplex during marriage; taxes, insurance and loan payments due during marriage were paid with community funds. Under the doctrine of inception of title, property is characterized based on the character of the first consideration given. So, the duplex was the husband's separate property. This means, traditionally, that all changes in value accrued to the husband's separate estate.

Does the community have any claim? Yes, because community funds were used to pay a "separate" (premarital) debt of the husband. This traditionally gives rise to a claim for "reimbursement"; the original prima facie amount of the claim would be the amount of community funds used to pay the loan, insurance and taxes. However, under traditional Texas reimbursement law, the amount of the community claim would be reduced by the value of any benefit the community enjoyed from the property. The "benefits" in this situation are the right to live in the duplex rent-free (and thereby avoiding the need to pay rent elsewhere) and the right to receive rent from the other unit (income from separate property being community property in Texas). In the "normal" case involving a house purchased before marriage, with house payments made by the community, courts frequently have estimated the "benefit" from living in the home as the amount allocated to the payment of interest, taxes, and insurance. So, the net community claim in such instances was the amount the principal amount of the loan was reduced during marriage.

This result was perceived by many to be unfair. In 1999, a new statutory "economic contribution" claim was created, in an attempt to increase the amount of the community claim in such instances. In 2009, the economic contribution statute was repealed, and was replaced by a more detailed statute dealing with reimbursement. See Tex. Fam. Code §3.402.

It is now clear that, after 2009, the only remedy that arises when one estate pays the debt of another is reimbursement.

The 2009 statute appears to change reimbursement analysis in some ways. For example, if community funds are used to make a house payment during marriage regarding a loan taken out before marriage, only the amount by which the principal balance is reduced creates a reimbursement claim. The community property reimbursement claim is not reduced for any community benefit if it is a "primary or secondary" residence. Tex. Fam. Code § 3.402. Reimbursement also arises due to capital improvements, with the measure of reimbursement the enhancement in value of the property as a result of the improvement. *See generally* J. Thomas Oldham, "Texas Abolishes Economic Contribution—Now What?" Houston Lawyer (Sept.–Oct. 2009).

There is a split of authority regarding whether the statutory examples of transactions creating reimbursement are an exhaustive list. *See Bigelow v. Stephens*, 286 S.W.3d 619 (Tex. App.—Beaumont 2009, no pet.).

Texas Family Code § 3.409(1) states that reimbursement does not arise for the payment of child support. This clearly applies to a situation when a spouse becomes a parent before the beginning of the current marriage, and is consistent with past Texas law. *See Pelzig v. Berkebile*, 931 S.W.2d 398 (Tex. App.—Corpus Christi 1996, no writ). It is less clear whether this is intended to apply to a situation where a spouse fathers a child during marriage with someone other than the wife and incurs a child support obligation. *See Butler v. Butler*, 975 S.W.2d 765 (Tex. App.—Corpus Christi 1998, no pet.) (distinguishing this situation). What should occur if a spouse gets involved in a legal dispute with a former spouse about custody or child support, and significant legal fees are incurred?

Is it fair not to allow reimbursement if community funds are used to pay a student loan incurred before marriage?

3. Equitable Limits to Inception of Title

Andrews v. Andrews
Texas Court of Appeals—Austin, 1984
677 S.W.2d 171, no writ

SHANNON, Justice.

Appellee Cynthia Mae Andrews filed suit in the district court of Travis County seeking a divorce from appellant John Dee Andrews. By her suit, appellee sought appointment as managing conservator of their daughter, Jamie Dee Andrews, an infant, an order requiring appellant to make child support payments, and a division of the community property.

John Andrews does not fault that part of the judgment granting the divorce, naming Cynthia Mae Andrews the managing conservator of the child, or setting the child support. Rather, he challenges that part of the judgment which disposes of the parties' property.

John Andrews claimed as his separate property the house at 2800 Hubbard Circle in Austin which the parties made their residence.

Among other things, the judgment of the district court imposed a constructive trust for the benefit of Cynthia Mae Andrews for a one-half interest in the real estate comprising the residence of the parties located at 2800 Hubbard Circle. The judgment also ordered John Andrews to execute a promissory note payable to his former wife in the sum of $45,000.00, the note being secured by a lien against certain personal and real estate awarded in the judgment of John Andrews as his separate property.

John Andrews complains initially of the imposition by the district court of the constructive trust for the benefit of his former wife of a one-half undivided interest in the parties' residence at 2800 Hubbard Circle. He insists that a constructive trust was not warranted because Cynthia Mae did not contribute to the down-payment for the purchase of the residence. Appellant maintains that the Hubbard Circle residence is his separate property and, at best, the community estate has only the right to reimbursement for sums spent upon the improvement of the residence.

In the autumn of 1975, the parties were living together in Dallas and were engaged to be married. They decided to move to Austin and to jointly buy a house. The parties made numerous trips to Austin, investigating the housing market, and ultimately decided to purchase the property at 2800 Hubbard Circle. John Andrews signed an offer to purchase the residence.

The parties agreed between themselves that they would buy the residence jointly, use the property as their mutual marital homestead, borrow funds sufficient to purchase said property, using their collective borrowing power and credit reputation, and jointly repay such indebtedness from funds they would later earn.

To assist in their qualification for the necessary long-term financing of the property, Cynthia Mae Andrews signed a loan application and delivered such application to John Andrews, at his request, for delivery to the lender. However, John Andrews delivered a different loan application for Cynthia Mae Andrews, typed but not signed, to the lender. The initial documents relating to the purchase of the residence reflected the names of Cynthia Mae Calvert and John Andrews as prospective co-borrowers and co-owners. Cynthia Mae did not pay any of the escrow money tendered the seller with the contract to purchase.

Before the closing of the purchase of the residence, appellant unilaterally informed the closing attorney that Cynthia Mae's name was to be stricken from such documents, and, as a result, title issued solely in the name of John Andrews. Only John Andrews signed the note and deed of trust. Appellant Andrews did not inform Cynthia of the changes directed to be made to the closing papers but did tell her that it was unnecessary for her to attend the closing, on March 2, 1976.

Upon disputed facts, the district court found that John Andrews knew that Cynthia Mae Andrews intended to be an equal, co-owner of the residence, and knew that she intended to share the cost of its debt service, maintenance and all improvements, as their marital abode. Such intent was formed before the ceremonial marriage, and long after the time when they had agreed to marry. The sale was closed on March 2, 1976, at a time when Cynthia was away from Austin.

On March 20, 1976, the parties were ceremonially married, and continued their cohabitation at 2800 Hubbard Circle, and thereafter treated it as their legal residence and it was, in fact, their domicile until separation. All sums borrowed to make the down-payment on the subject property were repaid, after their marriage, to the various lenders from community earnings of the parties.

After the parties marriage, they jointly improved and substantially enhanced the value of 2800 Hubbard Circle with community funds and significant community labor, and in all respects treated the property as equal owners. In 1980, Cynthia Andrews, for the first time, learned that the deed of conveyance to the residence reflected only the name of her husband as grantee.

The district court concluded that John Andrews, as constructive trustee, held an undivided one-half interest in the 2800 Hubbard Circle property for the benefit of Cynthia

Mae Andrews. The court reasoned that the constructive trust arose as a result of John Andrews' deliberate violation of their confidential relationship, which was likewise a fiduciary relationship, in direct fraud of Cynthia Mae Andrews' rights in the property. As a result, the district court concluded that the parties held equal undivided interests in the Hubbard Circle property as tenants-in-common.

In support of its imposition of the constructive trust, the district court reasoned that to fail to impose a constructive trust would result in an unconscionable and unjust enrichment of the husband's separate estate. The imposition of such trust and the resulting co-tenancy seemed to the district court to be the only fair and accurate way to evaluate the respective contributions of time, toil, labor and enhanced value of the residence. Any attempt to otherwise place a measure of reimbursement would be unnecessarily speculative and grounded on incomplete or disputed evidence. The district court concluded that the imposition of the constructive trust was not a divestiture of title, but instead an enforcement of the parties' agreement, made within the confidential and fiduciary relationship that existed prior to ceremonial marriage.

A constructive trust is the formula through which the conscience of equity finds expression. When property has been acquired under such circumstances that the holder of the legal title may not in good conscience retain the beneficial interest, equity converts him into a trustee.

Unlike an express trust, a constructive trust does not arise because of a manifestation of intention to create it; to the contrary, it is imposed by law because the person holding title to the property would profit by a wrong or would be unjustly enriched if he were permitted to retain title.

John Andrews argues that because Cynthia Mae Andrews did not contribute to the down-payment for the purchase of the residence, she cannot be the beneficiary of a resulting trust. This may be true. Nevertheless, this Court does not understand that appellee was required to prove a contribution to the down-payment for the purchase of the house as a condition for the imposition of a *constructive trust* as distinguished from a resulting trust. *Tolle v. Sawtelle*, 246 S.W.2d 916, 918 (Tex. Civ. App.—Eastland 1952, writ ref'd).

———————

4. Family Living Expenses

Trevino v. Trevino

Texas Court of Appeals—Corpus Christi, 1977
555 S.W.2d 792, no writ

YOUNG, Justice.

The Doctor [the husband] as well as Suzanne [the wife] were obligated to furnish support for community living, and if no community funds were available (as apparently was demonstrated by the testimony of Mr. Jones and petitioner's exhibit #76), he was required to use separate funds to provide for the community. It is the general rule that separate funds spent for community living are deemed a gift to the community for its well-being and use. Tex. Family Code Ann. Sec. 4.02; *Norris v. Vaughan*, 152 Tex. 491, 260 S.W.2d 676 (1953); *In re Marriage of Long*, 542 S.W.2d 712 (Tex. Civ. App.—Texarkana 1976, no writ).

———————

DISCUSSION

In *Trevino*, no community property existed when the separate property was used to pay the living expenses. A number of cases state that if no community property exists during marriage to pay family living expenses, separate property must be used to pay them, and no reimbursement is permitted. See, e.g., *Norris v. Vaughn*, 260 S.W.2d 676, 683 (Tex. 1953). The rationale and scope of this rule are unclear. First, it is clear that if separate property is used to pay expenses relating to a community property home, reimbursement is appropriate. So, the scope of "family expenses" for this purpose is unclear. Second, the rationale for the rule is rarely explained. Conceptually, the community estate is the net amount accumulated from the time, toil and talent of either spouse during marriage. Why should the separate estate not be reimbursed for satisfying a community obligation during marriage? This argument was accepted in *Brooks v. Brooks*, 612 S.W.2d 233 (Tex. Civ. App.—Waco 1981, no writ).

This general rule of *Trevino* is now codified in Tex. Fam. Code § 3.409. In *Winkle v. Winkle*, 951 S.W.2d 80 (Tex. App.—Corpus Christi, 1997, writ denied) the court discussed what falls within this category of "family living expenses."

Hilton v. Hilton

Texas Court of Appeals—Houston [14th Dist.], 1984
678 S.W.2d 645, no writ

DRAUGHN, Justice.

This is an appeal from a divorce decree relative to the property rights of the parties. Appellant, Patricia Hilton, asserts that the trial court erred in awarding appellee, Eric Hilton, 12,403 shares of Hilton Hotel Corporation stock as equitable reimbursement to appellee for utilizing his separate property to retire a community debt.

As an initial point, appellee has moved to dismiss this appeal because appellant has voluntarily accepted benefits (*i.e.* stock in various corporations) under the judgment. It is generally true that a party who has voluntarily accepted the benefits of a judgment, cannot afterward prosecute an appeal therefrom. This rule, however, is inapplicable where a reversal of the judgment on the grounds asserted by appellant could not possibly affect those benefits received. Under these circumstances, an appeal may be taken. *Carle v. Carle*, 149 Tex. 469, 234 S.W.2d 1002, 1004 (1950).

We proceed to consider the merits of the appeal. The trial court's judgment awarded appellee 12,403 shares of Hilton Hotel Corporation stock as reimbursement to his separate estate from the community estate. Upon request, the trial court made the following findings of fact: (1) Eric M. Hilton inherited 12,403 shares of Hilton Hotel Corporation stock; (2) on July 15, 1981, Eric M. Hilton sold the 12,403 shares of inherited Hilton Hotel stock to retire a community indebtedness, and (3) the separate estate of Eric M. Hilton and the borrowing power it allowed played a large part in his ability to build a significant community estate. The trial court's conclusions of law were (1) the 12,403 shares of Hilton Hotel Corporation stock inherited by Eric M. Hilton constitutes his separate property; and (2) Eric M. Hilton is entitled to equitable reimbursement to his separate estate for utilizing separate property to retire a community debt.

Appellant also contends under point of error one that appellee is not entitled to reimbursement because appellee failed to trace the funds obtained from the sale of his Hilton stock into some asset of the community estate. In this case, appellee proved that the community estate was benefited by the use of the proceeds of the sale of his stock to extinguish a community debt. This was all that was required of appellee to establish his reimbursement claim. Tracing is a means used to rebut the presumption that all property on hand at the dissolution of the marriage is community property. Tracing is not required for a claim of reimbursement based on the use of separate funds to retire a community debt. We overrule appellant's first point of error.

Appellant contends in her second point of error that appellee was not entitled to reimbursement to his separate estate because the original community debt that was partially retired by his separate stock sale represented funds which were used for living expenses, taxes and interest. Appellant asserts that these kinds of expenditures are not reimbursable. It is immaterial how the funds obtained from the incurrence of the community debt were spent. It is clear that the community estate benefited from the use of appellee's separate property to extinguish the community debt. Appellee is therefore entitled to reimbursement from the community estate. *Brooks v. Brooks*, 612 S.W.2d 233, 238 (Tex. Civ. App.—Waco 1981, no writ); *Bazile v. Bazile*, 465 S.W.2d 181 (Tex. Civ. App.—Houston [1st Dist.] 1971, writ dism'd). Point of error two is overruled.

Appellant contends in her fourth point of error that the trial court erred in awarding appellee 12,403 shares of Hilton Hotel Corporation stock as reimbursement to his separate estate because the trial court was without authority to award community property to satisfy the reimbursement claim. Appellee properly plead and proved his reimbursement claim. The trial court thus had authority to grant judgment for the claim. In most cases the trial court will grant the party entitled to reimbursement a money judgment. Here the trial court granted appellee judgment for 12,403 shares of Hilton stock from the community estate. Although the trial court's means of satisfying the reimbursement claim is somewhat unique, we find no legal precedent which denies the trial court's authority to use this means. Appellant is not prejudiced in any way by the trial court's decision to grant judgment in kind. If appellee had been granted a money judgment instead, appellee would have had the right to execute the judgment against the community property awarded to appellant. We hold that the trial court acted within its authority in awarding appellee judgment for the 12,403 shares of Hilton stock as reimbursement. Point of error four is overruled.

Appellant contends in her fifth point of error that appellee's reimbursement claim should have been limited to the amount of $300,000 because the Hilton stock distributed to appellee under his father's will was to have a value of $300,000. Appellant's contention is without merit. It was the value of the stock at the time the stock was sold to extinguish the community debt which set the limits of appellee's reimbursement claim. This is so because the increase in value of appellee's stock was his separate property. *Bakken v. Bakken*, 503 S.W.2d 315, 318 (Tex. Civ. App.—Dallas 1973, no writ). The stock which appellee sold to pay the community debt was sold for about $585,000. The trial court reimbursed appellee with 12,403 shares which had a value of $548,333 at the time of trial. Thus, the trial court actually awarded appellee stock with a value less than the amount of separate funds which he contributed toward the retirement of the community debt. Point of error five is overruled.

DISCUSSION

In *Hilton*, community funds were available when separate property was used to pay living expenses. Does this matter?

C. Other Acquisitions Over Time

In re Marriage of Garrett
Arizona Court of Appeals, 1983
683 P.2d 1166

JACOBSON, Chief Justice.

It is true that an attorney is not entitled to the full benefit of his contingency contract until the contingency upon which it is based is fulfilled. This does not mean, however, that valid enforceable contract rights do not exist regardless of its fulfillment. It is clear that a contingency fee contract does not involve a mere expectancy in which no enforceable rights exist in the holder of the expectancy. Based upon these considerations, we hold that an attorney's contingency fee contract is a valuable property right, though the contingency upon which it is based has not been fulfilled.

The question then becomes whether the community is entitled to an interest in that property right and if so, the value of that community interest. In answering this question, we reject the husband's contention that since the ultimate fee may not be acquired until after the dissolution, this automatically makes the fee separate property under A.R.S. Sec. 25-213 as property "acquired" while the husband is single. We have previously noted that a contingency fee contract has enforceable rights prior to its full performance. Therefore, considering the nature of a contingency fee contract (the performance of continuing services), it is not the existence of rights under that contract which must abide a future event, but an assessment of the value of those rights. The principle is recognized in those cases which hold that where community labor is expended in the acquisition of future pension benefits, whether the right to those benefits is vested or non-vested at the time of dissolution, the community is entitled to share in those benefits to the extent which community labor contributed to their acquisition.

The community is entitled to be reimbursed for the community labor expended in perfecting or protecting a future asset. In this regard, we reject a per se rule as to the ultimate character of the property being separate or community based upon when the contract was made. The community is not entitled to the services expended by one of its partners either before marriage or after the marriage has terminated. However, the community is entitled to such labors expended during marriage. Carrying these principles to their logical conclusion, it is theoretically immaterial if the contingency fee contract was entered into prior to marriage, if after marriage community labor was expended to bring it to fruition. For the same reasons, it is immaterial if the contract was entered into during marriage, but no community labor was expended to fulfill the contract. When the nature of the asset requires continuing services to reap an ultimate benefit (such as contingency fee contracts and pension plans) it is not when the inception of services begin (either before or after marriage) which is material in assessing the community interest, but rather the amount of community labor expended in perfecting the ultimate benefit.

Based upon this analysis, it is clear that the attorney's services performed during the marriage in fulfillment of the contract are community property and the community is entitled to what the percentage of the time expended as community labor bears to the time expended in reaching the ultimate recovery.

In this regard, we reject the husband's contention that the value of the community services is to be based upon a reasonable hourly rate. This overlooks the very nature of the contract—an all or nothing proposition. It is as unfair to require the attorney/spouse to pay the other spouse for reasonable services rendered when ultimately no fee is earned because the litigation was lost as it would be to require the non-attorney/spouse to accept a sum based upon an hourly fee when the attorney/spouse receives compensation far exceeding that amount. The contract sets the value of the services. Depending upon subsequent circumstances, the value of the services may be worth nothing, may be worth only a reasonable hourly fee, or may be worth the full value of the contract. In this regard, we approve of the trial court's continuing jurisdiction over this matter to monitor the value of the services.

We have held that only that portion of the labor expended during marriage in fulfillment of the contract is to be considered community property. The trial court, however, found that as to [one of the two contingency cases], all the labor necessary to bring the contract to fruition had been expended during the marriage and as to the [second case], that the contract could have been fulfilled during marriage if the husband had diligently applied himself. The wife argues that based upon these factual determinations, the trial court properly determined that the fees were "earned" during marriage and therefore subject to equal division.

We disagree. We are unaware of any community property principle which allows division of community property based upon a determination that the parties should have worked more diligently to increase the community assets. The law must necessarily presume that during the term of marriage the parties will expend their ultimate capabilities in obtaining community assets for their mutual benefit and welfare. However, the court is aware that at some point prior to the final termination of the marriage (the entry of a decree of dissolution), the motive to increase community assets for the mutual welfare of both parties may not only lessen, but cease, based upon the realization that the marriage will ultimately fail. Should the court embark upon an inquiry as to when this point was reached and the effect of this human characteristic upon the marshalling of assets? Should the court determine that one month prior to the decree of dissolution being entered, one of the spouses passed up a favorable investment opportunity which would have increased the community assets and awarded division of property based upon what could have been realized by this lost opportunity? We believe not. The concepts of waste and fraud adequately protected the community from the vindictive spouse without embroiling the fact finder in weighing motives for non-productivity or the result of that non-productivity.

Therefore, this matter must be remanded to the trial court for determination of the community interest in the contingent fee contracts based upon the percentage that the number of hours worked during the marriage bears to the total number of hours worked in earning the fee, the community being entitled to that percentage of the fee received.

Before leaving this subject, we touch briefly on the husband's contention that the trial court ignored the tax consequences that will flow to the husband by receiving income after dissolution, that is, that the entire fee will be taxable to him as separate property. We disagree. In our opinion, under existing tax decisions, each party must report and pay taxes upon the income we have declared by this opinion to be community property.

Finally, the husband contends that his overhead expenses should be figured into the division of the contingency fee contract. Again we disagree. First, out-of-pocket expenses are paid for by the plaintiffs. Second, to the extent that overhead expenses were incurred during the marriage, the husband has already had the benefit of those deductions during that marriage. Third, to the extent that the fee received is for services rendered after the dissolution decree, the husband will receive that portion of the fee as his separate property and must pay those expenses related to his separate income.

––––––––––

DISCUSSION

To date, Texas courts have applied the inception of title approach to all acquisitions over time other than pensions and other fringe benefits of employment. How would a Texas court characterize a spouse's right to a contingent fee that might be received after divorce? Is *Berry* relevant? What if the lawyer had filed the case before marriage and received the fee during marriage?

In *Licata v. Licata*, 11 S.W. 3d 269 (Tex. App.—Houston [14th Dist.] 1999, pet. denied) the court upheld the award of a percentage of potential contingent fees that might be recovered from pending cases originated during marriage, when there was no showing that any post-divorce effort would be required to generate the fees.

Garfein v. Garfein
California Court of Appeals, 1971
16 Cal. App. 3d 155

KINGSLEY, Justice

The husband is, and during the marriage was, a motion picture director; the wife is, and was, a motion picture actress [Carroll Baker]. During the marriage, the husband was active in procuring employment for the wife, including assisting in negotiating a "play or pay" contract for her with Paramount Pictures, under which she appeared in, and was paid for her appearance in, the motion picture "Harlow." The contract entitled Paramount to the services of the wife for six additional pictures, at the rate of one picture each twelve months,[2] commencing in May of 1966, and obligated Paramount to pay to her compensation (whether or not she was called to work) at the following rate:

Year 1 (until May 1966) $200,000
2 (until May 1967)   200,000
3 (until May 1968)   300,000
4 (until May 1969)   300,000
5 (until May 1970)   300,000
6 (until May 1971)   300,000

For reasons known to it, Paramount did not call on the wife to appear in any pictures after "Harlow" was completed. Litigation took place, resulting in a judgment declaring the obligation of Paramount to comply with the "pay" clauses of the agreement; thereafter, payments have been made as above provided.[3] The litigation cost the marital community in excess of $126,000 for attorney fees and costs.

––––––––––

2. Under the contract, plaintiff was obligated to appear in one picture a year, with a payment spread over ten calendar weeks; Paramount, at its option could require her to appear in a maximum of two pictures each year, with her compensation being thereby accelerated. Since she was never called on to make any picture after "Harlow" the exact details of the arrangements are not material on this appeal.

3. The trial and judgment were in 1969; both parties assume that the 1970 payment has been made and that the1971 payment will be made as provided in the contract.

The trial court held as a matter of law that the payments received by the wife after the separation were her own separate property. [H appeals.]

The judgment against Paramount was not one which, itself, called for the payment of any fixed sum; it established the validity and enforceability of that contract according to its terms. Those terms, so far as herein material, required the wife to hold herself available for service in one picture each twelve-month period; without the consent of Paramount she could not accept other potentially conflicting engagements, business or social.[4] Although counsel has not directed us to any cases directly on point, and although we have found none, we conclude that the trial court correctly held that the payments falling due after the date of separation (June 30, 1967) — *i.e., the* final $1,200,000 — were the separate property of the wife. Section 169 of the Civil Code (as it read at the time of trial) was as follows:

> The earnings and accumulations of the wife, while she is living separate from her husband, are the separate property of the wife.

The husband argues that the several payments were not "earnings" because the wife was entitled to them even though she did not "work" — *i.e.,* appear in any motion pictures. But appearance in a picture was only one alternative of her obligations to her employer under the contract. Under a "play or pay" contract, the employer secures: (1) an option on the performer's services; and (2) the assurance that a performer will not, without its consent, create competition for other pictures of the employer by performing for some other producer. We hold that the wife "earns" her agreed compensation by refraining from performing for anyone except the employer during the period of the contract, unless with the employer's consent. Since the payments made after June 1967, were "earned" after that date, they were separate property.[5]

The husband cites us to no authority that would require the trial court to prorate the community debts incurred in the Paramount litigation according to the ultimate division of the proceeds of the Paramount contract. A debt is community or separate at the time it is incurred; it does not change its character merely because the beneficial effect of the consideration received may survive the marital cohabitation.

The judgment is affirmed.

DISCUSSION

Would *Garfein* be decided the same way in Texas? In *Loaiza v. Loaiza*, 130 S.W.3d 894 (Tex. App. — Fort Worth 2004, no pet.) the court reached a conclusion consistent with *Garfein* in a case involving a professional athlete who signed a multi-year contract during marriage and divorced before the end of the contract term.

---

4. Under the contract, plaintiff could perform for another producer, provided she gave Paramount notice of her intent; in that event, Paramount was required either to consent or to schedule her for its own picture at the time or times involved.

5. The duty to pay, where no picture was made, did not accrue until the final day of each twelve-month period, since the wife was required to hold herself available for the full period. The compensation, thus, was not "earned" until that last day.

Chapter Nine

Rents and Profits

All increases in value of separate property during marriage due to natural enhancement remain separate property (subject to the claims outlined in chapter 10). Also, if separate property is exchanged during marriage for some other item of property, the "mutation" of the separate property remains separate. In Texas, "rents and profits" (income) generated by separate property during marriage are community property. It therefore becomes important to be able to distinguish between natural enhancement, a mutation, and rents and profits.

"Rents" are not difficult to understand. For Texas marital property rights purposes, the connotation of rents is the same as the normal understanding of the term — a payment received for the right to use property. For example, rents generated during marriage by separate property realty would be community property.

"Profits" are more complicated. For Texas marital property purposes, the term has a different connotation than the normal understanding of the term. For example, if a person buys one share of Exxon stock with $60 of separate property, and later sells it for $70, a normal human unexposed to Texas family law would conclude that the person had made a $10 profit. This is generally not true for purposes of Texas family law. Natural enhancement of separate property during marriage remains separate property. For purposes of Texas family law, the term "profit" generally does not include any increase in value of separate property due to natural enhancement.

There is one exception to the general rule referred to in the preceding paragraph. If a spouse's primary business is buying and selling the property involved, *all* increase in value of the separate property involved is a community property "profit," regardless of the reason for the increase in value. The investment is considered a proprietorship business. See chapter 10, *infra*. So, if a spouse's primary business is buying and selling stock, if a person buys a share of Exxon for $60 of separate property and sells it later for $70, that spouse has made a $10 community property profit.

Rents and profits are net concepts. So, all applicable expenses should be deducted before the community claim is calculated.

Common examples of rents and profits include profits from a proprietorship business, bank account interest and cash dividends from stock. Dividends in the form of stock, and stock splits, are considered separate property mutations and remain separate property. As *Wilson, infra,* shows, oil and gas royalties and bonus payments are considered separate property mutations of separate property realty; delay rentals are considered community property rents. In *Alsenz v. Alsenz*, 101 S.W.3d 648 (Tex. App. — Houston [1st Dist.] 2003, no pet.) the court held that royalties received during marriage on a patent received before marriage were community property income. In *LeGrand-Brock v. Brock*, 246 S.W.3d 318 (Tex. App. — Beaumont 2008, pet. denied) the court held that a cash liquidating distribution during marriage in connection with the dissolution of the husband's separate property corporation was separate.

There is some tension between the rule that "natural enhancement" of separate property remains separate, while income from separate property is community. For example, consider a spouse who has the option of investing separate property in a stock that doesn't pay dividends or buying a certificate of deposit. In Texas, the latter will create a community claim (to accrued interest), while the former will not. Is this distinction rational? See Andrews, *Income From Separate Property: Towards a Theoretical Foundation*, 56 Law & Contemp. Prob. 171 (1993) (arguing that it is not). In California, both income and natural enhancement remain separate.

The rule that income from separate property is community, coupled with the concept that mixing community property with separate property might well create a commingled mass of community property, suggests that lawyers, even if not family lawyers, need to discuss this matter when advising wealthy clients who are about to marry. If lawyers do not do this, is it malpractice? See *Mecom v. Vinson & Elkins*, No. 01-98-00280-CV, 2001 WL 493426 (Tex. App. — Houston [1st Dist.] May 10, 2001, pet. dism'd) (not designated for publication).

Stringfellow v. Sorrells

Supreme Court of Texas, 1891
18 S.W. 689

MARR, Justice.

Before and at the time of her marriage to W. J. Sorrells in the year 1884 the appellee, Mrs. C. V. Sorrells, owned in her own right, together with other separate property, two mules. These animals were then colts, and worth $35 each; and a portion of their present value, as a result of their growth and *avoirdupois* as the years rolled on, is the subject of this controversy. The appellant, in the year 1888, held a just debt, merged into a valid judgment, for a small sum against the husband of the appellee, and in satisfaction of which he caused a writ of execution to be levied upon these mules of the wife during that year. At the time of the levy the animals were grown, and each of them worth in the market $75, instead of $35, as originally. The husband had managed and cared for the mules since the marriage, and the community estate furnished the provender for the animals during the intermediate time. The appellee replevied the property, and duly made her claim thereto under the statute, "to try the rights of property." The case came up to the district court from a justice court, and the former court rendered a judgment in favor of the wife. The appellant insists that the enhanced value of the mules, which has resulted from the attention of the husband and the food furnished by the community since the marriage, and amounts to $80 is an increase of the separate estate of the wife, and consequently is community property, and liable to his execution. The equitable criterion, if any were admissible in cases like the present, should be the expenses to the husband or the community, regarded as an investment of rearing the mules, not the increased value, which may be due to other causes, subject to be offset by the value of their use, if anything. This would add to "confusion worse confounded." As applied to live-stock belonging to the wife, "the increase" of such property has been invariably ever since the decision of the supreme court in *Howard v. York*, 20 Tex. 670 (1858), recognized in the reported cases to denote the progeny of the original stock or their descendants. This construction comports with the etymology of the term, and accords with the universal understanding. The record therefore develops no "increase" of these particular mules in the sense that would add to or constitute a part of the community estate. They are still the same animals which the wife owned at the time of her marriage, and mule-like, they have stubbornly refused "to bring forth after their kind." The sex of these particular mules, nor their capacity for reproduction, if any, is not disclosed by the record, but the general rule, founded on common knowledge, with possibly some sporadic exceptions, must be recognized that mules do not "increase, multiply, and replenish the earth," according to the ordinary laws of procreation and the generic command. It would seem therefore, that there can be no "increase" of the wife's separate estate, if composed solely of specific mules at the time of her marriage. In cases of other live-stock, his interest, recognized by law, in the offsprings thereof, compensates the husband and the community, but the erratic mule standeth apart, "like patience on a monument, smiling at grief." It would tend to entirely destroy the corpus of the wife's estate, consisting of live personal property, to declare that an augmentation in weight or value should be deemed an "increase" of the property itself, so as to constitute a part of the community to that extent. We need only to add that the use of the mules, and the products of their labor, may be supposed to compensate the community for the provender consumed, and the husband would scarcely demand any recompense for the felicity of teaching them how "to work in the traces." We conclude that the judgment of the district court is a most righteous one, and ought to be affirmed.

DISCUSSION

If a spouse owns a certain number of cattle at the time of marriage, and the size of the herd has grown by the time of divorce, how many of the cattle are community property? See *Gutierrez v. Gutierrez*, 791 S.W.2d 659 (Tex. App.—San Antonio 1990, no writ). Should the answer to this question depend upon how many cattle died during the marriage?

Dixon v. Sanderson

Supreme Court of Texas, 1888
10 S.W. 535

[Creditors had obtained a judgment against H. In order to determine whether these creditors could reach certain property in the name of W, the court had to consider the character of certain lottery proceeds won by W.]

STAYTON, Chief Justice.

This is a suit brought by Mrs. Dixon to enjoin the sale of a house and lots under an execution issued against her husband. She claims and the evidence is sufficient to show that some time during her coverture, with one dollar which she had before her marriage, she bought a ticket in the Louisiana State Lottery on which a prize of $15,000 was drawn, and that with a part of this the lots in controversy were bought and the improvements thereon made.

It is further shown that the husband agreed at the time the lottery ticket was bought that whatever prize might be received on it should be the separate property of the wife; and that the money so drawn and property bought with it as between the husband and wife have been treated as her separate estate.

Dixon and wife both testified that at the time the property in controversy was bought he had ample means to pay all his debts, but neither of them state in what the means consisted, and it appears that the money received as a prize was placed on deposit in a bank in New Orleans in the name of Mrs. Dixon.

On the case thus made the court below dissolved the injunction and rendered a judgment for the defendant.

If the money with which the lots were bought was the separate property of Mrs. Dixon otherwise than through gift from her husband there can be no question of her right to an injunction, for the deed upon its face does not show it to be other than community property, and a sale under execution would cloud her title.

It is insisted that the money received as a prize became the separate property of Mrs. Dixon by reason of the fact that the lottery ticket on which it was drawn was bought with money owned by her in her separate right. The statute declares that "all property acquired by either husband or wife during marriage, except that which is acquired by gift, devise, or descent, shall be deemed the common property of the husband and wife." Rev. Stats., Sec. 2852.

That the prize came not by gift, devise, or descent is too clear. It came as the fortuitous result of a contract based on valuable consideration paid, and is but the profit on a return which, like other profit not resulting from the increased value of a thing bought with the separate means of one party to the marital union, becomes the common property of the husband and wife.

Property purchased with money the separate property of husband or wife, or taken in exchange for the separate property of either, becomes the separate property of the person whose money purchases or whose property is given in exchange, in the absence of some agreement express or implied to the contract, and if the thing purchased or taken in exchange increases in value this necessarily inures to the benefit of its owner.

Such a state of fact, however, is not before us, and we are constrained to hold that all profit realized on purchase of the lottery ticket became community property.

As between the husband and wife the facts are sufficient to show that the money received through the lottery ticket became the property of the latter through the gift of the husband, and the inquiry arises whether he was in condition lawfully to divert so much of the common property and thus place it beyond the reach of his creditors.

If the husband had ample means remaining within the reach of his creditors at the time he made the gift to satisfy all their claims, then the gift to his wife was not fraudulent and ought to be sustained.

The uncontradicted evidence of both husband and wife is that when she bought the property in controversy he had ample means to pay all his debts.

The judgment of the court below will be reversed, but as there is reason to believe that the case has not been developed as it may be, the cause will be remanded.

––––––––––

DISCUSSION

Is it clear that the proceeds of the lottery ticket purchased with separate property constitute a community property profit? Is any other argument possible?

Scofield v. Weiss

Unites States Court of Appeals
Fifth Circuit, 1942
131 F.2d 631

HUTCHESON, Chief Judge.

[H was one of the principal stockholders in the Popular Dry Goods Co., a Texas corporation, prior to his marriage in 1915.

During all of the period from 1917 to 1935, H devoted substantially all of his time and efforts to the business of the corporation. During the period 1917 to 1924 the corporation accumulated substantial earnings from which a stock dividend was declared, of which H received 2,900 shares. In 1933 he made a gift of 390 shares of this stock dividend to his children, and in 1935 he transferred 434 shares of the dividend to his wife. In both instances he paid the gift taxes as though the shares were his separate property. On his death in 1935 his widow qualified as executrix of his estate and brought this suit for refund of gift taxes paid on gifts of shares of corporate stock.]

The claim was that, though the original issue of stock was the separate property of the donor, the gift shares in question, having been issued as stock dividends to the donor during the existence of the community of himself and wife, were not separate but community property, and the payment of gift taxes on all instead of half of them was an overpayment. The district judge, agreeing with the plaintiff that the shares were community property and that the gift was, therefore, not of the whole but of one-half thereof, sustained the taxpayer's claim and gave judgment accordingly. The collector has appealed.

[I]t is well settled that an original issue of corporate stock, which was separate property when issued to the husband, retains its separate character, no matter how much it increases in value as a result of surplus accumulated out of the earnings of the corporation. *Commissioner v. Skaggs*, 5 Cir., 122 F.2d 721; *O'Connor v. Commissioner*, 5 Cir., 110 F.2d 652. And this is so, though the increased value is largely due to the efforts and activities of the husband as managing officer of the corporation, *Beals v. Fontenot*, 5 Cir., 111 F.2d 956. It is equally well settled that dividends paid in cash or property during the existence of coverture out of the earnings of a corporation on account of stock, the separate property of either spouse, are community property. The claim of the taxpayer here is that stock dividends paid during coverture are the same in actual and legal effect as cash or property dividends so paid, and are, therefore, community property. Entirely apart from the weight given by the decisions of the Supreme Court in *Eisner v. Macomber*, 252 U.S. 189, 40 S.Ct. 189, 64 L.Ed. 521, 9 A.L.R. 1570, and *Koshland v. Helvering*, 298 U.S. 441, 56 S.Ct. 767, 80 L.Ed. 1268, 105 A.L.R. 756, to the conclusion, that the declaration of a stock dividend works no change in the corporate entity and does not increase the actual interest of the shareholder in the assets of the corporation but merely increases the number of the units by which his interest is represented, we think it clear that under the settled jurisprudence of Texas, separate ownership of stock in a corporation may not be converted in part into community ownership by the device of declaring stock dividends. If this were so, a wife owning stock in a successful and prospering corporation might find the protection of her separate ownership taken away overnight and her property subjected to the claims of her husband's community creditors at any time that the directors decided to declare stock dividends. Nor is it any answer to say that the directors can do this by declaring cash dividends, for the two are not the same. Declaration of cash dividends above a normal rate depletes the assets and affects the security and strength of the corporation. The declaration of stock dividends has no effect upon it. The corporation's assets remain the same. Its strength is unimpaired. In *Beals v. Fontenot*, we pointed out the prime necessity under the community system of sticking to the general rule established by the jurisprudence that property owned separately before marriage does not through the increase of value after marriage become, either as to the original or the increased value, property of the community.

The judgment is reversed, and the cause is remanded with directions to enter judgment for the defendant.

DISCUSSION

Texas community property law borrows from corporate law when analyzing the character of an increase in value of a separate property business organization. The result is impacted by the type of business organization selected. If the business form is conceptualized as a separate entity, such as a corporation, income earned by the corporation during marriage is attributed to the business, not the owning spouse, unless and until the income is paid to the owning spouse as cash dividends. If the business is not considered a separate entity, such as a proprietorship, income earned by the business during marriage is attributed to its owners, and would be community property regardless whether it is actually paid to the owner.

The *Scofield* rule is quite important. Because of this rule, if a spouse starts a business before marriage (or, as we shall see, during marriage with separate property capital), and devotes all of her efforts to the business during marriage, all the increase in value during marriage is separate. The nature of the community claim is discussed in Chapter 10.

Commissioner of Internal Revenue v. Wilson

United States Court of Appeals
Fifth Circuit, 1935
76 F.2d 766

SIBLEY, Chief Judge.

The respondents were married men residing in Texas and under its matrimonial community laws during the years 1925 and 1926. Incomes received by them respectively as beneficiaries of the same trust were held by the Board of Tax Appeals to be community incomes and were thus taxed. The Commissioner here contends that such incomes were altogether the separate property of the respondents; but if not, so much of them as came from bonus and royalty payments from oil and gas properties were separate.

Income which accrues to the matrimonial community in Texas belongs equally to husband and wife and is to be taxed one-half to each. *Hopkins, Collector v. Bacon*, 282 U.S. 122, 51 S.Ct. 62, 75 L.Ed. 249. The community property embraces all acquisitions of either husband or wife during marriage except that which is the separate property of either. Article 4622. In 1917 (Acts 1917, c. 194, Sec. 1), an act was passed which added to the definition of the separate property of each the further words, "and the rents and revenues derived therefrom," and these changes made by the act were readopted in the Rev. Civil Stats. of 1925, arts. 4613, 4614. During 1925 the Supreme Court of Texas held the statutory effort to add to the wife's separate property the rents and revenues arising from it during marriage was contrary to the Constitution and void, *Arnold v. Leonard*, 114 Tex. 535, 173 S.W. 799. The rents and revenues of the wife's separate estate, therefore, still go to the community. It is nevertheless urged that since the Constitution does not define the husband's separate estate there is nothing to render ineffective the statutory extension of it.

We think otherwise. The whole course of legislation indicates a purpose to treat husband and wife alike in fixing their separate estates as against the community. Therefore, the ordinary rents and revenues of the separate property of the husbands here involved belong to their several communities. But their interests in the corpus of this trust are their separate property though acquired since marriage, because acquired by gift.

It is argued that the result should be otherwise because the husbands do not get the revenue directly from the property but through the hands of the trustee and subject to the expenditures which he is authorized to make. But the trustee is bound to act always for the benefit of the beneficiaries and to divide the net results among them. All net income and corpus ultimately go to them. The beneficiaries receive the income as income. The corpus is theirs in equity, the legal title being conveyed to the trustee expressly for their benefit. In *Irwin v. Gavit*, 268 U.S. 161, 45 S.Ct. 475, 69 L.Ed. 897, where the trust instrument did not expressly give the corpus to the beneficiary but only the income, it was held that the payments were taxable income from a corpus impliedly given. Income accruing from the separate equitable estates of the husbands during the marriage though collected and paid over by a trustee belongs to their respective communities.

The "delay rentals" on oil and gas leases are rents within the rule just announced. They accrue by the mere lapse of time like any other rent. They do not depend on the finding or production of oil or gas and do not exhaust the substance of the land. While having some likeness to a bonus payment which is held to be advance royalty, the delay rental is not paid directly or indirectly for oil to be produced, but is for additional time in which to utilize the land. We hold it to be rent.

On the other hand, royalties, including bonus, are not paid for time but for oil and gas taken out, and represent an actual removal and disposition of the contents of the soil. In some states, as for instance Louisiana, the law looks to the fugaciousness of oil and gas and considers that they belong to no one until captured and confined, so that an oil and gas lease is only a contract for the use of the land for the purpose of capture, and what is paid is rent. In Texas oil and gas in place in the soil are by the established rules of property a part of the realty and capable of separate ownership and conveyance. *Waggoner Estate v. Siegler Oil Co.*, 118 Tex. 509, 19 S.W.2d 27. When sold in the ground, the proceeds are the proceeds of sale of land and not the rents or revenues from it. The royalties under an ordinary oil lease are such proceeds and not rents. *State v. Hatcher*, 115 Tex. 332, 281 S.W. 192. By Texas law the lessee under the ordinary lease retaining a one-eighth royalty acquires a title to seven-eighths of the oil in the ground. When the oil is produced, the lessor owns, because he has never ceased to own, an undivided one-eighth. His oil has an added value at the surface, which value is the principal consideration received for the conveyance of the seven-eighths to the lessee. In the case last cited the lessor did not retain any oil, but the royalty was one-eighth of the value of the oil produced. Nevertheless, the money royalties paid were held to be the proceeds of corpus. In *Stephens v. Stephens* 292 S.W. 290 (Tex. Civ. App.—Amarillo 1927, writ dism'd), where royalty of one-eighth of the oil was reserved in a lease of the separate property of the wife and the issue was whether the proceeds of the oil were separate or community property, they were held to be separate. It is true that Texas royalties are held notwithstanding the local law not to be proceeds of sale but taxable income within the meaning of the federal Revenue Acts, so as to give a uniform nation-wide application of those acts. *Burnet, Commissioner v. Harmel*, 287 U.S. 103, 53 S.Ct. 74, 77 L.Ed. 199. But the question here is not the taxability of the royalties but the ownership of them. Whether the wife owns or does not own one-half of them in community depends directly on the state laws, the federal tax being imposed accordingly. *Poe, Collector v. Seaborn*, 282 U.S. 101, 51 S.Ct. 58, 75 L.Ed. 239.

Uniformity as respects taxation of community interest is not demanded by present tax laws, one result obtaining in California and another in Washington and Louisiana and Texas according to the laws of each state. *United States v. Robbins*, 269 U.S. 315, 40 S.Ct. 148, 70 L.Ed. 285; *Poe, Collector v. Seaborn, supra; Hopkins v. Bacon, supra; Bender v. Pfaff*, 282 U.S. 127, 51 S.Ct. 64, 75 L.Ed. 252. Therefore so much of the trust income of respondents as can be shown to be derived from royalties is their separate property. In the accounting, outlays by the trustee specially connected with these items are to be considered, and also a fair proportion of the general expenses of the trust, so as to ascertain what part of the net payment to the beneficiaries really came from royalties. The petitions for review are sustained and the Board of Tax Appeals is directed to proceed accordingly, hearing further evidence if necessary.

DISCUSSION

In *McElwee v. McElwee*, 911 S.W.2d 182 (Tex. App. — Houston [1st Dist.] 1995, writ denied), the court held that the sale of timber during marriage from a spouse's separate realty creates community property. Can you think of a reason why timber and oil would be treated differently?

Long v. Long

Texas Court of Appeals — Texarkana, 1976
542 S.W.2d 712, no writ

RAY, Justice.

This is a domestic relations case. Charles E. Long and Kathy Long, husband and wife, both petitioned the Domestic Relations Court of Gregg County to grant them a divorce. The cause was tried to the Court without the aid of a jury, and the trial court granted appellee, Charles E. Long, a divorce from Kathy Long. Appellant, Kathy Long, was appointed managing conservator of the couple's only child, and appellee was appointed the possessory conservator.

Kathy Long appeals from those parts of the judgment awarding her alimony; dividing the estate of the parties; obligating persons not standing in *loco parentis* to the minor child to pay child support; and awarding her inadequate attorney's fees. Eight points of error are presented for our consideration.

In 1954, H. L. Long and Bettye Virginia Long, parents of Charles E. Long, established an irrevocable trust consisting of oil and gas producing property naming their four children as beneficiaries, share and share alike. Under the terms of the trust, one-half of the corpus then in the trust for a child would be distributed upon the beneficiary attaining the age twenty-five, and the trust would terminate upon the distribution of the remaining one-half at age thirty. By 1961 the trust had discharged all indebtedness against the properties and was operating at a profit. From the period of January 1, 1961, to June 30, 1969, the trust had accumulated approximately $25,000.00 net income for each of the four beneficiaries. Charles attained age twenty-five on August 14, 1974, and was entitled to one-half of his share of the trust corpus. Suit for divorce was filed in April of 1975 and granted on October 7, 1975.

On June 26, 1969, Charles E. Long, then age twenty, and having completed two years at Kilgore College, married Kathy Johnson, age seventeen, who had completed ten years of formal education. Both Kathy and Charles worked at unskilled or semi-skilled jobs until they separated in June 1974. At the time of trial, Charles had been working as a reservation agent for an airline earning $850.00 per month (take-home pay of approximately $625.00) for one year. Prior to that he had been employed as a roustabout for Rusk County Well Service, a company owned by his mother, and operated a gymnasium owned by the trust. Kathy, on the other hand, at time of trial was enrolled in a vocational training program working 40 hours per week, earning $300.00 per month, and attending school to earn her high school equivalency diploma. Prior to that time, she had worked at various jobs including waitress, assembly line worker, and cashier in a retail store.

The Charles E. Long Trust will terminate August 14, 1979, at a time when Barbara Ann Long will be age seven.

Sometime after Charles attained the age of twenty-five, he orally stated his intent to allow the trustees of the Charles E. Long Trust to continue to manage his one-half share which the trustees were under an obligation to distribute within a reasonable time after August 14, 1974.

Charles E. Long had a present possessory interest in the trust at the time of trial. The trust had terminated as to one-half of the corpus of the trust. Charles was entitled to that one-half of the corpus and the income that had accumulated on that portion of the corpus following his having reached age twenty-five. The one-half of the corpus was his separate property but was appropriate for consideration by the trial court in dividing the estate of the parties. The accumulated income from his one-half of the corpus after reaching age twenty-five was community property and was subject to division by the court.

Income received by a married beneficiary on the trust corpus to which the beneficiary is entitled has been held to be community property, *Mercantile Bank at Dallas v. Wilson*, 279 S.W.2d 650, 654 (Tex. Civ. App.—Dallas 1955, writ ref'd n.r.e.), and has been taxed accordingly. *McFaddin v. Commissioner of Internal Revenue*, 148 F.2d 570 (5th Cir. 1945).

Trust income which a married beneficiary does not receive, and to which he has no claim other than an expectancy interest in the corpus, has been held not to be community property. *Currie v. Currie*, 518 S.W.2d 386 (Tex. Civ. App.—San Antonio 1974, writ dism'd).

The appellee contends that *Currie* is directly on point; the appellant contends that the *Mercantile Bank* case controls. The dispute is based upon the significance of the appellee's election not to seek a distribution of his one-half of the trust when he reached age twenty-five. By the terms of the trust, the income was to be accumulated until the beneficiary (appellee) reached age twenty-one. At that time, income was distributable solely at the discretion of the trustees. When the beneficiary reached age twenty-five the trust dictates that the trustees deliver and distribute unto the beneficiary one-half of the assets and property comprising the corpus of the trust. At age thirty, the beneficiary is to receive the remaining one-half. The appellee reached age twenty-five at a time after separation but before suit for divorce had been filed. The appellee decided to leave his half interest in the trust though he was entitled to withdraw approximately $85,000.00 in liquid assets exclusive of interests in real property.

The appellant does not claim a community interest in the entire $85,000.00, nor does she deny that such portion of this sum attributable to the corpus acquired by gift is separate property of the appellee. Kathy does contend that some $10,853.83 is attributable not to the corpus but to the income from the corpus. Outlined in appellant's brief is the income from interest, dividends, equipment rental and cattle sales which shows that from August 15, 1974, to July 31, 1975, there was accumulated $4,973.21. This is the only sum that we view to partially be community property from the sources named since the $4,973.21 represented income on the total Charles E. Long Trust. Only one-half of the

$4,973.21 was subject to distribution to Charles since the other one-half of such still belonged to the trust. It thus appears that $2,486.60 could be classed as community income to Charles and Kathy.

Unlike the situation in *Currie, supra,* the beneficiary in the case before us was entitled to a present possessory interest in one-half of the trust corpus and the income from that one-half. In the *Mercantile Bank* case, *supra,* undistributed income was in the hands of the trustees but the beneficiary had a present possessory interest in the funds. As in the *Mercantile Bank* case, we conclude that the income on the trust corpus should have been labeled community property.

DISCUSSION

Note that the income earned from the corpus after the spouse had the absolute right to the corpus was community property. Otherwise, income earned by the **trust** during marriage is not community property. The character of distributions of income is less clear. *In re Thurmond,* 888 S.W.2d 269 (Tex. App.—Amarillo 1994, writ denied); *Cleaver v. George Staton Company,* 908 S.W.2d 468 (Tex. App.—Tyler 1995, writ denied); *Sharma v. Routh,* 302 S.W.3d 355 (Tex. App.—Houston [14th Dist.] 2008, no pet.).

There is some question whether the rule should be the same if the spouse, not a third party, is the creator of the trust.

Chapter Ten

Business Interests

A. Corporations

1. In General

Allen v. Allen

Texas Court of Appeals—Fort Worth, 1986
704 S.W.2d 600, no writ

SPURLOCK, Justice.

This is an appeal from the trial court's division of property in a divorce action. May Marlene Allen, appellant, contests the property settlement on the grounds that the trial court abused its discretion by mischaracterizing the separate and community nature of certain properties.

In her first point of error, appellant claims that the trial court abused its discretion in treating "Marlene's Beauty Salon and Cuttery, Inc." as part of the community estate to be divided in the property settlement. Appellant admits that the beauty salon was incorporated during the period she was married to appellee, but she contends that this was an incorporation of her separate sole proprietorship, "Marlene's Beauty Salon." Appellant argues that the corporation's inception of title was in the sole proprietorship because it was an incorporation of an "ongoing business." Appellant presented evidence that the corporation was valued between $131,789 and $263,578 at the time of the parties' separation. According to appellant, the inclusion of the corporation in the estate of the parties resulted in an unjust division of the estate.

The characterization of marital property or community property is not a matter left to the discretion of the trial court, but is subject to the harmless error rule on appeal. Mere mischaracterization of property alone is not reversible as a matter of law; the mischaracterization may result in a manifestly unjust and unfair division of property, *King v. King*, 661 S.W.2d 252, 254 (Tex. App.—Houston [1st Dist.] 1983, no writ); *Munday v. Munday*, 653 S.W.2d 954, 957 (Tex. App.—Dallas 1983, no writ). It is not necessary, however, for us to determine whether there was harmful error in this case because appellant failed to meet her burden to show that the trial court erred in its treatment of the beauty salon as community property.

"Marlene's Beauty Salon" was a sole proprietorship and was owned and operated by appellant for about 17 years prior to August 21, 1978. On that date, a corporate charter was applied for under the name of "Marlene's Beauty Salon and Cuttery, Inc." by appellant. This act of incorporation occurred almost eight months after appellant's marriage to appellee. The corporation required an initial capitalization of $1,000. There was no evidence to show that this money was funded from anything other than the community estate. All of the physical assets of the sole proprietorship "Marlene's Beauty Salon" were retained in appellant's name and rented by her to the corporation. Appellant continued to operate the beauty salon in the same location it had been in for the previous six years although under the new corporate name. There was evidence that the management, employees, and clientele of the salon remained substantially the same following the incorporation. Appellant testified that her purpose in incorporating was to avoid having to purchase malpractice insurance.

The appellant's principal argument is that because this incorporation was of an ongoing business, the actual inception of title occurred at the acquisition of the sole proprietorship and therefore the corporation should be characterized as appellant's separate property. Appellant has not cited any authority for this "ongoing business" theory and we have not found any legal authority supporting this claim. Under Texas law, corporation does not exist until the issuance of a certificate of incorporation. Tex. Bus. Corp. Act Ann. art. 3.04 (Vernon 1980). It is undisputed that Marlene's Beauty Salon and Cuttery, Inc. was not incorporated until after the parties had married. We hold there can be no title to a corporation until it actually exists; consequently, the inception of title doctrine can only be applied to a corporation as of the date of incorporation.

The approach of Texas courts in determining the separate or community character of a corporation formed during a marriage has been to require the parties to clearly trace the separate and community property assets that were contributed during the formation of the corporation. See *Vallone v. Vallone*, 644 S.W.2d 455, 457 (Tex. 1982); *Marriage of York*, 613 S.W.2d 764, 769–70 (Tex. Civ. App.—Amarillo 1981, no writ). Corporations organized during marriage and capitalized entirely with traceable separate property of one spouse are characterized as the separate property of that spouse. *Holloway v. Holloway*, 671 S.W.2d 51, 56–57 (Tex. App.—Dallas 1983, writ dism'd).

Appellant in this case has failed to meet her burden to clearly trace her contribution of separate property in the formation of Marlene's Beauty Salon and Cuttery, Inc. The $1,000 used to capitalize the corporation is community property under the community property presumption. Tex. Fam. Code Ann. Sec. 5.02 (Vernon 1975). Appellant did not contribute any tangible assets to the corporation; the corporation rented all business property, equipment and furniture from appellant. The only contribution of separate property that appellant seems to claim is that the corporation continued to do business in the same location, with the same employees and the same clientele. Appellant appears to be claiming that she contributed goodwill to the corporation.

Although it is well established that goodwill is a property right which may be sold or transferred, appellant failed to meet her burden of clearly tracing this intangible asset as a contribution of her separate property to the corporation. While it is clear that the corporation took over the activities of appellant's sole proprietorship, there was no evidence presented at trial concerning the value of the goodwill contributed by the appellant at the time of incorporation.[1] Without this information, it is impossible for this court to trace the portion of the corporation created with appellant's separate property. Consequently,

---

1. This case is distinguishable from the line of cases that hold that goodwill of a professional practice which is attached to the person of the profession is not divisible as community property in a divorce proceeding. *Nail v. Nail*, 486 S.W.2d 761, 764 (Tex. 1972); *Austin v. Austin*, 619 S.W.2d 290, 291 (Tex. Civ. App.—Austin 1981, no writ). There was no evidence in this case that any professional goodwill attached to the appellant as a result of confidence in her skill and ability.

appellant has not met her burden of proving that the corporation is her separate property. Point of error number one is overruled.

———————

DISCUSSION

Allen reflects the manner in which Texas courts characterize corporate stock acquired during marriage. The marital status of the spouse at the time the shares are acquired is not determinative; the consideration given for the shares determines their character. The court suggests an argument for the wife that her lawyer apparently did not make. The goodwill of the ongoing separate property proprietorship could have been deemed a separate property contribution to the newly formed corporation. However, the lawyer did not establish the value of the goodwill at the time the corporation was formed, so this claim was lost. Did her lawyer commit malpractice?

Allen is an example of the careless manner in which most business lawyers incorporate a spouse's business during marriage. Because of this carelessness (coupled with the carelessness of the divorce lawyer) a separate property proprietorship worth at least $131,000 was transformed into community property. What could the lawyer incorporating the proprietorship have done to avoid this result? Was it malpractice not to have done this?

2. The Separate Property Corporation That Increases in Value During Marriage

If a corporation is formed during marriage and community funds are used to pay for the stock, the stock is community property, including all increase in value during marriage. If separate property is used to pay for the stock, the stock is separate property.

Separate property corporations have caused significant characterization confusion in Texas, since two different community property principles collide. On one hand, the inception of title doctrine states that the character of property is determined when it is purchased, and any later contributions merely create a reimbursement right. On the other hand, the community is supposed to reap the fruits of the time, toil and talent of each spouse, to the extent the services were rendered during marriage. If a spouse renders services during marriage to a separate property corporation, if the corporation (including all increase in value) is considered separate property, the community may not enjoy all the fruits of the spouse's efforts during marriage.

Other community property states have developed various approaches to deal with this separate property corporation problem. Cases from other states will first be considered, and then Texas rules will be compared.

a. Cases From Other States

Cockrill v. Cockrill

Supreme Court of Arizona, 1979
601 P.2d 1334

GORDON, Justice.

Appellant, Robert Cockrill, and Rose Cockrill, appellee, were married on June 15, 1974. At the time of the marriage, appellant owned, as his separate property, a farming operation known as Cockrill Farms. There seems to be no dispute that the net worth increase of the farm, during the two year and ten month marriage, after some credits, was $79,000. The trial court found that this increase was attributable primarily to the efforts of Mr. Cockrill and was, therefore, community property. Appellant contends that the net worth increase was primarily due to the inherent nature of his separate property, the farm, and was, therefore, also his separate property.

The profits of separate property are either community or separate in accordance with whether they are the result of the individual toil and application of a spouse or the inherent qualities of the business itself.

Seldom will the profits or increase in value of separate property during marriage be exclusively the product of the community's effort or exclusively the product of the inherent nature of the separate property. Instead, as in the instant case, there will be evidence that both factors have contributed to the increased value or profits. In Arizona, these "hybrid profits" have been governed by what can be labeled the "all or none rule." Pursuant to this rule, the profits or increase in value will be either all community property or all separate property depending on whether the increase is primarily due to the toil of the community or primarily the result of the inherent nature of the separate property.

This Court has also become disenchanted with the all or none rule. To implement the all or none rule and determine the primary source of the profits, the portion of the profits that resulted from each source must be calculated. Once this has been done, it is only logical to apportion the profits, or increased value, accordingly. To do otherwise will either deprive the property owner of a reasonable return on the investment or will deprive the community of just compensation for its labor.

We, therefore, also depart from the all or none rule and hold that profits, which result from a combination of separate property and community labor, must be apportioned accordingly.

There are several approaches to the problem of apportionment: "In making such apportionment between separate and community property our courts have developed no precise criterion or fixed standard, but have endeavored to adopt a yardstick which is most appropriate and equitable in a particular situation." *Beam v. Bank of America*, 6 Cal. 3d 12, 18 (1971).

In the case of real estate, the owner of the real property can be awarded its rental value, with the community being entitled to the balance of the income produced from the lands by the labor, skill and management of the parties. Another approach is to determine the reasonable value of the community's services and allocate that amount to the community, and treat the balance as separate property attributable to the inherent nature of the separate estate. [*Van Camp v. Van Camp*, 53 Cal. App. 17, 199 P. 885 (1921).] Finally, the trial court may simply allocate to the separate property a reasonable rate of return on the original capital investment. Any increase above this amount is community property. *Pereira v. Pereira*, 156 Cal. 1, 103 P. 488 (1909).

All of these approaches have merit, with different circumstances, requiring the application of a different method of apportionment. We, therefore, hold that the trial court is not bound by any one method, but may select whichever will achieve substantial justice between the parties.

The judgment of the Superior Court is reversed and the case remanded for the trial court to apportion the profits or increase in value of appellant's separate property between separate and community property.

DISCUSSION

Cockrill sets forth the two approaches used in most other community property states regarding separate property corporations. According to the *Pereira* approach, the value of the separate property corporation at the time of marriage is determined. This separate property component is then given a reasonable annual rate of return for each year of marriage, to compensate the separate estate for inflation and any other factors other than the services of the spouse. This initial separate property component is then combined with all amounts allocated to annual returns on the separate property to yield the total separate property component. The community share of the increase in value is the amount, if any, by which the value of the corporation at divorce exceeds the total separate property component.

Under *Van Camp*, the reasonable value of the spouse's services rendered during marriage is computed. Any salary received by the spouse during marriage from the corporation is deducted from this amount. The community is entitled to this net amount; the remainder of the corporation is separate property. If the spouse was adequately compensated, there will be no community claim under *Van Camp*. *See generally* Oldham, *Separate Property Businesses That Increase in Value During Marriage*, 1990 Wis. L. Rev. 585.

It is possible that the community will have no interest in the corporation under either theory, if the increase in value of the corporation during marriage is not significant.

Also, if the community has an equitable claim under either approach and if any of the stockholder's separate property was used to pay family living expenses during marriage, all amounts of separate property so expended should be offset against any community claim. *See Beam v. Bank of America*, 6 Cal. 3d 12, 490 P.2d 257 (1971).

Speer v. Quinlan
Supreme Court of Idaho, 1973
525 P.2d 314

McQUADE, Justice.

[After marrying W (Olive), H (Raymond) began working at his father's munitions manufacturing plant. In 1963, H became co-manager with his father. On December 31, 1963, H's parents gave him 320 of the total 500 shares of stock of the business, Speer, Inc., which they had just incorporated. Each share had a $100 par value. A further gift of 5 shares to H in 1970–71 gave him 65 percent ownership. In 1966, H became president of the corporation. At divorce in 1971, the trial court held W had a large community interest in the corporation. H appeals.]

The district court found that the book value of the stock per share had increased from $100.00 to $818.43. The court further found that as of August 31, 1971, the market value of the corporation had increased from no more than $400,000 in January of 1964, to $1,560,000 at the time of the trial, a net increase of $1,160,000. In all its years of incorporation, Speer, Inc. never declared any dividends on its stock nor issued any stock dividends.

During Raymond Speer's tenure as president of Speer, Inc., the company has accumulated undistributed after-tax earnings of $339,493. Raymond Speer devoted much time to his job, including some evening and weekend work. Olive Speer made some contributions to the conduct of the business by the entertaining of business guests.

The district judge concluded that justice required him to disregard the corporate form and to award Olive Speer a share in the enhanced value of the corporation. Since Raymond Speer had owned 64% of the stock in Speer, Inc., during the greater part of the period from January, 1964, until the time of trial, the district court found the community interest in the enhanced value of the corporation amounted to 64% of the net increase in fair market value, or $742,400. The court awarded Mrs. Speer a money judgment of $371,200, representing one-half of this community interest.

The principal issue in this case is whether Mrs. Speer is entitled to share in the increase in value of Speer, Inc., a close corporation, in which her husband was a majority stockholder and important employee during part of their marriage, on the ground that such increase resulted from community efforts, industry and other contributions. The authority from the other community property states on the subject of the enhancement in value of separate property businesses is conflicting. No pattern predominates.

[The court here discusses *Abraham v. Abraham* and *Beals v. Fontenot*, concluding that "the corporate form of ownership would not prevent the Louisiana court from finding a community interest in the enhanced value of corporate stock under some circumstances." Then after noting that California and Washington authorities are distinguishable because in those states rents and profits from separate property are also separate, the court reviews California's *Pereira* and *Van Camp* approaches and Washington's segregated-salary test. It is quite critical of the Washington rule requiring a spouse running a separately owned, unincorporated business to pay himself a salary in order to maintain a claim to separate profits.]

In 1954 in the case of *Gapsch v. Gapsch*, 76 Idaho 44, 277 P.2d 278 (1954), this Court promulgated rules relating to enhancement in value of separate property. The pertinent parts of the *Gapsch* case follow:

> As a general rule, the natural enhancement in value of separate property during coverture does not constitute community property; however, to the extent an enhancement in value is due to community efforts, labor, industry or funds, it falls into the community. Again, as a general rule, though not absolute, so-called profit or gain from the sale of separate property occasioned by a natural enhancement in the value of such property, constitutes a part of the separate estate.

In the instant case, we are dealing with the employment of one spouse in a separate property business in which he held an ownership interest and from which he received compensation in the form of salary, bonuses, and fringe benefits. Accordingly, we must ascertain the legislative intent regarding such a situation.

The community property system conceives of marriage as a cooperative enterprise in which assets acquired during the union are owned by both spouses in common. Besides tangible assets which a couple may acquire during a marriage, the marital community also possesses an important, though intangible, asset: the capability of both spouses to contribute to the material betterment of the community through their labor. It follows, therefore, that to the extent that either spouse is rewarded for his or her labor during the marriage, such reward is community property.

Accordingly, if community efforts and ability have been expended in the conduct of a separate property business, a proper inquiry upon the dissolution of that marriage is whether the community has received fair and adequate compensation for its labor. Such a rule strikes a balance between the legitimate claims of both the separate and community estates.

In determining whether the community has been adequately compensated for its labor over the period of the marriage, the trial court should take the following factors into consideration: the nature of the business, the size of the business, the number of employees, the nature and extent of community involvement in the conduct of the business, the growth pattern of the business. (Did it steadily enhance in value? Did periods of prosperity alternate with periods of decline?) Once these questions are answered, the proper inquiry is whether the over-all compensation received by the community for its contribution to the conduct of the business was equivalent to the compensation which the business would have had to pay to secure a non-owner employee to perform the same services which were rendered by the community. A relevant type of evidence for determining the adequacy of community compensation for its efforts would be evidence relating to the salaries of non-owner employees at the same level of responsibility in comparable types of businesses in the same area of the country. If it is found that the community has been deprived of adequate compensation for its services, the community would be entitled to a judgment against the owner-spouse equivalent to the difference between the income actually received by the community in the form of compensation from the business, and the income which the community would have received had the owner-spouse been justly compensated.

In the present case we look to the adequacy of compensation paid to Raymond Speer. We are dealing here only with the period of time subsequent to January 1, 1964, to the date of trial. Before January 1, 1964, Raymond Speer did not have an owner interest in the corporation. The only finding of fact made by the district court relative to the adequacy of Raymond Speer's salary, bonuses, and fringe benefits was that: "The value of community contributions of plaintiff and defendant to Speer, Inc. during the period of January 1, 1964 to date of the trial greatly exceeded the value of the compensation paid by Speer, Inc., to the community during that period." The district court made no finding as to whether Raymond Speer's salary and other emoluments would have secured an equally able employee to fill his position. The only evidence as to how Raymond Speer's compensation compared with that of similar employees on an industry-wide basis was his father's statement that Raymond's pay was "above the norm."

A determination of whether Raymond Speer received compensation comparable to that of a similar employee in his position is needed for a final resolution of this case.

By the time of the trial, Speer, Inc., had accumulated net after-tax earnings of $339,493, thus substantially increasing the "shareholders' equity" in the corporation, nor were any stock dividends issued. Raymond Speer testified that the $339,493 retained by Speer, Inc. was represented by "[v]arious assets such as [a]ccounts [r]eceivable, raw materials inventory, finished goods inventory, machinery, furniture and fixtures and the like." It is true, as respondent points out, that Raymond Speer's position as majority stockholder as well as president and general manager of Speer, Inc., gave him substantial influence over the decision to retain the net earnings or to disburse them in the form of cash dividends. However, no contention is made that retention of the net earnings was unreasonable from a business point of view or that the earnings were retained to defraud the Raymond Speer community.

Had part or all of the earned surplus been distributed by the corporation in the form of cash dividends, such dividends as were attributable to Raymond Speer's stock would have been community property. Presumably, the Speer community would have received 65% of the hypothetical dividend distribution, in proportion to Raymond Speer's ownership of 65% of the corporate stock. Because the net earnings were never disbursed by the corporation, they cannot be considered to be "income" or "rents and profits." Therefore, the retention of the earnings in the business does not present a case of community funds being invested in a separate property business. Nevertheless, the fact remains that, because of business exigencies, monies that might otherwise have been distributed to the community as cash dividends, instead remained in the business in which Raymond Speer holds separate property ownership interest.

Discretionary division [at divorce] of community property is one mechanism by which any inequities may be rendered. As part of its re-examination of the amount of community property to be divided between Mr. and Mrs. Speer, the district court should determine the extent to which the community would have been benefited, had 65% of the distributable earnings of the corporation been received by the community in the form of dividends. At least two factors must be taken into consideration in determining what proportion of the retained earnings would have been available for distribution in the form of cash dividends. First, on remand it is possible that the district court may determine that Raymond Speer was under-compensated for his labor in the corporation. To the extent that the district court finds that the Speer community was entitled to additional compensation for Raymond's labor, the amount of potentially distributable earnings here under consideration must be reduced. This is because any salary payments to Raymond Speer would have been deducted from the income of the corporation in the process of arriving at the figure for net earnings. The amount of retained net earnings under consideration should also be reduced to the extent that the salary of the other employee-stockholder, Forrest Luthy, was inadequate. Consideration should be given toward the maintenance of the corporate solvency.

An attempt to compensate Mrs. Speer for detriment that the community may have experienced because of the retention of the earned surplus must, of necessity, be inexact. Nevertheless, such a procedure would be no more lacking in precision than awarding damages for pain and suffering, which has been accomplished satisfactorily by the courts for many years. Because of its decision regarding the distribution of property, the district court denied an award of alimony to Mrs. Speer. In view of this opinion, the district court on remand may reconsider the issue of alimony.

Reversed and remanded for further proceedings.

DISCUSSION

What approach does the Idaho court apply to determine the community claim to the increased value of the business?

In order to determine the community claim, how should the reasonableness of the spouse's compensation be determined? Should this computation be affected by the actual success of the business?

In addition to the adequacy of the husband's compensation during marriage, the *Speer* court is concerned about the adequacy of the company's dividends paid during marriage. If a separate property corporation makes a profit, this profit remains an asset of the corporation and increases the value of the separate property stock. The profit is still considered owned by the corporation, and is not considered a "rent or profit" of the separate property stock. If some of the profit is paid out to the shareholders in the form of cash dividends, however, this profit paid by the separate property corporation to the stockholder becomes a community property "profit" in states like Idaho and Texas where "rents and profits" of separate property are community. In separate property corporations where the spouse controls the dividend policy, the spouse has the ability to determine whether corporate profits will be paid to the shareholders. This gives the owning spouse the power to reduce, or eliminate altogether, the community claim to any corporate profits.

Speer attempts to establish a mechanism to ensure that the community will retain a claim to a reasonable amount of the profits of the corporation. Is this mechanism workable? How should a court determine the amount of "distributable earnings"? Does this mean the annual profits of the business or something else? Should the *Speer* dividend analysis be made whenever a spouse owns stock that is separate property? What if the husband owned stock in IBM?

Simplot v. Simplot

Supreme Court of Idaho, 1974
526 P.2d 844

McQUADE, Justice.

[When he married W in 1953, H owned 610 of the 2,262 shares outstanding of Apex Corp., a holding company, which in turn owned 22,622 of 72,622 shares outstanding of J. R. Simplot Co., so that in effect H owned 8.4% of Simplot. From the date of H's marriage in 1953 to the divorce in 1971, Simplot Co.'s retained earnings increased from $6 million to over $44 million. The divorce court held all of H's interest in the corporations to be his separate property, and W appeals.]

[A]ll property acquired before marriage remains the separate property of the acquiring spouse. Since the 610 shares of Apex were acquired before the marriage, they are the respondent's separate property.

It is the appellant's position that the respondent's proportionate share of the increase in retained earnings during the marriage is rent and profit of his separate property and is therefore community property.

First, it must be determined whether separate property stock's proportionate share of an increase in a corporation's retained earnings is rent and profit or natural enhancement. The record establishes that there has been a dramatic increase in J. R. Simplot Company's retained earnings, but the respondent has no means of obtaining the use or control over his proportionate share of the retained earnings.

The retained earnings of J. R. Simplot Company are not accumulated as a cash account, but rather the corporation's earnings have been reinvested in the expansion of the business through the purchase of plant and equipment. The decision of the directors to reinvest the earnings is a matter of business judgment, and the growth of the J. R. Simplot Company demonstrates that it was a sound decision. For this Court to declare that the respondent is entitled to a portion of the retained earnings would be in effect to require the J. R. Simplot Company to declare a dividend and then require Apex Corporation to declare a dividend and thus, substitute its judgment for the business judgment of the directors of both the Simplot and Apex Corporations. Since the respondent has no legal right to the retained earnings and since there is no guarantee that they will ever become of economic benefit to him, they are not income or rents and profits. Respondent owned 610 unencumbered shares of Apex before the marriage; there were no changes in his ownership during the marriage; at the dissolution of the marriage the respondent should still own 610 unencumbered shares of Apex stock to be consistent with the right to own and maintain separate property. If the increase in retained earnings allowable to the 610 shares of Apex stock is held to be community property, the result will be to divide and distribute part of the respondent's stock owned as separate property. The increase in retained earnings in this action must be considered natural enhancement and not income or rents and profits in order to preserve the right to own and hold separate property.

The appellant contends that if retained earnings are not held to be a profit, then the husband may deny the community his business earnings by incorporating the business. In this action the respondent has served on the board of directors of J. R. Simplot Company, but the appellant does not allege that the retention of earnings has been fraudulent or intended to deprive the community of funds. There is no evidence that the respondent did not receive an adequate salary in relationship to his responsibilities. Furthermore, there is no evidence that the respondent used the corporate structure to deprive the community of earnings. The courts must be vigilant to protect the community from the use of business organizations to deprive the community of earnings that are the result of community labor, but there is no allegation or evidence in this action of an attempt to prevent the community from enjoying earnings of community labor.

The second issue involved in the determination of the character of retained earnings is whether the increase in retained earnings was due to community labor. In its findings of fact, the trial court held:

> Plaintiff Don J. Simplot is now, and has been during a substantial portion of the time since his marriage to the defendant an officer of the J. R. Simplot Company; plaintiff was not shown to possess any special skills, knowledge, or talent or to have received any formal education or training in the types of business and industries conducted by the J. R. Simplot Company or its subsidiaries or in the fields of business administration, finance, accounting, or corporate management; that the offices which plaintiff has held and now holds have been in large part sinecures, and plaintiff has during said period received adequate, ample and full compensation for his services rendered to J. R. Simplot Company; that the efforts, labor and industry of the plaintiff, or the community, have not contributed to any increase in the value of the company assets or the stock of J. R. Simplot Company or Apex Corporation during the marriage of the parties.

[The court concluded that the community had no interest in the stock.]

DISCUSSION

Does the Idaho Supreme Court apply the same analysis in *Simplot* and *Speer* regarding the companies' retained earnings? Is there any explanation for the different analysis? Why does the *Simplot* court ignore whether the corporation had any distributable earnings? Does *Simplot* overrule *Speer*?

b. Texas Cases

Vallone v. Vallone
Supreme Court of Texas, 1982
644 S.W.2d 455

RAY, Justice.

This is an appeal from a division of property in a divorce action. At issue is whether the trial court abused its discretion by not specifically considering the community's interest, if any, in the increase in value of the separate property portion of stock in a closely-held corporation in which all of the corporation's stock was issued in the husband's name. The stock was originally received in exchange for both community and separate assets. The court of civil appeals held that the trial court, "in making a division of the estate, did not take into consideration the large increment to [the husband's] separate property by reason of community labor and as a result the division of the estate was manifestly unfair to [the wife]." 618 S.W.2d 820, 824. We reverse the judgment of the court of civil appeals and affirm the judgment of the trial court.

The holding of the court of civil appeals in this case conflicts with the holding in *Hale v. Hale*, 557 S.W.2d 614 (Tex. Civ. App.—Texarkana 1977, no writ). In *Hale*, the court held that a contribution of community labor should not be taken into account in determining the amount of reimbursement that may be owing to the community by the benefited separate estate.

Tony and Leslie Vallone were married in 1966. During the first years of their marriage, Tony worked in a restaurant owned and operated by his father as a sole proprietorship. In January 1969, the assets of the restaurant were transferred to Tony from his father as a gift. Tony operated the restaurant as a sole proprietorship until its incorporation in August 1969. The initial capitalization consisted of $19,663 in assets. Included in the initial capital was the used restaurant equipment given to Tony by his father, valued at $9,365 (or slightly over 47% of the initial capital).

During the period beginning with the incorporation of the restaurant until the couple divorced, the business prospered. The restaurant business constituted the major asset of both the community estate and the husband's separate estate. Tony received approximately $200,000 per year as salary and bonus from the corporation. Many of the couple's personal transactions were handled through the corporation.

The court found the business to be worth $1,000,000. Finding that 47% of its initial capitalization was traceable to Tony's separate estate, the trial court set aside a proportionate share of the corporate stock as Tony's separate property. The trial court then awarded Leslie 70% of the remaining stock as her share of the community interest in the corporation, subject to redemption provisions. The decree ordered Tony's Restaurant, Inc., to purchase Leslie's share of the stock for a cash payment of $77,000 and a $300,000 note personally guaranteed by Tony and secured by all of the stock in Tony's. The court of civil appeals calculated that Leslie received 51.4% of the net estate. Tony was ordered to assume all tax liabilities.

Leslie appealed the division of property. The court of civil appeals determined that the transfer of restaurant equipment from father to son was a gift, not a sale, and that the corporation was not operated as Tony's alter ego. But while further affirming the trial court's finding that 47% of the corporate stock was Tony's separate property, the court of civil appeals sustained Leslie's point of error that the trial court's division of the property was so manifestly unfair as to amount to an abuse of discretion, determining "that the court, in making a division of the estate, did not take into consideration the large increment to appellee's separate property by reason of community labor." 618 S.W.2d at 824.

The case comes to us in the following posture: Did the trial court abuse its discretion by ignoring community rights and equities which might have existed in the corporation?

At trial, Leslie asserted that the increase in the value of the corporation's stock should be considered as part of the community, alleging that the corporation existed as Tony's alter ego. She further requested reimbursement if, to quote from her pleadings, "(1) money or property of one of the petitioner's estates (separate or community); (2) has been used or expended to benefit the receiving estate (separate or community); (3) for which Petitioner's contributing estate received no *quid pro quo*; (4) thereby unjustly enriching the receiving estate."

Consideration of whether a corporation is an alter ego for purposes of determining whether assets held in the corporation's name should be treated as community property is an issue of fact from which the status of the property is determined. The trial court and the court of civil appeals found that the restaurant corporation was not Tony's alter ego. No error of law has been correctly preserved on this point.

Characterization of property as separate, however, does not necessarily preclude the right to reimbursement. Questions concerning the right to reimbursement do not concern which estate owns legal or equitable title in certain property.

When separate property is combined with community time, talent and labor, and both the community and the separate estate make claim upon the increment, the courts are confronted with conflicting principles of marital property law. It is fundamental that any property or rights acquired by one of the spouses after marriage by toil, talent, industry or other productive faculty belongs to the community estate. Nevertheless, the law contemplates that a spouse may expend a reasonable amount of talent or labor in the management and preservation of his or her separate estate without impressing a community character upon that estate. *Norris v. Vaughn*, 152 Tex. 491, 260 S.W.2d 676 (1953).

The rule of reimbursement is purely an equitable one. *Golden v. Alexander*, 141 Tex. 134, 171 S.W.2d 328 (1943). It obtains when the community estate in some way improves the separate estate of one of the spouses (or vice versa). The right of reimbursement is not an interest in property or an enforceable debt, per se, but an equitable right which arises upon dissolution of the marriage through death, divorce or annulment.

A right of reimbursement arises when the funds or assets of one estate are used to benefit and enhance another estate without itself receiving some benefit. We hold it also arises when community time, talent and labor are utilized to benefit and enhance a spouse's separate estate, beyond whatever care, attention, and expenditure are necessary for the proper maintenance and preservation of the separate estate, without the community receiving adequate compensation.[2] To the extent that *Hale v. Hale, supra,* held that the expenditure

---

2. Other community property states have formulated rules which permit the community to seek reimbursement for uncompensated community labors. Washington follows the rule that where a salary is paid to the spouse by a closely held corporation of which he owns all or substantially all of the stock, it is presumed that the community has been compensated for the services that spouse may have rendered. The enhanced value retains a separate character. See *Hamlin v. Merlino,* 44 Wash. 2d 851, 272 P.2d 125, 129 (1954). In Arizona, the salary paid to the spouse must be fair and adequate, otherwise the entire increment in value will be deemed community property. See *Nace v. Nace,* 104 Ariz. 20, 448 P.2d 76 (1968). California applies either of two rules which provide for (1) allocation of a reasonable rate of return on the separate property to the separate estate and apportioning the remainder to the community, or (2) awarding the reasonable value of the spouse's services to the community. See *Beam v. Bank of America,* 6 Cal. 3d 12, 98 Cal. Rptr. 137, 490 P.2d 257 (1971). Nevada courts likewise apply both California tests. See *Johnson v. Johnson,* 89 Nev. 244, 510 P.2d 625 (1973). As a rule, New Mexico reimburses or allocates *to the community* the reasonable value of the spouse's labors. See *Katson v. Katson,* 43 N.M. 214, 89 P.2d 524 (1939). Idaho courts are in accord. They consider a number of factors to determine if the salary paid the spouse is a fair compensation for labor expended, including the nature and size of the incorporated business, number of employees, and extent of the spouse's involvement and the growth pattern of the business. If the spouse has not taken an adequate compensation from the corporation, the courts will award the community the difference

of community time, talent and labor may under no circumstances give rise to an equitable right of reimbursement in the community's favor, it is hereby disapproved.

The party claiming the right of reimbursement has the burden of pleading and proving that the expenditures and improvements were made and that they are reimbursable. By her first cause of action, Leslie prayed for equitable reimbursement if community funds or property were used to benefit the separate estate of Tony to which end no compensation was had or received, thereby resulting in an unjust enrichment. As to this particular theory of recovery, the trial court found: "(3) The profits from ... Tony's Restaurant, Inc., have been used, in large measure, for the benefit of the community estate and to build the community estate." Leslie objected to this finding of fact. Her several objections to the findings of fact and conclusions of law, together with those she urged the court to adopt, are in no way referable to the theory of reimbursement due to time, talent and labor expended by Tony on behalf of his separate estate to the detriment of the community estate. The only other causes of action pleaded by Leslie referable to reimbursement are those of constructive fraud arising out of Tony's alleged operation of the corporation as his alter ego.

Reimbursement is not available as a matter of law, but lies within the discretion of the court. In the absence of pleadings either specifically for or referable to reimbursement premised on uncompensated time, talent or labor, such recovery is waived and the failure of the trial court to consider the matter does not constitute error.

We have carefully considered the entire record of this case to determine whether the trial court abused its discretion in dividing the community estate of the parties and have found no such abuse. We therefore reverse the judgment of the court of civil appeals and affirm the judgment of the trial court.

Jensen v. Jensen
Supreme Court of Texas, 1984
665 S.W.2d 107

ON MOTION FOR REHEARING

WALLACE, Justice.

This court's opinion and judgment of November 9, 1983, are withdrawn and the following opinion is substituted therefor.

Petitioner, Robert Lee Jensen, and Respondent, Burlene Parks Jensen, were divorced on May 21, 1980. The decree of divorce provided that 48,455 shares of stock in RLJ Printing Co., Inc., acquired by Mr. Jensen four months prior to marriage, together with any increase in value in such stock which occurred during marriage, were the separate property of Mr. Jensen, and denied Mrs. Jensen any interest in the stock or its increased value. The court of appeals reversed and remanded, holding that the community should be compensated for an enhancement in value of the stock because such appreciated value had been due primarily to the time, toil and effort of Mr. Jensen. 629 S.W.2d 222. We remand to the trial court for determination of the amount, if any, of reimbursement to the community.

---

between the compensation received and what the corporation would have had to pay an employee to perform the same services. See *Speer v. Quinlan*, 96 Idaho 119, 525 P.2d 314 (1974).

On March 21, 1975, Mr. Jensen formed the RLJ Printing Company, Inc. (RLJ) and for $1.56 per share acquired 48,455 of the 100,000 shares outstanding. On May 16, 1975, RLJ acquired Newspaper Enterprises, Inc., in what the trial court found to be a "unique business opportunity." The Jensens were married on July 21, 1975, separated on June 3, 1979, and divorced on May 21, 1980. At all pertinent times, Mr. Jensen was the key man in the operation of RLJ, which was a holding company whose sole assets consisted of all of the stock of Newspaper Enterprises, Inc. Mr. Jensen's compensation from RLJ, consisting of salary, bonuses and dividends, was $64,065.97 in 1976, $95,426.00 in 1977, $106,143.00 in 1978 and $115,000.00 in 1979.

The record does not reflect that any evaluation of the RLJ stock was made as of the date of the marriage. At trial, the per share value of the stock was $13.48 according to Mr. Jensen's expert and $25.77 according to Mrs. Jensen's expert.

The findings of fact and conclusions of law made by the trial court are as follows:

FINDINGS OF FACT

1. The RLJ Printing Company, Inc. was created by Respondent before the marriage of the parties.

2. RLJ Printing Company, Inc. acquired the stock of Newspaper Enterprises, Inc., 64 days before the marriage of the parties in a unique business opportunity.

3. RLJ Printing Company, Inc. is not an alter ego of the Respondent.

4. RLJ Printing Company, Inc. was not created in fraud of the rights of the community estate.

5. The salary paid Respondent has been adequate and reasonable.

6. The dividends paid Respondent have been adequate and reasonable.

7. The bonuses paid Respondent have been adequate and reasonable.

8. Respondent was the key man in the operation of RLJ Printing Company,Inc.

9. The successful operations of RLJ Printing Company, Inc. were primarily due to the time, toil and effort of Respondent.

CONCLUSIONS OF LAW

1. The community was not the equitable owner of any shares of RLJ Printing Company, Inc.

2. The community was not entitled to receive the value of the appreciation in shares of RLJ Printing Company, Inc. that was due to the successful operations of the company.

3. The community was not entitled to receive the value of the appreciation in shares of RLJ Printing Company, Inc., that was due to the time, toil and effort of Respondent.

The point of first impression squarely before us is how to treat, upon divorce, corporate stock owned by a spouse before marriage but which has increased in value during marriage due, at least in part, to the time and effort of either or both spouses.

The community property states have adopted variations of either "reimbursement" or "community ownership" theories. Common to both theories is the general concept that the community should receive whatever remuneration is paid to a spouse for his or her time and effort because the time and effort of each spouse belongs to the community.

Though sharing a common conceptual basis, the two theories diverge when it comes to the valuation of the community's claim against separately owned stock that has appreciated by virtue of a spouse's time and effort. The "reimbursement" theory provides that the stock, as it appreciates, remains the separate property of the owner spouse. Under this theory, the community is entitled to reimbursement for the reasonable value of the time and effort of both or either of the spouses which contributed to the increase in value of the stock. The "community ownership" theory, on the other hand, holds that any increase in the value of the stock as a result of the time and effort of the owner spouse becomes community property.

A consideration of the writings of various scholars in this field, the treatment of the issue by our sister community property states, and the constitutional, statutory and case law of Texas leads to the conclusion that the reimbursement theory more nearly affords justice to both the community and separate estates. This theory requires adoption of the rule that the community will be reimbursed for the value of time and effort expended by either or both spouses to enhance the separate estate of either, other than that reasonably necessary to manage and preserve the separate estate, less the remuneration received for that time and effort in the form of salary, bonus, dividends and other fringe benefits, those items being community property when received.

This rule is a reasonable means of assuring that the community will be fully reimbursed for the value of community assets, *i.e.*, time and effort expended, while at the same time providing that the property interest of the separate estate is also protected and preserved. As a practical matter, this rule will obviate the need for the trial court to undertake the onerous and quite often impossible burden that would be placed on it under the community ownership theory of attempting to determine just what factors actually contributed to the increase in value of the stock and in what proportion. The reimbursement theory of compensation is also consistent with the laws of Texas as found in the Texas Constitution, statutes and Supreme Court opinions set out below.

The Texas Constitution, art. XVI, Section 15, provides that property owned by a spouse before marriage remains the separate property of that spouse during marriage. In *Welder v. Lambert*, 91 Tex. 510, 44 S.W. 281 (1898), this Court decided that all property held by either a husband or a wife before marriage remains the separate property of such spouse and the status of the property is to be determined by the origin of the title to the property, and not by the acquisition of the final title. *Ibid.* This Court has consistently adhered to the rule expressed in *Welder*. The shares of RLJ stock thus remain the separate property of Mr. Jensen, subject only to the right of reimbursement, if any, proven by Mrs. Jensen.

The trial court found that Mr. Jensen was adequately and reasonably compensated for his time and effort expended in enhancing the value of the RLJ shares. This finding, if sustained, precludes Mrs. Jensen's right to reimbursement because that compensation was community property.

The only evidence offered at trial to establish the reasonableness of Mr. Jensen's compensation was the testimony of Mr. T. Wesley Hickman. Mr. Hickman was an expert in the field of corporate evaluation. It was his opinion that Mr. Jensen was reasonably compensated, but he based that opinion "primarily upon Mr. Jensen's percentage of the stock ownership." He further stated that without the stock ownership he seriously doubted that Mr. Jensen would have stayed with RLJ. His opinion as to reasonable compensation was primarily based upon Mr. Jensen's stock ownership and not upon the salary, bonuses and dividends received by the community due to the time, toil and effort of Mr. Jensen. Therefore the trial court's finding that Mr. Jensen's compensation was reasonable is without adequate support. Without that finding of fact there is no basis for the trial court's finding that "the community was not entitled to receive the value of the appreciation in shares of RLJ Printing Company, Inc. that was due to the time, toil and effort of Respondent."

Upon retrial of this case the burden of proving a charge upon the shares of RLJ owned by Mr. Jensen will be upon the claimant, Mrs. Jensen. *Welder, supra.* The right to reimbursement is only for the value of the time, toil and effort expended to enhance the separate estate other than that reasonably necessary to manage and preserve the separate estate, for which the community did not receive adequate compensation. *Vallone v. Vallone*, 644 S.W.2d 455, 459 (Tex. 1982). However, if the right to reimbursement is proved, a lien shall not attach to Mr. Jensen's separate property shares. Rather, a money judgment may be awarded.

It has long been the rule of this court to remand to the trial court rather than to render judgment when the ends of justice will be better served thereby. Such remanding has often been ordered to supply additional testimony or to amend pleadings.

Therefore, pursuant to T.R.C.P. Sec. 505, we remand this cause to the trial court for the limited purpose of determining the amount of reimbursement, if any, due to the community as a result of the time, toil and talent expended by Mr. Jensen toward enhancement of the stock of RLJ. From the value of the time, toil and talent expended is to be subtracted the compensation paid to Mr. Jensen for such time, toil and talent in the form of salary, bonuses, dividends and other fringe benefits. Any remainder is the reimbursement due the community. This reimbursement, if any, shall be distributed by the trial court in addition to the property division heretofore made to the parties.

DISCUSSION

Jensen announces that when a spouse during marriage renders more than a reasonable amount of management services to a separate property corporation, the community is entitled to "the value of the time and effort" expended by the spouse during marriage to benefit the corporation. How is this to be determined? Does this method of calculating the community claim resemble any other method previously encountered in this chapter?

The Court suggests that the time, toil, and talent claim involves subtracting the value of time needed to "manage and preserve" the property from the overall value of the services contributed during marriage. No appellate case since 1984 has clarified how one might determine the amount of time necessary to "manage and preserve" the property. The 2009 reimbursement statute merely states there is a reimbursement claim if the spouse is "inadequately compensated for time, toil, and talent contributed to a business"; no exception for time needed to "manage and preserve" is mentioned. Tex. Fam. Code § 3.402(a)(2).

In *Jensen*, the court states that all salary received during marriage from the corporation, as well as all dividends paid to the spouse during marriage, are to be offset against any community reimbursement claim. Is it clear that both of these offsets are appropriate?

What happens if the non-owning spouse renders services to the corporation? Can this ever create a community reimbursement claim? If so, what kinds of services should be considered? In *Gutierrez v. Gutierrez*, 791 S.W.2d 659 (Tex. App. — San Antonio

1990, no writ) the wife argued that she should be reimbursed for the value of the services she devoted to managing the husband's separate property. The court concluded that she had not established that the services she provided exceeded what was necessary to maintain and preserve the husband's property; for this reason, as well as others, the court rejected her reimbursement claim. Do you agree with this analysis? If the wife could have established a prima facie reimbursement claim, are any offsets potentially appropriate?

Note that *Jensen* applies to reimbursement claims at either death or divorce.

What does *Jensen* say about judicial review of the corporation's dividend policy?

Thomas v. Thomas
Texas Court of Appeals—Houston [1st Dist.], 1987
738 S.W.2d 342, no writ

DUNN, Justice (Concurring and dissenting).

On May 29, 1979, the Coca-Cola Bottling Co. borrowed $2,000,000 at a maximum interest rate of the prime rate + 1.35%, from the Guaranty Bank of Trust Co. of Alexandria, Louisiana. This loan was to be used to purchase land and construct improvements at the Coca-Cola bottling facility. The improvements were completed sometime in August 1980. On September 1, 1981, the Guaranty Bank and Trust Co. entered into an agreement, effective October 14, 1981, with the Industrial Development Board of the Parish of Rapides, Inc. for the issuance of industrial revenue bonds in the amount of $2,200,000 for the purpose of refinancing the May 29, 1979 loan to the Coca-Cola Bottling Co. Also on September 1, 1981, both the Coca-Cola Bottling Co. and the appellant and the appellee entered into agreements with Guaranty Bank and Trust Co. guaranteeing the payment of the principal and interest on the bonds. The purpose of this refinancing agreement was to reduce Coca-Cola Bottling Co.'s interest costs on its loan. The maximum interest rate payable on the bonds was 70% of the prime rate, with a total savings to the corporation of approximately $638,000.

Neither the parties' research nor ours has revealed a Texas case deciding the question of whether the community has a right to reimbursement for the use of its credit to secure a loan to refinance the husband's separate property debts. However, I am not willing to state, at this time, that this new reimbursement theory is without merit. I would analogize this situation to cases where separate debts are discharged with community funds. See *Villarreal v. Villarreal*, 618 S.W.2d 99 (Tex. Civ. App.—Corpus Christi 1981, no writ); *Hawkins v. Hawkins*, 612 S.W.2d 683 (Tex. Civ. App.—El Paso 1981, no writ). However, there is an important difference between the case before us and cases involving the discharge of a separate debt with community funds. When a debt is refinanced with the community acting as a guarantor, the cost to the community is not so readily ascertainable. In the latter situation expert testimony would be required on the percentage risk undertaken by the community, and a dollar value would have to be assigned to that risk.

DISCUSSION

Loans to closely-held businesses frequently are personally guaranteed by the owner. Should the community estate have no reimbursement claim for the guarantee (if the loan is repaid by the business and the community suffers no actual loss)? If the community would be entitled to reimbursement, how would such a reimbursement claim be computed?

Young v. Young

Texas Court of Appeals—Dallas, 2005
168 S.W.3d 276, no pet.

ONEILL, Justice.

Gary Paul Young (Husband) appeals from the trial court's divorce decree. In three points of error, Husband contends the trial court erred in: (1) characterizing certain assets as community that he claims are his separate property; (2) assessing the value of certain assets; and (3) awarding Wife certain equitable liens. We sustain Husband's third point of error to the extent he contends the trial court erred in imposing an owelty of partition on partnership property. We reform the trial court's judgment to delete the owelty of partition provision. In all other respects, we affirm the trial court's judgment.

Background

Husband and Wife were married on June 28, 1994. Approximately seven years later, Wife filed for divorce. Prior to the marriage, Husband had formed DAX Enterprises, Inc. During the marriage, Husband and Wife entered into various business ventures. The source of the investment funds used in forming these businesses was contested at trial. Several assets that Husband claimed were his separate property were also in dispute.

Following trial, the trial court orally rendered judgment. Wife filed a motion for reconsideration. The trial court granted Wife's motion and the parties presented additional testimony as to the value of certain assets. The trial court signed a final judgment on January 7, 2004. The trial court rendered judgment that DAX was the alter ego of Husband. In addition to dividing the property, the trial court awarded Wife a money judgment and placed liens on community property awarded to Husband to secure that judgment. The trial court made findings of fact and conclusions of law. This appeal timely followed....

Characterization

In his first point of error, Husband contends the trial court erred in characterizing six items as community assets. He contends these assets are his separate property....

1. DAX Enterprises, Inc.

Husband contends the trial court erred in its finding that DAX Enterprises, Inc. was his alter ego. DAX was Husband's separate property because he owned it prior to the marriage. *See* TEX. FAM. CODE ANN. § 3.001 (Vernon 1998).

Under certain circumstances, a spouse may be able to reach the assets of the other spouse's separately owned corporation. A finding of alter ego allows piercing of the corporate veil. Piercing the corporate veil, in turn, allows the trial court to characterize as community property assets that would otherwise be the separate property of a spouse. *Lifshutz v. Lifshutz*, 61 S.W.3d 511, 516 (Tex. App.—San Antonio 2001, pet. denied). In the divorce context, piercing the corporate veil allows the trial court to achieve an equitable result. *Id.*

In a divorce case, a finding of alter ego sufficient to justify piercing the corporate veil requires: (1) unity between the separate property corporation and the spouse such that the separateness has ceased to exist; and (2) the spouse's improper use of the corporation damaged the community estate beyond that which might be remedied by a claim for reimbursement. *Lifshutz v. Lifshutz*, 61 S.W.3d at 517. In *Lifshutz*, the trial court pierced the corporate veil of the husband's corporation. The appeals court reversed. Although there was some evidence of unity between the corporation's and the husband's finances, the court held there was no evidence that the husband's misuse and dominance of the corporation resulted in a transfer of community property to the corporation. *Lifshutz*, 61 S.W.3d at 517–18.

In another case, the appellate court held the trial court's conclusion that the husband's corporation was not his alter was against the great weight and preponderance of the evidence. *See Zisblatt v. Zisblatt*, 693 S.W.2d 944, 955 (Tex. App. — Fort Worth 1985, writ dism'd). In *Zisblatt*, the husband had a separately owned corporation. The home purchased by the couple was in the corporation's name. The furniture in the couple's home was paid for and owned by the corporation. *Id.* at 947. The husband's income came from the corporation. He deposited his earned income into the corporate account. *Id.* at 955. In finding the husband's management of his separately owned corporation to constitute a fraud on the community, the court stated, "to uphold the fiction of [the corporation] as an entity separate from [the husband] would be a clear and material prejudice to the rights of [the wife] and the community estate and an evasion of an existing legal obligation of [the husband] to devote his time, talent, and industry to the community." *Id.*

Turning now to the facts of this case, the first requirement for piercing the corporate veil is unity between the spouse and the corporation. Husband was the sole employee of DAX. He alone was in charge of the day-to-day finances of the corporation. Wife put her income into the parties' personal account. Instead of doing the same, Husband kept his income in the DAX account. Wife testified that Husband routinely used the DAX account to pay personal expenses. Husband admitted to this practice. He argues, however, that such expenditures benefited the community estate. To the extent these personal expenses were community debts, the community did benefit. Husband, however, paid many debts for which he alone was responsible. He used the DAX account to pay for the daycare expenses for his daughter from a former marriage and make car payments and payments on a house he owned individually. Roger Johnson, a business partner of the Youngs testified that, in his opinion, Husband and DAX were one in the same. We conclude the evidence establishes a unity between Husband and DAX.

We turn now to the second requirement that the spouse's misuse of the corporation damaged the community estate. From 1995 through 2000, DAX's gross earnings amounted to $992,000. During this five-year period, Husband reported officer income of $40,000, officer loans of $31,260, and personal checks from the DAX account of $145,000. Near the time of the marriage the parties agreed to purchase a house. Husband told Wife the house would be in both of their names. Husband instead put the house in the corporation's name. Testimony at trial showed that many charges had been made on the DAX credit cards from locations where DAX had previously done work. However, Husband claimed that he had not been working during this time and that there were no invoices to produce showing income to DAX.

According to corporate records, there is a substantial amount of money unaccounted for. Husband's practice of commingling his income with that of the corporation supports the trial court's fraud finding. During the course of the marriage, Husband dedicated most of his time and talent to DAX. Essentially, the benefit received by the community from Husband's time and talent was the payment of some of its expenses. Labeling the vast majority of income as belonging to DAX, was an effective tool to enhance his separate property. Like the husband in *Zisblatt*, Husband placed many community assets in the corporation's name. Husband also paid himself a relatively small salary in relation to the income received by DAX. Moreover, he put his earned income, a community asset, right back into DAX.

We conclude the evidence in this case reveals Husband misused DAX to the extent it damaged the community estate. The evidence supports the trial court's finding that DAX was the alter ego of Husband....

5. Boat Slip/Condominium

Husband contends the boat slip and condominium (collectively "boat slip") are his separate property because he had the lease on the boat slip since 1988 when he purchased the boat. He testified that he *believed* he signed a lease that automatically renewed from year to year. He did not produce a copy of the lease. Following the marriage, the Youngs paid the lease payments from both the DAX account and their personal account.

Depending upon the language in the lease, a holdover tenancy may be a new tenancy rather than a continuation of the original lease. *Bockelmann v. Marynick,* 788 S.W.2d 569, 571 (Tex. 1990). In *Bockelmann,* a husband and wife leased a duplex. Prior to the lease's expiration, the wife moved out of the duplex. The husband continued to occupy the duplex after the lease expired and became delinquent on the rent. The lessors sued both the husband and wife for the unpaid rent. The trial court found the husband liable but not the wife. The court of appeals held the husband and wife were liable for the unpaid rent because her joint obligation under the lease continued through her husband's holdover period. *Id.* at 571. The supreme court, looking to the language of the lease, reversed. The lease in *Bockelmann* provided that if a tenant remained in possession of the leased premises after the lease expired, "a *new* tenancy from year to year shall be created ..." *Id.* at 570. The supreme court held that the wife was not liable for the unpaid rent because she was not a tenant when the holdover term began and the new tenancy was created. *Id.* at 572.

If the boat slip lease provides that a holdover tenancy creates a new tenancy, then the leasehold interest would have been acquired during the marriage and, therefore, constitutes community property. It was Husband's burden to establish by clear and convincing evidence that the boat slip was his separate property. Husband did not produce a copy of the lease. Because the lease's language is controlling, Husband failed to establish the boat slip as his separate property.

We overrule Husband's first point of error....

Liens

In his last point of error, Husband contends the trial court erred in placing liens on certain assets to secure the money judgment to Wife.

A trial court may impose an equitable lien against community property to secure one spouse's obligation to pay a monetary award that represents the consideration for the other spouse's relinquishment of his or her interest in the marital estate. *Magallanez v. Magallanez,* 911 S.W.2d 91, 94 (Tex. App.—El Paso 1995, no writ). The trial court awarded Wife an equitable lien in certain community assets that the trial court awarded to Husband. The purpose of the lien was to secure the money judgment awarded to Wife. We conclude the trial court did not err in placing a lien on assets it found to belong to the community.

Husband also contends the trial court erred in placing an owelty of partition on the entire 69 RV property. We agree.

Partnership property is owned by the partnership itself and not by the individual partners. *Marshall v. Marshall,* 735 S.W.2d 587, 595 (Tex. App.—Dallas 1987, writ ref'd n.r.e.). A partner's partnership interest, the right to receive his share of the profits and surpluses from the business, is the only property right a partner has that is subject to a community or separate property characterization. *Id.*

The trial court found that 69 RV was partnership property. The trial court awarded the community interest in 69 RV to Husband. Accordingly, Husband owns one-half of the partnership and Tim Armstrong owns the other half. Because 69 RV belongs to the partnership, the trial court erred when it placed an owelty of partition against the entirety of the partnership property....

Lifshutz v. Lifshutz

Texas Court of Appeals — San Antonio, 2001
61 S.W.3d 511, pet. denied

Kymberly contends the trial court was correct when it pierced the corporate entities to characterize one-third of the Companies' assets as part of the community estate. Her complaint on appeal is that the trial court erred by awarding her only twenty-five percent of all the community property. The Companies attack the trial court's finding of alter ego and its decision to pierce the corporate veil.

A. The application of alter ego and piercing the corporate veil in community property division

The doctrine of alter ego, in a traditional business context, allows the trial court to set aside the corporate structure of a company, or "pierce the corporate veil," to hold individual shareholders liable for corporate debt. *Castleberry v. Branscum,* 721 S.W.2d 270, 271–72 (Tex. 1986). Alter ego has two elements: (1) "such unity between corporation and individual that the separateness of the corporation has ceased," and (2) a finding that "holding only the corporation liable would result in injustice." *Id.* at 272. Traditionally, courts pierce the corporate structure to hold an individual officer, director, or stockholder liable for the debts of the corporation only where "it appears that the individuals are using the corporate entity as a sham to perpetrate a fraud, to avoid personal liability, avoid the effect of a statute, or in a few other exceptional situations." *Zisblatt,* 693 S.W.2d at 950. Mere domination of corporate affairs by a sole stockholder or financial unity between shareholder and corporation will not justify disregard of the corporate entity. *Id.* at 950.

In exceptional circumstances, the principles of alter ego and piercing the corporate veil have been applied to divorce cases in what could be termed "reverse piercing." *See Zisblatt,* 693 S.W.2d at 952. Piercing the corporate veil in a divorce case allows the divorce court to characterize as community property corporate assets that would otherwise be the separate property of one spouse. *Id.; accord Vallone v. Vallone,* 644 S.W.2d 455, 458 (Tex. 1982) (alter ego is issue of fact from which the status of property as community or separate is determined). Unlike traditional piercing in which the stockholder is held liable for debts of the corporation, piercing in the divorce context allows the trial court to move assets out of the corporation and divide them between spouses as part of the shareholder's community estate. *See Zisblatt,* 693 S.W.2d at 955. The concepts of alter ego and piercing are applied in divorce cases to achieve an equitable result, that is, a just and right settlement of the marital estate.

Generally, the trial court pierces in a divorce case to avoid leaving the community estate with virtually no property. *Id.* at 953 (wife awarded separate corporate property because husband attempted to change the character of earned income by forming a corporation and depositing his income into corporate accounts, creating a fraud on the community); *Spruill v. Spruill,* 624 S.W.2d 694, 695–96 (Tex. App.—El Paso 1981, writ dism'd) (wife awarded corporate stock and assets where corporation owned the parties' home, furniture, automobiles and other assets, and corporation even paid food and other costs of living). Other courts have considered whether the conduct of the stockholder resulted in fraud upon the other spouse or third parties. *See Bell v. Bell,* 513 S.W.2d 20, 22 (Tex. 1974); *Southwest Livestock & Trucking Co. v. Dooley,* 884 S.W.2d 805, 810 (Tex. App.—San Antonio 1994, writ denied); *Humphrey v. Humphrey,* 593 S.W.2d 824, 826 (Tex. Civ. App.—Houston [14th Dist.] 1980, writ dism'd).

Thus to properly pierce in a divorce case, the trial court must find something more than mere dominance of the corporation by the spouse.[1] At the least, a finding of alter ego sufficient to justify piercing in the divorce context requires the trial court to find: (1) unity between the separate property corporation and the spouse such that the separateness of the corporation has ceased to exist, and (2) the spouse's improper use of the corporation damaged the community estate beyond that which might be remedied by a claim for reimbursement.[2]

B. Sufficiency of the evidence

Having defined the minimum requirements for piercing, we review the sufficiency of the evidence to support the trial court's finding of alter ego. The evidence is conflicting but there is at least some evidence James disregarded the corporate form and used corporate funds for personal dealings. Therefore, we defer to the trial court's implied finding of unity between the corporations and James' personal finances. *See Jauregui,* 695 S.W.2d at 263.

Regarding the second requirement, however, James's alleged dominance of the corporation and disregard of the corporate entity is not enough to justify piercing in this case. The conduct which arguably supports the trial court's finding of alter ego is not conduct which harmed the community estate by converting community assets to separate corporate property. The trial court found James breached his fiduciary duty to the corporations by paying personal expenses through the businesses, failing to follow formalities, and purchasing notes for himself and Kymberly in contravention of his duty to the businesses. This activity actually enhanced the community at the expense of the corporations. There is no evidence James's alleged dominance and misuse of the corporate businesses resulted in a transfer of community property to the separate property corpo-

---

1. *See Goetz v. Goetz,* 567 S.W.2d 892, 896 (Tex. App.—Dallas 1976, no writ) (wife not entitled to award of separate property corporate assets even though husband was sole shareholder and committed some improprieties, where husband's improper use of corporation did not damage community estate). In the case before this court, the trial court held the proponent of alter ego need not show intent or fraud, only that an inequitable result will occur if piercing is not applied. We hold this statement is overbroad and misleading. It may be true the evidence need not show intent to defraud, but the inequity that justifies "reverse piercing" in a divorce case must stem from an improper transfer of community assets to the corporation.

2. The Companies assert there is a third element—a finding the corporate spouse is the sole shareholder or the existence of other shareholders is a sham. *See, e.g., Vallone,* 644 S.W.2d at 457; *Bell,* 513 S.W.2d at 21; *Eikenhorst v. Eikenhorst,* 746 S.W.2d 882, 887 (Tex. App.—Houston [1st Dist.] 1988, no writ); *Zisblatt,* 693 S.W.2d at 953–55 (husband was sole owner and his attempt to transfer stock to sister would be fraud on the community); *Humphrey,* 593 S.W.2d at 826; *Goetz,* 567 S.W.2d at 896; *Uranga v. Uranga,* 527 S.W.2d 761, 765 (Tex. Civ. App.—San Antonio 1975, writ dism'd); *Dillingham v. Dillingham,* 434 S.W.2d 459, 462 (Tex. Civ. App.—Fort Worth 1968, writ dism'd). We need not address this contention because Kymberly has not established the second element necessary for piercing.

rations. The evidence does not reflect the egregious circumstances that have led other courts to pierce the corporate veil and characterize separate property corporate assets as community property. We hold the trial court improperly pierced the corporate entities. Because of the piercing, the trial court considered more property in making its division than was available to the community estate.

C. Application to partnership interest

Liberty Properties Partnership argues piercing is not appropriate for a partnership. Under the Texas Revised Uniform Partnership Act, a trial court may not award specific partnership assets to the non-partner spouse in the event of a divorce. TEXAS REVISED PARTNERSHIP ACT, Tex. Rev. Civ. Stat. Ann., art. 6132b-5.01, -5.02, -5.03, -5.04 (Vernon Supp. 2001); *McKnight v. McKnight,* 543 S.W.2d 863, 867–68 (Tex. 1976). The trial court may only award the spouse an interest in the partnership. Kymberly argues as a matter of policy that a partnership should be treated the same as a corporation. However, the comment of the bar committee to section 6132b-5.01 specifically notes the statute incorporates the limitation that "a partner's spouse has no community property right in partnership property."[3] Tex. Rev. Civ. Stat. Ann. art. 6132b-5.01 cmt. Because legislative intent is clear and the Texas Supreme Court has followed that dictate, we hold the trial court improperly pierced Liberty Properties Partnership.

Conclusion

Accordingly, we affirm the trial court's judgment dissolving the marriage and establishing custody and maintenance of the children. We reverse and remand for new trial on the division of community property.

DISCUSSION

Note that *Lifshutz* suggests that the rules for piercing in a divorce case might differ from piercing rules in other types of cases. In *Young v. Young,* 168 S.W.3d 276 (Tex. App.— Dallas 2005, no pet.), the court applied the same alter ego test as suggested in *Lifshutz.*

B. Partnerships and Proprietorships

Under Texas law, profits earned during marriage from a separate property proprietorship business are community property "rents and profits," regardless whether they are distributed to the owner. No separate entity exists, so the profits are attributed to the spouse. In contrast, profits earned during marriage by a separate property corporation remain the property of the corporation, unless and until they are paid to the shareholder as a dividend. If a spouse has a separate property partnership interest, for marital property rights purposes, should it be treated as a corporation or a proprietorship?

---

3. The statute reads: "A partner is not a co-owner of partnership property and does not have an interest that can be transferred, either voluntarily or involuntarily, in partnership property." Tex. Rev. Civ. Stat. Ann., art. 6132b-5.01; *see also* Tex. Rev. Civ. Stat. Ann., art. 6132b-5.04 (in divorce, spouse is treated as transferee of partnership interest).

Marshall v. Marshall

Texas Court of Appeals — Dallas, 1987
735 S.W.2d 587, writ ref. n.r.e.

STEWART, J.

Arlene O. Marshall and J. W. "Woody" Marshall sued each other for divorce.

ARLENE'S REIMBURSEMENT CLAIMS

In her first point of error, Arlene argues that the trial court incorrectly characterized the disbursements by the partnership to Woody as his separate property and that, as a result, the trial court abused its discretion in denying her claim that Woody should be ordered to reimburse the community for (1) $125,375.50 of community funds used to pay Woody's 1982 taxes, a separate debt incurred before the marriage, and (2) $63,325.58 of community funds that Woody gave to his daughter during the marriage.

EXTENT OF COMMUNITY EARNINGS

To resolve Arlene's contentions, we must first determine the extent of the community earnings during the marriage. The partnership disbursed $542,315.72 to Woody during the marriage. The partnership records and Woody's tax returns reflect that some amounts were distributed as "salary" and other amounts were distributed as "distributions of profits." Woody argues that only $22,400 of the amount disbursed was salary and that the rest was a return of capital and, therefore, his separate property. Arlene argues that all the disbursements were either salary or distributions of profits and, therefore, community.

Arlene first argues that all partnership disbursements to Woody during marriage were community property because they were acquired during the marriage, Tex. Fam. Code Ann. Sec. 5.01(b) (Vernon 1975), and, therefore, are presumed to have been community property. *Id.*, Sec. 5.02. She further contends that whatever is earned from the labor and effort of either spouse is community property, *Givens v. Girard Life Insurance Co.*, 480 S.W.2d 421, 423 (Tex. Civ. App. — Dallas 1972, writ ref'd n.r.e.); thus, all the disbursements are community property because they are compensation for Woody's labor and effort on behalf of the partnership. Finally, she maintains that the partnership distributions are revenues and profits from Woody's separate property, thereby making them community property, *Arnold v. Leonard*, 114 Tex. 535, 273 S.W. 799 (1925); consequently, whether classified as "distributions of profits" or "salary," all disbursements are community....

Woody's ... response is that the distributions from the partnership, other than the salary in the partnership agreement, were from his capital account and were, therefore, his separate property. We develop Woody's argument and the reasons why we disagree with it below.

The partnership engaged in the business of exploring for, developing, and producing oil and gas. The partnership acquired all its oil and gas leases before the second marriage. The partnership agreement provides that it will pay Woody $700 in salary per month. For the duration of the marriage, the amount comes to $22,400. The partnership agreement also provides that all other distributions are from the distributee's share of the profits. The partnership disbursed $542,315.72 to Woody during the marriage. Woody maintains that only $22,400 was community property and that the rest was a return of capital.

The Texas Uniform Partnership Act (UPA) provides that unless the partners agree otherwise, no partner is entitled to remuneration for acting in the partnership business and that each partner is to share equally in the profits. Tex. Rev. Civ. Stat. Ann. art 6132b,

Sec. 18(1)(a) and (f) (Vernon 1970). Because the agreement is controlling, Woody concedes that the $22,400 is community.

Woody next points to *Norris v. Vaughan*, 152 Tex. 491, 260 S.W.2d 676 (1953). In *Norris*, the husband owned a separate determinable fee interest in the Pakan wells and an interest in a separate partnership that was in the sole business of acquiring gas wells, drilling under lease agreements, and selling the gas. The Texas Supreme Court held that the proceeds from the production and sale of oil and gas from the Pakan wells and from the three leases acquired by the partnership before the husband's marriage were the husband's separate property. The supreme court applied the aggregate theory of partnership and treated the individual partners as owners of the partnership property. Thus, the court characterized partnership property as separate or community, depending upon whether the partnership acquired its property rights before or after the marriage of the partner/husband. Because the husband had acquired his interest in the partnership before the marriage, that interest was his separate property. Likewise, because the partnership had owned its interest in three producing gas wells prior to the husband's marriage, the court held that the husband's interest in the three wells was his separate property and the gas produced from them was "an invasion of the assets comprising (husband's) separate estate." *Id.*, 260 S.W.2d at 681. The court further held that the proceeds from the sale of oil and gas produced from separate property remains separate so long as the oil and gas can be definitely traced and identified. The court reasoned that, since oil and gas in place are part of the corpus of the land, when they are produced, they simply undergo a mutation. Similarly, when the oil and gas production is sold, the proceeds are derived from the piecemeal sale of a separate asset, the corpus of land, and remain separate property. *Id.* at 679–80.

Woody contends that the *Norris v. Vaughan* analysis is applicable in this case because it is undisputed that his partnership interest is his separate property, that the primary business of the partnership is production of oil and gas, that all the partnership leases were acquired prior to marriage, and that the proceeds from the sale of oil and gas are simply mutations of the oil and gas in place, and, therefore, all partnership proceeds form these sales distributed during the marriage remain his separate property.

Arlene has two responses. First, she argues that the adoption of the Uniform Partnership Act in 1961 has amended *Norris*. Second, she contends that because Woody's tax returns and the partnership's own records reflect that Woody received $334,891 in salary for the years 1983 and 1984, Woody cannot now gainsay them. Arlene emphasizes that whether the distributions are for salary or from partnership profits makes no difference, since both salary and profits from separate property become community property. *Trawick v. Trawick*, 671 S.W.2d 105, 109 (Tex. App.—El Paso 1984, no writ).

With the passage of the Uniform Partnership Act in 1961, Texas discarded the aggregate theory and adopted the entity theory of partnership. Under the UPA, partnership property is owned by the partnership itself and not by the individual partners. In the absence of fraud, such property is neither community nor separate property of the individual partners. A partners' partnership interest, the right to receive his share of the profits and surpluses from the business, is the only property right a partner has that is subject to a community or separate property characterization. Tex. Rev. Stat. Ann. at art. 6132b, Sections 8, 26, and 28-A; Note, Community Rights and the Business Partnership, 57 Tex. L. Rev. 1018 (1979); Bromberg, Commentary on the Texas Uniform Partnership Act, 17 Tex. Rev. Civ. Stat. Ann. 300–01 and 321 (Vernon 1970). Further, if the partner receives his share of profits during marriage, those profits are community property, regardless of whether the partner's interest in the partnership is separate or community in nature. Tex.

Fam. Code Ann. Sec. 5.01(b) (Vernon 1975); *Arnold v. Leonard*, 273 S.W. at 799; Note, 57 Tex. L. Rev. at 1032.

The supreme court recognized the changes in partnership law wrought by the adoption of the UPA in *McKnight v. McKnight*, 543 S.W.2d 863 (Tex. 1976). There the court determined that the only partnership-related property a trial court can award upon dissolution of a partner's marriage is the partnership interest. *Id.* at 867–68; see *Haney v. Fealey, Bate, Deaton & Porter*, 618 S.W.2d 541, 542 (Tex. 1981).

Initially, we note that according to the partnership records, Woody's distributions were a series of draws allocated to him, Arlene, and Debra (Woody's daughter), many of which were based on payments by the partnership to personal creditors on behalf of one of these three. The major "distinction" each year was the partnership's payment of Woody's individual income tax liability. It is true that a portion of the distributions was closed to Woody's capital account at the end of the year, but this was simply a bookkeeping entry after the fact.

The amount closed to the capital accounts of both partners, Woody and his ex-wife, Ruby, was based on the total of their draws for the year. In this manner the accountant determined their personal income and their income tax thereon; the accountant then had the partnership pay their personal income tax. These amounts are reflected on the partnership returns as "withdrawals and distributions" in the reconciliation of the partners' capital accounts. Woody's draws throughout each year at issue, and historically, always exceeded Ruby's. Consequently, Woody's excess draws were allocated to salary for Woody on the partnership books and reported as "guaranteed payments for partners" on the partnership tax returns. Woody reported all disbursements received from the partnership, either directly or indirectly, as ordinary income on the spouses' joint tax returns for 1983 and 1984.

Woody apparently relies on the rule that mutations of separate property remain separate if properly traced. *Norris*, 260 S.W.2d at 679. However, a withdrawal from a partnership capital account is not a return of capital in the sense that it may be characterized as a mutation of a partner's separate property contribution to the partnership and thereby remain separate. Such characterization is contrary to the UPA and implies that the partner retains an ownership interest in his capital contribution. He does not; the partnership entity becomes the owner, and the partner's contribution becomes partnership property which cannot be characterized as either separate or community property of the individual partners. Tex. Rev. Civ. Stat. Ann. art. 6132b, Sections 8, 25, and 28-A(1) (Vernon 1970); Bromberg, 17 Tex. Rev. Civ. Stat. Ann. at 300–01. Thus, there can be no mutation of a partner's separate contribution; that rule is inapplicable in determining the characterization of a partnership distribution from a partner's capital account.

Further, the *Norris v. Vaughan* characterization of proceeds from the production of oil and gas is inapplicable to a partnership receipt of such proceeds, for they are simply partnership property and are not subject to characterization as separate or community property. Tex. Rev. Civ. Stat. Ann. art. 6132b Sections 8, 25, and 28-A(1) (Vernon 1970); *McKnight v. McKnight*, 543 S.W.2d 867; Bromberg, 17 Tex. Rev. Civ. Stat. Ann. at 300–01. In this case, all monies disbursed by the partnership were made from current income. The partnership agreement provides that "any and all distributions ... of any kind or character over and above the salary here provided ... shall be charged against any such distributee's share of the profits of the business." Under these facts, we hold that all of the partnership distributions that Woody received were either salary under the partnership agreement or distributions of profits of the partnership.

Although the partnership utilized the bookkeeping device of allocating to salary Woody's withdrawals that were in excess of Ruby's, that device does not make such distributions "salary" contrary to the partnership agreement. The withdrawals nevertheless were distributions of partnership income or profits and, thus, community. We hold that all distributions by the partnership to Woody during the course of the second marriage were community property. Woody's second argument in support of the trial court's separate characterization of the partnership distributions is overruled.

DISCUSSION

As *Marshall* suggests, a partnership is now viewed as an entity; all the spouse owns is an "interest in partnership." Even if the interest is community, that is all the divorce court may divide; it is reversible error to attempt to divide property owned by the partnership. *Gibson v. Gibson*, 190 S.W.3d 821 (Tex. App.—Fort Worth 2006, no pet.).

If the partnership makes a distribution during marriage, it may be significant whether it was a liquidating distribution. Compare *Lifshutz v. Lifshutz*, 199 S.W.3d 9 (Tex. App.—San Antonio 2006, pet. denied), with *LeGrand-Brock v. Brock*, 246 S.W.3d 318 (Tex. App.—Beaumont 2008, pet. denied).

If *Marshall* is not accepted and separate property partnerships are to be treated differently from separate property corporations, how should a court treat a separate property S corporation, which is a corporation but is taxed like a partnership? *Thomas v. Thomas*, 738 S.W.2d 342 (Tex. App.—Houston [1st Dist.] 1987, writ denied) held that this should be treated like any other corporation.

C. A Note Regarding Business Valuation

A business started during marriage with community funds is a community asset. So, the value of the business, including any non-personal goodwill, is community property. Business valuation is a complicated topic, but any serious family lawyer needs to know something about it. For a general overview of this subject, see the materials prepared by Ike Vanden Eykel for the Spring 1995 University of Houston Family Law Practice Seminar, Chapter C, as well as those prepared by Oldham for the 1994 Texas Bar Advanced Family Law Course, Chapter J.

Businesses may be valued by various mechanisms. For example, one might focus on the net asset value of the business. This is in some ways the simplest approach. Under this approach, aggregate liabilities are subtracted from the current value of the assets to arrive at a valuation. A rough estimate of the net asset value approach may be found from a balance sheet. Additional investigation is necessary, however, because the values attributed to assets on the balance sheet reflect historic cost and can be grossly inaccurate for current valuation purposes.

A net asset valuation will undervalue most businesses, however, because that approach ignores the value of the business as a going concern. For this reason most appraisals include an analysis of the earnings or cash flow of a business.

Chapter Eleven

Management Powers

A. In General

In Texas, property can either be sole management or joint management property. Sole management property can be sold or encumbered by one spouse acting alone. Joint management property cannot generally be sold or encumbered without the consent of both spouses.

1. Sole Management Property

Separate property is the sole management property of the owner. Tex. Fam. Code § 3.101. Community property can be either sole management or joint management property. Tex. Fam. Code § 3.102. Sole management community property includes the property accumulated by the spouse during marriage "that he or she would have owned if single...." Tex. Fam. Code § 3.102(a). Although this appears to encompass almost all property that could be accumulated by a spouse during marriage, the Texas Supreme Court in *Cockerham v. Cockerham, infra*, has limited the scope of 3.102(a) property.

2. Joint Management Property

Property that is not 3.102(a) property is 3.102(b) or (c) joint management community property, unless the parties have agreed that the property could be managed solely by one spouse. Tex. Fam. Code § 3.102(b), (c). Can this agreement be oral?

The spouses' homestead is joint management property, regardless whether it is separate or community property. Tex. Fam. Code § 5.001.

Joint management property requires the consent of both spouses to convey or encumber it. What is required to evidence such consent? If one spouse acquiesces in the other's action, does this suffice? *See* Oldham, *Management of the Community Estate During an Intact Marriage*, 56 Law & Contemp. Prob. 99 (1993).

The Texas Constitution and the Family Code provide that a sale of the family "homestead" is a joint management transaction. *See* Tex. Fam. Code § 5.001. If only one spouse signs a listing agreement with a real estate broker, is this enforceable? *See Peters v. Coleman*, 263 S.W.2d 639 (Tex. Civ. App.—Ft. Worth 1953, writ ref'd n.r.e.); *Ryan v. Long*, 183 S.W.2d 473 (Tex. Civ. App.—Galveston 1944, no writ).

A few cases have considered the effect of one spouse's attempt to convey joint management property.

Vallone v. Miller

Texas Court of Appeals—Houston [14th Dist.], 1983
663 S.W.2d 97, writ ref'd n.r.e.

ROBERTSON, Justice.

This appeal is from a judgment that the appellant recover nothing on his suit seeking specific performance of a contract to convey real property or, alternatively, for damages. Under the authority of Tex.R.Civ.P. Sec. 307 and 377(d), the appeal is limited to the question of whether the jury's responses to the special issues support the judgment entered. We affirm.

Appellant's Second Amended Original Petition alleged that a completed written agreement to convey property had been executed by appellant as purchaser and appellee James B. Miller as seller. Appellant also alleged that appellee Elaine Miller's interest in the property was covered by this written agreement and should be conveyed to appellant because "Mr. Miller had the right to manage this property and she is bound by his signature on the earnest money contract or because Mr. Miller was authorized to act for her in the transaction made the subject of this suit." The contract was attached to the petition as an exhibit and constitutes the entire statement of facts before this court. The document is entitled "Earnest Money Contract" and is a printed form with blanks that have been filled in. In the blank for the name of the "sellers" are the names "James B. Miller & Elaine R. Miller." Appellant's name appears in the space for "purchaser." The next blank has been filled with a description of the property. At the bottom of the printed form are the signature lines. Appellant's signature appears on the line reserved for purchaser. Instead of having the signatures of both James B. Miller and Elaine R. Miller, only Mr. Miller's signature appears in the space for the seller's signatures. Mrs. Miller's signature is not on the document.

The answers for both appellees: denied that James B. Miller had the authority to act on behalf of Elaine R. Miller in selling the property; contended that the property was joint management community property which could not be conveyed or encumbered by one spouse alone; and asserted the contract was incomplete on its face and it had no force or effect because Mrs. Miller's signature did not appear on the document.

The case was submitted to the jury on fifteen special issues. In response to the jury's finding that the property was joint management community property, the trial judge entered judgment in favor of appellees. In two points of error appellant contends the trial court erred in: (1) entering judgment in favor of appellees on the verdict returned and (2) failing to enter judgment in favor of appellant on the verdict returned. We believe the answer to special issue number one was determinative and the trial court did not err by entering judgment for the appellees.

It is clear that a husband has the right to convey his one-half interest in non-homestead joint management community property without the signature of his wife on the conveyance. *Williams v. Portland State Bank*, 514 S.W.2d 124 (Tex. Civ. App.—Beaumont 1974, writ dism'd). Appellant argues that under *Williams*, he has the right to compel the husband alone to specifically perform the contract. However, in order to maintain a suit to compel the husband to convey that interest, there must be a valid and complete contract to convey. In *Williams* documents were drawn up for both the husband and wife to execute but the wife refused. New documents were prepared for the husband alone to execute. The operative documents involved in *Williams* were not the incomplete ones that the wife refused to execute but rather the documents that were later drawn up for the husband alone to execute.

Unlike *Williams*, we do not have such a contract in the case before us. The earnest money contract is incomplete on its face and is not capable of being enforced by specific performance. While both husband and wife are named as sellers only the husband's signature appears on the contract. The description of the property to be sold is not in terms of the husband's "undivided one-half interest" or other words to indicate that only Mr. Miller's interest was involved. From the terms of the document it is evident the parties intended that the agreement would be effective only upon execution by both Mr. and Mrs. Miller as sellers. Once there was the proper execution, the contract was to involve the interests of both of the Millers. There is no basis for a finding that James B. Miller alone must specifically perform the incomplete contract as to his undivided one-half interest. The question remains whether the signature of one spouse was binding upon both husband and wife.

The jury, in response to special issue number one, found that this property was joint management community property. One spouse cannot alone convey or encumber joint management community property unless the spouses have otherwise agreed. Tex. Fam. Code Ann. 5.22(c). Appellant has failed to present a statement of facts from which it could be determined whether such an agreement existed. Without a "power of attorney in writing or other agreement" to the contrary, James B. Miller had no authority to contract to dispose of the entire joint management community property without his wife joining in the contract.

Based upon the "contract" made the basis of this suit and the jury's response to special issue number one, the trial court entered the correct judgment. Appellant's two points of error are overruled.

The judgment is affirmed.

DISCUSSION

The *Vallone* court, in dictum, states that a spouse has the right to convey a one-half interest in joint management community property without the consent of the other spouse. Wouldn't this make joint management property equivalent to a tenancy in common? Would that be a good idea? Compare *Dalton v. Don J. Jackson*, 691 S.W.2d 765 (Tex. App. — Austin 1985, no writ).

B. Reliance Upon Title

Cumming v. Johnson

United States Court of Appeals
Ninth Circuit, 1979
616 F.2d 1069

GOODWIN, Circuit Judge.

Glendon Johnson appeals a judgment of specific performance of an oral stock transfer agreement between Johnson's brother Franklin, who was acting as Johnson's agent, and the plaintiff, Ian Cumming. Johnson asserts that his wife's community property interest in the disputed stock could not be transferred under the trial court's order. We affirm the district court.

Johnson and his wife, Bobette Johnson, are Texas residents. Cumming is a Utah resident. All three are shareholders in Terracor, Inc., a Utah corporation. Cumming has been a director of Terracor since March 1970 and president of the corporation since September 1971.

In 1973 Terracor was involved in litigation with Avco Financial Services, Inc. Avco and other plaintiffs brought three actions against Terracor, naming Glendon, Franklin, and Bobette Johnson and others as individual codefendant-guarantors. In order to settle this litigation, Franklin Johnson reached an oral agreement with Cumming. Under this agreement, Glendon and Franklin Johnson and Roger Boyer, a third Terracor shareholder named in the Avco litigation, promised to transfer their Terracor stock to Cumming in return for Cumming's personal undertaking to settle the Avco suits.

Cumming had not been named as a defendant in the Avco litigation, but his personal participation in the settlement negotiations became a necessary condition of Avco's agreement to settle. One of the terms of this settlement required Cumming to personally pledge to Avco 400,000 shares of Terracor stock that he owned and to give Avco a $550,000 note in return for various considerations and property. As part of the settlement, the parties to the Avco litigation also executed an Agreement of Dismissal and Release.

After the final settlement of the Avco litigation, Franklin Johnson and Roger Boyer transferred their Terracor shares to Cumming. Glendon Johnson, however, refused to transfer the 132,563 shares of Terracor stock, represented by Terracor share certificate No. 1005, that are registered in his name, arguing that his brother Franklin lacked the authority to bind him under the November 1973 oral agreement and that, even if Franklin Johnson was authorized to act as his agent, the oral agreement was unenforceable.

Cumming filed this diversity action to obtain possession of certificate No. 1005, which was in escrow in a Los Angeles bank. The district court in due course entered the challenged judgment divesting Johnson of title to the Terracor shares and vesting title in Cumming.

Johnson argues that the district court could not order specific performance of the stock transfer agreement, because his wife Bobette has a community property interest in the disputed shares that could not be conveyed without her consent, and because Mrs. Johnson was not a party to this litigation. As will be seen, the success of these arguments hinges on whether Cumming had actual or constructive notice of any interest Bobette Johnson had in share certificate No. 1005.

Bobette Johnson had a presumptive community property interest in the Johnson Terracor shares. "Property possessed by either spouse during or on the dissolution of marriage is presumed to be community property." Tex. Fam. Code Ann. Sec. 5.02 (Vernon 1974). Glendon Johnson possessed the shares during his marriage. Because Cumming offered no evidence that Johnson acquired the shares with premarriage assets, or other rebuttal, the statutory presumption controls. Not only did Mrs. Johnson have a community property interest in the disputed shares, but she had a joint control interest as against her husband. Texas Family Code Sec. 5.22 defines the instances, as between spouses, in which community property is under the sole management of one spouse, and none of those exceptions applies here.

The purpose of Section 5.22 of the Texas Family Code was to eliminate unilateral conveyance and virtual representation of one spouse's community property interests by another. *See* Comment, 6 Tex. Tech. L. Rev. 1185 (1975); Note, 52 Texas L. Rev. 1410 (1974). Thus, in most cases, one spouse cannot transfer the other's interests in property without his or her consent, and a court cannot determine the status of community property in the absence of either spouse. *See Williams v. Saxon*, 521 S.W.2d 88 (Tex. Civ. App. — San Antonio 1975, writ ref'd n.r.e.); *Cooper v. Texas Gulf Industries*, 513 S.W.2d 200 (Tex. 1974).

If our inquiry were to end here, the district court could not compel the transfer of the Terracor shares. While Franklin Johnson's power of attorney allowed him to act for both Glendon and Bobette Johnson, he contracted with Cumming only to convey Mr. Johnson's shares. The record shows no mention of Mrs. Johnson's interest in the oral agreement, and, as noted, Mrs. Johnson was not joined as a party defendant in these proceedings.

There are, however, exceptions to the statutory presumption of joint control which apply not between spouses, but between spouses and innocent third parties. The district court relied on one of these exceptions, Tex. Fam. Code Sec. 5.24(a), which raises a counter-presumption of sole control if property is held in one spouse's name. The court found that, for purposes of oral agreement between Cumming and Franklin Johnson, Terracor certificate No. 1005 was community property under Glendon Johnson's sole control. It is not disputed that the Terracor shares were registered in appellant's name alone and that certificate No. 1005 bore only his signature. Consequently, a presumption of sole control, allowing Johnson to unilaterally convey and virtually represent his wife's interest, arises.

Johnson attempts to overcome this presumption by showing that Cumming was not an innocent third party entitled to invoke the statutory presumption of sole control because he had "actual or constructive notice" of Johnson's lack of authority over the shares. Tex. Fam. Code Ann. Sec. 5.24(b)(1)(B) (Vernon 1974). Johnson contends that Cumming had notice of Mrs. Johnson's interest in the Terracor stock both because of his position as Terracor's chief executive officer and because of his membership on an executive committee which sent Glendon and Bobette Johnson two letters promising them defense and indemnification in the Avco litigation. Johnson argues that the Terracor executive committee would not have addressed such letters to his wife unless its members believed that she was a Terracor shareholder.

While it is difficult to define what combination of facts constitutes actual or constructive notice in a given case, the facts relied upon by Johnson are not "of such a nature as to have reasonably excited the suspicions of a reasonably cautious man" under Texas law. *Houston Oil Co. of Texas v. Griggs*, 181 S.W. 833, 838 (Tex. Civ. App. 1915), affirmed, 213 S.W. 261 (Tex. 1919). A review of Texas cases in other contexts reveals a strong presumption that "[s]tatutes regulating the general subject of notice are construed most liberally in favor of the party who is affected by the notice." *Exxon Corp. v. Raetzer*, 533 S.W.2d 842, 847 (Tex. Civ. App.—Corpus Christi 1976, writ ref'd n.r.e.). Two examples of this presumption appear in cases in which Texas courts concluded that third parties were without notice. *Houston Oil Co. of Texas v. Griggs, supra; Exxon Corp. v. Raetzer, supra*. In *Griggs*, the court held that a bank which purchased land from a Mrs. E. O. Griggs was not put on notice by the vendor's use of "Mrs." that the land might be encumbered by a community property interest; the court reasoned that use of the title "Mrs." on vendor's original deed did not necessarily mean that Mrs. Griggs was married at the time she acquired the land—she might have been widowed. *Raetzer* reflects an even more narrow concept of notice. There, a court concluded that a letter from a shareholder to a corporation stating that certain irregularities in handling the shareholder's investments had been discovered and that the issuer should advise the shareholder of "any change of ownership or status of the shares" did not give the issuer notice that the stock certificates had been lost or stolen.

In light of these precedents, appellant's argument that Cumming had notice of Mrs. Johnson's interest must be rejected. The fact that Cumming was president of Terracor does not, without more, give him notice that a shareholder's wife has a community property interest. As in *Houston Oil Co. of Texas v. Griggs, supra*, Cumming could reasonably have concluded that the shares had been purchased before the Johnsons' marriage or were bought with noncommunity assets. Similarly, Cumming's role in sending the Avco litigation indemnity letter to the Johnsons does not support a finding of notice; there could be any number of reasons for Mrs. Johnson's participation as a defendant-guarantor in the Avco litigation, including protection of "her husband's interest" in Terracor.

Without evidence that Cumming had notice of Mrs. Johnson's interest, the statutory presumption of sole control is decisive. For purposes of the stock transfer agreement, the Terracor shares were under Glendon Johnson's sole management. He could unilaterally convey the whole community property interest in the stock to Cumming, through his agent, and he could virtually represent his wife's interest in the district court. Bobette Johnson's community property interest in the disputed shares does not prevent specific performance of the oral agreement.

AUTHOR'S QUESTION

How might a careful lawyer attempt to avoid the problems encountered in *Vallone* and *Cumming*?

C. Duties of the Manager

Under Texas law, one spouse can have sole management power over community property. So, he (or she) is managing property for the benefit of the other spouse, who owns a one-half interest in the property. This raises the question whether the managing spouse should be held to a fiduciary standard when managing the community estate.

Andrews v. Andrews
Texas Court of Appeals — Austin, 1984
677 S.W.2d 171, no writ

SHANNON, SMITH and GAMMAGE, Justices.

[The husband here challenged the manner in which the trial court divided the community estate.] Cynthia Mae Andrews suggests that the unequal distribution of the community was warranted by her former husband's "waste, mismanagement, or outright conversion of community funds." As authority for such proposition, appellee relies upon *Grothe v. Grothe*, 590 S.W.2d 238 (Tex. Civ. App. — Austin 1979, no writ) and *Reaney v. Reaney*, 505 S.W.2d 338 (Tex. Civ. App. — Dallas 1974, no writ).

In *Grothe v. Grothe, supra*, the judgment recited that the former spouse wrongfully and willfully converted substantial amounts of community funds for his own personal use with the intention of depriving the former wife of her community interest in those funds. The former spouse failed to challenge that finding. In the absence of an attack upon the finding of conversion of community funds, this Court held that the finding of conversion justified an unequal distribution of the remaining community estate. In *Reaney v. Reaney, supra*, the former husband admitted that he "squandered" $53,000.00 in community funds. He lost some of the money gambling, he gave some of it away, and he spent some of the money "very foolishly." As this Court understands *Reaney*, the husband's profligacy must have been viewed by the Court as a fraud on the community estate.

There are no facts or findings in this appeal which are similar to those in either *Grothe* or *Reaney*. Without dispute John Andrews made some poor investments of community funds. Also without doubt, he used community income to purchase with his mother some of the parcels of real estate. Cynthia Mae knew that her husband made payments on notes executed in such transactions. In fact, in at least one of the real estate transactions she wrote many of the checks for the monthly payments. Neither *Grothe* nor *Reaney* is authority for the proposition that a spouse's good faith, but unwise, investment of community funds resulting in losses to the community estate justifies an unequal distribution of remaining community property. Absent a fraud on the community, the court may not order reimbursement for gifts of community property made during the marriage to a stranger. *See* Geer, *Gifts in Fraud of the Rights of the Wife*, 26 Baylor L. Rev. 85 (1974). There are no findings by the district court that Andrews' investment of community funds in the purchase of the real estate was tantamount to a fraud on the community.

[The court reversed and remanded the division of community property by the trial court.]

DISCUSSION

Andrews concludes that a spouse's "good faith, but unwise investment of community funds" is not actionable. Why is the court reluctant to review the management decisions of the spouses? Some commentators have urged courts to place some restrictions upon the managing spouse's discretion. *See* Riley, *Women's Right in the Louisiana Matrimonial Regime*, 50 Tulane L. Rev. 557, 570 (1976). Under normal principles of trust law, a trustee can be liable to beneficiaries for negligence. *See In re Rowe*, 712 N.Y.S.2d 662 (App. Div. 2000). Should a managing spouse be treated like a trustee?

In *Grossnickle v. Grossnickle*, 935 S.W.2d 830 (Tex. App.—Texarkana 1996, writ denied), the wife was allowed to live in the house while the divorce was pending. She didn't repair leaks in the roof and the house was severely damaged. Would the logic of *Andrews* mean she shouldn't be liable to the community for the loss?

In Texas, management power over community property is frequently vested in one spouse. If this is so, and the other cannot challenge expenditure decisions in most instances, is this consistent with the norm that each spouse owns a "vested, 50% interest" after acquisition? If not, how could the Texas system be changed to be more congruent with the community property model? Other states have adopted an equal management system for most community property. Under this type of system, either spouse may manage property.

Should a spouse be liable for negligent investment decisions? *See* Oldham, *Management of the Community Estate During an Intact Marriage*, 56 Law & Contemp. Prob. 99 (1993). If not, what should be the standard for reviewing investment or expenditure decisions? Can a spouse ever be held accountable for unwise expenditures of community funds? In *Gademski v. Gademski*, 664 N.Y. S.2d 886 (App.Div. 1997) the court held a spouse responsible for losses due to very speculative investments made while the marriage was breaking down. Should a special rule be created for investments during that period?

If a spouse could be held liable for dissipation of funds, where would the line be drawn? For example, what if a spouse buys a mink coat, or takes an expensive trip to Europe? To date, courts have been quite reluctant to review the consumption decisions of the spouses during marriage. Should extravagant expenditures of community funds after separation be subject to a stricter review? Courts seem to agree on one issue—if a spouse uses community funds for "dates" before or after separation, the community estate should be reimbursed for all amounts spent on the date.

Marriage of Williams, 927 P.2d 679 (Wash. App. 1996) considers whether losing $12,000 gambling is actionable. The appellate court upheld a finding that this was not actionable, noting that the gambling spouse had a substantially higher income than the other. Should this be relevant?

In *Beard v. Beard*, 49 S.W.3d 40 (Tex. App.—Waco 2001, no pet. h.), the wife alleged that the husband had spent $12,000 community funds in strip clubs and requested reimbursement. The trial court denied this request.

In *Schweitzer v. Schweitzer*, 915 P2d 575 (Wash. App. 1996) the wife used community funds, over the husband's objection, to pay the college expenses for her son from a prior marriage. At divorce, should she have to reimburse the community estate?

What should occur if a spouse commits a crime during marriage, which necessitates the expenditure of community funds for a lawyer and may result in lost community income (due to jail time, etc.)?

If a spouse has both separate property and community property available to make an investment, does the spouse have a duty to use the community funds? In *Somps v. Somps*, 58 Cal. Rptr. 304 (Cal. App. 1967), the court said no.

In *Marriage of Hokanson*, 80 Cal.Rptr.2d 699 (Cal. App. 1998) the wife was ordered to sell the house "as expeditiously as possible for the best price reasonably obtainable." The market was weakening at the time. In March 1994 she was told that by a broker that a reasonable price would be $525,000. By June 1995, when the divorce terms were finalized and she was ready to list the house, the broker advised a list price of $499,000. She told the broker to list it for substantially more. The wife agreed in February 1996 to drop the price to $499,000. The house eventually sold in June 1996 for $430,000. The court held the wife liable for the amount the community lost due to delay in the sale (because the market continued to deteriorate). Is this consistent with *Andrews*?

Arrington v. Arrington

Texas Court of Appeals—Ft. Worth, 1981
613 S.W.2d 565, no writ

HUGHES, Justice.

Albert C. Arrington has appealed the judgment which divorced him from his wife, Ruby D. Arrington, divided their property and made Mrs. Arrington managing conservator of Bonnie Lou, their dog.

In point of error no. 5 Mr. Arrington says that the trial court erred in considering the $28,419.00 cash "he drew out of" his account at Rauscher Pierce while this divorce suit was pending because of no and insufficient evidence that such property existed at the time of trial. Since he admitted withdrawing such amount of money between May 27, 1977 and April 20, 1979 in the face of a restraining order and an injunction of the trial court, he does not appear to be in a very good position to urge a lack of evidence. His concealing or disposing of the funds under such circumstances would sustain sufficiently the order of the trial court allowing him the $28,419.00 cash withdrawal as part of his share.

Courts have a wide discretion in making a division of community and separate property. *Baxla v. Baxla*, 522 S.W.2d 736 (Tex. Civ. App.—Dallas 1975, no writ). *Grothe v. Grothe*, 590 S.W.2d 238 (Tex. Civ. App.—Austin 1979, no writ). We overrule point of error no. 5.

A dog, for all its admirable and unique qualities, is not a human being and is not treated in the law as such. A dog is personal property, ownership of which is recognized under the law. 3 Tex. Jur. 3d 513, Sections 4 & 5, "Animals as Property" (1980). There was testimony that Bonnie Lou was given to Mrs. Arrington over ten years ago.

DISCUSSION

What is the difference between the claim of the wife in this case and the claim of the wife in *Andrews, supra*? Do you agree with this distinction?

Mazique v. Mazique

Texas Court of Appeals—Houston [1st Dist.], 1987
742 S.W.2d 805, no writ

EVANS, J.

This is an appeal from a monetary award in a final decree of divorce.

The appellee, Sylvia Yvonne Mazique, sued appellant, Emory Edwin Mazique, for a divorce alleging, among other things, that the appellant had fraudulently deprived her of a portion of the community estate. After a non-jury trial, the court made a monetary award to the appellee in the amount of $30,000 as actual damages, and $5,000 as exemplary damages. Findings of fact were requested, but if findings were made, they were not brought forward as part of the appellate record. In two points of error, the appellant challenges the actual and punitive awards, contending that there is no evidence or insufficient evidence to support the court's finding that the appellant committed fraud on the community.

The parties were married in June 1961, and ceased living together as husband and wife in February 1986. They have three children, all of whom live at home with the appellee. Their daughter, Kicha, is 22 years old and a student at the University of Houston; their older son, Mark, is 21 years old and a student at Rice University; and their younger son, Marlon, is 17 years old and a student at St. John's High School in Houston. The appellant is a licensed physician in private practice specializing in internal medicine, and the appellee is a health educator for the City of Houston.

The appellant admitted having sexual relationships with at least 5 women during the course of his 25-year marriage, the first occurring within several weeks following his marriage. These relationships lasted from a few weeks to several years. The appellant admitted that he spent varying sums of money on these women to pay for trips out of town, meals, gifts, dresses, and local hotels. The appellant testified that he usually arose about 10:30 to 11 o'clock each morning, went to his office and made hospital rounds during the afternoon, and then socialized at the Groovy Cafe or some other lounge until 2 to 4 o'clock in the morning. He conceded that he was not around the children when they were going to or from school, and that he was not usually home in the evenings. By the appellant's own admission, he could not recall exactly how many extramarital affairs he had during his marriage, the names of all the persons with whom he had affairs, or how much money he had spent on his various sexual activities.

The appellant testified that some of his patients paid for his professional services in cash, and that he usually collected about $100 in cash each day when he was in the office. He said that he used some of the cash for his daily spending money and estimated that he took from $30 to $100 from the cash receipts each day. He estimated that during the last several years of his marriage, he had taken cash out of the business from the time he first began his practice in the mid-1960s. He admitted that his deposits of over $130,000 to his bank account in 1984 reflected his earnings, although he only reported about $93,000 in cash receipts on his 1984 income tax return. He admitted that he had never accounted to his wife for the money he had taken, and that on one occasion he told his wife she would never know how much he had taken from the business.

Although the appellant blamed his extramarital sexual activities on his wife's refusal to engage in sex with him, the trial court, as the trier of fact, was not bound to accept his version of the facts. Because of the appellant's continuous withdrawal of cash receipts, without any attempt to account to his wife, to the federal government, or to the mortgage company, the court necessarily had to apply a broad yardstick to measure the extent to which the appellant's conduct had damaged the community estate. The court's award of actual damages was within the range of the evidence showing the amount of cash that the appellant had taken from the community funds, and for which no accounting was ever made. In the absence of fraud on the other spouse, the managing spouse has the sole right of control and disposition of the community property as he or she sees fit. *Krueger v. Williams*, 163 Tex. 545, 359 S.W.2d 48, 50 (1962). Thus, it is unnecessary for the managing spouse to obtain the approval or agreement of the other spouse to dispositions of the managing spouse's special community property. *Horlock v. Horlock*, 533 S.W.2d 52, 55 (Tex. Civ. App. — Houston [14th Dist.] 1975, writ dism'd w.o.j.). But a trust relationship exists between a husband and wife as to that portion of the community property controlled by the managing spouse, *Carnes v. Meador*, 533 S.W.2d 365, 370 (Tex. Civ. App. — Dallas 1975, writ ref'd n.r.e.); *Brownson v. New*, 259 S.W.2d 277, 281 (Tex. Civ. App. — San Antonio 1953, writ dism'd w.o.j.), and a presumption of fraud arises when a spouse unfairly disposes of the other spouse's one-half interest in the community. *Carnes*, 533 S.W.2d at 370. If the managing spouse violates his or her duty to the other spouse, a personal judgment for damages may provide a means for recoupment of the value lost to the community as a result of the constructive fraud. *Belz v. Belz*, 667 S.W.2d 240, 247 (Tex. App. — Dallas 1984, writ ref'd n.r.e.); *Swisher v. Swisher*, 190 S.W.2d 382, 384 (Tex. Civ. App. — Galveston 1945, no writ).

The managing spouse may make moderate gifts for just causes to persons outside the community. *Hartman v. Crain*, 398 S.W.2d 387, 390 (Tex. Civ. App. — Houston 1966, no writ). But a gift of community funds that is capricious, excessive, or arbitrary may be set aside as a constructive fraud on the other spouse. *Horlock*, 533 S.W.2d at 55; *see also Givens v. Girard Life Ins. Co. of America*, 480 S.W.2d 421, 424–25 (Tex. Civ. App. — Dallas 1972, writ ref'd n.r.e.).

The burden is on the managing spouse to prove that a gift or disposition of community funds was not unfair to the rights of the other spouse. *Jackson v. Smith*, 703 S.W.2d 791, 795 (Tex. App. — Dallas 1985, no writ); *Redfearn v. Ford*, 579 S.W.2d 295, 297 (Tex. Civ. App. — Dallas 1979, writ ref'd n.r.e.). Thus, constructive fraud will usually be presumed unless the managing spouse proves that the disposition of the community funds was not unfair to the other spouse. *Carnes*, 533 S.W.2d at 370.

When the fairness of the transaction is brought into question, the non-managing spouse does not have to prove that the gift to a third party was motivated by actual fraudulent intent or that the gift was otherwise unfair. *Murphy v. Metropolitan Life Ins. Co.*,

498 S.W.2d 278, 282 (Tex. Civ. App.—Houston [14th Dist.] 1973, writ ref'd n.r.e.). In considering the fairness of the transaction, the courts may look to the relationship between the managing spouse and the person to whom the gift was made; whether there were any special circumstances tending to justify the gift; and whether the community funds used for the gift were reasonable in proportion to the community estate remaining. *Redfearn,* 579 S.W.2d at 297. Similarly, where the managing spouse has received community funds, and the time has come to account for such funds, the managing spouse has the burden of accounting for their proper use. *Maxwell's Unknown Heirs v. Bolding,* 36 S.W.2d 267, 268 (Tex. Civ. App.—Waco 1931, no writ).

We hold there is legally and factually sufficient evidence to support the trial court's award of actual damages, and that its award is not against the great weight and preponderance of the evidence.

The first point of error is overruled.

The appellant challenges the award of exemplary damages solely on the ground that the evidence is legally and factually insufficient to support the award of actual damages. Because we have found the evidence sufficient to support the award of actual damages, we also overrule the second point of error.

The judgment of the trial court is affirmed.

DISCUSSION

What made the expenditures by the husband actionable? If he merely went out drinking with various friends and spent a great deal of money, would the result have been different? What is the holding of this case?

In *Osuna v. Quintana,* 993 S.W. 2d 201 (Tex. App.—Corpus Christi 1999, no writ), the wife obtained a judgment against her husband's mistress for the amount of community funds given to her by the husband.

Devine v. Devine

Texas Court of Appeals—Amarillo, 1993
869 S.W.2d 415, writ denied

POFF, Justice.

After 48 years of marriage, John DeVine [Jack] sued his wife Antoinette [Rita] for divorce. Following a trial to a jury, the court granted the divorce, finding that Rita had committed adultery. By ten points of error, Rita challenges certain jury findings, the court's award of various damages and the court's division of the parties' community estate.

Jack and Rita [collectively, the DeVines] were married in 1942. They had two daughters and a son. For most of their marriage, Jack was employed as an airline pilot while Rita did not work outside the home. Jack retired in 1977. At the time of the divorce, Jack was 72 years of age and Rita was 67 years of age.

In the early 1970s, the DeVines began investing in real estate in Dallas. Their investments proved to be quite successful; at one time they owned as many as 50 condominiums.

In 1983, the DeVines invested $25,000 in a development called Turtle Creek Place that was to be a "big high rise luxurious hotel health club." One of the principal developers of Turtle Creek Place was a man named Jack Counts [Counts]. Counts developed real estate in Dallas and Denver and he owned several nursing homes. The DeVines met Counts through their daughter, Sandy DeVine [Sandy], who was employed as a nurse at one of Counts' nursing homes.[1] Rita was interested in getting involved in Turtle Creek Place. After meeting Counts, the DeVines made their $25,000 investment in Turtle Creek Place. Due to a lack of financing, however, the development never materialized and the DeVines lost their $25,000 investment.

The DeVines were not the only persons who lost money on Turtle Creek Place; Counts lost $5 million he had invested in the development, forcing him into bankruptcy. Counts continued to make investments after his bankruptcy, however, by investing in the name of his wife, Jane Counts [Jane]. Jack and Rita were often co-investors.

[The court then discusses various investments made by the DeVines in Counts' projects.]

The DeVines never made a penny investing in Counts' various schemes. In fact, they lost a total of $151,000. Each time an investment was made in a Counts enterprise, Jack testified Rita encouraged and persuaded him to join in the venture.

In late 1989, Jack became aware that Rita was sexually involved with Counts. The record is not entirely clear as to when Rita and Counts first began their sexual relationship. Counts testified that he first had sex with Rita in May 1988. Sandy testified that although her sexual relationship with Counts lasted until December 1987, she suspected her mother was having sex with Counts as early as August 1986. Rita moved out of the bedroom she shared with Jack in 1986 and refused to have sex with him thereafter.

Regardless of when Rita became sexually involved with Counts, it is clear that Rita shifted her allegiance from her husband to Counts in 1985. Rita had stayed in frequent contact with Counts since their initial meeting in late 1983. In July 1985, Counts invited Rita to use an office at the Creatview Nursing Home in Dallas. Counts also maintained an office there. This was the beginning of a daily working relationship between Rita and Counts that developed into much more.

Rita testified that a big change took place in her life in 1985. The change had to do with her study of astrology. A tape recording of a September 15, 1987 conversation between Rita and her astrologer, Laura Carlson [Carlson] was played for the jury. In that tape recording, Rita stated that she separated from her husband in her heart, although not physically, in October 1985. Rita's exploration of astrology led to an experience on May 16, 1987, in which Rita claimed to have been contacted by a spirit entity named Master Korr. This spirit was her master.[2] Rita is known to Master Korr as Beth.

Although Rita did not relate this event to her husband, she did share the experience with Counts. Counts had dabbled in astrology for nearly 30 years. From May 16, 1987 for-

---

1. Sandy had since 1982 been engaged in an adulterous sexual relationship with Counts. Sandy had informed her mother of her relationship with Counts. Rita disapproved, however, of Sandy's relationship with Counts because Counts was a married man. At the time of trial, Sandy and Rita were still estranged.

2. According to the book "Black Diamonds" (discussed later in this opinion):

Master Korr was created with her soul mate "in the beginning." [sic] She lived many lives during that period of the first million years of man on earth, sometimes as a male and sometimes as a female. Somewhere along the line she became a healer. She remembers lives in Lemura as a male physician. She remembers lives in the first Atlantis as a fisherman and as a physician. She remembers a life in the Andes as an Indian Chief's wife during the sixth world when the tops of the Andes were only 10,000 feet high. She remembers a life time in Israel during the life of Jesus Christ as a physician and a shepherd. Her last life on earth was in 1600 when she was a tall, black-robed gentleman with gray hair and a gray beard carrying a large crystal ball. Again, she was a healer and a prophet.... Today, Korr works from the house of Opals on the fifth plane and she is a healer. She comes to Beth [Rita] to heal through her.

ward, Rita and Counts held several "channeling" sessions each week in which they contacted Master Korr. Counts would assist Rita in going into a trance. Then Master Korr, using Rita's voice, would speak. Hundreds of these channeling sessions were tape-recorded and the recordings were transcribed.

In August 1987, Rita and Counts were able to contract Counts' master — Master Todlee — through a Ouija board. Counts is known to his master as Able. On October 5, 1987, Master Todlee began speaking through Rita.[3] Counts and Rita continued to contact both spirits over the course of the succeeding two years. The spirits instructed Rita and Counts to put the transcribed recordings in book form. Rita and Counts did so, publishing the book "Black Diamonds" in July 1989.

Through their masters, Rita and Counts learned that they had shared several lives together through the ages. In fact, Master Todlee told them they had been romantically involved with each other in other lives dating back 400 million years to the time Counts and Rita were both in a clam shell. It is clear that by the summer of 1987, Rita considered Counts to be her soul mate and her true partner. In her September 1987 tape-recorded session with the astrologer Carlson, Rita and Carlson discussed how Jack was a thorn in Rita's side and a disruptive influence in her efforts to contact Master Korr. Carlson told Rita that because Jack was born a Scorpio in 1917, he had a fear of the occult. Indeed, Jack testified he did not believe in the occult. Carlson informed Rita that she had "honed in" on the right partner for her in 1985 or 1986 and that she would "hook up" with her new partner by the end of 1988. This new partner, Counts, was, according to Carlson, the type of man that Rita should have been with all along. Rita told Carlson there was bad karma at her home and that she wanted to be away from home as much as possible. During 1988 and 1989, it was Rita's daily practice to leave for her office about 5:30 a.m., return home 12 hours later, cook a quick dinner for Jack and then retire to her bedroom until the next morning.

In her first point of error, Rita contends there is no evidence, or in the alternative, factually insufficient evidence to support the jury's findings that (1) she committed actual fraud with respect to Jack's community property rights and that (2) $100,000 would fairly compensate the DeVines' community estate for her actual fraud. We will first resolve Rita's no evidence claim. In doing so, we must examine the record in the light most favorably to the finding to determine if there is any probative evidence, or reasonable inferences therefrom, which support the finding, and we must disregard all evidence or reasonable inferences therefrom to the contrary.

In the present case, the jury was instructed in accord with the following pattern jury charges.

> A spouse commits [actual] fraud if that spouse transfers community property or expends community funds for the primary purpose of depriving the other spouse of the use and enjoyment of the assets involved in the transaction. Such fraud involves dishonesty of purpose or an intent to deceive.[4]

> A relationship of confidence and trust exists between a husband and wife with regard to that portion of the community property that each controls. This rela-

---

3. Master Todlee is described in "Black Diamonds" as an "alien" from the planet "Iris".... Today, Todlee works from the house of Black Diamonds on the fifth plane and from his planet Iris which he visits periodically by thought. His mission is to bring the book [Black Diamonds] to mankind and keep Able [Counts] alive to write it. He also tells Able [Counts] he is here to assist him in building those structures Abe [Counts] is destined to build on earth before he leaves this time.

4. This jury charge is an accurate statement of the law. See *Horlock v. Horlock*, 533 S.W.2d 52, 55 (Tex. App. — Houston [14th Dist.] 1975, writ dism'd).

tionship requires that the spouses use the utmost good faith and frankness in their dealings with each other.

Because of the nature of the spousal relationship, conduct of a spouse affecting the property rights of the other spouse may be fraudulent even though identical conduct would not be fraudulent as between non-spouses.

Rita did not object to the court's charge. Thus, even if, *arguendo*, the court's instructions did not accurately state the law, any compliant concerning the instructions was waived. Tex. R. Civ. P. 274.

The record clearly contains evidence that Rita did not "use the utmost good faith and frankness" in dealing with Jack. In encouraging and persuading Jack to invest in Counts' various projects, she did not tell Jack of her close personal involvement with Counts. It is entirely reasonable to infer from the evidence that Rita was sexually involved with Counts at the time she and Jack invested $56,000 in Denver Suites, $25,000 in Denver Plaza, $20,000 in Sundance Trading and $25,000 in 140 Place. It can also be readily inferred that Jack would not have agreed to invest in the foregoing projects had Rita informed him of the true nature of her relationship with Counts. Jack testified that his wife strongly influenced his decision to invest. It is evident that Jack relied on his wife's judgment, included by any ulterior motives, in making his investment decisions.[5] There is no question the jury had evidence before it by which it could have rightfully concluded that Rita's conduct evidenced an intent to deceive and was outright dishonest. By persuading her husband to invest community funds in Counts' various schemes without informing Jack of her true relationship with Counts, Rita perpetrated an actual fraud.

In its charge, the court instructed the jury that if it found Rita to have committed an actual fraud on the DeVines' community estate then to determine "[w]hat sum of money, if any, should be awarded against Rita DeVine as exemplary damages?" The jury found that sum to be $3,000. In her fifth point of error, Rita contends that the trial court erred as a matter of law in submitting the exemplary damage question. In her fourth point of error, Rita argues that the trial court erred as a matter of law in awarding exemplary damages against her for an economic tort committed against the community estate. We need not reach the merits of either of these points of error, however, because Rita failed to object to the submission of the exemplary damages issue at trial.

---

5. On direct examination, Jack testified as follows:
    Q. Did your wife encourage you to make these investment
    A. I think she influenced me very much.
    Q. Did she —
    A. She pushed me into them I am convinced.
    Q. Did you usually sign the actual checks?
    A. Pardon?
    Q. Would you often actually sign the checks?
    A. I signed them, she signed them, yes.
    Q. Well, why would you sign those checks. Mr. DeVine?
    A. Why did I sign them?
    Q. Yes, sir.
    A. She wanted me to get into those schemes, these investments.
    Q. Did you always do what your wife wanted you to do?
    A. Pretty much so.
    Q. Did you know at the time that you were making these investments that your wife was involved in an affair with Jack Counts?
    A. I did not.

[The court concluded that the $100,000 loss to the community due to Rita's fraud should be added back into the community and allocated to Rita as part of her share of the community.]

DISCUSSION

What did Rita do that constituted actual fraud? If she alone had invested sole management community funds in Counts' ventures, would that also constitute fraud? Is this case different from *Andrews, supra*?

Fields v. Michael

California Court of Appeals, 1949
205 P.2d 402

SHINN, Presiding Justice.

This is an appeal from a judgment in favor of defendant after an order sustaining a demurrer to plaintiff's complaint without leave to amend.

The complaint set forth the following allegations: Defendant is the duly appointed and acting executrix of the estate of W. C. Fields, who died on December 25, 1946. Plaintiff married decedent in California on April 8, 1900, and was his first wife at all times thereafter until his death. At the time of the marriage decedent had no assets or estate of any kind whatsoever, and all of the estate which he acquired subsequent to marriage was from compensation for personal services rendered during marriage together with the increment thereon. Several years subsequent to their marriage, decedent deserted plaintiff. He never discussed his financial affairs with her and willfully withheld from her all information concerning the extent of his assets and any gifts or transfers made by him out of the community property. Solely from his personal earnings for services rendered during marriage, decedent secretly and without plaintiff's knowledge or consent made extensive transfers of money by way of gifts. Ten separate gifts in stated amounts, made to named individuals are set out, all of which "were illusory and were transferred and set over by said decedent willfully and fraudulently, secretly and clandestinely, from the community property of plaintiff and said decedent with intent to defraud plaintiff of her interest in her and his estate." The total amount of these gifts was $482,450. Upon information and belief, six additional gifts in unknown amounts to fictitiously named defendants are alleged. The complaint states that "plaintiff has not at any time consented to the making of said gifts or to any one or more of them and said gifts and each of them were made without her knowledge and approval and are all disaffirmed by plaintiff"; and alleges that plaintiff did not learn of any of the gifts until after the death of her husband.

On July 23, 1947, plaintiff duly and regularly filed her "Creditor's Claim and Disaffirmance" with defendant as executrix setting forth substantially the same facts related above and claiming the sum of $241,225 due to plaintiff as her community interest in the unauthorized gifts. The claim was rejected.

This action was thereafter brought against the estate for the reason that "many of said donees are deceased and that those remaining alive reside at diverse places, some of them away from the State of California, and that they have used up and dissipated the sums of money by way of gift transferred and set over to them as aforesaid, and would not be able to pay a judgment, if one were rendered against them for return to plaintiff of said gifts or of some part thereof. Plaintiff is without any means of collecting in full from said donees those portions of said gifts which she is entitled to." It is also alleged that defendant executrix has possession and control of the financial records and papers of decedent; that she has refused to permit plaintiff to inspect them; and that these records disclose to a large extent detailed information concerning the alleged gifts of money as to which plaintiff is without information. The prayer for relief was twofold: (1) "By reason of plaintiff's disaffirmance of the gifts hereinbefore described, that defendant pay the plaintiff the sum of $241,225.00." (2) An accounting be had to determine the amount of any additional gifts made by decedent from community funds, and upon such accounting judgment be rendered for plaintiff to the extent of her interest therein.

Defendant's demurrer set forth some seven grounds upon which it was claimed the complaint was insufficient. The written opinion of the trial judge, which this court is entitled to consider on appeal (*see Union Sugar Co. v. Hollister Estate Co.*, 3 Cal. 2d 740, 750, 47 P.2d 273, and cases cited; cf. Rules on Appeal, rule 5(a), and which is set forth in full in respondent's brief, discloses that the sole ground upon which the demurrer was sustained was that the complaint did not state a cause of action maintainable against defendant as executrix of the estate of W. C. Fields. The paramount issue presented is whether plaintiff may proceed directly against the estate of her husband to secure relief from his dissipation of the community funds through secret and unauthorized inter vivos gifts, or must seek recourse solely against the donees.

Section 574 of the Probate Code provides that "any person, or the personal representative of any person, may maintain an action against the executor or administrator of any testator or intestate who in his lifetime has wasted, destroyed, taken, or carried away, or converted to his own use, the property of any such person...."

The facts alleged in the complaint are in our opinion sufficient to bring the action within these provisions. Even before the husband was forbidden by statute to make a gift of community property without his wife's consent, his power of disposition had never been deemed to include the privilege of acting in fraud of the rights of the wife in the community property. *Smith v. Smith*, 12 Cal. 216, 225, 73 Am. Dec. 533; *Lord v. Hough*, 43 Cal. 581,585. Where actual fraud is alleged, as it is here, it would seem clear that a husband who has made unauthorized gifts of a large share of the community property may be held accountable to the offended wife as in the case of any other person who has wrongfully disposed of the property of another.

The position of the husband, in whom the management and control of the entire community estate is vested by statute, Civ. Code, secs. 161a, 172, 172a, has been frequently analogized to that of a partner, agent, or fiduciary. *In re Estate of McNutt*, 36 Cal. App. 2d 542, 552, 98 P.2d 253; *Grolemund v. Cafferata*, 17 Cal. 2d 679, 684, 111 P.2d 641; *Lynam v. Vorwerk*, 13 Cal. App. 507, 509, 110 P. 355; 1 de Funiak, *Principles of Community Property*, sec. 95, p. 263. Section 2219 of the Civil Code provides: "Everyone who voluntarily assumes a relation of personal confidence with another is deemed a trustee ... as to the person who reposes such confidence...." It is clear that, being a party to the confidential relationship of marriage, the husband must, for some purposes at least, be deemed a trustee for his wife in respect to their common property. *Cf. Vanasek v. Pokorney*, 73 Cal. App. 312, 320, 238 P. 798; *Arnold v. Leonard*, 114 Tex. 535, 273 S.W. 799, 804. Fundamental principles governing trust relationships are set forth in sections 2228 and 2229 of the Civil Code: "In all matters connected with his trust, a trustee is bound to act in the highest good faith toward his beneficiary, and may not obtain any advantage therein over the latter by the slightest misrepresentation, concealment, threat, or adverse pressure of any kind. A trustee may not use or deal with the trust property for his own profit, or for any other purpose unconnected with the trust, in any manner." Section 2234 declares: "Every violation of the provisions of the preceding sections of this article [i.e., sections 2228 through 2233] is a fraud against the beneficiary of a trust." Disregarding the allegations of intent to defraud, it is abundantly clear from those remaining that Fields must be held to have consummated a fraud against plaintiff. Nine years prior to their marriage, section 172 of the Civil Code was amended to provide that the husband could not make a gift of community property without the written consent of his wife. Stats. 1891, p. 425. Fields' disregard of this affirmative duty imposed upon him as manager of the community estate was a violation of his fiduciary obligations as defined in sections 2228 and 2229 of the Civil Code, supra. Even if good faith were to be shown, he would nevertheless be subject to personal liability for disposing of trust property in an unauthorized manner. Civ. Code, sec. 2238.

It is well settled, of course, that a gift made in violation of section 172 is, as against the donee, voidable by the wife in its entirety during the husband's lifetime, *Matthews v. Hamburger*, 36 Cal. App. 2d 182, 97 P.2d 465; *Lynn v. Herman*, 72 Cal. App. 2d 614, 165 P.2d 54, and to the extent of one-half after his death. *Trimble v. Trimble*, 219 Cal. 340, 26 P.2d 477; *Ballinger v. Ballinger*, 9 Cal. 2d 330, 70 P.2d 629. The beneficiary of a trust, however, is not required to pursue the trust property, but may elect to hold the trustee (or after his death, his estate) personally liable, *McElroy v. McElroy*, 32 Cal. 2d 828, 831, 198 P.2d 683; *Lathrop v. Bampton*, 31 Cal. 17, 23, 89 Am. Dec. 141; and the latter may not escape such liability by showing that the trust property has been dissipated. 54 Am. Jur., sec. 253, p. 196. Manifestly, a wife whose community property rights have been violated, as plaintiff alleges hers have been, is entitled to pursue whatever course is best calculated to give her effective relief. Where the amount of the gifts and identity of the donees are known, and the property can be readily reached, the former remedy may be decidedly more advantageous to the plaintiff than an action against the husband's estate, since the assets of the latter may be insufficient to satisfy a judgment. On the other hand, where recourse against the donees would be ineffective to give relief, as in the present instance, a denial of the alternative remedy would not only be in disregard of rudimentary principles applicable to persons acting in a fiduciary capacity, insofar as the husband stood in that relation, but would also amount to a concession that the law is powerless to accord to the wife's community interest the full protection which section 172 was evidently designed to ensure. We think the law is not so toothless. Whether the action is viewed as one based upon actual fraud, or as one based upon a violation of a statutory limitation upon the husband's power of control and management, is immaterial, for the dissipation of community assets by means of unauthorized gifts is in either view a conversion of the "property" of the wife such as would subject the husband's estate to suit under section 574 of the Probate Code. The statutory language is sufficiently comprehensive to include any wrongful conduct resulting in a loss of "property" to another.

No question was raised either here or in the trial court as to whether plaintiff should have proceeded in the probate court to claim as her share of the community property an amount equal to one-half of all sums previously given away without her consent, in addition to her share in the assets presently remaining in the estate. *See* McKay, *Community Property*, 2nd ed., secs. 734, 735, p. 494; 1 de Funiak, ibid., sec. 232, p. 600. We have nevertheless considered the question of jurisdiction and think it is clear that the present action, being one on a rejected claim based upon a personal liability arising out of the breach of a fiduciary duty, is within the general jurisdiction of the superior court, 11a Cal. Jur., secs. 500, 600, pp. 706, 842; Probate Code, sec. 714.

The sole question we decide is that the complaint states a cause of action for compensatory relief. If plaintiff should prevail it will be for the trial court to decide the form the judgment should take and for the court in probate to give proper effect to it in exercising its jurisdiction with relation to claims to the community property.

The judgment is reversed with directions to overrule the demurrer and permit defendant to answer.

D. Expenditure of Community Funds for Separate Debts

Debts incurred during marriage generally are incurred for family living expenses, and it is appropriate to use community funds to pay such debts.

Debts incurred before marriage are considered separate debts. It is normally not considered appropriate to utilize community funds for such debts; if community funds are used to pay such debts, the community should be reimbursed, unless the community has enjoyed an offsetting benefit from any property subject to the debt. For example, if a spouse uses community funds to pay credit card bills incurred prior to marriage for meals and a vacation, reimbursement would be appropriate.

TFC §§ 3.402 and 3.409 address reimbursement claims. Section 3.409 bars reimbursement for the payment of child support or spousal maintenance as well as for the payment of a student loan.

What if a spouse gets in litigation during marriage about the amount of child support to be paid to a child of a former relationship? *See Farish v. Farish*, 982 S.W.2d 623 (Tex. App.—Houston [1st Dist.] 1998, no writ) (permitting the divorce court to consider this when dividing the community estate). What if a spouse pays his former spouse more than he was ordered by the divorce court because the former spouse had additional financial needs? *See Knight v. Knight*, 301 S.W.3d 723 (Tex. App.—Houston [14th Dist.] 2009, no petition) (finding it was an abuse of discretion not to order reimbursement).

E. Gifts of Community Property

Under Texas law, a spouse can make a gift of a "reasonable" amount of community property. Some states do not allow one spouse to make a gift of any community property without the consent of the other spouse. What arguments could be made in favor of each system?

How should a court determine whether a gift is reasonable? Most courts agree that this determination depends upon the relationship between the spouse and the donee, the need of the donee, and the amount of the gift, compared to the size of the community estate. So, for example, gifts to "misters" or mistresses normally do not pass the appropriate relationship hurdle, while gifts to family members or charities do. The trickiest issue pertains to the maximum percentage of the community estate that will be deemed reasonable. This normally will be a function of the need of the donee and the financial resources of the non-donor spouse.

Why should spouses be able to give away more than a negligible amount of community property without the consent of the other spouse? Doesn't this undercut the vested, equal ownership rights of the non-manager spouse? If the donor spouse owns liquid separate property and makes a gift of community property, isn't this even less acceptable?

If one spouse discovers that an unreasonable gift of community property has been made by the other spouse, the objecting spouse can attempt to recover the gift from the donee for the benefit of the community. If the objecting spouse discovers the gift after the death of the donor spouse, 50% of the gift could be recovered as the separate property of the objecting spouse. *Fields, supra,* is one of the few cases that discusses whether the objecting spouse can sue the donor spouse if the gift cannot be recovered from the donee.

Chapter Twelve

Creditors' Rights

Management rights of the spouses can be altered by agreement. This can affect the rights of the contract creditors of one spouse.

LeBlanc v. Waller
Texas Court of Appeals — Houston [14th Dist.], 1980
603 S.W.2d 265, no writ

PRESSLER, Justice.

This is an appeal from the judgment in a divorce action wherein appellee, as an alleged creditor of the community, intervened, seeking enforcement of debts incurred during the marriage of appellant and her former husband. Appellant's former husband is not a party to this appeal. We affirm in part and reverse and render in part.

Appellant and Mr. LeBlanc were separated on or about September 15, 1978. At that time, they orally agreed to a division of their modest estate. There was no written partition agreement as contemplated by Tex. Fam. Code Ann. Sec. 5.42 (Vernon 1975). The presumption is, therefore, that all of the assets were community property. Tex. Fam. Code Ann. Sec. 5.02 (Vernon 1975). Immediately following the separation, Mr. LeBlanc became an independent plumbing contractor and, pursuant to such business, incurred an indebtedness to appellee for materials to be used in his plumbing business. The record reflects that appellant never had any contact with appellee prior to the divorce proceedings, was not a party to the transactions between Mr. LeBlanc and appellee, in no way benefited from those transactions, and did not in fact become aware of the indebtedness until shortly before the hearing for the divorce. She further testified that she was living alone at the time the debts were incurred and was financially supporting herself.

The debt having been incurred prior to the termination of the marriage, is presumed to be a community debt. *Cockerham v. Cockerham*, 527 S.W.2d 162 (Tex. 1975). However, appellant contends that Tex. Fam. Code Ann. Sec. 5.61 (Vernon 1975) insulates her from liability for this debt allegedly incurred by her former husband. Section 5.61 provides in part:

(1) Unless both spouses are liable by other rules of law, the community property subject to a spouse's sole management control, and disposition is not subject to:

(2) any nontortious liabilities that the other spouse incurs during marriage.

Appellant claims that all of the community property which was in her possession from the time the debt arose until the date of the divorce judgment was subject to her sole management, control, and disposition and therefore not subject to any nontortious liability incurred by Mr. LeBlanc subsequent to the time she gained sole management, control, and disposition of the assets. Neither party contends that any other "rules of law" are applicable to this situation.

Tex. Fam. Code Ann. Sec. 5.22 (Vernon 1975), which sets forth the guidelines for determining what constitutes community property subject to the sole management, control, and disposition of one spouse provides:

> (a) During marriage, each spouse has the sole management, control, and disposition of the community property that he or she would have owned if single, including but not limited to:
>
> (1) personal earnings;
>
> (2) revenue from separate property
>
> (3) recoveries for personal injuries; and
>
> (4) the increase and mutations of, and the revenue from, all property subject to his or her sole management, control, and disposition.
>
> (c) Except as provided in Subsection (a) of this section, the community property is subject to the joint management, control, and disposition of the husband and wife, *unless the spouses provide otherwise by power of attorney in writing or other agreement.* [Emphasis added.]

This "agreement" referred to in subsection (c) is not a partition agreement of the community, but rather an agreement to transfer the power of management, control, and disposition over certain community property assets from one spouse to the other. Appellant contends that the oral agreement for division of their property falls within the "other agreement" provision of subsection (c) above. We agree. Prior to 1974, Section 5.22(c) read, "... unless the spouses provide otherwise by power of attorney or other agreement in writing." In 1973 that section was amended to read, "... unless the spouses provide otherwise by power of attorney in writing or other agreement." This amendment became effective on January 1, 1974. Applying the standard rules of statutory construction, it is apparent that the Texas Legislature chose to remove the requirement that such an agreement be in writing.

In the case of *Evans v. Muller*, 510 S.W.2d 651 (Tex. Civ. App. — Austin) rev'd per curiam, 516 S.W.2d 923 (Tex. 1974), the Court of Civil Appeals concluded that a Section 5.22(c) oral agreement had been entered into, that there was no evidence that said agreement was designed to delay, defraud or hinder creditors, and that the property subject to that agreement was, therefore, insulated from liability by Section 5.61(b)(2). The Texas Supreme Court, in reversing the Court of Civil Appeals, *supra*, did not criticize its reasoning or interpretation of Section 5.22(c), but reversed simply on the basis that the agreement and trial were prior in time to the date on which the amendment removing the requirement for a written agreement became effective. The agreement having been made subsequent to the amendment, we hold that the oral agreement in this cause meets the requirements of Section 5.22(c).

However, it must also be determined whether the liability in question was incurred by Mr. LeBlanc alone or, instead, was a joint liability. Tex. Fam. Code Ann. Sec. 5.61(b)(2). The Texas Supreme Court, in *Cockerham v. Cockerham, supra*, has stated the applicable rule as follows:

> To determine whether a debt is only that of the contracting party or if it is instead that of both the husband and wife, it is necessary to examine the totality of the circumstances in which the debt arose. Of particular importance in the in-

stant case is the consideration of implied assent to the debt by the noncontracting party, the husband.

The Court pointed out that, in the absence of some evidence that the creditor agreed
to look solely to the separate estate of the contracting spouse for satisfaction, the debt, incurred during marriage, is presumed a community liability. The Court emphasized, however, that "[c]haracterization of the debts as community liabilities is only one aspect of
the circumstances to be considered in determining whether the debts are joint." The other
factors which the Court considered in determining whether the debts were joint liabilities were: (1) who advanced the capital necessary to pay for the initial and additional inventory; (2) statements by the parties as to their willingness to pay the debt; (3) who
signed the checks to pay for operational expenses; and (4) the treatment of depreciation
deductions and shop losses on the parties' joint income tax return.

In the case before us, the noncontracting spouse had no knowledge of the liability
until shortly before the inception of this action, did not participate in the business, did
not realize any gain from it, nor have the opportunity to do so. There is no evidence of
assent, implied or expressed, on appellant's part to incurring this debt. While the evidence reflects that appellee never agreed to look solely to Mr. LeBlanc's separate estate
for satisfaction of this debt, that circumstance alone will not support the conclusion that
it is a joint liability. There are no other circumstances reflected in the record, and therefore, no evidence to rebut the conclusion that the liability was incurred by Mr. LeBlanc
alone. Consequently, neither the community property under appellant's sole management, control, and disposition, nor her separate property is subject to this liability according
to the terms of Section 5.61(a) and (b)(2). As the record reflects that there are no assets
in appellant's possession or under her control which do not fall into one of those categories, appellant is not liable for this debt.

Affirmed in part and reversed and rendered in part.

DISCUSSION

Texas creditors' rights rules are found in Tex. Fam. Code § 3.202. For contract debts,
Texas has a "management" system. That is, a contract creditor of a spouse can attach all
property over which the spouse has sole or joint management power. For purposes of
creditors' rights, it does not matter whether the debt arose before or during marriage.
(However, the community may be entitled to reimbursement if community property is
used to pay a separate debt.) If the obligor has management power over both separate
and community property, attachment priority is governed by Section 3.203. The separate estates of both spouses, as well as all of the community estate, can be attached if
both spouses were obligated to pay the debt. Read through Section 3.202; do you understand how the statute establishes the system described above? Given these rules, what
advice would you give a person who plans to marry someone with substantial premarital debts?

Tort claims are more complicated than contract claims for creditors' rights issues. If
the liability was "incurred" during marriage, all community property can be attached, as
well as the separate property of the tortfeasor. If the liability was "incurred" prior to marriage, only property over which the defendant has management power can be attached.
It is not clear when a tort liability is "incurred." In another context, the court in *Williams
v. Adams*, 74 S.W.3d 437 (Tex. App.—Corpus Christi 2002, pet. filed) held that a tort liability was incurred at the time of the injury.

[handwritten: CREDITOR AGREE) TO only book to Spouse for repayment property]

Diagram of Marital Property Liability

	Husband's Separate Property	Husband's Sole Mgmt. Com. Prop.	Joint Mgmt. Com. Prop.	Wife's Sole Mgmt. Com. Prop.	Wife's Separate Property
Husband's Separate Debt*	■				
Husband's Pre-Marital Liabilities	■	■	■		
Husband's Non-Tortious Liabilities During Marriage	■	■	■		
Husband's Tortious Liabilities During Marriage	■	■	■	■	
Wife's Tortious Liabilities During Marriage		■	■	■	■
Wife's Non-Tortious Liabilities During Marriage			■	■	■
Wife's Pre-Marital Liabilities			■	■	■
Wife's Separate Debt*					■
Joint Liabilities of Spouses	■	■	■	■	■

* A person's "separate debt" is one incurred during marriage where the creditor agrees to look only to the debtor's separate estate for payment.

Under Section 3.202, it is clear that a spouse's separate property is never attachable for the contract debts or torts committed by the other spouse.

These creditors' rights rules are the rules applicable if the creditor has not limited his or her rights. Of course, if the creditor's rights are limited in the instrument involved, the creditor's rights would be subject to such a limitation. For example, if the creditor agreed to collect a loan only from the separate estate of the obligor, only the obligor's separate estate could be attached. *See Brazosport Bank of Texas v. Robertson*, 616 S.W.2d 363 (Tex. Civ. App.—Houston [14th Dist.] 1981, no writ).

The general creditors' rights rules set forth in this discussion assume that a spouse is not liable for the act of the other spouse based on some legal theory other than spousal liability. For example, one spouse can be liable for the act of the other if that spouse is acting as an agent for the other spouse.

There is another exception to the general rules set forth above. Tex. Fam. Code § 2.501 provides that each spouse has the duty to support the other, and if a spouse "fails to discharge the duty of support," the spouse is liable to any person who provides "necessaries" to the other spouse. Because of this obligation, if a creditor provides a "necessity" to one spouse, all of the property of the other spouse can be attached to collect such a debt. *See* Tex. Fam. Code § Sec. 3.201. However, before this obligation arises, it must be established that the spouse "failed to discharge the duty of support." It is unclear whether this requires the spouse to ask the other spouse to purchase the necessity, and have been refused, before the spouse has the right to purchase the necessity and obligate the other spouse to pay. Cases to date do not appear to require this. *See Daggett v. Neiman-Marcus*, 348 S.W.2d 796 (Tex. Civ. App.—Houston 1961, no writ).

Before one spouse can be liable under this doctrine for the purchase by the other, it must be established that the item purchased was a "necessity." The term "necessity" is obviously vague, but even a restrictive interpretation would include food and medical care. The "station of life" of the couple affects how a court defines a necessity in a particular case. For example, where the standard of living was fairly high a court has determined that the wife's clothing bills from Neiman-Marcus amounting to $2,000 were necessaries. *See Daggett v. Neiman-Marcus, supra.*

Cockerham v. Cockerham
Supreme Court of Texas, 1975
52 S.W.2d 162

JOHNSON, Justice.

This is a divorce case in which the wife's trustee in bankruptcy has intervened. The trial court granted the divorce and made the property division to be discussed hereinafter. The court of civil appeals affirmed with one justice dissenting. 514 S.W.2d 150. We affirm the judgment of the court of civil appeals in part and reverse and render in part.

Petitioner Dorothy Cockerham brought this suit for divorce against her husband, respondent E. A. Cockerham. Petitioner Theodore Mack, trustee in bankruptcy of Dorothy Cockerham, intervened seeking to require the payment of indebtedness due the bankruptcy creditors out of the community property prior to its division between husband and wife.

The property at issue in the trial, which is relevant to this appeal, included (1) a 198-acre tract claimed to be the homestead of the husband and wife, (2) a 320-acre tract on which the husband operated a dairy, and (3) a dairy business consisting of cattle, farm equipment and machinery, a milk base and milking equipment. Several claims were asserted against these properties. First, community debts totaling $47,985, which includes the sum of $36,200 due on indebtedness secured by a lien on the 198-acre tract, were alleged. Second, the trustee in bankruptcy asserted a claim for $68,933.99 to pay the wife's bankruptcy creditors and the bankruptcy expenses. These debts arose out of the operation of a dress shop by the wife during the last two years of the marriage. Finally, the husband alleged the wife had made fraudulent gifts of community assets in the amount of $19,317.14 to DeRay Houston.

Trial on the property rights of the parties was to the court which made findings of fact and conclusions of law.[1]

The judgment of the trial court set aside the 198-acre homestead tract, along with household goods and furnishings, to the husband. The 320-acre tract was adjudicated to be one-half the separate property of the husband and one-half community property. The court required the $47,985 "community debts," which included the $36,200 due on the debt secured by a lien on the 198-acre tract, to be paid out of the community interest in the 320 acre tract of land and the other community property, consisting of the dairy business. After the community debts were paid the community property was to be divided equally between the parties. However, the husband was also awarded $9,658.57 (one-half of the $19,317.14 of community property which the trial court found to be fraudulently given by the wife to DeRay Houston) out of the wife's share of what remained of that equally divided property after payment of the community debts. The $68,933.99 due the trustee was to be satisfied out of the wife's share after the payment of all community debts and after further reducing her interest by the above-mentioned amount of $9,658.57.

Both Dorothy Cockerham and the trustee appealed from the judgment adjudicating the property rights to the court of civil appeals. That court affirmed the trial court's judgment, making, among others, the following determinations:

---

1. The findings of fact are substantially as follows:

(1) The court held the 198-acre tract was the homestead of the parties and had an existing debt of $36,200 against it. The parties in addition owed $11,785 of other community debts for a total community indebtedness of $47,985.

(2) As to the 320-acre tract, the findings recite "… that one-half thereof is community property and one-half the separate property of the said E. A. Cockerham by reason of his ownership to an undivided one-half interest thereof prior to his marriage with Dorothy Cockerham" and that the partition suit "was but a means of convenience provided by law to complete the purchase of the whole and secure a loan thereon."

(3) The court made a finding which is contrary to the jury's answer to special issue number three, as above quoted. The court's gifts of community assets to DeRay Houston in at least the sum of $19,317.14 in fraud of the community. The court further found that "this sum should be charged to the proportionate share owned by the said Dorothy Cockerham but subject to the community debts above set out."

(4) The court found the dairy business, along with one-half of the 320 acres of land, to be community property and held the parties would take same subject to the community debt.

(5) As to priority, the court found "that the property rights of the said Dorothy Cockerham set out herein are subject first to the judgment of this Court, and then subject to the rights of the Intervenor Trustee in Bankruptcy."

Included in the conclusions of law were the following:

(1) "The act of Dorothy Cockerham, over the protest of E. A. Cockerham, in using community funds in her store adventure; and having a joint bank account with a third party male; and in transferring inventory from her store to the supposed store of the third party male without accounting for same, was a fraud upon the rights of E. A. Cockerham, and for which she is entitled to have charged against her interest."

(2) The estate is subject to the community debts ($47,985) and that Dorothy's share of the community property is chargeable with gifts made in fraud of the community.

(3) One-half of the 320 acres is the separate property of E. A. Cockerham and one-half is the community property of E. A. Cockerham and Dorothy Cockerham.

(4) As a final conclusion, the court stated, "The share or portion of Dorothy Cockerham is subject to the divisions of this Court, and the rights of the Intervenor Trustee in the order as set out."

1. An undivided one-half of the 320-acre tract was E. A. Cockerham's separate property by reason of his prior ownership before marriage; the other undivided one-half of the 320-acre tract was the community property of E. A. and Dorothy Cockerham. Thus, there was a tenancy in common with respect to the 320-acre tract between the separate estate of E. A. Cockerham and the community estate.

2. The dairy business operated by the husband on the 320-acre tract was under the sole management and control of the husband, E. A. Cockerham, "and under Texas Family Code Section 5.61, community property consisting of an undivided one-half of the 320 acres, the milking equipment, cattle, milk base, and farm equipment, was not subject to the nontortious liabilities of the wife, Dorothy Cockerham, same being the claims of the bankruptcy creditors of Dorothy Cockerham...."

3. The trial court had the power to disregard the jury's finding that the wife did not make gifts to DeRay Houston because the jury findings regarding the division of property were advisory only. There was evidence to support the trial court's finding that the property was fraudulently conveyed by the wife; the trial court acted within its discretion in charging the wife's share with the amounts given.

4. The trial court acted within its discretion in requiring the indebtedness secured by a lien on the 198-acre homestead tract to be paid out of the community property prior to the wife's bankruptcy creditors.

5. The division of community property was not so disproportionately favorable to the husband as to be an abuse of discretion.

Both Dorothy Cockerham and the trustee have filed applications for writ of error. Their contentions will be discussed separately.

APPLICATION OF THE TRUSTEE

The trustee brings fifteen points of error to this court. Basically he asserts error on the part of the court of civil appeals in not subjecting the whole 320-acre tract and all of the community property to the claims of the bankruptcy creditors, and in relegating those creditors to an inferior position with regard to priority. His initial contention is that the entire 320-acre tract was community property. Alternatively he argues that even if an undivided one-half interest in the 320-acre tract is the husband's separate property, the husband made a gift of one-half of his separate property interest to his wife. The trustee further argues that even if some part of the property is the separate property of the husband, it is nevertheless liable for the debts incurred in the operation of the dress shop.

The 320-Acre Tract as Community or Separate Property

When the Cockerhams were married on May 16, 1949, the husband, E. A. Cockerham, owned an undivided one-half interest in the 320-acre tract and his brother, Herman Cockerham, owned the other undivided one-half interest. The brothers conducted a farming and cattle raising operation on this property. A number of years later, in 1955, Herman Cockerham wanted to sell his undivided one-half interest in the 320 acres, and his brother, E. A. Cockerham, wanted to buy him out. However, E. A. Cockerham had to get a loan on the property in order to pay his brother for his half. In order to accomplish these things, the two brothers went to a lawyer who filed a partition suit on behalf of E. A. and wife against Herman and wife and secured the court appointment of receiver. The receiver thereupon sold the 320-acre tract to E. A. and Dorothy Cockerham at private sale under the orders of the district court. The receiver's deed indicates a total consideration of $22,700, of which $11,400 cash was recited to have been paid by E. A. and Dorothy Cockerham and $11,300 cash furnished by John Hancock Mutual Life Insurance Company, who reserved a vendor's lien on the land. It was undisputed, however, that E. A. and Dorothy Cockerham actually made no cash payment at all. It is also undisputed that the amount recited to have been paid in cash by E. A. Cockerham in this transaction ($11,400) was approximately the value of his undivided one-half interest in the property. The receiver's deed was a conveyance to E. A. and Dorothy Cockerham, in both names as grantees. All Dorothy seemed to know about this transaction was that her husband was buying his brother out of the 320-acre tract. The trial court held that these facts were sufficient to establish that an undivided one-half of the 320-acre tract was separate property of E. A. Cockerham "by reason of his ownership of an undivided one-half interest thereof prior to his marriage." The court of civil appeals affirmed, holding that there was a tenancy in common between the separate property of E. A. Cockerham and the community property. The trustee attacks this holding, asserting that the evidence is insufficient to support the conclusion of the court of civil appeals that E. A. Cockerham adequately traced his prior separate property ownership in the 320-acre tract.

"Property possessed by either spouse during or on dissolution of marriage is presumed to be community property." Section 5.02. In order to overcome this presumption, the party asserting separate ownership must clearly trace the original separate property into the particular assets on hand during the marriage.

In the instant case it was undisputed that the husband owned an undivided one-half interest in identifiable real property prior to marriage. The partition suit and sale was, as found by the trial court, only "a means of convenience provided by law to complete the purchase of the whole and secure a loan thereon." In addition, the cash consideration ($11,400) recited to have been paid by E. A. Cockerham in this transaction was the approximate value of his prior undivided interest in the property. No cash, however, actually changed hands. These facts are sufficient to justify the trial court in finding that E. A. Cockerham put up the interest he owned prior to marriage as partial consideration for the purchase. Since the interest he owned prior to marriage was an undivided one-half of the 320-acre tract, such undivided one-half interest remained his separate property.

The trustee alternatively contends that if the husband had a separate property interest in the 320 acres, the record shows he made a gift of an undivided one-half of such separate property interest to his wife. In support of this position the trustee points out that title to the whole 320 acres was taken in the name of E. A. Cockerham and wife, Dorothy Cockerham, and asserts that it is well established that when a husband uses separate property consideration to pay for land acquired during the marriage and takes title to the land in the name of husband and wife, it is presumed he intended the interest placed in his wife to be a gift. *Smith v. Strahan*, 16 Tex. 314 (1856); *Carriere v. Bodungen*, 500 S.W.2d 692 (Tex. Civ. App.—Corpus Christi 1973, no writ); *Hampshire v. Hampshire*, 485 S.W.2d 314 (Tex. Civ. App.—Fort Worth 1972, no writ). This presumption, however, can be rebutted by evidence clearly establishing there was no intention to make a gift. *Smith v. Strahan, supra.*

In the instant case Dorothy Cockerham testified she never paid any attention to the purchase of the 320 acres; in fact, she claimed she never even saw the deed to the property until the preparation for the instant litigation. Her attitude toward the 320-acre tract has, until the instant suit, been largely one of complete disinterest—the 320 acres and the dairy business on it were her husband's business to which she paid little, if any, attention. She offered no testimony in support of the presumption that her husband meant to make a gift to her of part of his interest in the 320-acre tract. There is nothing in her testimony which would indicate any understanding that a gift had been made to her. The husband's testimony also tends to negate any idea that he intended a gift to his wife. The structure of the transaction whereby he bought his brother's interest in the 320-acre tract was of no concern to him; he left the transaction entirely to his lawyer. All he knew was that one day he went to the courthouse and then, "I just owned 160 acres worth of land." At trial he took the position that the whole 320 acres had always been his land. Moreover, the husband's brother, Herman, from whom he bought the property, corroborated the testimony that the purchase was structured as it was solely to enable the husband to buy the property. Based upon this evidence the trial court entered two findings of fact which relate to whether the husband intended a gift to the wife. First, the court found the method used to purchase the 320 acres was but a "means of convenience" to complete the purchase. Second, the court entered a finding that "one-half [of the 320-acre tract] is community property and one-half the separate property of E. A. Cockerham." By entering these findings the court impliedly found that the presumption the husband intended a gift to the wife was sufficiently rebutted and that, in fact, there was no such intention. This finding must be upheld if it finds any support in the evidence. *Langlotz v. Citizens Fidelity Insurance Company*, 505 S.W.2d 249 (Tex. 1974); *Butler v. Hanson*, 455 S.W.2d 942 (Tex. 1970). Considering the record before us, we are unable to say there is no evidence to uphold the implied finding of the trial court that E. A. Cockerham did not intend to make a gift to his wife.

Since E. A. Cockerham adequately traced his prior separate interest in an undivided one-half of the 320-acre tract and sufficiently rebutted the presumption which arises from the fact that title was taken in the name of himself and his wife, a tenancy in common exists in the 320-acre tract between the undivided one-half separate property interest of E. A. Cockerham and the undivided one-half community property interest. *Gleich v. Bongio*, 128 Tex. 606, 99 S.W.2d 881 (1937).

The Trustee's Claim Against the Community Property

As noted above, the community owned an undivided one-half interest in the 320acre tract as tenants in common. In addition, the dairy business, which was purchased during marriage with community funds, is indisputably community property.

The trustee claims the community interest in the 320-acre tract and the community property dairy business is subject to the dress shop obligations.

The trustee argues, first, that the community property was subject to joint management, control and disposition and is thus liable for the debts incurred by Dorothy Cockerham in the operation of the dress shop under Section 5.61(c). Alternatively, the trustee contends that even if the dairy business was under the sole management of the husband within Section 5.61(b) the debts incurred in the operation of the dress shop are joint liabilities of the husband and wife and thus the dairy business is not insulated from liability by Section 5.61(b)(2), which protects sole management property only from nontortious liabilities incurred by the other spouse. Thus the trustee argues the dairy business would be subject to these joint liabilities under Section 5.61(c), which provides that property subject to the sole management of a spouse is subject to liabilities incurred by that spouse.[2]

---

2. The reference to liabilities "incurred by him or her" in Section 5.61(c) is interpreted to mean liabilities incurred by the spouse referred to in that section.

The Community Property as Joint or Sole Management Property

Resolution of the issue of whether community property is joint or sole management property depends upon the construction and interpretation of Section 5.22, which pertains to the management of community property. At the time this case was tried that section read as follows:

> (a) During marriage, each spouse has the sole management, control, and disposition of the community property that he or she would have owned if single, including but not limited to:
>
> (1) personal earnings;
>
> (2) revenue from separate property;
>
> (3) recoveries for personal injuries; and
>
> (4) the increase and mutations of, and the revenue from, all property subject to his or her sole management, control, and disposition.
>
> (b) If community property subject to the sole management, control, and disposition of one spouse is mixed or combined with community property subject to the sole management, control, and disposition of the other spouse, then the mixed or combined community property is subject to the joint management, control, and disposition of the spouses, unless the spouses provide otherwise by power of attorney or other agreement in writing.
>
> (c) Except as provided in Subsection (a) of this section, the community property is subject to the joint management, control, and disposition of the husband and wife, unless the spouses provide otherwise by power of attorney or other agreement in writing.[3]

The court of civil appeals pointed out that the dairy business on the 320-acre tract was operated solely by E. A. Cockerham; that it was near but not contiguous to the homestead tract3; that it was in possession and control of the husband; and that the wife took no part in its operation. Thus, reasoned the court of civil appeals, the community property dairy business along with the undivided one-half community property interest in the 320 acres upon which the business was located was under the sole management of E. A. Cockerham within the meaning of Section 5.22(a). The trustee disputes this holding, contending the dairy business does not fit into any of the specifically enumerated classifications of sole management property listed in Section 5.22(a). Since Section 5.22(c) provides that all property except property included in Subsection (a) is joint management property, the trustee reasons the dairy business and the community tract are thus subject to the joint management of the husband and wife.

With regard to the 320-acre tract, the record reveals E. A. Cockerham and his wife in effect borrowed the cash necessary to purchase the community interest by giving a note secured by a deed of trust on the property in return. Title to the property was taken in the name of both husband and wife; both husband and wife were obligated on the note. Under virtually identical circumstances these facts were considered sufficient to establish that the community interest was subject to the joint management of the husband and wife in *Cooper v. Texas Gulf Industrials, Inc.*, 513 S.W.2d 200 (Tex. 1974). We therefore hold that the community interest in the undivided one-half of the 320-acre tract was subject to the joint management of E. A. Cockerham and his wife. Section 5.22(c).

---

3. Effective January 1, 1974 Subsection (c) was changed to allow spouses to eliminate the requirement that an agreement to alter managerial powers be in writing.

The situation with respect to the dairy business is somewhat more complicated. As has been noted, the dairy is located on the 320-acre tract, which is one-half separate property of the husband and one-half community property. The dairy was acquired during the marriage when the husband converted his cattle operation into a dairy business. Over the years the proceeds from the business were invested in additional machinery and equipment causing the business to increase in size and worth. It is asserted that the proceeds from the dairy business are "personal earnings" of the husband within Section 5.22(a)(1); that these earnings alone have caused the dairy business to grow and thus the business is the "increase and mutation" of the husband's personal earnings and is under the sole management of the husband. Section 5.22(a)(4). We do not agree. The income from the dairy business was produced not only by the labor of the husband but also by the use of the land on which the business was located. Personal earnings, on the other hand, are earnings solely by physical or mental labor, unaided by capital, except insofar as may be necessary to supply the means of such labor as, for example, the ax of a woodcutter or the pen and paper of a writer. *First Nat. Bank v. Davis*, 5 S.W.2d 753 (Tex. Com. App. 1928, holding approved); 1 Speer's *Marital Rights in Texas* Sec. 421 at 625 (4th ed. 1961). We conclude the income produced by the dairy business was not "personal earnings" of the husband within Section 5.22(a)(1). The husband has not shown that this is property which he "would have owned if single." Section 5.22(a). The use of community assets was an integral part of the dairy business. We therefore hold the dairy business was thus under the joint management, control and disposition of the husband and wife under Section 5.22(c).

Since both the community interest in the 320-acre tract and the community dairy business were under the joint management of both E. A. Cockerham and his wife, they will be liable for the dress shop debts whether those debts are considered obligations of only the husband, of only the wife, or joint obligations of both the husband and wife. Section 5.61(c).

The Trustee's Claim Against the Husband's Separate Property

The trustee also seeks to hold the husband's separate property interest in an undivided one-half of the 320-acre tract liable for the dress shop debts. He argues that Section 5.61(a) does not insulate the husband's separate property from liability for the dress shop debts. He contends, first, that the dress shop debts are joint liabilities for which both spouses are liable. Alternatively, he claims that even if the dress shop debts are liabilities of the "other spouse" (wife) within Section 5.61, the husband is nevertheless also liable under "other rules of law" within the meaning of that statute. We sustain the trustee's first contention and thus find it unnecessary to consider his alternative argument.

The Character of the Dress Shop Debts

In 1969 Dorothy Cockerham opened a dress shop in Hurst, Texas. The evidence is conflicting as to E. A. Cockerham's attitude toward this enterprise—she claimed he urged her to open the shop; he claimed he opposed the move but realized that not allowing her to open the shop would cause a divorce. Notwithstanding his alleged opposition, however, the wife did, in fact, open the shop using approximately $4,000 which was advanced to her by the husband.

Dorothy had financial difficulties from the beginning and in 1970 she moved the shop to Burleson, Texas in an attempt to improve sales. The business continued to flounder, however, and eventually resulted in bankruptcy. The debts asserted by the trustee represent, primarily, credit purchases of inventory for the store.

THIS IS WEAK.

E. A. Cockerham never took part in the conduct or operation of the dress shop and all purchases for the shop were made by Dorothy. The husband claims this fact alone establishes that the debts incurred were solely those of his wife. The fact of physical operation of a business, however, is not wholly determinative of the character, as sole or joint, of the debts incurred in its operation. This is especially true since both husband and wife have full capacity to contract. Section 4.03.

To determine whether a debt is only that of the contracting party or if it is instead that of both the husband and wife, it is necessary to examine the totality of the circumstances in which the debt arose. Of particular importance in the instant case is the consideration of implied assent to the debt by the noncontracting party, the husband.

The debts in the instant case arose, of course, during marriage. It is well established that debts contracted during marriage are presumed to be on the credit of the community and thus are joint community obligations, unless it is shown the creditor agreed to look solely to the separate estate of the contracting spouse for satisfaction. *Broussard v. Tian*, 156 Tex. 371, 295 S.W.2d 405 (1956); *Gleich v. Bongio, supra*. There is no evidence that the parties who extended Dorothy Cockerham credit agreed to look solely to her separate estate for satisfaction, and thus, there are no facts to rebut the presumption that these debts are community liabilities. Though this would establish the community character of the debts, the fact that the debts are community liabilities would not, without more, necessarily lead to the conclusion that they were joint liabilities. Characterization of the debts as community liabilities is only one aspect of the circumstances to be considered in determining whether the debts are joint.

In the instant case the record is replete with factors which point to the conclusion that the dress shop debts were joint liabilities of both the husband and the wife. For example, it was the husband who advanced the wife the necessary capital to pay for the initial inventory of the store. In addition, it was the wife's practice, acquiesced in by her husband, to write checks for personal and family expenses on his personal checking account by signing his name rather than hers; this was done because the parties did not have a joint account. Their bank knew of this practice and honored the checks written by the wife on her husband's account. After the wife opened the dress shop, she continued to write checks on her husband's account and often paid for merchandise for the store in this manner. The husband never forbade her to do so nor did he stop payment on any of the checks. On one occasion, as the business began to encounter difficulties, he borrowed $5,000 to pay off some of the dress shop debts because, in his words, "... I have always paid my debts." It is clear that he recognized these as his obligations. Though the husband now claims he did not authorize the dress shop liabilities, his actions were consistent with an implied assent to their establishment. In addition, there is some evidence of an expressed assent in that there was at least one instance in which he himself signed a check in the sum of $1,400 which was used to pay operational expenses of the dress shop. Moreover, the joint income tax returns of Dorothy and her husband for the years Dorothy had the dress shop reveal they took depreciation deductions on the dress shop equipment and wrote off substantial losses because of the dress shop operation. Because of this, the Cockerhams paid very little, and in some years no, federal income tax even though the husband had a substantial income from his dairy business.

In view of the record presented to this court, we hold the dress shop debts are joint liabilities of both the husband and the wife. Since they are not liabilities of the "other spouse," Section 5.61(a) does not insulate the husband's separate property from liability for these debts. A joint liability is an obligation of both parties; the husband's separate property is therefore subject to the dress shop debts. *See e.g.*, 4 *Corbin on Contracts*, Sec. 928 (1951).

As noted above, the trial court found that Dorothy Cockerham had fraudulently taken community property and made gifts to DeRay Houston. This finding was in disregard of the jury's refusal to find that Dorothy had made such fraudulent gifts. As recognized by the court of civil appeals, the testimony was sharply conflicting on this issue and there was certainly at least some evidence to support the jury's answer. The court of civil appeals, however, held that the trial court had the power to disregard the jury's answer because answers of the jury regarding disposition of property are advisory only. Though the trial court has wide discretion in dividing the property of the spouses as it feels just and in disregarding advisory answers of the jury, it may not ignore the jury's answers which extend to issues of fact from which the status of property is determined. *Stafford v. Stafford,* 41 Tex. 111 (1874); *Rice v. Rice,* 21 Tex. 58 (1858); *Baker v. Baker,* 104 S.W.2d 531 (Tex. Civ. App.—San Antonio 1936, no writ). This is particularly true when the disposition of the property to the husband or wife is based solely on its status. In the instant case, the award of part of the wife's share of community property to the husband was based only on the findings of the trial court that the property was property which had been fraudulently disposed of by the wife. This was directly related to the status of the property. The action of the trial court in disregarding the jury's answer regarding the status of the property was in error. There was no basis for the award to the husband.

We hold that the husband did not make a gift of an undivided one-half interest in his separate property interest in the 320-acre tract to the wife; that the 320-acre tract is one-half the separate property of the husband and one-half the community property of the husband and the wife; that a tenancy in common exists on the 320-acre tract between the undivided one-half community property interest and the undivided one-half separate property interest of the husband; that the undivided one-half community property interest in the 320-acre tract was under the joint management of the husband and the wife and is subject to the dress shop debts; that the dairy business was community property under the joint management of the husband and the wife and is liable for the dress shop debts; that the dress shop debts are joint obligations rendering the husband's separate property interest in the 320 acres liable for these obligations; that the bankruptcy creditors and the community creditors have an equal right to be satisfied out of the community property; that the trial court erred in disregarding the jury's answer regarding the status of the property allegedly given by the wife to DeRay Houston, and the courts below erred in ordering a reduction in the wife's share of the community property in the sum of $9,658.57, and that the trial court's division of the property was not so disproportionate as to amount to an abuse of discretion.

The judgment of the court of civil appeals is accordingly affirmed in part and reversed and rendered in part in accordance with this opinion. The case is further remanded to the trial court for determination, pursuant to Section 5.62, of the order in which the property of the parties shall be subject to execution.

REAVLEY, Justice (dissenting).

I disagree with the Court's holding that E. A. Cockerham is personally liable for, and his separate property subject to, the debts incurred by Dorothy Cockerham in the operation of the dress shop. It is a long step through fact and law from the decision of the trial court that E. A. Cockerham is not liable personally for those debts, incurred by Dorothy "in her store adventure" which used community funds "over the protest of E. A. Cockerham," to the decision by this Court that he is personally liable.

I had supposed that the Texas Family Code as enacted and amended by the 61st, 62nd and 63rd Legislatures places a creditor who deals with one spouse in a position where, in the event of subsequent unpaid debts and liabilities, he might not be able to reach that community property which is not held solely in the name of the spouse with whom he deals. Section 5.24 protects the creditor to the extent that he can assume the spouse has sole management of property in that spouse's name. However, the other community property may well be under the sole management of the other spouse by the terms of Sec. 5.22, which so specifies for property that the other spouse "would have owned if single" and which also gives effect to agreements between the spouses, whether or not the agreement is known to the creditor. If the other spouse has sole management, under Sec. 5.61 that property is beyond the creditor's reach. If that state of the law was disturbing to creditors, they can now relax while spouses with separate estates do the worrying. The Court today seems to hold that a wife (or husband) who assents to the husband (or wife) spending community funds in a venture thereby subjects her (or his) total estate to any liability that the husband's (or wife's) venture may precipitate.

GREENHILL, Chief Justice and WALKER, Justice, join in this dissent.

DISCUSSION

The *Cockerham* holding is not in itself surprising. If the husband ratifies his wife's contract debts, his separate property, as well as his 3.102(a) community property, is available to the creditors. However, certain loose language in the *Cockerham* opinion caused confusion in Texas creditors' rights law for more than a decade. The court in *Cockerham* refers to a "community debt," and suggests that this term has some significance in connection with Texas creditors' rights rules. A review of Tex. Fam. Code § 3.202 will reveal that the concept of "community debt" has no application to creditors' rights rules. *See generally* Tom Featherston & Allison Dickson, "Dispelling the Myth of Community Debt," 73 Tex. Bar. J., No. 1 at 16 (January 2010).

In Texas, for purposes of creditors' rights, there are only two types of contract debts: the debts of one spouse and the debts of both. For the former, as long as the debt is not a necessity, the creditor may only attach the separate property of the debtor, as well as all joint management community property and the debtor's 3.102(a) community property. For the latter, the creditor may attach all non-exempt property owned by either spouse. Note: the above rules are applied regardless whether the debt is incurred before or during marriage. The concept of "community debt" has no relevance to creditors' rights issues. It <u>does</u> have meaning for purposes of reimbursement, however. So, if community property is levied upon to collect a spouse's premarriage debt (a "separate" debt), the community would have a prima facie claim for reimbursement. For more than a decade, Texas courts seemed disinclined to read the Family Code to determine the extent of creditors' rights. After *Cockerham*, some courts concluded that a debt incurred by one spouse during marriage was a "community debt," which to these courts meant it was a joint liability; in other words, both spouses (and all of their property) were personally liable for the contract debts of either spouse incurred during marriage. *See Wileman v. Wade*, 665 S.W.2d 519 (Tex. App.—Dallas 1983, no writ). Creditors were, of course, delighted with this turn of events; the only hitch was that this interpretation was not consistent with the Texas Family Code. In an attempt to clarify this situation, Section 3.202 of the Family Code was amended, and Section 3.201 was added. This appears to have worked. For example, *Nelson v. Citizens Bank and Trust Co.*, 881 S.W.2d 128 (Tex. App.—Houston [1st Dist.] 1994, no writ) involved a situation where a husband, but not the wife, guaranteed a debt during marriage. The creditor sued both the husband and the wife during marriage. The court correctly applied Texas law, stating that the wife would only be personally liable if the husband were acting as her agent when he signed the guarantee or if the debt was a necessity. Because the creditor could establish neither of these grounds, she was not personally liable; the creditor could attach only all joint management community property and the husband's 3.102(a) community property (as well as his non-exempt separate property).

Patel v. Kuciemba

Texas Court of Appeals — Corpus Christi, 2002
82 S.W.3d 589, pet. denied

Opinion by Justice AMIDEI.

This is an appeal from an adverse jury verdict and judgment in a cause of action by appellees Anthony Richard Kuciemba ("Tony") and Dorothy Kuciemba ("Dorothy") against appellant Ilaben M. Patel ("Ilaben"), individually on four promissory notes.

Ilaben, as Independent Executrix of the Estate of Manubhai G. Patel ("Manu"), deceased, Kailash Patel, Manu Enterprises, Inc. and HMI Enterprises, Inc., defendants in the trial court did not appeal.

The jury found in favor of appellees on all questions. Ilaben only contests the findings in questions 6 and 7 which found Manu had apparent authority to sign the notes as Ilaben's agent, and that Ilaben ratified Manu's execution of the notes.

Factual Background

Manu owned and operated five convenience stores until March, 1997 when he was killed. In the beginning Manu leased a convenience store at 13745 Chrisman Road, Houston, Texas, for about five years until September 1990 when the owners, Tony and Emrik Nowak sold the store to DAS. DAS is a corporation owned by a general partnership consisting of Ilaben and Kailash Patel, the general partners. The purchase price balance was evidenced by a note and secured by a deed of trust lien executed by DAS. The payments were made on the deed of trust note until Manu's death. The deed of trust was posted for foreclosure. Prior to the foreclosure, DAS conveyed the real estate to Manila by a deed wherein Manila agreed to assume the existing deed of trust lien indebtedness. However, the real estate note was paid in full by DAS prior to a foreclosure sale. DAS paid Tony and Emrik Nowak the purchase money from Manila for their release of the deed of trust lien.

In addition to the real estate note discussed above there were four promissory notes signed and executed by Manu on the dates and for the amounts as follows:

1. Note # 1: October 1, 1990 $ 35,000 Plaintiffs' Exhibit # 1

2. Note # 2: November 15, 1992 60,000 Plaintiffs' Exhibit # 3

3. Note # 3: April 19, 1994 20,000 Plaintiffs' Exhibit # 4

4. Note # 4: September 1, 1996 50,000 Plaintiffs' Exhibit # 7

Manu and Ilaben were married at all relevant times but Ilaben did not sign any of the notes and did not have any knowledge that Manu had signed the notes. Tony agreed that Manu only pay interest on the notes. The interest on the notes was 12 percent. By agreement the interest payments on the notes were consolidated so that Manu made only one interest payment each month in the amount of $ 1,650 on all four notes until his death in March 1997. Ilaben continued the $ 1,650 monthly payments until December 1997. At that time, Ilaben denied the debts and wanted proof of their validity. Appellees filed suit on the notes and sought to null and void the deed from DAS to Manila on the grounds it was a fraudulent transfer.

Issues Presented

Ilaben contends in issue number one that the trial court erred in entering judgment against her because there was neither legally nor factually sufficient evidence to support the jury findings of apparent authority and ratification.

Ilaben objected to the charge on the ground there was legally and factually insufficient evidence of apparent authority and ratification to support jury questions numbers 6 and 7, and repeated such objections in her motion for new trial.

The conclusions and arguments by appellees as to evidence to support the jury findings that Manu had apparent authority to sign the notes as agent for Ilaben and our response thereto are as follows:

1. The fact that Manu and Ilaben were married. We disagree. As a matter of law, this cannot be evidence of apparent authority because a spouse does not act as an agent for the other spouse solely because of the marriage relationship. *See Nelson v. Citizens Bank & Trust*, 881 S.W.2d 128, 131 (Tex. App.—Houston [1st Dist.] 1994, no writ); *Carr v. Houston Bus. Forms, Inc.*, 794 S.W.2d 849, 852 (Tex. App.—Houston [14th Dist.] 1990, no writ). At the time the four notes were made, appellees were charged with knowledge that the marital relationship alone is insufficient evidence that a spouse acts as agent for the other spouse because section 4.031(c) [now section 3.201(c)] of the Texas Family Code specifically provided that a spouse does not act as an agent for the other spouse solely because of the marriage relationship. TEX. FAM. CODE ANN. §3.201(c). The case *Cockerham v. Cockerham*, 527 S.W.2d 162 (Tex. 1975), cited by appellees to support the findings of agency and ratification, is distinguishable because in that case the husband and wife were both clearly active in the wife's dress shop, whereas in this case Ilaben did not have an actual involvement in Manu's businesses other than operating two of the convenience stores which did not include decisions or knowledge of Manu's business borrowing. Also, *Cockerham* was decided prior to the enactment of section 4.031(a) [now section 3.201(a)(1)] of the Texas Family Code which provided as follows:

A person is personally liable for the acts of the person's spouse only if:

(1) the spouse acts as the agent for the person;....

TEX. FAM. CODE ANN. §3.201(a)(1).

Other cases have distinguished *Cockerham* in a similar fashion before and after section 4.031(a) was enacted in 1987; Nelson, 881 S.W.2d at 131; *Pope Photo Records, Inc. v. Malone*, 539 S.W.2d 224, 227 (Tex. Civ. App.—Amarillo 1976, no writ).

2. The two checks on the Patels' joint account used to secure two of the notes. We disagree. The checks were signed by Manu but were not signed by Ilaben; the checks were never cashed; and there was no proof that Ilaben had any knowledge of the checks. Apparent authority in Texas is based on estoppel. *Ames v. Great S. Bank*, 672 S.W.2d 447, 450 (Tex. 1984). "It may arise either from a principal knowingly permitting an agent to hold himself out as having authority or by a principal's actions which lack such ordinary care as to clothe an agent with the indicia of authority, thus leading a reasonably prudent person to believe that the agent has the authority he purports to exercise." *Id*. "A prerequisite to a proper finding of apparent authority is evidence of conduct by the principal relied upon by the party asserting the estoppel defense which would lead a reasonably prudent person to believe an agent had authority to so act." *Id*. There was no evidence that

Ilaben intentionally and knowingly permitted Manu to use the two checks as he did, or by any want of due care by Ilaben which led Tony to believe Manu had authority to sign the checks as her agent. A reasonably prudent person would not have believed Manu had authority to act as Ilaben's agent as claimed merely because checks with both Manu's and Ilaben's names were printed thereon when Ilaben had not signed the checks. Manu's conduct in using the checks as he did is not evidence of apparent authority to act as Ilaben's agent. "A court may consider only the conduct of the principal leading a third party to believe the agent has authority in determining whether an agent has apparent authority." *Sociedad De Solaridad Social "El Estillero" v. J. S. McManus Produce Co.*, 964 S.W.2d 332, 334 (Tex. App.—Corpus Christi 1998, no pet.). The two checks cannot be evidence to support jury question number six regarding apparent authority.

4. The statement by Manu to Tony not to worry about the money he loaned to Manu because if anything happened to him, then Ilaben would repay all of the loans with his life insurance proceeds. We disagree. The statement was made by Manu, not Ilaben, and cannot be evidence of apparent authority of Manu to sign the notes in question as Ilaben's agent. *See Ames*, 672 S.W.2d at 450. Even if Manu made the statement, he could not bind Ilaben because any insurance proceeds the wife receives at her husband's death are her separate property not subject to her husband's debts unless the proceeds have been assigned as collateral security therefor. *Pope Photo Records*, 539 S.W.2d at 226. There is nothing in the record showing that the proceeds of a life insurance policy on Manu's life was assigned either as collateral security of the note in question, or otherwise assigned to the appellees. To the contrary, Tony believed Ilaben would first receive the insurance proceeds from the insurance company, and then pay him out of the proceeds. No mention was made of an assignment.

12. Tony demanded payment of the principal for all four notes from Ilaben so she knew what she was ratifying by paying the interest. We disagree. During the time interest payments were made after Manu's death, appellees did not prove Ilaben had full knowledge of all the material facts concerning the four loans, and the checks paying the interest were from Manu Enterprises, a corporation which is a part of Manu's estate, and Manu's estate. Ilaben was independent executrix of Manu's estate and properly could make payments for the estate, but she was not personally linked to the four notes by the payments of interest. *Frazier v. Wynn*, 472 S.W.2d 750, 753 (Tex. 1971). The cash payments were made to Tony when he would show up at a store where Ilaben was working until she told him to stop. The source of the cash which was paid was not proven.

13. Ilaben retained the benefits of the loans through the inventory and equipment the money purchased as well as the continued recycling of the money for her check cashing business (an implied ratification). We disagree. Appellees did not prove any remaining benefits such as inventory, equipment, and money for cashing checks from the loans in question. Manu used the borrowed money for a number of years before he died. The bookkeeper testified the name Kuciemba did not appear in the Patel records. Even if there were benefits from the loans when made, there was nothing to give Ilaben notice she was retaining any benefits from the loans, or that she had full knowledge of all the material facts. Id. Before she could be held to have voluntarily assented to the loans, the Kuciembas were required to prove Ilaben knew the terms of the notes. *Taylor v. Gilbert Gertner Enters*, 466 S.W.2d 337, 340 (Tex. Civ. App.—Houston [1st Dist.] 1971, writ ref'd n.r.e.).

The trial court erred in submitting jury questions 6 and 7, and in rendering judgment against Ilaben, individually, based on the jury's answers thereto because there was no evidence that Manu acted as Ilaben's agent in executing the promissory notes under apparent authority or that Ilaben ratified the promissory notes.

The trial court judgment: (1) against Ilaben, individually, is reversed and judgment is rendered that appellees take nothing against Ilaben, individually.

Inwood National Bank of Dallas v. Hoppe

Texas Court of Appeals — Texarkana, 1980
596 S.W.2d 183, writ ref'd n.r.e.

HUTCHINSON, Justice.

Inwood National Bank of Dallas, appellant, by this suit against Patricia Hoppe, appellee, seeks to recover the unpaid balance of the principal, accrued interest and attorney fees as provided for in a certain promissory note executed by her former husband and his business partner. The trial court sustained appellee's exceptions to appellant's Third Amended Original Petition and granted her Plea in Abatement and Bar and assessed the costs against the appellant.

From the record here it appears that on September 29, 1972, Robert Hoppe, then husband of appellee, and his business partner obtained a loan from appellant. No security was given to secure the loan, but Hoppe and his business partner personally guaranteed the payment of the loan note and submitted their personal financial statements. Hoppe's statement listed community property of himself and appellee. Payment of the original note evidencing the loan became due on March 29, 1973, and a renewal note was executed. This renewal note was due on June 29, 1973. Neither of the notes was executed by appellee. The Hoppes' suit for divorce was heard on June 18, 1973, and the formal judgment of divorce was signed and entered on July 13, 1973. The division of the community property as agreed upon by the Hoppes was approved by the court and reflected in the entered judgment. The note payable to appellant was to be discharged by Mr. Hoppe. In 1974, Mr. Hoppe was adjudged to be bankrupt and was discharged from any further liability on the note payable to appellant. Appellant participated in the bankruptcy proceeding as a creditor and received a partial payment on the note. This suit was instituted on November 14, 1975. Neither the original petition nor the first two amended petitions made reference to the renewal note of March 29, 1973. The first allegation of its execution was made in the Third Amended Original Petition filed September 15, 1978. Appellee's special exceptions and plea in abatement and bar were sustained on October 13, 1978.

Appellant alleged that the debt sued upon was a community debt of appellee and her former husband. Appellee does not challenge appellant's allegation that the original note was executed during her marriage to Robert Hoppe. However, Mrs. Hoppe did not sign the note. Being contracted for during marriage, the debt evidenced by the note is presumed to be upon the credit of the community and therefore a community debt. *Cockerham v. Cockerham*, 527 S.W.2d 162 (Tex. 1975). Even though the court in granting the divorce and making a division of the community property ordered Mr. Hoppe to pay the community debts, such order could have no legal effect whatsoever upon the rights of appellant. *Broadway Drug Store of Galveston v. Trowbridge*, 435 S.W.2d 268 (Tex. Civ. App. — Houston [14th Dist.] 1968, no writ); *Swinford v. Allied Finance Company of Casa View*, 424 S.W.2d 298 (Tex. Civ. App. — Dallas 1968, writ dism'd), cert. denied, 393 U.S. 923, 89 S.Ct. 253, 21 L.Ed.2d 259 (1968). Appellant, as a creditor of the community, had the right to resort to the entire non-exempt community property, and this right was in no way affected by the divorce decree. *First National Bank of Brownwood v. Hickman*, 89 S.W.2d 838 (Tex. Civ. App. — Austin 1935, writ ref'd). Appellant's petition alleged a sustainable cause of action.

The question next to be considered is whether or not this cause of action is barred by reason of the discharge in bankruptcy of appellee's former husband. This question has heretofore been answered by the case of *Swinford v. Allied Finance Company of Casa View, supra*. The discharge in bankruptcy of appellee's former husband did not have the effect of canceling or releasing her joint liability for a community debt to the extent of the community property set aside to her by the divorce decree. Appellee was not a party to the bankruptcy proceeding and that portion of the community estate awarded to her by the divorce judgment was not subject to such proceeding. In order for the community creditors to have reached the former community property awarded to her by the divorce judgment, appellee would have to have been made a party to the bankruptcy proceeding or, as here, be sued in her individual capacity.

The trial court erred in sustaining all of the exceptions to appellant's pleading and in granting the plea in abatement and bar. The cause is therefore reversed and remanded to the trial court.

DISCUSSION

Another related issue regarding creditors' rights is the effect of divorce. Obviously, divorce can have no effect on the personal liability of each spouse for debts incurred during marriage. So, for example, if both spouses signed a note during marriage, even if the divorce court orders one spouse to pay the note, the creditor may sue the other spouse after divorce for nonpayment.

However, divorce might have a more subtle effect. Divorce ostensibly changes community property into the separate property of each spouse. Does this affect creditors' rights? To answer this question, one needs to be aware of certain somewhat recent changes in Article XVI, Section 15 of the Texas Constitution. For example, the prior version stated that spouses could partition community property into separate property without prejudice to preexisting creditors. The current version states that the spouses may do this without the intention to defraud preexisting creditors. Cases construing the prior version of the Texas Constitution generally agree with *Hoppe* that the creditor of one spouse may pursue after divorce property placed in the hands of the other by the divorce court, if the creditor could have attached this property before divorce. Would the new version of Article XVI, Section 15 dictate a different result? See Professor Paulsen's comments in 1994 Texas Bar Advanced Family Law Course, Chapter G. In *Mock v. Mock*, 216 S.W.3d 370 (Tex. App.—Eastland 2006, pet. denied.), the court infers that the holding in *Hoppe* remains unchanged.

Pope Photo Records v. Malone

Texas Court of Appeals—Amarillo, 1976
539 S.W.2d 224, no writ

REYNOLDS, Justice.

A creditor sought to recover the balance of a debt incurred by a deceased husband from the lump sum proceeds of his life insurance received by his surviving widow. The trial court denied recovery. The insurance proceeds became the widow's separate property not shown to be subject to the debt. Affirmed.

When James Pat Malone died on 20 November 1973, eight insurance policies, the beneficiaries of which he had the contractual right to change, were in force on his life. He had gratuitously named his wife, Roberta E. Malone, as the beneficiary of each policy. One of them was issued prior to their marriage and none of its premiums was paid with community funds. The remaining seven policies were issued during the marriage and Mrs. Malone was named the beneficiary at the time each was issued. Six of the seven policies were issued prior to 1 January 1970 and all premiums on them were paid monthly or annually with community funds. The remaining policy was issued on 1 May 1971 in the face amount of $25,000 as an incident to Malone's employment on that date as president of the First National Bank in Hereford, Texas. The bank paid the monthly premium after deducting $15 per month from Malone's salary to apply toward the premium. The proceeds from the eight policies were paid to Mrs. Malone in lump sums aggregating $83,458.27.

Mrs. Malone qualified as the independent executrix of Malone's estate. She filed an inventory and appraisement omitting the insurance proceeds and reflecting that the community debts and claims against the estate exceeded the assets.

During his lifetime on 27 March 1970, James Pat Malone executed, and thereafter made two payments on, his interest bearing promissory note in the principle sum of $9,000 payable on demand to the order of National Litho & Printing Company. The note was transferred and assigned to Pope Photo Records, Inc. Following Malone's death, the balance due on the note was reduced to a judgment against, and a claim was made on, his estate. One payment was made on the debt from the estate assets and, after the assets were exhausted without payment of the debt in full, Pope Photo Records, Inc., proceeded against Roberta E. Malone individually. The suit, from which this appeal stems, sought the recovery of $4,416.73 as the principal due on the debt, together with interest and reasonable attorney's fees.

There was a bench trial. In addition to the development of the foregoing facts, there was testimony by the president of National Litho & Printing Company and sole owner of the stock of Pope Photo Records, Inc., that he made a loan to Malone in order for Malone to pay a bank note placed for collection, and that he had never talked with Mrs. Malone about the existence of the debt. After Malone's death, he referred the note to his attorney to get in touch with Mrs. Malone, who testified that she did not know about the debt until after her husband's death. Mrs. Malone conceded that the community estate was insolvent at the date of her husband's death, but she did not know when it first became insolvent. There was and is no contention that the estate was insolvent on 27 March 1970, the date of the debt, or on 1 May 1971, the date of the latest insurance policy naming Mrs. Malone as the beneficiary. At the conclusion of the trial, the court, later making and filing findings of fact and conclusions of law, rendered a take-nothing judgment from which Pope Photo Records, Inc., has appealed.

Pope initially contends the trial court erred in legally concluding that the insurance proceeds received by Mrs. Malone are not subject to its debt. It should be observed that presently in Texas when a husband insures his life with community funds, the right to receive the future insurance proceeds is community property in the nature of a chose in action maturing at the death of the husband. Consequently, the matured proceeds are community in character, "except where the named beneficiary is in fact surviving in which case a gift of the policy rights of such beneficiary is presumed to have been intended and completed by the death of the insured." *Brown v. Lee*, 371 S.W.2d 694, 696 (Tex. 1963). The corollary is that by naming the wife the beneficiary, the husband manifests the intent to make a gift to her. Huie, *Community Property Laws as Applied to Life Insurance*, 17 Tex. L. Rev. 121, 123–24 (1939). Long standing is the coexisting rule that the insurance proceeds she receives at her husband's death are her separate property not subject to the husband's debts unless the proceeds have been assigned as collateral security therefor.

San Jacinto Bldg., Inc. v. Brown, 79 S.W.2d 164, 166 (Tex. Civ. App.—Beaumont 1935, writ ref'd).

From these principles Pope argues that because the gratuitous gift of the insurance proceeds to Mrs. Malone was not completed until Malone's death when the community estate was insufficient to pay the existing debts, the intended gift was voided by Sec. 24.03 of the Texas Business and Commerce Code (1968). Because that statute, as material here, does void a gratuitous transfer of property as to an existing creditor unless at the time of the transfer the debtor has enough property in this state subject to execution to pay all of his existing debts, the argumentative inference is that the insurance proceeds retained their community character, making them liable for the debt.

After an in-depth consideration, the very same argument, made under circumstances strikingly similar to those we review and also in reliance on the "gift ... is ... completed by the death of the insured" language in *Brown v. Lee, supra*, was rejected in *Parker Square State Bank v. Huttash*, 484 S.W.2d 429 (Tex. Civ. App.—Fort Worth 1972, writ ref'd n.r.e.). The holding indispensable to the rejection was that the controlling date of the transfer meant in V.T.C.A., Bus. & C. Sec. 24.03, was the date the beneficiary was designated. In context, the holding is not, as Pope asserts that it is, in direct conflict with the *Brown v. Lee, supra*, language that the gift is "completed by the death of the insured." At least, the Supreme Court, after reviewing the *Huttash* opinion quoting that language from *Brown v. Lee, supra*, in connection with its consideration of the application for writ of error, did not reverse *Huttash* as it was authorized to do by Rule 483, Texas Rules of Civil Procedure, if the holding were in conflict with the *Brown v. Lee, supra*, decision. *See e.g.,* Calvert, *Application for Writ of Error, Appellate Procedure in Texas*, Sec. 22.9. Thus, applied here in the absence of any contention that the Malones' community estate was insolvent on or before the last date Mrs. Malone was designated a beneficiary, the *Huttash* holding negates the applicability of V.T.C.A., Bus. & C. Sec. 24.03, to void the gift to Mrs. Malone.

Next, Pope seeks to neutralize the trial court's factual finding that Malone became insolvent on or about 1 November 1973, but presents no point of error that insolvency on an earlier date was established conclusively or as a matter of law. The neutralization is sought as a predicate for an attack on the court's legal conclusion that no portion of the insurance proceeds is subject to Pope's debt even though a portion of the premiums was paid when Malone was insolvent. The two-prong challenge is viable only if Texas law permits the claimed right of recovery from the proportional part of the proceeds generated by premiums paid from the community when it was insolvent. The challenge is unavailing because it has been settled, again under circumstances similar to those in the case at bar, that Texas law does not sanction such recovery absent fraud in the formation of the insurance contract which is not alleged here. *San Jacinto Bldg., Inc. v. Brown, supra*, at 166–67. The only Texas case which Pope cites for its proposition is *Red River Nat. Bank v. De Berry*, 47 Tex. 96, 105 S.W. 998 (1907), where that holding is clearly based on a specifically pleaded Arkansas statute exempting from the claims of the husband's creditors only the insurance purchased by premiums not exceeding a set amount annually. The opinion in *San Jacinto Bldg., Inc. v. Brown, supra*, in discussing *De Berry* and stating that it actually is authority for the conclusion reached in *San Jacinto Bldg., Inc. v. Brown, supra*, that Texas law does not allow the husband's creditors to recover from the widow's insurance proceeds attributable to premiums paid during insolvency, points out that there is no like statute in Texas limiting or regulating in any manner the amount one may expend on premiums or that would render such payments transfers of property in fraud of creditors.

Finally, Pope assigns error to the denial of judgment on its theory that its debt is a jointly incurred community debt to which Mrs. Malone's separate property is subject. The Sec. 5.61(a) provision of the Texas Family Code (1975) is that a spouse's separate property is not subject to liabilities of the other spouse unless both spouses are liable by other rules of law. To escape the efficacy of the proviso, Pope proposes the application of the rule of *Cockerham v. Cockerham*, 527 S.W.2d 162 (Tex. 1975).

In *Cockerham*, a divorce case, the court subjected the husband's separate property to the debts incurred by the wife in her operation of her business during the marriage when the court found that the husband had impliedly, and to some extent expressly, consented to the establishment of the debts as joint liabilities. There, among other circumstances, the husband advanced the wife the necessary capital for the business inventory, the wife wrote checks on the husband's bank account to pay for merchandise, at least on one occasion the husband wrote a check to pay the operational expenses, and the husband borrowed money to pay some of the business debts which he recognized as his obligations.

But the facts of *Cockerham* are readily distinguishable from the facts before us, and the Supreme Court made it clear in *Cockerham* that an examination of the totality of the circumstances giving rise to the debt is necessary to determine joint liability. Here, Malone incurred the debt at issue to pay his prior bank note. The use made of the money represented by the bank note is merely speculated. It is undisputed that Mrs. Malone did not know of the debt until after her husband's death more than three and one-half years later. The totality of these circumstances, without more, is insufficient to remove the insulation installed by V.T.C.A., Family Code Sec. 5.61(a), to protect Mrs. Malone's separate property from the debt incurred by her husband.

Each facet of Pope's points of error has been considered whether specifically mentioned or not. None of the points presents reversible error.

The judgment is affirmed.

Mock v. Mock

Texas Court of Appeals—Eastland, 2006
216 S.W.3d 370, pet. denied

This appeal arises from a divorce proceeding. Martha Davis Mock raises two points of error. In the second point, appellant argues that the trial court erred in ordering her to pay credit card debts that appellee incurred in his name. We affirm.

Credit Card Debt

In her second point, appellant complains that the trial court erred in ordering her to pay credit card debts that were solely in appellee's name. The evidence showed that, during the marriage, appellee acquired several credit cards solely in his name. Appellant said that she did not sign any contracts relating to appellee's credit cards. Appellee had credit card debt of about $32,000 when he and appellant separated; and, by the time of trial, appellee's credit card debt had risen to about $55,000. The trial court ordered appellant to pay $26,204 in credit card debts and loans that appellee incurred in his name.

Appellant relies on Section 3.201 of the Family Code in arguing that the trial court erred in ordering her to pay appellee's credit card debts. *See* TEX. FAM. CODE ANN. § 3.201 (Vernon 1998). Section 3.201 limits spousal liability for debts incurred during the marriage. However, appellant's argument fails to recognize the distinction between community liability for a debt and personal liability for a debt. *See Cockerham*, 527 S.W.2d at 171.[4] If a spouse is not personally liable for a debt, the creditor may not reach that spouse's separate property to satisfy the debt. TEX. FAM. CODE ANN. §§ 3.201–.202 (Vernon 1998). Unless it is shown that the creditor agreed to look solely to the separate estate of the contracting spouse for satisfaction, Section 3.201 has no effect on the long-standing presumption that debts contracted during the marriage are presumed to be on the credit of the community and, thus, are joint community obligations. *See Cockerham*, 527 S.W.2d at 171; *Kimsey v. Kimsey*, 965 S.W.2d 690, 702 (Tex. App.—El Paso 1998, pet. denied).

Appellant does not dispute that appellee incurred the debts at issue during the marriage. Therefore, the debts are presumptively community obligations. While the trial court ordered appellant to pay some of appellee's credit card debts, the trial court also awarded community property to appellant. Section 3.202(c) of the Family Code provides that "community property subject to a spouse's sole or joint management, control, and disposition is subject to the liabilities incurred by the spouse before or during marriage." Thus, community property that was under appellee's sole or joint management during the marriage may be reached to satisfy debts incurred solely by appellee. Section 3.202; *see also Anderson v. Royce*, 624 S.W.2d 621, 623 (Tex. App.—Houston [14th Dist.] 1981, writ ref'd n.r.e.). Section 3.102 of the Family Code defines sole management and joint management community property. TEX. FAM. CODE ANN. § 3.102 (Vernon 1998). The record does not demonstrate that the community property awarded to appellant did not include property subject to appellee's sole management or joint management during the marriage. Therefore, we find that the trial court did not err in ordering appellant to pay debts that were solely in appellee's name. We overrule appellant's second point.

This Court's Ruling

We affirm the judgment of the trial court.

Broday v. United States
United States Court of Appeals
Fifth Circuit, 1972
455 F.2d 1097

RONEY, Circuit Judge.

Frank Broday married his present wife, Billie Shipman Broday, on June 7, 1966. As of that date, Billie Shipman was liable for income taxes assessed against her and her former husband, Joe Shipman (now deceased), for the taxable year 1962. In an effort to collect this tax, the District Director of Internal Revenue levied upon a checking account which held funds received as dividend income from Mr. Broday's separate property. Mr. Broday paid his wife's income tax liability and then filed a claim for refund on the ground that there was a wrongful levy upon the bank account. Holding that under Texas community property law the wife possessed a property right in the dividend income from the separate property of her husband, which property right is subject to a federal tax lien for

---

4. Appellant cites a number of cases in which creditors attempted to collect debts. These cases did not involve the division of community liabilities upon divorce, and, therefore, the cases do not apply.

prenuptial income taxes of the wife, we must reverse the decision of the lower court which awarded a refund to Mr. Broday.

The basic issue involved in this appeal is whether, under Texas property law, the community property bank account of which the husband had sole right to management and control is subject to levy for a federal tax debt of the wife incurred prior to marriage. The government is entitled to a lien for the tax plus interest upon all of the wife's "property and right to property."[1] The question of whether and to what extent the wife has property and right to property is determined under the applicable state law. *Aquilino v. United States*, 363 U.S. 509, 512–513, 80 S.Ct. 1277, 4 L.Ed.2d 1365 (1960); *Morgan v. Commissioner of Internal Revenue*, 309 U.S. 78, 82, 60 S.Ct. 424, 84 L.Ed. 585 (1940). However, once it has been determined under state law that the taxpayer owns property or rights to property, federal law is controlling for the purpose of determining whether a lien will attach to such property or rights to property. *United States v. Bess*, 357 U.S. 51, 56–57, 78 S.Ct. 1054, 2 L.Ed.2d 1135 (1958).

There is no question that the bank account upon which the government levied constituted community property of Mr. and Mrs. Broday under Texas law. This point is made clear by the decision of this Court in *Commissioner of Internal Revenue v. Chase Manhattan Bank*, 259 F.2d 231, 239 (5th Cir. 1958), cert. den., 359 U.S. 913, 79 S.Ct. 589, 3 L.Ed.2d 575 (1959), in which we said: "All property accumulated during marriage is community property, unless it is received by gift, devise, or inheritance. In Texas even income derived from separate property belongs to the community, including interest and dividends from separately owned securities."

See Warren v. Schawe, 163 S.W.2d 415 (Tex. Civ. App.—Austin 1942, writ ref'd). As community property, Mrs. Broday had a present vested interest therein equal and equivalent to that of her husband.

The taxpayer contends that article 4620 of Vernon's Texas Civil Statutes Annotated, as amended by Acts of 1967, 60th Legislature, p. 738, ch. 309, Section 1,[2] which by its terms would operate to exempt the particular community property here in issue from the antenuptial debts of Mrs. Broday, is effective to prevent attachment of a federal tax lien on her vested present interest in such property. Taxpayer concedes that mere state exemption statutes are ineffective against a statutory lien of the federal government for federal taxes. *United States v. Hoper*, 242 F.2d 468 (7th Cir. 1957). However, he argues that article 4620 gives a property right in the husband which transcends the federal tax law.

---

1. Section 6321 of the Internal Revenue Code of 1954.
Lien for taxes
If any person liable to pay any tax neglects or refuses to pay the same after demand, the amount (including any interest, additional amount, addition to tax, or assessable penalty, together with any costs that may accrue in addition thereto) shall be a lien in favor of the United States upon all property and rights to property, whether real or personal, belonging to such person.
2. The community property subject to sole or joint management, control and disposition to a spouse shall be subject to the liabilities of that spouse incurred before or during marriage. The community property subject to the sole management, control and disposition of a spouse shall not be subject to any liabilities of the other spouse incurred before marriage or nontortious liabilities incurred by the other spouse during marriage unless both spouses are liable by other rules of law. All the spouses' community property is subject to liability for all torts committed by either spouse during marriage.
Effective Jan. 1, 1970, article 4630 was repealed by Acts of 1969, p. 2707, ch. 888, 6. However, similar language now appears in the new Texas Family Code, ch. 5.

When the district court granted the taxpayer summary judgment in this case, it did not have the advantage of the *United States v. Mitchell*, 403 U.S. 190, 91 S.Ct. 1763, 29 L.Ed.2d 406 (1971), in which the Supreme Court by unanimous decision reversed the decisions of this Court in *Mitchell v. Commissioner of Internal Revenue*. 430 F.2d 1 (5th Cir. 1970) and *Angello v. Metropolitan Life Ins. Co.*, 430 F.2d 7 (5th Cir. 1970). This Supreme Court decision controls the instant case. Indeed, it is pointed out in the government's brief that the taxpayer's brief in support of his motion for summary judgment before the trial court relied upon this Court's decisions in *Mitchell, Angello* and *Ramos v. Commissioner of Internal Revenue*, 429 F.2d 487 (5th Cir. 1970) as presenting the identical issue as the case at bar, and argued that those decisions were controlling. The decision in *Ramos* was based upon the *Mitchell* and *Angello* cases, and therefore was effectively overruled by the Supreme Court in *Mitchell*. Although those cases involved Louisiana community property law, while this case involves Texas law, it was properly conceded below by the taxpayer that the law of Texas is identical to the law of Louisiana as to whether the community fund is liable for the wife's separate debts incurred before marriage.

In *Mitchell*, the Supreme Court held that under the laws of Louisiana a married woman has a present vested interest in community property equal to that of her husband and therefore is personally liable for federal income taxes on her one-half share of the community income, notwithstanding her subsequent election under state law to renounce all of her rights in the community. The Court rejected the contention that the taxpayers involved should not be personally liable for community debts because under Louisiana law their husbands had complete control over the community property.

Since a married woman in Louisiana or Texas has a vested interest in, and is the owner of a half share of the community income sufficient to require her to pay income taxes thereon, it follows a fortiori that she has "property" or "rights to property" to which a federal tax lien would attach under Section 6321 of the Code.

We think that the taxpayer must fail in his argument that article 4620 of Vernon's Texas Civil Statutes should be characterized in a different manner than an exemption statute. The Ninth Circuit cases of *United States v. Overman*, 424 F.2d 1142 (9th Cir. 1970) (relating to the law of the State of Washington) and *In re Ackerman*, 424 F.2d 1148 (9th Cir. 1970) (relating to the law of Arizona), which held against the taxpayer in cases similar to this one, were specifically approved in the opinion of the Supreme Court in *Mitchell*. In *Overman* the taxpayer advanced the argument that the state statute in issue was not merely an exemption statute but instead was one which defined property rights and therefore was controlling. In rejecting this argument, the Court noted "all that Section 6321 requires is that the interest be 'property' or 'rights to property.' It is of no statutory moment how extensive may be those rights under state law, or what restrictions exist on the enjoyment of those rights." 424 F.2d at 1145. It appears clear from the decision in *Mitchell* that the right of the United States to enforce its liens does not depend upon state laws which regulate the rights of creditors generally and does not depend upon whether the "exemption" label is attached to the particular statute in question.

The only cases cited by the taxpayer in his brief in support of his position are *Bice v. Campbell*, 231 F.Supp. 948 (N.D. Tex. 1964) and *Mulcahy v. United States*, 251 F.Supp. 783 (S.D. Tex. 1966). It is apparent that these decisions are now incorrect because they are fundamentally incompatible with the decisions in *Mitchell, Overman* and *Ackerman, supra*.

Reversed.

DISCUSSION

There is a "heads I win, tails you lose" aspect to litigation with the IRS. *Broday* determined that, where Texas creditors' rights law was more restrictive than federal rules, federal creditors' rights rules governed. In *Medaris v. United States*, 884 F.2d 832 (5th Cir. 1989), the husband owed taxes. The IRS sued, and the court considered how much of the husband's and wife's earnings could be attached. The District Court concluded that the IRS could only attach 50% of the earnings of each, in light of the wife's interest in each. The Fifth Circuit reversed, and concluded that the IRS could attach 50% of the wife's 3.102(a) community property (*Broday*), as well as 100% of the husband's 3.102(a) community property (as provided by Texas law). The court decided that, as to each issue, the IRS should never have less expansive rights than as provided under Texas law.

The effect of the Supremacy Clause upon Texas marital property rights will be discussed in more detail in the next chapter.

State Board of Equalization v. H.Y. Woo
California Court of Appeals, 2000
98 Cal. Rptr.2d 206

HANLON, P.J.

Doreen H.Y. Woo (appellant) appeals from an earnings withholding order for taxes. The underlying tax liability stems from delinquent sales taxes in the amount of $35,504.43 owed by James K. Ho, appellant's husband, to respondent State Board of Equalization. Appellant contends that a marital agreement she entered into with Ho transmuting the couple's community property to the separate property of each spouse precludes respondent from garnishing her wages. We affirm.

FACTUAL BACKGROUND

In 1992, respondent determined that Ho owed taxes, interest and penalties in the amount of $37,419.90, which represented the unpaid sales taxes of the Monsoon Restaurant. In September 1996, Ho filed a complaint seeking a refund of certain payments made towards that tax liability. The trial court sustained respondent's demurrer to the complaint without leave to amend and entered judgment against Ho. This court affirmed that judgment in an unpublished opinion.

In July, 1995, respondent notified appellant that it would seek an earnings withholding order against her to pay Ho's tax debt. On November 5, 1995, appellant and Ho entered into a marital agreement transmuting their future earnings to separate property. Appellant subsequently became employed by Wells Fargo Bank, earning approximately $500,000 per year.

On July 27, 1999, respondent filed an application for an earnings withholding order for taxes. In support of the order, respondent argued that the marital agreement between appellant and Ho did not bar garnishment of her wages because the agreement was fraudulent and unenforceable under Family Code section 851 and Civil Code section 3439.04. Appellant contended that the marital agreement did not constitute a fraudulent transfer because she was not employed by Wells Fargo Bank at the time the agreement was executed and that her future earnings were a mere expectancy that could not be transferred. Following a hearing, the trial court entered an earnings withholding order for taxes directing Wells Fargo Bank to withhold and pay to respondent the sum of $3,000 per month from appellant's earnings.

DISCUSSION

Civil Code section 3439.06, subdivision (d) provides that "[a] transfer is not made until the debtor has acquired rights in the asset transferred." Relying on Civil Code section 3439.06, subdivision (d), appellant contends that the marital agreement did not constitute a fraudulent transfer of community property because Ho had no property interest in her potential future earnings. This contention lacks merit.

Contrary to appellant's argument, Ho had a present interest in appellant's future earnings at the time he executed the marital agreement. It is well settled that earnings of either the husband or the wife acquired during the marriage constitute community property. (Fam. Code, § 760.) And, a spouse's respective interests "in community property during continuance of the marriage relation are present, existing, and equal interests." (Fam.Code, § 751.) Ho's interest in appellant's earnings was thus not dependent on whether she was employed at the time she executed the agreement.

Further, appellant's attempt to transmute the community property earnings to her separate property constituted a fraudulent transfer. Family Code section 851 provides that "[a] transmutation is subject to the laws governing fraudulent transfers." Civil Code section 3439.04 subdivision (a) provides that a transfer is fraudulent as to a creditor if it is made "[w]ith actual intent to hinder, delay, or defraud any creditor of the debtor." Here, appellant does not dispute that the community estate was liable for Ho's tax debt. Nor does she dispute that she entered into the marital agreement after learning that respondent intended to garnish her wages. Given these facts, the trial court did not err in rejecting appellant's argument that there was no fraudulent transfer. Ho had a present interest in appellant's earnings at the time the agreement was executed. Appellant's attempt to transmute that interest to avoid Ho's tax debt constituted a fraudulent transfer in violation of Family Code section 851 and Civil Code section 3439.04, subdivision (a).

The order is affirmed.

DISCUSSION

Calmes v. U.S., 926 F. Supp. 582 (N.D. Tex. 1996) is a somewhat similar case where a court enforced a premarital agreement that recharacterized each spouse's income as separate property. As a result, the government was not able to attach the wife's earnings to collect the husband's tax debt. Here, though, the couple signed the premarital agreement years before the tax problem arose.

Chapter Thirteen

Constitutional Limits

A. State Constitution

1. The Scope of Separate Property

Arnold v. Leonard

Supreme Court of Texas, 1925
273 S.W. 799

GREENWOOD, Justice.

[H contracted what the court calls a "community indebtedness," and his creditor obtained judgment against him. Creditor sought to levy execution on the rents and revenues from W's separate property on the ground they were community property and liable for H's debt. The trial court granted W's prayer for an injunction, based on article 4621, and the creditor appealed, contending article 4621 of the Texas Revised Statutes of 1911 was unconstitutional. It had been amended in 1917 and 1921 to provide that rents and revenues of W's separate property were also separate. The Court of Civil Appeals held that the case turned on whether the amendments to article 4621 violated the Texas Constitution. It certified the question to the Texas Supreme Court.]

Section 15 of article XVI of the Constitution declares:

> All property, both real and personal, of the wife, owned or claimed by her before marriage, and that acquired afterward by gift, devise or descent, shall be her separate property; and laws shall be passed more clearly defining the rights of the wife, in relation as well to her separate property as that held in common with her husband. Laws shall also be passed providing for the registration of the wife's separate property.

This section is found, without a single word changed, in the Constitutions of 1845, 1861, and 1866.

Prior to the adoption of the Constitution of 1845, the wife's separate property had been so defined by the act approved January 20, 1840, as to include the lands and slaves owned or claimed by the wife at the time of her marriage and the lands and slaves acquired by her during coverture by gift, devise, or descent, together with the increase of such slaves, and her paraphernalia.

It is undeniable that under the Act of 1840 all property other than that specifically defined as separate property of the wife was intended to belong to the separate estate of the husband or to become common property of the husband and wife. Such is the express provision of the Act. Section 19 of article VII of the Constitution of 1845 was essentially an enlargement of the wife's separate estate. Under the Act of 1840 all the wife's right to personal property passed to the husband, with the solitary exception of slaves and their increase. By the constitutional provision, *all* property, both real and personal, owned or claimed by the wife before marriage and that acquired by the wife afterwards by gift, devise, or descent, became her separate property. We can conceive of no sound reason for concluding that the terms of the Constitution of 1845 were not meant to furnish the sole measure of the wife's separate estate, as had the Act of 1840, with its less liberal provision for the wife. Whatever the language of Section 19 of article VII meant in the Constitution of 1845, that language has the same signification in Section 15 of article XVI of the Constitution of 1876.

The plain and obvious import of the language of the Constitution is to prescribe a test by which to determine when an acquest by the wife becomes a portion of the wife's separate estate. The test during coverture relates to the method by which the property is acquired. If the method be by gift, devise, or descent, to the wife, then the Constitution makes the property belong to the wife's separate estate. If the method of acquiring during marriage be different, then the property falls without the class of separate estate of the wife as fixed by the Constitution. We think the Supreme Court was doing no more than giving effect to the words of the Constitution when it said, through Chief Justice Willie, "But of the property which a wife may acquire during marriage, none becomes her separate estate, except such as is derived by gift, devise, or descent." *Ezell v. Dodson*, 60 Tex. 332.

We have no doubt that the people in adopting the Constitution in 1845, as in 1876, understood that it was intended to put the matter of the classes of property constituting the wife's separate estate beyond legislative control. Thereby both the wife and the husband were given constitutional guaranty of the status of all property derived by means of or through the wife.

Since rents and revenues derived from the wife's separate lands are entirely without the constitutional definition of the wife's separate property, and since the Legislature can neither enlarge nor diminish such property, it follows that the portions of the Acts of 1917 and 1921, which undertake to make rents and revenues from the wife's separate lands a part of her separate estate, are invalid.

By an Act approved March 21, 1913, it was provided that "neither the separate property of the wife nor the rents from the wife's separate real estate, nor the interest on bonds and notes belonging to her, nor dividends on stocks owned by her, nor her personal earnings shall be subject to the payment of debts contracted by the husband; and the Act committed the classes of property enumerated as exempt from payment of the husband's debts to "the control, management, and disposition of the wife alone," provided the joinder of the husband was necessary in an incumbrance or conveyance of the wife's separate lands, and in a transfer of her stocks and bonds, unless she was authorized to act alone by an order of the District Court, and provided that the husband and wife must join in a conveyance of the homestead. The Acts of 1917 and 1921 retain each and all of the above provisions of the Act of 1913.

There can be no doubt that the Act of 1913 left the rents and revenues of the wife's separate lands assets of the community estate. Nor can there be any doubt that the Act of 1913 and the subsequent acts intended to exempt rents of the wife's separate lands from payment of a community debt contracted by the husband. The provision of the Acts of 1917 and 1921, declaring the exemption, is separate and distinct from the portions of the Acts undertaking to change the ownership of rents and revenues from the wife's separate lands. Hence such provision might be operative in each Act despite failure of the purpose to make the rents separate property of the wife.

The Supreme Court of the United States upholds the validity of legislation conferring on the wife not only the right to manage but the right to dispose of community property, so long as the husband's interest attaches to the proceeds of such property.

Speaking through Chief Justice White, the Court states its conclusions as follows: The legislature could as well have provided that the wife could convey, as the husband; and if it had power to say that either could dispose of the community interest of the other, could say that neither could do so. Changing the manner of conveyance did not alter the status of ownership. It could not make the interest of either spouse in community lands greater or less.

> It is a misconception of [the community] system to suppose that because power was vested in the husband to dispose of the community acquired during marriage, as if it were his own, therefore by law the community property belonged solely to the husband. The conferring on the husband the legal agency to administer and dispose of the property involved no negation of the community, since the common ownership would attach to the result of the sale of the property.

Warburton v. White, 176 U.S. 484, 44 L.Ed. 555.

To the same effect is *Arnett v. Reade*, 220 U.S. 318, 55 L.Ed. 477, 36 L.R.A. (N.S.) 1040.

These conclusions harmonize with the conceptions, underlying the Texas decisions, that the wife's capacity to own and hold property is as complete as that of the husband; that each marital partner owns an estate in the community property equal to that of the other partner; and that statutes empowering the husband to manage the wife's separate lands and community assets make the husband essentially a trustee, accountable as such to the separate estate of the wife, or to the community. The sum of our conclusions is: the Legislature, in defining the wife's rights in and to her separate property and property held in common with her husband, could lawfully deprive the husband of the power granted him for many years to manage and control the wife's separate property and portions of the community which were derived from use of the wife's separate property or from her personal exertions, and could confide the management, control, and disposition thereof to the wife alone, and could exempt not only her separate property but said portions of the community from payment of the husband's debts. In making this grant of enlarged rights to the wife and working the corresponding diminution in rights to be exercised by the husband, the Legislature was lawfully defining the wife's rights in both her separate estate and common property, as expressly authorized by the Constitution. But, the Legislature could not divest the husband of all interest in and to property which, under the Constitution, was guaranteed either to the community or to the husband's separate estate and use the same to enlarge the wife's separate estate beyond its constitutional limits.

We, therefore, answer to the certified questions that so much of the Act of 1917 and of the Act of 1921 as undertook to declare the rents and revenues of the wife's separate realty to be her separate estate was violative of Section 15 of article XVI, and of Section 35 of article III of the Constitution, but that the provisions of said Acts, and of the prior Act of 1913, are valid, which render the rents and revenues of the wife's separate lands free from liability to forced sale for the payment of debts contracted by the husband.

Graham v. Franco

Supreme Court of Texas, 1972
488 S.W.2d 390

GREENHILL, Chief Justice.

[W was injured by the concurrent negligence of H and defendant Graham. In W's tort suit, Graham raised the imputed negligence defense. Prior to the accident, the legislature had enacted former art. 4615, Tex.Civ.Stats., now Tex. Fam. Code Sec. 3.001 (3), declaring recovery for injury, pain and suffering to be separate property. The trial court rendered judgment for defendant. The intermediate appellate court reversed, holding the statute not to be violative of the state constitution, even though a tort recovery did not arise from "gift, devise or descent."]

The basic question is the interpretation of Section 15 of article 16 of the Texas Constitution. With the key words underscored by us, it provides, "All *property*, both real and personal, of the wife, *owned* or claimed by her before marriage, and that *acquired* afterward by gift, devise or descent, shall be the separate property of the wife...."

This Court in *Arnold v. Leonard*, 114 Tex. 535, 273 S.W. 799 (1925), held unconstitutional a statute which attempted to declare as separate property the rents and revenues from the wife's separate realty. The holding of that case is so limited; and in view of the history of our community property system and laws, it was a correct decision. The language of the opinion, however, is broad. The reasoning of the court in *Arnold v. Leonard*, and of cases following it, is one of implied exclusion; *i.e.*, if property was acquired during marriage by any other means than gift, devise, or descent, it was and is necessarily community.

A much later case of this Court reverted to a test more akin to that prevailing under the Spanish and Mexican law, and several early opinions of this Court, dealing with community property. It applied an affirmative test; *i.e.*, that property is community which is acquired by the work, efforts or labor of the spouses or their agents, as income from their property, or as a gift to the community. Such property, acquired by the joint efforts of the spouses, was regarded as acquired by "onerous title" and belonged to the community. *Norris v. Vaughan*, 152 Tex. 491, 260 S.W.2d 676 (1953). Under this reasoning, it is clear that the personal injuries to the wife are not "acquired" by the efforts of the spouses and would not belong to the community. Thus in *Norris v. Vaughan*, *supra*, Justice Smith wrote for this Court that: "the principle which lies at the foundation of the whole system of community property is, that whatever is acquired by the joint efforts of the husband and wife, shall be their common property."

It is not necessary, however, to here make a decision on the correctness or applicability of *Norris v. Vaughan* and related cases and the concept of "onerous title."

[In an omitted portion of the opinion the court attempts to establish that, when the Texas constitution was adopted, a personal injury chose in action was not regarded as "property." Hence, the constitutional provision does not apply to such a right of action.]

Assuming that a chose in action arising out of a personal injury to a spouse is, or created, "property," the character of the "property" was personal to the one spouse injured at common law.

Similarly under Spanish law, an injury to the wife gave rise to rights in *her*, for her separate estate, not to the community. A recognized authority in this area, de Funiak, writes in *Principles of Community Property*, Section 81, that:

There is no question that this ["delictus" or "delict"] included the wife as a person wronged ... with the right to be made whole so nearly as was possible.... Thus, the injury to the person of a wife was compensable to her to the extent that she was wronged or dishonored by such injury.

That authority concludes that injuries to the wife were her separate right under the Spanish and Mexican law upon which our system of community property law was based.

[A]ble scholars have reasoned that the body of the wife brought into the marriage was peculiarly her own; and that if any "property" was involved in a personal injury to the wife, it was peculiarly hers. If her house, her separate property, were set afire and destroyed by a third person, the recovery should be her separate property. If an automobile were owned by the wife before marriage and was injured or destroyed, the recovery should go to repay the loss or damage to her separate property. So, the reasoning continues, if the arm of the wife is cut off, the recovery for the loss because of disfigurement and for the attendant pain and suffering should go to the wife. The reasoning is that the recovery is a replacement, in so far as practicable, and not the "acquisition" of an asset by the community estate.

In the light of the foregoing, it is our conclusion that, in adopting the provisions of Section 15 of article 16 of our constitution, the people did not intend to change the common law or the Spanish law under which Texas operated so as to make a cause of action for injuries to the wife an asset of the community. A personal injury, and the chose in action created, was not "property" at common law as then understood, and it was not property "acquired" by any community effort. If it was "property" under the common law, the Spanish law, or the Texas law, its character was separate, or personal, to the wife.

Our holding is that, independent of the statute involved, recovery for personal injuries to the body of the wife, including disfigurement and physical pain and suffering, past and future, is separate property of the wife. And, of course, a statute which provides that such recovery shall be the separate property of the wife is constitutional.

DISCUSSION

In *Arnold*, the supreme court concluded that the definition contained in article XVI, Section 15 of the Constitution was exhaustive, and could not be expanded by the legislature. Although *Arnold* was not overruled by *Graham*, in that later opinion the court certainly seemed more willing to construe the constitutional provision flexibly. If the legislature enacted a statute that classified wages received after permanent separation as the separate property of the recipient, would the statute be constitutional?

Does any policy concern support the holding of the court in *Arnold*?

In *Lack v. Lack*, 584 S.W.2d 896 (Tex. Civ. App.—Dallas 1979, writ ref'd n.r.e.), the court attempted to characterize the nature of certain death benefits payable under the City of Dallas pension plan. The decedent's first wife sought a portion of the death benefits. The benefits were payable to the "widow" of the employee. The decedent had married a second wife before he died. The court held that, since the benefits were statutory, the legislature could determine to whom they would be payable. The court concluded that the death benefits were payable to the second wife. Given *Arnold*, can this be correct?

Note that the rationale of *Arnold* casts a shadow over the ability of spouses to reclassify property. (That is, if the legislature can't reclassify property, how could spouses?) This will be discussed in a later section.

2. Property Divisible at Divorce

Before the Family Code was enacted, divorce courts could divide separate personalty, if necessary, but not separate realty. Section 3.63 (now 7.001) of the new Family Code was somewhat different from the prior property division statute, so the question arose whether the Family Code had affected the types of property that could be divided at divorce. Because of the language of the new section, it was not clear whether all separate property was now divisible, no separate property was divisible, or only separate personalty was divisible. The ambiguity has been clarified, at least for now, in *Eggemeyer* and *Cameron*.

Eggemeyer v. Eggemeyer
Supreme Court of Texas, 1977
554 S.W.2d 137

POPE, Justice.

The question presented by this appeal is whether a trial court may in a divorce decree divest one spouse of his separate realty and transfer title to the other spouse. The court of civil appeals in reversing the judgment of the trial court has ruled that Section 3.63 of the Family Code does not authorize such a divestiture of one's title to separate property. 535 S.W.2d 425. We affirm that judgment.

This trial court granted Virginia Eggemeyer a divorce from Homer Eggemeyer and named her managing conservator of their four minor children. The trial court also awarded Virginia all of the community interest in the small family farm. Homer owned as his separate property an undivided one-third interest in the farm by reason of a gift from his mother. The trial court divested him of that interest and transferred his title to Virginia. The farm was already subject to a $20,101.80 debt owing to the Federal Land Bank of Houston as well as a second lien in the amount of $5,200. In divesting title from Homer, the court created and imposed still another lien against the property in the sum of $10,000 which was ordered payable to Homer by Virginia on July 16, 1982, the date when the youngest of the four children reaches age eighteen. The trial court ordered Homer to pay one hundred dollars per child per month until each reaches eighteen. The court of civil appeals in reversing the divestiture of title followed the well-reasoned decision of *Ramirez v. Ramirez*, 524 S.W.2d 767 (Tex. Civ. App.—Corpus Christi 1975, no writ), and several previous decisions by this court.

It has long been the law that upon divorce the rents, revenues, and income from a spouse's separate property may be set aside for the support of the minor children. In support of that principle, the court of civil appeals properly cited *Hedtke v. Hedtke*, 112 Tex. 404, 248 S.W. 21 (1923); *Rice v. Rice*, 21 Tex. 58 (1858); *Fitts v. Fitts*, 14 Tex. 443 (1855), and Section 14.05(a) of the Texas Family Code. The trial court could have but did not set over the father's separate interest in the farm to the mother for the support of the children during their minority. The court of civil appeals did remand the cause to the trial court to consider such an arrangement. That arrangement would have satisfied the law's command that Homer Eggemeyer must support his minor children without divesting Homer of his title in his separate property.

Article 4639a, enacted in 1935, for the first time authorized divorce courts to inquire into the financial circumstances of the parties and to make orders for child support. Prior to this article's enactment, the Texas courts fashioned a method for enforcing the parents' legal duty to provide child support. The parents' property, whether community or separate, was subjected to a trust or some other form of interim management to insure the payment of child support. *Cunningham v. Cunningham*, 120 Tex. 491, 40 S.W.2d 46 (1931); *Fitts v. Fitts, supra*. When the duty of support to the minor was fulfilled, the property was freed from the trust. This method did not divest nor transfer to another person the owner's fee title.

Virginia Eggemeyer states that Section 3.63 of the Family Code authorizes the divestiture of Homer's separate realty and its vesting in her because the trial court can make such an order when it is "just and right." The statute is, of course, wholly silent about that matter. The argument is that the earlier article 4638 specifically prohibited the divestiture of title[1] where as the Family Code does not.[2] From this omission, she argues the legislature intended to change the law and to authorize a divestiture. This is not a correct result for several reasons.

The legislative commentary which accompanied the section when it was being considered by the legislature stated: "This is a codification of present law." McKnight, *Commentary on Sec. 3.63*, 5 Tex. Tech. L. Rev. 337 (1974). The legislature believed it was making no change but was carrying forward the law as it then existed.

Section 14.05(a) of the Family Code supplies additional evidence of the legislature's intent to keep the law unchanged and as it was under article 4638. In construing Section 3.63, Section 14.05(a) has apparently escaped the consideration of the parties. As appears from the section's second sentence, Section 14.05(a) carried forward into the Family Code what was well established by judicial precedent:

Sec. 14.05. Support of Child

> (a) The court may order either or both parents to make periodic payments ora lump-sum payment, or both, for the support of the child until he is 18years of age in the manner and to the persons specified by the court in the decree. In addition, the court may order a parent obligated to support a child to set aside property to be administered for the support of the child in the manner and by the persons specified by the court in the decree.

The legislature expressly authorized the setting aside of property "to be administered," not divested, and "for the support of the child," but not for the support of a spouse. That was a codification of existing law. Section 3.63 does not expressly authorize the divestiture of separate realty, but Section 14.05 does expressly authorize an interim administration of a spouse's property to assure the payment of child support. The reasonable conclusion is the legislature in enacting Section 14.05 was codifying existing law.

Other evidence of legislative intent is derived from that part of Section 3.63 which declares a divorce decree shall order "a division of the estate of the parties in a manner that the court deems just and right." The only "estate of the parties" is community property. Under former article 4638, we construed "the estate of the parties" to mean community property. *Reardon v. Reardon*, 359 S.W.2d 329 (Tex. 1962); *Hailey v. Hailey*, 160 Tex. 372, 331 S.W.2d 299 (1960); *Mansfield v. Mansfield*, 308 S.W.2d 80 (Tex. Civ. App.—El Paso

---

1. Article 4638. [4634] [2864] Division of property. The court pronouncing a decree of divorce shall also decree and order a division of the estate of the parties in such a way as the court shall deem just and right, having due regard to the rights of each party and their children, if any. Nothing herein shall be construed to compel either party to divest himself or herself of the title to real estate. [P.D. 3452.]

2. Section 3.63: "In a decree of divorce or annulment the court shall order a division of the estate of the parties in a manner that the court deems just and right, having due regard for the rights of each party and any children of the marriage."

1958, writ dism'd). The community estate may logically be the subject of "a division." The statute does not authorize a division of the "estates" of the parties. McKnight, *Commentary on Sec. 3.63*, 5 Tex. Tech. L. Rev. 338 (1974).

A constitutional problem also arises from the trial court's decree that the husband's separate property shall become the separate property of the divorced wife. The nature of property is fixed by the Texas Constitution, and not by what is "just and right." Culpability may, despite no-fault divorce, be a basis for the dissolution of the marriage, but it is no basis for a redefinition of property at variance with the Texas Constitution. Section 15, article XVI of the Texas Constitution declares that a wife's property, owned or claimed by her before marriage, and that acquired afterward by gift, devise or descent shall be the separate property of the wife.[3] By reason of legislation, the husband's property is classified the same way.[4] If one spouse's separate property may by a divorce decree be changed from the separate property of the one spouse into the separate property of the other, there is a type of separate property which is not embraced within the constitutional definition of the term. This question has never been confronted by this court, and as Professor McKnight has written: "Thus a constitutional issue that has never been raised needs resolution." McKnight, *Matrimonial Property*, 27 Sw. L. J. 37, 38 (1973).

This court held in *Arnold v. Leonard*, 114 Tex. 535, 273 S.W. 799 (1925), and again in *Graham v. Franco*, 488 S.W.2d 390, 392 (Tex. 1972), that the constitutional definition of separate property was intended to be exclusive and that it may not be altered or enlarged by an act of the legislature. This court has also held that the legislature cannot transform one type of constitutionally defined property into another type of property. *Williams v. McKnight*, 402 S.W.2d 505 (Tex. 1966). We said in *Hilley v. Hilley*, 161 Tex. 569, 342 S.W.2d 565, 567–68 (1961):

> All marital property is thus either separate or community. If acquired before marriage by any method, or after marriage by gift, devise or descent, it is separate; otherwise, it is community.... Property purchased with separate funds is separate ... and community property partitioned in the manner provided in articles 4624a and 881a-23, becomes separate property.

There is another constitutional problem. The protection of one's right to own property is said to be one of the most important purposes of government. That right has been described as fundamental, natural, inherent, inalienable, not derived from the legislature and as preexisting even constitutions. *Pennsylvania Coal Co. v. Mahon*, 260 U.S. 393, 43 S.Ct. 158, 67 L.Ed. 322 (1922); 28 A.L.R. 1321 (1924); 16 Am.Jur.2d, *Constitutional Law*, 362 (1964). Article I, Section 19, of the Texas Constitution[5] explains that no citizen of this state shall be deprived of his property except by the due course of the law of the land. The due course that protects citizens requires not only procedural but also substantive due course. See Interpretive Commentary after Section 19, art. I, Tex. Const., p.

---

3. "All property, both real and personal, of the wife, owned or claimed by her before marriage, and that acquired afterward by gift, devise or descent, shall be the separate property of the wife."

4. Section 5.01. Marital Property Characterized. (a) A spouse's separate property consists of: (1) the property owned or claimed by the spouse before marriage; (2) the property acquired by the spouse during marriage by gift, devise, or descent; and (3) the recovery for personal injuries sustained by the spouse during marriage, except any recovery for loss of earning capacity during marriage. (b) Community property consists of the property, other than separate property, acquired by either spouse during marriage.

5. "No citizen of this State shall be deprived of life, liberty, property, privileges or immunities, or in any manner disfranchised, except by the due course of the law of the land." Tex. Const. art. 1, Sec. 19.

448, Vernon's Tex. Const. "One person's property may not be taken for the benefit of another private person without a justifying public purpose, even though compensation be paid." *Thompson v. Consolidated Gas Co.,* 800 U.S. 55, 80, 57 Ct. 364, 376, 81 L.Ed. 510 (1936). This court quoted and relied upon that statement from *Thompson* in *Marrs v. Railroad Commission,* 142 Tex. 298, 177 S.W.2d 941, 949 (1944). There is no contention that the taking of Homer's separate property and its transfer to Virginia is justified by any benefit to the public welfare. The taking was not grounded upon the police power; consequently, the taking from Homer would not have been a constitutional act even if the legislature had expressly authorized the divestiture of one person's property and its vesting in another person.

The court of civil appeals, as stated above, held correctly that the trial court may set aside either spouse's separate real property, its income, rents, or revenues for the support of the minor children. Chief Justice Hemphill, writing in *Rice v. Rice,* 21 Tex. 58, 71 (1858) said:

> The separate property may be divided in cases of necessity; or the whole, both separate and community, may be kept together as in this case, for the benefit of the children; but the decree must not divest either party of their title in the lands or slaves. It will be no breach of the statute to decree the use of property, for some period, to the use of the children, reserving the fee of the property in the husband to be enjoyed by him after the expiration of the trust estate for the children.

The basis for the holding was the duty of the parent to support his children whether from the community or the separate estate. The trial court judgment which was approved in *Rice* was that a receiver under bond would take charge of the property, collect the proceeds, and apply them to the support, education, and maintenance of two minor children. *Rice, supra,* 64.

The correct rule, as stated by the court of civil appeals in this case, is that a parent owes a duty to support his child and that duty can be enforced against the parent and his separate property. A receiver or trustee may be named to assure compliance with the order for support. The fee to the separate property, however, may not be divested.

We affirm the judgment of the court of civil appeals reversing the trial court's divestiture of the husband's separate property and remanding the cause to the trial court to determine whether an interim arrangement for the support of the children should be made.

ON MOTION FOR REHEARING

STEAKLEY, Justice, dissenting.

The dissenting opinion delivered May 18, 1977 is withdrawn, and the following is substituted therefor.

This case presents a narrow and easily articulable question: Does Section 3.63 of the Texas Family Code authorize the divestiture of title to a spouse's separate real property where such action is necessary to effect a "just and right" division of the marital property of divorcing spouses? In the instant case the Court of Civil Appeals held the trial court did not have such authority, citing *Ramirez v. Ramirez,* 524 S.W.2d 767 (Tex. Civ. App. — Corpus Christi 1975, no writ). *Eggemeyer v. Eggemeyer,* 535 S.W.2d 425 (Tex. Civ. App. — Austin 1976). A majority of this Court affirms that holding. I would reverse the judgment of the Court of Civil Appeals and affirm that of the trial court, the effect of which would be to divest Homer Eggemeyer of a one-third undivided interest in the family farm, an interest which was his separate property by virtue of a gift from his mother.

Section 3.63 of the Texas Family Code provides: "In a decree of divorce or annulment the court shall order a division of the estate of the parties in a manner that the court deems just and right, having due regard for the rights of each party and any children of the marriage." Tex. Family Code Ann. Sec. 3.63 (1975). The predecessor statute repealed by the enactment of the Family Code was article 4638. It provided:

> The court pronouncing a decree of divorce shall also decree and order a division of the estate of the parties in such a way as the court shall deem just and right, having due regard to the rights of each party and their children, if any. *Nothing herein shall be construed to compel either party to divest himself or herself of the title to real estate.* [Emphasis added.]

See Tex. Laws 1841, *An Act Concerning Divorce and Alimony*, Sec. 114, at 19–22, 2 H. Gammel, *Laws of Texas* 483–486 (1898). The italicized sentence in article 4638, and in all its predecessor statutes, was not carried forward in Section 3.63. Notwithstanding, the majority here holds that Section 3.63 does not authorize the trial court to divest a divorcing spouse of his or her separate real property when ordering a division of the marital estates. Accord, *Ramirez v. Ramirez, supra; contra, Wilkerson v. Wilkerson*, 515 S.W.2d 52 (Tex. Civ. App.—Tyler 1974, no writ). Established principles of statutory construction require the opposite result. Furthermore, such a result does not contravene either the United States or Texas Constitution.

I.

The majority construes the phrase "estate of the parties" to mean only the community property of the spouses. Such a construction, while perhaps grammatically sound, is contrary to well-established Texas law and practice. In *Hedtke v. Hedtke*, 112 Tex. 404, 248 S.W. 21 (1923), this Court reiterated the parameters of a trial court's discretion in dividing the property of divorcing spouses. Construing the language of article 4638, the Court wrote:

> "The estate subject to division, under the statute, include[s] all property of the parties whether community property or separate property. The meaning of the statute is not different from what it would have been had the word 'property' been substituted in its phraseology for the word 'estate.'"

Id. at 22. The construction adopted by the Court in *Hedtke* has been accepted and adhered to ever since. *See e.g., In re Marriage of Jackson*, 506 S.W.2d 261 (Tex. Civ. App.—Amarillo 1974, writ dism'd); *Dorfman v. Dorfman*, 457 S.W.2d 417 (Tex. Civ. App.—Texarkana 1970, no writ); *Earnest v. Earnest*, 223 S.W.2d 681 (Tex. Civ. App.—Amarillo 1949, no writ); Smith, *Family Law*, 26 Sw. L. J. 51, 55 & n.30 (1972). The phrase "estate of the parties" was carried forward into Section 3.63. In construing a statute we must assume the Legislature was aware of prior judicial interpretations, and reenactment of a statute or portion thereof without a change in its language indicates approval of such prior judicial interpretations. Thus, I would construe "estate of the parties," in accordance with established Texas law, to mean all property of the parties, whether real or personal, separate or community.

The pronouncements of this Court in *Hedtke* and *Hailey* established the parameters of article 4638 within which a trial court could exercise its discretion in dividing the property of a divorcing husband and wife. In *Hedtke* this Court construed "estate of the parties" to mean all property of the parties, community and separate. In *Hailey* we held the prohibition against divestiture of title to real estate applied only to the separate real property of the spouses and did not prohibit the division of community realty upon divorce.

At the time of the enactment of Section 3.63 the law was clear—a court dividing the marital properties was authorized to award community realty, community personalty, and separate personalty to either spouse upon a determination that such was "just and right." It could not, however, award one spouse's separate realty to the other because the last sentence of article 4638 prohibited it.

There is no difference in the constitutional classification of separate real and separate personal property. It is therefore unmistakably implicit in the decisions of this Court and the various courts of civil appeals that absent the statutory prohibition against the divestiture of title to real estate, an award of separate realty would also within the authority of the trial court in ordering a division of the estate of the divorcing parties. It was precisely this prohibition that was removed by the Legislature in the enactment of Section 3.63. Ordinarily, the fact "that significant words are omitted from the reenactment or amendment of a statute imports a conclusive presumption that the Legislature intended to exclude the object theretofore accomplished by the abandoned words." *Gateley v. Humphrey*, 151 Tex. 588, 254 S.W.2d 98 (1952). Stated differently, there is a presumption that if a change occurs in legislative language, a change was intended in legislative result.

Where the language of a statute is plain and clear, it must be given effect as written. would give effect to the language of Section 3.63 and hold that a trial court adjudicating a divorce has the authority to divide all the marital properties, whether real or personal, separate or community.

II.

The majority holds that a trial court's divestiture of title to one spouse's separate property and subsequent investiture of title in the other spouse would violate substantive due course, *i.e.*, would be a taking of private property unjustified by a resultant benefit to the public welfare.

There is a public purpose served by the statutory investiture of trial courts with the broad power to divide the divorcing spouses' separate and community real and personal property as they deem "just and right." That purpose is to insure that one spouse does not, through artful management of the marital property, accumulate a separate estate of substantial value at the expense of the separate estate of the other spouse or at the expense of the community and then, upon divorce, retain that separate estate and relegate the other spouse to his or her separate estate and to the potentially depleted community estate. By prohibiting the invasion of a spouse's separate property where necessary to effect a just and right property division, the majority sanctions and promotes the societal disharmony resulting from inequitable property settlements upon divorce. In my view the Legislature sought to avoid this potential injustice by granting the trial court broad discretion in dividing the property of the marriage. The holding of the majority narrowly circumscribes that discretion and, in my opinion, is neither mandated by the Constitution nor comports with the statutory provisions.

III.

To reiterate, I would hold that Section 3.63 authorizes a trial court to divest title to one spouse's separate real property and to award that property to the other spouse as his or her separate property. The Constitution does not prohibit such statutory authorization, and the clear language of the statute demands such an interpretation. I recognize that as a general rule separate property, whether real or personal, should be restored to its owner and the community property of the marriage divided as seems just and right. *Fitts v. Fitts*,

14 Tex. 443 (1855); *Fuhrman v. Fuhrman*, 302 S.W.2d 205 (Tex. Civ. App.—El Paso 1957, writ dism'd). As this Court wrote in *McElreath v. McElreath*, 162 Tex. 190, 345 S.W.2d 722 (1961), each spouse primarily "must look to the community property for her [his] share of the material gains incident to an ill-starred marriage." *Id.* at 724. Furthermore, the conceptual basis of community property is the notion that spouses should share as equal partners in the benefits and burdens of the marriage. When the marriage is terminated, the primary fund to be divided is that comprised of assets acquired by the spouses as a community. The invasion of the separate property of one spouse for the benefit of the other can be justified only in exceptional circumstances. This is illustrated by the action of the Court of Civil Appeals in *Cooper v. Cooper,* 513 S.W.2d 229 (Tex. Civ. App.—Houston [1st Dist.] 1974, no writ).

Cameron v. Cameron

Supreme Court of Texas, 1982
641 S.W.2d 210

POPE, Justice.

The questions presented concern the trial court's division of military retirement pay and United States Savings Bonds between divorcing spouses in Texas. The property was acquired in states that do not have a community property system. The trial court awarded the wife thirty-five percent of the gross military retirement funds received in the future by the divorced husband and fifty percent of the United States Savings Bonds. Considerable other property was divided about which there is no dispute. The court of civil appeals reversed the judgment in part and held that the retirement pay and savings bonds, acquired by the spouses in a common law property state, were the husband's separate property and, thus, not subject to division. 608 S.W.2d 748. We reverse the judgment of the court of civil appeals with respect to the military retirement pay; we reverse the judgment of the court of civil appeals and affirm the trial court's judgment dividing the savings bonds.

Paul Cameron joined the United States Air Force on June 22, 1954. While in the military, Paul married Sue Akers in Midland, Texas, on September 29, 1957, and the couple immediately moved to California. The Camerons remained in California, a community property state, for only three months. During the balance of Mr. Cameron's military service, the two lived in Arkansas, Indiana, Maryland, Nebraska, Ohio and Oklahoma, all of which observe the common law property system. The Camerons' move to Texas in August, 1977, coincided with Paul's retirement from the Air Force. At the time the divorce suit was filed in 1978, both spouses lived in Texas.

I. THE MILITARY RETIREMENT PAY

In awarding a fraction of Paul Cameron's military retirement pay to his wife, the trial court followed a number of Texas decisions approving such a division upon divorce. *Taggart v. Taggart*, 552 S.W.2d 422 (Tex. 1977); *Cearley v. Cearley*, 544 S.W.2d 661 (Tex. 1976). While this cause was on appeal, the United States Supreme Court held that the supremacy clause of the United States Constitution, article VI, precludes a state court from dividing military nondisability retirement pay on divorce. *McCarty v. McCarty*, 453 U.S. 210, 101 S.Ct. 2728, 69 L.Ed.2d 589 (1981). In the wake of *McCarty*, we held that the supremacy clause effectively foreclosed the division of military retirement benefits under Texas community property laws. *Trahan v. Trahan,* 626 S.W.2d 485, 487 (Tex. 1981).

Mrs. Cameron urged that we should remand the cause to afford the trial court an opportunity to increase her award from the community property as a means of offsetting her loss of thirty-five percent of the future retirement pay. The United States Supreme Court had also closed the door to that remedy. *McCarty,* 453 U.S. at 228–29 n. 22, 101 S.Ct. at 2739 n. 22. *See also Hisquierdo v. Hisquierdo,* 439 U.S. 572, 588, 99 S.Ct. 802, 811, 59 L.Ed.2d 1 (1979).

On September 9, 1982, the President signed into law the Uniformed Services Former Spouses' Protection Act, Pub. L. No. 97252, 96 Stat. 730 (1982). The purpose of the act was to reverse the effect of the McCarty decision. Under the act, a divorce court may divide military retirement pay between the spouses in accordance with the law of the jurisdiction of that court. The act limits such division of retirement pay to periods beginning after June 25, 1981. *Id.* Sec. 1002(a) [to be codified at 10 U.S.C. Sec. 1408(c)(1)].

Paul Cameron served in the military for more than nineteen years of his twenty-one and a half year marriage to Sue Cameron. Under the Act, Sue Cameron is entitled to receive a portion of Paul Cameron's retirement pay. The divorce decree, dated March 29, 1979, awards Sue Cameron "thirty-five percent (35%) of the gross present and future Military Retirement presently being received." Sue Cameron is entitled to recover that thirty-five percent, but not for the period from March 29, 1979, to June 25, 1981. Therefore, we affirm that part of the trial court judgment awarding Sue Cameron thirty-five percent of the military retirement pay, but only for the period beginning after June 25, 1981.

II. THE U.S. SAVINGS BONDS

The court of civil appeals characterized the funds earned by Mr. Cameron in common law jurisdictions as his separate property and, through tracing principles, decided the bonds acquired with the common law funds belonged in his separate, Texas estate. As a part of Mr. Cameron's separate estate, the bonds, according to the court of civil appeals, could not be divested by the trial court. Sue Cameron seeks to uphold the trial court's disposition of the bonds by arguing that we should overrule our decision in *Eggemeyer v. Eggemeyer,* 554 S.W.2d 137 (Tex. 1977), or, alternatively, treat separate personalty differently than separate realty. Although we view the nature of the savings bonds acquired in common law jurisdictions in a different light than the court of civil appeals, we first address these arguments advanced by Mrs. Cameron.

A. Eggemeyer *Correctly States the Law*

Since the early days of the Republic of Texas, Texas has carefully drawn a line between the separate and community property of spouses in an attempt to preserve the distinctions between and the integrity of the two classes of property. Any judicial divestiture of separate property would essentially disregard the constitutionally mandated distinction. At times pertinent to this action, the Texas Constitution has provided: "All property, both real and personal, of the wife, owned or claimed by her before marriage, and that acquired afterward by gift, devise or descent, shall be the separate property of the wife...." Tex. Const. art. XVI, Sec. 15. In interpreting this provision, the court in *Arnold v. Leonard,* 114 Tex. 535, 273 S.W. 799 (1925), ruled that the constitution contained the exclusive definition of separate property and that the legislature could neither alter nor enlarge upon it. Section 3.63 of the Family Code authorizes a "just and right" division of the estate of the parties, but it does not provide authority for the transmutation of one spouse's separate property into the other spouse's separate property. Allowing a trial court to divest separate property from one spouse and award it to the other spouse as part of the latter's separate estate would impermissibly enlarge the exclusive constitutional definition of separate property. *See Eggemeyer, supra*, at 140.

In addition to this constitutional reason for disallowing the divestiture of separate property on divorce, the statutory construction of Section 3.63, Tex. Fam. Code Ann., does not imbue our courts with the authority to divest separate property. The Fourth Congress of the Republic of Texas approved in 1840 an "Act adopting the Common Law of England ... and to regulate the Marital [sic] Rights of Parties." 1840 Laws of the Republic of Texas, at 3–6, 2 H. Gammel, *Laws of Texas* 177–180 (1898). In defining separate and community property, the congress decreed that land or slaves acquired before marriage or afterward by gift, devise or descent constituted separate property. All other marital acquisitions fell into the common or community estate of the spouses. One year later, the Fifth Congress of the Republic of Texas approved an act "Concerning Divorce and Alimony." The statute authorized a divorce court to "order a division of the estate of the parties ... as shall seem just and right," and added, "that nothing herein contained shall be construed to compel either party to divest him or herself of title to real estate or to slaves." 1841 Laws of the Republic of Texas, *An Act Concerning Divorce and Alimony*, Section 4, at 20, 2 H. Gammel, *Laws of Texas* 484 (1898); *see* McKnight, *Commentary on Sec. 3.63*, 5 Tex. Tech. L. Rev. 337–38 (1974). The divorce statute made clear it was "the estate of the parties,"—the common property—that the court had the power to divide. In contrast, the congress directed that real estate and slaves—separate property as defined one year earlier by the Fourth Congress—should remain inviolate on divorce. The Fifth Congress, thus, forbade the divestiture of a spouse's separate property, as then defined, by the courts on divorce. Consequently, division of property by a divorce court was limited to the community estate.

The phrase "estate of the parties" has been carried forward in Texas divorce laws and now appears in Tex. Fam. Code Ann. Section 3.63(a). This court in *Eggemeyer, supra*, at 139, affirmed the construction that the phrase referred only to community property.[6] Four years after *Eggemeyer*, the 67th Texas Legislature amended Section 3.63, but left undisturbed this court's decision that "estate of the parties" refers only to community property. In addition, the scheme enacted by the legislature in Section 3.63(b) of the Family Code builds upon the law that property acquired before marriage or afterward by gift, devise or descent cannot be divided by Texas courts.[7] To now hold that the "estate of

---

6. The Arizona Supreme Court in construing its divorce statute providing for a "division of the property of the parties as to the court shall seem just and right," also determined that the phrase "property of the parties" referred only to the community property. *Collier v. Collier*, 73 Ariz. 405, 242 P.2d 537, 541 (1952).

7. Amended Section 3.63 now provides:

Section 3.63 Division of Property.

(a) In a decree of divorce or annulment the court shall order a division of the estate of the parties in a manner that the court deems just and right, having due regard for the rights of each party and any children of the marriage.

(b) In a decree of divorce or annulment the court shall also order a division of the following real and personal property, wherever situated, in a manner that the court deems just and right, having due regard for the rights of each party and any children of the marriage;

(1) property that was acquired by either spouse while domiciled elsewhere and that would have been community property if the spouse who acquired the property had been domiciled in this state at the time of the acquisition; or

(2) property that was acquired by either spouse in exchange for real or personal property, and that would have been community property if the spouse who acquired the property so exchanged had been domiciled in this state at the time of its acquisition.

the parties" encompasses separate as well as community property would thwart the intent of this most recent pronouncement by the legislature.

Section 3.63(a), moreover, authorizes a "division" of the parties' estate, but provides no authority for a court to "divest" a divorcing spouse's separate property. Castleberry, *Constitutional Limitations on the Division of Property Upon Divorce*, 10 St. Mary's L. J. 37, 4855 (1978). As early as in the 1841 divorce statute discussed above, the Texas Congress drew a distinction between allowing courts to "order a *division* of the estate of the parties" while at the same time forbidding them "to compel either party to *divest* him or herself of the title to real estate or slaves." 1841 Laws of the Republic of Texas, *An Act Concerning Divorce and Alimony*, Sec. 4, at 20, 2 H. Gammel, *Laws of Texas* 484 (1898) (emphasis added). The 1981 amendment to Tex. Fam. Code Ann. Sec. 3.63 continues the use of the term "division" when addressing the courts' power to order a disposition of marital property. In *Hailey v. Hailey*, 160 Tex. 372, 331 S.W.2d 299 (1960), this court recognized and explained the difference between a "division" of property and a "divestiture" of property. A division of the community is similar to a partition of property and "is not a divesting of title of either owner...." *Id*. at 377, 331 S.W.2d at 303. The division, we said, does not effect a conveyance or transfer of title; the transaction only dissolves the tenancy in common. One year later in *McElreath v. McElreath*, 162 Tex. 190, 345 S.W.2d 722 (1961), we repeated our holding in *Hailey*:

> Under our laws, permanent alimony is not recognized, nor is a Texas court authorized to divest either spouse of his or her title to separate property, *Hailey v. Hailey*, Tex. Sup., 331 S.W.2d 299, but the wife, in the main, must look to the community property for her share of the material gains incident to an ill-starred marriage.

Id. at 193, 345 S.W.2d at 724. Thus, the terminology utilized first by the Texas Congress and carried forward to the present day by the Texas Legislature reinforces our decision that separate property is not subject to divestiture by courts on divorce.

It is also suggested that separate property may be divested and granted to the non-owning spouse as an exercise of the police power. The Texas Legislature, however, has not seen fit to exercise this power in favor of divestiture of spouses' separate property on divorce. Presently, Section 3.63(a) of the Family Code is silent on the courts' power to take one spouse's property and give it to the other on divorce. In comparison, the California statute concerning the disposition of property on divorce, Cal. Civ. Code Sec. 4800,

---

Tex. Fam. Code Ann. Section 3.63. The Bill Analysis for H.B. 753 prepared for the House Committee on the Judiciary stated:

Division of Property. Two separate systems of marital property regimes exist in the various states; common law and community property. Each regime provides for the welfare and estate of both spouses upon dissolution of marriage. The end is similar while the nomenclature is different. In community property states, like Texas, each spouse has legal title in property accumulated during the marriage. In common law states, the same property may belong to one spouse, but the other spouse is found to have acquired an equitable interest that can be vested upon dissolution of the marriage.

* * *

Suggested solutions would be to allow Texas courts to find an equitable interest in separate property, or to allow the courts to consider as community property that property which would have been community had it been acquired by someone domiciled in Texas at the time of acquisition.

* * *

Section 1 amends Family Code, Section 3.63, to allow Texas courts to divide all property before them in a marriage dissolution suit which according to Texas law would be considered community property if the acquiring spouse had been domiciled in Texas at the time of acquisition. House Comm. On the Judiciary, 67th Legislature Of Texas, Bill Analysis To H.B. 753, p. 1 (1981).

like Tex. Fam. Code Ann. Sec. 3.63(a), neither expressly prohibits nor provides for divestiture of separate property on divorce. Yet the California courts have consistently refused to interpret the statute as authorizing its courts to divest spouses of their separate property. One California court has explained:

> The jurisdiction of the court with respect to property in a divorce action is found in Section 137 *et seq.* of the Civil Code. As a general rule and subject to certain exceptions not material here, the power of the court is limited to a disposition of the community property and a court is without power to pass upon a dispute as to separate property or the disposition of the same.

Roy v. Roy, 29 Cal. App. 2d 596, 85 P.2d 223 (Dist. Ct. App. 1938). As recently as 1981 when the Texas Legislature considered and substantially amended Tex. Fam. Code Ann. Sec. 3.63,[8] it failed to assert any intention to use the police power it might have as a means of divestiture. We do not see, therefore, that the state has authorized the use of any power it might have to take separate property on divorce.

Texas property law contains a rich tradition of respect for the constitutional, Tex. Const. art XVI, Section 15, and statutory, Tex. Fam. Code Ann. Section 5.01, boundaries between community and separate property. Our state's courts have steadfastly guarded these estates from, and have been alert to rectify fraudulent encroachment by one estate upon the other. The integrity of each estate has been protected by developed principles of law and accounting by which funds or assets may be traced. *Tarver v. Tarver,* 394 S.W.2d 780 (Tex. 1965). The law of reimbursement between separate and community estates of spouses at divorce has been recognized since an early date. *Rice v. Rice,* 21 Tex. 58 (1858). A decision that would throw all separate and community property of the divorcing spouses into a hotchpotch so a trial judge could divide the mass without regard to when or how it was acquired would raze much of our developed community property law.

As we look beyond the boundaries of Texas, we find our holding in *Eggemeyer* that separate property may not be divested puts Texas in conformity with the law in six of the seven other community property states. In Arizona, "the court in pronouncing the decree of divorce had no authority to compel either party to divest himself or herself of the title to separate property." *Wiltbank v. Wiltbank,* 18 Ariz. 435, 162 P. 60, 61 (1917).

In California, the court may not assign the separate property of one spouse to the other, nor require one to pay the other any amount in lieu of an assignment or divestiture. *Fox v. Fox,* 18 Cal. 2d 645, 117 P.2d 325 (1941).

The Idaho Supreme Court, interpreting that state's divorce laws, stated, "The court has the power to divide the community property between the parties, but has no power or authority to award the wife's separate property, or any of it, to the husband." *Radermacher v. Radermacher,* 61 Idaho 261, 100 P.2d 955 (1940).

Nevada courts cannot divest separate property and award it to a spouse in fulfillment of the statutory power to make an equitable disposition of the marital property. *Stojanovich v. Stojanovich,* 86 Nev. 789, 476 P.2d 950 (1970). The New Mexico law regarding divestment of title parallels that of Nevada. *Ridgway v. Ridgway,* 94 N.M. 345, 610 P.2d 749 (1980). Louisiana also maintains a distinction on divorce between a couple's community and separate estates. See generally *Curtis v. Curtis,* 403 So. 2d 56 (La. 1981); *Lane v. Lane,* 375 So. 2d 660 (La. Ct. App. 1978), writ denied, 381 So. 2d 1222 (La. 1980). The Nevada, New Mexico, and Louisiana legislatures have imposed upon spouses a continuing legal duty

---

8. *See* note 7, *supra.*

to provide support for a divorced spouse through alimony. While prohibiting divestment for property settlements, those states expressly permit a transfer in discharge of the legislatively enunciated duty to provide support. *See* La. Civ. Code Ann. art. 160; Nev. Rev. Stat. Sec. 125.150(3); N.M. Stat. Ann. Sec. 40-4-7.B(1).

The State of Washington is the only community property jurisdiction that holds contrary to *Eggemeyer* and the rule in all other community property states. Even so, Washington permits divestment only in exceptional circumstances. *Morris v. Morris*, 69 Wash.2d 506, 419 P.2d 129 (1966).

The undercurrent of arguments to this court in support of the divestment of separate property is that Texas does not allow permanent alimony.[9] Section 3.59, Tex. Fam. Code Ann. authorizes support of a spouse only until a final decree. *See Eichelberger v. Eichelberger*, 582 S.W.2d 395, 402 (Tex. 1979). The policy against permanent alimony is so strong that the Texas Legislature has stated that the duty of support will be honored under the laws of other states except that the rule "shall not include alimony for a former wife."[10] Tex. Fam. Code Ann. Sec. 21.21; *see McElreath v. McElreath*, 162 Tex. 190, 228–29, 345 S.W.2d 722, 747 (1961).

One reason that Texas denies permanent alimony is that more than a century and a half ago, the state, along with Louisiana, took the lead to give wives equality with their husbands in the ownership of property they acquired during coverture. The common law recognized the wife's existence only through the husband, who upon marriage became the owner of the wife's property. In addition, spouses share the gains of their marriage equally under our community property legacy from Spain. Common law jurisdictions are yielding to this equal system of marital property ownership.

It is urged that we, by indirection, should resolve the problem of the state's lack of alimony laws by allowing our courts to divest a spouse of separate property and award it to the other spouse. In so doing, it is argued that we would be insuring the state that a worthy spouse would receive the financial support necessary to keep him or her from being a charge of society. As noted earlier, New Mexico currently allows its courts to transfer spouses' separate property on divorce, but the statute permitting such expressly notes that the transfer is considered alimony. N.M. Stat. Ann. Sec. 40-4-7.B(1). Divestiture of separate property for reason of financial support is nothing less than alimony. Our legislature has not authorized Texas courts to grant permanent alimony, and we do not perceive that it is our function to legislate in its stead.

Whatever may be the reasons for the strong Texas legislative policy against permanent alimony, this court will respect it. To do otherwise requires this court to disregard the rules of statutory construction, the history of the law prohibiting divestment of separate property, and the developed law of the other community property states. It would wipe out the legal distinctions between property, generate unnecessary constitutional prob-

---

9. Texas is the only state that forbids an award of alimony. In 1980, Pennsylvania reformed its law to permit alimony, but at the same time, the state's reform statute excluded "separate" property from the term "marital property." Separate property is defined as that which is acquired before marriage and that which is acquired during marriage by gift, bequest, devise or descent. Only marital property is divisible upon divorce. *See* Freed & Foster, *Divorce in the Fifty States: An Overview*, 14 Fam. L. Q. 230–31 (1981).

10. The parental duty to support children is not here involved. That duty exists independent of the character of property a spouse owns and may be enforced and secured by setting aside property, separate or community, to assure the children's support. *Eggemeyer v. Eggemeyer*, 554 S.W.2d 137 (Tex. 1977); *Cunningham v. Cunningham*, 120 Tex. 491, 40 S.W.2d 46 (1931); *Hedtke v. Hedtke*, 112 Tex. 404, 248 S.W.2d (1923).

lems about the classification and taking of property, create a new cycle of problems in construing amended article 3.63(b) of the Family Code, and would be contrary to the directions the law is taking in both common and community property law states as well as in the provisions of the Uniform Marriage and Divorce Act. The rules stated in this cause and in *Eggemeyer* harmonize these problems and keep the Texas community law consistent with the law of the other community property states. If there is a need for permanent alimony, it must come from the legislature where the policy arguments can be fully addressed by the whole public.

B. Separate Personal Property; Like Separate Real Property, May Not Be Divested.

The court in *Eggemeyer* was unanimous in its decision, as stated by the dissent, that the "estate of the parties" includes both real and personal property. In 1969, article 4638, later to become Section 3.63 of the Family Code, was amended to eliminate the statutory prohibition concerning divestment of realty. As previously written, there was a question whether article 4638 meant that separate personalty could be divested. The Texas Legislature by its 1969 amendment of Section 3.63 removed this provision, and as now written, the statute avoids the charge that it violates the due course of law, Tex. Const. art I, Sec. 19, equal protection, Tex. Const. art. I, Sec. 3, and the constitutional classifications of property, Tex. Const. art. XVI, Sec. 15.

Sue Cameron argues that *Eggemeyer* stands only for the narrow rule that separate realty may not be divested; separate personalty, she argues, may be divested. Only realty was involved in *Eggemeyer*, but, on the issue concerning an unconstitutional classification between realty and personalty, the entire court agreed that realty and personalty must be treated alike.[11] To hold that the owner of separate realty may not be divested of his property, but that the owner of vendor's lien notes secured by the same realty or that the owner of stock in a corporation owning the realty could be divested would be an unreasonable classification of property. *Railroad Commission v. Miller*, 434 S.W.2d 670 (Tex. 1968).

Our construction of the statute corresponds with the law that prevails in community property states. Arizona holds that there may be no divestment of either separate realty, *Porter v. Porter*, 67 Ariz. 273, 195 P.2d 395 (Ct. App. 1966). California denies a divestment of separate realty, *Reid v. Reid*, 112 Cal. 274, 44 P. 564 (1896), and treats separate personalty in the same manner, *Donovan v. Donovan*, 223 Cal. App. 2d 691, 36 Cal. Rptr. 225 (Dist. Ct. App. 1963). Idaho held the same in *Simplot v. Simplot*, 96 Idaho 239, 526 P.2d 844 (1974). In Nevada, neither the separate realty, *Thorne v. Thorne*, 74 Nev. 211, 326 P.2d 729 (1958), nor the separate personalty, *Zahringer v. Zahringer*, 76 Nev. 21, 348 P.2d 161 (1960), may be divested in settling marital property rights. We can find no justifiable reason for treating separate personalty in a different manner than separate realty in divorce proceedings. As a result, we reject Sue Cameron's argument to allow the divestiture of separate personalty upon divorce.

C. "Separate" Property Under Common Law and Community Property Regimes

Mr. Cameron acquired most of the U.S. Savings Bonds here at issue during his marriage to Sue Cameron while the couple was domiciled in common law states. Reviewing the action of the trial court, which had awarded Mrs. Cameron one-half of the bonds, the court of civil appeals characterized the bonds earned by Mr. Cameron in the common law jurisdictions as his separate property and held that the trial court could not divest a

---

11. The dissent stated: "There is no difference in the constitutional classification of separate real and separate personal property." *Eggemeyer, supra,* at 144 (Steakley, J., dissenting).

spouse's separate personalty, 608 S.W.2d at 751. We recognize that property acquired in common law jurisdictions has historically been termed "separate" property, but we hold that the property spouses acquire during marriage, except by gift, devise or descent should be divided upon divorce in Texas in the same manner as community property, irrespective of the domicile of the spouses when they acquire the property.

Characterization of the common law marital estate as separate property comes from the common law concept that the wife possessed no legal identity apart from her husband in whom legal title to the couple's property vested. *See* Oldham, *Property Division in a Texas Divorce of a Migrant Spouse: Heads He Wins, Tails She Loses?* 19 Hous. L. Rev. 1, 3–15 (1981); *see generally Dickson v. Strickland*, 114 Tex. 176, 201–02, 265 S.W. 1012, 102–22 (1924). Beginning with the enactment of the various Married Women's Property Laws throughout the nation during the nineteenth and early twentieth centuries, common law jurisdictions began to modify statutorily their archaic treatment of wives' rights in marital property. *See* Glendon, *Matrimonial Property: A Comparative Study of Law and Social Change*, 49 Tul. L. Rev. 21, 28–35 (1974). As a result of the statutes, courts in thirty-nine of the forty-two common law property states[12] now possess power to fashion upon divorce an equitable distribution of property acquired during marriage. *See* Freed & Foster, *Divorce in the Fifty States: An Overview*, 14 Fam. L. Q. 229, 249–52 (1981). A husband in a common law state may now have full paper title to property, but the non-acquiring wife holds valid and substantial rights to an equitable share of the "separate" marital property on divorce.

Common law jurisdictions have been compelled to recognize the justness of a community property system which recognizes the rights of both the husband and wife during the period of their acquisition of real and personal property. Common law marital property is not and should not be regarded by Texas courts as "separate" property in the context of our community property law on divorce. *See* Tex. Const. art. XVI, Sec. 15. Four of the eight community property states in recent years have addressed this difference in meanings of terms and have recognized the distinctions between the community and common law property concepts of "separate" property. Each court has looked behind the label when dividing marital property, that which was acquired during marriage.

In *Hughes v. Hughes*, 91 N.M. 339, 573 P.2d 1194 (1978), the New Mexico Supreme Court considered the disparate natures of separate property in common law and community property states. The court held that New Mexico courts should not treat separate property as recognized in common law jurisdictions the same as separate property under community property laws. *Id.* at 1201–02. The court further held that the bare legal principle that a wife has no legal title in her husband's separate common law marital property could not be accepted in light of the benefits, incidents, and immunities recognized as attaching to marital property in a wife's favor by courts in common law property states. *Id.* at 1197–99.

In *Rau v. Rau*, 6 Ariz.App. 362, 432 P.2d 910 (1967), the court of appeals in Arizona confronted a judgment in which an Arizona trial court had equally divided personalty (savings bonds) and realty (a farm) that the Raus bought with funds they acquired during their marriage in Illinois, a common law state. The court determined that a spouse in Illinois holds an equitable interest upon divorce to a fair and just division of jointly earned marital property even though title to such property rests in the name of only one spouse.

---

12. Even in those three states—Mississippi, Virginia, and West Virginia—the wife has some of the "bundle of sticks." Any injustice that accrues to divorcing parties from one of those three states, is the problem of their own archaic and unfair laws.

Comparing the definition of separate property under Arizona statutory law[13] with the nature of separate property as found in Illinois, the court maintained that Arizona's prohibition against divestiture of spouses' "separate" property would preclude a division of the Illinois common law separate property. *See also Braddock v. Braddock*, 91 Nev. 735, 542 P.2d 1060 (1975). We agree with the New Mexico, Idaho, Arizona, and Nevada courts that substantively distinguish common law marital property from the separate property of community property jurisdictions.

The 67th Texas Legislature last year adopted this sensible approach when it authorized a division, on divorce, of common law property acquired during marriage in a manner like they would divide community property on divorce. This amendment to Tex. Fam. Code Ann. Sec. 3.63 provides as follows: [the statute is set forth]. The bill analysis accompanying the subsequently adopted statute correctly explained:

> Two separate systems of marital property regimes exist in the various states: common law and community property. Each regime provides for the welfare and estate of both spouses upon dissolution of marriage. The end result is similar while the nomenclature is different. In community property states, like Texas, each spouse has legal title in property accumulated during the marriage. In common law states, the same property may belong to one spouse, but the other spouse is found to have acquired an equitable interest that can be vested upon dissolution of the marriage.

House Comm. on the Judiciary, 67th Legislature of Texas, Bill Analysis to H.B.753, p. 1 (1981). In enacting subsection (b) of Tex. Fam. Code Ann. Sec. 3.63, the legislature established a workable, uncomplicated framework for effecting just divisions of common law marital property on divorce in Texas. The amendment, however, applies only to suits for divorce or annulment in which a hearing has not been held before September 1, 1981. 1981 Tex. Gen. Laws, Ch. 712, Sec. 3, at 2656. The trial court rendered a judgment divorcing the Camerons in 1979. Rather than returning in this cause to the now discredited approach of assuming the equivalence of "separate" property under community property systems and common law "separate" property, and rather than embarking upon a cumbersome conflict of law approach[14] which produces essentially the same result, we judicially adopt Tex. Fam. Code Ann. Sec. 3.63(b) as part of the substantive law of this state.

It has been suggested that Section 3.63(b) may run afoul of this court's decision in *Eggemeyer*, because the statute may unconstitutionally authorize trial courts to interfere with the rights of a spouse holding legal title to common law marital property. *See* Oldham, *supra*, at 37–46.

As stated above, divorce courts in all but three of the common law jurisdictions may effect an equitable distribution of the marital assets upon divorce. The New Mexico

---

13. The court in *Rau* cited Arizona's community property definition of separate property, and except for its treatment of the increases, rents, issues and profits from separate property, it is the same definition we have in Texas.

Compare Ariz.Rev.Stat. Ann. Sec. 25-213: A. "All property, real and personal, of the husband, owned or claimed by him before marriage, and that acquired afterward by gift, devise or descent, and also the increase, rents, issues and profits thereof, is his separate property"; with Tex. Const. art. XVI, Sec. 15: "All property, both real and personal, of a spouse owned or claimed before marriage, and that acquired afterward by gift, devise or descent, shall be the separate property of that spouse."

14. Professor J. Thomas Oldham has thoughtfully developed this viable concept in Oldham, *Property Division in a Texas Divorce of a Migrant Spouse: Heads He Wins, Tails She Loses*, 19 Hous. L. Rev. 1 (1981).

Supreme Court explained in *Hughes*: "[T]he wife, in many common law states, has inchoate equitable rights to her husband's separate property where she has made contributions to preserving and bettering that property, whereas in a typical community property state she has no such rights since she has community property rights instead." *Hughes, supra,* at 1199. A Texas court that makes a distribution on divorce of the common law marital estate equivalent to what would occur in the common law jurisdiction where the couple was domiciled when they acquired the property, does not impair the rights of spouses in the common law marital property. No divestment transpires because the acquiring spouse loses no more in a Texas divorce than he loses in a judgment rendered in an equitable distribution common law state. Our judicial adoption of the quasi-community property amendment to Tex. Fam. Code Ann. Sec. 3.63 does not violate article I, Section 19 of the Texas Constitution.

III. CONCLUSION

The framework for the Spanish community property system of marital property builds upon a distinction between spouses' community and separate estates. This distinction springs from a reality that property acquired during marriage other than by gift, devise or descent is the product of a unique, joint endeavor undertaken by spouses. That is the concept of matrimony. Community property owes its existence to the legal fact of marriage, and when the parties to that compact determine their relationship should end, property acquired during marriage is and should be divided among them in a just and right manner. By way of contrast separate property, in the community property setting, owes its existence to wholly extramarital factors, things unrelated to the marriage. In relation to that property, the parties are, in essence, strangers; they are separate. Any property that arises independently of marriage as a means of "equitably" balancing the spouses' positions on divorce cannot be justified. Such a view rejects the viability of the community property system and ignores the carefully hewn jurisprudence that attempts to preserve the integrity of the two estates. The vast majority of common law property states have demonstrated that they too recognize the special nature of property acquired through the corroborative efforts of spouses. In adopting Tex. Fam. Code Ann. Sec. 3.63(b) as the substantive law of the state, we continue the national trend endorsing the use of marital property as the means of settling the equities between divorcing spouses.

We reverse that part of the judgment of the court of civil appeals that denied Sue Cameron fifty percent of the savings bonds and affirm the judgment of the trial court ordering the equal division.

We reverse that part of the judgment of the court of civil appeals that reversed the trial court's judgment that Sue Cameron receive thirty-five percent of the military retirement pay, and we render judgment awarding Sue Cameron her share of the military retirement pay, but only from June 25, 1981.

Costs are adjudged against the respondent.

DISCUSSION

Although it seems fairly clear that *Cameron's* discussion of separate personalty was dictum, Texas courts have accepted the view that no separate property (personalty or realty) can be divided in a Texas divorce. Parties may agree in a separation agreement to divide separate property; *Eggemeyer/Cameron* only bar the court from ordering such a division in a decree. *See Boyett v. Boyett*, 799 S.W.2d 360 (Tex. App.—Houston [14th Dist.] 1990, no writ).

Because of the standard announced in *Eggemeyer/Cameron* that separate property cannot be divided at divorce, the primary dispute in Texas divorces now pertains to the character of the property. In *Love v. Bailey-Love*, 217 S.W.3d 33 (Tex. App.—Houston [1st Dist.] 2006, no petition) the divorce court ordered the husband to pay the wife's student loan incurred before marriage. The appellate court ruled *Eggemeyer/Cameron* barred the court from ordering one spouse to pay the other's "separate" debt.

One justification for the *Cameron* holding stemmed from the Texas policy of barring post-divorce alimony. Now that Texas has accepted alimony, does this affect *Cameron*? Division of military retirement benefits will be discussed in more detail later in the chapter.

After *Eggemeyer* and *Cameron,* courts have considered what constitutes an unlawful taking of separate property.

Duke v. Duke

Texas Court of Appeals—El Paso, 1980
605 S.W.2d 408, writ dism'd

PRESLAR, Chief Justice.

The judgment ordered Appellant to execute a deed of trust lien on Lot 3, Block 11, Colonia Verde, Unit Two, City of El Paso, which the Court had found to be Appellant's separate property. This appears to be contrary to the Supreme Court's decision in *Eggemeyer v. Eggemeyer, supra*. It was there held that the estate to be divided, within the meaning of Section 3.63 of the Tex. Family Code, is the community estate, and the title to the separate realty of one spouse may not be divested and awarded to the other. In the case before us, the Court has placed a deed of trust lien on the husband's separate property for the benefit of the wife. If that lien is to have any meaning and be enforced, then he can be, by such enforcement, divested of his realty. If it is not enforced or foreclosed, it still divests him of some title in his realty for it is unmarketable while under such lien.

We conclude that the Court erred in ordering the deed of trust on Appellant's separate realty. *Campbell v. Campbell* followed *Eggemeyer v. Eggemeyer,* and holds that a party may not be divested of his personal property in a property division decree under Section 3.63. We apply the same reasoning as we did on the realty and hold that the Court erred in placing Appellant's separate personal property, acquired prior to marriage, under a security agreement for Appellee's benefit.

DISCUSSION

Rider v. Rider, 887 S.W.2d 255 (Tex. App.—Beaumont 1994, no writ) appears to disagree with *Duke*, holding that a divorce court could impose an equitable lien on a spouse's out of state separate realty to secure a property division obligation. *See also, Jones v. Jones,* 804 S.W.2d 623 (Tex. App.—Texarkana 1991, no writ). Courts have upheld the granting of a lien if the community claim related to the property to which the lien attached. *See Johnson v. Johnson,* 804 S.W.2d 296 (Tex. App.—Houston [1st Dist.] 1991, no writ).

If property is partly separate and partly community, the court may order the sale of the property, as long as the holder of the separate property portion receives at least that fraction of the sales proceeds. *Mogford v. Mogford*, 616 S.W.2d 936 (Tex. Civ. App.—San Antonio 1981).

Cohen v. Cohen

Texas Court of Appeals—Waco, 1982
632 S.W.2d 172, no writ

McDONALD, Justice.

This is an appeal by plaintiff Jay Howard Cohen from an order of the trial court sustaining defendant Helene Renee Cohen's plea in abatement and dismissing plaintiff's cause of action.

On January 31, 1975, the trial court rendered a judgment of divorce between the parties herein, from which plaintiff did not appeal. Thereafter in December, 1980, almost six years after the divorce judgment was rendered, plaintiff filed this case, a "Petition for a Declaratory Judgment," seeking to hold void two provisions of the property award in such divorce judgment.

In the portion of the judgment plaintiff attacks, defendant was awarded:

Out of cash on hand, $219,600, to be paid … as follows:

(a) $27,000 in cash within 10 days.

(b) $192,000 due and payable on or before February 1, 1985. Until such sum has been paid, Jay Howard Cohen shall pay Helene Renee Cohen interest on the remaining unpaid principal balance of said sum at the rate of 10% per annum beginning on February 1, 1975. If the entire sum has not been paid by February 1, 1978, the principal sum outstanding on February 1, of each succeeding year shall be increased or decreased … [according to the] *Implied Price Deflator for Personal Consumption Expenditures* (1958 = 100) published by the Bureau of Economic Analysis of the United States Department of Commerce.

Defendant filed a plea in bar (denominated a plea in abatement) asserting the Texas Declaratory Judgment Act "does not allow a declaratory judgment as a remedy against a previous judgment of this court or any other court."

After hearing the trial court sustained the plea and rendered judgment dismissing plaintiff's cause of action.

Plaintiff appeals asserting the trial court erred in sustaining defendant's plea in abatement and in dismissing plaintiff's suit because the declaratory judgment proceeding was proper to state and declare rights and responsibilities of parties to a judgment where one party claimed rights under void portions of the judgment.

Plaintiff contends the provision for interest at 10% is void because at the time the judgment was entered the law of Texas provided that all judgments shall bear interest at 6% after date of judgment; and further that the provision for increase or decrease of the principal amount awarded defendant based on a cost of living index is void in that it is a deprivation of property without due course of law under the Texas and United States Constitutions.

We overrule plaintiff's point and affirm the judgment of the trial court.

Moreover the complained of portion of the 1975 judgment is not void on its face. The record reflects the parties owned a great deal of real and personal property. The money plaintiff was awarded out of the cash on hand was only one of the items of property awarded defendant. The terms of the decree merely provided a method by which plaintiff would be allowed to use the funds in exchange for paying 10% interest. The 10% interest was not interest on the judgment as such. The same reasoning applies to the cost of living increase or decrease in the amount awarded defendant. Plaintiff could avoid this (or have avoided this) by paying in cash the money awarded plaintiff.

A divorce judgment unappealed and regular on its face is not subject to collateral attack in a subsequent suit. *Hardin v. Hardin*, 597 S.W.2d 347. And the judgment of a court of general jurisdiction is not subject to collateral attack except on the ground that it had no jurisdiction of the person of a party or his property, no jurisdiction to enter the particular judgment. *Austin I.S.D. v. Sierra Club*, 495 S.W.2d 878.

Here the trial court had jurisdiction of the parties, of the subject matter, and the judgment is not void on its face.

Plaintiff's point is overruled.

AFFIRMED.

3. Discrimination Based upon Sex

Texas has enacted a form of the Equal Rights Amendment. *See* Tex. Const., art. I, § 3a. The marital property rights sections of the Texas Family Code make no distinctions based upon sex, so this provision has little effect upon Texas family law.

Glud v. Glud

Texas Court of Appeals — Waco, 1982
641 S.W.2d 688, no writ

HALL, Justice.

Family Code Sec. 14.01(b) provides in part as follows: "In determining which parent to appoint as managing conservator, the court shall consider the qualifications of the respective parents without regard to the sex of the parent." The purpose and effect of this statute was the elimination of the prior existing rule of preference for the mother on the issue of child custody and the placing of both parents on an equal plane on this issue insofar as their sex is concerned.

In our case, in announcing the decision to award custody of the children to the mother, the trial court stated to the parties:

> In my opinion I think it would be detrimental looking at it from a man's standpoint, and I'm a man and father, Mr. Glud, I think it would be very difficult for a man to raise two boys like a woman can. Therefore, I'm going to name her as managing conservator of the children.

Appellant asserts that under the facts of our case this comment by the trial judge affirmatively shows that the judge's award of custody of the children to appellee was based upon his personal bias in favor of the mother on the child custody issue in violation of the provisions of Sec. 14.01(b). We sustain this contention. Our record shows a close and loving relationship by both parents for their children and by both children for their parents. It shows that both parents are equally capable of caring for the children and providing for their moral, physical and educational needs and well-being. Appellee conceded in her testimony that appellant was capable of caring for the children. Family Code Sec. 14.07(a) provides that the best interest of the child shall always be the primary consideration of the court in determining the question of custody, and that in determining the best interest of the child the court shall consider the circumstances of the parents. Nevertheless, this decision of custody must not be based upon the sex of the parents. Sec. 14.01(b). In our case, after expressing his opinion that "it would be very difficult for a man to raise two boys like a woman can," the trial court ruled that "therefore, I'm going to name her as managing conservator of the children." This comment affirmatively shows that the trial court's determination of custody was based upon the consideration of the sex of the parents, and thus deprived appellant of his right to have his qualifications as custodian of the children considered without regard to his sex, all in violation of Family Code Sec. 14.01(b). Under the record, we cannot say that this error was harmless to appellant. Therefore, we must reverse the child custody order.

---

4. Retroactivity of Changes in the Law

Addison v. Addison
Supreme Court of California, 1965
399 P.2d 897

PETERS, Justice.

[Morton (H) and Leona (W) moved from Illinois to California, and he brought with him considerable wealth earned in Illinois that was quasi-community property as defined in the predecessor to California Civil Code Section 4803, *supra*. W divorced H in California. The divorce court held it would be an unconstitutional taking of H's property to award W pursuant to what is now Civil Code Section 4800, *supra*, half of H's quasi-community property. She appeals. In a prior case, *Estate of Thornton*, 1 Cal. 2d 1, 33 P.2d 1 (1934), the court had invalidated a statute, former Civil Code Section 164, which was construed as converting English common-law separate property to community property as soon as the couple established a California domicile, if such property would have been community if acquired by a California spouse. This was held in *Thornton* to constitute a taking of a share of the acquiring spouse's property without due process of law and to abridge that spouse's constitutionally protected privileges and immunities by penalizing her or him for change of domicile].

[T]he correctness of the rule of *Thornton* is open to challenge. But even if the rule of that case be accepted as sound, it is not here controlling. This is so because former Section 164 of the Civil Code has an entirely different impact from the legislation presently before us. The legislation under discussion, unlike old Section 164, makes no attempt to alter property rights merely upon crossing the boundary into California. It does not purport to disturb vested rights "of a citizen of another state, who chances to transfer his domicile to this state, bringing his property with him." Instead, the concept of quasi-community property is applicable only if a divorce or separate maintenance action is filed here after the parties have become domiciled in California. Thus, the concept is applicable only if, after acquisition of domicile in this state, certain acts or events occur which give rise to an action for divorce or separate maintenance. These acts or events are not necessarily connected with a change of domicile at all.

Clearly the interest of the state of the current domicile in the matrimonial property of the parties is substantial upon the dissolution of the marriage relationship.

In this case at bar it was Leona who was granted a divorce from Morton on the ground of the latter's adultery and hence it is the spouse guilty of the marital infidelity from whom the otherwise separate property is sought by the operation of the quasi-community property legislation. We are of the opinion that where the innocent party would otherwise be left unprotected the state has a very substantial interest and one sufficient to provide for a fair and equitable distribution of the marital property without running afoul of the due process clause of the Fourteenth Amendment. For the same reasons Sections 1 and 13 of article I of the California Constitution, substantially similar in language, are not here applicable.

Aside from the due process clause, already held not to be applicable, *Thornton* may read as holding that the legislation there in question impinged upon the right of a citizen of the United States to maintain a domicile in any state of his choosing without the loss of valuable property rights. As to this contention, this distinction we have already noted between former Civil Code Section 164 and quasi-community property legislation is relevant. Unlike the legislation in *Thornton*, the quasi-community property legislation does not cause a loss of valuable rights through change of domicile. The concept is applicable only in case of a decree of divorce or separate maintenance.

[T]he judgment is reversed.

In re Marriage of Bouquet

Supreme Court of California, 1976
546 P.2d 1371

TOBRINER, Justice.

Harry Bouquet appeals from certain provisions of an interlocutory judgment dissolving the marriage and determining the property rights of the parties.

Harry Bouquet and Ima Nell Bouquet married on June 9, 1941, and separated on March 2, 1969. On April 20, 1971, Ima petitioned for dissolution of marriage and determination of the property rights of the spouses. After trial on May 17 and 18, 1972, the court entered an interlocutory judgment dissolving the marriage and determining the property rights of the spouses on May 16, 1972.

On March 4, 1972, after the filing of the petition but before the entry of the interlocutory judgment, Civil Code, Section 5118, as amended in 1971, took effect. The amended legislation provides that the earnings and accumulations of both spouses while they live apart constitute separate property. Prior to the amendment of Section 5118, the earnings and accumulations of the wife while the spouses lived apart were separate property although those of the husband were community property. With the trial court's permission, the husband amended his original response and insisted at trial that his earnings and accumulations subsequent to March 2, 1969, the date of separation, were his separate property. The trial court rejected the husband's contention and held that only the earnings and accumulations he acquired after March 4, 1972, the effective date of the amendment, constituted his separate property.

This case squarely poses an issue of first impression, namely, whether amended Section 5118 governs property rights acquired prior to the effective date of that amendment that have not been finally adjudicated by a judgment from which the time of appeal has elapsed. In resolving this question affirmatively we conclude that the amendment, properly construed, requires retroactive application and that such application does not constitute an unconstitutional deprivation of the wife's property.

We first address the issue of statutory construction: does the amendment to Section 5118 of the Civil Code govern property acquired prior to its effective date. The central inquiry, therefore, is whether the Legislature intended the amendment to Section 5118 to operate retroactively.

The language of the amendment does little to reveal the Legislature's intent regarding the amendment's prospective or retroactive application. The issue in the present case is a close one, but we conclude that the Legislature did intend the amendment to Section 5118 to apply retroactively.

Although the constitutionality of former Section 5118 is not directly before us in this case, we can nonetheless observe that it would be subject to strong constitutional challenge. Prior to the amendment, Section 5118 blatantly discriminated against the husband during periods of separation: the earnings of the wife were her separate property while those of the husband belonged to the community. It seems doubtful that the state could conjure a rational relation between this unequal treatment and any legitimate state interest. It is even less likely that the state could sustain the greater showing required by our recognition that sex based classifications are inherently suspect.

The probable constitutional infirmity of the former law does lend some support to the conclusion that the Legislature intended the amendment to have retroactive effect. We assume that the Legislature was aware of judicial decisions; we thus assume that the Legislature knew of the dubious constitutional stature of the sexually discriminating old law. We may reasonable infer, therefore, that the Legislature wished to replace the possibly infirm law with its constitutionally unobjectionable successor as soon as possible. While this inference is hardly conclusive, it is of some value in ascertaining the Legislature's intent.

We must now determine whether the retroactive application of amended Section 5118 constitutes an unconstitutional deprivation of the property of the wife. The status of property as community or separate is normally determined at the time of its acquisition. Consequently, the wife gained vested property rights when, prior to the effective date of amended Section 5118, her husband earned income. The retroactive application of the amendment deprives the wife of her half share of the income that her husband had accumulated during that period. Notwithstanding the fact that it denudes the wife of certain vested property rights, we uphold the retroactive application of the amendment.

Retroactive legislation, though frequently disfavored, is not absolutely proscribed. The vesting of property rights, consequently, does not render them immutable:

> Vested rights, of course, may be impaired "with due process of law" under many circumstances. The state's inherent sovereign power includes the so called "police power" right to interfere with vested property rights whenever reasonably necessary to the protection of the health, safety, morals, and general well being of the people.... The constitutional question, on principle, therefore, would seem to be, not whether a vested right is impaired by a marital property law change, but whether such a change reasonably could be believed to be sufficiently necessary to the public welfare as to justify the impairment.

Addison v. Addison, 62 Cal. 2d at p. 566, 43 Cal. Rptr. at p. 102, 399 P.2d at p. 902.

In determining whether a retroactive law contravenes the due process clause, we consider such factors as the significance of the state interest served by the law, the importance of the retroactive application of the law to the effectuation of that interest, the extent of reliance upon the former law, the legitimacy of that reliance, the extent of actions taken on the basis of that reliance, and the extent to which the retroactive application of the new law would disrupt those actions.

The parties agree that amended Section 5118 can be applied retroactively if such a retroactive application is necessary to subserve a sufficiently important state interest. The wife, however, contends that the retroactive application of this amendment serves no such interest. We disagree.

Addison involved a factual pattern almost identical to that of the present case; it conclusively established the constitutionality of applying amended Section 5118 retroactively. Prior to 1961, a wife could not, upon obtaining a decree of divorce or separate maintenance, secure any interest in property that her husband had acquired in a common law state. California's 1961 quasi-community property legislation effectively reclassified as community property any common law separate property that would have been community property if it had been acquired by a California domiciliary. *Addison* upheld the constitutionality of applying that legislation to spouses who came to California, resided here, and then separated prior to the effective date of the legislation, so long as the trial was held subsequent to that date.

The application of the quasi-community property legislation to property acquired before its effective date clearly impaired the husband's vested property rights; prior to the enactment of the legislation he had been the sole owner of certain property and afterwards the property belonged to the community. Nevertheless, we deemed the retroactive application of the legislation a proper exercise of the police power. The state's paramount interest in the equitable distribution of marital property upon dissolution of the marriage, we concluded, justified the impairment of the husband's vested property rights.

The infringement of the wife's vested property rights in this case finds support in the same state interest that justified the retroactive application of the legislation in *Addison*; here, as in *Addison*, the legislature reallocated property rights in the course of its abiding supervision of marital property and dissolutions. Moreover, the legislation sprang in both cases from an appreciation of the rank injustice of the former law. The calculus of the costs and benefits of the retroactive application of amended Section 5118, therefore, does not differ significantly from that implicit in *Addison*. This peculiar congruence between the present case and *Addison* permits us to sustain the retroactive application of amended Section 5118 without protracted discussion. The divestiture of the wife's property rights in the instant case is no more a taking of property without due process of law than was the divestiture of the husband's property rights in *Addison*. The state's interest in the equitable dissolution of the marital relationship supports this use of the police power to abrogate rights in marital property that derived from the patently unfair former law.

In sum, we hold that amended Section 5118 governs all property rights, whenever acquired, that have not been finally adjudicated by a judgment from which the time to appeal has lapsed.

We reverse the judgment below and remand the case for proceedings consistent with the views expressed herein.

DISCUSSION

Amendments to statutory schemes, if given full retroactive effect, can affect property acquired before the effective date of the law. Sometimes these changes are challenged as an unconstitutional "taking" of property. *Addison* and *Bouquet* set forth the normal police power analysis. The taking is lawful if the change is "sufficiently necessary to the public welfare to justify the impairment." What public welfare concerns were addressed in the statutes involved in these cases? Note that retroactive application of community property rules is not always constitutional. *See In re Fabian*, 224 Cal. Rptr. 333 (Cal. 1986); *In re Marriage of Heikes*, 899 P.2d 1349 (Cal. 1995).

Tex. Fam. Code § 7.002 is essentially identical to the California statue involved in *Addison*. Is Section 7.002 retroactive? If so, is it constitutional?

B. Federal Constitution

1. Jurisdiction

Hoffman v. Hoffman

Court of Appeals of Texas—Ft. Worth, 1992
821 S.W.2d 3, no writ

OPINION

HILL, Justice.

Henry Daniel Hoffman III appeals from the trial court's order sustaining the special appearance of Shirley Darlene Hoffman, the appellee, and dismissing his divorce action for want of jurisdiction.

In three points of error, Henry contends that the trial court erred by placing the burden of proof at the special appearance hearing on him and by sustaining the special appearance, because the evidence clearly showed that he was a domiciliary of the State of Texas and a resident of Denton County for ninety days prior to the filing of his petition, and because the pleadings and the evidence clearly showed that the court had jurisdiction.

We reform the trial court's order sustaining special appearance to provide that Shirley Darlene Hoffman's special appearance is sustained but that the cause is not dismissed, because we hold that the trial court has jurisdiction over the marital status of its citizens that is not defeated by its lack of personal jurisdiction over their spouses. We affirm the order as reformed and, because the order is therefore interlocutory in nature, we remand this cause for further proceedings.

We agree with Henry that the trial court has jurisdiction over the divorce. Where the trial court in a divorce proceeding has no personal jurisdiction over the respondent, the trial court has the jurisdiction to grant the divorce, but not to divide property outside the State of Texas. *Comisky v. Comisky*, 597 S.W.2d 6, 8 (Tex. Civ. App.—Beaumont 1980, no writ). It may also lack jurisdiction to divide property within the state. *See Shaffer v. Heitner*, 433 U.S. 186, 212, 97 S.Ct. 2569, 2584, 53 L.Ed.2d 683 (1977). Therefore, the trial court erred in dismissing Henry's divorce petition for want of jurisdiction, even though it might not have jurisdiction to deal with the property of the parties. The special appearance should only have been granted to the extent of the trial court's recognition that it does not have personal jurisdiction over Shirley and therefore may not divide the property of the parties located outside the State of Texas and possibly that located within the State of Texas.

In support of her contention that the trial court properly dismissed the entire proceeding for want of jurisdiction, Shirley relies on *Comisky*, but an examination of the opinion in that case supports the result that we reach here. Her reliance on *Scott v. Scott*, 554, S.W.2d 274 (Tex. Civ. App.—Houston [1st Dist.] 1977, no writ) and *Fox v. Fox*, 559 S.W.2d 407 (Tex. Civ. App.—Austin 1977, no writ) are likewise misplaced, for there is nothing in either opinion that conflicts with our results here. As noted in *Scott*, a state has jurisdiction in a divorce action when one of the parties alone becomes a domiciliary of that state because the divorce action is *quasi in rem*. *Scott*, 554 S.W.2d at 278. In *Fox*, the court also noted the ability of the district court to award a divorce and divide property located within the state, even though the court might not have personal jurisdiction over the respondent, because those are *in rem* proceedings. *Fox*, 559, S.W.2d at 410. These authorities all show that TEX. FAM. CODE ANN. sec. 3.26 relates to obtaining personal jurisdiction over a nonresident respondent and does not in any way take away from the trial court's *in rem* jurisdiction to grant a divorce and divide property located within this state. Even though the United States Supreme Court in *Shaffer*, in some cases eliminated the distinctions between *in personam, in rem,* and *quasi in rem* as they related to a state's ability to deal with the rights of nonresidents, the Court in that opinion appeared to recognize adjudications of status as an exception to the "minimum contacts" requirement of *International Shoe Co. v. Washington*, 326 U.S. 310, 66 S.Ct. 154, 90 L.Ed. 95 (1945) *Shaffer*, 433 U.S. 208 n. 30, 97 S.Ct. 2578 n. 30. *See also Perry*, 604 S.W.2d at 315.

We reform the trial court's order to reflect that Shirley Darlene Hoffman's special appearance is sustained in that the trial court does not have personal jurisdiction over her, but that the divorce action is not dismissed. We affirm the order sustaining special appearance as reformed and remand this cause for further proceedings.

DISCUSSION

The concept of "divisible divorce" is now accepted in American family law. Under this view, the state where one spouse is domiciled can divorce the parties, regardless of the contacts, if any, the other spouse has with the state. However, if the state wishes to divide the parties' property or award child support, the court must have in personam jurisdiction over both parties. *See Kulko v. U.S.*, 436 U.S. 84 (1978); *Shaffer v. Heitner*, 433 U.S. 186 (1977). If property is located in the forum, that state will almost always have sufficient contacts with the property and the parties to exercise jurisdiction regarding that property.

Burnham v. Superior Court, 110 S. Ct. 2105 (1990) has muddied the personal jurisdiction waters. The Supreme Court there announced that transient personal jurisdiction (jurisdiction based upon service within the state) is not subject to *International Shoe* "minimum contacts" analysis. So, unless a spouse is fraudulently enticed into a forum, personal jurisdiction is possible based upon personal service within the forum, regardless of the contacts between the served spouse and the forum. *See In re Gonzalez*, 993 S.W.2d 147 (Tex. App.—San Antonio 1999, no writ).

In re S.A.V., 837 S.W.2d 80 (Tex. 1992) discusses the distinction between contacts necessary for jurisdiction to order child support and the requirements for child custody jurisdiction. For child support, *Kulko, supra*, requires personal jurisdiction over the obligor. In contrast, *S.A.V.* holds that a court does not need personal jurisdiction over both parents to render a custody determination. The rules for custody jurisdiction are set forth in TFC Sec. 152.003.

So, for example, if a Texas divorce court without personal jurisdiction over an absent spouse awarded a money judgment against that spouse, that portion of the judgment would not be entitled to full faith and credit. *Dillard v. Dillard*, 611 NYS2d 590 (N.Y. App. Div. 1994).

Dawson-Austin v. Austin

Supreme Court of Texas, 1998
968 S.W.2d 319

The issues we address in this divorce action are whether the district court had in personam jurisdiction over the wife, and if not, whether the court nevertheless had jurisdiction to divide the marital estate. The court of appeals upheld personal jurisdiction. 920 S.W.2d 776. We disagree.

I

Since 1970, William Franklin Austin has been the president, chief executive officer, sole director, and sole stockholder of Starkey Laboratories, Inc., a Minnesota corporation in the business of manufacturing and distributing hearing aids. In 1977, Austin met Cynthia Lee Dawson at a seminar in Oregon, where she was living, and persuaded her to come to work for Starkey at its headquarters in Minnesota. Austin was 35 years old and divorced, and Dawson was 30 years old and separated from her husband. Dawson soon moved into Austin's Minnesota home and continued working for Starkey. On a business trip to China in 1980, Austin and Dawson recited marriage vows in a Beijing restaurant. Two years later they filed a marriage certificate in Minnesota. At some point Dawson assumed the surname, Dawson-Austin.

Dawson-Austin worked for Starkey until shortly after she and Austin separated in 1992. Over the years the business had grown. In 1980 Starkey was worth about $ 1.5 million with some $ 12 million in net revenues. By 1992 the company had become the second largest manufacturer of hearing aids in the world with sales totaling more than $ 200 million and a net worth of at least $40 million.

Throughout the marriage the couple's principal residence was in Minnesota, although they also owned homes elsewhere, including one they acquired in California in 1984. They never resided in Texas, and neither of them ever came to the state except on business, and then only a few times. When they separated in February 1992, Dawson-Austin was living in their California home, and she remained there. Austin moved to Texas on March 10. On April 10 Dawson-Austin filed for divorce in California but did not serve Austin until October 16. Austin filed for divorce in Texas on September 10, the first day he could do so under Texas law, TEX. FAM. CODE § 6.301 (formerly TEX. FAM. CODE § 3.21), and served Dawson-Austin four days later.

Dawson-Austin filed a special appearance and an amended special appearance, both of which the district court overruled. Dawson-Austin requested the court in dividing the couple's property to apply Minnesota law, under which she contends she would be entitled to a part of the increase in value of petitioner's Starkey stock attributable to the efforts of either spouse. The court refused and instead applied Texas law, holding that the stock was Austin's separate property subject only to any right of reimbursement of the community estate. The court awarded Dawson-Austin 55.59% of the community—a little over $ 2 million.

Dawson-Austin appealed. The court of appeals in its initial opinion reversed the decree, holding that Minnesota law should have been applied in dividing the marital estate.

On rehearing, however, a divided court of appeals affirmed the decree in all respects. 920 S.W.2d 776.

III

A

[T]he district court erred in overruling Dawson-Austin's amended special appearance. Section 6.305(a) of the Family Code provides:

> If the petitioner in a suit for dissolution of a marriage is a resident or a domiciliary of this state at the time the suit for dissolution is filed, the court may exercise personal jurisdiction over the respondent or over the respondent's personal representative although the respondent is not a resident of this state if:
>
> (1) this state is the last marital residence of the petitioner and the respondent and the suit is filed before the second anniversary of the date on which marital residence ended; or
>
> (2) there is any basis consistent with the constitutions of this state and the United States for the exercise of the personal jurisdiction.

TEX. FAM. CODE § 6.305(a) (formerly TEX. FAM. CODE § 3.26(a)). Austin had been domiciled in Texas exactly six months to the day when he filed suit for divorce. See id. § 6.301 ("A suit for divorce may not be maintained in this state unless at the time the suit is filed either the petitioner or the respondent has been ... a domiciliary of this state for the preceding six-month period....") (formerly TEX. FAM. CODE § 3.21). Dawson-Austin, however, neither was nor ever had been a Texas resident. Thus the district court did not have in personam jurisdiction over Dawson-Austin unless it was under Section 6.305(a)(2).

The United States Constitution permits "a state court [to] take personal jurisdiction over a defendant only if it has some minimum, purposeful contacts with the state, and the exercise of jurisdiction will not offend traditional notions of fair play and substantial justice." *CMMC v. Salinas*, 929 S.W.2d 435, 437 (Tex. 1996) (citing cases); *International Shoe Co. v. Washington*, 326 U.S. 310, 90 L. Ed. 95, 66 S. Ct. 154 (1945). Dawson-Austin had no "minimum, purposeful contacts" with Texas. At the time Austin filed suit, Dawson-Austin resided in California, as Austin's petition itself alleged. She was served in California. At the hearing on her amended special appearance, she testified unequivocally and without contradiction from Austin that her only contact with the State of Texas had been to attend a business convention nine or ten years earlier. She had never lived in Texas, and Austin had not lived here before March 1992. There was no basis for the district court to exercise personal jurisdiction over Dawson-Austin, and Austin does not contend otherwise.

B

Even though the district court did not have in personam jurisdiction over Dawson-Austin, it is possible under the United States Constitution, and thus under Texas law, for the court to have had jurisdiction to divide the marital estate located in Texas. The property in Texas in which the parties claimed an interest was Austin's Dallas home and Texas bank accounts, which the parties agreed was community property, and the stock certificate evidencing Austin's shares in Starkey. As we have previously stated, Austin contends that his Starkey stock is separate property, while Dawson-Austin claims that she is entitled under Minnesota law to part of the increase in value of the stock attributable to her and Austin's efforts during marriage.

In *Pennoyer v. Neff*, 95 U.S. 714, 24 L. Ed. 565 (1877), the United States Supreme Court held that a state court could exercise jurisdiction over property within the state's borders and determine the rights and interests of non-residents. But in *Shaffer v. Heitner*, 433 U.S. 186, 53 L. Ed. 2d 683, 97 S. Ct. 2569 (1977), the Court abandoned this position and concluded instead that jurisdiction over property, like jurisdiction over persons, must be based on minimum, purposeful contacts and must not offend traditional notions of fair play and substantial justice:

> The fiction that an assertion of jurisdiction over property is anything but an assertion of jurisdiction over the owner of the property supports an ancient form without substantial modern justification. Its continued acceptance would serve only to allow state-court jurisdiction that is fundamentally unfair to the defendant.

> We therefore conclude that all assertions of state-court jurisdiction must be evaluated according to the standards set forth in International Shoe and its progeny.

433 U.S. at 212. *Shaffer* was a shareholder derivative suit against officers and directors of two Delaware corporations. A Delaware court sequestered defendants' stock in the corporations, even though neither defendants nor their stock were physically present in Delaware, basing its jurisdiction to do so on a Delaware statute that deemed Delaware the situs of ownership of all stock in Delaware corporations, *see Shaffer*, 433 U.S. at 192. The Supreme Court held that neither defendants nor their stock had sufficient contacts with Delaware to justify the state court's exercise of jurisdiction over them. *Shaffer*, 433 U.S. at 213–217.

In the present case, the location in Texas of property that either is or is claimed to be part of the marital estate does not supply the minimum contacts required for the court to exercise jurisdiction over Dawson-Austin. Austin bought his Dallas home, opened his Texas bank accounts, and brought his Starkey stock certificate to Texas after he separated from Dawson-Austin. We do not believe that one spouse may leave the other, move to another state in which neither has ever lived, buy a home or open a bank account or store a stock certificate there, and by those unilateral actions, and nothing more, compel the other spouse to litigate their divorce in the new domicile consistent with due process. One spouse cannot, solely by actions in which the other spouse is not involved, create the contacts between a state and the other spouse necessary for jurisdiction over a divorce action. *See In the Interest of S.A.V.*, 837 S.W.2d 80, 83–84 (Tex. 1992) (holding that without personal jurisdiction over one parent, a court could still decide custody of a child living in the State, but could not determine support and visitation). Moreover, Dawson-Austin's claim to a part of the value of the Starkey stock is completely unrelated to the situs of the certificate; rather, it is based on the parties' efforts to increase the value of Starkey, most of which occurred in Minnesota. In no sense can it be said that Dawson-Austin ever "purposefully availed" herself of the privilege of owning property in this State. *See Burger King Corp. v. Rudzewicz*, 471 U.S. 462, 475, 85 L. Ed. 2d 528, 105 S. Ct. 2174 (1985) (citing *Hanson v. Denckla*, 357 U.S. 235, 253, 2 L. Ed. 2d 1283, 78 S. Ct. 1228 (1958)).

Thus, the district court lacked jurisdiction to adjudicate Dawson-Austin's claim to part of the value of the Starkey stock or to divide the marital estate.

The district court had jurisdiction only to grant a divorce and not to determine the parties' property claims. Accordingly, the judgment of the court of appeals is reversed and the case is remanded to the district court for rendition of judgment divorcing Austin and Dawson-Austin and dismissing all other claims for relief for want of jurisdiction.

2. Property Located Outside the State

There is authority for the view that a court's divorce decree which purports to affect title to foreign realty is not entitled to full faith and credit. *See Fall v. Estin*, 215 U.S. 1 (1909). To circumvent this problem, courts normally require the parties, while they are before the court, to execute deeds regarding the subject property. This is within the court's power. *Eckard v. Eckard*, 636 A.2d 455 (Md. 1994). Personalty located in another state may be divided by the divorce court, if the court has personal jurisdiction over both spouses.

3. Federal Preemption

Pursuant to the Supremacy Clause of the U.S. Constitution, federal law can preempt state law. Federal courts have recently been increasingly inclined to conclude that certain types of federal benefits were intended by Congress to be the separate property of the employee, even though the benefits were earned pursuant to services rendered during marriage. If a court reaches this conclusion, the benefits are deemed the separate property of the employee; normal Texas marital property rules are preempted.

a. Military Retirement

McCarty v. McCarty
Supreme Court of the United States, 1981
453 U.S. 210

BLACKMUN, Justice.

[During marriage H served in the U.S. Army 18 of the 20 years necessary to earn retirement pay. A California divorce court awarded to W a fraction of the future retirement benefits H might receive, holding the benefits earned during marriage were either community property or, because the spouses were domiciled outside California at various times, quasi-community. The California appellate courts rejected H's contention that federal law mandated that all military retirement pay was his separate property. H appealed to the United States Supreme Court.]

Under current law, there are three basic forms of military retirement: nondisability retirement; disability retirement; and reserve retirement. For our present purposes, only the first of these three forms is relevant. Since each of the military services has substantially the same nondisability retirement system, the Army's system may be taken as typical. An Army officer who has 20 years of service, at least 10 of which have been active service as a commissioned officer, may request that the Secretary of the Army retire him. An officer who requests such retirement is entitled to "retired pay." This is calculated on the basis of the number of years served and rank achieved. An officer who serves for less than 20 years is not entitled to retired pay.

The nondisability retirement system is noncontributory in that neither the service member nor the Federal Government makes periodic contributions to any fund during the period of active service; instead, retired pay is funded by annual appropriations. In contrast, since 1957, military personnel have been required to contribute to the Social

Security System. Upon satisfying the necessary age requirements, the Army retiree, the spouse, and ex-spouse who was married to the retiree for at least 10 years, and any dependent children are entitled to Social Security benefits.

Military retired pay terminates with the retired service member's death, and does not pass to the member's heirs. The member, however, may designate a beneficiary to receive any arrearages that remain unpaid at death. In addition, there are statutory schemes that allow a service member to set aside a portion of the member's retired pay for his or her survivors. The first such scheme, now known as the Retired Serviceman's Family Protection Plan (RSFPP), was established in 1953. Under the RSFPP, the military member could elect to reduce his or her retired pay in order to provide, at death, an annuity for a surviving spouse or child. Participation in the RSFPP was voluntary, and the participating member, prior to receiving retired pay, could revoke the election in order "to reflect a change in the marital or dependency status of the member of his family that is caused by death, divorce, annulment, remarriage, or acquisition of a child." Further, deductions from retired pay automatically cease upon the death or divorce of the service member's spouse.

Because the RSFPP was self-financing, it required the deduction of a substantial portion of the service member's retired pay; consequently, only about 15% of eligible military retirees participated in the plan. In order to remedy this situation, Congress enacted the Survivor Benefit Plan (SBP) in 1972. Participation in this plan is automatic unless the service member chooses to opt out. The SBP is not entirely self-financing; instead, the Government contributes to the plan, thereby rendering participation in the SBP less expensive for the service member than participation in the RSFPP. Participants in the RSFPP were given the option of continuing under that plan or of enrolling in the SBP.

We need not decide today whether federal law prohibits a State from characterizing retired pay as deferred compensation, since we agree with appellant's alternative argument that the application of community property law conflicts with the federal military retirement scheme regardless of whether retired pay is defined as current or as deferred compensation. The statutory language is straightforward: "A member of the Army retired under this chapter is entitled to retired pay." In *Hisquierdo v. Hisquierdo*, 439 U.S. 572 (1979), we emphasized that under the Railroad Retirement Act a spouse of a retired railroad worker was entitled to a separate annuity that terminated upon divorce. In contrast, the military retirement system confers no entitlement to retired pay upon the retired service member's spouse. Thus, unlike the Railroad Retirement Act, the military retirement system does not embody even a limited "community property concept." Indeed, Congress has explicitly stated: "Historically, military retired pay has been a personal entitlement payable to the retired member himself as long as he lives."

Appellee argues that Congress' use of the term "personal entitlement" in this contest signifies only that retired pay ceases upon the death of the service member. But several features of the statutory schemes governing military pay demonstrate that Congress did not use the term in so limited a fashion. First, the service member may designate a beneficiary to receive any unpaid arrearages in retired pay upon his death. The service member is free to designate someone other than his spouse or ex-spouse as the beneficiary; further, the statute expressly provides that "[a] payment under this section bars recovery by any other person of the amount paid." In *Wissner v. Wissner*, 338 U.S. 655 (1950), this Court considered an analogous statutory scheme. Under the National Life Insurance Act, an insured service member had the right to designate the beneficiary of his policy. *Wissner* held that California could not award a service member's widow half the proceeds of a life insurance policy, even though the source of the premiums—the member's army pay—

was characterized as community property under California law. The Court reserved the question whether California is "entitled to call army pay community property," *id.* at 657, n. 2, since it found that Congress had "spoken with force and clarity in directing that the proceeds belong to the named beneficiary and no other." *Id.* at 658. In the present contest, Congress has stated with "force and clarity" that a beneficiary under Section 2771 claims an interest in the retired pay itself, not simply in proceeds from a policy purchased with that pay.

Second, the language, structure, and legislative history of the RSFPP and the SBP also demonstrate that retired pay is a "personal entitlement." While retired pay ceases upon the death of the service member, the RSFPP and the SBP allow the service member to reduce his or her retired pay in order to provide an annuity for the surviving spouse or children. Under both plans, however, the service member is free to elect to provide no annuity at all, or to provide an annuity payable only to the surviving children, and not to the spouse. Here again, it is clear that if retired pay were community property, the service member could not so deprive the spouse of his or her interest in the property. But we need not rely on this implicit conflict alone, for both the language of the statutes and their legislative history make it clear that the decision whether to leave an annuity is the service member's decision alone because retired pay is his or her personal entitlement. It has been stated in Congress that "[t]he rights in retirement pay accrue to the retiree and, ultimately, the decision is his as to whether or not to leave part of that retirement pay as an annuity to his survivors." H. R. Rep. No. 92-481, p. 9 (1971). California's community property division of retired pay is simply inconsistent with this explicit expression of congressional intent that retired pay accrue to the retiree.

Moreover, such a division would have the anomalous effect of placing an ex-spouse in a better position than that of a widower or a widow under the RSFPP and the SBP. Appellee argues that "Congress' concern for the welfare of soldiers' widows sheds little light on Congress' attitude toward the community treatment of retirement benefits," quoting *Fithian*, 10 Cal. 3d, at 600, 517 P.2d, at 454. But this argument fails to recognize that Congress deliberately has chosen to favor the widower or widow over the ex-spouse. An ex-spouse is not an eligible beneficiary of an annuity under either plan. In addition, under the RSFPP, deductions from retired pay for a spouse's annuity automatically cease upon divorce, so as "[t]o safeguard the participant's future retired pay when ... divorce occurs."

Third, and finally, it is clear that Congress intended that military retired pay "actually reach the beneficiary." *See Hisquierdo*, 439 U.S., at 584. Retired pay cannot be attached to satisfy a property settlement incident to the dissolution of a marriage. In enacting the SBP, Congress rejected a provision in the House bill, H. R. 10670, that would have allowed attachment of up to 50% of military retired pay to comply with a court order in favor of a spouse, former spouse, or child. Although this provision passed the House, it was not included in the Senate version of the bill. Thereafter, the House acceded to the Senate's view that the attachment provision would unfairly "single out military retirees for a form of enforcement of court orders imposed on no other employees or retired employees of the Federal Government."

Subsequently comprehensive legislation was enacted. In 1975, Congress amended the Social Security Act to provide that all federal benefits, including those payable to members of the armed services, may be subject to legal process to enforce child support or alimony obligations. In 1977, however, Congress added a new definitional section providing that the term "alimony" "does not include any payment or transfer of property in compliance with any community property settlement, equitable distribution of property, or other division of property between spouses or former spouses."

Hisquierdo also pointed out that Congress might conclude that this distinction between support and community property claims is "undesirable." Indeed, Congress recently enacted legislation that requires that Civil Service retirement benefits be paid to an ex-spouse to the extent provided for in "the terms of any court order or court-approved property settlement agreement incident to any court decree of divorce, annulment, or legal separation." In an even more extreme recent step, Congress amended the Foreign Service retirement legislation to provide that, as a matter of federal law, an ex-spouse is entitled to a pro rata share of Foreign Service retirement benefits. Thus, the Civil Service amendments require the United States to recognize the community property division of Civil Service retirement benefits by a state court, while the Foreign Service amendments establish a limited federal community property concept. Significantly, however, while similar legislation affecting military retired pay was introduced in the 96th Congress, none of those bills was reported out of committee. Thus, in striking contrast to its amendment of the Foreign Service and Civil Service retirement systems, Congress has neither authorized nor required the community property division of military retired pay. On the contrary, that pay continues to be the personal entitlement of the retiree.

[I]t is manifest that the application of community property principles to military retired pay threatens grave harm to "clear and substantial" federal interests.

In the first place, the community property interest appellee seeks "promises to diminish that portion of the benefit Congress has said should go to the retired [service member] alone." *See Hisquierdo*, 439 U.S., at 590. State courts are not free to reduce the amounts that Congress has determined are necessary for the retired member. Furthermore, the community property division of retired pay may disrupt the carefully balanced scheme Congress has devised to encourage a service member to set aside a portion of his or her retired pay as an annuity for a surviving spouse or dependent children.

The potential for disruption of military personnel management is equally clear. [T]he military retirement system is designed to serve as an inducement for enlistment and reenlistment, to create an orderly career path, and to ensure "youthful and vigorous" military forces. While conceding that there is a substantial interest in attracting and retaining personnel for the military forces, appellee argues that this interest will not be impaired by allowing a State to apply its community property laws to retired military personnel in the same manner that it applies those laws to civilians. Yet this argument ignores two essential characteristics of military service: the military forces are national in operation; and their members, unlike civilian employees, *cf. Hisquierdo*, are not free to choose their place of residence. Appellant, for instance, served tours of duty in four States and the District of Columbia. The value of retired pay as an inducement for enlistment or reenlistment is obviously diminished to the extent that the service member recognizes that he or she may be involuntarily transferred to a State that will divide that pay upon divorce.

The interference with the goals of encouraging orderly promotion and a youthful military is no less direct. Here, as in the Railroad Retirement Act context, "Congress has fixed an amount thought appropriate to support an employee's old age and to encourage the employee to retire." *See Hisquierdo*, 439 U.S., at 585. But the reduction of retired pay by a community property award not only discourages retirement by reducing the retired pay available to the service member, but gives him a positive incentive to keep working, since current income after divorce is not divisible as community property. Congress has determined that a youthful military is essential to the national defense; it is not for States to interfere with that goal by lessening the incentive to retire created by the military retirement system.

The judgment of the California Court of Appeal is reversed, and the case is remanded for further proceedings not inconsistent with this opinion.

Segrest v. Segrest

Supreme Court of Texas, 1983
649 S.W.2d 610

RAY, Justice.

This is an appeal from a suit filed for a declaratory judgment by a former husband seeking a determination of the validity and enforceability of a portion of a 1974 divorce decree. The decree incorporated a property settlement agreement treating military retirement benefits as part of the community estate of the parties. The trial court determined that pre-1981 divisions of military retirement pay are void and unenforceable in light of the United States Supreme Court decision in *McCarty v. McCarty*, 453 U.S. 210, 101 S.Ct. 2728, 69 L.Ed.2d 589 (1981). The court of appeals affirmed. We reverse the judgments of the courts below, dismiss Claude Segrest's cause of action and remand Patsy Segrest's counterclaim to the trial court for proceedings in accordance with our opinion.

Claude and Patsy Segrest were divorced on February 12, 1974. The decree of divorce incorporated a contractual property settlement agreement dividing Mr. Segrest's non-disability military retirement benefits. On June 26, 1981, the United States Supreme Court held that military retirement benefits were not divisible as community property in a state court. *McCarty v. McCarty*, 453 U.S. 210. Thereafter, on or about August 1, 1981, Mr. Segrest discontinued payments to his former wife as required by the settlement agreement. The present proceedings were instituted on October 16, 1981. Mrs. Segrest counterclaimed, seeking enforcement on the pre-divorce contractual settlement agreement.

The trial court rendered judgment declaring both the portion of the 1974 decree awarding Patsy Segrest an interest in Claude Segrest's retirement pay and the incorporated pre-divorce property settlement agreement to be void and unenforceable. No statement of facts was filed in anticipation of appeal. The court of appeals summarily affirmed the trial court's judgment without addressing any of the points of error raised by Patsy, stating "[i]n the absence of a statement of facts, it must be presumed on appeal that the evidence introduced at the trial supports the findings and judgment of the court."

The court of appeals erred in not considering Mrs. Segrest's points of error. Tex. R. Civ. P. 451. Rule 371 requires that a statement of facts be filed only where necessary to the appeal. Tex. R. Civ. P. 371. The rule applies to issues which require reference to the evidence and not to matters which are strictly questions of law. No issues of fact were raised at trial. While the court of appeals has not disposed of the points raised by petitioner, these points present only questions of law. We may, therefore, dispose of them now instead of requiring the parties to go back to the court of appeals and then possibly return here with a second application for writ of error. *McKelvy v. Barber*, 381 S.W.2d 59, 65 (Tex. 1961).

Patsy Segrest, the petitioner, raises two points of error concerning the propriety of her husband's suit. By her first point, Mrs. Segrest contends that a suit for declaratory judgment may not be used to collaterally attack a final judgment. It is well established that a voidable judgment is not open to collateral attack, but can only be corrected by direct review. *Ex parte Sutherland*, 526 S.W.2d 536 (Tex. 1975). Moreover, the right to declaratory relief is subject to the rule of res judicata. *Cornell v. Cornell*, 413 S.W.2d 385 (Tex. 1967). We must, therefore, determine the validity of the 1974 decree before determining the propriety of Mr. Segrest's action and the applicability of the doctrine of res judicata. By her second point of error, Mrs. Segrest contends that the *McCarty* decision does not command retroactive application, and as such the portion of the 1974 divorce decree dividing the military retirement benefit is merely voidable, not void. We agree.

A review of the relevant United States Supreme Court decisions indicates that *McCarty* was not intended to be retroactive. None of the cases involving the question of federal law preemption of state community property law indicate an intent to invalidate or otherwise render unenforceable in retroactive fashion all prior valid and subsisting state court judgments. *See Ridgway v. Ridgway*, 454 U.S. 46 (1981); *McCarty v. McCarty*, 453 210 (1981); *Hisquierdo v. Hisquierdo*, 439 U.S. 572 (1979); *Yiatchos v. Yiatchos*, 376 U.S. 306 (1964); *Free v. Blank*, 369 U.S. 663 (1962); *Wissner v. Wissner*, 338 U.S. 655 (1950); *McCune v. Essig*, 199 U.S. 382 (1905).

In *Chevron v. Huson*, 404 U.S. 97, 92 S.Ct. 349, 30 L.Ed.2d 296 (1971), the Supreme Court set out a three-pronged test for determining whether and to what extent a judicially modified or abrogated rule of law should be given retroactive operation: (1) whether the holding in question "decid[ed] an issue of first impression whose resolution was not clearly foreshadowed" by earlier cases; (2) "whether retrospective operation will further or retard [the] operation" of the holding in question; and (3) whether retroactive application "could produce substantial inequitable results" in individual cases. 404 U.S. at 105–08. *See also Northern Pipeline Construction Co. v. Marathon Pipe Line Co.*, ___U.S.___, 102 S.Ct.___, 73 L.Ed.2d 598 (1982); *Ciprano City of Houma*, 395 U.S. 701 (1969); *Linkletter v. Walker*, 381 U.S. 618 (1965); *Chicot County Drainage District v. Baxter State Bank*, 308 U.S. 371 (1940); *Great Northern Railway Co. v. Sunburst Oil & Refining Co.*, 287 U.S. 358 (1932).

The question as to what effect should be given a division of military benefits awarded in a final divorce decree was discussed in *Erspan v. Badgett*, 647 F.2d 550, reh. denied en banc, 659 F.2d 26 (5th Cir. 1981), and *Wilson v. Wilson*, 667 F.2d 497 (5th Cir. 1982), cert. denied, ___U.S.___, 102 S.Ct. 3485 (1982). *Erspan* involved an appeal from a judgment enforcing a decree finalized before *McCarty* was decided, and which divided retirement benefits. Relying on *Federated Department Stores, Inc. v. Moitie*, 452 U.S. 394 (1981), the federal court of appeals held that the divorce decree was entitled to its usual res judicata effect. A final judgment settles not only issues actually litigated, but also any issues that could have been litigated. That the judgment may have been wrong or premised on a legal principle subsequently overruled does not affect application of res judicata. 659 F.2d at 28. *See Federated Department Stores, Inc. v. Moitie*, 452 U.S. at 398–99; *Trahan v. Trahan*, 626 S.W.2d 485, 487–88 (Tex. 1981).

The holding of the Fifth Circuit Court of Appeals was the same in *Wilson*. The Wilsons were divorced in a Texas state court in 1970. Pursuant to an agreed property settlement agreement (as we have in the instant case), the trial court awarded Mrs. Wilson $226.25 per month from her husband's military retirement pay, which was to commence in 1971. No appeal was made from that judgment. Mrs. Wilson never received a payment, and brought a successful suit in federal court. On appeal, Mr. Wilson urged the same *McCarty* argument Mr. Segrest now presents to us. Citing 28 U.S.C.A. Sec. 1738, which requires that final state judgments be accorded full faith and credit, the court of appeals concluded that the Texas state court judgment was res judicata of the suit at bar. 667 F.2d at 498.

Within the parameters established by *Chevron* and *Federated Department Stores*, we are persuaded to follow the decisions of the Fifth Circuit Court of Appeals in *Erspan* and *Wilson*. The decision in *McCarty* does not command retroactive application as to divorce decrees which were final before the Supreme Court announced its decision and which treat military retirement benefits as community property. The *McCarty* decision, being a case of first impression, could not have been foreseen. Retroactive application would place an inequitable burden upon those ex-spouses for whom divisions of the community estate were based upon the assumption that military retirement benefits constituted a community asset.

Having determined that *McCarty v. McCarty*, 453 U.S. 210 (1981), does not operate retroactively, the Segrests' 1974 divorce decree should be viewed as being erroneous or voidable, as opposed to void. *Austin Independent School District v. Sierra Club*, 495 S.W.2d 878, 882 (Tex. 1973). Consequently, the rule of res judicata is applicable. Mr. Segrest's suit for declaratory judgment is therefore not a remedy available to him to set aside the final decree of divorce rendered in 1974. *Sutherland v. Sutherland*, 560 S.W.2d 531, 533 (Tex. Civ. App.—Texarkana 1978, writ ref'd n.r.e.). Being a final, unappealed and valid judgment, Mr. Segrest's suit for declaratory judgment constitutes both an improper as well as impermissible collateral attack upon the 1974 decree of divorce.

The judgments of the court below are reversed and judgment is rendered dismissing Claude Segrest's suit for declaratory judgment. That part of the judgment is severed. The portion of the case concerning Patsy Segrest's counterclaim for enforcement of the settlement agreement is remanded to the trial court to determine the amounts owed to her.

DISCUSSION

McCarty concluded that Congress intended military retirement benefits to be the separate property of the employee. *Segrest* clarified that *McCarty* would not be given retroactive effect; it would only apply to actions not yet final when the decision was announced. *See also Trahan* v. *Trahan*, 626 S.W.2d 485 (Tex. 1981).

McCarty was not enthusiastically received. A little over a year after *McCarty* was announced, Congress enacted a statute (the Uniform Services Former Spouse's Protection Act) clarifying that non-disability military retirement could be divided by a state divorce court. This law was effective February 1, 1983. After this law was enacted, there were three types of Texas divorces involving military retirement: those that became final before *McCarty*; those that became final after *McCarty* but before February 1, 1983; and those that became final after February 1, 1983. The second type of divorce has been referred to as a "gap" divorce.

Under USFSPA, a state court may divide military retirement benefits only if the military member resides in or is a domiciliary of the state, or if the member consents to the court's jurisdiction. 10 U.S.C. § 1408(c)(4).

Voronin v. Voronin

Texas Court of Appeals—Austin, 1983
662 S.W.2d 102, writ dism'd

SMITH, Justice.

The wife, appellant, contends that the trial court erred: in awarding appellee all his non-disability military retirement benefits on the theory that it (the court) was obliged to do so under *McCarty v. McCarty*, 453 U.S. 210, 101 S.Ct. 2728, 69 L.Ed.2d 589 (1981); in abusing its discretion by dividing the estate unequally in favor of the husband; and in its unequal division of the property because such a division was not supported by any evidence, or in the alternative, was supported by insufficient evidence. For the reasons herein stated, we reverse the judgment of the trial court and remand the cause.

The parties married February 19, 1955, and separated in January 1982. Appellee filed suit February 12, 1982, and the case was heard September 3, 1982, at which time appellee was forty-eight years of age. The decree of divorce, signed by the court on January 31, 1983, was subsequently re-dated February 1, 1983.

Appellee enlisted in the United States Marine Corps on December 13, 1951. He retired in June, 1975, after having served 282 months; thus the parties were married for a total of 244 months during the period of appellee's creditable military service.

In the division of property, the parties agree that the two major assets requiring division by the court were the homestead (valued by the appellant at $38,000 net, and by the appellee at approximately $44,000) and the non-disability military retirement benefits of appellee. Appellee was also receiving military disability payments which are conceded to be his separate property. Appellant sought division of the community property interest and appellee's non-disability military retirement benefits. The record shows that the trial court awarded such benefits to appellee on the premise that under *McCarty v. McCarty, supra*, he was bound to award all the retirement benefits to appellee. This Court must determine whether, at the time of the signing of the divorce decree, or during the time when the trial court had absolute control of the divorce decree, the military pension benefits earned during marriage were property subject to division upon divorce, and if so, whether the trial court abused its discretion in awarding all of the benefits to appellee.

The law in Texas was well established that military benefits earned during marriage were property subject to division. *Taggart v. Taggart*, 552 S.W.2d 422 (Tex. 1977); *Cearley v. Cearley*, 544 S.W.2d 661 (Tex. 1976); *Busby v. Busby*, 457 S.W.2d 551 (Tex. 1970). However, in *McCarty v. McCarty*, 453 U.S. 210, 101 S.Ct. 2728, 69 L.Ed.2d 589 (1981), the United States Supreme Court held that the supremacy clause of the United States Constitution, article VI, precluded a state court from dividing military non-disability retirement pay on divorce. In *Trahan v. Trahan*, 626 S.W.2d 485, 487 (Tex. 1981), the Supreme Court of Texas held that the supremacy clause effectively foreclosed the division of such military retirement benefits.

In *Trahan*, the wife brought suit in 1977 for partition of vested Air Force retirement benefits which had not been divided by property settlements in either of two divorce cases. The trial court concluded that 77.92% of the retirement pay was community property not considered at either divorce proceeding, and awarded the wife 38.96% of benefits accrued to the date of judgment and those which would be paid in the future. On appeal, the Court of Civil Appeals upheld the division of the benefits, but reformed the trial court's judgment relating to the method of the ex-wife's collection of the money judgment for past accrued benefits due her. See *Trahan v. Trahan*, 609 S.W.2d 820 (Tex. Civ. App. 1980). The judgment of the trial court and that of the Court of Civil Appeals both preceded *McCarty*. The Supreme Court of Texas, in its opinion handed down November 18, 1981, held that *McCarty* controlled its decision on appeal, even though the *McCarty* decision was dated June 26, 1981, stating that "it is clear that *McCarty* controls the disposition of this case." *Trahan v. Trahan, supra*, at 487. That is, the Supreme Court gave effect to *McCarty*, even though the trial court and the Court of Civil Appeals had handed down their respective judgments before the decision in *McCarty*. The Supreme Court, in so holding, said "no final adjudication regarding Jack Trahan's military retirement benefits, therefore, has or will be made until this Court renders its opinion." *Trahan v. Trahan, supra*, at 488.

To determine whether *McCarty* controls this case, we look to the record and the latest decision of the Texas Supreme Court. This divorce case was filed February 12, 1982. The case was heard by the trial court on September 3, 1982. The decree of divorce was originally dated January 31, 1983, six and one-half years after appellee retired and began drawing his non-disability retirement benefits. (Appellant concedes that the January 31, 1983 date of the judgment should be considered as a proper date for this appeal.) The trial judge made it absolutely clear that he was awarding the retirement benefits to appellee because he felt that he was bound to do so by *McCarty*. The court said: "Now, I'm just not going to go against *McCarty*, gentlemen, and I am going to award the military and the retirement and disability benefits to Mr. Voronin."

The record shows that the judge and the parties were aware, at time of trial and the court's judgment, of legislation passed by Congress and awaiting the signature of the President, which would overturn the effect of the *McCarty* decision. When asked to find in the decree that he "was compelled by the *McCarty* decision and therefore did not consider the military retirement as far as dividing the property is concerned," the court refused to do so, and again said "I've told you that I'm not going against *McCarty* ... and as far as I am concerned, the court is concerned, it's the law."

We hold that *Cameron v. Cameron*, 641 S.W.2d 210, 212–13 (Tex. 1982) is dispositive of this case. In *Cameron*, Paul Cameron joined the U.S. Air Force on June 22, 1954. He married Sue Akers September 29, 1957, and retired from the Air Force in August, 1977. The divorce suit was filed in Texas in 1978. On March 29, 1979, the trial court awarded the wife thirty-five percent of the gross military retirement funds received by the husband. Noting that under *McCarty*, the Supreme Court had held that the supremacy clause of the United States Constitution foreclosed the division of military non-disability retirement pay on divorce, the Supreme Court of Texas then held:

> On September 9, 1982, the President signed into law the Uniform Services Former Spouse's Protection Act, Pub.L. No. 97-252, 96 Stat. 730 (1982). The purpose of the act was to reverse the effect of the *McCarty* decision. Under the Act a divorce court may divide military retirement pay between the spouses in accordance with the law of the jurisdiction of that court. The Act limits such division of retirement pay to periods after June 25, 1981. *Id.* 1002(a) [to be codified as 10 U.S.C.A. 1408(c)(1)].

The divorce decree, dated March 29, 1979, awards Sue Cameron "thirty-five percent (35%) of the gross present and future military retirement presently being received." Sue Cameron is entitled to receive that thirty-five percent, but not for the period from March 25, 1979, to June 25, 1981. Therefore, we affirm that part of the trial court judgment awarding Sue Cameron thirty-five percent of the military retirement pay, *but only for the period beginning after June 25, 1981* (emphasis added).

The Texas Supreme Court correctly recognized that the purpose and intent of the quoted language of subsection (c)(1) of the Act—indeed the whole Act—is "to reverse the effect of the *McCarty* decision." *Cameron v. Cameron, supra*, at 212. That purpose is affirmed in the Congressional Conference Report. U.S. Code Cong. & Admin. News (1982), 1570.

As was true in *Trahan v. Trahan, supra*, the judgment of the trial court in the instant case was not final. Following *Trahan v. Trahan, supra*, at 488, we hold that no final adjudication regarding appellee's military retirement benefits in this case has or will be made until this Court renders a decision. *Cameron v. Cameron, supra*, controls. In this case the trial court still had control of its judgment when *McCarty* was overturned by the Act. The appellee, in his brief, concedes this to be true, but argues that the trial court considered the Act in its division of community property and, having considered the change in the law, made a fair and equitable division of the community property. To the contrary, in the last pages of the statement of facts, the trial judge makes it clear that he was bound by *McCarty* and on that basis, awarded appellee all the retirement benefits. We hold that the trial court erred in holding that the community estate had no divisible interest in the military non-disability retirement payments of appellee. The community interest in such benefits in this case equaled the months of marriage while the appellee was in the military, divided by the number of months of creditable military service of appellee. Thus the community interest was 86.525%.

We reverse the judgment of the trial court and remand this cause.

Allison v. Allison
Supreme Court of Texas, 1985
700 S.W.2d 914

PER CURIAM.

This is a partition suit brought by a former spouse of a military serviceman to obtain division of military retirement benefits. The trial court rendered summary judgment for the serviceman, and the court of appeals affirmed that judgment. 690 S.W.2d 340. The parties were divorced in September, 1981. The divorce decree expressly awarded all military retirement benefits to the serviceman.

The parties' divorce decree was rendered after the date of the United States Supreme Court's opinion in *McCarty v. McCarty*, 453 U.S. 210, 101 S.Ct. 2728, 69 L.Ed.2d 589 (1981), and before the effective date of the Uniform Services Former Spouses Protection Act, 10 U.S.C. 1408 [February 1, 1983]. The USFSPA makes *McCarty* nugatory with respect to its application to judgments rendered after the date of that decision. *Segrest v. Segrest*, 649 S.W.2d 610, 613 n. 2 (Tex. 1983); *Cameron v. Cameron*, 641 S.W.2d 210, 212–13 (Tex. 1982). Accordingly, the rules of law applicable to the partition of military retirement benefits which controlled prior to the rendition of the *McCarty* decision control the disposition of partition suits brought after the effective date of the USFSPA.

Partition is available as a means of dividing property formerly held by spouses as community property which is not divided upon divorce and is later held by the former spouses as tenants in common. *Harrell v. Harrell*, 692 S.W.2d 876 (Tex. 1985). However, the disposition of retirement benefits in the express terms of a divorce decree renders those benefits not subject to later partition. *Constance v. Constance*, 544 S.W.2d 659, 660–61 (Tex. 1976). In the present case, the divorce decree made an express disposition of William Allison's military retirement benefits. The court of appeals' opinion is consistent with our opinion in *Constance v. Constance* and, therefore, we refuse petitioner's application for writ of error, no reversible error. Tex. R. Civ. P. 483.

Eddy v. Eddy
Texas Court of Appeals—Austin, 1986
710 S.W.2d 783, writ ref'd n.r.e.

CARROLL, Justice.

Peggy Eddy appeals from a take-nothing judgment entered in a suit for partition of military non-disability retirement benefits accrued by her former spouse, Clarence Eddy. We will reverse the judgment of the trial court.

The Eddys were married on July 4, 1964, and were divorced on October 23, 1981. Mr. Eddy served a total of 119 months in the military before the marriage, and 195 months in the military during the marriage. The record also reflects that Mr. Eddy had retired from the military before the entry of the final decree of divorce.

The final decree of divorce: (1) dissolved the marriage; (2) divided certain community property of the parties; and (3) assigned liability for certain debts. All relief requested and not expressly granted in the divorce decree was denied. No specific reference was made in the divorce decree regarding Mr. Eddy's military retirement benefits. The divorce decree was not appealed and became final.

On July 26, 1983, Mrs. Eddy filed the instant suit. She alleged that the military retirement benefits Mr. Eddy accumulated during their marriage constituted community property which had not been partitioned by the divorce decree. After a bench trial, the district court determined that "at the time the decree of divorce was entered, that is October 23, 1981, Clarence Eddy's military retirement benefits were not subject to Texas community property laws by virtue of the decision of the United States Supreme Court in the case of *McCarty v. McCarty*, 543 [453] U.S. 210 [101 S.Ct. 2728, 69 L.Ed.2d 589] (1981)," and entered a take-nothing judgment against Mrs. Eddy. The district court concluded that the doctrine of res judicata now barred relitigation of community property issues.

On appeal, Mrs. Eddy contends that the Uniform Services Former Spouses Protection Act (the Act), 10 U.S.C.A. Sec. 1408 (West 1983 & Supp. 1986), passed some 18 months after *McCarty*, effectively overruled that case and permitted the division of military retirement benefits pursuant to state law as it existed before *McCarty*. Under the provisions of the Act, Mrs. Eddy argues that res judicata does not bar her suit for partition of military retirement benefits from a divorce decree that became final during the "gap" period, that is, after *McCarty* but before passage of the Act.

Before *McCarty*, under Texas law, all military retirement benefits which accrued during a marriage were community property. *Busby v. Busby*, 457 S.W.2d 551 (Tex. 1970). Where the divorce decree failed to provide for a division of military retirement benefits, the husband and wife became tenants in common with respect to the benefits, and this property was subject to a later suit for partition. *Id.*

On June 26, 1981, the United States Supreme Court handed down the *McCarty* case which held that the supremacy clause of the United States Constitution, article 6, precluded a state court from dividing military non-disability retirement pay on divorce. In the wake of *McCarty*, the Texas Supreme Court concluded that the supremacy clause effectively foreclosed the division of military retirement benefits under Texas community property laws. *Trahan v. Trahan*, 626 S.W.2d 485 (Tex. 1981). Thus, *McCarty* forced Texas courts to characterize military retirement benefits as separate property upon divorce. *Id.*

On September 9, 1982, the President signed the Act into law. It provided that a divorce court could divide military retirement pay between the spouses in accordance with the law of the jurisdiction of that court. *Cameron v. Cameron*, 641 S.W.2d 210 (Tex. 1982). In other words, if a state's law treated military retirement benefits as community property before *McCarty*, then the Act once again made these benefits community property.

The Texas Supreme Court has acknowledged that the Act "makes *McCarty* nugatory with respect to its application to judgments rendered after the date of that decision." *Allison v. Allison*, 700 S.W.2d 914, 915 (Tex. 1985). As a consequence, the rules of law applicable to the partition of military retirement benefits which controlled before *McCarty*, once more control the disposition of partition suits brought after the effective date of the Act. *Id.* According to the *Allison* opinion, we must treat *McCarty* as if it never existed.

Partition is available as a means of dividing property formerly held by spouses as community property not divided upon divorce. *Allison v. Allison, supra.* The former spouses hold this omitted property as tenants in common, and it may be partitioned at a later date. *Harrell v. Harrell,* 692 S.W.2d 876 (Tex. 1985). On the other hand, community property, including retirement benefits, specifically allocated by the express terms of a divorce decree is not later subject to partition. *Allison v. Allison, supra,* at 915, citing *Constance v. Constance,* 544 S.W.2d 659 (Tex. 1976).

Thus, where military retirement benefits are not allocated by the express terms of a divorce decree that became final during the "gap" period, the Act negates any effect that *McCarty* had on the characterization of this property at the time of divorce. The parties become tenants in common with respect to this omitted community property, and the property is subject to later partition. *See Busby v. Busby, supra.* In contrast, if the final divorce decree had contained express language from which one could reasonably conclude that the divorce court actually and expressly adjudicated ownership of the military retirement benefits, res judicata would bar a subsequent suit for partition of the military retirement benefits. *Constance v. Constance, supra.*

At the time of trial of this cause, the district court did not have the benefit of the *Allison* opinion. It is now evident that *Allison* is dispositive of the issue in this appeal.

After reviewing *Allison,* we conclude that Mrs. Eddy's suit for partition was not barred by the doctrine of res judicata. The Eddys' divorce became final during the "gap" period. The Eddys' final divorce decree did not mention or dispose of military retirement benefits. After passage of the Act, the Eddys became tenants in common with respect to military retirement benefits which accrued during their marriage. This property is subject to a later partition.

We reverse the judgment and remand this cause to the trial court for determination of amounts due Mrs. Eddy in accordance with this opinion.

DISCUSSION

After the adoption of Section 9.203 of the Family Code, if military retirement benefits earned during marriage are not mentioned in the decree, in a later partition action they will be divided in a manner deemed "just and right" by the divorce court. *See Haynes v. McIntosh,* 776 S.W.2d 784 (Tex. App.—Corpus Christi 1989, writ den.).

A 1990 amendment to USFSPA provided that a state divorce court cannot treat military retirement as divisible property if the decree was issued before June 25, 1981 and did not treat the retirement as part of the marital estate. The statute further stated that it governed all judgments issued before, on or after November 5, 1990. The court considered this provision in *Havlen v. McDougal,* 22 S.W.3d 343 (Tex. 2000) Here the spouses divorced in 1976 and the decree did not mention the retirement benefits. The non-military spouse filed a partition action in 1996. The Supreme Court concluded that the new law governed this case, and held that federal law barred the award of any retirement benefits to the nonmilitary spouse.

A related issue is presented if the non-military spouse filed a post-divorce partition action regarding a pre-*McCarty* silent decree and obtained a final judgment before the 1990 amendment. The enacting legislation provides that such judgments are not valid after November 5, 1992. Two courts have concluded that this federal statute did not preempt such a valid final Texas judgment, and that the judgment remained valid. *Trahan v. Trahan*, 894 S.W.2d 113 (Tex. App.—Austin 1995, writ denied); *Ex Parte Kruse*, 911 S.W.2d 839 (Tex. App.—Amarillo 1995, n.w.h.).

The U.S. Supreme Court has clarified that *McCarty* still has some vitality after the adoption of the Uniformed Services Former Spouses Protection Act. The Court held in *Mansell v. Mansell*, 490 U.S. 581 (1989), that the USFSPA bars the division of military disability benefits. "Disposable retired or retainer pay," which the USFSPA establishes state divorce courts may divide, is defined to exclude disability benefits. The Court therefore concluded that divorce courts could not divide such benefits. This is true even if retirement pay is waived in order to receive disability benefits. *See Gallegos v. Gallegos*, 788 S.W.2d 158 (Tex. App.—San Antonio 1990, n.w.h.); *Thomas v. Piorkowski*, 286 S.W.3d 662 (Tex. App.—Corpus Christi 2009, no pet.).

After *Mansell*, it is clear that only "disposable" retirement benefits may be divided at divorce. "Disposable" benefits are defined in the statute as a net concept, computed after deducting such things as retirement pay waived to receive disability benefits. *See Gallegos.* In *Limbaugh v. Limbaugh*, 71 S.W.3d 1 (Tex. App.—Waco 2002, not pet. h.) the trial court ordered the military spouse to pay the non-military the amount of disposable pay that would be lost if the military spouse waived disposable pay to get disability benefits. The appellate court ruled that this was barred by *Mansell. See also, Loria v. Loria*, 189 S.W.3d 797 (Tex. App.—Houston [1st Dist.] 2006, no pet.). Other courts have disagreed. *See Danielsen v. Evans*, 36 P.3d 749 (Ariz. App. 2001).

The Texas Supreme Court has construed the retroactivity of *Mansell* in the same manner as *McCarty*. A decree that divided military disability benefits that became final before *Mansell* was decided is not affected by *Mansell. See Berry v. Berry*, 786 S.W.2d 672 (Tex. 1990, writ denied).

b. Other Federal Benefits

Preemption obviously does not apply only to military retirement. If the federal benefit in question does not specifically state that the benefit is divisible in a divorce action, a court will attempt a *McCarty* analysis of whether Congress intended the benefit to be the separate property of the employee.

Ryan v. Ryan
Texas Court of Appeals—Beaumont, 1981
626 S.W.2d 103, writ ref'd n.r.e.

KEITH, Justice.

The primary question presented in this appeal is: Do the provisions of the Employee Retirement Income Security Act, commonly known as ERISA [29 U.S.C., 1001, *et seq.*], preempt state law and prohibit the division of the pension and retirement plan in a partition of the community property?

We find no merit to the first contention that ERISA, by preemption, has deprived the wife of all of her community interest earned through her twenty-two years participation in creating this estate. Primary reliance is placed upon *McCarty v. McCarty*, 453 U.S. 210, 101 S.Ct. 2728, 69 L.Ed.2d 589 (1981). *McCarty* involved military retirement benefits created and governed by federal statutes, and the Court held that there was a conflict between the state-created community property interest and the benefits the Congress intended for the retired military man. (101 S.Ct. at 2741, 69 L.Ed.2d at 605). Thus the

Supremacy Clause in the Constitution prevailed over state law. *See also, Trahan v. Trahan,* 626 S.W.2d 485 (Tex. 1981), following *McCarty, supra.*

Great reliance also has been placed in the Court's recent opinion in *Hisquierdo v. Hisquierdo,* 439 U.S. 572, 99 S.Ct. 802, 59 L.Ed.2d 1 (1979), relating to Railroad Retirement benefits. *See also, Eichelberger v. Eichelberger,* 582 S.W.2d 395 (Tex. 1979), following *Hisquierdo, supra.*

We answer the question in the negative. There has been no federal preemption by ERISA.

We overrule the husband's first point of error contending that ERISA preempts state law and prohibits division of the pension and retirement plan.

DISCUSSION

Congress later adopted an amendment to ERISA that clarified that ERISA was not intended to preempt the division of private retirement benefits in a divorce proceeding.

Kamel v. Kamel

Court of Appeals of Texas — Tyler, 1986
721 S.W.2d 450 appeal after remand, 760 S.W.2d 677, writ den.

BILL BASS, Justice.

In his fourth point of error the appellant argues that the trial court erred in awarding to the appellee a percentage of all retirements benefits arising out of the appellant's employment with Cotton Belt Railroad. The appellant points to section 101 of the Railroad Retirement Act of 1974, 45 U.S.C.A. Sec. 231m (West Pam. Supp. 1986), and an amendment thereto under the Railroad Retirement Solvency Act of 1983, Pub. L. No. 9876, Sec. 419(a), 97 Stat. 438, in support of his argument that federal law precludes the trial judge from dividing all of the benefits or, in the alternative, from dividing a portion of the benefits. We sustain.

Under the railroad retirement system, retirement benefits are calculated on the basis of several statutory components. *See* 45 U.S.C.A. Sec. 231b (West Pam. Supp. 1986). The basic component is described in section 231b(a), and is designed to provide benefits equivalent to those under social security. See H. R. Rep. No. 30(I), 98th Cong., 1st Sess., reprinted in 1983 U. S. Code Cong. & Ad. News 729, 730–34. Section 231m of the statute provides that "[N]o annuity or supplemental annuity shall be assignable or be subject to any tax or to garnishment, attachment, or other legal process under any circumstances whatsoever, nor shall the payment thereof be anticipated." The United States Supreme Court in *Hisquierdo v. Hisquierdo,* 439 U.S. 572, 99 S. Ct. 802, 59 L. Ed. 2d 1 (1979), held that benefits payable under the Railroad Retirement Act were not subject to division by a state court on divorce, citing the provisions of section 231m. The Texas Supreme Court followed the *Hisquierdo* decision in *Eichelberger v. Eichelberger,* 582 S.W.2d 395 (Tex. 1979), holding that "the [Supreme Court's] opinion makes it clear that such benefits are not to be treated as "property" and future benefits are not subject to division upon divorce as property." 582 S.W.2d at 401.

Under the Railroad Retirement Solvency Act of 1983, cited above, Congress added a subsection to section 231m after the *Hisquierdo* and *Eichelberger* decisions were handed down. The amendment expressly permits characterization of certain components of the benefits as community property. *See* 45 U.S.C.A. Sec. 231b (West Pam. Supp. 1986). The basic component of the benefits under Sec. 231b(a), however, remains free of a trial court's division under the amendment.

The record reflects that no evidence was adduced as to the value of each of the components of the appellant's retirement benefits. There was therefore no evidence as to what part of the benefits were susceptible to division by the court. It seems clear that the benefits were not calculated to exclude the exempt component set forth in section 231b(a). The trial court lacked the power to divide all of the appellant's retirement benefits and its attempt to do so was beyond its discretion. The appellant's fourth point of error is sustained.

In his fifth point of error the appellant argues that the trial court erred in awarding the appellee sixty percent of the cash value of an insurance policy issued under the National Service Life Insurance Act. The appellant's insurance policy is issued by the Veteran's Administration and is governed by the provisions of Title 38 of the United States Code. *See* U.S.C.A. Secs. 701–726 (West 1979 & Supp. 1986). Title 38 contains a provision establishing the nonassignability and exempt status of benefits issued under that title:

> Payments or benefits due or to become due under any law administered by the Veterans' Administration shall not be assignable except to the extent specifically authorized by law, and such payments made to, or on account of, a beneficiary … shall not be liable to attachment, levy, or seizure by or under any legal or equitable process whatever, either before or after receipt by the beneficiary.

38 U.S.C.A. Sec. 3101 (West 1979). Accordingly, our courts have consistently held that Veterans' Administration benefits are not divisible property on divorce. Appellant's fifth point of error is sustained.

That portion of the decree dividing the property of the parties is reversed and remanded for further proceedings. In all other respects, the judgment is affirmed.

Richard v. Richard

Texas Court of Appeals — Tyler, 1983
659 S.W.2d 746, no writ

McKAY, Justice.

This is a divorce case in which petitioner, Deon Richard, appeals from the portion of the judgment which divested him of one-half of his monthly Social Security disability benefits. The issue on this appeal is whether the trial court erred in characterizing the husband's Social Security disability benefits as community property and awarding one-half of all future payments to the wife.

Appellant, Deon Richard, was discharged from the military in 1969. Sometime thereafter he began receiving military disability checks. Deon Richard married Roberta Richard in 1973 several months after the birth of their daughter. During the marriage, Deon converted his military disability payments to Social Security disability payments. At the time of the divorce in 1981, Deon, Roberta, and their daughter were all receiving Social Security checks as a result of Deon's disability.

Trial was to the Court. The trial court granted the divorce and awarded custody of the daughter to Roberta. The trial court awarded Roberta one-half of Deon's Social Security disability payments as part of the division of their community property. Roberta Richard also continued to receive the Social Security check that she had received prior to the divorce. The trial court decreed that the Social Security check that the daughter received prior to the divorce should continue to be paid to Roberta for the daughter's benefit, in lieu of child support. Deon Richard appeals from the portion of the judgment that divested him of one-half of his Social Security disability benefits. No findings of fact or conclusions of law were requested or filed.

The question on appeal is whether the Supremacy Clause of the United States Constitution preempts a division by the state court of Texas of a spouse's Social Security disability benefits under the federal Old Age Survivors and Disability Insurance Family Benefit Plan (OASDI), 42 U.S.C. Sec. 402, *et seq.*

State law which conflicts with a federal statute is invalid under the Supremacy Clause of the United States Constitution. Although this particular question has not been answered by Texas courts, other community property jurisdictions have held that Social Security benefits are not community property, and a state court's attempted disposition would conflict with federal law, disrupting a "uniform federal scheme of benefits" by producing results which would vary "depending upon the community property law of various states." *In re Marriage of Kelley*, 64 Cal. App. 3d 82, 98, 134 Cal. Rptr. 259, 268 (1976). In a recent California decision, the court stated, "While there are numerous similarities between Social Security and private pension plans, there are also peculiarities in the statutory plan which make it impossible to characterize and divide the benefits as community property." *Hillerman v. Hillerman*, 109 Cal. App. 3d 334, 341, 167 Cal. Rptr. 240, 243 (1980). California courts have repeatedly refused to recognize any community property interest in Social Security benefits. *In re Marriage of Nizenkoff*, 65 Cal. App. 3d 136, 135 Cal. Rptr. 189 (1976); *In re Marriage of Cohen*, 105 Cal. App. 3d 836, 164 Cal. Rptr. 672 (1980). These decisions have been based on federal cases which, for purposes of federal law, characterized Social Security as a general public benefit creating no legally recognized property or contract right. *Fleming v. Nestor*, 363 U.S. 603, 610, 80 S.Ct. 1367, 1372, 4 L.Ed.2d 1435 (1960). In *Fleming*, the Court stated, "To engraft upon the Social Security system a concept of 'accrued property rights' would deprive it of the flexibility and boldness in adjustment to everchanging conditions which it demands. It was doubtless out of an awareness of the need for such flexibility that Congress included in the original Act, and has since retained, a clause expressly reserving to it [t]he right to alter, amend, or repeal any provision of the Act, 42 U.S.C. Sec. 1304."

In the past, Texas courts have held that military retirement payments are community property and divisible upon divorce. *Busby v. Busby*, 457 S.W.2d 551 (Tex. 1970); *Cearley v. Cearley*, 544 S.W.2d 661 (Tex. 1976). In 1981, the United States Supreme Court held in *McCarty v. McCarty*, 453 U.S. 210, 101 S.Ct. 2728, 69 L.Ed.2d 589 (1981), that nondisability military retirement benefits were not subject to division under community property or other variations of marital property laws. However, Congress enacted the Uniformed Services Former Spouses' Protection Act, 10 U.S.C. Sec. 1408, *et seq.*, effective February 1, 1983, which reversed the effect of the *McCarty* decision. Although the statute had the effect to restore the prior law that allowed state courts to apply state divorce property law to military retirement pay, federal law has established the right for state courts to divide the federal benefits.

In *Hisquierdo v. Hisquierdo*, 439 U.S. 572, 99 S.Ct. 802, 59 L.Ed.2d 1 (1979), the Court established the test to determine the federal preemption question. In *Hisquierdo*, the Court stated that "the pertinent questions are whether the right as asserted conflicts with the express terms of federal law and whether its consequences sufficiently injure the objectives of the federal program to require nonrecognition." 439 U.S. at 583, 99 S.Ct. at 809, 59 L.Ed.2d, at 12.

The *Hisquierdo* Court held that benefits under the Railroad Retirement Act are not community property and are not subject to division by a state court as "property" upon divorce. The Court held that California community property law was preempted by the express terms of the Railroad Retirement Act. The Court noted that the anti-attachment clause demonstrated the Congressional intent to preclude claims based on marital and family obligation as well as those of ordinary creditors. The anti-attachment provision ensures that the benefits actually reach the beneficiary. The anti-attachment clause, 45 U.S.C.A. Sec. 231m, provides as follows:

> Notwithstanding any other law of the United States, or of any State, territory, or the District of Columbia, no annuity or supplemental annuity shall be assignable or be subject to any tax or to garnishment, attachment, or other legal process under any circumstances whatsoever, nor shall the payment thereof be anticipated.

42 U.S.C.A. Sec. 407 of the Social Security Act contains similar language against attachment and assignment:

> The right of any person to any future payment under this subchapter shall not be transferable or assignable, at law or in equity, and none of the moneys paid or payable or rights existing under this subchapter shall be subject to execution, levy, attachment, garnishment, or other legal process,or to the operation of any bankruptcy or insolvency law.

The rationale in *Hisquierdo* is applicable to Social Security benefits in that the language in 42 U.S.C.A. Sec. 407 manifests a Congressional intent of preemption of state law. The Texas Supreme Court in *Eichelberger v. Eichelberger*, 582 S.W.2d 395, 401 (Tex. 1979), held that Railroad Retirement benefits are not to be treated as "property" for purposes of division upon divorce.

A similar result has been reached with regard to Veterans Administration disability benefits. In the case of *Ex parte Johnson*, 591 S.W.2d 453, 456, the Texas Supreme Court held that an award of the husband's Veterans Administration disability benefits to the wife upon divorce, conflicts with the clear intent of Congress that these benefits be solely for the use of the disabled veteran. The Court stated that the *Hisquierdo* holding was determinative of the question even though the *Hisquierdo* case involved Railroad Retirement benefits and this case involved Veterans Administration benefits. The Court analogized that both statutes contained prohibitions against attachment and anticipation of benefits. Likewise, the Social Security Act (OASDI) 42 U.S.C.A. Sec. 407 contains a non-attachment provision. Also, the Court concluded that both Veterans Administration benefits and Railroad Retirement benefits are not contractual. Social Security benefits are not contractual either.

The Court held in *Ex parte Johnson* that *Hisquierdo* controlled the decision by analogy and that Veterans Administration benefits were not subject to division as community property due to federal preemption. Accordingly, *Hisquierdo* controls the case at bar.

In the Texas Supreme Court case of *Ex parte Burson*, 615 S.W.2d 192 (Tex. 1981), the court held that Veterans Administration benefits are not divisible property. In deciding that Burson's military disability retirement pay was divisible upon divorce, but Veterans Administration benefits were not, the Court stated that the statutes control the property characterization of each and the fact of or lack of federal preemption of each. Therefore, viewing the Social Security Act in light of *Hisquierdo*, Texas community property law is preempted by the Supremacy Clause of the United States Constitution.

Appellee, Roberta Richard, cites the case of *Brownlee v. Brownlee*, 573 S.W.2d 878 (Tex. Civ. App. — El Paso 1978, no writ), for the proposition that disability benefits including Social Security benefits, are community property. In *Brownlee*, the husband received Veterans Administration and Social Security Administration benefits for a disability rating. The Court held that the benefits were community property and subject to division upon divorce. The decision in *Ex parte Johnson* overrules the *Brownlee* decision.

Additional reasoning indicating Congressional intent to preempt state community property is shown by the fact that Congress expressly provides in 42 U.S.C. Sec. 402(b)(1) for certain benefits for divorced spouses so that a divorced spouse would not have to depend upon a particular state's system of marital property law. The benefit payable to a divorced spouse of a covered worker does not reduce the benefit payable to the worker. 42 U.S.C. Sec. 403(a)(3). The *Nizenkoff* court, *supra* at 65 Cal. App. 3d 136, 140, 135 Cal. Rptr. 189, 191, concluded that Congress demonstrated an intention to preserve the federal character of the Social Security system in the face of "variations and idiosyncrasies of local law." In addition, the amount of an employee's "contributions" or earning does not necessarily determine the quantum of his benefits under OASDI. *In re the Marriage of Kelley, supra*, 64 Cal. App. 3d 82, 97, 134 Cal. Rptr. 259, 268.

Railroad Retirement benefits and Veterans Administration disability benefits have been held not to be subject to division under community property laws due to federal preemption. Social Security disability benefits are similar and are likewise not subject to division under community property laws due to federal preemption.

We reverse that part of the trial court's judgment that awards appellee, Roberta Richard, one-half of Deon Richard's Social Security disability benefits and remand the cause to the trial court for a complete redistribution of the estate of the parties under Section 3.63 of the Texas Family Code. The remainder of the trial court's judgment is affirmed.

DISCUSSION

This case involves Social Security disability benefits. Almost all courts agree that a divorce court also cannot divide Social Security longevity benefits.

As these cases suggest, if a divorce case involves a federal benefit, the possibility of preemption must be considered. Some statutes expressly state that the benefit can be divided at divorce. For example, the statutes pertaining to military retirement or railroad retirement contain such express language, as does a statute pertaining to civil service retirement. *See Naydan v. Naydan*, 800 S.W.2d 637 (Tex. App. — Dallas 1990, no writ). If the civil service retirement is not divided at divorce, post-divorce partition is possible. *Buys v. Buys*, 898 S.W.2d 903 (Tex.App. — San Antonio 1994). If the statute does not expressly provide that the benefit is divisible at divorce, a *McCarty/Hisquierdo* analysis is necessary.

c. ERISA Preemption

Barnett v. Barnett

Supreme Court of Texas, 2001
67 S.W.3d 107

Justice Owen delivered the opinion of the Court in Parts I, II, III, and V, in which Justice Hecht, Justice Enoch, Justice Jefferson, and Justice Rodriguez joined, and an opinion in Part IV in which Justice Hecht, Justice Jefferson, and Justice Rodriguez joined.

Justice Enoch filed a concurring opinion. Justice Hankinson filed a concurring and dissenting opinion, in which Chief Justice Phillips, Justice Baker and Justice O'Neill joined.

The principal issues in this case are whether a life insurance policy obtained through an employee benefit plan was community property and, if so, whether the Employee Retirement Income Security Act (ERISA) preempts a surviving wife's community property rights or the imposition of a constructive trust on policy proceeds to remedy a constructive fraud on the community. The court of appeals held that the policy was community property and that ERISA does not preempt the wife's state-law claims. While we agree that the policy was community property, we hold that the wife's claim for constructive fraud on the community and a constructive trust are preempted by ERISA. We accordingly reverse the court of appeals' judgment in part to eliminate recovery by Marleen Barnett of the proceeds of the policy at issue. The judgment of the court of appeals is otherwise affirmed, and this case is remanded to the trial court for further proceedings.

I

Christopher Barnett had been employed by a company formerly known as Houston Industries for eleven years when he married Marleen Barnett. The parties and the court of appeals referred to Christopher's employer as HL&P, which was a subsidiary of Houston Industries, and we follow their lead to avoid confusion. As part of an ERISA employee benefits plan, HL&P procured life insurance policies for Christopher throughout his employment. The first was a policy issued by Great Southern Life. That policy was allowed to expire after several years when HL&P changed carriers and the terms of coverage. HL&P obtained a new policy from Metropolitan Life. When Christopher and Marleen were married, that policy was in effect. During the marriage, however, that policy was not renewed by HL&P, and a new policy was issued by Metropolitan Life with different terms. Then, again during the marriage, HL&P did not renew the Metropolitan Life policy and instead procured insurance from Prudential Life Insurance Company. The Prudential policy, like the one it replaced, was a term life policy. The premiums for the Prudential policy were paid by deductions from Christopher's payroll. While the Prudential policy was in effect, Christopher and Marleen began to experience marital discord, they separated, and divorce proceedings were commenced. Christopher changed the beneficiary of the life insurance policy at issue from Marleen to his estate. He also executed a new will in which he named his mother Dora Barnett as the executrix and principal beneficiary of his estate. Other than a bequest to his sister of certain real property and a devise of $1.00 to each of his two children to be paid on their eighteenth birthdays, Christopher bequeathed his estate to his mother.

Before the divorce proceedings between Christopher and Marleen concluded, Christopher died. The Prudential policy proceeds were $169,770.93. Marleen brought suit asserting that the policies were community property, that Christopher committed a fraud on the community when he gave all the proceeds to Dora under his will, and that a constructive trust should be imposed on one half of all policy proceeds. Among Marleen's other claims was a request for a family allowance under the Texas Probate Code, and she sought to recover attorney's fees from Dora in connection with a claim that Dora had converted and wasted community property. Dora disputed all of Marleen's claims, except her claim for reimbursement of one half the community funds spent to pay the premiums on Christopher's insurance policies. The defendants contended that all the life insurance policies, including the Prudential policy, were Christopher's separate property. They further asserted that even if the policies were community property, Marleen's community property interest and her claim for fraud on the community were preempted by ERISA.

Marleen moved for partial summary judgment. She asked the trial court to declare that the policies were community property, that ERISA did not preempt her interest in the policies, and that a constructive fraud had been committed. Dora also moved for partial summary judgment with regard to the insurance policies, asserting that they were separate property and that ERISA preempted any community interest. The trial court denied Marleen's motion and granted the defendants' motions. The case then proceeded to a jury trial. At the close of Marleen's evidence, the trial court granted a directed verdict in favor of Dora on the constructive trust issue.

Marleen and Dora, appealed. The court of appeals reversed the trial court's judgment with regard to the Prudential policy. The court of appeals held that the policy was community property, and that ERISA did not preempt Marleen's claims. The court then held that Christopher's gift of the proceeds of the Prudential policy to Dora was constructive fraud, and that Marleen was entitled to summary judgment against all defendants, jointly and severally, for one half the proceeds. The court also concluded that section 286 of the Probate Code required the trial court to establish a family allowance for Marleen, and it remanded that claim to the trial court. The court of appeals affirmed the award of attorney's fees to Marleen. Dora Barnett filed petitions for review in this Court, which we granted. We first consider whether the Prudential policy was separate or community property.

II

The facts in this case are undisputed. The Prudential policy was a term life policy issued during the marriage of Christopher and Marleen Barnett. It was not a renewal of the Great Southern or Metropolitan Life policies that had been issued when Christopher was single, nor was it a renewal of the second Metropolitan Life policy that was issued after Christopher married Marleen. The premiums on the Prudential policy were paid with community funds. Dora and Marleen agree that Christopher's employer was the actual owner of all the policies, but that Christopher was the beneficial owner.

Dora contends, however, that the Prudential policy was a mutation of the prior policies that Christopher had obtained through his employer when he was a single man. We disagree. The policies issued from time to time insuring Christopher's life had no value once they were terminated. They provided coverage only during the time that they were in effect. There was no property remaining when the policies terminated. The premiums that Christopher paid when he was a single man for the Great Southern and Metropolitan Life policies purchased coverage only for the time that those policies were in effect. When those policies were not renewed, there was nothing which could mutate into other separate property. When the Prudential policy was acquired during the marriage, it took effect from its inception date, not from an earlier date when Christopher was single. We therefore conclude that the Prudential policy was not a mutation of prior policies for purposes of marital property law. The court of appeals did not err in holding that the Prudential policy was community property. We turn to the ERISA preemption issue.

III

Christopher Barnett's life insurance policy was part of an employee welfare benefit plan covered by ERISA. ERISA preempts any state laws that "relate to" covered employee benefit plans: "[T]he provisions of this subchapter shall supersede any and all State laws insofar as they may now or hereafter relate to any employee benefit plan described in section1003(a) of this title and not exempt under section1003(b) of this title." Under Texas law, Marleen Barnett has a cause of action for fraud on the community. Neither Dora nor any of the other defendants challenged the court of appeals' holding that a fraud on the community occurred in this case. Marleen's state-law remedy is to impose a constructive trust on one half of the proceeds of the Prudential policy that insured the life of her estranged husband. Dora Barnett and the other petitioners (hereinafter Dora, unless otherwise indicated) contend that Marleen's state-law claim is preempted by ERISA. Dora argues that federal law requires ERISA plans to be administered in accordance with the documents and instruments governing the plan. She asserts that the plan's administrator is therefore required by federal law to honor an employee's designation of a beneficiary. Thus, she contends, ERISA extinguishes all community property rights in a life insurance policy provided under an ERISA plan, and community property rights "do not spontaneously spring into being," she argues, after the life insurance proceeds are distributed as part of an estate. Dora asserts that the effect of ERISA is no different than if her son had designated her as the beneficiary of his life insurance policy rather than his estate. The result in either case, Dora contends, is that ERISA preempts community property rights.

Marleen counters that ERISA is not implicated since her husband's welfare benefit plan paid the life insurance proceeds to his designated beneficiary, which was her husband's estate, and her suit is against the executrix of the estate and those to whom the executrix then gave the policy proceeds, rather than against the ERISA plan administrator. The purposes of ERISA, Marleen argues, remain undisturbed because Congress had no interest in what happens to plan benefits once they are paid to a designated beneficiary.

Marleen's contention that there is no preemption because her suit is against the beneficiary of an employee benefit plan rather than the plan administrator is disposed of by *Boggs v. Boggs*, 520 U.S. 833. The Supreme Court reasoned that preemption does not turn on whether state-law community property claims are asserted against the beneficiary after plan benefits have been disbursed rather than against the plan's administrator. The Court held that when there is a clash between community property rights and the purposes of ERISA, state-law rights are preempted even though they were asserted against the beneficiary of an ERISA plan after the plan's administrator had paid the benefits to the designated beneficiary. The Court further explained that when there is preemption, "[r]eading ERISA to permit nonbeneficiary interests, even if not enforced against the plan, would result in troubling anomalies."

The question we must resolve, therefore, is whether Marleen's claim for fraud on the community "relate[s] to" her husband's employee benefit plan within the meaning of ERISA's general preemption provision.

A

The United States Supreme Court has formulated a two-part inquiry to determine if there is preemption by virtue of the "relate to" provision. A state law relates to an employee benefit plan if it has (1) a connection with or (2) a reference to such a plan. In spite of this formulation, the Supreme Court has said in recent years that the term "relate to" as used in ERISA's preemption clause is "'unhelpful text.'" In *Dillingham*, 519 U.S. 316, Justice Scalia recounted the Court's struggle to bring clarity to the law in this area, noting that as of the date of that opinion, the Court had decided "no less than 14 cases to resolve conflicts in the Courts of Appeals regarding ERISA preemption" and had accepted two more ERISA preemption cases for decision that term.

In *Dillingham*, the Court reviewed its holdings as to when a state law refers to a plan. In order to reference a plan, a state law must actually mention ERISA or plans covered by ERISA, depend on the existence of an ERISA plan, or act immediately and exclusively on ERISA plans. Based on these precedents, we have no difficulty in concluding that a common-law cause of action for constructive fraud when one spouse has transferred a disproportionate share of community property to someone other than his or her mate does not have reference to an employee benefit plan. Nor does a common-law cause of action for constructive fraud expressly mention ERISA or ERISA plans, depend on the existence of an ERISA plan, or act exclusively on ERISA plans. Whether a state law has a "connection with" a covered employee benefit plan is a more complex inquiry. To place meaningful limits on preemption in determining if a state law has a connection with an employee benefit plan, the Supreme Court has directed courts to look to the objectives of ERISA and the nature of the effect of the state law on ERISA plans.

B

Were we to decide this case without the benefit of the United States Supreme Court's recent decision in *Egelhoff*, 532 U.S. 141 (2001), we would be inclined to conclude that based on the prior decisions in *Mackey v. Lanier Collection Agency & Service, Inc.*, 486 U.S. 825, *Guidry v. Sheet Metal Workers National Pension Fund*, 493 U.S. 365, and *Boggs v. Boggs*, Marleen Barnett's claim for fraud on the community and correspondingly a constructive trust is not preempted by ERISA. Those cases explain that there is a difference for preemption purposes between benefits that can be alienated and those that cannot. Under ERISA pension plan benefits are subject to anti-alienation provisions, but welfare benefits are not. Life insurance policies provided pursuant to an employee benefit plan are welfare plan benefits, not pension plan benefits, and ERISA's anti-alienation provisions do not apply.

In *Egelhoff*, David Egelhoff obtained a divorce but did not change the designation of his former wife as the beneficiary of a life insurance policy. Upon Egelhoff's death, his ERISA plan administrator paid the policy proceeds to his former wife. His children then sued her to recover those proceeds. The Egelhoff children relied on a state statute that revoked a designation of a spouse as the beneficiary of a life insurance policy upon divorce. The Supreme Court held that ERISA preempts state law in this regard. The Court reasoned that the state law was at odds with ERISA's directives that a plan administrator must make payments to the beneficiary designated by the plan participant:

In particular, [the Washington statute] runs counter to ERISA's commands that a plan shall "specify the basis on which payments are made to and from the plan," § 1102(b)(4), and that the fiduciary shall administer the plan "in accordance with the documents and instruments governing the plan," § 1104(a)(1)(D), making payments to a "beneficiary" who is "designated by a participant, or by the terms of [the] plan." § 1002(8).

The Supreme Court further reasoned that one of the primary goals of ERISA is uniformity and that "[u]niformity is impossible, however, if plans are subject to different legal obligations in different States." The Court then concluded that uniformity was threatened because plan administrators could not rely on a beneficiary designation but would instead have to learn state laws. The burden on administrators would be compounded when the employer, plan participant, and the participant's former spouse were each in a different state. The goals of ERISA would be undermined, the Court concluded:

Requiring ERISA administrators to master the relevant laws of 50 States and to contend with litigation would undermine the congressional goal of "minimiz[ing] their administrative and financial burden[s]." ... [D]iffering state regulations affecting an ERISA plan's "system for processing claims and paying benefits" impose "precisely the burden that ERISA pre-emption was intended to avoid."

The Court's determination that state law was preempted was unaffected by the fact that the plan administrator in *Egelhoff* had already paid the proceeds to David Egelhoff's former wife, and that the suit was against her, not the plan administrator.

Nor was it an answer, the Supreme Court reasoned, that the state statute protected an administrator who made payments to a former spouse without actual knowledge that the marriage had been dissolved. First, an administrator faces the risk that it could be found to have actual knowledge of the divorce. Second, if the administrator awaited the results of litigation before making payment, the costs of delay, uncertainty, and litigation would ultimately be borne by the beneficiaries: "If they instead decide to await the results of litigation before paying benefits, they will simply transfer to the beneficiaries the costs of delay and uncertainty." The Supreme Court concluded that one of ERISA's purposes is efficient, low-cost administration of employee benefit plans, and that purpose would be frustrated:

The dissent observes that the Washington statute permits a plan administrator to avoid resolving the dispute himself and to let courts or parties settle the matter. This observation only presents an example of how the costs of delay and uncertainty can be passed on to beneficiaries, thereby thwarting ERISA's objective of efficient plan administration.

C

The United States Supreme Court said in *Egelhoff* that it granted the petition for certiorari in that case to resolve a conflict between decisions finding preemption, which the Court identified as federal Circuit Court decisions in *Manning v. Hayes*, 212 F.3d 866 (5th Cir. 2000), and *Metropolitan Life Insurance. Co. v. Hanslip*, 939 F.2d 904 (10th Cir. 1991), and decisions finding no preemption, which the Court identified as the Ninth Circuit's opinion in *Emard v. Hughes Aircraft Co.*, 153 F.3d 949, and the Washington Supreme Court's decision in *Egelhoff*, 989 P.2d 80. The United States Supreme Court resolved the conflict in favor of *Manning* and *Hanslip*. Although neither *Manning* nor *Hanslip* concerned community property law, *Emard* did.

In both *Manning* and *Hanslip*, the decedent had failed to change the beneficiary designation after divorce, and the dispute was between the decedent's former wife as the designated beneficiary and the decedent's estate. Neither the heirs nor the former wife asserted community property claims. The heirs relied on state statutes that voided the designation of a former spouse as beneficiary. Both courts held that these state laws were preempted, and the former spouse was entitled to the proceeds.

In *Emard*, two state statutes specifically addressed and purported to void nonprobate transfers of community property without the written consent of the affected spouse. The court in *Emard* held that the surviving spouse's common-law and statutory community property rights were not preempted. The Supreme Court's decision in *Egelhoff* decision implicitly rejected the result and the reasoning in *Emard*, in which the Ninth Circuit embraced many of the arguments that Marleen Barnett advances in this case.

In *Emard*, the decedent had been divorced and had remarried. Gary Emard, her surviving husband, contended that his wife had failed to change the beneficiary of her life insurance policy before her death by mistake, and that in the absence of that mistake, he would be entitled to all the proceeds under California law. He sought a constructive trust on those proceeds. Relying on *Mackey* and *Guidry*, the Ninth Circuit held that "ERISA does not preempt California law permitting the imposition of a constructive trust on insurance proceeds after their distribution to the designated beneficiary."

The Ninth Circuit concluded that the community property laws in question did not conflict with any specific ERISA provision, that California law would not frustrate any of ERISA's purposes, and that Congress had not indicated an intent to occupy the field so completely that these California laws were preempted.

As noted above, the arguments that carried the day in *Emard* are strikingly similar to those advanced by Marleen Barnett in this case. But the United States Supreme Court was unpersuaded by the rationale of *Emard*. The United States Supreme Court concluded that a state law that would have the direct or indirect effect of causing a plan administrator to pay other than in accordance with plan documents is preempted. The Supreme Court resolved the conflict between *Emard* and other decisions in favor of the holdings in *Manning* and *Hanslip*. *Manning* held that there was "no doubt" that ERISA preempted a Texas statute rendering a life insurance beneficiary designation of no effect after divorce. *Hanslip* held that ERISA preempted a similar Oklahoma statute.

D

A host of other federal circuit court decisions have held that ERISA preempts state marital property laws, including divorce decrees that are not "qualified domestic relations orders" (QDROs) within the meaning of ERISA, that purport to resolve competing claims to ERISA life insurance proceeds. Two of these decisions, *Brown*, 934 F.2d 1193 (11th Cir. 1991), and *Pettit*, 164 F.3d 857 (4th Cir. 1998) involved claims similar to Marleen's. A divorce decree required the former husband to maintain life insurance designating his former wife as beneficiary. He did not comply. He named his new wife as beneficiary. Upon the husband's death, his former wife sued, attempting to erect a constructive trust on the life insurance proceeds. The courts in each case held that the divorce decree was preempted by ERISA because it was not a qualified domestic relations order (QDRO) under ERISA. The constructive trust claims were preempted as well. The court in *Pettit* explained that it had "no trouble determining that the constructive trust claim, which is based upon the terms of a property settlement agreement entered to effect a property division upon divorce, meets the ERISA definition of state law," and had "a connection with an ERISA plan."

IV

A few courts have recognized the inequities that can result from preemption of state marital property law, particularly when ERISA preempts a state statute that revokes the designation of a spouse as beneficiary upon divorce, or when a divorce decree does not qualify as a QDRO. Those courts have applied federal common law to ameliorate those inequities. Federal common law regarding waiver is most typically applied. Some courts have sought to determine whether the former spouse waived his or her interest in plan benefits under the terms of a divorce decree, even though the decree was not a QDRO. However, the Second and Sixth Circuits have held that a beneficiary designation in plan documents governs and that federal common law cannot be applied to override that designation.

Egelhoff did not expressly resolve the division among these authorities. The question of whether there was a waiver under federal common law was raised in the lower state courts, but was not directly addressed by either the Washington Supreme Court or the United States Supreme Court. The United States Supreme Court reversed the judgment of the Washington Supreme Court in *Egelhoff* and remanded for further proceedings "not inconsistent" with the United States Supreme Court's decision. The United States Supreme Court did not expressly say whether the Washington state courts could still determine that the deceased's former wife, Samantha Egelhoff, waived her rights to policy proceeds under federal common law and that the life insurance proceeds must be paid to the children of her former husband.

In other ERISA contexts, federal courts have recognized that although Congress 'intended that the courts would "develop a 'federal common law of rights and obligations under ERISA-regulated plans,'"' they have also recognized that federal common law must be applied only "when it is 'necessary to effectuate the purposes of ERISA,'" and cannot be fashioned or applied to conflict with ERISA's statutory provisions or threaten to override the explicit terms of an established ERISA benefit plan. For example, some federal courts have recognized that a federal common-law formulation of unjust enrichment may be applicable. In *Provident Life*, a plan administrator was permitted to recover sums advanced to an employee under the terms of the plan to pay medical expenses she incurred from an accident that was unrelated to her work, even though she did not agree in writing, as contemplated in the plan, to repay those sums. But the court in *Provident Life*, 906 F2d 985 (4th Cir. 1990) recognized that unjust enrichment should be not be utilized to override a contractual provision in an employee benefit plan. And courts cannot create rights "under the rubric of federal common law" to thereby "'use state common law to re-write a federal statute.'"

(The Court discusses some earlier U.S. Supreme Court cases.)

While these authorities provide some support for Marleen Barnett's position, we are bound to follow the United States Supreme Court's most recent pronouncement of the preemptive effect of ERISA. We cannot extrapolate from decisions construing other statutes when to do so would contravene what the Supreme Court has said in construing ERISA. The decision in *Egelhoff* identified specific goals and concerns of ERISA and concluded that state family law was preempted.

The state law embodied in the statute at issue in *Egelhoff* was far easier for a plan administrator to discern and follow and far less fact intensive in applying than the community property law of Texas that gives rise to a claim for a constructive trust. The state statute under scrutiny in *Egelhoff* provided in a straightforward manner that upon divorce, the designation of a former spouse as the beneficiary of a life insurance policy was automatically revoked. But the United States Supreme Court nevertheless concluded that this statute "interferes with nationally uniform plan administration." The Court concluded that the state law clashed with one of "the principal goals of ERISA," which is "'to establish a uniform administrative scheme, which provides a set of standard procedures to guide processing of claims and disbursement of benefits.'" The state law threatened the purposes of ERISA because "[p]lan administrators cannot make payments simply by identifying the beneficiary specified by the plan documents." The state law also impermissibly burdened plan administrators because they would have to familiarize themselves with state statutes so that they could determine whether the named beneficiary's status had been "'revoked' by operation of law." If administrators decide "to await the results of litigation before paying benefits, they will simply transfer to the beneficiaries the costs of delay and uncertainty." The Court continued, "[r]equiring ERISA administrators to master the relevant laws of 50 States and to contend with litigation would undermine the congressional goal of 'minimiz[ing] the administrative and financial burden[s]' on plan administrators-burdens ultimately borne by the beneficiaries." All these conclusions and observations apply with equal if not greater force to community property laws that would require an administrator to pay benefits in a manner different from that prescribed by plan documents

In the face of this reasoning, we are constrained to conclude that federal common law would not be crafted to permit community property law to provide a means for a spouse to effectively negate the beneficiary designation made under an ERISA plan. It is for the United States Supreme Court, not this Court, to draw a distinction between the statute at issue in *Egelhoff* and state community property laws. Unless and until the Supreme Court does so, we must apply the rationale of *Egelhoff.*

Moreover, federal common law should be uniform in this area. As the Fourth Circuit said in *Singer,* 964 F.2d 1449 (4th Cir. 1992) "[i]n fashioning federal common law, courts do not look to the law of a particular state, but rather should apply common-law doctrines best suited to furthering the goals of ERISA. Consequently, federal common law should be consistent across the circuits." The elements of a constructive fraud on the community are derived, of course, from community property law. The majority of the fifty states are not community property states. The concept of constructive fraud on the community is not a uniform one that readily lends itself to the application of uniform federal common law. Constructive fraud on the community is not the equivalent of common-law fraud.

We conclude that fraud on the community, absent actual common-law fraud, is the type of claim that Congress intended to preempt under ERISA and that fraud on the community has no counterpart in federal common law. Requiring plan administrators to weigh the factors identified above in deciding whether to honor a designated beneficiary is the type of administrative burden that ERISA sought to eliminate. Accordingly, we hold that Marleen Barnett's claim for constructive fraud on the community and her corresponding claim for a constructive trust are preempted by ERISA.

V

For the foregoing reasons, we reverse the judgment of the court of appeals in part and remand this case to the trial court for further proceedings.

DISCUSSION

Note that this was a 5–4 discussion, and Justice Enoch did <u>not</u> join in part IV of the opinion, which discusses whether federal common law could provide a remedy for Marleen Barnett. The Fifth Circuit has held that, under this federal common law approach, a divorce decree can effectively change a beneficiary designation. *Clift v. Clift,* 210 F.3d 268 (5th Cir. 2000). And note that the U.S. Supreme Court in *Egelhoff* did not address the federal common law issue.

Note that *Egelhoff* and *Barnett* probably impact the holding of *Allard v. Frech* (Chapter 4).

Manning v. Hayes

U.S. Court of Appeals
Fifth Circuit, 2000
212 F.3d 866

DeMOSS, Circuit Judge.

In this insurance dispute, the estate of a deceased ERISA plan participant and the decedent's ex-wife are battling over the proceeds to an ERISA plan providing life insurance benefits. The district court granted summary judgment in favor of Defendant-Appellee Audrey Allison Hayes, who is both the decedent's ex-wife and the named beneficiary under the policy. Plaintiff-Appellant Sylvia Manning, in her capacity as executor of the estate of

Houghton H. West, appeals. We affirm, although for reasons that are substantially different than those employed by the district court.

I.

On February 15, 1993, Unum Life Insurance Company of America issued a life insurance policy to Houghton H. West through his employer, the Amherst Securities Group. On December 22, 1994, West and Audrey Allison Hayes, in light of their impending marriage, executed a prenuptial agreement titled the Separate Property Preservation and Definition Agreement. As suggested by the title of the document, the primary purpose of the agreement was to define the substantial separate assets held by both West and Hayes, and to memorialize their agreement that neither party had or would have an equitable or legal interest in property separately owned by the other. The agreement provided that, in the event the marriage was terminated, neither party would assert any claim for such things as reimbursement, aid, comfort, or support and maintenance, and further, that neither party would assert any claim in accounts held solely in the name of the other. The agreement recognized that community property would be acquired during the marriage, primarily from earnings, and that such property would be subject to a just and equitable distribution. Finally, the agreement contained representations that each party would attempt to avoid commingling community property with separate property or the proceeds of separate property owned by the other. Although the agreement included a non-exhaustive list of each of the parties assets, the agreement made no mention of employee benefits or insurance proceeds generally, or the Unum policy in particular.

Five days later, on December 27, 1994, West and Hayes were married. Almost one year later, on December 15, 1995, West voluntarily designated Hayes as the beneficiary on the Unum policy. West did not designate any alternative beneficiaries.

Six months later, on June 26, 1996, West and Hayes were divorced. There were no children born to the marriage. The final divorce decree holds that "no community property other than personal effects has been accumulated by the parties," and that such property is "awarded to the party having possession." The decree then states that the foregoing division was "made pursuant to the terms of the Separate Property Preservation and Definition Agreement." The divorce decree does not otherwise refer to the terms of that or any other agreement concerning the division of property or refer specifically to the Unum policy.

Less than one month later, on July 29, 1996, West died of pancreatic cancer. After West's death, Hayes claimed benefits as the named beneficiary of the Unum policy. West's estate disputed Hayes' entitlement to those benefits, arguing that Texas Family Code § 9.301 required the proceeds to be paid to the estate. Texas Family Code § 9.301 provides, in relevant part:

(a) If a decree of divorce or annulment is rendered after an insured has designated the insured's spouse as a beneficiary under a life insurance policy in force at the time of rendition, a provision in the policy in favor of the insured's former spouse is not effective unless:

(1) the decree designates the insured's former spouse as the beneficiary;

(2) the insured redesignates the former spouse as the beneficiary after rendition of the decree; or

(3) the former spouse is designated to receive the proceeds in trust for, on behalf of, or for the benefit of a dependant of either former spouse.

The dispute between West's estate and Hayes was not settled, and in February 1998, Manning sued Hayes and Unum on behalf of the estate in Texas probate court, seeking a declaratory judgment that the estate was entitled to the proceeds. Unum removed on the basis of ERISA preemption. *See* Employee Retirement Income Security Act, 29 U.S.C. § 1001 et seq. Shortly thereafter, Unum interpleaded the proceeds of the policy into the registry of the district court and was dismissed, leaving only Manning, on behalf of the estate, and Hayes as parties to the suit.

In November 1998, both Manning and Hayes moved for summary judgment. Manning argued that this Court's opinion in *Brandon v. Travelers Ins. Co.,* 18 F.3d 1321 (5th Cir.1994), which dealt with similar facts, adopted Texas Family Code § 9.301 for purposes of the federal common law applicable in similar ERISA actions. Manning therefore argued that both *Brandon* and § 9.301 dictated a result in favor of the estate. Hayes argued that *Brandon* was both wrongly decided at the time, because inconsistent with ERISA provisions governing competing claims for life insurance proceeds, and subsequently undermined by the Supreme Court's decision in *Boggs v. Boggs,* 520 U.S. 833, 117 S.Ct. 1754, 138 L.Ed.2d 45 (1997), which applied an expansive preemption analysis. Alternatively, Hayes argued that *Brandon* did not purport to adopt the rule codified in Texas Family Code § 9.301 for similar ERISA actions, and that the facts at issue in *Brandon* were distinguishable, such that *Brandon* did not dictate a result in favor of the estate in this case.

The district court considered these motions, eventually concluding that Hayes, as the named ERISA beneficiary, was entitled to the proceeds of the life insurance policy. Manning timely appealed. We review the district court's grant of summary judgment de novo. *Clift v. Clift,* 210 F.3d 268, at 269–70 (5th Cir. 2000).

II.

Congress passed ERISA in 1974 to establish a comprehensive federal scheme for the protection of the participants and beneficiaries of employee benefit plans. *See* 29 U.S.C. § 1001; *see also Pilot Life Ins. Co. v. Dedeaux,* 481 U.S. 41, 107 S.Ct. 1549, 1551, 95 L.Ed.2d 39 (1987); *Shaw v. Delta Air Lines Inc.,* 463 U.S. 85, 103 S.Ct. 2890, 2896, 77 L.Ed.2d 490 (1983). ERISA broadly preempts "any and all State laws insofar as they may now or hereafter relate to any employee benefit plan." 29 U.S.C. § 1144(a). A law "relates to" an employee benefit plan when the law has "a connection with or reference to such a plan." *Shaw,* 103 S.Ct. at 2900. The scope of the ERISA preemption provisions is "deliberately expansive," and they are consistently construed to accomplish the congressional purpose of insuring certain minimum standards in the administration of employee benefit plans. *See Pilot Life Ins.,* 107 S.Ct. at 1552.

There is no doubt that Manning's claim on behalf of the estate is preempted, to the extent that it relies upon the Texas beneficiary redesignation statute. Almost every circuit court to consider the issue, including this one, has determined that a state law governing the designation of an ERISA beneficiary "relates to" the ERISA plan, and is therefore preempted. *See Dial v. NFL Player Supplemental Disability Plan,* 174 F.3d 606, 611 (5th Cir. 1999); *Brandon,* 18 F.3d at 1325; *see also Metropolitan Life Ins. Co. v. Pettit,* 164 F.3d 857, 862 (4th Cir. 1998); *Mohamed v. Kerr,* 53 F.3d 911, 913 (8th Cir. 1995); *Krishna v. Colgate Palmolive Co.,* 7 F.3d 11, 15 (2d Cir. 1993); *Metropolitan Life Ins. Co. v. Hanslip,* 939 F.2d 904, 906 (10th Cir. 1991); *Brown v. Connecticut General Life Ins. Co.,* 934 F.2d 1193, 1195 (11th Cir. 1991); *McMillan v. Parrott,* 913 F.2d 310, 311 (6th Cir. 1990); *Fox Valley & Vicinity Constr. Workers Pension Fund,* 897 F.2d 275, 278 (7th Cir. 1989). But *see Emard v. Hughes Aircraft Co.,* 153 F.3d 949, 961 (9th Cir.1998) (holding that ERISA does not preempt California constructive trust or community property law in a dispute between a surviving and former spouse over life insurance benefits), *cert. denied sub nom.,* 525 U.S. 1122, 119 S.Ct. 903, 142 L.Ed.2d 902 (1999).

The more difficult issue is whether, having established that the state law is preempted, the federal law governing the resolution of this and similar cases may be reasonably drawn from the text of ERISA itself, or must instead be developed as a matter of federal common law. There is presently a circuit split on this issue. A majority of the circuit courts to have considered the issue have recognized that ERISA does not expressly address the circumstances, if any, in which a non-beneficiary may avoid the payment of life insurance benefits to the named beneficiary. For that reason, these courts have held that the issue is governed by federal common law. *See, e.g., Clift,* 210 F.3d 268, at 269–71; *Brandon,* 18 F.3d at 1325–26; *see also Hill v. AT&T Corp.,* 125 F.3d 646, 648 (8th Cir.1997); *Mohamed,* 53 F.3d at 913.

With respect to a former spouse's claim as a designated beneficiary, this Court has specifically held that the former spouse may waive his or her beneficiary status in a subsequent divorce decree or agreement, provided the waiver is explicit, voluntary and made in good faith. *Clift,* 210 F.3d 268, at 270–71; *Brandon,* 18 F.3d at 1326–27. In *Brandon,* we held that the former spouse effectively waived her beneficiary status by virtue of explicit language in the divorce decree depriving her of any interest in the participant's employee benefit plans. *See id.* at 1323, 1327. Thus, in this Circuit, the determination of who is entitled to the proceeds of an ERISA plan providing life insurance benefits may depend upon more than merely the plan documents, and may be properly defined by reference to the federal common law of waiver as applied to the particular facts of the case.

Hayes urges a contrary rule. Hayes contends that ERISA § 1104(d) expressly requires that plan benefits be paid directly to the ERISA designated beneficiary, and further, bars any inconsistent federal common law permitting a broader inquiry. Hayes thus argues that the preemption issue is one of conflict preemption, rather than preemption under the "relates to" clause of § 1144(a).

The Sixth Circuit is the only circuit to unambiguously employ this minority approach. *See McMillan v. Parrott,* 913 F.2d 310 (6th Cir.1990); *see also Metropolitan Life Ins. Co. v. Marsh,* 119 F.3d 415 (6th Cir.1997); *Metropolitan Life Ins. Co. v. Pressley,* 82 F.3d 126 (6th Cir.1996). The decisions of that circuit hold that ERISA § 1104(d), which simply provides that plan administrators are to discharge their duties "in accordance with the documents and instruments governing the plan," expressly provides the statutory rule for resolving competing claims to insurance proceeds. Indeed, the Sixth Circuit construes this statutory subsection to set forth a "clear mandate" that plan administrators determine the beneficiary with reference to the plan documents, and only the plan documents. *See Marsh,* 119 F.3d at 420 ("ERISA itself supplies the rule of law for determining the beneficiary."); *Pressley,* 82 F.3d at 130 (Section 1104(d) establishes "a clear mandate that plan administrators follow plan documents to determine the designated beneficiary."); *McMillan,* 913 F.2d at 312 (holding that § 1104(d) establishes the exclusive rule for determining beneficiary status). Thus, under the Sixth Circuit's minority rule, the named beneficiary must always prevail, without regard to any other circumstances or provisions of law.

Hayes relies upon this analysis, as well as the Supreme Court's recent disposition in which involved a clear case of conflict preemption in a different context, for the proposition that ERISA precludes any reliance upon federal common law when resolving a dispute between a named ERISA beneficiary and another claimant. The district court essentially accepted these arguments, holding that the controlling ERISA law was to be drawn directly from ERISA § 1104(a) rather than the federal common law. The district court repudiated this Court's analysis in *Brandon* and opined that it was wrongly decided. The district court likewise relied upon stray language from the Supreme Court's decision in *Boggs* as additional support for the proposition that the federal common law can have no place when determining the beneficiary of an ERISA life insurance policy.

III.

We conclude that the district court erred. The rule announced by this Court in *Brandon* and recently reaffirmed *Clift* in is the law in this Circuit. Neither the district court nor a panel of this Court is at liberty to change that rule. Moreover, we are not persuaded, in the context of this case and premised upon the arguments made by these parties, that the rule requires any correction.

Section 1104 defines the fiduciary duties owed by the plan administrator to plan participants and beneficiaries. That section does not either expressly or implicitly purport to establish any methodology for determining the beneficiary of an ERISA plan or for resolving competing claims to insurance proceeds. Thus, considered in isolation, § 1104(d) is a very thin reed upon which to find complete conflict preemption with respect to competing claims to life insurance proceeds. While we can certainly appreciate the simplicity of the bright line rule embraced by the Sixth Circuit, that simplicity comes at too great a cost. As we noted in *Brandon* the law of family relations, which includes an individual's right to expressly apportion property upon divorce, has traditionally been a fairly sacrosanct enclave of state law. *See Brandon*, 18 F.3d at 1327. Similarly, the Sixth Circuit's bright line rule that a beneficiary designation cannot be challenged would supplant what is a fairly uniform set of state laws providing that a named beneficiary who kills a plan participant in order to obtain the plan benefits is not entitled to recover those proceeds. *See Emard*, 153 F.3d at 959 n. 11 (noting that forty-four states and the District of Columbia have such laws in effect). While ERISA requires the conclusion that the state law governing such matters is itself preempted when it relates to an ERISA plan, we have no trouble concluding, as have many of the courts that have addressed the issue, that the traditional deference given to state law in these areas supports our decision to borrow from state law when determining the federal common law that should control such claims. *See, e.g., Clift*, 210 F.3d 268, at 270–71; *Mohammed*, 53 F.3d at 913; *Brandon*, 18 F.3d at 1325. In sum, ERISA is broad enough in its preemptive scope to accomplish the purposes of ERISA; namely the imposition of adequate safeguards with "respect to the establishment, operation, and administration" of employee benefit plans for the benefit of ERISA plan participants and beneficiaries. *See* 29 U.S.C. § 1001(a). There is no additional need to breathe imaginary preemptive effect with respect to competing claims for life insurance benefits into general provisions addressing another topic altogether.

Neither is a contrary approach required by *Boggs*. In *Boggs* two parties asserted competing claims to the pension benefits of one Isaac Boggs after his death in 1989. Boggs' sons from a prior marriage claimed entitlement to the pension benefits by virtue of their deceased mother's testamentary transfer of her state law community property interest in Boggs' undistributed pension benefits. Boggs' surviving wife claimed entitlement to the pension benefits by virtue of ERISA § 1055, which mandates that covered pension plans protect the interests of surviving spouses by providing benefits in the form of a qualified joint and survivor annuity, and ERISA § 1056, which provides that the benefits due under a covered pension plan are inalienable and unassignable, absent a qualified domestic relations order (QDRO) meeting certain statutory requirements.

Recognizing that *Boggs* was positioned "at the intersection of ERISA pension law and state community property law," 117 S.Ct. at 1760, the Supreme Court held that "[t]he surviving spouse annuity and QDRO provisions, which acknowledge and protect specific pension plan community property interests, give rise to the strong implication that other community property claims are not consistent with the statutory scheme," 117 S.Ct. at 1763. The Supreme Court noted that Congress significantly strengthened the specific statutory protection afforded surviving spouses against competing interests by amending the statute in 1984. *See id.* at 1761. The Supreme Court then employed a conflict preemption analysis to hold that Louisiana community property law permitting a testamentary transfer of a former spouse's community property interest in the undistributed pension benefits of her former spouse, who remarried prior to death, was completely preempted by contrary provisions of ERISA that were plainly intended to provide an income stream to surviving spouses that was both inalienable and immune to competing interests absent compliance with the specific statutory framework for preserving such interests with a QDRO. *See id.* at 1763–66.

Hayes maintains, and the district court at least implicitly held, that *Boggs* somehow undermines this Court's analysis and reliance upon federal common law in *Brandon*. We disagree. The principles at work in *Boggs* are clearly inapplicable in this case. As an initial matter, this case does not involve either pension benefits or the express provisions of ERISA ensuring special protection to surviving spouses in the context of pension benefits. Both ERISA § 1055 and ERISA § 1056 are facially limited in application to pension plans, and neither section purports to have any application with respect to competing claims to benefits under a non-pension employee welfare plans, such as the life insurance policy at issue here. *See* 29 U.S.C. §§ 1055,1056; *see also Brandon,* 18 F.3d at 1324 (characterizing employer-provided life insurance policies as "welfare plans" within the meaning of 29 U.S.C. § 1002 (1)). Of equal importance, this case does not involve the assertion of any community property interest. Hayes is not asserting a community property interest. To the contrary, Hayes is the designated beneficiary under the plan. For that reason, those ERISA provisions that have been construed to protect those interests of a former spouse that are inconsistent with plan documents or other ERISA provisions, provided those interests are preserved in a QDRO, are simply inapplicable to this dispute. Likewise, the estate does not claim entitlement on the basis of a community property interest. Rather, the estate seeks to void West's designation of beneficiary by virtue of the statutory presumption erected by Texas Family Code § 9.301, and then to rely instead upon Texas law governing the distribution of assets in the absence of such a designation. As should be apparent, *Boggs* dealt with a clearly distinguishable situation involving explicit ERISA provisions addressing an issue plainly within the express regulatory provisions of the statute. In sum, we are not persuaded that *Boggs* requires any more expansive view of the discrete ERISA preemption issue presented in *Brandon.*

The district court's broad reliance upon § 1104 for the proposition that ERISA expressly requires payment to a named beneficiary without regard any other circumstances and without resort to federal common law reflects nothing more than an inappropriate reliance upon the Sixth Circuit's minority position, which has been soundly rejected by this Circuit and a majority of other circuits to consider the issue. Similarly, the district court's reliance upon *Boggs* is without support; *Boggs* does not provide any rule of law that may be applied to this case. For the foregoing reasons, we conclude a reconsideration of the legal principles set forth in *Brandon* and recently reaffirmed in *Clift* is neither appropriate nor desirable.

IV.

Having ascertained that our Circuit follows the majority approach by applying federal common law to disputes between a non-beneficiary claimant and the named ERISA beneficiary to life insurance proceeds, and that neither the express language of ERISA nor the Supreme Court's decision in *Boggs* require that we abandon that approach, we must now determine the content of the applicable federal common law.

Manning correctly notes that federal common law may be determined by reference to analogous state law. *See Wegner v. Standard Ins. Co.,* 129 F.3d 814 (5th Cir. 1997; *Sunbeam-Oster Co., Inc. Group Benefits Plan for Salaried and Non-Bargaining Hourly Employees v.*

Whitehurst, 102 F.3d 1368, 1374 n. 18 (5th Cir. 1996); *Jones v. Georgia Pacific Corp.*, 90 F.3d 114,115 (5th Cir. 1996); *Todd v. AIG Life Ins. Co.*, 47 F.3d 1448, 1451 (5th Cir. 1995). Manning then argues on behalf of the estate that this Court incorporated the requirements of the Texas redesignation statute, Texas Family Code 9.301, into the federal common law in *Brandon*.

We disagree. While it is true that we used the Texas statute as a starting point, holding that we would "adopt the Texas rule creating a presumption of waiver absent redesignation following divorce," *Brandon*, 18 F.3d at 1326 we recognized that "wholesale adoption of the Texas redesignation statute" would not "sufficiently protect the interests of [ERISA] beneficiaries," *id.* at 1326. We therefore modified that rule by requiring that any waiver by a designated beneficiary of ERISA life insurance proceeds be "explicit, voluntary, and made in good faith." *Id.* at 1327. Moreover, we measured the adequacy of the asserted waiver under this modified standard with reference to the existing federal, rather than state, common law. *See Brandon*, 18 F.3d at 1326–27 discussing *Lyman Lumber Co. v. Hill*, 877 F.2d 692 (8th Cir. 1989) and *Fox Valley & Vicinity Constr. Workers Pension Fund*, 897 F.2d 275 (7th Cir. 1989)). We therefore reject Manning's argument that necessarily requires a result in favor of the estate because we incorporated the Texas redesignation statute into the federal common law when deciding that case. To the contrary, whether the estate is entitled to the proceeds of the life insurance policy must be determined with reference to the express contractual language purporting to establish Hayes' waiver, as well as any other factual circumstances bearing upon whether that waiver was intentionally and voluntarily made in good faith. *See Brandon*, 18 F.3d at 1322, 1327 (discussing divorce decree provisions as well as other facts bearing upon the issue of waiver).

V.

Brandon provides the rule of federal common law applicable to this dispute. That rule is that a named ERISA beneficiary may waive his or her entitlement to the proceeds of an ERISA plan providing life insurance benefits, provided that the waiver is explicit, voluntary, and made in good faith. The final question requiring our consideration is whether Hayes in fact waived her beneficiary status.

There does not appear to be any issue relating to whether the parties acted voluntarily or in good faith when signing the prenuptial agreement that is made the basis of Manning's waiver argument. To the contrary, the sole issue appears to be whether the express provisions of that agreement establish Hayes' explicit waiver of her status as the named ERISA beneficiary under the Unum policy as a matter of law.

Manning asserts that Hayes waived her interest in the policy as a matter of law by signing the prenuptial agreement, which was later made the basis of the property division ordered by the divorce decree. Hayes responds that the prenuptial agreement is incompetent to waive her interest in the policy because it was executed prior to the creation of her interest as a designated beneficiary and because the document does not explicitly waive her interest in either West's employee benefit plans or the Unum policy in particular.

In deciding this issue, we are guided by the treatment given analogous waiver language in the existing precedent. In *Brandon* and *Clift*, we held that former spouses effectively waived their interest in the proceeds of ERISA life insurance policies by virtue of explicit language appearing in the divorce decrees. In *Brandon* the divorce decree expressly divested the former spouse of any interest in or claim to:

"Any and all sums, whether matured or unmatured, accrued or unaccrued, vested or otherwise, together with all increases thereof, the proceeds therefrom, and any other rights relating to any profit-sharing plan, retirement plan, pension plan, employee stock option plan, employee savings plan, accrued unpaid bonuses, or other benefit program existing by reason of Petitioner's past, present, or future employment." *Brandon*, 18 F.3d at 1323. In *Clift*, a more obvious case of waiver, the divorce decree expressly divested the former spouse of any interest in or claim under "any and all policies of life insurance (including cash value) insuring the life" of her former husband. *Clift*, 210 F.3d at 269.

Underlying the result in each of these cases is a focus upon the specificity or explicitness of the language used to affect the alleged waiver. *Clift* presents the easiest case, given that the former spouse expressly waived any interest in life insurance policies insuring the life of her former husband. The case is also instructive because in *Clift*, we did not distinguish between an interest in the life insurance policy and beneficiary status under that policy. Indeed *Clift*, expressly declined the Seventh Circuit's lead in this regard, by rejecting a former spouse's invitation to hold that magic words, such as a right to "proceeds" or a "beneficiary interest" must be included in a valid waiver. The Court explained that, while waiver will not be presumed in the absence of fairly explicit language setting forth the waiver, neither is any particular formulation required. *See Clift*, 210 F.3d 268, at 270–72. Rather, the Court clarified that the Court "will only find waiver if, upon reading the language in the divorce decree, a reasonable person would have understood that" the beneficiary was "waiving [his or] her beneficiary interest in the life insurance policy at issue." *Id.* at 271–72. *Brandon* and *Fox Valley* serve as examples of less obvious, but nonetheless adequate, waivers. In both of those cases, the courts were persuaded by divorce decrees that explicitly divested the former spouse of any interest arising from the employment of the participant spouse. Thus, although we must eschew any mechanistic formulation of the language required to cause a valid waiver, the inclusion of language explicitly divesting a former spouse of an interest in any and all employee benefit plans of the other is probably sufficient to support an alternative beneficiary's claim that the former spouse waived his or her beneficiary status.

Applying these principles to this case, we find no waiver. The prenuptial agreement was executed prior to the time that Hayes was designated as beneficiary under the policy. The clear purpose of the document, as reflected by the title, was to define and provide for the preservation of separate property brought to the marriage. The broad language waiving West's and Hayes' interests in the other's "property" does not in any manner either explicitly or implicitly contemplate waiver of a subsequently acquired beneficiary interest in a life insurance policy.

Manning suggests that the prenuptial agreement was incorporated into the divorce decree, such that the terms of that agreement were revived and applied to the parties' then-existing interests. We disagree. As an initial matter, the divorce decree does not purport to incorporate or revive the terms of the prenuptial agreement. To the contrary, the divorce decree provides that there is no community property to be divided aside from personal effects, and that that property would be awarded to the person in possession. The divorce decree then provides that the foregoing division, i.e., that each party retained their own personal effects, was made pursuant to the Separate Property Preservation and Definition Agreement. The divorce decree does not provide that either West's or Hayes' interests were otherwise being divided in accordance with that agreement.

Moreover, even if we agreed that the divorce decree effectively divides the parties' after-acquired interests in accordance with the prenuptial agreement, we would still find no waiver here. While the prenuptial agreement is broadly drafted, there is nothing in that agreement either implicitly or explicitly addressing either insurance or employee benefits. Likewise, and as set forth above, there is nothing in the agreement that would have placed a reasonable person on notice that Hayes was waiving her after-acquired beneficiary interest in the Unum life insurance policy. *See Clift*, 210 F3d 268, at 271–72.

To conclude, we have not found any cases holding that an agreement negotiated prior to marriage for the purpose of defining and preserving separate property is effective to negate an insured spouse's subsequent and voluntary decision to designate the other spouse as a named beneficiary under an ERISA plan. We do not say that such an agreement would never suffice, but something substantially more than the tangential and obscure references to each of the parties "property" rights would have to be present to support a finding of waiver. The divorce decree in this case is likewise inadequate to revive the preclusive effect of the agreement, if any. The divorce decree relies upon and invokes the agreement solely for the purpose of clarifying that there is no community property and therefore no property to be divided by the family court. The divorce decree does not purport to revive the various provisions of the agreement for the purpose of precluding Hayes' claim to benefits pursuant to her status as the designated beneficiary of West's life insurance policy. For these reasons, we find no waiver of Hayes' interests, and affirm the district court's holding that Hayes is entitled under ERISA and subject to the terms of the plan to recover the proceeds of the Unum life insurance policy.

CONCLUSION

The district court is affirmed.

DISCUSSION

In *Keen v. Weaver*, 121 S.W.3d 721 (Tex. 2003), the Texas Supreme Court held that, where a spouse waived her rights in connection with a divorce in her husband's pension plan, and she was still designated as the beneficiary when he died, ERISA did not require the benefits to be paid to the beneficiary. The Court held that, based on *Egelhoff*, Tex. Fam. Code § 9.301 was preempted. However, based on federal common law, the Court held that a waiver in a divorce decree could effectively revoke the beneficiary designation made during marriage.

In *Estate of Kennedy v. Plan Administration for Dupont Savings*, 129 S.Ct 865 (2009), the Supreme Court considered a similar issue relating to the rights to the funds in a pension plan when the employee died after divorce. The employee had designated his wife as beneficiary during marriage. He did not change the beneficiary designation, but the wife waived her rights to the benefits in connection with their divorce. The husband later died. The Supreme Court held that ERISA required that the benefits be paid to the beneficiary. It did not decide, however, whether the employee's estate could sue the beneficiary after payment by the plan.

Branco v. UFCW-Northern California Employers Joint Pension Plan

U.S. Court of Appeals
Ninth Circuit, 2000
279 F.3d 1154

RAWLINSON, Circuit Judge.

This case sits at the intersection of the Employee Retirement Income Security Act ("ERISA") and California's community property statutes. We must decide whether ERISA preempts a state law which allows a predeceased spouse's interest in her ex-husband's pension plan to pass to her heirs. In this case of first impression, we hold that state law must yield. Accordingly, we REVERSE and REMAND.

BACKGROUND

Alfred Branco ("Branco") is a participant in the UFCW-Northern California Employers Joint Pension Plan (the "Plan"). On July 1, 1998, Branco was eligible for retirement benefits in the amount of $594.17 per month. Branco and his former wife, Anna Branco ("Anna"), had previously stipulated to a court order granting Anna a 47.07% community property interest in Branco's pension benefits. The order required payments to continue "for so long as they were payable to or on behalf of [Branco]." Anna died before any pension payments were payable to Branco. Anna was survived by Steven and Edward Branco ("Steven and Edward"), her two adult sons.

Based upon its interpretation of the court order and applicable law, the Plan paid Branco the sum of $314.49 per month in pension benefits, after deducting Anna's community property interest as awarded in the court order.

Branco filed his original complaint against the Plan in state court alleging breach of contract, seeking payment of the entire benefit amount without deduction.

DISCUSSION

ERISA Preemption

The preemption doctrine, which has its roots in the Supremacy Clause, U.S. Const., Art. VI, cl. 2, requires us to examine Congressional intent. Preemption may be either express or implied, and "is compelled whether Congress' command is explicitly stated in the statute's language or implicitly contained in its structure and purpose." *Jones v. Rath Packing Co.,* 430 U.S. 519, 525, 97 S.Ct. 1305, 51 L.Ed.2d 604, (1977) (citation omitted). ERISA's express preemption clause states that the Act "shall supersede any and all State laws insofar as they may now or hereafter relate to any employee benefit plan...." 29 U.S.C. § 1144(a). However, like the Supreme Court in *Boggs v. Boggs,* "[w]e can begin, and in this case end, the analysis by simply asking if state law conflicts with the provisions of ERISA or operates to frustrate its objects." 520 U.S. 833, 841, 117 S.Ct. 1754, 138 L.Ed.2d 45 (1997).

Analysis

In reaching its decision, the district court concluded that California's community property law was not preempted because it did "not operate to deprive Plaintiff, or any other ERISA participant or beneficiary, of benefits to which he would otherwise be entitled" because Branco was already "deprived of that interest" under the court order. Accordingly, the district court narrowed the issue to whether the Plan or Anna's estate is entitled to the benefits. Having to decide between these two potential recipients, the court concluded that permitting Anna to devise her interest in Branco's pension benefits would not frustrate ERISA's purpose to protect plan participants and beneficiaries. The court went on to note that its ruling would protect the community property interest conferred upon Anna by the court order, while also requiring the Plan to meet its obligation to pay out the total amount of earned benefits. Accordingly, the district court decided that Anna's estate was entitled to the benefits, and rendered a tentative ruling in favor of Branco if he could show that he was properly assigned those benefits from the beneficiaries of Anna's estate.[1] In reaching its decision, the district court distinguished *Boggs v. Boggs*, 520 U.S. 833, 117 S.Ct. 1754, 138 L.Ed.2d 45, and *Ablamis v. Roper*, 937 F.2d 1450 (9th Cir.1991), on the grounds that the present case involves a divorced spouse who predeceased the plan participant, whereas those cases involved only a predeceased spouse.

Contrary to the district court's ruling, we are of the view that the reasoning of *Boggs* and *Ablamis* and their applications of ERISA persuasively inform our analysis.

ERISA dictates that "[e]ach pension shall provide that benefits provided under the plan may not be assigned or alienated." 29 U.S.C. § 1056(d)(1). The limited exception to this anti-alienation provision is a pension benefit conferred through a Qualified Domestic Relations Order ("QDRO"). 29 U.S.C. § 1056(d)(3)(A).[2] Unless the court order between Branco and Anna meets the requirements of a QDRO, Anna's pension interests are subject to the anti-alienation provision, and cannot pass to her intestate heirs. Whether the order "constitutes a valid QDRO under ERISA is a question of law for this court to determine de novo." *Stewart v. Thorpe Holding Co. Profit Sharing Plan*, 207 F.3d 1143, 1150 n. 5 (9th Cir.2000).

In reaching its decision, the district court assumed, without analysis, that the state court order was a QDRO. However, in order to qualify as a QDRO, a Domestic Relations Order (DRO) must "relate[] to the provision of child support, alimony payments, or *marital property rights to a spouse, former spouse*, child, or other dependent of a participant...." 29 U.S.C. § 1056(d)(3)(B)(ii)(I).

Payments to Anna as a deceased spouse are not authorized under ERISA's definition of a qualifying recipient because, at that point, the QDRO does not relate to marital property rights of a spouse or former spouse. Despite the district court's ruling to the contrary, *Ablamis* is directly applicable on this point. In *Ablamis*, we held that the death of the spouse "divests her of the title of 'spouse or other dependent,'" thereby rendering her an unqualified recipient under ERISA. *Ablamis* at 1456. When Anna died she was divested of her qualified status under ERISA. The fact that Anna was divorced from Branco before she died does not alter the analysis. If the term "spouse" does not include a deceased spouse, the term "former spouse" does not include a deceased former spouse. *Id.*[3]

Anna's estate and/or heirs are similarly precluded as qualified beneficiaries. ERISA permits payment of pension benefits to a third party only if that individual falls within ERISA's statutory definitions of "beneficiary" or "alternate payee." 29 U.S.C. §§ 1002(8),

---

1. The district court subsequently ruled that Branco failed to offer credible evidence on this claim, and granted summary judgment to the Plan. Branco argues that he did offer sufficient proof on this claim. This issue need not be resolved given our decision that the district court failed to apply the correct substantive law.

2. QDRO is defined in section 1056 as follows:

(i) the term "qualified domestic relations order" means a domestic relations order—

(I) which creates or recognizes the existence of an alternate payee's right to, or assigns to an alternate payee the right to, receive all or a portion of the benefits payable with respect to a participant under a plan, ...

(ii) the term "domestic relations order" means any judgment, decree, or order (including approval of a property settlement agreement) which—

(I) relates to the provision of child support, alimony payments, or marital property rights to a spouse, former spouse, child, or other dependent of a participant, and

(II) is made pursuant to a State domestic relations law (including a community property law). 29 U.S.C. § 1056(d)(3)(B)(i),(ii).

3. In *Ablamis*, we noted that "[i]n legal parlance, however, the term 'former spouse' does not include a deceased spouse." *Id.*

1056(d)(3)(J),(K). Anna's estate and heirs do not fall within these statutory definitions.[4] *See Ablamis,* at 1456 ("An estate, even of a deceased spouse, certainly does not fall within even the most liberal construction of the phrase 'spouse, former spouse, child or other dependent of the participant.'"). Nor were these alternate payees specifically listed in the DRO, as ERISA requires. *See* 29 U.S.C. § 1056(d)(3)(C)(i) ("A domestic relations order meets the requirements of this subparagraph only if such order *clearly specifies*— ... the name and mailing address of each alternate payee covered by the order....").

An extension of payments to Anna's estate or heirs is akin to the disapproved probate transfer at issue in *Ablamis.* "ERISA's express statutory language and legislative history make it clear that Congress did not intend to classify state court orders effecting Testamentary transfers as QDROs." *Ablamis* at 1455; *see also Boggs* at 852, 117 S.Ct. 1754 (noting that it would be "inimical to ERISA's purposes to permit testamentary recipients to acquire a competing interest in undistributed pension benefits").

We recognized in *Ablamis* that "Congress' fundamental purpose was evident throughout—to ensure that both spouses would receive sufficient funds to afford them security during their lifetimes, not to arrange for an opportunity for a predeceasing non-employee spouse to leave a part of her surviving husband's pension rights to others." *Ablamis,* 937 at 1457. Similarly, in *Boggs* the Supreme Court ruled:

> The QDRO provisions, as well as the surviving spouse annuity provisions, reinforce the conclusion that ERISA is concerned with providing for the living. The QDRO provisions protect those persons who, often as a result of divorce, might not receive the benefits they otherwise would have had available during retirement as a means of income. In the case of a predeceased spouse, this concern is not implicated. The fairness of the distinction might be debated, but Congress has decided to favor the living over the dead and we must respect its policy.

Boggs at 854, 117 S.Ct. 1754. Given ERISA's concern for the living, it is consistent to conclude that the QDRO exception to ERISA's anti-alienation provision was not intended to subject significant portions of pension benefits to transfer by a predeceased spouse.

In *Egelhoff v. Egelhoff,* 532 U.S. 141, 121 S.Ct. 1322, 149 L.Ed.2d 264 (2001), the Supreme Court held that a Washington statute providing for automatic revocation, upon divorce, of any designation of one's spouse as the beneficiary of nonprobate assets was preempted, as it applied to ERISA benefit plans, because of a direct conflict with ERISA's requirement that plans be administered, and benefits be paid, in accordance with plan documents. The Court reached its decision by reasoning that the Plan should not be required to "pay the benefits to the beneficiaries chosen by state law, rather than those identified in the plan documents." *Id.* at 1327. The court further reasoned that "[r]equiring ERISA administrators to master the relevant laws of 50 states and to contend with litigation would undermine the congressional goal of 'minimiz[ing] the administrative and financial burden[s]' on plan administrators—burdens ultimately borne by the beneficiaries." *Id.* at 1329 (citation omitted).

---

4. 29 U.S.C. § 1002(8) defines beneficiary as "a person designated by a participant, or by the terms of any employee benefit plan, who is or may become entitled to a benefit thereunder." 29 U.S.C. § 1056(d)(3)(K) defines "alternate payee" as "any spouse, former spouse, child, or other dependent of a participant who is recognized by a domestic relations order as having a right to receive all, or a portion of, the benefits payable under a plan with respect to such participant." While Steven and Edward may be Anna's intestate heirs, it does not appear that they would fit under the definition of alternate payee, since they are not children or dependents.

The Supreme Court's concerns in *Egelhoff* apply equally to the present case. Acceptance of the district court's ruling would impermissibly require the Plan Administrators to master California's probate law; to pay benefits to the beneficiaries chosen by state law (California's intestate scheme); and/or to await the conclusion of probate litigation to establish Anna's lawful heirs. Such eventualities clearly contravene *Egelhoff's* holding.

Because there is no QDRO in effect, *Egelhoff* directs us to section 8.04 of the Plan, which provides: "Benefits are payable ... to Participants...." As the Plan Participant, Branco is entitled to payment of the entire benefit, without reduction.

CONCLUSION

Because the state court order was not a QDRO, it impermissibly alienated Branco's pension benefits to Anna as a deceased former spouse. The language of the court order requiring payments to continue "for as long as they are payable to or on behalf of [Branco]," conflicts with ERISA's anti-alienation provision and is therefore preempted. Accordingly, the district court erred in entering judgment on behalf of the Plan, and denying Branco's motion for summary judgment.

Because we have ruled in Branco's favor on the assignment issue, his remaining claims need not be addressed.

REVERSED and REMANDED for entry of judgment in favor of Branco.

PREGERSON, Circuit Judge, Dissenting.

The majority reaches its holding by relying on our decision in *Ablamis v. Roper*, 937 F.2d 1450 (9th Cir.1991), and two recent Supreme Court decisions, *Boggs v. Boggs*, 520 U.S. 833, 117 S.Ct. 1754, 138 L.Ed.2d 45 (1997) and *Egelhoff v. Egelhoff*, 532 U.S. 141, 121 S.Ct. 1322, 149 L.Ed.2d 264 (2001). The District Court, however, already properly distinguished *Ablamis* and *Boggs*, and *Egelhoff* is likewise distinguishable.

In each of these three cases, a plan participant or beneficiary, upon the death of their spouse, suddenly saw their interest in benefits they expected at that time divested and defeated by state law. *Ablamis*, 937 F.2d at 1452; *Boggs*, 520 U.S. at 836–37, 117 S.Ct. 1754; *Egelhoff*, 121 S.Ct. at 1325–26. The circumstances in the present case are different. Neither when Anna died nor at any later point in time did California state law suddenly divest Alfred of any benefits he expected at that time. On the contrary, Alfred had long ago given up any expectation in these benefits when he stipulated to the divorce settlement order explicitly granting Anna 47.07% of the benefits "for as long as they are payable to or on behalf of" Alfred. Under these circumstances, the majority's holding not only does not advance the purpose of ERISA's anti-alienation clause to "guarantee that retirement funds are there when a plan's participants and beneficiaries expect them." *Boggs*, 520 U.S. at 852, 117 S.Ct. 1754. The majority's holding also undermines community property law's "commitment to the equality of husband and wife and ... the real partnership inherent in the marital relationship." *Id.* at 840, 117 S.Ct. 1754.

I respectfully dissent.

Chapter Fourteen

Representing the Divorce Client

This book primarily deals with the technical and policy concerns surrounding marital property rights issues. However, a significant aspect of the family lawyer's job is the manner in which the lawyer interacts with the client.

In many types of practice, lawyers represent people who are experiencing traumatic events. This is particularly true in family law. Because of this, a family lawyer must be, by necessity, a decent counselor as well as a technician. Unfortunately, from the comments of many dissatisfied former clients, it appears that many family lawyers do not competently fulfill the counseling function. The author encourages any student who is considering a family law practice to enroll in programs that will enhance counseling skills. Certain common counseling problems will be mentioned below.

A. The First Interview

It is important to structure the first interview in a professional manner. An attorney can significantly influence the actions of the family law client, so it is important that the lawyer ascertain what action appears to be in the client's best interest.

First of all, is it clear that the client wants a divorce? Clients frequently decide to divorce without significant deliberation or after a recent argument with a spouse. In such instances it normally is desirable to encourage the client to consider marriage counseling, or merely to wait a short period, to be sure that the client has reached a final decision to initiate a divorce.

In my view, a lawyer needs to ask some probing questions and provide some information to the client before a lawyer can decide whether the client has made a final and informed decision to divorce. First, the lawyer might want to describe the probable outcome of the divorce process to the client. For example, if the client is the husband/father and the client does not want custody of the children, does he accept that he will no longer live with the children, and will, in all likelihood, have visitation periods as set forth in the TFC standard possession order? Similarly, the lawyer might want to show the client the Texas child support guidelines. Is the client prepared to make the payments set forth in the guidelines until the child reaches majority? Similarly, if the client is a female and has not worked outside the home for a significant period, is she aware that it is unlikely she will receive substantial post-divorce alimony in Texas? Will she be able to be economically self-sufficient after the community property is divided? Also, if there are minor children and the female client is likely to be awarded custody, is she willing to be a single parent for an indefinite period? Could she support the household with her earnings and the amount of child support calculated from the guidelines?

Once a lawyer determines that the client has made a final decision to divorce, a number of other determinations must be made. First, does the client need interim support for herself or any children? Also, is spousal violence a potential problem? If so, steps need to be taken to ensure the parties' safety. Other important matters involve determining who will stay in the family home and who will have temporary custody of any children. After the divorce action has been initiated, temporary orders can be obtained regarding these matters.

Divorce clients are quite upset about the unknown ramifications of the divorce process. A good lawyer will explain to the client how the divorce process works. How long will it take? Can you suggest a range of how much will it cost? How will the client's life be affected? Many clients have never hired a lawyer or been in court before, and frequently need a great deal of reassurance.

The manner in which a divorce action is initiated can significantly affect the level of hostility in the divorce. For example, before a spouse is served with divorce papers, to facilitate an amicable divorce it is important that the spouse be aware that the other spouse is initiating a divorce. Also, it is usually wise to attempt to get the spouse (or the spouse's lawyer) to agree to accept service, rather than humiliating the spouse by serving the spouse at work.

As in any matter, the lawyer must clarify the fee arrangement with the client. Do you plan to charge by the hour, or the task? Also, the lawyer should inform the client whether the client will be charged for the first interview. A client may well want to be quoted a fixed fee for representation in a family law matter. Can you think of any risks inherent in such an arrangement?

Contingent fees are generally not appropriate in family law matters. In *Twyman, supra,* the Texas Supreme Court stated that a contingent fee arrangement could be appropriate for representation in connection with a spousal tort claim. What is different about a tort claim and a divorce action that would justify a contingent fee in one but not the other?

It is generally advisable to have written fee agreements. How would you draft your fee arrangements?

Another decision the lawyer needs to make at the first interview is whether to agree to be retained by the client. Many lawyers choose not to represent certain types of clients who are very difficult to satisfy. For example, if the client has been represented by others and has been dissatisfied with their work, this is a signal that they may well be quite critical of your work. Also, clients with unrealistic expectations of what you can accomplish will be difficult to satisfy. Clients whose primary motive is revenge on the other spouse can also be very difficult. If a client makes objections to proposed fee arrangements, and these objections are unreasonable in light of the client's situation, this also suggests future problems.

B. Handling the Case

Lawyers can significantly affect the tenor and cost of the divorce. Each family lawyer must make his own decision regarding what role is appropriate. Most discover that it is in everyone's best interest to attempt to be reasonable. Clients should not be encouraged to do damaging things, such as looting bank accounts or going on wild shopping sprees.

This type of activity generally infuriates that other spouse, establishes a terrible environment for the divorce, and does not impress many family court judges. If the spouses have liquid assets like bank accounts that could be dissipated, it might be wise to advise your client to remove 50% from all such accounts and put them in another account in the client's name, so the client will have control of 50% of the spouses' funds. This frequently is a nice compromise that protects your client from the other spouse's rash actions and does not create a hostile atmosphere. Temporary orders are also possible to discourage the other spouse from dissipating the community estate.

The parties themselves sometimes can work out some disputed issues. For parties who can still deal rationally with each other, mediation of disputed points can be useful. Some criticize mediation as a process that disadvantages a spouse without significant business experience. Others contend that men can dominate women. For this reason, many lawyers support mediation only if lawyers are either present at the mediation or are available for consultation before an agreement is signed. Additionally, it would be reckless to enter into a mediated agreement before adequate discovery has been completed.

Divorce clients frequently suffer from guilt, and this affects their decisions during the divorce process. For example, a guilty spouse may say, "I don't want any property, I merely want a divorce." This spouse may later conclude that this was not a wise decision, and criticize or even sue a divorce lawyer for approving such a settlement. If a client is willing to agree to an extremely disproportionate arrangement, the lawyer needs to emphatically tell the client that the settlement may not be fair to him and be sure that the client understands the ramifications of the settlement. Written documentation of this advice would also be prudent.

Dating during separation is a subject the lawyer must discuss with the client. Some judges may consider this behavior negatively in connection with the divorce property division or custody determination. This is particularly true if the spouse has overnight guests with children present. In any event, dating can embarrass the other spouse, so care should be taken to begin a social life in a manner that considers the feelings of the former spouse. For example, it would be unwise, at least soon after separation, to take a date to a family holiday party that the former spouse will attend.

C. Counseling the Client

Lawyers unfortunately do not receive much training in counseling. Many lawyers find it very useful to learn more about counseling; this is doubly true for family lawyers. First, remember that the client will be talking to you about very personal, and possibly embarrassing and terrifying, matters. At a minimum, emphasize the confidentiality of your discussions. You may also want to make a short statement to new clients about how many clients find the divorce process embarrassing and scary.

A good counselor is a good listener. For this reason, many lawyers are lousy counselors. When talking to a client, even in a first interview, many of us have a tendency to be thinking about how we are going to handle the case and what information we will need to draft the petition, etc. STOP! It is imperative that the client believe that you are listening and that you care about the case and how it will affect his/her life. How can you do this? First, look at the client. Really. Don't look out the window, look at your watch, yawn, or play with a paper clip. Don't take phone calls except in emergencies. Another good listening technique is sometimes called the Columbo technique. This involves paraphrasing what the client has just told you. "What I hear you saying is that you are scared that your husband might take the kids to another state over Christmas." In many instances, you will find that you did not hear the client correctly or that the client then adds additional helpful information.

D. Maintaining Good Client Relations

Family law representation generates many grievance claims and many unhappy clients. Is this because family lawyers are incompetent technicians? No. However, family lawyers frequently do not pay enough attention to the personal aspect of family law representation. Part of this has to do with the lack of listening skills mentioned above. Also, clients need to get a sense that their case is important and that the lawyer is doing all he/she can. How can this be accomplished? First, send the client copies of all incoming and outgoing correspondence and court filings relating to the case. You may also want to talk to the client when any significant action is being taken so the client understands what is happening. If the case has been dormant for a while, call the client or send a letter explaining why it has been dormant and what the next step will be.

When planning how to organize your law practice, it might be useful for you to think about your reaction to professional services provided by others. What has generated a *Texas Marital Property Rights* strong response from you when you went to the doctor? If the doctor finds time to see you in an emergency, you probably feel that the doctor cares about you and your problems; if the earliest appointment available is in two weeks, you might have the opposite response. Similarly, if the doctor keeps you waiting in the reception area for a long time, this does not very successfully communicate that you are important. While regulating appointments is not per se part of the practice of medicine, it is a part of the practice that can significantly affect the way the patient feels about the doctor. When you practice law, be aware of what you can do to convey to each client that he or she is important.

Family law clients frequently need someone to talk to, and they often contact their lawyer. Many lawyers feel uncomfortable in this situation. First, they feel awkward charging a significant fee for talking about nonlegal problems. Second, if they don't feel they can charge for the call, they get restless and don't listen very compassionately to the client. Some lawyers have tried to solve this problem by hiring staff whose primary job is to talk to clients. These staff can be billed at a much lower rate than the lawyer, and can transfer the call to the lawyer if a legal question is involved.

Family lawyers sometimes are tempted to establish a sexual relationship with a client. This can create conflicts of interest for the lawyer and substantially complicate the lawyer-client relationship. Wise family lawyers would, at a minimum, wait until the case is complete before contemplating an intimate relationship.

Other guidelines are helpful for successful legal representation. First, return every phone call every day. If you are out of town or unavailable, have someone in your office return the call. Return your most difficult calls first. When communicating with clients, tell the truth. Many lawyers are reluctant to tell clients "bad news." It is always better to be the one who tells the client about case developments, rather than have the client learn it from someone else in an awkward setting. Also, send regular bills. Clients are more willing to pay smaller bills shortly after work has been performed than large bills long after.

Finally, take care of yourself and those who love you. If you are healthy and alert, you will be a better lawyer. If you take time and nurture important relationships in your life, you will be a happier lawyer.

E. Collaborative Law

Some lawyers have been concerned that, due to judge's needs to move their docket, they have been pressured to take a litigation stance, before the parties have had a reasonable period to try to teach an amicable settlement without litigation. For this reason, a "collaborative" track was established in 2001 in Tex. Fam. Code § 6.603. This gives the parties two years to settle the case without litigation, if parties choose this route.

Chapter Fifteen

Dividing the Community Estate at Divorce

Texas Family Code § 7.001 prescribes that the parties' community estate should be divided at divorce "in a manner the court deems just and right, having due regard for the rights of each party and any children of the marriage." This is obviously less than a precise rule.

A. Fault

Young v. Young
Texas Court of Appeals—Dallas, 1980
594 S.W.2d 542 (writ history revealed in Discussion)

CARVER, Justice.

Husband appeals from a part of a divorce decree making a division of the parties' estate and assessing the wife's attorneys fees to the husband. We reverse and remand the division of the estate of the parties because the trial court erroneously considered (1) the needs of a disabled adult son in making the division and (2) the fault of the husband in causing the termination of the marriage.

The evidence shows that the parties were married in 1942 and separated in 1970. Two children were born to the marriage and both were past the age of 18 when this suit was filed in 1975. The husband testified that he was earning about thirteen thousand dollars a year, and the wife testified she was earning about five thousand dollars a year. The only significant item of community property possessed by the parties was the prospective enjoyment of two pension plans arising from the husband's long-term employment by Kentron Incorporated and from the husband's active and reserve duty with the United States Navy. The trial court awarded 70% of the pensions to the wife and 30% of the pensions to the husband, plus an additional monetary judgment to the wife against the husband in the amount of ten thousand dollars. The testimony of a witness from Kentron Incorporated gave the private pension's prospects as commencing, at the earliest, in 1985 with an amount payable then of $255.20 for the remainder of his life. The prospects of the Navy pension were described by husband as commencing, at the earliest, in 1983 and the amount payable then as less than $200 per month for his life.

The wife argues that a disparate division was "just and fair" because of the trial court's finding of "fault" on the part of the husband in causing the divorce. We cannot agree. Section 3.63, as well as its predecessor statutes back to 1841, contains no word or words warranting the imposition of either a penalty or a forfeiture on either party to a divorce action for "fault."

"Fault" as a factor to be considered in property division upon divorce of spouses is unsatisfactory for at least two reasons. First, the charge of the statute to the trial judge is that the division be "fair and just" and the supreme court adds "having due regard to the probable future necessities" of the spouses. *See Hedtke v. Hedtke, supra.* Should "fault" also be considered, it would deny one spouse probable future necessities and give the other spouse an excess. This lopsidedness, great or small, cannot be "fair and just" nor in fact equate to the "probable future necessities" of either spouse. Second, "fault," when sought to be employed to justify a division of property, seems to be urged as against only one of the spouses when, in the reality of human nature, fault must lie with both spouses in a divorce situation varying only in degree.

We see no usefulness in arriving at a fair and just division to require a trial judge to assess each and every bicker, nag and pout, as well as greater faults, of each spouse. To the contrary, we anticipate that in doing so there is even less likelihood that the division will be "fair" or "just" or, in fact, provide for the spouses' "probable future necessities." We hold that "fault" may not be considered in dividing the community estate of the parties. It follows that "fault" cannot be considered to justify the disparate division of the estate of the parties before us. Our holding does not prevent the trial court from requiring each spouse to account for the estate of parties which may have been secreted or fraudulently transferred in order that the true estate may be determined before it is "fairly and equitably" divided by the decree.

We hold that the trial court abused its discretion in making the division of the pensions and in awarding to the wife a ten thousand dollar judgment because: it took into consideration the "fault" of the husband. Accordingly, the judgment is reversed and remanded.

DISCUSSION

This opinion reflects the American majority view that the parties' behavior is not relevant to the divorce property division. On one hand, it is difficult to determine who really was "at fault" when a marriage does not work. One person might have had an affair, but this may have stemmed from the other spouse's extreme criticism or other cruelty, or from the spouse's continued absence from the home due to work or other friendships. Also, the fault determination process severely undermines the general goals of the divorce process, which are to facilitate a separation of the spouses in a manner not traumatic to either, and to dissipate the enmity between the spouses. Finally, the fault determination has little to do with the crucial social goal of attempting to ensure that both spouses and any dependent children will have sufficient financial resources after divorce.

The *Young* opinion set forth above was reversed by the Texas Supreme Court. *See* 609 S.W.2d 758 (Tex. 1980). The court held that in a fault-based divorce, evidence of "fault" could be considered by a court in connection with the division of the community estate. After *Young*, in a fault-based divorce Texas courts do not have to consider fault, but they may, if they choose.

What conceivable rationale supports the supreme court's decision? What kind of behavior should be punished? In *Young*, the supreme court noted the spouse's alleged "cruelty, adultery and desertion." The court approved the consideration of these matters. After *Young*, the Texas Supreme Court has abolished spousal tort immunity. Does this undermine the *Young* rationale?

In *Brown v. Brown*, 187 S.W.3d 143 (Tex. App. — Waco 2006, pet. dism'd.), the court held that fault could be considered in connection with the property division in a no-fault divorce.

What is accomplished by a consideration of fault? On one hand, conduct contributing to the divorce could be the focus. If this is the case, conduct after separation would be irrelevant. Still, if the goal of considering fault is also to encourage parties to behave reasonably during separation, behavior during this period should also be considered.

What if both spouses are considered at fault?

What is "desertion"? If one spouse moves out of the marital residence, has that spouse "deserted," or is something more required? Does it make any sense to punish this kind of behavior? Possibly a spouse must both leave the residence and shirk support responsibilities to the other spouse (and children) before "desertion" has occurred.

Adultery occurs when a married person has sexual relations with a person other than his or her spouse. Does it make sense to punish all adultery? What about sexual activity after the parties have separated?

What is "cruelty"? *See Martin v. Martin*, 561 So.2d 787 (La. App. 1990) (suggesting that a refusal to engage in sexual intercourse is cruelty); *Hausler v. Hausler*, 636 S.W.2d 874 (Tex. App. — Waco 1982, no writ) (suggesting that leaving the home, refusing to attempt reconciliation, and engaging in a sexual relationship with another after the separation occurred is some type of fault). In *Phillips v. Phillips*, 75 S.W.3d 564 (Tex. App. — Beaumont 2002, no pet. h.), the court held that, if the divorce is sought solely based on the "no-fault" ground of insupportability, the court may not consider fault in the property division.

Brown v. Brown
Texas Court of Appeals — Amarillo, 1986
704 S.W.2d 528, no writ

COUNTISS, Justice.

This is a divorce case. Appellant Dawn Marie Richards Brown appeals from a judgment granting appellee Horace Brown a divorce, on grounds of cruelty, and voiding two post-marital agreements. Dawn Marie attacks the judgment by questioning the sufficiency of the evidence of support findings that (1) she was guilty of cruel treatment and (2) the agreements are void. We affirm.

Horace was a 70 year old retired widower from West Texas with several hundred thousand dollars in the bank and several hundred acres of farmland. Dawn Marie was a 46 year old divorcee from Denver. They met by correspondence through a pen pal club and married after a whirlwind courtship. Unfortunately, the marriage lasted only slightly longer than the courtship.

Horace sued for divorce, alleging cruelty by, and incompatibility with, Dawn Marie. He testified that her treatment of him, and the rapidity with which she spent his money, made him ill.[1] He also testified that there were some aspects of the post-marital agreement, by which he bestowed certain financial benefits on Dawn Marie, that he didn't understand.

---

1. According to Horace's calculations, Dawn Marie spent an average of $675 per day during the time they lived together.

After hearing the evidence, the trial court found, as pertinent here:

1. That Respondent [Dawn Marie] is guilty of cruel treatment toward Petitioner [Horace] of a nature that renders further living together insupportable.

. . . .

7. That Respondent has not proven by clear and convincing evidence that Petitioner gave informed consent and that the [post-marital] Agreements were not procured by fraud, duress or overreaching.

The court then granted the divorce, voided the post-marital agreements and granted other relief.

By her first point of error, Dawn Marie says the trial court erred in finding that she was guilty of cruel treatment toward Horace because "the alleged cruelty was of a most tenuous and minor nature." We construe the point to be an attack upon the factual sufficiency of the evidence to support the finding that she was guilty of cruel treatment.

The cruelty for which we are seeking evidence was defined in various pre-Family Code cases as willful and persistent infliction of unnecessary suffering, whether in realization or apprehension, whether of mind or body, *Gentry v. Gentry*, 394 S.W.2d 544 (Tex. Civ. App.—Corpus Christi 1965, no writ) and as acts that endanger or threaten life, limb or health of the aggrieved party and inflict mental anguish. *Gentry v. Gentry, supra; McDonald v. McDonald*, 316 S.W.2d 780 (Tex. Civ. App.—Fort Worth 1958, no writ). There being nothing in the Texas Family Code or subsequent case law to suggest that those definitions are no longer viable, we will use them to measure the activities described in this record.

Horace testified that the marriage encountered problems from the outset and was a stormy situation most of the time. Although Dawn Marie did not physically abuse him, he said she talked to him like he was dirt, hurt his feelings, made him nervous, refused at times to let him touch her, did little or no housekeeping or cooking, didn't like visits from the neighbors, and was very extravagant with his money. As a result, they quarreled and he developed stomach trouble. Horace's doctor corroborated Horace's testimony about his stomach trouble, stating that upon examining Horace soon after the marriage he found Horace to be weak and nervous, with acid irritation of the stomach and gastritis. The problems were caused, said the doctor, by situational stress. A neighbor also described Horace as depressed, nervous and shaky soon after the marriage.

When Dawn Marie was asked whether she made Horace nervous, she said, "No, sir. Far to the contrary." She also denied quarreling over money, speaking to him like dirt, fussing about the neighbors, or spending extravagantly.

The trial court was entitled to believe the evidence tendered by Horace, his doctor, and his neighbor, and was entitled to conclude from it that Dawn Marie had inflicted upon Horace willful and persistent unnecessary suffering and mental anguish, endangering Horace's health. Thus, we cannot conclude that the evidence is insufficient or the finding clearly wrong and unjust. Point of error one is overruled.

Our disposition of point one renders point two moot. The post-marital agreements in question state that they are "null and void" if the marriage is terminated because Dawn Marie is guilty of cruelty as set out in Chapter 3 of the Family Code. Because Dawn Marie must be fault-free in order to enforce the agreements, all counsel agreed at oral argument that any discussion of the agreements is immaterial unless Dawn Marie prevails on her first point. She has not; accordingly, point of error two is overruled.

The judgment is affirmed.

B. Other Equitable Concerns

Murff v. Murff

Supreme Court of Texas, 1981
615 S.W.2d 696

SPEARS, Justice.

In this divorce case, petitioner, Wanda Faye Murff, was granted a divorce by the trial court from respondent, John Samuel Murff, after a non-jury trial. John Murff was dissatisfied with the trial court's division of the community property and appealed to the court of civil appeals. That court reversed the judgment of the trial court and remanded the cause for a new trial, holding that the trial court abused its discretion in the division of the parties' estate. 601 S.W.2d 116.

We granted Mrs. Murff's Application for Writ of Error on all five asserted points of error. We have jurisdiction of the case because the holding of the court of civil appeals on the issue of whether fault may be considered in dividing the property, conflicts with *Duncan v. Duncan*, 374 S.W.2d 800 (Tex. Civ. App.—Eastland 1964, no writ) and on the issue of whether disparity in earning power or capacity may be considered in dividing the property, with *In re Marriage of McCurdy*, 489 S.W.2d 712 (Tex. Civ. App.—Amarillo 1973, writ dism'd). We reverse the judgment of the court of civil appeals and affirm the judgment of the trial court and hold the trial court did not abuse its discretion in dividing the parties' property.

Mrs. Murff sought the divorce on three grounds: "no-fault" insupportability, and alternatively, adultery and cruel treatment, both "fault" grounds. Although the Decree of Divorce did not specify upon which ground the divorce was granted to Mrs. Murff, the Findings of Fact filed by the court stated that she had proved grounds under all three alternative grounds. In its division of the community estate of the parties, the trial court awarded the wife property valued by the trial court at $78,901, plus attorney's fees of $8,500, and awarded the husband property valued at $73,600, plus $30,000 of husband's claimed separate property. The trial court further found that by alternatively valuing the wife's retirement and annuity at $47,090.55 instead of $8,000, the property awarded the wife would be $117,991.55, plus attorney's fees of $8,500. The court of civil appeals found that the trial court abused its discretion in six particulars: (1) in giving consideration to "fault" of a spouse to justify a disparate division of the community property; (2) in giving consideration to disparity of "income" between spouses instead of considering a disparity of "need" between spouses; (3) in failing to consider an award of attorney's fees to the wife against the husband as an element of the court's division; (4) in failing to declare the identity of separate property and fix any charge thereon in favor of the community; (5) in failing to evaluate correctly the pension plans; and (6) in failing to *divide* the spouses' property and in imposing an inequitable money judgment in lieu of division.

Mr. and Mrs. Murff had been married over 22 years at the time of the divorce hearing. They had a 21-year old daughter who attended college at the time. The wife was 46; the husband 47. Both spouses had worked full-time during their marriage. At the time of the divorce, the wife's annual gross salary was $14,750 or $1,229 per month; her net monthly take-home pay was $927 per month. The husband's annual gross salary was $26,715; his gross pay per month was approximately $2,200 from which deductions were made for taxes, insurance and retirement; however, taking into consideration the added "service incentive pay," the husband's gross pay per month was almost $3,000 per month. Both husband and wife were members of a pension plan with their employers.

Mrs. Murff's first point of error is that the court of civil appeals erred in holding that the trial court could not consider fault in the breakup of the marriage in arriving at a "just and right" division of the community estate. We sustain this point, having recently ruled on the same question in *Young v. Young*, 609 S.W.2d 758 (Tex. 1980). We there held that in a divorce granted on a fault basis, the trial court may consider the fault of one spouse in breaking up the marriage when making a property division. In the instant case, the divorce was based upon both no-fault and fault grounds, thus *Young* is applicable. As we said in *Young*, however, "this does not mean that fault must be considered, only that it may be considered."

In her second point of error, Mrs. Murff attacks the holding of the court of civil appeals that the trial court erred in considering a disparity in the income of the spouses. The court of civil appeals has held that only the cure of the "necessitous circumstances" or "probable future necessities" may be considered in arriving at a just and right division.

The Texas Family Code Sec. 3.63 provides for the division of the parties' property upon divorce: "In a decree of divorce or annulment the court shall order a division of the estate of the parties in a manner that the court deems just and right, having due regard for the rights of each party and any children of the marriage."

The trial court has wide discretion in dividing the estate of the parties and that division should be corrected on appeal only when an abuse of discretion has been shown. *Hedtke v. Hedtke*, 112 Tex. 404, 248 S.W. 21 (1923).

Numerous courts of civil appeals decisions have recognized that a trial court may consider the disparity of incomes or of earning capacities of the parties in dividing the estate of the parties. The cases cited in the margin recognize that community property need not be equally divided. In exercising its discretion the trial court may consider many factors and it is presumed that the trial court exercised its discretion properly. *Bell v. Bell*, 513 S.W.2d 20, 22 (Tex. 1974). These cases further indicate that the trial court may consider such factors as the spouses' capacities and abilities, benefits which the party not at fault would have derived from continuation of the marriage, business opportunities, education, relative physical conditions, relative financial condition and obligations, disparity of ages, size of separate estates, and the nature of the property. We believe that the consideration of such factors by the trial court is proper in making a "just and right" division of the property. Likewise, the consideration of a disparity in earning capacities or of incomes is proper and need not be limited by "necessitous" circumstances.

We next address Mrs. Murff's contention that the court of civil appeals erred in holding that the trial court's award of a money judgment of $7,500 to her was an abuse of discretion because it was not used as a "device to avoid fractionating items in the estate to be divided." We disagree with the court of civil appeals that the trial court abused its discretion. There was evidence that the wife had only $300 in funds on hand, but that the husband had substantial sums in savings before the separation that had disappeared by the time of trial. Some $1,400 of the money judgment represented unpaid court-ordered temporary alimony for the wife from the pendency of the divorce action prior to trial. We find no abuse of the trial court's discretion under these facts.

Mrs. Murff next complains of the holding of the court of civil appeals that the trial court should have considered the attorney's fees awarded her as a factor in achieving a just and right division of the property. In *Carle v. Carle*, 149 Tex. 469, 234 S.W.2d 1002, 1005 (1950), this court, in responding to a certified question, said:

> In practical effect, a decree that the husband pay all of the wife's attorney's fees may be to award him less of the community estate than that awarded to the wife, but that alone does not condemn it. The attorney's fee is but a factor to be considered by the court in making an equitable division of the estate, considering the conditions and needs of the parties and all of the surrounding circumstances.

We agree with the statement of the court of civil appeals in this case that it is not clear whether the award of attorney's fees to the wife was taken into consideration by the trial court; however, there is likewise no indication in the trial court's judgment, findings of fact or conclusions of law that it did not take them into consideration in making its division. The failure to list the attorney's fees as "property" in the list of property awarded to the wife is no indication that they were not considered in the division, only that it was not considered "property." In either event, in applying the *Carle* standard, we find no abuse of discretion in awarding to the wife her attorney's fees under the circumstances of this case.

The trial court in a divorce case has the opportunity to observe the parties on the witness stand, determine their credibility, evaluate their needs and potentials, both social and economic. As the trier of fact, the court is empowered to use its legal knowledge and its human understanding and experience. Although many divorce cases have similarities, no two of them are exactly alike. Mathematical precision in dividing property in a divorce is usually not possible. Wide latitude and discretion rests in these trial courts and that discretion should only be disturbed in the case of clear abuse.

Accordingly, the judgment of the court of civil appeals is reversed and the judgment of the trial court is affirmed.

DISCUSSION

Murff outlines the general laundry list of things a court can consider at divorce when dividing the spouse's property. Most are not too surprising. Some do raise an eyebrow, however. What does the court mean when it states that the court can consider "the benefits which the party not at fault would have derived from the continuation of the marriage"?

As you might guess, due to the vagueness of the "just and right" standard it is quite difficult to predict how a judge will divide the community estate, unless the lawyer is familiar with the manner in which the judge normally divides the community estate. If you were a family court judge, when would you divide the community estate in disproportionate shares?

Upon request, the judge must state in writing its findings of facts and conclusions of law concerning (1) the characterization of each party's assets, and (2) the value or amount of the community estate's assets and liabilities. Tex. Fam. Code §6.711.

Some community property states divide the community estate equally. Would this be a good idea in Texas? Should there at least be a presumption that the community estate should be divided equally?

It is quite difficult to challenge a property division on appeal. The appellate court must find that the trial court abused its discretion in dividing the community estate. This conclusion is reached by appellate courts only when the trial court's decision is impossible to justify.

A final property division decree may not be modified. However, an ambiguous decree may be clarified under Tex. Fam. Code § 9.008.

An improper property division must be appealed directly; collateral attack generally is not effective.

Putegnat v. Putegnat

Texas Court of Appeals — Corpus Christi, 1986
706 S.W.2d 702, no writ

KENNEDY, Justice.

Appellant, plaintiff below, appeals a summary judgment rendered in favor of the defendant below. The parties hereto were formerly husband and wife. They were divorced in Brazoria County, Texas, in 1976. The divorce decree awarded appellee 25% of the property which appellant "will receive through inheritance or otherwise from the Sarita Kenedy East Estate" as her separate property. No appeal was taken from the entry of the decree and a subsequent bill of review filed by appellant was dismissed for want of prosecution.

The action which resulted in the summary judgment below was filed by appellant in Kenedy County, which is the location of the disputed property. Appellant sought to declare void the award of his separate property to appellee in the original divorce proceedings, alleging therein that the divestiture was of appellant's separate property, that it was not constitutional, and, therefore, was void as beyond the power of the court. This appeal turns on this one point, *i.e.*, whether the disputed portion of the divorce decree was void. Carried further, can this divorce decree be the object of a collateral attack? We affirm the judgment of the trial court.

The case of *Stinson v. Stinson*, 668 S.W.2d 840 (Tex. App. — San Antonio 1984, writ ref'd n.r.e.) is on point herein. *Stinson* also involved a collateral attack on a divorce decree which purported to divest the appellant of his separate property. The *Stinson* court held:

> That the divorce court may have awarded appellant's separate property to appellee and that the divorce court may have rendered judgment without the joinder of the life tenant, even if the judgment was erroneous in these respects, does not render the judgment void. If the trial court erred, the error was one of substantive law to be remedied by appeal.

Id. at 841; *see Williams v. Williams*, 620 S.W.2d 748 (Tex. Civ. App. — Dallas 1981, writ ref'd n.r.e.).

To collaterally attack a judgment rendered in a prior proceeding, the judgment attacked must be void. *Stinson*, 668 S.W.2d at 841; *Williams*, 620 S.W.2d at 749. Any error of the trial court was of substantive law to be remedied by appeal, and, therefore, not void nor the proper subject of a collateral attack. *Stinson*, 668 S.W.2d at 841; *Williams*, 620 S.W.2d at 749.

Appellant relies on *Donias v. Quintero*, 227 S.W.2d 252 (Tex. Civ. App. — El Paso 1949, no writ) to support his position that the divorce decree was void and may be attacked collaterally. In *Donias*, the divorce decree attempted to divest the party of his title to separate property realty, in direct contravention of Tex. Rev. Civ. Stat. Ann. art. 4638 (repealed 1969). The El Paso Court of Appeals held that part of the divorce decree void and subject to collateral attack. Based on *Hardin v. Hardin*, 597 S.W.2d 347 (Tex. 1980), we think the *Donias* holding is erroneous. "It is well established in Texas that a divorce judgment, unappealed, and regular on its face, is not subject to a collateral attack in a subsequent suit." *Id.* at 350. Notwithstanding *Hardin* and assuming *Donias* is correct, the present case is distinguishable from *Donias*. Pursuant to Tex. Fam. Code Ann. Sec. 3.63 (Vernon Supp. 1986) which reads, "In a decree of divorce or annulment the court shall order a division of the estate of the parties in a manner that the court deems just and right, having due regard for the rights of each party and any children of the marriage," the trial court entered the present decree.

However, not until *Eggemeyer v. Eggemeyer*, 554 S.W.2d 137 (Tex. 1977), which was subsequent to the divorce decree in the case before us, did the Supreme Court hold that the phrase "estate of the parties" means community estate and refused to permit a divestiture of a party's separate property in a divorce action. Following the *Donias* rationale, at the time the divorce decree was entered herein (1976 and pre-*Eggemeyer*), it was not a void decree. Therefore, notwithstanding the subsequent changes brought about by *Eggemeyer*, the decree before us was not void nor subject to collateral attack.

The judgment of the trial court is affirmed.

DISCUSSION

Later cases have reaffirmed the *Putegnat* holding. *See Lawrence v. Lawrence*, 911 S.W.2d 450 (Tex. App.—Texarkana 1995, writ denied); *Reiss v. Reiss*, 118 S.W.3d 439 (Tex. 2003). An unappealed decree that divests separate property is not void.

When dividing the community estate, courts attempt to divide the estate in a sensible manner, considering the talents and needs of the spouses. For example, a spouse without significant earning capacity should not be given assets that have a negative cash flow, if possible; such spouses need income-generating assets. A closely-held business run by one spouse should not be given to the other spouse. In general, it is undesirable to make the spouses co-owners of property, since many spouses do not enjoy continuing contact with former spouses. If necessary, the court can award a spouse a money judgment from the other spouse to compensate one spouse for the community property interest. Not surprisingly, it has been held to be an abuse of discretion for a divorce court merely to award each spouse 50% of each item of community property. *Walston v. Waltson*, 971 S.W.2d 687 (Tex. App.—Waco 1998, writ den.). The idea is to divide the estate in a matter that, when possible, will reduce the need for continued contact.

Some property is only of use to one spouse. For example, one spouse might enjoy guns or a recreational vehicle, but the other has no interest in the property.

Cluck v. Cluck

Texas Court of Appeals—San Antonio, 1982
647 S.W.2d 338, writ dism'd

REEVES, Justice.

Appellant, by his fourth point of error, challenges the authority of the trial court in awarding a membership in the San Antonio Country Club to appellee. The San Antonio Country Club is a voluntary association organized as a non-profit corporation. Membership in the club is by invitation of the Board of Governors and the Board has the authority to terminate membership. The bylaws of the club provide, in part:

> Upon the death of any stockholding member of the club, or upon the resignation or dismissal of any member or upon such member being dropped for any cause from membership of the club, or upon acceptance by the Board of an application for a senior membership, or upon acceptance to become an associate member, or upon transfer to a non-resident member, the Board of Governors shall have the prior right to purchase for the corporation, the share or shares of stock held by such member for $1,000.00, provided, however, the widow or widower or adult son or daughter of a deceased member may have the deceased member's share transferred to their name without payment of initiation fee, upon being invited to stockholding membership by the Board of Governors. Upon the certificate evidencing such share of stock issued or transferred, there shall be endorsed the following:

> The stock is nonnegotiable and nontransferable except on the books of the club, and only after the club has been afforded an opportunity to exercise its option to purchase the same for $1,000.00 per share.

Appellant, upon paying his initiation fee, was granted membership in the club in his name only.

The divorce decree provided:

> Petitioner, Margaret Cluck, is awarded the following property as her sole and separate property and estate, and respondent, Elwood Cluck, is hereby divested of all right, title and interest in and to such property, to-wit:

> ....

> M. All right, title, interest, equity and ownership in and to the San Antonio Country Club, San Antonio, Texas, currently standing in the name of Elwood Cluck; Elwood Cluck is hereby divested of any membership or ownership rights in said stock and such membership and ownership rights are hereby transferred to Margaret Cluck, and all rights and privileges in connection with said stock heretofore standing in Elwood Cluck shall be and are hereby assigned and transferred to Margaret Cluck.

Since the membership stock has a contingent redeemable value of $1,000.00, the trial court could and did take into consideration this as an asset of the community in dividing the community estate of the parties. However, we are of the opinion that the trial court had no authority to divest the appellee of membership in the club. We view the stock certificate as merely an *indicia* of the right to membership analogous to a membership card in any voluntary association, and personal only to the appellant. Courts have been reluctant to interfere with the internal management of a voluntary association.

The San Antonio Country Club, as a voluntary association, has the sole right to determine who will be members of their club. We note that, according to its bylaws, even a spouse of a decedent member stockholder needs the approval of the Board of Governors prior to becoming a stockholder member of the club. Our Supreme Court has stated: "A voluntary association has the power to enact rules governing the admission of members and prescribing certain qualifications for membership; and such rules will be enforced, unless they are against good morals or violate the laws of the state." *Cline v. Insurance Exchange of Houston*, 140 Tex. 175, 166 S.W.2d 677 (1942).

We therefore hold that the trial court erred in divesting the appellant of his membership in the country club.

Patt v. Patt

Texas Court of Appeals—Houston [1st Dist.], 1985
689 S.W.2d 505, no writ

DUGGAN, Justice.

This is an appeal from that portion of a divorce decree dividing the parties' community property.

The parties had been married for over 31 years before their separation in June, 1982. The divorce was granted on the basis of irreconcilable differences without regard to fault of either party. The eleven children of the marriage were all over eighteen years of age at trial time in February 1984.

The community estate consisted of a homestead valued by the parties at $40,000 (subject to a mortgage of approximately $8,000), a 1977 Grand Prix automobile, and household furniture and fixtures purchased originally for between $1,500 and $2,200, and situated in the homestead residence. Neither party owned separate property. The court awarded each party (1) an undivided one-half interest in the homestead, and (2) ownership as separate property of the household furnishings, appliances, fixtures, wearing apparel, jewelry, and other personal property in his or her own possession or control. The court further awarded the appellee, Almatine Patt, the automobile and the exclusive use and possession of the home during the remainder of her life, subject to her timely payment of the house note, taxes, insurance, and reasonable maintenance and upkeep. All of the household furnishings, appliances and fixtures were situated in the homestead residence and thereby became the separate property of the appellee wife.

Appellant urges by his points of error one, two, three, and six, that (1) the trial court divided the community property in a manner that was "disproportionate, inequitable, and manifestly unjust and unfair," because the effect of the decree was to award all of the personalty and realty to the wife; and (2) there is no evidence to support such a division.

At the time of trial, the appellee wife was 51 years of age. Four of the parties' eleven children were still living with her at home. The youngest child was an unemployed eighteen year-old high school student, and the three older children were employed. Appellee testified that she had received no financial assistance from appellant since he left the house (other than the worker's compensation settlement sum discussed in point of error four), that the children had helped her by paying the house notes and other bills, that she was not employed, and that she had no source of income. There was no testimony that she had ever worked outside the home, or that she possessed any marketable job skills.

While there was no testimony as to appellant's age, appellee's original petition for divorce, filed December 1, 1982, alleged that appellant was 49 years of age. Appellant testified that he had been living with his sister for about two years; that he pays her $100 per month from his only source of income, a monthly social security disability check in the amount of $406; and that he is unable to work because of his physical disability. He testified that since leaving the parties' home, he has remained under a doctor's care for an emphysema condition; that he was hospitalized for his condition after his workers' compensation settlement; but that since the separation he has not had any further attacks that have required hospitalization.

Neither party has any separate property, and their only significant community asset is the home and its furnishings and fixtures. Taking into consideration appellant's age and physical condition, it is highly possible, as he asserts in his brief, that he will never receive anything more than the remainder interest awarded by the court in the residence property, the most valuable item of community property owned by the parties.

In considering the needs of the parties and the surrounding circumstances, the trial court appears to have shown a primary and realistic concern that each spouse have current living expenses. The court apparently concluded that the appellant's subsistence needs are met by his $406 monthly social security disability benefit, which provides him current funds that, after payment of $100 to his sister for room and board, leaves him $306 monthly for other living expenses. The court's award of the exclusive use of the house to the appellee/wife provides her a place of residence and the means to earn current income by renting either to her children or other persons. Although testimony showed that three adult children living at home presently provide the appellee her sole current income, the court may have recognized that the adult children's living arrangement was temporary. If the children move, appellee might be able to rent a portion of the house to other persons to earn current living expenses. Should she be unable to do so, and be unable to satisfy mortgage, tax, insurance and maintenance payments on the residence premises, the property would have to be sold, at which time appellant would receive payment for his community one-half interest. Appellant's equity would have increased in value because of interim current monthly payments made by appellee. We are unable to say that the trial court's division of the estate constituted, in the circumstances, an abuse of discretion.

LeBlanc v. LeBlanc

Texas Court of Appeals — Corpus Christi, 1988
761 S.W.2d 450, writ denied

OPINION

SEERDEN, Justice.

Appellant contests the property division and child support award in a divorce action tried to the court, and further claims error in the trial court's failure to grant him a continuance and denial of his motion for a new trial. We affirm the trial court's decree in part, but reverse and remand for a redetermination of the property issues.

Appellant's points one through three attack the property division. By point one he claims that the trial court abused its discretion in divesting him of his separate real property in violation of the holding in *Eggemeyer v. Eggemeyer*, 554 S.W.2d 137 (Tex. 1977). By point two, he claims that the award of a life estate to appellee violated his due process rights under Article 1, Section 19 of the Texas Constitution. By point three, he claims the division was not "just and right" as Tex. Fam. Code Ann. Sec. 3.63 (Vernon Supp. 1988) requires.

The trial court has wide discretion in dividing the property. We presume the trial court exercised its discretion properly. The test for abuse of discretion is not whether, in the opinion of the reviewing court, the facts present an appropriate case for the trial court's action, but whether the court acted arbitrarily or unreasonably.

The court may consider many factors in arriving at a "just and right" division of the property. These factors include fault in the breakup of the marriage, disparity in earning capacities or incomes, spouses' capacities and abilities, benefits which a party not at fault would have derived from continuation of the marriage, business opportunities, education, relative physical conditions, relative financial condition and obligations, disparity of ages, size of separate estates, and the nature of the property. Appellee introduced considerable evidence of fault.

We first consider the disposition of the tract on which the couple lived. Appellee's petition requested the homestead be awarded to her. In the decree, the trial court awarded appellee "the exclusive use and benefit ... for her lifetime" of the 24-acre tract upon which the couple had lived.

Appellant had purchased the land in his name before the parties married. Although appellee documented that she had provided $45,000 of the $46,000 purchase price from her separate money, and testified to extensive community improvements, she does not contest his separate ownership, or argue fraud or constructive trust. Appellant argues that Eggemeyer does not permit appellee to gain a life interest in the tract because it was his separate property. We agree that the interest the court awarded was greater than a homestead right and had the effect of divesting him of a fee interest in the tract.

A court may set aside property as the homestead of the wife and children for a period of time even though it is the husband's separate property. *Villarreal v. Laredo National Bank*, 677 S.W.2d 600, 606 (Tex. App.—San Antonio 1984, writ ref'd n.r.e.); *see Hedtke v. Hedtke*, 112 Tex. 404, 248 S.W.21, 23 (Tex. 1923). In appropriate circumstances the court can award use and benefit of one spouse's community real property to the other spouse, whether or not there are minor children. *Patt v. Patt*, 689 S.W.2d 505, 508 (Tex. App.—Houston [1st Dist.] 1985, no writ). The court may not divest a spouse of separate property, real or personal. *Cameron v. Cameron*, 641 S.W.2d 210, 220 (Tex. 1982).

Appellee relies on *Hedtke* to support her claim. *Eggemeyer* distinguishes Hedtke because in that case, homestead was awarded, not title. *Eggemeyer*, 554 S.W.2d at 141–142. The decree specifically stated "Possession of said land to revert to said defendant, J.G. Hedtke, at the termination of said homestead rights...." *Hedtke*, 248 S.W. at 22. We believe that the homestead is a community interest which the court may award either party, while a life estate is part of appellant's separate interest in the land. Though similar, these interests are not identical.

> In this State, homestead interest of each spouse or the surviving spouse in the homestead property constitutes an estate therein, and is treated as a life estate, *so long as the property retains its homestead character*. This is true, whether the fee title to the homestead property belongs to the separate estate of either or both spouses, or to their community estate.

Sparks v. Robertson, 203 S.W.2d 622, 623 (Tex. Civ. App.—Austin 1947, writ ref'd) [emphasis added]. The homestead character, and the homestead right, can be lost through abandonment. *Fiew v. Qualtrough*, 624 S.W.2d 335, 337 (Tex. App.—Corpus Christi 1981, writ ref'd n.r.e.). As written, the award in this case would give appellee property rights in appellant's separate property tract even if she abandoned it as a homestead. This is not permissible.

Appellee, by motion, volunteers that in the alternative, if we cannot sustain the award of the use and benefit of the 24-acre tract beyond the time that her youngest child reaches eighteen years of age, she would remit the remaining years under the decree and consent to a reformation of the decree. *McKnight v. McKnight*, 543 S.W.2d 863, 866 (Tex. 1976), held that the appellate court has no authority to render a judgment dividing property, but must remand if it finds an abuse or discretion. It distinguished cases in which remittitur would be made. However, in *Jacobs v. Jacobs*, 687 S.W.2d 731, 732 (Tex. 1985), the Supreme Court made no exception to its holding that an appellate court must remand the entire community property estate for a new division when it finds reversible error which materially affects the trial court's "just and right" division. The opinion condemns piecemeal editing of the property division. *Jacobs*, 687 S.W.2d at 732.

There is no question that disposition of the disputed property is material to the division. However, the parties can be spared the time and expense of an additional evidentiary hearing because the only error we found is an error of law by the trial court. We deny the motion and sustain appellant's points one and two.

DISCUSSION

I do not believe *LeBlanc* is correct in its suggestion that a divorce court can grant a non-owning spouse a post-divorce "homestead right" in the other spouse's separate realty. However, if *LeBlanc* is accepted, this could provide a useful alimony substitute in some situations.

C. Characterization Errors

Texas divorce courts may divide only the community estate. If a court mischaracterizes separate property as community property and divides it, this automatically is reversible error. However, if the court merely mischaracterizes property, this is not automatically reversible error, according to most courts.

McElwee v. McElwee
Texas Court of Appeals—Houston [1st Dist.], 1995
991 S.W.2d 182, writ denied

Hutson-Dunn, Justice.

Trial courts have broad discretion in making a "just and right" division of the community estate, and this discretion is not disturbed on appeal unless a clear abuse of discretion is shown. *Murff v. Murff*, 615 S.W.2d 696, 698 (Tex. 1981). When a court mischaracterizes *separate* property as *community* property, the error requires reversal because the subsequent division divests a spouse of his or her separate property. *Eggemeyer*, 554 S.W.2d at 140.

The issue of whether a court commits reversible error by mischaracterizing *community* property as *separate* property has not been directly decided by our supreme court. However, the high court has held that "[o]nce reversible error affecting the 'just and right' division of the community estate is found, the court of appeals must remand the entire community estate for a new division." *Jacobs v. Jacobs*, 687 S.W.2d 731, 733 (Tex. 1985). Only the trial court may make a just and right division of community property. Tex.Fam.Code Ann. §3.63 (Vernon 1993). The appellate court's role is to determine only if the trial court abused its discretion in making the division. *See Jacobs*, 687 S.W.2d at

732–33; *McKnight v. McKnight,* 543 S.W.2d 863, 866–68 (Tex.1976). If the trial court mischaracterizes community property as separate property, then the property does not get divided as part of the community estate. If the mischaracterized property has value that would have affected the trial court's just and right division, then the mischaracterization is harmful and requires the appellate court to remand the entire community estate to the trial court for a just and right division of the properly characterized community property. If, on the other hand, the mischaracterized property had only a *de minimis* effect on the trial court's just and right division, then the trial court's error is not an abuse of discretion.

We recognize that some appellate decisions have held that a trial court's error in mischaracterizing community property as separate property does not require reversal unless the appellate court finds that the trial court would have made a different division if the property had been properly characterized. *See King v. King,* 661 S.W.2d 252, 254 (Tex. App.—Houston [1st Dist.] 1983, no writ); *see also Bradley v. Bradley,* 725 S.W.2d 503, 505 (Tex. App.—Corpus Christi 1987, no writ); *Cook v. Cook,* 679 S.W.2d 581, 585 (Tex. App.—San Antonio 1984, no writ); *McLemore v. McLemore,* 641 S.W.2d 395, 398 (Tex. App.—Tyler 1982, no writ); *Smith v. Smith,* 620 S.W.2d 619, 623 (Tex. Civ. App.—Dallas 1981, no writ). In general, the cases hold that reversal is required only if the appellant shows that, due to the trial court's legal error, the resulting division constituted an abuse of discretion. *King,* 661 S.W.2d at 254; *Bradley,* 725 S.W.2d at 505. Although this Court has not revisited this rule since *Jacobs,* other courts have continued to apply the rule without analyzing it in light of *Jacobs. See Iglinsky v. Iglinsky,* 735 S.W.2d 536, 539 (Tex. App.—Tyler 1987, no writ); *Bradley,* 725 S.W.2d at 505. We disagree with these courts.

The facts of this case illustrate why this Court cannot presume that the trial court would have made the same division despite the mischaracterization. At rendition, the trial court judge stated that he had made an approximately 61%/39% division[1] in Mary's favor. Because the division did not consider the approximately $45,000 in mischaracterized property, the court actually made an approximately 64%/36% division in Mary's favor.[2] We do not suggest that, under the facts of this case, the trial court judge did not have the power to make a more or less disproportionate division. However, under *Jacobs*

---

1. Mary has argued that we should ignore this statement because it was a mere finding of fact recited in the judgment which conflicts with findings of fact which were later filed by the trial court. Under rule 299a, if findings of fact are recited in a judgment and are in conflict with the findings of fact made pursuant to rules 297 and 298, the latter findings are controlling for appellate purposes. Tex.R.Civ.P. 299a. However, the allegedly conflicting findings Mary cites are conclusions of law, properly filed under the heading "CONCLUSIONS OF LAW." Rule 299a simply does not apply.

2. The trial court found the community estate to be valued at $534,300. We assume the court meant $534,700 because the court awarded Edward assets amounting to $209,900, and awarded Mary assets amounting to $324,800 ($209,900 + $324,800 = $534,700). Therefore, the trial court found that it awarded 39.2% of the community estate to Edward and 60.8% to Mary.

The trial court did not assess a value for the annuity because Edward did not offer a value at trial. Edward has asked this Court to take judicial notice of his calculated value of the annuity. We decline to do so. However, assuming without deciding the annuity was valued at $21,602.20, as he suggests, the total value of the mischaracterized properties amounts to $45,413.80 ($7,553.43 + $4489.73 + $2796.96 + $8971.37 + $21602.20 = $45,413.80). Adding the value of the mischaracterized assets to the total value of the community estate found by the trial court, the correct value of the community estate is $580,113.80 ($534,700 + 45,413.80 = $580,113.80).

Therefore, Mary received community property valued at $370,213.80 ($324,800 + $45,413.80 = $370,213.80). Edward received community property valued at $209,900. Thus, the court awarded approximately 64% of the community estate to Mary ($370,213.80 / $580,113.80 = .64). The court awarded Edward 36% of the community assets ($209,900/$580,113.80 = .36).

and *McKnight,* only the trial court has the power to make a just and right division of the community estate. *Jacobs,* 687 S.W.2d at 733; *McKnight,* 543 S.W.2d at 865 (stating "a court of civil appeals has no authority to render its own property division"). To hold that this Court may not remand the case unless we determine that the distribution actually made by the trial court, considering the mischaracterization, is not an abuse of discretion effectively permits this Court to award a completely new division of the community estate —a 64%/36% division, rather than a 61%/39% division. Yet, this Court does not have the power to render a new division. Therefore, in light of *Jacobs,* we rule that when a mischaracterization has more than a mere *de minimis* effect upon the trial court's division, the appellate court must remand the community estate to the trial court for a just and right division based upon the correct characterization of the property.

In this case the trial court's error affected the court's property division. Hence, we reverse and remand the cause for a just and right division of the community estate. In addition, because the value of the America United Life annuity has not yet been determined, the trial court must assess the value, if any, of the annuity before disposing of the property.

DISCUSSION

The *McElwee* opinion discusses what should happen if community property is mischaracterized by the trial court as separate. The court mentions the different rules courts of appeal have applied.

It is not automatic reversible error if separate property is mischaracterized as community and the property is awarded to the owner. *Magill v. Magill,* 816 S.W.2d 530 (Tex. App.—Houston [1st Dist.] 1991, writ denied). It would be automatic reversible error, however, if the property would be awarded to the non-owner. *Tate v. Tate,* 55 S.W.3d 1,7 (Tex. App.—El Paso 2000, no pet. h.).

Jacobs v. Jacobs
Supreme Court of Texas, 1985
687 S.W.2d 731

RAY, Justice.

This is a divorce case in which only the property division is challenged on appeal. The court of appeals, after finding that the trial court had erred in determining what was properly a part of the community estate, reversed and rendered judgment as to part of the property division; reversed and remanded as to another part; and affirmed the trial court's judgment as to the remainder. 669 S.W.2d 759. We reverse that part of the court of appeals judgment which limits the remand to specific properties, substitute therefore a remand of the entire community estate for a new division and affirm the remainder of the judgment. We hold that a court of appeals must remand the entire community estate for a new division when it finds reversible error which materially affects the trial court's "just and right" division of the property.

The trial court found the value of the community estate to be between $1,300,000 and $1,500,000. About one-half of this value was attributable to reimbursement claims. The trial court found the community estate entitled to reimbursement for the time, toil and effort expended by husband on behalf of his separate property corporation, for certain community expenditures which benefited husband's separate estate and for certain income earned by husband, but diverted from the community estate to third parties.

Husband appealed the property division contending that the trial court had erred in awarding reimbursement to the community estate, had mischaracterized certain property and had erred in awarding wife her attorney's fees upon appeal. The court of appeals held that the trial court had erred in the following respects: (1) by awarding reimbursement to the community estate for the time, toil and effort of husband on behalf of his separate property corporation, (2) by awarding reimbursement to the community estate for income allegedly due husband, but diverted by him to third parties, (3) by characterizing as wholly community property certain properties in which husband had a separate property interest, (4) by characterizing as wife's separate property certain properties belonging to the community estate, and (5) by awarding wife her attorney's fees on appeal regardless of outcome.

Regarding the two reimbursement claims enumerated above, the court of appeals rendered judgment holding there was no evidence to support the first claim and no pleadings to support the second. The court of appeals also rendered judgment vacating wife's claim for attorney's fees on appeal. Regarding the mischaracterized property, the court of appeals remanded that part of the cause that affected the properties for a new division. The remainder of the property division was affirmed.

Under a single point of error, husband argues that the court of appeals has erred in failing to remand the entire property division to the trial court for a new division. Husband contends that the court of appeals' piecemeal editing of the property division made by the trial court is contrary to *McKnight v. McKnight*, 543 S.W.2d 863 (Tex. 1976). We agree.

In *McKnight*, the appellate court found the trial court had abused its discretion in how it divided the community estate and rendered a new division of the property. In reversing this judgment and remanding to the trial court, we held that an appellate court could not substitute its discretion for that of the trial court because a "just and right" division of the community estate was a matter lying solely within the discretion of the trial court. *McKnight v. McKnight*, 543 S.W.2d at 867.

In the present case, the court of appeals modified the trial court's property division by rendering judgment on the two reimbursement claims while limiting its remand to specific properties found to have been mischaracterized. *McKnight*, however, dictates a remand to the trial court of the entire community property division for a new division. Although the court of appeals appears to recognize in its opinion that the reimbursement claims materially influenced the property division, the court simply attempts by some unarticulated method to expunge the value of such claims from the community property division. The result, if it could be achieved, would be to alter the trial court's plan for a "just and right" division of the community estate.

It is, however, probably impossible to excise the reimbursement claims from the community property division, absent a remand of the community property division, because such claims are not represented in the divorce decree by any specific, identifiable award of money, nor are they traceable to any specific properties. Even if the reimbursement claims could be identified in the trial court's property division, the court of appeals could not simply modify the decree by striking the reimbursement awards "because to do so would be to make a new division of the estate of the parties, a matter within the discretion of the trial court." *Faulkner v. Faulkner*, 582 S.W.2d 639, 642 (Tex. Civ. App.—Dallas 1979, no writ).

The Texas Family Code requires the trial court to "order a division of the estate of the parties in a manner that the court deems just and right, having due regard of the rights of each party." Tex. Fam. Code Ann. Sec. 3.63. The trial court has wide discretion in dividing the "estate of the parties," but must confine itself to the community property; the only property subject to division under Section 3.63. *Eggemeyer v. Eggemeyer*, 554 S.W.2d 137, 139 (Tex. 1977). Whether the trial court abuses its discretion in dividing the property, as in *McKnight*, or commits reversible error in defining what property is properly a part of the community estate and therefore subject to division, as in the present case, the principle to be applied is the same. Once reversible error affecting the "just and right" division of the community estate is found, the court of appeals must remand the entire community estate for a new division.

That part of the court of appeals judgment limiting remand to specific properties is reversed and the cause is remanded to the trial court for a new division of the community estate. In all other respects, the judgment of the court of appeals is affirmed.

D. Miscellaneous Property Division Issues

When dividing the community estate, courts consider who will have the custody of any minor children, and the needs of those children. The needs of the children can be satisfied via a child support award or the property division.

Hourigan v. Hourigan
Texas Court of Appeals — El Paso, 1981
635 S.W.2d 556, no writ

PRESLAR, Justice.

This is a divorce case in which the only issue on appeal is with respect to the division of property. We affirm the judgment of the trial court.

The parties were married on February 26, 1956, and separated on June 6, 1979. The husband filed this suit based on the grounds of insupportability and abandonment. The wife cross-actioned on the ground of insupportability. They have one minor child, a girl, who was born in September, 1971. There is no dispute as to the custody of their minor child, and the Court appointed the husband as managing conservator. The husband earns approximately $1,415.36 net each month as an engineer. The wife earns a monthly net income of about $720.00 as a secretary. Both parties are in good health.

In a non-jury trial, the Court awarded the husband the homestead appraised at $27,800.00, all the household goods valued at $2,100.00, a 1974 Toronado automobile worth about $1,800.00, a $500.00 U.S. bond, $4,300.00 from the savings account, and a pension plan valued at $5,720.00. Additionally, the Court ordered that the child be named as beneficiary of the four insurance policies and ordered the husband to pay the premiums. The court further awarded to the husband a rental home, net value of $19,000.00, which was to be administered by him in support of their daughter. When the obligation to support ceased, the rental home was to be sold and the wife was to receive the first

$10,000.00 of the cash proceeds. The husband was ordered to pay all transportation expenses incurred when the parties' daughter visited her mother in Alaska. The wife was awarded the 1977 Aspen automobile and her personal property.

There are no findings of fact and conclusions of law in this case, and in the absence thereof we must presume that the trial Court took into consideration the entire circumstances of the parties in dividing their property. *Musslewhite v. Musslewhite*, 555 S.W.2d 894, 897 (Tex. Civ. App.—Tyler 1977, writ dism'd). Further, the evidence and all reasonable inferences must be drawn in a light most favorable to the Appellee. *Robbins v. Robbins*, 601 S.W.2d 90, 91 (Tex. Civ. App.—Houston [1st Dist.] 1980, no writ).

Appellant's single point of error complains that the trial court abused its discretion in the division of the community property. When a divorce is based upon both no fault and fault grounds, the trial court may consider the fault of one spouse in breaking up the marriage when making a property division. *Murff v. Murff*, 615 S.W.2d 696, (Tex. 1981.) In this case, there was evidence presented that the wife abandoned her husband and child which the court could properly consider.

When dividing the property, the trial court considered the parties' duty of support of their eight-year old daughter. The wife testified that she could not afford to make child support payments. She also said that she should not have to make such payments since the husband's salary was almost twice as much as her own. Each parent has the duty to support his or her minor child. Tex. Fam. Code Ann. Sec. 4.02 (Supp. 1980). In order to enforce this duty, the court may order either or both parents to make periodic payments or lump sum payments, or both, for the child's support until the child reaches eighteen years of age. Tex. Fam. Code Ann. Sec. 14.05(a). Although the duty of support is imposed equally between both parties, the court need not divide this obligation equally in terms of monetary contributions. The relative value of non-monetary services of the parent who is appointed managing conservator, as well as the relative capabilities of the parties, should be considered in ordering a payment of child support. *Hazelwood v. Jinkins*, 580 S.W.2d 33, 36 (Tex. Civ. App.—Houston [1st District] 1979, no writ).

From the record and the judgment, the trial court in this case indicated that the wife's duty of support would be in a lump sum payment from her share of the community property in lieu of periodic payments. Although the wife may have had difficulty in making periodic child support payments from her current income, her share of the community assets could be reached in order to discharge her duty of support. *Musick v. Musick*, 590 S.W.2d 582, 586 (Tex. Civ. App.—Tyler 1979, no writ).

The fact that the husband could support their child from his current earnings without any outside contribution does not relieve the wife of her obligation of support. *See Grandinetti v. Grandinetti*, 600 S.W.2d 371, 372 (Tex. Civ. App.—Houston [14th Dist.] 1980, no writ). The record shows that tuition is being paid for private school, and also reveals the cost of clothing, lunches, transportation and housing for an eight-year-old child. There was testimony that the cost of raising their daughter until eighteen years of age would be the discounted figure between $45,000.00 and $46,000.00. Moreover, in this instance, the husband was appointed managing conservator, and, from the evidence in the record, he provides most of the non-monetary services. These services are a very real and important part of the support of their child.

Consequently, we conclude that the wife failed to show any abuse of discretion of the trial court. The appellant's point of error is overruled.

The judgment of the trial court is affirmed.

Gordon v. Blackmon

Texas Court of Appeals — Corpus Christi, 1984
675 S.W.2d 790, no writ

SEERDEN, Justice.

This is an original mandamus proceeding wherein Carol Ann Gordon asks this Court to direct the Honorable Judge Jack R. Blackmon of the 117th District Court of Nueces County to vacate an order denying certain pre-trial discovery and enter its order directing Judge Blackmon to allow the discovery and permit relator to take the deposition of the real adverse party in interest, William Thomas Gordon.

This dispute arises out of a divorce suit originally filed by relator in February 1981. After discovery was completed, a trial was had before the court resulting in a divorce decree being entered on December 29, 1981. Relator appealed the trial court's decree solely on issues relating to division of the property owned by the parties. No complaint was made of the granting of the divorce or of the management or support provided for the minor child of the parties.

On September 22, 1983, this Court, noting that on February 1, 1983, the Uniformed Services Former Spouses' Protection Act took effect, 10 U.S.C.A. Sec. 1408(c)(1) (West 1983) and that William Thomas Gordon's military retirement was subject to the act and had not been considered by the trial court in dividing the property of the parties, we reversed the judgment of the trial court insofar as it divided the property of the parties and remanded it for a new trial.

On remand, relator filed an amended petition for divorce raising or attempting to raise a variety of new issues and requesting a new division of the community estate of the parties. She specifically requested the court to reimburse the community estate for the funds or assets received by William Thomas Gordon from his military retirement since December 29, 1981, and alleged that such funds "have been expended by the community estate to benefit or enhance the Respondent's (William Gordon's) separate estate."

Relator now seeks to take the deposition of William Thomas Gordon and have him produce all business records relating to his income and the property he may have acquired since December 29, 1981. In addition to requesting records as to military retirement statements, relator has itemized twelve other broad categories of records and documents, none of which related to the property owned by the parties on December 29, 1981, but only to property acquired by Mr. Gordon since that date.

The trial date quashed the notice to take Mr. Gordon's deposition, and it is this action which gives rise to the petition for writ of mandamus.

In order to determine the relevancy of the materials relator seeks to discover, it is necessary to determine the effect of the partial remand by this Court on the status of the parties and their property. While relator seems to concede that the bonds of matrimony were severed by the original decree of December 29, 1981, it appears to be her argument that our remand had the effect of extending the marital status as to the property until the decree is final after the remand.

Tex. Fam. Code Ann. Sec. 5.01(b) (Vernon 1975) provides that community property consists of the property, other than separate property, acquired by either spouse during marriage. It seems clear, then, that, if the effect of this Court's judgment of September

22, 1983, prolongs the marriage relationship, Judge Blackmon abused his discretion by refusing relator's request for additional discovery. If, on the other hand, the decree of December 29, 1981, dissolved the marriage of the parties, the extent and nature of their property was fixed at that time and had already been discovered, and we cannot say that Judge Blackmon abused his discretion by refusing additional discovery.

Neither the briefs of the parties nor our research have revealed any precedent resolving the question before us. Tex. Fam. Code Ann. Sec. 3.63 (Vernon Supp. 1984) provides that in a decree of divorce the court shall order a division of the estate of the parties. It has been held that a divorce decree which does not divide the estate of the parties is interlocutory and not a final, appealable order.

At the same time, Tex. R. Civ. P. 434 permits a remand for a partial retrial where it appears "that the error affects a part only of the matter in controversy and that part is clearly *separable* without unfairness to the parties…." It is noted that, in 1976, this rule was amended in part to substitute the words "and that such part is clearly separable without unfairness to the parties" for "and the issues are severable." The reason for this rule change, as well as similar changes in Rule 320 as relates to trial courts and Rule 503 as relates to the Supreme Court, is to provide each court with some discretion in ordering a partial new trial when the issues are clearly separable.

All of the issues in this case, including the marital status of the parties, were fairly tried and resolved in the original trial of this case, except for the property issue. We see no legitimate practical or legal reason why the marital status of the parties should have been preserved beyond the date of the original decree. The division of property is clearly separable from the marital status of the parties, without any unfairness to either of them. While Mr. Gordon may have added to his property in this instance, situations can as easily be conceived where either party's community estate could have been diminished during the appeal to the detriment of the other party. It is in the interest of justice that, once a party has had a fair trial on such a question, uncomplained of and unaffected by error, there should not be another trial.

We hold that the relator and her husband were divorced effective December 29, 1981, and that the nature and extent of their property was fixed as of that date. Judge Blackmon did not abuse his discretion by denying additional discovery by relator.

The petition for mandamus is denied.

DISCUSSION

Texas law regarding the issue raised in *Gordon* is somewhat confused. This confusion stems from the general rule that the issue of divorce and property division may not be severed. If a party appeals an issue relating to the division of the community estate and the matter is remanded to the trial court, what is the marital status of the parties during this period? In *Vautrain v. Vautrain*, 646 S.W.2d 309 (Tex. App.—Ft. Worth 1983, writ dism'd) the court held that the divorce was *not* final and parties continued to accumulate community property. There is no Texas Supreme Court opinion clarifying this. However, *Parker v. Parker*, 897 S.W.2d 918 (Tex. App.—Fort Worth 1995, no writ) and *Herschberg v. Herschberg*, 994 S.W.2d 273 (Tex. App.—Corpus Christi 1999, no writ) suggest that *Gordon* currently is the accepted rule, as to whether parties continue to accumulate community property when a divorce property division (and not the divorce itself) is appealed.

Leal v. Leal

Texas Court of Appeals—San Antonio, 1982
628 S.W.2d 168, no writ

KLINGEMAN, Justice.

Delia Leal, the Petitioner in a divorce suit, appeals only from that portion of the divorce action making a partition of the community property. In a non-jury trial the court granted the divorce and divided the property between the parties and also awarded attorney's fees to Petitioner in the sum of $3,000.00.

Petitioner's single point of error is that the trial court abused its discretion when dividing the community estate by failing to consider monies spent by Respondent [appellee], Hector Leal, during the pendency of the divorce. Appellee by cross-point asserts that there is no evidence to support the trial court's award of attorney's fees to Petitioner in the sum of $3,000.00.

We first consider appellant's point of error that the trial court abused its discretion in making the division of the community estate of the parties. It is well settled that Texas courts are given wide discretion in making division of the property of the parties and that such division will not be disturbed on appeal unless the court has clearly abused its discretion. *Bell v. Bell*, 513 S.W.2d 20, 22 (Tex. 1974); *Hedtke v. Hedtke*, 112 Tex. 404, 248 S.W. 21 (Tex. 1923). Section 3.63 of the Texas Family Code provides that in a decree of divorce the court shall order a division of the estate of the parties in a manner that the court deems just and right, having due regard for the rights of each party and any children of the marriage. Tex. Fam. Code Ann. Sec. 3.63 (Vernon 1975). The provisions of Section 3.63 do not require that the property division be equal, and appellate courts have held that it must be presumed that the trial court exercised its discretion properly and that a case should be reversed only where there is a clear abuse of that discretion. *In re McCurdy*, 489 S.W.2d 712 (Tex. Civ. App.—Amarillo 1973, writ dism'd); *Hensley v. Hensley*, 496 S.W.2d 929 (Tex. Civ. App.—El Paso, 1973, no writ).

Appellant's basic complaint as to the property division is that the court abused its discretion when making such property division in failing to consider monies spent by the Respondent during the pendency of the divorce. Appellant relies heavily on *Reaney v. Reaney*, 505 S.W.2d 338 (Tex. Civ. App.—Dallas 1974, no writ), where the court held that a fair and just division of community property could not be made without taking into account the admitted dissipation of community assets, and *Posey v. Posey*, 561 S.W.2d 602 (Tex. Civ. App.—Waco 1978, no writ), where the court held that the trial court must view the case in its entirety in making a division that is just and right between the parties.

These differ materially from the case before us. For instance, in *Reaney* the husband [appellant] admitted that he squandered the money, gave some of it away, spent it very foolishly, lost it on gambling, and at the time of the trial he did not have any of it. In *Posey* the appellant testified that he put $2,000.00 of the community funds in a hole in the apartment the date the suit was filed; thereafter he put another $1,000.00 into a hole; and further put $1,000.00 in his pockets. He also admitted that on the date the suit was filed he withdrew $2,000.00 of community funds from the Lakewood State Bank.

The testimony here is entirely different. Appellant testified that the husband had a girlfriend upon whom he spent community funds and that he generally dissipated some of the community funds during the period of time the divorce was filed until the divorce was granted. However, she was unable to produce any definite proof of amounts spent or any evidence as to how much of the community estate, if any, was dissipated. The husband generally denied her testimony and testified that the money he spent was for living and business expenses. At the most we have conflicting testimony. In the cases relied on by appellant the husbands admitted either dissipation of or fraudulent concealment of community property.

Moreover, at a "hearing on court's ruling on the division of community property," appellant requested the court to make some sort of ruling for the husband to pay her back some of the money he had spent. In response the court stated that it had made a fair decision. The inference is, at least, that the court had taken into consideration any dissipation of community property, if it found any, in making the property division. In other words, if the trial court found that appellee spent community funds for other than living or business expenses, such was taken into account when the court exercised its discretion in dividing the community estate. It is also to be noted that in the *Reaney* and *Posey* cases the Court of Civil Appeals affirmed the trial court's judgment, finding that the trial court had made a fair and just division of the property. The Court of Civil Appeals thus found no abuse of discretion. Appellant here is trying to prove an abuse of discretion; therefore, her burden is entirely different.

Applying the applicable rules set forth in *Bell v. Bell, supra,* and other cases we have cited, we find no abuse of discretion by the trial court. Appellant's point of error is overruled.

DISCUSSION

As *Leal* shows, spouses have great discretion regarding the manner in which community funds should be spent prior to divorce, unless a court order is obtained that limits that freedom. Courts only become concerned when money is totally squandered during separation or when money is spent on dates.

Archambault v. Archambault

Texas Court of Appeal—Beaumont, 1988
763 S.W.2d 50, no writ

BURGESS, Justice.

Shanna Malene Archambault filed suit for divorce in May of 1985. In her Third Amended Original Petition, she added a third party, TexasBanc Savings Association. The trial court granted the TexasBanc's motion for a separate trial, and proceeded to trial on the action against appellee. The case was submitted to the jury on special issues inquiring into the following: the proportionate division of the community estate, the amount of child support to be paid by the husband, the fair market value of items of community property, and the amount of reasonable attorney's fees for the wife's attorney. In response to the special issues, the jury found the proportionate division should be 60% to the wife and 40% to the husband, found the husband should pay $1200 per month as child support, placed values on fifty-three items of community property and found the reasonable amount of attorney's fees to be $20,000 for the trial and $2,500 for appeal to this court.

The trial court entered a judgment which states, in part, "The case was submitted to the jury concerning several advisory issues and the jury returned answers to the advisory issues...." The judgment dissolved the marriage, made conservatorship orders, ordered the husband to pay $800 per month as child support and divided the community estate. The wife appeals urging four points of error.

The first point of error asserts the trial court erred in making a disproportional division of the community estate. Appellant alleges this division to equal an 81.71% share to the husband and 18.29% to her. She claims the trial court treated the values set by the jury as advisory and disregarded them, effectively denying her the right to trial by jury. In response, the husband argues the trial court did not disregard the values as established by the jury, but made the division based upon the net values. Unfortunately, we have no findings of fact concerning the property division; we only have the judgment itself. The judgment makes no orders concerning liabilities. Therefore, the husband's argument about net values is not supported by the record. In reviewing the division under the judgment, both parties' briefs allege the husband was awarded $432,400 worth of property using the market values found by the jury. Using the same findings, the wife was awarded $155,983 of property. This equates to 73.49% to the husband and 26.51% to appellant.

If the trial court treated the jury's findings of market value as advisory, this was error. A jury's determination of value is binding upon the trial court. The division of the estate, however, is properly determined by the court, and the jury's 60–40 proportionate division was advisory only. It is not required that a division be equal, and abuse of discretion is the standard of review. Although the division does not have to be equal, an unequal division must be supported by some reasonable basis. We find no such reasonable basis under this record. The division as evidenced by the judgment is grossly disproportionate so as to constitute a manifestly unfair or unjust judgment. Point of error number one is sustained.

Point of error number two avers the trial court erred in failing to order the husband to pay $1200 per month as child support in light of the jury's answer and in failing to make findings pursuant to Rule 7 of the Child Support Guidelines promulgated by our Supreme Court. The jury's finding on the amount of child support is advisory only and not binding on the trial court. Tex. Fam. Code Ann. sec. 11.13(b) (Vernon 1986); *Havis v. Havis*, 657 S.W.2d 921, 924 (Tex. App.—Corpus Christi 1983, writ dism'd). A trial court has broad discretion in setting the amount of child support and its decision should not be disturbed unless the record demonstrates a clear abuse of discretion. We find no such abuse of discretion.

Abrams v. Abrams

Texas Court of Appeals—Corpus Christi, 1986
713 S.W.2d 195, no writ

UTTER, Justice.

This is an appeal from a divorce decree dissolving the marriage of appellee and appellant. Appellant has limited his appeal to issues regarding the amount of child support ordered by the trial court and an award of attorney's fees. We reform the judgment of the trial court, and as reformed, affirm.

The parties were divorced on June 6, 1985. Support orders were entered regarding their three minor children. The trial court ordered that appellant pay child support of $500.00 per month per child, increased to $600.00 per month per child when the first child reaches age eighteen or is otherwise emancipated, and further increased to $800.00 per month for the youngest child until he reaches age eighteen or is otherwise emancipated.

By his third and fourth points of error, appellant contends that the trial court erred in entering a child support order which provides for periodic increases in the amount of child support which he is obligated to pay. Appellant contends that "[t]here must be some material change in the conditions of the parties and a trial court cannot anticipate such changes." We agree. Any increase in child support must be supported by evidence that the circumstances of the child or a person affected by the order have materially and substantially changed since the entry of the order. Tex. Fam. Code Ann. Sec. 14.08(c)(2) (Vernon Supp. 1986). In order to increase child support, the trial court should examine the circumstances of the child and the parents at the time the prior decree was rendered in relation to circumstances existing when the modification is sought. Although each case must stand on its own facts, and the trial court has wide discretion in determining the amount of child support payments, the determination of that amount must be supported by evidence that the children's needs are as much as the amounts specified in the order.

The only evidence in the record which goes to the future needs of any of the children is testimony given by appellee. She testified that "Jenny [the second oldest child] needs braces and dental work and it's going to be expensive." She further testified that such dental work would cost approximately $3,000.00. There is no testimony as to when the dental work would begin. It could be that Jenny's dental work could be commenced and completed before the first child attained the age of eighteen or was otherwise emancipated. If so, then under the record before us, the need for any increases in child support would be obviated. Any child support order which anticipates the future needs of children and incorporates such anticipated needs into periodic increases in child support payments must be based upon legally sufficient evidence, specific as to not only the amounts of any needed increases but also as to the times such increases are needed. The record before us presents no such evidence. The child support order requiring appellant to increase child support payments periodically is arbitrary, unreasonable, and not based upon the facts. We find that, under the law in effect at the time of its decision, the trial court abused its discretion in ordering such periodic increases. We recognized that in the future such matters will be governed by the Supreme Court's Child Support Guidelines and that the trial court may fashion a child support order providing for periodic increases consistent with the percentage guidelines set forth by our Supreme Court. Appellant's third and fourth points of error are sustained. The judgment of the trial court is REFORMED to delete those provisions ordering periodic increases in child support.

AUTHOR'S COMMENT

Divorcing spouses can, by agreement, incorporate automatic adjustments to child support. *See Cisneros v. Cisneros*, 787 S.W.2d 550 (Tex. App.—El Paso 1990, n.w.h.).

DeGroot v. DeGroot

Texas Court of Appeals—Dallas, 2008
260 S.W.3d 658, no pet.

Opinion By Justice LANG.

Katherine Diane DeGroot appeals the trial court's January 24, 2007 final decree of divorce. She raises three issues on appeal, arguing the trial court erred when it: (1) signed the January 24, 2007 divorce decree, replacing its July 19, 2006 divorce decree, because the trial court's plenary power had expired.

We conclude the trial court erred when it signed the January 24, 2007 divorce decree because the trial court's plenary power had expired and, because it exceeds the trial court's limited, post-judgment jurisdiction to clarify that divorce decree, it is void. The trial court's January 24, 2007 divorce decree is vacated. The July 19, 2006 divorce decree is reinstated.

I. FACTUAL AND PROCEDURAL BACKGROUND

On October 25, 2005, Ms. Degroot filed a petition for divorce from her husband, Richard Douglas DeGroot. On July 19, 2006, the trial court signed the final decree of divorce. In the July 19, 2006 divorce decree, the trial court stated the DeGroots had entered into a written agreement, which was incorporated in the decree, noted they stipulated the agreement was enforceable as a contract, and approved the agreement as contained in the decree. The deadline was August 18, 2006, to file a motion to modify or for new trial of the July 19, 2006 divorce decree. Mr. DeGroot claims on August 18, 2006, he mailed to the trial court his motion for clarification of the July 19, 2006 divorce decree. That motion was actually filed on August 23, 2006.

On October 5, 2006, the DeGroots filed a joint motion for appointment of an "arbitrator," in which they claimed there is a reasonable expectation that several post-divorce disputes may be resolved by the use of the "alternative dispute resolution procedure of arbitration." On October 13, 2006, the trial court ordered the appointment of an arbitrator for the "pending disputes" between the DeGroots "as to the unresolved issues regarding the Agreed Decree of Divorce entered on July 18, 2006 [sic] be arbitrated." In a handwritten statement at the bottom of the order, it states the arbitration award will be binding on the parties. However, on appeal, the DeGroots agree the ordered arbitration was non-binding. In a separate order, the trial court administratively closed the case pending the arbitration, but retained jurisdiction, including the authority to vacate the order administratively closing the case, if cause was shown that further litigation was necessary. On November 1, 2006, Ms. DeGroot filed a petition for enforcement of the July 19, 2006 divorce decree.

On December 18, 2006, at the conclusion of the arbitration, the arbitrator signed an "arbitration order" that set out the results of the arbitration. The "arbitration order" changed some of the property-division terms of the July 19, 2006 divorce decree. Also, the "arbitration order" states the DeGroots "arbitrated the remaining issues for the preparation of the Final Decree of Divorce," and that Ms. DeGroot "is awarded the specific items as requested in her Motion for Enforcement."

On January 18, 2007, Mr. DeGroot filed a motion requesting the trial court to set aside the July 19, 2006 divorce decree, confirm the December 18, 2006 "arbitration order," and sign a new final decree of divorce incorporating the "arbitration order." On January 16, 2007, after her counsel withdrew, Ms. DeGroot filed a pro se "motion to enter a [QDRO]" and a pro se "motion for review of arbitrator's order." On January 24, 2007, without signing an order vacating its October 13, 2006 order administratively closing the case, the trial court held a hearing where it orally denied all of Ms. DeGroot's motions and her petition for enforcement, and announced a new divorce decree would be signed. Subsequent to the hearing, the trial court signed the new, written divorce decree dated January 24, 2007.

On February 20, 2007, Ms. DeGroot filed a motion for new trial, which was denied without a hearing on February 21, 2007. On March 9, 2007, Ms. DeGroot filed her notice of appeal. Also, on March 9, 2007, the trial court signed written orders denying Ms.

DeGroot's "motion for a review of arbitrator's order," motion to enter a QDRO, and petition for enforcement.

II. TRIAL COURT'S PLENARY JURISDICTION

In issue one, Ms. DeGroot argues the trial court erred when it signed the January 24, 2007 divorce decree, replacing its July 19, 2006 divorce decree, because the trial court's plenary jurisdiction had expired. Also, in her brief, she asserts the January 24, 2007 divorce decree substantially revises the division of property, exceeding the trial court's power to clarify its original decree.

Mr. DeGroot responds there are several reasons the trial court had jurisdiction to replace the July 19, 2006 divorce decree with the decree of January 24, 2007. First, he asserts his motion for clarification, filed-stamped August 23, 2006, was mailed on August 18, 2006, the final day to file a motion to modify. According to Mr. DeGroot, under the "mailbox rule" in Texas Rule of Civil Procedure 5, his mailing of the motion on August 18, 2006 effected timely filing. *See* Tex. R. Civ. P. 5. Second, he contends that, although his motion was called a "motion for clarification," it requests a substantive change to the July 19, 2006 divorce decree so it qualifies as a motion to modify, which extends the trial court's plenary power. Third, he claims the trial court's October 13, 2006 order appointing an arbitrator actually vacated the July 19, 2006 divorce decree or granted a new trial because it was based on his "motion for clarification." Finally, he claims the trial court's order administratively closing the case states the trial court "retains complete jurisdiction," which shows the order appointing an arbitrator actually vacated the July 19, 2006 divorce decree or granted a new trial.

A. Applicable Law

To promote the amicable settlement of disputes in a suit for divorce, the spouses may enter into a written agreement concerning the division of the property, liabilities of the spouses, and maintenance of either spouse. Tex. Fam. Code Ann. § 7.006(a) (Vernon 2006). If the court finds that the terms of the written agreement in a divorce are just and right, those terms are binding on the court. *See id.* § 7.006(b). Property adjudications in a divorce decree become final the same as other judgments relating to title and possession of property. The date the judgment is signed determines the beginning of the periods prescribed for the trial court's plenary power to grant a new trial or to vacate, modify, correct, or reform a judgment, and for filing the various motions and documents authorized by the Texas Rules of Civil Procedure. Tex. R. Civ. P. 306a.

A motion for new trial or a motion to modify, correct, or reform a judgment shall be filed within thirty days after the judgment is signed. Tex. R. Civ. P. 329b(a), (g). A motion to modify, correct, or reform a judgment shall be in writing, signed by the party or his attorney, and specify the respects in which the judgment should be modified, corrected, or reformed. Tex. R. Civ. P. 329b(g). A timely filed post-judgment motion that seeks a substantive change in an existing judgment qualifies as a motion to modify under rule 329b(g), extending the trial court's plenary jurisdiction and the appellate time table. *Lane Bank Equip. Co. v. Smith S. Equip., Inc.*, 10 S.W.3d 308, 314 (Tex. 2000). During the period of a trial court's plenary power, its power to modify its judgment is virtually absolute. *See Stallworth v. Stallworth*, 201 S.W.3d 338, 349 (Tex. App.—Dallas 2006, no pet.). The trial court's plenary power to grant a new trial or to vacate, modify, correct, or reform a judgment is limited to a maximum of one hundred and five days after the judgment is signed. *In re Nguyen*, 155 S.W.3d 191, 193 (Tex. App.—Tyler 2003, orig. proceeding). After the trial court's plenary power expires, the trial court may not alter, amend, or modify the substantive division of the property in the divorce decree. *See* TEX. FAM. CODE ANN. § 9.007 (Vernon 2006).

A court that rendered a divorce decree generally retains continuing subject-matter jurisdiction to enforce and to clarify the divorce decree's property division. *See* TEX. FAM. CODE ANN. §§ 9.002, 9.008; *Gainous v. Gainous*, 219 S.W.3d 97, 106 (Tex. App. — Houston [1st Dist.] 2006, pet. denied). Texas Family Code sections 9.002, 9.006, 9.008, 9.101, 9.103, and 9.104 provide for limited, post-judgment jurisdiction that may be invoked only in particular circumstances, rather than for plenary, original jurisdiction. *Gainous*, 219 S.W.3d at 108.

A party may seek clarification of a divorce decree through a suit for enforcement or a motion to clarify. *See* TEX. FAM. CODE ANN. §§ 9.001, 9.006, 9.008. In a suit to enforce the decree, a court has continuing jurisdiction to render further orders to enforce the division of the property made in the decree of divorce to assist in the implementation of or to clarify the prior order. *See id.* § 9.006(a); *Gainous*, 219 S.W.3d at 106. Similarly, on the request of a party or on the court's own motion, the court has continuing jurisdiction to render a clarifying order setting forth specific terms to enforce compliance with an original division of property on a finding that the original division of property is not specific enough to be enforceable by contempt. *See* TEX. FAM. CODE ANN. § 9.008; *Gainous*, 219 S.W.3d at 106.

However, there are limitations on the enforcement and clarification powers of the court that rendered the divorce decree. *Gainous*, 219 S.W.3d at 106. A court may not amend, modify, alter, or change the division of property made or approved in the divorce decree. *See* TEX. FAM. CODE ANN. § 9.007(a); *Shanks v. Treadway*, 110 S.W.3d 444, 449 (Tex. 2003). An order that amends, modifies, alters, or changes the divorce decree's property division is beyond the power of the court. *See* TEX. FAM. CODE ANN. § 9.007(b); *Gainous*, 219 S.W.3d at 106–07. Accordingly, section 9.007 of the Texas Family Code is jurisdictional and orders violating its restrictions are void. *Gainous*, 219 S.W.3d at 108.

B. Application of the Law to the Facts

In his "motion for clarification of final divorce decree," Mr. DeGroot noted that a final decree of divorce was signed, an agreement was reached between the parties for settlement of all issues in the matter, including an agreement that each party would be responsible for the portion of debt he or she incurred since October 2005, and the parties agreed to the entry of an order clarifying the division of that debt. Mr. DeGroot's motion for clarification specifically requested:

> [t]he court [to] clarify the Final Decree of Divorce that was entered by th[e] Court on or about July 19, 2006 and specifically divide the debt in accordance with the division as set out in the attached Exhibit B ... so as to make said Final Decree of Divorce clear and specific enough so that it may be enforced by th[e] Court.

Also, in the event the trial court granted Mr. DeGroot's motion for clarification, he requested attorney's fees.

Mr. DeGroot argues his motion for clarification should be considered a motion to modify because he requested a substantive change in the July 19, 2006 divorce decree. He asserts the July 19, 2006 divorce decree allocated $5,000 of the debt to Ms. DeGroot and provided the remaining debt would be allocated fifty percent to each. He claims the remaining debt was in the amount of $138,717 and, pursuant to the terms of the July 19, 2006 divorce decree, $66,858.50 of the debt should have been allocated to Mr. DeGroot and $71,558.50 of the debt should have been allocated to Ms. DeGroot. However, Mr. DeGroot argues that, in his motion for clarification, he requested the debt to be allocated in accordance with Exhibit B, which requested that $63,723 of the debt be allocated to Mr. DeGroot and $74,394 of the debt be allocated to Ms. DeGroot.

Although Ms. DeGroot's calculation may not be exactly correct, even based on his argument, Mr. DeGroot's motion for clarification specifically requested the trial court to "clarify the Final Decree of Divorce that was entered by th[e] Court on or about July 19, 2006" and "to make said Final Decree of Divorce clear and specific enough so that it may be enforced by th[e] Court." Mr. DeGroot's motion for clarification does not request a substantive change in the July 19, 2007 divorce decree. *See* Tex. R. Civ. P. 329b(g) (motion to modify should specify respects in which judgment should be modified, corrected, or reformed); *Lane Bank*, 10 S.W.3d at 314 (timely filed post-judgment motion seeking substantive change in judgment qualifies as motion to modify under Rule 329b(g)). Rather, the substance of Mr. DeGroot's motion for clarification shows it is a motion for clarification under section 9.008 of the Texas Family Code. *See* Tex. Fam. Code Ann. § 9.008. Accordingly, the trial court's plenary power expired on August 18, 2006, thirty days after it signed the July 19, 2006 divorce decree, and that decree was final. The January 24, 2007 divorce decree was signed after the trial court's plenary power expired. Further, the January 24, 2007 divorce decree modified the property-division terms of the July 19, 2006 divorce decree, exceeding the trial court's limited, post-judgment jurisdiction to clarify that divorce decree and is void. *See Gainous*, 219 S.W.3d at 106–08.

Ms. DeGroot's first issue is decided in her favor.

V. CONCLUSION

The trial court did not have plenary power to enter the January 24, 2007 final decree of divorce. Further, the January 24, 2007 divorce decree modified the property-division terms of the July 19, 2006 divorce decree, exceeding the trial court's limited, post-judgment jurisdiction to clarify that divorce decree and is void. Accordingly, the trial court's January 24, 2007 final decree of divorce is vacated. The July 19, 2006 final decree of divorce is reinstated.

E. Independent Claims in a Divorce Action

Spouses apparently may now bring tort actions against one another. These actions apparently may be brought either in connection with the divorce action, or in a separate action. The most common type of action is assault and battery. *See Mogford v. Mogford*, 616 S.W.2d 936 (Tex. Civ. App.—San Antonio 1981, writ ref'd n.r.e.). Should other tort claims be permitted? (Remember *Schlueter v. Schlueter* in chapter 8.)

There has been increasing acceptance of various types of claims that can be brought by one cohabitant against the other. What if spouses cohabited before marriage? Can a cohabitation claim be joined with the divorce action?

Are any other claims permitted in a divorce action? For example, could a spouse add a claim in *quantum meruit* for uncompensated household services rendered during the marriage? What policy concern does this present?

F. Death Abates a Divorce Action

If a spouse dies while the divorce action is pending, this normally abates the divorce action, and the decedent's property passes according to the rules governing marriage dissolution by death.

In re Marriage of Joyner
Texas Court of Appeals — Texarkana, 2006
196 S.W.3d 883, pet. denied

1. Statement of the Case

The trial court announced, "your divorce is granted." The question presented is whether that pronouncement was the rendition of a final judgment in a divorce and child conservatorship case when the parties had previously entered a mediated settlement agreement complying with statutory provisions which made the agreement immediately binding and irrevocable on the parties and entitled them to a judgment on the agreement. We find the trial court rendered judgment by its oral pronouncement.

On May 29, 2001, Belinda Joyner filed for divorce from Thomas Joyner. At the end of their third mediation April 7, 2003, the parties signed a mediated settlement agreement that delineated and partitioned most of their property and conservatorship and support of their minor son. The parties met for their "final hearing" on July 2, 2003, to argue the few personal property issues they had been unable to resolve in mediation.

On July 3, 2003, the day after the final hearing, Thomas purchased a winning lottery ticket worth $2,080,000.00. Almost a year later, on May 7, 2004, Belinda filed a motion for final trial setting, claiming the divorce had never been finalized, she was still married to Thomas, and the $2,080,000.00 should be divided as community property. On June 28, 2004, the court signed a "Final Decree of Divorce," which stated the divorce had been judicially pronounced and rendered on July 2, 2003. Belinda appeals, claiming the divorce was not final until June 28, 2004.

2. Issues Presented

The issue in this case is whether the trial court's actions on July 2, 2003, constituted an oral rendition of judgment on the Joyners' divorce. A decision on this issue directly affects the categorization of the lottery winnings as Thomas' separate or the Joyners' community property.

Belinda contends the trial court did not render a final judgment on the three issues before it (the divorce, the property division, and the custody of their son) until June 28, 2004. She claims the trial court was required to specifically render judgment on each of these issues before she and Thomas could be deemed divorced. In the alternative, Belinda asserts even if the trial court rendered the parties divorced, it did not render final judgment because it did not render a decision on the property issues, relying on case law that a court cannot sever the divorce from the property. She contends she and Thomas were still married when he won the lottery, and therefore she is entitled to a just and right division of those winnings.

3. Analysis

a. The Dissolution of the Marriage

A judgment is rendered when the court makes an official announcement, either in writing or orally in open court, of its decision on the matter submitted for adjudication. *James v. Hubbard*, 21 S.W.3d 558, 561 (Tex. App.—San Antonio 2000, no pet.); *In re Bland*, 960 S.W.2d 123, 124 (Tex. App.—Houston [1st Dist.] 1997, no pet.). Once a judgment is rendered by oral pronouncement, the entry of a written judgment is purely a ministerial act. *Keim v. Anderson*, 943 S.W.2d 938, 942 (Tex. App.—El Paso 1997, no pet.); *see also Dunn v. Dunn*, 439 S.W.2d 830, 832–33, 12 Tex. Sup. Ct. J. 441 (Tex. 1969) (oral rendition of divorce constituted as final judgment even though judgment not signed until after spouse's death).

In order to be an official judgment, the trial court's oral pronouncement must indicate intent to render a full, final, and complete judgment at that point in time. *S & A Rest. Corp. v. Leal*, 892 S.W.2d 855, 858, 38 Tex. Sup. Ct. J. 303 (Tex. 1995); *In re Marriage of Ellsworth*, No. 07-01-0072-CV, 2001 Tex. App. LEXIS 6588, at *8 (Tex. App.—Amarillo Sept. 28, 2001, no pet.) (not designated for publication). The trial court's words, whether spoken or written, must evince a present, as opposed to future, act that effectively decides the issues before the court. *Woods v. Woods*, 167 S.W.3d 932, 933 (Tex. App.—Amarillo 2005, no pet.). Compare *Hubbard*, 21 S.W.3d at 561 (judge's statement he was "going to grant the divorce" once the final decree was on his desk did not suffice as a rendering), with *Baize v. Baize*, 93 S.W.3d 197, 200 (Tex. App.—Houston [14th Dist.] 2002, pet. denied) (judge's statement "I'll grant your divorce today" was found to be sufficient rendition of judgment). Whether a particular action constitutes a rendition of judgment is a question of fact. *Bockemehl v. Bockemehl*, 604 S.W.2d 466, 469 (Tex. Civ. App.—Dallas 1980, no writ).

In this case, the words granting a divorce are undeniably there. Belinda argues the trial court did not render judgment, did not pronounce officially that it had made a legal determination as to the divorce, and did not use the word "render." The statement by the trial court was made in open court while officiating as the presiding judge after all evidence had been presented and in the presence of all parties and attorneys. During the process of ruling on some rings and other personal property items, the court recognized that Thomas acknowledged a gift of a diamond ring to his son because he knew that was his (Thomas') mother's wish; however, he did not recognize a similar gift of a ring to his daughter because he did not hear his mother make such a statement. The court then stated,

> There is evidence, and, you know, probably credible evidence that your mother made a similar statement in regard to this lady's ring, broach, and broach guard, in regard to your daughter, but since you didn't hear it yourself, you've elected not to make yourself a gift of these items to your daughter. And that's your prerogative. You have every legal right to do so. And it may be—that your divorce is granted—so I'll now say—your former wife has made all this up.

We interpret that as a clear statement granting the divorce. The trial court then referred to Belinda as "your former wife." Belinda argues that the court said only that it "may be" that "your divorce is granted." However, from the context it is clear that the "may be" language refers to the possibility "it may be that" his "former wife" had fabricated the story about his mother's desire to give the daughter the ring. The present intent to grant a divorce by oral pronouncement is clear to us.

Moreover, the trial court's word choice throughout the hearing manifested intent this would be the last time these parties would argue as husband and wife. The trial court started the hearing by stating it was the court's understanding that almost everything had been settled and that there were only a handful of matters the court needed to decide. Later, the trial court requested clarification as to what was in contention, and thus before the court, as opposed to matters that had already been decided in the parties' mediated settlement agreement.

Perhaps the most telling were the trial court's comments at the close of arguments. The court started its ruling by simply stating:

> I'll tell you what I'm going to do. I'm going to rule, and then I'll allow y'all to make of record your exceptions to my rulings. And in so doing, you can ask for a, I guess in effect, a judgment N.O.V., a motion for rehearing, or whatever you want to call it, and tell me why you are entitled to it.

This statement denoted clear, present intent; the judge was going to rule immediately and when the ruling was complete, he was going to ask for exceptions. He went on to state how each piece of disputed property was to be divided and then asked for exceptions. The comment that exceptions should be made in the form of a judgment N.O.V. or motion for rehearing adds depth to this statement, since these motions are only made after final judgment has been rendered. Further, the trial court closed the ruling with a simple, "So it's yours, and I'm so finding. And that's my ruling." In light of the tone of the court throughout the day, the language "your divorce is granted" expressed present intent to render judgment.

As is often the case, it is this Court's duty to take words written on a page and decipher their precise meaning. However, in this case there is some assistance from the speaker. The trial court's final decree from June 28, 2004, listed the date of judgment for the divorce as July 2, 2003. While Belinda properly points out that this is not dispositive, it is merely additional information this Court can use to decipher the trial court's intention on July 2, 2003. No matter which parts of the hearing this Court points to as present intent to render judgment, there is ample evidence the court had more than mere cognition to render a judgment on July 2, 2003.

b. Division of Property

A judgment is final only when it disposes of all issues before it and settles the controversy between the parties, although further proceedings may be required to carry the judgment into effect. *R.R. Comm'n of Tex. v. Home Transp. Co.*, 654 S.W.2d 432, 434, 26 Tex. Sup. Ct. J. 564 (Tex. 1983). Belinda contends that the court did not render judgment on the property and custody issues and that this omission is fatal to any potential oral decree of divorce. Belinda further asserts the trial court did not officially rule on any of the property, and therefore the court, inadvertently, severed the divorce from the property, which it cannot do. *See Herschberg v. Herschberg*, 994 S.W.2d 273, 277 (Tex. App.—Corpus Christi 1999, no pet.).

1. Disputed Property

The "final hearing" was conducted because there were a few items of property not included in the mediated settlement agreement, of which the court needed to make a just and right division. Thomas provided the court with a list of the five items in controversy: (1) ring, broach and broach guard; (2) large diamond; (3) baseballs; (4) two watches; and (5) pearls. This list was fortified when Belinda was prevented from discussing a tennis bracelet that was not on the list, and thus not at issue before the court. The court clearly and explicitly decided who would have ownership of each of these items. The disputed property was undeniably settled in this hearing and therefore not severed from the divorce.

2. Settlement Agreement

Keeping in mind a written decree is merely a ministerial act once an oral decree has been pronounced, we move to the issue of the mediated settlement agreement (Agreement). The Agreement was formed under Sections 6.602 and 153.0071 of the Texas Family Code. *See* Tex. Fam. Code Ann. §§ 6.602, 153.0071 (Vernon Supp. 2005). By satisfying the requirements of these sections, all parties are bound to the agreement and are entitled to a judgment on the agreement. Tex. Fam. Code Ann. § 6.602(b), (c); *see also Cayan v. Cayan*, 38 S.W.3d 161, 165 (Tex. App.—Houston [14th Dist.] 2000, pet. denied). Compliance with Section 6.602 makes the agreement an exception to Sections 7.001 and 7.006, which allow revision and repudiation of settlement agreements. Tex. Fam. Code Ann. §§ 7.001, 7.006 (Vernon 1998); *Cayan*, 38 S.W.3d at 165. Via Section 6.602, the parties elect to make their agreement binding at the time of execution rather than at the time of rendering, thus creating a procedural shortcut for the enforcement of those agreements. *Cayan*, 38 S.W.3d at 165–66. Additionally, a Section 6.602 agreement may be ruled on without a determination by the trial court that the terms of the agreement are just and right. *Id.* at 166. After all, the purpose of mediation is to let parties settle their property as they see fit, keeping those matters out of the courtroom. *Id.*

a) Parties Were Bound to the Agreement

The Agreement was binding on the parties as of April 7, 2003, because it (1) prominently displayed a statement in boldface, underlined, capital letters that the agreement was not subject to revocation, (2) was signed by both parties to the agreement, and (3) was signed by the parties' attorneys. *See* Tex. Fam. Code Ann. § 6.602(b). By meeting the requirements of Section 6.602, the Agreement became more binding than a basic written contract; nothing either party could have done would have modified or voided the Agreement once everyone had signed it. *Cayan*, 38 S.W.3d at 165–66. While Section 6.602 cannot be imposed on the parties, once affirmative steps are taken to comply with that section, neither party can repudiate the agreement. *Id.* at 166.

Further, Belinda and Thomas both asked the court to accept the Agreement. Once a party asks the court to accept a settlement agreement and render judgment, they may not later attack that judgment. *Mailhot v. Mailhot*, 124 S.W.3d 775, 777 (Tex. App.—Houston [1st Dist.] 2003, no pet.). Belinda and Thomas were not trying to find a way to avoid the Agreement, but rather taking one more step to ensure its enforcement. The binding nature of the Agreement should be no surprise to either party, since the language throughout the Agreement clearly indicated intent of finality. Primarily, paragraph 21 contained the explicit language which caused the Agreement to fall under Section 6.602.[1] Both of the parties' attorneys signed the Agreement and should have recognized the repercussions of the inclusion of that section of the Texas Family Code. The Agreement further provided:

---

1. As well as Section 153.0071.

The parties agree that this Mediated Settlement Agreement is effective immediately.

....

2. Scope of the Agreement

The parties agree to settle all claims and controversies between them, asserted or assertable, in this case.

....

15. Release

Each party releases the other from all claims, demands, and causes of action each may have against the other, save and except those covenants, duties, and obligations set forth in this agreement.

16. Full Disclosure

Each party represents that he or she has made a fair and reasonable disclosure to the other of the property and financial obligations known to him or her.

17. Final Documents

1. The terms of this agreement will be incorporated in a decree that will follow the forms published in the Texas Family Law Practice Manual (2d ed.).

....

20. Court Appearance

The parties agree to appear in court at the first available date to present evidence and secure rendition of judgment in accordance with this agreement.

Last, it should be reiterated that the court ruled and then asked for exceptions. While Belinda asked for clarification on one piece of disputed property, no comment was made regarding the Agreement on which they had both requested the court to rule. Everyone involved recognized the binding nature of the Agreement, and no one objected to or questioned its enforceability.

b) Parties Were Entitled to Judgment

Not only was there nothing the parties could do to void or modify the Agreement once it had been signed, there was also little to nothing the trial court could do in regard to the Agreement. Section 6.602(c) states, "If a mediation settlement agreement meets the requirements of this section, a party is *entitled* to a judgment on the mediated settlement agreement notwithstanding Rule 11, Texas Rules of Civil Procedure, or another rule of law." TEX. FAM. CODE ANN. §6.602(c) (emphasis added). The statute requires the trial court to render judgment on a Section 6.602 agreement, even if one party attempts to withdraw consent. *In re Circone*, 122 S.W.3d 403, 406–07 (Tex. App.—Texarkana 2003, no pet.); *Alvarez v. Reiser*, 958 S.W.2d 232, 234 (Tex. App.—Eastland 1997, pet. denied).

Section 6.602 does not authorize the trial court to substitute its judgment for the mediated settlement agreement entered by the parties if the mediation agreement complies with the statutory requirements making it irrevocable and granting the parties the entitlement to a judgment thereon. A trial court is not required to enforce a mediated settlement agreement if it is illegal in nature or was procured by fraud, duress, coercion, or other dishonest means. *Boyd v. Boyd*, 67 S.W.3d 398, 403 (Tex. App.—Fort Worth 2002, no pet.); *see also In re Kasschau*, 11 S.W.3d 305, 314 (Tex. App.—Houston [14th Dist.] 1999, no pet.) (mediated settlement agreement voided for requiring the criminal act of destruction of evidence). The court is not allowed to modify Section 6.602 agreements as it sees fit, and it has no authority to enter a judgment that varies from their terms. *Circone*, 122 S.W.3d at 406; *Garcia-Udall v. Udall*, 141 S.W.3d 323, 330 (Tex. App.—Dallas 2004, no pet.). Here, no one urged that the mediated settlement agreement was illegal or was procured by fraud, duress, coercion, or other dishonest means. To the contrary, both parties requested that the trial court approve the agreement.

Section 6.602 has been classified as a "procedural shortcut" for enforcement of mediated settlement agreements in divorce cases. *Cayan*, 38 S.W.3d at 166. It contrasts with agreements incident to divorce in that the mediated agreement is binding and irrevocable at the time of its execution rather than at the time divorce is rendered, the parties are entitled to judgment on it, and the trial court does not have to determine that it is "just and right." *Id.* at 164–66. The mediated settlement agreement places this case in a different posture than those cases in which an agreement incident to divorce in accordance with Section 7.006 of the Texas Family Code was presented without objection, because in such cases (not based on mediation), the trial court was required to examine the agreement to determine if it was "just and right" before approving the agreement.[2] Here, the parties were entitled to a judgment incorporating the provisions of the mediated settlement agreement and, since no allegation was presented that the agreement was illegal, or procured by fraud, duress, or coercion, and there is no indication the trial court sua sponte questioned the legality of the agreement, the trial court was required to enter a judgment based on the mediated agreement. Considering the hearing's tone of finality, the lack of any argument concerning the agreement's illegality, the limited actions the court could have taken on the matter, and this State's policy of encouraging alternative dispute resolution with "special consideration" given to disputes involving parent-child relationships (*see* TEX. CIV. PRAC. & REM. CODE ANN. § 154.002 (Vernon 2005)), allowing the absence of a specific statement rendering judgment on this binding Agreement to void the divorce is unwarranted. We hold that the judgment granting the divorce was rendered July 2, 2003, and since the trial court had no authority (absent an issue on illegality, duress, etc. raised either by the parties or the court sua sponte) to do otherwise, the mediated settlement agreement was a part of the divorce rendition.

c) The Custody Portion of the Mediated Settlement Agreement

The Joyners and their attorneys entered a mediated settlement agreement which addressed property issues as well as child conservatorship, possession and access, and child support. As explained earlier, two statutes exist governing mediated settlement agreements—Section 6.602 for property matters and Section 153.0071 for child conservatorship. The wording of the statutes is identical as to the requirements for entering an irrevocable, immediately binding agreement. Before June 18, 2005, there was no provision requiring the trial court to conduct an evidentiary hearing to determine if the agreement entered into by the parties was in the child's best interest. The Dallas Court of Appeals has held that a trial court had no authority to enter a judgment, regarding conservatorship, that varied from the terms of the mediated settlement agreement and to do so was an abuse of discretion. *Garcia-Udall*, 141 S.W.3d at 331–32. The Garcia court noted that the trial court made no findings that the agreement was illegal or violated pub-

---

2. *See Markowitz v. Markowitz*, 118 S.W.3d 82, 89 (Tex. App.—Houston [14th Dist.] 2003, pet. denied)("Texas law requires a finding by the trial court that the terms of a written agreement for the division of assets and liabilities are just and right [TEX. FAM. CODE ANN. § 7.006(b)] ... Thus, without approval from the trial court, there was no longer a written agreement capable of being enforced.").

lic policy. *Id.* at 332. The Houston First Court of Appeals has held that the trial court may, but is not required to conduct an evidentiary hearing to determine whether the parents' custody mediated agreement is in the best interest of the child. *Beyers v. Roberts*, No. 01-04-00619-CV, 199 S.W.3d 354, 2006 Tex. App. LEXIS 3511, at *11 (Tex. App.—Houston [1st Dist.] Apr. 27, 2006, no pet. h.). ("Nothing in the statute requires that a trial court conduct a best interest hearing before entering an order pursuant to a mediated settlement agreement ... Furthermore, nothing in the common law creates a duty to determine best interest in every case in which the parents have reached a settlement of their custody disputes."). Here, the parties both testified the agreement was in the child's best interest, neither filed any motion contesting the agreement on any basis, and the trial court did not sua sponte find the agreement to be illegal or void for public policy reasons such as being contrary to the child's best interest. We note that the Legislature has now amended Section 153.0071 authorizing a trial court to decline to enforce a mediated settlement agreement if it finds the agreement is not in the child's best interest. *See* TEX. FAM. CODE ANN. § 153.0071(e-1)(2). However, the judgment in this case was signed June 28, 2004, and the amendment to the statute does not apply. As in Garcia, the trial court was required to enter judgment on the mediated settlement agreement. Therefore, when the trial court announced it was granting the divorce judgment, the mediated settlement agreement was incorporated as a part of the judgment.

IV. Conclusion

Once a couple is divorced, they can no longer accumulate community property, for there is no longer a community. By looking at the record of the hearing in its entirety, we conclude the trial court rendered an oral pronouncement granting a judgment of divorce which necessarily incorporated the terms of the binding mediated settlement agreement. The judgment of the trial court is affirmed.

———————

G. Alimony

Until 1995, Texas was the only state that did not allow a court to order post-divorce alimony for a spouse. Only temporary support was permitted until the divorce became final. Tex. Fam. Code § 6.502; *Massey v. Massey*, 813 S.W.2d 605 (Tex. App.—Houston [1st Dist.] 1991, no writ). What is the rationale for alimony? Should either spouse ever have a post-divorce support obligation to the other spouse? When? For conflicting views, see J. Eekelaar and M. MacLean, *Maintenance after Divorce* (1986); L. Weitzman, *The Marriage Contract* (1981); Oldham, *Is the Concept of Marital Property Outdated?*, 22 J. Fam. L. 263 (1984).

As you can see, the new alimony statute was a compromise. Some supported a broader statute that would permit alimony in any divorce, while others favored a continuation of the complete bar. The enacting legislation stated that its purpose was "to provide spousal maintenance primarily as a temporary rehabilitative measure for a divorced spouse whose ability for self-support is lacking or has deteriorated through the passage of time while the spouse was engaged in homemaking activities and whose capital assets are insufficient to provide support. * * * Spousal support should be terminated in the shortest possible time, not to exceed three years, in which the former spouse is able to be employed or to acquire the necessary skills to become self-supporting. Only in circumstances in which the former spouse cannot become self-supporting by reason of incapacitating physical or mental disability should maintenance be extended beyond this period."

So, the new statute primarily is a rehabilitative, short-term remedy to allow dependent spouses in certain situations some breathing room until they have to become self-sufficient financially. Note some important things about the new statute. First, alimony cannot be ordered unless the marriage lasted ten years or the payor has been convicted of family violence. Tex. Fam. Code § 8.051. (The parties don't have to *live together* for 10 years. *Hipolito v. Hipolito*, 200 S.W.3d 805 (Tex. App.—Dallas 2006, pet. denied).) Even in these situations, alimony is not possible unless the spouse requesting alimony lacks earning ability "to provide support for the spouse's minimal reasonable needs." Tex. Fam. Code § 8.051. (It is not totally clear that this requirement applies if the spouse has been convicted of family violence.) Is this term "minimal reasonable needs" clear? Consider a nurse earning $30,000 annually who divorces a doctor who earns $300,000 annually. If there is not a substantial amount of community property, should the nurse be entitled to alimony?

Alimony normally cannot continue for more than three years, regardless of the continuing need of the recipient, unless the recipient suffers from "an incapacitating physical or mental disability." Tex. Fam. Code § 8.054. What situations should be included in this category?

A spouse can agree to pay contractual alimony. This is done for tax purposes, and will be discussed in more detail *infra*. The court can approve the contract, and incorporate by reference the contract into the decree, but the court cannot order the spouse to pay alimony, unless the alimony order is authorized by the new alimony statute.

In re Green
Supreme Court of Texas, 2007
221 S.W.3d 645

PER CURIAM

Alvin Green argues he cannot be imprisoned for nonpayment of a contractual alimony obligation incorporated into his divorce decree. We agree that a court order to pay spousal support is unenforceable by contempt if the order merely restates a private debt rather than a legal duty imposed by Texas law. Because the district court's decree was not "spousal maintenance" ordered under the Family Code but rather was issued solely on the basis of the parties' private alimony contract, we grant Alvin's writ of habeas corpus and order him discharged.

Alvin and Brenda Green divorced in 2004, and the district court's final divorce decree includes this "spousal maintenance" language:

> The Court finds that ALVIN R. GREEN has agreed contractually to pay BRENDA KAY GREEN spousal maintenance, as owelty and to affect [sic] a fair division of the community estate. Accordingly, ALVIN R. GREEN is ordered to pay as spousal maintenance the sum of $1,950.00 per month to BRENDA KAY GREEN....

The decree specifies that the $1,950 payments shall continue from February 2004 until April 1, 2005, and then drop to $1,450 per month until January 19, 2016.

Chapter Eight of the Texas Family Code provides for court-ordered spousal "maintenance" under certain circumstances. Section 8.057(c) allows for modification of maintenance orders upon a showing of "a material and substantial change in circumstances of either party." Several months after the 2004 divorce decree was signed, Alvin sought a reduction in his spousal support obligations on grounds of inability to pay. The same district court that entered the divorce decree, but with a different judge, denied the motion, stating:

> The Court finds that the spousal maintenance requested to be modified is not "spousal maintenance" ordered by the court under Texas Family Code § 8 et seq., but rather that the payments are contractual alimony agreed by the parties to affect [sic] a fair division of the community estate. As such, the Court finds that payments are not subject to modification as plead.

In January 2006, Brenda filed a "Second Motion for Enforcement and First Motion to Revoke Suspension of Commitment," arguing that Alvin had failed to make spousal support payments and to maintain health insurance for their children as required by the divorce decree, and requesting that Alvin be held in contempt and incarcerated.

After a hearing, the district court granted this motion. The court signed an order prepared by Brenda, but crossed out some of the language. The order states that Alvin failed to maintain the children's health insurance as ordered by the divorce decree during certain months, but the court six times crossed out Brenda's proposed language finding Alvin "in contempt of court for this failure to maintain health insurance as ordered." The order goes on to state that Alvin did not pay the required spousal support during several months, and that this failure amounted to contempt of court. In the decretal portion of the order, as modified by the district court, the court adjudged Alvin in contempt for seven instances of failure to make spousal support payments. Again, the court crossed out Brenda's proposed language—for a seventh time—that would have adjudged Alvin in contempt for failure to provide health insurance for the children. The order then contains commitment orders. As punishment for criminal contempt, it commits Alvin to the county jail for 180 days for the seven instances of failure to pay spousal support. In a section styled "Civil Contempt," the order then states:

> IT IS ORDERED that Respondent, Alvin Green, is committed to and shall be confined in the county jail of Dallas County, Texas, until he complies with the following:
>
> 1. Payment of $ 32,384.92 to Ms. Brenda K. Green.
>
> 2. Proof of current health insurance coverage for the children.

Alvin was thereupon incarcerated. He sought habeas corpus relief in the court of appeals, which denied relief without opinion. He then sought a writ of habeas corpus in this Court. We granted temporary relief and ordered him released on $ 3,000 bond pending review of his petition. We hold that Alvin cannot be incarcerated for failure to make the contractual spousal payments specified in the divorce decree. The failure to pay a private alimony debt, even one referenced in a court order, is not contempt punishable by imprisonment.

Article I, section 18 of the Texas Constitution states: "No person shall ever be imprisoned for debt." Construing this succinct, eight-word provision—our lengthy Constitution's shortest section—we have held that a failure to pay support promised under a prenuptial agreement is not punishable by contempt. *Ex parte Hall*, 854 S.W.2d 656, 656–57, 36 Tex. Sup. Ct. J. 733 (Tex. 1993). In *Hall*, we recognized that "[t]he obligation which the law imposes on spouses to support one another and on parents to support their children is not considered a 'debt' within Article I, section 18, but a legal duty arising out of the status of the parties." *Id.* at 658. We noted, for example, that an order requiring temporary support payments under the Family Code fell under this duty. *Id.* "However, a person may also contract to support his spouse and children, and that obligation, to the extent it exceeds his legal duty, is a debt." *Id.* We held that an order of support is enforceable by contempt only if it was entered on the authority of the Family Code. *Id.* at 659.

In this case, the spousal payments were payments Alvin voluntarily agreed to make as part of the divorce. As the district court stated in the order quoted above, the payments were contractual and not ordered under the Family Code's provision for spousal maintenance.

Under Chapter Eight of the Family Code, the court in a divorce matter may order spousal maintenance, broadly defined to include "an award in a suit for dissolution of a marriage of periodic payments from the future income of one spouse for the support of the other spouse." TEX. FAM. CODE § 8.001(1). However, a spouse can only be ordered to pay maintenance if (1) the spouse has committed a recent act of family violence, or (2) the marriage lasted at least ten years and the receiving spouse cannot support himself or herself due to disability, is the full-time custodian of a disabled child of the marriage, or "clearly lacks earning ability in the labor market adequate to provide support for the spouse's minimum reasonable needs, as limited by Section 8.054." *Id.* § 8.051. Under section 8.054, unless the receiving spouse is disabled or the custodian of a disabled child, the maintenance cannot exceed three years, and under section 8.056, the obligation terminates if the receiving spouse remarries.

In the pending case, the support Alvin agreed to pay falls outside of Chapter Eight. The payment obligation exceeds three years, and there were no findings that Brenda was herself disabled, was caring for a disabled child, or lacked sufficient earning ability. Nor did the decree state that payments terminate upon Brenda's remarriage. And as noted above, the district court has held explicitly that the maintenance "is not 'spousal maintenance' ordered by the court under Texas Family Code § 8 et seq., but rather that the payments are contractual alimony agreed by the parties...." Under *Hall*, the support was not entered "on the authority of the Family Code," 854 S.W.2d at 658, and thus cannot be enforced by contempt.

Brenda argues that the district court could hold Alvin in contempt under section 8.059(a) of the Family Code, which provides: "The court may enforce by contempt the court's maintenance order or an agreement for the payment of maintenance voluntarily entered into between the parties and approved by the court." This provision and the remainder of the original version of Chapter Eight became law in 1995, after our decision in *Hall*. See Act of May 26, 1995, 74th Leg., R.S., ch. 655, § 10.02, 1995 Tex. Gen. Laws 3543, 3577–80.

Section 8.059(a) can be read two ways. Brenda's interpretation is that any agreement to pay spousal support is enforceable by contempt. The alternative interpretation is that a maintenance obligation, whether contractual or court-imposed, is punishable by contempt only if it meets Chapter Eight's other requirements. We reject Brenda's construction for several reasons.

First, such a reading would make "maintenance" under section 8.059(a) inconsistent with the requirements of maintenance elsewhere in Chapter Eight. Maintenance under this chapter must be of limited duration, must terminate on remarriage, and must be to support a spouse with special needs or in special circumstances. Second, reading section 8.059(a) as applying to all contractual alimony agreements would clash head-on with section 9.012(b), which provides generally that "[t]he court may not enforce by contempt an award in a decree of divorce or annulment of a sum of money payable in a lump sum or in future installment payments in the nature of debt." As one treatise explains:

The traditional agreement to pay alimony incorporated into a divorce decree falls within the Family Code's ban on enforcement by contempt [citing §9.012(b)]. The obligation typically assumed in an alimony agreement is not a legal duty to pay but is, plain and simple, a debt, nonpayment of which cannot result in imprisonment [citing Hall and other authorities]. It could be argued that the 1995 enactment of the spousal maintenance statute changes the situation.... A better reasoned approach is to distinguish the traditional alimony promise (to pay money to balance the property division and minimize taxes, without regard to the spouse's ability to be self-supporting) from the legal obligation to support an ex-spouse who is incapable of gainful employment. While a legal obligation of support is enforceable by contempt, the promise to pay contractual alimony creates nothing more than a debt.

Third, reading section 8.059(a) as requiring imprisonment for breach of a contractual arrangement would surely make that section unconstitutional. We held in *Hall*, and reaffirm today, that one spouse's voluntary agreement to support the other, to the extent it exceeds a legal duty, is a contractual debt that cannot be enforced by contempt. 854 S.W.2d at 658–59; *see also Allen v. Allen*, 717 S.W.2d 311, 313, 29 Tex. Sup. Ct. J. 536 (Tex. 1986) ("A marital property agreement, although incorporated into a final divorce decree, is treated as a contract and its legal force and meaning are governed by the law of contracts, not the law of judgments."). We must of course avoid a construction of a statute that renders it unconstitutional. *See* TEX. GOV'T CODE §311.021(1). Brenda may certainly attempt to enforce the parties' contract via other legal mechanisms—execution or attachment of real property—but Alvin cannot be jailed unless his obligation arises from a legal duty with a statutory or constitutional basis. There can be no imprisonment absent such authority.

There remains the question of whether Alvin can be incarcerated under the contempt order for failure to provide health insurance for his children. Brenda does not argue that Alvin can be imprisoned for this reason, nor does Alvin argue the contrary. Regardless, as described above, the contempt order purports to keep Alvin in jail for civil contempt until he makes spousal payments and provides proof of current health insurance for his children.

A failure to provide child support, including a failure to provide health insurance under a voluntary agreement, is punishable by contempt. *See* TEX. FAM. CODE §§154.124(c), 157.002(b)(2), 157.166(b). But Alvin cannot validly be confined absent a proper order of commitment, and this contempt order omits two indispensable things: (1) a written judgment of contempt for neglecting to maintain his children's health insurance, and (2) a written order of commitment for that failure. "It is well established that both a written judgment of contempt and a written order of commitment are required by due process to imprison a person for civil constructive contempt." *Ex parte Hernandez*, 827 S.W.2d 858, 858, 35 Tex. Sup. Ct. J. 588 (Tex. 1992) (per curiam); accord *Ex parte Lee*, 704 S.W.2d 15, 16, 29 Tex. Sup. Ct. J. 213 (Tex. 1986); *Ex parte Barnett*, 600 S.W.2d 252, 256, 23 Tex. Sup. Ct. J. 352 (Tex. 1980). As described above, the order Brenda originally proposed contained such language, but the district court crossed out that portion of the contempt judgment relating to Alvin's failure to provide health insurance and every factual finding that would have supported such a judgment. However, the court-modified and -signed order, while lacking findings and a written judgment of contempt concerning health insurance, does contain an order of confinement that says Alvin must remain in jail until he pays past due spousal support and provides "[p]roof of current health insurance coverage for the children." Thus, the commitment order purports to make such insurance coverage a condition of Alvin's release, if not a basis for his confinement (a fine distinction, to be sure). This passing reference is not enough under our governing precedent. At the very least, the district court's multiple strike-outs of insurance-related language makes the order ambiguous as to whether the court intended Alvin's failure to provide health insurance, standing alone, to serve as a sufficient basis for a judgment of contempt and resulting commitment. A contempt order "cannot contain uncertainty or susceptibility of more than one construction or meaning." *Ex parte Glover*, 701 S.W.2d 639, 640, 29 Tex. Sup. Ct. J. 31 (Tex. 1985); *see also Ex parte Shaklee*, 939 S.W.2d 144, 145, 40 Tex. Sup. Ct. J. 365 (Tex. 1997) (per curiam) (holding that a contempt order must clearly state in what respect the court's earlier order has been violated and "must clearly specify the punishment imposed by the court").

Accordingly, we grant the writ of habeas corpus and order the relator discharged.

Price v. Price
Texas Court of Appeals — Tyler, 1979
591 S.W.2d 601, no writ

MOORE, Justice.

Appellee, Betty Price, instituted this suit against appellant, Scottie Price, seeking a divorce and a division of the property. After a trial before the court, sitting without a jury, judgment was rendered dissolving the marriage. The community property, which consisted only of household and kitchen furniture, was divided between the parties. In addition, the trial court also awarded Mrs. Price a judgment against appellant for the sum of $4,000.00 as well as a $1,000.00 attorney's fee. Appellant perfected this appeal and brings eight points of error attacking only that portion of the judgment dividing the property.

We affirm.

Appellant asserts by his first point of error that the award of $4,000.00 personal judgment in favor of Mrs. Price constitutes permanent alimony and is therefore contrary to the public policy of this state. By his second point, appellant contends that even if the $4,000.00 personal judgment in favor of Mrs. Price does not constitute alimony, the trial court nevertheless abused its discretion in dividing the property, because the personal judgment rendered against him had the effect of awarding appellee his separate property to the extent of $4,000.00 without just cause. We fail to find any merit in either contention.

The term "alimony" has come generally, in legal parlance, to include an allowance, whether periodical or in gross, judicially made to a wife upon an absolute divorce. The statutes and public policy of this state do not sanction alimony for the wife after a judgment of divorce has been entered. *Francis v. Francis*, 412 S.W.2d 29 (Tex. 1967).

In applying the above definition, the courts have generally held that the trial court may require one party to make monetary payments to the other after a divorce, so long as a division was referable to the rights and equities of the parties in and to the properties at the time of the dissolution of the marriage. In such a case, the courts have held that the division is not an allowance of permanent alimony in violation of the established public policy. *Francis v. Francis, supra; Garrett v. Garrett*, 534 S.W.2d 381, 383 (Tex. Civ. App.—Houston [1st Dist.] 1976, no writ).

In our opinion the evidence supports the trial court's award of the $4,000.00 judgment to Mrs. Price as being referable to the rights and equities of the parties in the properties at the time of the divorce hearing. Consequently, we hold that appellant failed to establish that the monetary judgment awarded Mrs. Price was in the nature of alimony.

DISCUSSION

In *Siefkas v. Siefkas*, 902 S.W.2d 72 (Tex. App.—El Paso 1995, no writ) the court held that ordering the husband to make payments after divorce on a home improvement loan taken out during marriage was not alimony.

H. Tax Consequences of Divorce

1. Alimony and Child Support

1984 amendments to the Internal Revenue Code greatly simplified the tax ramifications of divorce. These amendments did not change the general principle that "alimony" is deductible by the payor, and income to the payee, and that "child support" is neither deductible nor income. This distinction can be useful for spouses if their marginal tax rates after divorce will be significantly different. The payor normally will be willing to make higher payments to the custodial parent if the payments can be characterized as alimony and not child support.

If the spouses' respective incomes are substantially different and their post-divorce marginal tax rates will also be different, if the spouses have a minor child it might be sensible to consider contractual alimony. Assume the highest tax rate for individuals is about 40%. If the obligor is in the 40% marginal tax bracket and the recipient is in the 15% tax bracket, for example, there could be some significant negotiating room. For example, every $100 in alimony is costing the obligor $60 (after tax) but is worth $85 to the recipient (after tax). However, contractual alimony can have disadvantages. For example, it must stop when the recipient dies. Such payments cannot stop exactly when the child reaches majority. (See the discussion below about when support payments will be considered "fixed" to a child.)

If payments to a former spouse (i) are made under a divorce and separation instrument, (ii) are in cash, (iii) will terminate upon the death of the recipient, (iv) are not referred to as child support and are not fixed to any minor child of the spouses, and (v) the spouses are not the members of the same household when the payment is made, the payment is alimony for tax purposes. If these requirements are not met, the payment is child support for tax purposes. Certain recapture provisions might apply if the annual amount of alimony decreases by more than $15,000 during the first three post-separation years. Note that alimony no longer must be a periodic payment. A lump-sum payment therefore appears to be deductible, subject to possible recapture.

The 1984 amendments changed the test for taxable alimony in one important respect. Before 1984, courts would not look beyond the language of the decree. In other words, the payment would not be considered child support as long as the decree did not say it was child support. The current rule is different. An award will be considered child support if it is "fixed" to a child. An analysis of whether a payment is fixed to a child now requires more than a review of the decree. A court may now look beyond the decree to determine whether a payment is in reality child support. Under current IRS rules, if the parties had one child and the payments end (or are reduced) within six months of the child's eighteenth birthday, the amount the payment is reduced is presumptively considered child support (even if the decree does not say it is child support).

For post-1984 decrees, the custodial spouse is entitled to the dependency exemption, unless both spouses agree in writing that the other spouse should be given the deduction. Such agreements can be made annually or for a longer period. The amount of actual support provided is irrelevant.

Either spouse may deduct medical expenses incurred on behalf of the children. Only the custodial parent may claim a child care credit.

2. Dividing the Property

After the 1984 amendments, there generally is no taxable event in connection with a divorce property division. There obviously would be a taxable event if property is sold to a third party and the proceeds divided. However, if the spouses' property is merely divided between them at the time of divorce, there generally is no taxable event as a result of the property division.

This does not mean that a family lawyer can ignore tax issues relating to the property division. After divorce, the property received by a spouse under the property settlement retains its prior basis. Low basis appreciated property is worth less than high basis property, since the low basis property has hidden potential tax liability associated with it. (Tax will have to be paid on the difference between the basis and the proceeds received at the time of sale.) If the spouse does not intend to sell the property, this issue is not very important. However, if the spouse plans to sell the appreciated property after divorce, the client should be informed that there will be tax liability at the time of sale.

Under prior case law, the court was advised to consider the tax consequences of the property division. This normally was limited to any tax liability that would result from the property division itself. After 1984, there rarely will be a taxable event directly stemming from the property division. It is unclear whether Texas courts now will ignore tax concerns when dividing property. If Texas courts choose this approach, this would be quite unrealistic. At divorce, the court is trying to make a fair financial adjustment. If property has inchoate tax liability, this should be an important factor in trying to determine the actual value of the property. In *Harris v. Holland*, 867 S.W.2d 86 (Tex. App.—Texarkana 1993, no writ) the appellate court reversed a trial court judgment that apparently gave the husband credit for the tax liability the husband would have incurred if he had sold the property awarded him in the divorce, even though the husband said he had no plans to sell the property. This ruling seems quite sensible. Still, when fashioning an equitable division of property at divorce, the court should be able to consider the potential post-divorce tax consequences. *See Goldman v. Goldman*, 646 A2d 504 (N.J. App. Div. 1994).

Complicated tax issues can arise in connection with a divorce property division. For example, pension payments divided at divorce (if the plan is a qualified plan) are taxed to the recipient <u>if the order is a qualified domestic relations order</u>. In *Hawkins v. Commissioner*, 102 T.C 61 (1994), the court determined that the decree awarding the non-employee spouse $1,000,000 from the employee's pension plan was not a QDRO, so the distribution to the nonemployee was taxed to the employee. Such potential malpractice minefields explain why most family lawyers have divorce decrees involving significant property reviewed by competent tax counsel.

Other non-obvious tax issues can arise at divorce. For example, in *Kochansky v. Commissioner*, 92 F.3d 957 (9th Cir. 1996) the husband had some pending contingent fee cases at divorce. He assigned to his wife 50% of any net contingent fees that would be generated by the cases after divorce. The court concluded that, based on the "assignment of income" doctrine, that the husband had to pay income tax on all the fees recovered (including the amount paid to the wife).

Remember that both spouses are liable after divorce for any tax deficiency later determined to be due during the marriage. If your client was not very familiar with the couple's finances, the lawyer might try to add a provision to the settlement agreement that the client would be indemnified by the other spouse if the client would be required to pay any such deficiency.

3. Income Tax Planning at Divorce

In a community property state, for income tax purposes, spouses are deemed to each earn one-half of the aggregate income earned by the couple during marriage. If the spouses divorce during the year, each spouse will have to pay tax at the end of the year on one-half the couple's aggregate earnings through the date of the divorce, plus the spouse's post-divorce earnings through the end of the year. For this reason, it is important to negotiate who will be responsible for paying these income taxes for the year the divorce occurred. Remember also that the spouses' tax returns for prior years could be audited and additional tax payments could be required. It is important that the settlement agreement address this issue. Of course, if the settlement agreement says that the other spouse will bear all such taxes, this would not limit the power of the IRS.

A spouse's marital status for income tax purposes is determined by his or her status on December 31. Tax liability can vary significantly depending upon whether the spouse will be considered single or married for the year. If the final date of the divorce will be at about the end of the year, lawyers may wish to consider whether to expedite the divorce process to be sure that the divorce will be final before the end of the year, so the parties can file as single adults for that year.

If only one spouse works outside the home, it is advantageous for tax reasons to stay married. For example, if one spouse earns $50,000 and the other has no income, and if there are no children and they take the standard deduction, as a single person the employee would owe $7,767.06 for 2002, while the couple would owe $4,822.50 as a married couple filing jointly. In contrast, if both spouses work, it frequently is advantageous from a tax standpoint to be single. For example, if each spouse earns $25,000 annually, they each would owe $2,295 as single adults for 2002. As a married couple filing jointly, they would owe $4,822.50, $232.50 more than their aggregate tax as single adults.

I. Collection Concerns

Family law clients obviously would like to be sure that marital settlement obligations will be fulfilled. Two tools that help assure fulfillment of family law obligations are garnishment and contempt. These remedies will be discussed in the next chapter.

Family lawyers must be aware of the spector of bankruptcy. An individual normally may file for bankruptcy relief at any time. It appears that after the most recent amendments to the Bankruptcy Code family law obligations generally cannot be discharged in bankruptcy. Due to concerns about bankruptcy discharge, as well as collection difficulties in Texas, it is always wise to attempt to obtain security for payment obligations whenever possible.

J. Other Matters to Remember

When a person divorces, he may want to revise his will and change beneficiary designations on life insurance policies or other death benefits. If a person does not change his will at the time of divorce and the will at the time of death includes a bequest to a former spouse, the Probate Code assumes this is not intended and treats such a bequest as void. Tex. Prob. Code § 69.

Chapter Sixteen

Drafting the Settlement Agreement and Divorce Decree

A. Settlement Agreement

In connection with a divorce, parties normally negotiate a settlement agreement which sets forth the terms of the dissolution. This settlement agreement frequently is incorporated by reference into the divorce decree.

The settlement agreement must set forth the agreement of the parties in sufficient detail so that later disputes will be minimized.

Garza v. Garza

Texas Court of Appeals — San Antonio, 1983
666 S.W.2d 205, writ ref'd n.r.e.

TIJERINA, Justice.

The decree of divorce was entered following a hearing before the trial court. As part of the decree, the property of the parties was divided as required by Tex. Fam. Code Ann. Sec. 3.63 (Vernon 1975). Simon Garza was divested of the real property at 8122 and 8106 Hausman Road, Bexar County, Texas, and the property was awarded to Carmen Keever de Garza as her sole and separate property, subject to the payment of the balance due on the note secured thereby and subject to an "option" granted to Mr. Garza "to buy this item of real property ... for the sum of One Hundred Eleven Thousand Six Hundred and No/100 Dollars ($111,600.00) and the assumption of the debt thereon, which ... must be exercised within ninety (90) days after the entry of [the decree]...." If the "option" was not exercised within the time period, the award of the property to Mrs. Garza was to be complete and final.

On September 3, 1980, Mr. Garza, through his attorney of record, filed with the trial court, a "Notice of Exercise of Option," with a copy served on Mrs. Garza through her attorney of record.

On March 31, 1981, Mr. Garza filed a motion to enforce judgment in an attempt to compel Mrs. Garza to convey the Hausman Road property to him. Following a hearing on the matter, the trial court entered an order enforcing judgment, requiring Carmen to execute all instruments necessary to effect the conveyance.

Appellant's initial point of error alleges the trial court erred in finding in its order of enforcement that Mr. Garza had a valid and binding option to purchase the real property on Hausman Road. Appellant argues the invalidity of the option based on a lack of authority of the trial court to so divide the property.

Tex. Fam. Code Sec. 3.63 (Vernon Supp. 1982–1983) provides that: "(a) In a decree of divorce … the court shall order a division of the estate of the parties in a manner that the court deems just and right, having due regard for the rights of each party.…"

The specific and principle issue of the case at bar concerns the option, granted by the court, that appellee husband could purchase the real property on Hausman Road. The relevant and pertinent part of the final judgment and decree of divorce provides as follows:

> It is therefore ordered, adjudged and decreed that the following properties be and the same are hereby set aside and awarded to the respondent, Carmen Keever de Garza, as her sole and separate property, subject to the further orders of this court with respect thereto as set forth herein below.
>
> ....
>
> 3. The real property at 8122 and 8106 Hausman Road (legal description omitted).
>
> The award of this item of real property to respondent is made to her subject to an option hereby granted to petitioner, Simon T. Garza, to buy this item of real property from respondent, Carmen Keever de Garza, for the sum of one hundred eleven thousand six hundred and no/100ths dollars ($111,600.00) and the assumption of the debt thereon, which option must be exercised within ninety (90) days after the entry of judgment, if such option is not exercised within that period of time, the award of this item of real property to respondent, Carmen Keever de Garza, shall be complete and final.

Appellant contends that the trial court did not have authority to delegate to the husband the right to decide who would receive the property on Hausman Road. We do not agree, for such is not the true import of the divorce decree. The final judgment and decree of divorce is not included in this record but we have a copy attached as an exhibit which indicates that it was rendered and filed June 6, 1980. On September 3, 1980, appellee filed with the trial court the "notice of exercise of option," with a copy served on appellant through her attorney of record.

The notice sent to the trial court and appellant's attorney was sufficient. The tender of funds necessary was a prerequisite to a transfer of title and not for exercising the option.

In making a division of property in a divorce proceeding, the trial judge is given wide discretion which will not be disturbed on review unless there is a clear showing of abuse. We find no abuse of discretion in the division of the Garza property and in the option given Mr. Garza.

DISCUSSION

Could the agreement and decree in *Garza* have been drafted in such a way that this dispute would not have arisen?

Stewart v. Stewart

Missouri Court of Appeals, 1987
727 S.W.2d 416

CRIST, Judge.

Respondent (father) filed a motion to cite appellant (mother) for contempt for failing to pay him his equity in the marital residence after their youngest son had reached his majority, as provided by their separate agreement and dissolution decree. Father also asked the trial court for its order to sell the residence to satisfy his claim to the equity. Mother filed an answer asking that father be cited for contempt for failing to pay past child support. The trial court denied both motions for contempt, but ordered the sale of the residence with father to get one-half of the equity of such residence as of the time of sale. We reverse and remand with directions.

The seminal issue is whether father was to get one-half the equity at the time of sale, or whether he was to get one-half the equity at the time of the dissolution decree on October 22, 1975. The equity in the real estate has increased in value from approximately $12,000 to at least $38,000.

At the time of the divorce, the parties were joint owners of the marital residence. The terms of the dissolution decree referred to a written separation agreement incorporated therein. A portion of the separation agreement provides:

> Party of the First Part (mother) shall be entitled to the Parties' home located at 119 Flesher in Ellisville, Missouri. At the time the Parties' youngest son, Steven Paul Stewart, shall reach the age of majority or be fully emancipated, it shall become the obligation of the Party of the First Part to pay to the Party of the Second Part (father) a sum of money equal to one-half (1/2) of the current equity in the said real estate less all proper expenses of selling said home, taxes and other fees. It is further agreed that the fair market value of said property as of the signing of this Agreement is Twenty Eight Thousand ($28,000) Dollars.

At no time since the dissolution has there been any conveyance of the marital residence, and title continues in both mother and father. Their youngest son became twenty-one years of age on January 28, 1984. Father testified he thought he was to receive one-half of the equity valued at the time of the sale. Mother testified he was to receive one-half of the equity, valued at the time of the dissolution decree. There was little evidence on the question of the intention of the parties at the execution of the separation agreement.

Excepting for the words "less all proper expenses of selling said home, taxes and other fees," there can be little question about the intention of the parties at the time of the execution of their agreement. The parties would not have used the term "current equity" or provided that "the fair market value ... as of the signing ... is twenty-eight thousand dollars," unless the equity to be paid to father was to be calculated based upon the value of the home at the time of the dissolution decree.

Mother was to get the marital residence. When their youngest son reached his majority, mother had to pay father a sum of money equal to one-half of the equity value at the time of dissolution, which was approximately $12,000. We do not know why the parties chose to add the words "less all proper expenses of selling said home, taxes and other fees," and no reasonable explanation is offered by the parties; but we are not permitted to make an agreement other than that of the parties. In any event, the parties agree that if the property must be sold, each must share the payment of the sale expenses.

The wording of the agreement regarding the proceeds of the marital residence is not ambiguous. The parties are bound by its terms.

The judgment of the trial court that "current equity" was to be measured as of the time mother's obligation to pay had matured rather than the time of the dissolution decree is reversed. The separation agreement shall be interpreted to mean father may receive his "current equity" measured as of the time of the dissolution decree. Mother shall have the right to pay the equity due father in lieu of sale of the marital residence. In all other respects, the judgment of the trial court is affirmed. The trial court is directed to enter an order in accordance with this opinion.

Judgment reversed and remanded.

DISCUSSION

This case may be a good example of the difficulty a lawyer confronts when trying to draft a clear and unambiguous document. At first glance, a phrase employed seems clear. However, a careful lawyer reviews a document many times in an attempt to foreclose future disputes about ambiguous provisions. Read the divorce decree. Does "current equity" seem ambiguous to you? What do you think the parties intended? What could have been added to clarify the meaning of this term? Even if the time the property was to be valued had been made more clear, is there anything else that needed to be clarified to avoid a future dispute?

General contract principles apply when determining whether a settlement agreement is enforceable. In *Chavez v. McNeely*, 287 S.W.3d 840 (Tex. App.—Houston [1st Dist.] 2009, no pet.) in the agreed decree of divorce the wife agreed, after divorce, to provide "as much toward the care and providing for the needs, of [her former husband] limited only by her financial situation." The former husband sued his former wife a few years later for inadequate support. The trial court rendered a judgment in favor of the former husband for $950,000. Should the former wife appeal? If so, on what grounds?

Herbert v. Herbert

Texas Court of Appeals—Ft. Worth, 1985
699 S.W.2d 717, writ granted

FENDER, Chief Justice.

This is an appeal from a take-nothing judgment rendered against Appellant, Dorothy Herbert, in her suit to enforce the property settlement agreement and judgment in a prior divorce decree between the parties. Appellee, Hansel Kay Herbert, counterclaimed that appellant had breached the agreement herself, thereby excusing further performance of the contract on his part, *i.e.*, payment to appellant of one-half of appellee's military retirement benefits. Upon the jury's finding that appellant had not substantially complied with the settlement agreement, the trial court rendered a take-nothing judgment against appellant. From this judgment appellant raises seven points of error.

We reverse.

However, inasmuch as this cause is remanded for a new trial, in the interest of justice we shall discuss what we perceive to be the applicable law on retrial. Basically, appellee's major assertion is that the law of contracts applies in this suit to enforce the property settlement agreement/judgment, and therefore appellee's affirmative defense that appellant materially breached (failed to substantially comply with) the contract would excuse appellee's compliance therewith. Appellant's position on appeal is that the property settlement agreement/judgment is a final judgment and the law of judgments should apply in the instant case, thereby precluding appellee from raising this impermissible contractual defense so as to collaterally attack the divorce judgment. For reasons stated herein, we agree with appellant's position.

Property settlement agreements entered into by the parties incident to a divorce are given the effect of a contract. *McGoodwin v. McGoodwin*, 671 S.W.2d 880, 882 (Tex. 1984);

Francis v. Francis, 412 S.W.2d 29, 33 (Tex. 1967). However, once the agreement has been approved by the court and incorporated into its judgment, "the agreement is no longer merely a contract between private individuals but is the judgment of the court." *Ex parte Gorena*, 595 S.W.2d 841, 844 (Tex. 1979). The fact that the judgment may be by consent of the parties does not render it any less force and validity.

Texas cases are in unison that contractual defenses which assail the validity of the underlying property settlement agreement/judgment between divorced parties are impermissible collateral attacks. *See Peddicord v. Peddicord*, 522 S.W.2d 266 (Tex. Civ. App. — Beaumont 1975, writ ref'd n.r.e.). In *Peddicord*, a suit to enforce a property settlement agreement/judgment, the defendant asserted the defenses of lack and failure of consideration, duress in executing the agreement, and lack of mental capacity to contract, all defenses pertaining to the *inception* of the property settlement agreement/judgment. The Court held that the trial court properly refused to allow the defendant to interpose contractual defenses, inasmuch as this would be to allow a collateral attack upon the judgment. *Id.* at 267.

In support of his theory that his affirmative defense in the instant case is proper, appellee places primary reliance on three cases. *McGoodwin v. McGoodwin*, 671 S.W.2d 880, 882 (Tex. 1984), *Conner v. Bean*, 630 S.W.2d 607 (Tex. App. — Houston [1st Dist.] 1981, writ ref'd n.r.e.), and *Sorrels v. Sorrels*, 592 S.W.2d 692, 697 (Tex. Civ. App. — Amarillo 1979, writ ref'd n.r.e.), which appellee contends all state that the *law of contracts* should govern a situation such as ours, and, therefore, events occurring subsequent to the entry of the divorce decree are not collateral attacks, and are permissible defenses.

In *McGoodwin*, at the time of the parties' divorce the court approved a property settlement agreement reached by the parties, and divided their property according to that agreement. The husband was awarded certain acreage and the wife was to receive a sum of money as consideration for the conveyance of her one-half interest in the land. The husband did not pay this consideration, but asserted full ownership, whereupon the wife brought a suit to subject the land to forced sale to satisfy her claim for the unpaid consideration. The issue to be decided was whether the divorce decree which approved the property settlement agreement implied a vendor's lien in favor of the wife. Prior to deciding this issue in the affirmative, the Court held as follows:

> Correct resolution of the question presented requires first an understanding of the effect given a marital property settlement agreement by Texas law. *Such an agreement, though incorporated into a final divorce decree, is treated as a contract, and its legal force and its meaning are governed by the law of contracts, not by the law of judgments.* [Citations omitted.] The property settlement provision now considered is one that directs the payment of money as consideration for the conveyance of the interest in real estate. Its construction, therefore, is dictated by the law regarding contracts for the sale of land. [Emphasis added.]

McGoodwin, 671 S.W.2d at 882.

Notwithstanding the above quoted language, we find that *McGoodwin* is not directly on point and therefore not controlling in the case at bar inasmuch as it dealt with the legal construction and effect of a property settlement agreement/judgment, and it did *not* deal with the situation wherein one party is attempting to raise subsequent defenses to the enforcement of that judgment.

The two Court of Appeals' cases upon which appellee relies both hold: 1) that actions to enforce a property settlement agreement/ judgment are governed by the law of contracts rather than judgments, and that any defenses which attack the validity of the agreement at inception, execution or approval by the trial court of the divorce decree, are collateral attacks and are barred; but 2) that defenses which are grounded upon subsequent events are not barred. *See Sorrels*, 592 S.W.2d at 697; *Conner*, 630 S.W.2d at 699–700.

In *Sorrels*, the ex-husband sought to avoid liability for almost ten years of spousal support which had gone unpaid when the Sorrels remarried each other. *Sorrels*, 592 S.W.2d at 694. The trial court granted the ex-husband's motion for summary judgment. *Id.* The Amarillo Court of Appeals reversed, holding Mr. Sorrels could establish the defenses of waiver, limitations and payment, but that he had not done so as a matter of law so as to be entitled to a summary judgment. *Id.* at 697–98. The Court reasoned that *Peddicord* only forbade using contractual defenses that challenged the inception, execution and approval by the court of the property settlement agreement, and that any defense to the contract based upon the occurrence of events subsequent to that point was permissible. *Id.* at 697.

The only case to date which has followed *Sorrels* is *Conner v. Bean*, 630 S.W.2d at 697. The former husband in *Conner* sought to defend his non-payment of contractual alimony by raising several contractual defenses. *Conner*, 630 S.W.2d at 699. The appellate court refused to allow Mr. Conner to raise contractual defenses of no consideration and no acceptance of his offer since they are impermissible collateral attacks on the final judgment. *Id.* However, he *could* raise the condition subsequent of his wife's remarriage as a defense. *Id.* at 699–700. However, the ex-husband did not prevail because he failed to properly present the question of condition subsequent to the jury and court. *Id.* at 700.

There is no Texas case on all fours with our situation wherein one party sought to raise an affirmative defense which would have the effect of totally abrogating the prior final judgment of the trial court. We do not disagree that under the *Conner* and *Sorrels* cases *some* conditions subsequent to the property settlement agreement/judgment may result in permissible contractual defenses which may be asserted in an attempt to defeat a later suit to enforce the property settlement agreement/judgment. However, these defenses are directed toward explaining the non-performing party's inaction under certain provisions of the property settlement agreement/judgment, and even if found to be true, *the finality of the property settlement agreement/judgment is not altered.* In the instant case, appellee seeks to totally abrogate the property settlement agreement/judgment by asserting the defense of material breach of contract. We will not extend the holdings of *Conner* and *Sorrels* so as to violate well-established legal principles regarding the finality of a judgment; therefore, we point out to the trial court on retrial that the specific affirmative defense which was raised by appellee in this case was an impermissible collateral attack on the finality of the property settlement agreement/judgment, and should not be allowed upon retrial.

The cause is reversed and remanded for a new trial. Costs of this appeal are assessed against appellee.

DISCUSSION

In a very strange opinion, the Texas Supreme Court reversed the court of appeals in *Herbert*. 754 S.W.2d 141 (Tex. 1988). The Texas Supreme Court upheld the trial court's determination that, if the jury failed to find, by a preponderance of the evidence, that the wife had substantially complied with the duties and obligations required under the settlement agreement, the husband was excused from his obligation to convey to the wife 50% of military retirement benefits received. The Court did not discuss why it treated this question as one pertaining to contract rights, rather than on pertaining to rights accruing from a final judgment.

The Texas Supreme Court decision in *Herbert* did little to clarify this area of Texas law. In *Spradley v. Hutchison*, 787 S.W.2d 214 (Tex. App. — Ft. Worth 1990, writ denied), the Ft. Worth Court of Appeals reiterated its analysis announced in *Herbert*, when the court was presented with a very similar issue.

Cayan v. Cayan

Texas Court of Appeals — Houston [14th Dist.], 2000
38 S.W.3d 161, no writ

OPINION

Richard H. Edelman, Justice

In this divorce case, William Cayan ("Bill") appeals a judgment in favor of Amalia Cayan ("Amy") on the grounds that the trial court erred in signing their divorce decree based on a mediated settlement agreement which Bill had repudiated because: (1) section 6.602 of the Texas Family Code does not create a procedural shortcut for enforcement of mediated settlement agreements; (2) a trial court is not required to enter judgment on a mediated settlement agreement merely because it technically complies with section 6.602; and (3) automatic enforcement of a mediated settlement agreement pursuant to section 6.602 violates the open courts and equal protection provisions of the Texas and United States Constitutions. We affirm.

Background

After the parties filed for divorce in 1997, Amy hired Barbara McKittrick, a CPA, to assist her in identifying and valuing the assets and liabilities of the community estate and to advise her on the tax consequences of the settlement options. In December of 1998, the parties attended a mediation session and entered into a "Rule 11 Stipulation and Mediated Settlement Agreement" (the "agreement") to divide the community assets and liabilities. Both parties and their attorneys signed the agreement, and on January 14, 1999, the associate judge of the trial court approved it. On February 16, Amy filed a motion for the court to sign and enter a final divorce decree based on the agreement. The motion was set for hearing on March 1, but Bill filed a motion that day to revoke the agreement, alleging error, mistake, and misrepresentation because he had entered into it based upon McKittrick's incorrect characterizations of his retirement benefits. After a brief hearing, the District Judge signed Amy's proposed final decree (the "decree") on March 1.

Section 6.602

Bill's first point of error argues that because section 6.602 is silent regarding enforcement of mediated settlement agreements, the agreement in this case must be enforced in the same manner as any other written contract. Bill thus asserts that following his revocation of the agreement Amy could enforce it only by amending her pleadings and suing for breach of contract. He further asserts that a trial court may enter judgment on such a repudiated settlement agreement only by way of a summary judgment proceeding or trial, neither of which occurred in this case. Bill thus contends that when the Legislature enacted section 6.602, it did not create a procedural short-cut for enforcement of Rule 11 mediated settlement agreements in family law cases.

Bill's second point of error contends that if a trial court cannot reject a mediated settlement agreement that complies with section 6.602 (a "section 6.602 agreement"), then that section directly conflicts with: (1) the requirement under sections 7.002 and 7.006 of the Texas Family Code that a court find a property division to be "just and right" before approving it; (2) the portion of section 7.006 allowing parties to revise or repudiate a property division agreement until rendition of the divorce; and (3) article XVI, section 15 of the Texas Constitution, which prevents a trial court from divesting a spouse of separate property. Bill's third point of error similarly asserts that if a trial court cannot reject a section 6.602 agreement, then that section also violates the open courts and equal protection clauses of the Texas Constitution.

With few exceptions, a complaint, including a constitutional challenge, must be raised in the trial court to be preserved for appellate review. In this case, because Bill failed to raise the contentions asserted in his second and third points of error in the trial court, those complaints present nothing for our review. However, as will be discussed with regard to Bill's first point of error, we do not believe that section 6.602 is in conflict with any of the statutory or constitutional provisions cited by Bill.

In a final decree of divorce, a trial court is generally required to order a division of the community and quasi-community property that the court deems "just and right." *See* TEX. FAM. CODE ANN. §§ 7.001, 7.002 (Vernon 1998 & Supp. 2000). Where parties enter into an agreement concerning the division of their property, the agreement may be revised or repudiated before rendition of the divorce *"unless the agreement is binding under another rule of law." Id.* § 7.006(a) (emphasis added). If the court finds that the terms of a property division agreement are just and right, those terms are binding on the court; if not, the court may request the parties to submit a revised agreement or may set the case for a contested hearing. *See id.* § 7.006(b), (c). Once a court renders judgment on a settlement agreement, consent to the agreement cannot be revoked. *See id.* § 7.006(a) (the agreement may be revised or repudiated before rendition of the divorce).

In contrast to the above provisions, section 6.602 provides that where a mediated settlement agreement meets its requirements: (1) the agreement "is binding on the parties"; and (2) a party is "entitled to judgment on the ... agreement *notwithstanding Rule 11, Texas Rules of Civil Procedure, or another rule of law." Id.* § 6.602(b), (c) (emphasis added). In construing this language, we presume the Legislature intended the plain meaning of its words. The plain meaning of section 6.602 could hardly be more clear: a section 6.602 agreement is binding, *i.e.*, irrevocable, and a party to one is entitled to judgment based on the agreement. Because section 7.006(a) expressly recognizes that a settlement agreement can be made binding before rendition of the divorce under another rule of law, and because section 6.602 expressly entitles a party to a section 6.602 agreement to judgment notwithstanding other law, we interpret section 6.602 simply as an exception to section 7.006(a) whereby parties to a divorce may elect to make their agreement binding as of the time of its execution rather than at the subsequent time the divorce is rendered. In addition to reflecting the plain meaning of section 6.602, this interpretation is indicated by other considerations as well.

First, the Legislature is presumed to have acted with knowledge of cases interpreting a statute. Therefore, when the Legislature amended section 6.602 in 1999, we presume that it was aware of the cases holding that judgments should be entered on settlement agreements which complied with section 153.0071 despite attempts by parties to withdraw their consent.

Secondly, we presume the Legislature enacts statutes with knowledge of existing law. We thus assume the Legislature enacted section 6.602 with knowledge of section 154.071 of the Civil Practice & Remedies Code which provides that a written settlement agreement is enforceable in the same manner as any other written contract. *See* TEX. CIV. PRAC. & REM. CODE ANN. § 154.071 (Vernon 1997). Moreover, we do not lightly presume that the Legislature did a useless act. To adopt Bill's contention that section 6.602 agreements are only enforceable in the same manner as other written contracts would render section 6.602 meaningless relative to section 154.071 and thus treat its enactment as a useless act.

Thirdly, the purpose of alternative dispute measures is to keep parties out of the courtroom. *See generally* George B. Murr, *In the Matter of Marriage of Ames and the Enforceability of Alternative Dispute Resolution Agreements: A Case for Reform*, 28 TEX. TECH L. REV. 31, 35 (1997). Where a mediated settlement agreement is not summarily enforceable, the trial court is then faced with litigating the merits of not only the original action but also the enforceability of the settlement agreement, thereby generating more, not less, litigation. Enforcing mediated agreements as of the time they are entered rather than later also encourages parties to avail themselves of mediation by giving them greater assurance of a prompt and final resolution. Further, parties are more likely to mediate in good faith if they know their agreement will be enforced. Therefore, effecting the plain meaning of section 6.602 is supported by public policy.

Thus, contrary to Bill's contentions, the language of section 6.602 reflects that when the Legislature enacted that section, it definitely and deliberately created a procedural shortcut for enforcement of mediated settlement agreements in divorce cases. Equally apparent is that section 6.602 does not conflict with, but is an exception to, section 7.006. We are similarly persuaded that section 6.602 is also an exception to sections 7.001 and 7.006 in allowing a judgment to be entered on a section 6.602 agreement without a determination by the trial court that the terms of the agreement are just and right. Importantly, however, section 6.602 cannot be imposed on parties against their wishes. Rather, they remain free to enter mediated settlement agreements that do not fall within section 6.602 and, in fact, must take affirmative steps to qualify for section 6.602 treatment.

Bill further complains that section 6.602 violates: (1) the constitutional prohibition against divesting a spouse of separate property; (2) the open courts provision of the Texas Constitution by depriving him of the common law defense of fraud in the inducement to avoid being divested of separate property under the agreement; and (3) constitutional equal protection rights in that litigants who mediate family law disputes are afforded less protection than other litigants who file common law claims for fraud. We first note that the prohibition against divesting a spouse of separate property applies only to judicial, *i.e.*, unagreed divestitures and does not restrict parties from dividing separate property by agreement. *See, e.g., Boyett v. Boyett*, 799 S.W.2d 360, 363 (Tex. App.—Houston [14th Dist.] 1990, no writ). In addition, as noted above, section 6.602 agreements operate differently from non-section 6.602 agreements only with regard to the *time* at which parties become irrevocably bound, not the *extent* to which they become bound. Once the point of becoming bound is reached, a party is no more deprived of their rights to open courts or equal protection by section 6.602 agreements than non-section 6.602 agreements.

In any event, neither the open courts nor equal protection provision prevents a party from waiving a procedural or substantive claim by agreement (or inadvertence). In this case, the consequences of entering into a section 6.602 agreement are unequivocally stated on the face of both the statute and a section 6.602 agreement. If a party fails to exercise diligence in investigating facts or law or otherwise enters into a section 6.602 agreement inadvisedly, he will not be rewarded for doing so with a reprieve from the agreement. Conversely, if a party is wrongfully induced to enter into a section 6.602 agreement, he has the same recourse as one who discovered such a circumstance after judgment was entered on a non-section 6.602 agreement.

Because the agreement in this case complied with section 6.602, the trial court was required to enter judgment on it despite Bill's attempted repudiation. Accordingly, we overrule Bill's points of error and affirm the judgment of the trial court.

DISCUSSION

Courts have reopened a mediated settlement agreement when a party made a material misrepresentation in the negotiations. *See Boyd v. Boyd*, 67 S.W.3d 398 (Tex. App.—Ft. Worth 2002, no pet.).

A "mediated" agreement requires a third-party neutral. *Lee v. Lee*, 158 S.W.3d 612 (Tex. App.—Ft. Worth 2005, no pet.). In *Haynes v. Haynes*, 180 S.W.3d 927 (Tex. App.—Dallas 2006, no pet.) the court held that the divorce court may add terms to the mediated agreement "to effectuate and implement" the agreement.

B. Drafting the Decree

Once the property division and all support arrangements have been agreed upon, the next concern of the family law attorney is enforcement of the agreement. If the settlement is memorialized in a written agreement, normal breach of contract remedies will be available. These remedies have serious problems, however. On one hand, the most that can normally be obtained for breach of contract is a money judgment. This remedy is expensive, time-consuming and frequently worthless in Texas. Most clients do not want to rely on breach of contract remedies to assure compliance with family law orders.

Two powerful additional remedies are available to the family law attorney. Child support now may be collected by income withholding. *See* Texas Family Code Chapter 158. Thus, a procedure can be established so that child support is taken from the parent's wages before receipt and forwarded to the custodial parent. (A "turnover" order can also be useful.)

Contempt is also available to enforce a correctly drawn order. Tex. Fam. Code § 157.002. It is not available to enforce an incorrectly drawn order. Adults can be encouraged to do a great number of things they are not otherwise inclined to do if jail is the remedy for noncompliance. The threat of contempt can be quite effective enforcement insurance.

A court order can be the subject of a contempt action only if the order clearly specifies who, what, how, when, and where to the party who has been ordered to act. The cases below illustrate how lawyers sometimes have difficulty drafting an appropriate order.

Ex parte Slavin

Supreme Court of Texas, 1967
412 S.W.2d 43

POPE, Justice.

Relator, Eugene L. Slavin, brought this original habeas corpus proceeding after the district judge held him in contempt and committed him to jail for three days and until he purged himself of contempt by paying $212.00 which the court found was the amount he had not paid under a child-support order. The question presented for decision is whether the terms of the child-support order are definite and certain enough to be enforced by contempt. Our opinion is that the order is ambiguous, and, therefore, the relator should be discharged.

Relator and his wife Gloria Slavin were divorced on February 8, 1963. The divorce decree awarded custody of the three minor children to Gloria. They were at that time aged four, nine and fourteen. The portion of the decree which ordered relator to pay support and which is in question is:

> The Defendant is further ORDERED to pay the sum of ONE HUNDREDFIFTY AND No/100 DOLLARS ($150.00) per month for the care, support and maintenance of the three minor children until said children attain the age of eighteen years, that the Defendant, EUGENE L. SLAVIN, shall pay the sum of THIRTY-SEVEN AND 50/100 DOLLARS ($37.50) each week for the care, support and maintenance of his minor children beginning with the 7th day of February, 1963, and shall pay a like sum on the Thursday of each succeeding week thereafter.

The decree was sufficiently certain as long as all three of the children were less than eighteen years of age. Relator urges, however, that the order became reasonably subject to either one of two constructions after one of the children reached eighteen. Relator paid the monthly support of $150.00 until one year after the oldest of the three children reached eighteen. He then reduced the support payments proportionately and began paying $100.00 for the two children who were still less than eighteen. He urges that art. 4639a, 1, Vernon's Ann. Civ. Stat., authorizes a court to order a parent to make payments for benefit "of such child or children, until same have reached the age of eighteen (18) years ..." Relator says that by his payment of $150.00 monthly for a year after the oldest child reached eighteen, he actually paid $318.00 more than he was required by law to pay. He says this construction of the support order is a reasonable one and is consistent with innocence.

The order is subject to another construction, one that would support the order of contempt. That construction is that the court which ordered relator to pay support intended that he would pay the fixed monthly sum of $150.00 until the youngest of the three children reached the age of eighteen. By such a construction, the father would continue to pay $150.00 to the two children beneath the age of eighteen, and when the second child reached that age, the sum would continue until the youngest child reached eighteen.

It is an accepted rule of law that for a person to be held in contempt for disobeying a court decree, the decree must spell out the details of compliance in clear, specific and unambiguous terms so that such person will readily know exactly what duties or obligations are imposed upon him. The underlying reason for this rule is that:

> The rights of the parties under a mandatory judgment whereby they may be subjected to punishment as contemnors for a violation of its provisions, should not

rest upon implication or conjecture, but the language declaring such rights or imposing burdens should be clear, specific and unequivocal so that the parties may not be misled thereby.

Plummer v. Superior Court of the City and County of San Francisco, 20 Cal. 2d 158, 124 P. 2d 5 (1942).

Texas decisions hold that an order of a court, such as an "injunction decree must be as definite, clear and precise as possible and when practicable it should inform the defendant of the acts he is restrained from doing, without calling on him for inferences or conclusions about which persons might well differ and without leaving anything for further hearing." *San Antonio Bar Ass'n. v. Guardian Abstract & Title Co.*, 156 Tex. 7, 291 S.W.2d 697 (1956); *Villalobos v. Holguin*, 146 Tex. 474, 208 S.W.2d 871 (1948). In *Ex parte Kottwitz*, 117 Tex. 583, 8 S.W.2d 508 (1928), the court stated the measure of certainty required to sustain the validity of a contempt order. The reasons for certainty in such an order are similar to those required of the order which one is charged with violating. The court said:

> Where, as in the instant case, the order does not state that the commitment is until the defendant shall do or perform certain acts in compliance with the orders of the court, but simply states in indefinite language that he is committed until he purges of contempt, the order is too indefinite, and is void.

In *Garza v. Fleming*, 323 S.W.2d 152 (Tex. Civ. App. — San Antonio 1959, writ ref'd n.r.e.), the court of civil appeals held that an order which provided that the father should pay "$100.00 per month ... for the support of said minor children until David E. Garza shall reach his eighteenth birthday" was certain enough for enforcement by contempt. David was the youngest of three children. The order was definite in that it made clear to the father that his payments would be the same fixed sum until David, the youngest child, reached eighteen. The order in the present case lacks that clarity. It orders, on the one hand, that the support is for "the three minor children," but, on the other, it limits the support payments by the further provision, "until said children attain the age of eighteen years." It is uncertain whether this means that relator must support his oldest child after reaching eighteen, or whether the support is to continue unreduced for the other two children, or whether the support payments should be proportionately reduced.

The language of the support order in the present case is equivocal. When the commands of the order and the provisions of art. 4693a are read together, we are unable to say that the order can be readily understood. The ambiguity of the support order renders it unenforceable.

The relator is discharged from custody.

———

DISCUSSION

What was the difference between the decree in *Slavin* and the decree in *Garza v. Fleming* referred to in *Slavin* that was enforceable by contempt?

An order to pay child support, with the amount of support determined by the judge after considering all relevant facts, is enforceable by contempt, if the order is drafted correctly. However, if the level of support is set at a higher amount, based on a provision in a prenuptial agreement, this obligation cannot be enforced by contempt. *See Ex parte Hall*, 854 S.W.2d 656 (Tex. 1993).

Even if the decree is ambiguous, some courts require the person to comply with one reasonable construction of the order to avoid contempt. *See Ex parte Linder*, 783 S.W.2d 754 (Tex. App.—Dallas 1990, no writ).

An indigent defendant in a contempt action is entitled to a court-appointed attorney. *In re Aarons*, 10 S.W.3d 833 (Tex. App.—Beaumont 2000, no pet.).

Ex parte Bible

Texas Court of Appeals—Houston [14th Dist.], 1980
596 S.W.2d 207, no writ

SALAZAR, Justice.

This is an original proceeding for habeas corpus instituted by John Bible, Relator, contending that he was illegally deprived of his liberty by an order of contempt.

On September 28, 1979, the 328th Family District Court of Fort Bend County, Texas, entered a judgment and decree of divorce against Relator, ordering him to execute a good and sufficient deed to specified property "within ten (10) days from the signing of [the] Decree." Relator willfully disobeyed this order and duly perfected an appeal of the judgment. On October 12, 1979 (fourteen days after divorce had been decreed and judgment entered), the district court ordered John Bible to appear on October 26, 1979, to show cause why he should not be held in contempt. The Notice of Hearing to Show Cause, the Show Cause Order, and the Citation were simultaneously delivered to John Bible on October 12, 1979. Relator filed an answer to the Motion for Contempt but did not personally appear at the contempt hearing on October 26. Relator was held in contempt by an order signed on October 31 and was restrained by virtue of a Writ of Attachment and Commitment.

Relator complains that the contempt order is void and therefore his detention is illegal. We agree, based on the fact that Relator was held in contempt of a judgment that had not yet become final.

Our authority for so holding is *Ex parte Valdez*, 521 S.W.2d 724 (Tex. Civ. App.—Houston [14th Dist.] 1975, no writ). In that matter the Court of Domestic Relations entered judgment on December 30, 1974, against Respondent Valdez, awarding certain real estate to the wife and ordering him to vacate the premises by January 31, 1975. On January 9, Valdez filed a motion for new trial, complaining of the division of the estate. The motion for new trial was overruled by operation of law on February 24, 1975. Meanwhile, Valdez did not vacate the premises, and a contempt order was entered against him on February 5, 1975. This court held that the contempt order was void since the judgment had not yet become enforceable as a final judgment.

We have almost exactly the same facts before us now. The only difference is that Relator Bible actually perfected an appeal whereas Valdez moved for a new trial. The same rule applies in either case: a judgment regarding property division may not be enforced by orders of contempt before the judgment as to the property has become final.

The writ of habeas corpus is granted and the Relator is ordered discharged.

———

DISCUSSION

Bible sets forth the basic rule that only final judgments can be the subject of contempt. This is not true for child support orders, however. *See Ex parte Swearingen*, 574 S.W.2d 585 (Tex. Civ. App.—Beaumont 1978, no writ).

Ex parte Choate

Texas Court of Appeals—Beaumont, 1979
582 S.W.2d 625, no writ

KEITH, Justice.

This is a continuation of a domestic relations dispute between Alton Choate and his former wife, Juanita Choate, and for convenience we will refer to the parties by their Christian names.

Alton has invoked our original jurisdiction seeking relief from an order adjudging him to be in contempt of court for the violation of several provisions in a final decree of divorce. We granted leave to file the petition, admitted Alton to bail pending a hearing, and now review the contempt proceeding.

The *nunc pro tunc* judgment which partitioned the community property— after the granting of the divorce—became final because no appeal was perfected there from. This judgment contained several paragraphs material to our disposition of this cause, the decretal paragraph containing these provisions:

> Petitioner Juanita Holley Choate shall receive as her sole and separate property the following, and Respondent is hereby divested of all right, title and interest in and to such property:
>
> 1.   The home located at 2911 Nashville, Nederland, Jefferson County, Texas, more specifically described as Lot 19, Block 13, Helena Park IV Subdivision to the City of Nederland, Jefferson County, Texas;
>
> 2.   All contents of home [not material to this proceeding];
>
> 3.   The Oldsmobile automobile;
>
> 4.   150 shares of Texaco stock, now held in the Texaco Savings Plan, in the name of Respondent [Alton];
>
> 5.   Division of pension rights—not material to this proceeding].

It was ordered further that Juanita's firm of attorneys "be and is hereby awarded the sum of $3,750.00 for legal services rendered. Said judgment is hereby awarded against Respondent." Another paragraph read: "It is decreed that both parties shall execute all instruments necessary to accomplish final execution and disposition of this judgment."

Finally, all costs were adjudged against our Relator "for which let execution issue."

After this judgment became final, Juanita filed her motion seeking an order holding Alton in contempt of court for his failure and refusal to comply with the terms of the decree. At the conclusion of the hearing, Alton was found guilty of contempt upon several specifications and ordered confined in jail for a period of one day and until he purged himself of contempt. We set out the four separate paragraphs of the order:

> 1. Sign and execute any required instruments necessary to convey 150 shares of Texaco stock to Juanita Holley Choate, and sign and execute any required instruments necessary to transfer title of the 1978 Oldsmobile automobile from Respondent to Movant, Juanita Holley Choate.
>
> 2. Sign and execute a deed to the home located at 2911 Nashville, Nederland, Jefferson County, Texas, more particularly described in the judgment herein, said deed being necessary to convey title of the property from Respondent to Movant, Juanita Holley Choate.

3. Pay the sum of $89.00 to the District Clerk of Jefferson County, Texas, for costs incurred in the divorce proceedings in this cause.

4. Pay the sum of $3,750.00, for legal services rendered, to the law firm of Provost, Umphrey, Doyle & McPherson [Juanita's attorneys].

We will consider each of the adjudications separately. As to the first, we point out that it contains two separate acts on the part of Relator:

(1) Sign and execute any required instruments necessary to convey 150 shares of Texaco stock ... and

(2) [S]ign and execute any required instruments necessary to transfer title of the 1978 Oldsmobile.

We note that even in the contempt order authorizing the imprisonment, there is no description of the particular action required of Alton. He is imprisoned until he signs the "required instruments." Moreover, this order can have as its base only the language in the decree requiring the parties to "execute all instruments necessary to accomplish final execution and disposition of this judgment."

We are of the opinion that the first section of the order holding Alton in contempt is void. Neither the judgment nor the order holding him in contempt spelled out specifically just what Alton was to sign.

In *Ex parte Slavin*, 412 S.W.2d 43, 44 (Tex. 1976), the Court reviewed the cases on the subject and held:

It is an accepted rule of law that for a person to be held in contempt for disobeying a court decree, the decree must spell out the details of compliance in clear, specific and unambiguous terms so that such person will readily know exactly what duties or obligations are imposed upon him.

Slavin has been followed by many courts and its basic holding has not been challenged.

Indeed, it was followed in *Ex parte Carpenter*, 566 S.W.2d 123, 124 (Tex. Civ. App.—Houston [14th Dist.] 1978, no writ), where the relator was adjudged in contempt for failure to comply with a decree requiring that he "timely pay" medical expenses, the court holding:

Relator urges that the medical expenses provision of the divorce decree is vague and indefinite. We agree. The word "timely" is imprecise and subjective; it does not readily inform the person of the duty imposed upon him. Such an order is unenforceable and cannot support a contempt judgment. *Ex parte Slavin*, 412 S.W.2d 43 (Tex. 1967).

Alton can secure his release only by signing the "required instruments" and this is as vague and indefinite as the Boy Scouts' motto, "Be prepared." The words of the judgment and the contempt order are so vague and imprecise that the order of incarceration is void as to the first finding and adjudication.

Under the same line of authorities, and for the same reasons, the second adjudication—requiring Alton to "[s]ign and execute a deed" to the home place—is void. It is readily apparent that no particular type of deed is mentioned. Would compliance be attained by delivery of a quitclaim deed?—Or perhaps, by a special warranty deed? Or, is Alton required to execute a general warranty deed when there may be an outstanding purchase money lien on the property? Again, as noted earlier, the command is imprecise and vague—and, more importantly, void.

Ex parte Myrick, 474 S.W.2d 767, 769 (Tex. Civ. App.—Houston [1st Dist.] 1971, no writ), found the court holding void an order of commitment for failure to "execute all notes and instruments, to carry this agreement into full force and effect" by the refusal to execute a specific trust agreement. Following *Ex parte Slavin, supra,* the court held the commitment order to be void because of the indefinite nature of the original decree. We follow the holdings in *Slavin* and *Myrick.* A person may not be deprived of his liberty under the vague and imprecise language used in the judgment.

The portion of the order holding Alton in contempt for failure to pay Juanita's attorney's fees is void under the holding in *Wallace v. Briggs,* 162 Tex. 485, 348 S.W.2d 523, 525, 526 (1961), where the court held:

> The court has the power on the final disposition of the case to award attorneys' fees to the wife, the reasonableness of which are to be determined by the trier of the facts, and they are then entered as a part of the final judgment. *Even then there is no authority for the judge to summarily order them paid or attempt to enforce that order by* contempt proceedings. (Emphasis supplied).

Accord, *McCauley v. McCauley,* 374 S.W.2d 719, 723 (Tex. Civ. App.—Waco 1964, writ dism'd).

There was no showing made that the attorneys' fees or court costs were payable out of property in possession of Alton at the time of the entry of the *nunc pro tunc* judgment. To allow such enforcement by imprisonment for contempt would amount to imprisonment for debt in violation of Tex. Const. art. I, Sec. 18. *Ex parte Duncan,* 462 S.W.2d 336, 338 (Tex. Civ. App.—Houston [1st Dist.] 1970, no writ). *Cf. Ex parte Harwell,* 538 S.W.2d 667, 671 (Tex. Civ. App.—Waco 1976, no writ).

In habeas corpus proceedings, we are limited to a determination of whether or not the order of commitment is void. *Ex parte Hosken, supra* (482 S.W.2d at 20), and authorities therein cited. Having held the order void as to each of the four separate adjudications, we forego a discussion of all other questions apparent on the face of the record.

It is the order of this Court that our Relator, Alton Choate, be discharged from compliance with the contempt judgment entered on the 12th day of April, 1979.

DISCUSSION

How could the order have been drafted regarding the transfer of title to the home so that the order could have been enforced by contempt?

Choate illustrates that an order to pay money in the future cannot be enforced by contempt unless the order is tied to certain money in existence at the time the order is rendered. Can you think of any policy reason for this distinction?

Can an order to (i) pay house payments or (ii) pay attorneys' fees be enforceable by contempt? *See In re Lozano,* 263 S.W.3d 87 (Tex. App.—Houston [1st Dist.] 2006, pet. denied); *Tracy v. Tracy,* 219 S.W.3d 527 (Tex. App.—Dallas 2007, no pet.).

Ex parte Gorena

Supreme Court of Texas, 1979
595 S.W.2d 841

GREENHILL, Chief Justice.

This is an original habeas corpus proceeding. It arises from an order committing Juan J. Gorena to the Bexar County jail for contempt of court in failing to make, pursuant to a divorce decree, monthly payments of a portion of his military retirement benefits to his former wife.

Mr. Gorena's main contentions are: (1) that the trial court lacked jurisdiction to enter the contempt order because the divorce decree on which the order was based is an "agreed judgment"; and (2) that the decree is too vague and indefinite to be enforced. Also presented is the question as to whether he is imprisoned for debt.

We overrule all of the contentions and remand Mr. Gorena to the custody of the Bexar County Sheriff.

On February 7, 1978, Juan J. Gorena and Elvia Gorena, now Elvia Barber, were divorced. The divorce decree recites that the parties had reached an agreement concerning custody and support of the children as well as the disposition of property. Pursuant to this agreement, the court issued the following order in the divorce decree:

> It is decreed that Respondent [Mr. Gorena] shall pay to Petitioner [Ms. Barber], as her portion of the community retirement pay received by Respondent as a result of his retirement from the United States Air Force, 42.5% of Respondent's gross retirement pay per month, with the first payment due and payable 1 March 1978 and like payments due and payable on the 1st day of each month thereafter.

Mr. Gorena made these payments until July, 1978, but he has not made payments since that time.

Mr. Gorena's contention is that the trial court's contempt order is void because it is based on a violation of a divorce decree that is indefinite and ambiguous. He is correct in his assertion that for a person to be held in contempt for disobeying a court decree, "the decree must spell out the details of compliance in clear, specific and unambiguous terms so that such person will readily know exactly what duties or obligations are imposed upon him." *Ex parte Slavin*, 412 S.W.2d 43 (Tex. 1967).

The divorce decree in this case orders Mr. Gorena to pay 42.5 percent of his "gross retirement pay per month." The order further states that the first date for payment is March 1, 1978. Mr. Gorena contends that the term "gross" renders the decree ambiguous. We disagree. "Gross" means the "overall total exclusive of deductions." Webster's Third International Dictionary 1002 (1966). The decree clearly requires that the 42.5 percent to be paid to Ms. Barber be calculated on the basis of the total pay, exclusive of deductions, that Mr. Gorena receives from the government; and the decree is not indefinite as to the time for payment. The payments are to be made monthly, commencing on March 1, 1978. *Ex parte Anderson*, 541 S.W.2d 286 (Tex. Civ. App. — San Antonio 1976, no writ).

During oral argument, the question was raised from the bench whether the contempt order is void in that it constitutes imprisonment for debt in violation of article I, Section 18, of the Texas Constitution. The thrust of the argument appears to be that an order requiring one to pay money to another, rather than requiring one to remit the money to the registry of the court, amounts to imprisonment for debt. The decree in this case directs Mr. Gorena to make the payments directly to his former wife.

Mr. Gorena cites *Ex parte Yates*, 387 S.W.2d 377 (Tex. 1965). *Yates* involved a divorce decree which, in effect, ordered the husband to pay to the wife $67,920.75 of a debt of the Gordon Yates Lumber Company to Gordon L. Yates, the husband. The payments to the wife were to be made in monthly installments of $500.00 plus interest. The wife sought to enforce the divorce decree by contempt proceedings. The trial court held the husband in contempt for failure to make the monthly payments and for pledging the note evidencing the debt to a bank. This court held that the husband could not be held in contempt for failure to make the payments. The court reasoned:

> The order itself reveals that the money which Yates was being ordered to pay to Mrs. Yates was not property found to be owned by Mrs. Yates and in the possession of Yates, but was money to be earned by Yates in the future. The order does not ... make a division of the property and direct a surrender to the clerk of the court property held by Yates. The record clearly shows that Yates is being imprisoned for debt in violation of the Texas Constitution.

387 S.W.2d at 380.

We consider the controlling factor in the *Yates* decision to be the fact that Mr. Yates was required to pay money that he had not yet earned. Although the court in *Yates* mentioned the fact that the husband was not directed to pay the money to the clerk of the court, the court's opinion in no way indicates that that fact was controlling of its decision.

The court of civil appeals in *Ex parte Anderson*, 541 S.W.2d 286 (Tex. Civ. App.— San Antonio 1976, no writ), cited above, was directly confronted with this problem of an order directing payment directly to the wife rather than to the registry of the court. In *Anderson*, the husband was held in contempt for violating a divorce decree that ordered him to pay his former wife $105.00 each month out of his military retirement pay. The court of civil appeals denied the husband's petition for writ of habeas corpus. In holding that the contempt order did not constitute imprisonment for debt, the court reasoned that the husband was not being required to pay a debt to his former wife but was, instead, being required to surrender to her property that already belonged to her by virtue of the divorce decree. *See Ex parte Sutherland*, 526 S.W.2d 536 (Tex. 1975). The court likened the husband's position to that of a trustee. Numerous cases in other jurisdictions have affirmed a trial court's order holding a trustee or other fiduciary in contempt for failure to turn property, including money, over to third persons. Annotation, 134 A.L.R. 927 (1941). The court further noted the tremendous burden that would be placed on district clerks were they required to receive and disburse all such monthly payments. We think the decision and reasoning in *Anderson* are correct; and, accordingly, we hold that Mr. Gorena is not being imprisoned for debt.

Juan J. Gorena is remanded to the custody of the Sheriff of Bexar County.

———

AUTHOR'S QUESTION

Do you understand why *Gorena* and *Anderson* are distinguished from *Yates*?

Ex parte Harris

Texas Court of Appeals — Corpus Christi, 1983
649 S.W.2d 389, no writ

GONZALEZ, Justice.

Relator has brought an original habeas corpus proceeding in this Court seeking his discharge from the custody of the Sheriff of San Patricio County. Upon presentation of his application, this Court directed the issuance of the writ and ordered his release upon the posting of the bond fixed by us.

Relator was found guilty of contempt of court by the 156th Judicial District Court of San Patricio County for allegedly violating its order in failing to make monthly payments for the support of a child as ordered in a divorce decree entered on September 8, 1982.

The divorce decree, so far as is material here reads:

After presentation of the testimony, evidence and argument of counsel, and after examination of the record, the Court finds:

. . . .

f. That the parties have entered into a written agreement containing provisions for conservatorship and support of the child, a copy of which is filed in this proceeding; the agreement is in the best interest of the child and is made a part of the order of this Court. . . .

Then, in the decretal portion of the decree the Court states:

Based on such findings, it is DECREED and ORDERED:

. . . .

2. That the property settlement agreement of the parties be incorporated into this divorce decree.

3. That the agreement of the parties concerning conservatorship and support of the minor child is in the best interest of the child and accordingly is incorporated into this divorce.

The Agreement Incident to Divorce provides in part:

6.01. Cash Payments. The parties agree that Donald Patrick Harris shall pay to Bettye Warren Harris child support in the amount of $300.00 per month, with the first installment due and payable on the 1st day of August, 1982, and a like installment due and payable on the first day of the month thereafter until the child reaches the age of eighteen or is otherwise emancipated.

Mr. Harris did not make child support payments in October and November of 1982, and only a partial payment of $50.00 for the month of December and no payments in January and February of 1983. (Other matters alleged by Mrs. Harris in the motion for contempt were waived by her at the time of the hearing.) Mrs. Harris filed a motion for contempt and after a hearing, the trial court found Mr. Harris in contempt and assessed punishment at 30 days in the county jail and a $250.00 fine. The trial court also ordered that Harris thereafter be confined in the county jail until he purged himself of the contempt by paying the arrearage in the amount of $1,450.00 plus court costs and attorney's fees. He thereafter filed this proceeding.

It is Relator's contention that the trial court was without power to hold him in contempt because the divorce decree which formed the basis for contempt failed to command him to do or refrain from doing any act pertaining to the payment of child support. He submits that since there is no order of the court which he could have violated, the judgment of contempt and commitment order entered by the court are void. We agree.

In *Ex parte Slavin,* 412 S.W.2d 43, 44 (Tex. 1967), the Court said:

> It is an accepted rule of law that for a person to be held in contempt for disobeying a court decree, the decree must spell out the details of compliance in clear, specific and unambiguous terms so that such person will readily know exactly what duties or obligations are imposed upon him....

The court went on to hold, citing, *Ex parte Duncan,* 42 Tex. Cr. R. 661, 62 S.W. 758 (1901), that:

> Where the court seeks to punish either by fine, arrest, or imprisonment for a disobedience of an order or command, such order or command must carry with it no uncertainty and must not be susceptible of different meanings or constructions, but must be in the *form of a command,* and, when tested by itself, must speak definitely the meaning and purpose of the court in ordering. (Emphasis added.)

An inspection of the divorce decree reveals that the trial court failed to order or command Relator to make any child support payments whatsoever. Even though the decree did "incorporate into the divorce" the agreement of the parties which contained provisions for support of the child, such a decree cannot be enforced by contempt absent language ordering, decreeing, adjudging or otherwise directing that Relator make the child support payments.

The divorce decree failed to set out the provisions for support of the child in the decree and also failed to order that the parties comply with any order of the court or agreement of the parties. As such, the trial court's divorce decree is not enforceable by contempt.

The trial court did recite in paragraph (f.) of the decree its finding "that the parties have entered into a written agreement containing provisions for conservatorship and support of the child, a copy of which is filed in this proceeding; the agreement is in the best interest of the child and is made a part of the order of the Court." This recital does not specifically order Relator to perform any act and absent language in the nature which we discussed above, cannot form the basis for a finding of contempt.

The judgment of contempt and commitment order are void and unenforceable. It is the order of this Court that Relator be discharged from the contempt judgment and that relator's sureties on the bond furnished for his release pending our decision are released from further liability.

DISCUSSION

It appears the *Harris* holding has been overruled by Tex. Fam. Code §§ 153.007 (c). So, child support provisions in an agreement incorporated by reference into a decree may be enforced by contempt. The Texas Supreme Court reiterates the basic point of *Harris* (about the necessity of command language in the decree to permit a contempt remedy) in *In re Coppock,* 277 S.W.3d 417 (Tex. 2009).

Ex parte Barnes

Texas Court of Appeals—San Antonio, 1987
730 S.W.2d 46, writ dism'd

OPINION

Relator seeks relief from the coercive portion of a contempt order ordering his incarceration for failure to make child support payments in accordance with the provisions of the divorce decree. The court below ordered relator imprisoned for 30 days and thereafter until he paid $7,000.00 in child support arrearages and attorney's fees in the sum of $758.00. Relator has served more than 30 days and now seeks relief from this Court after his application for writ of habeas corpus was denied by a district court.

Relator's contention is that he is presently unable to purge himself of contempt by complying with the coercive portion of the order because he does not have the $7,000.00, nor any part of such amount.

After this Court heard oral argument, we ordered the trial court to conduct a hearing to determine relator's ability to comply with the purge condition. The trial court conducted the hearing and made findings of fact which were filed with this court along with a transcript of the evidence heard by the trial court. The real party in interest agrees that the evidence conclusively establishes relator's present inability to pay the child support arrearages and attorney's fees because he has no resources of his own, is unable to borrow from any relatives and has been refused loans by various lending institutions to which he has made application.

It appears that at the original contempt hearing relator's ex-spouse made a prima facie showing of relator's ability to make the required payments and that relator did not claim inability to comply with the support provisions of the divorce decree.

While the cases agree that where it is not within a person's power to perform the act which alone will purge him of contempt he may not be imprisoned for an indefinite term for an offense already committed, there is language in some of the cases which indicates the inability to perform the required act must be established at the time of the contempt hearing. However, it is apparent that keeping a person until he performs an act which is beyond his power to perform is no more acceptable when the inability arises after he is imprisoned than it would be if the inability existed at the time the imprisonment began.

In *Ex parte Ramzy*, 424 S.W. 220 (Tex. 1968), the court in a divorce case temporarily enjoined the spouses from disposing of property. A motion to hold the husband in contempt, alleging that he had disposed of certain gold coins, was filed by the wife. After a hearing held on September 25, 1967, the Court denied his application for habeas corpus, relator filed an application in the trial court on October 10, 1967, and a hearing was held the same day. A statement of evidence was prepared by the trial court and filed in the Supreme Court on October 11, 1967.

On October 12, 1967, relator filed a motion for rehearing on his application for habeas corpus in the Supreme Court, which was granted the same day. The significant feature of the case is that the Supreme Court considered both the evidence produced at the contempt hearing and that introduced at the October 10, 1967, hearing. The Supreme Court found that relator was unable to comply with certain of the purge conditions and upheld the commitment order only as to those purge conditions which were within relator's power to perform. It is clear that we are not limited to a consideration of the evidence introduced at the contempt hearing but may consider the evidence at the subsequent hearing ordered by this Court.

Since the evidence properly before us conclusively establishes that the relator is unable to comply with the purge condition in this case, we order him discharged from custody. Our order in this case does not relieve relator of his liability for the child support arrearages.

Ex parte Shelton

Texas Court of Appeals—Dallas, 1979
582 S.W.2d 637, no writ

GUITTARD, Chief Justice.

These two applications for habeas corpus present the question of whether a provision in a divorce decree ordering one of the parties to pay future medical expenses for the children, but without specifying them or prescribing any procedure for determining the amount, is enforceable by contempt and confinement in jail. We hold that such an order lacks the certainty required for such enforcement. Accordingly, we have granted the writs applied for in both cases, and we now state the reasons for our decision.

The test of the certainty required of an order enforceable by contempt is that it must spell out the details of compliance in clear, specific, and unambiguous terms so that the person affected by the order will readily know exactly what obligations are imposed on him. *Ex parte Slavin*, 412 S.W.2d 43, 44 (Tex. 1967). By that test, neither of these decrees are sufficiently specific. In one case the relator was ordered to pay the medical and dental bills of the three minor children until they should reach the age of eighteen years. In the other, the relator was ordered to maintain a medical and hospitalization insurance policy covering the children until they should reach age eighteen and to pay, as additional child support, the premiums in such policy and all other medical and hospitalization expenses for the children not covered by insurance.

Enforcement of such provisions as these in particular cases would necessarily give rise to many questions. Are dental expenses included? Orthodontic services? Plastic surgery? Prescription or non-prescription drugs? Who determines the necessity of treatment or the level of services? To whom is payment to be made? How much time is allowed to raise the money before a contempt charge is proper? Is the party charged with contempt permitted to question the necessity of the treatment or reasonableness of the amount? Does presentation of a bill raise a presumption of necessity of treatment and reasonableness of charges? May the obligated parent be held in contempt for failure to pay a bill which has been disallowed by the insurer?

None of these questions can be determined from the decrees in question. We conclude that they do not spell out the details of compliance in such clear, specific, and unambiguous terms that persons affected by them will readily know exactly what obligations are imposed. Consequently, they are not enforceable by contempt.

Writs of habeas corpus granted.

DISCUSSION

An appropriately drafted visitation order is enforceable by contempt. This is true for both the managing conservator and the parent exercising visitation rights. *See Ex Parte*

Morgan, 886 S.W.2d 829 (Tex. App.—Amarillo 1994, no writ). If the order provides that the spouses will later agree regarding the appropriate visitation schedule or allows other informal modification of the schedule set forth in the decree, the contempt remedy is not available. *See Ex parte Brister*, 801 S.W.2d 833 (Tex. 1990).

In *Marriage of Alford*, 40 S.W.3d 187 (Tex. App.—Texarkana 2001, no pet. h.), the decree awarded the wife "200,000 miles from [the husband's] frequent flier miles with Lufthansa." Is this order enforceable by contempt?

Unclear decrees may be clarified after divorce pursuant to § 9.008 of the Texas Family Code. *Dechon v. Dechon*, 909 S.W.2d 950 (Tex. App.—El Paso 1995, no writ).

Another good enforcement mechanism for post-divorce payment obligations is security of some sort. *Winkle v. Winkle*, 951 S.W.2d 80 (Tex. App.—Corpus Christi 1997, writ denied).

In re Small

Texas Court of Appeals—Houston [14th Dist.], 2009
286 S.W.3d 525, no pet.

OPINION ON REHEARING

Relator's motion for rehearing is granted. The opinion issued on February 26, 2009, is withdrawn. This opinion is substituted in its place.

On November 25, 2008, relator, John W. Small, filed a petition for writ of mandamus in this court. *See* Tex. Gov't Code Ann. § 22.221 (Vernon 2004); *see also* Tex. R. App. P. 52. In the petition, relator asks this court to compel the Honorable Mary Nell Crapitto, presiding judge of County Court at Law No. 1 of Galveston County, to set aside her October 31, 2008 order finding relator in contempt for failing to pay court-ordered temporary spousal support to real party in interest, Murriah S. McMaster, and to reverse her November 1, 2005 order awarding temporary spousal support to McMaster. We conditionally grant the petition for writ of mandamus.

BACKGROUND

In April 2005, a jury found that relator and McMaster had entered a common law marriage on December 25, 1991. On May 17, 2005, the trial court entered an interlocutory judgment adopting the jury's finding. On November 1, 2005, after holding hearings on July 20, 2005 and September 12, 2005, the trial court signed an order directing relator to pay McMaster monthly temporary support in the amount of $4,000.00.

On March 8, 2006, the trial court held a hearing on McMaster's first motion for enforcement of temporary spousal support. On April 20, 2006, the trial court signed an order, finding relator in contempt for failing to pay temporary support from November 1, 2005 through March 1, 2006.

On May 1, 2006, relator filed a petition for writ of mandamus in this court, requesting that we direct the trial court to deny any motion for enforcement of temporary support filed by McMaster, reverse its April 20, 2006 contempt and commitment order, and modify the November 1, 2005 order for temporary support. On June 1, 2006, this court denied relator's petition for writ of mandamus.

In October 2007, the trial court held a second jury trial on issues of community property. The jury made findings regarding which properties were community property, relator's separate property, or third party property, and findings regarding the value of the community property. The jury further found that relator had committed fraud with respect to the community property rights of McMaster. On October 26, 2007, the trial court granted McMaster's motion for appointment of joint receivers. On November 8, 2007, relator filed for bankruptcy.

On February 15, 2008, the bankruptcy court entered an order granting partial relief from the bankruptcy stay. *See* 11 U.S.C.A. § 362(a)(1) (West 2004) (filing of bankruptcy petition stays commencement or continuation of judicial proceeding against debtor). The bankruptcy court modified the stay to allow the trial court to (1) enter judgment from the October 2007 trial "consistent with the evidence and the jury verdict," (2) enter a divorce between relator and McMaster, (3) determine the amount of any future support owed by relator to McMaster so long as such support is paid from relator's future earnings and not from property of the bankruptcy estate, (4) determine the amount of any monetary damages claim held by McMaster against relator, (5) enter any other order against any non-debtor parties, and (6) allocate the community estate between relator and McMaster. The order also allows any party to the underlying proceeding to "prosecute any appeal of the orders and/or judgments" of the trial court.

On October 29, 2008, the trial court held a hearing on McMaster's fifth motion to enforce in which McMaster asked the trial court to direct relator to pay the $20,000 in arrears previously ordered on April 20, 2006, and $124,000 in arrears through October 1, 2008. On October 31, 2008, the trial court entered an order, finding that relator was able to pay temporary monthly spousal support in the amount of $4,000.00 from April 1, 2006 through October 1, 2008, and is in arrears in the amount of $124,000.00 for that period. The trial court found relator in contempt for each violation and assessed confinement in Galveston County jail for 179 days, but probated the sentence for one year provided that relator paid the $124,000.00 in arrears in four installments of $31,000.00 each on or before December 1, 2008, January 3, 2009, February 2, 2009, and March 2, 2009. The trial court also assessed attorney's fees and costs in the amount of $8,694.15 against relator and directed that he pay such amount on or before March 2, 2009. The trial court further ordered relator to pay the $20,000.00 in arrears, as directed in the April 20, 2006 contempt order, and $25,000.00 in attorney's fees, as directed in the November 1, 2005 order, on or before March 2, 2009.

In his motion for rehearing, relator argues, for the first time, the October 31, 2008 contempt order is void because it violates the automatic bankruptcy stay. "Because in Texas we recognize that a judgment entered in violation of the bankruptcy stay is void for lack of jurisdiction, this is a fundamental error that can be recognized by the appellate court, sua sponte, or raised for the first time on appeal by a party." *Houston Pipeline Co. LP v. Bank of Am., N.A.*, 213 S.W.3d 418, 429 (Tex. App.—Houston [1st Dist.] 2006, no pet.). Therefore, we will address this issue.

STANDARD OF REVIEW

Because relator is not restrained, petition for writ of mandamus, rather than habeas corpus, is relator's only possible relief. *In re Long*, 984 S.W.2d 623, 625 (Tex. 1999) (orig. proceeding) (per curiam); *Rosser v. Squier*, 902 S.W.2d 962, 962 (Tex. 1995) (orig. proceeding) (per curiam). To be entitled to the extraordinary relief of a writ of mandamus, the relator generally must show that the trial court clearly abused its discretion and he has no adequate remedy by appeal. *In re Team Rocket, L.P.*, 256 S.W.3d 257, 259 (Tex. 2008) (orig. proceeding). A trial court clearly abuses its discretion if it reaches a decision so arbitrary and unreasonable as to amount to a clear and prejudicial error of law. *Walker v. Packer*, 827 S.W.2d 833, 839 (Tex. 1992) (orig. proceeding). When a challenged order is void for lack of jurisdiction, the relator is not required to establish that he has no adequate remedy by appeal. *In re S.W. Bell Tel. Co.*, 35 S.W.3d 602, 605 (Tex. 2000) (per curiam).

Section 6.502 of the Texas Family Code provides for temporary support while a suit for dissolution of a marriage is pending. Tex. Fam. Code Ann. § 6.502(a)(2) (Vernon 2006). Generally, a person who willfully disobeys a valid court order is guilty of contempt and subject to imprisonment for a prescribed period until he complies with the order. *Ex parte Hall*, 854 S.W.2d 656, 658 (Tex. 1993) (orig. proceeding). An order requiring temporary support payments is enforceable by contempt. *Id.*

BANKRUPTCY STAY

The filing of a bankruptcy petition stays:

> [T]he commencement or continuation, including the issuance or employment of process, of a judicial, administrative, or other action or proceeding against the debtor that was or could have been commenced before the commencement of the case under this title, or to recover a claim against the debtor that arose before the commencement of the case under this title.

11 U.S.C.A. § 362(a)(1). An automatic stay is triggered when a bankruptcy petition is filed, whether or not a party or the non-bankruptcy court learns of the bankruptcy prior to taking action against the debtor. *Darr v. Altman*, 20 S.W.3d 802, 806–07 (Tex. App.—Houston [14th Dist.] 2000, no pet.); *Paine v. Sealey*, 956 S.W.2d 803, 805 (Tex. App.—Houston [14th Dist.] 1997, no pet.). The automatic bankruptcy stay abates any judicial proceeding against the debtor, depriving state courts of jurisdiction over the debtor and his property until the stay is lifted or modified. *Baytown St. Bank v. Nimmons*, 904 S.W.2d 902, 905 (Tex. App.—Houston [1st Dist.] 1995, writ denied); *S. County Mut. Ins. Co. v. Powell*, 736 S.W.2d 745, 748 (Tex. App.—Houston [14th Dist.] 1987, orig. proceeding). An action taken in violation of the automatic bankruptcy stay is void, not merely voidable. *Howell v. Thompson*, 839 S.W.2d 92, 92 (Tex. 1992) (order); *Continental Casing Corp. v. Samedan Oil Corp.*, 751 S.W.2d 499, 501 (Tex. 1988) (per curiam). The terms of an order modifying the automatic stay must be strictly construed. *Stephens v. Hemyari*, 216 S.W.3d 526, 529 (Tex. App.—Dallas 2007, pet. denied) (citing *Casperone v. Landmark Oil & Gas Corp.*, 819 F.2d 112, 114 (5th Cir. 1987)).

Section 362(b)(1) provides the filing of a bankruptcy petition does not operate as a stay "of the commencement or continuation of a criminal action or proceeding against the debtor; ..." 11 U.S.C. § 362(b)(1) (emphasis added). Thus, the commencement or continuation of a criminal contempt action is not automatically stayed by filing a bankruptcy petition. *In re Wiese*, 1 S.W.3d 246, 249 (Tex. App.—Corpus Christi 1999, orig. proceeding). "'This exception is consistent with the strong federal policy against federal interference with state court criminal prosecutions.'" *In re Roussin*, 97 B.R. 130, 132 (D. N.H. 1989) (quoting 2 Collier on Bankruptcy P 362.05, at 62–44 (15th ed. 1988)). We must determine whether the order at issue is for criminal or civil contempt.

The distinction between civil and criminal contempt is based on the nature and purpose of the penalty imposed. *Ex parte Johns*, 807 S.W.2d 768, 770 (Tex. App.—Dallas 1991, orig. proceeding). In a civil contempt proceeding, the court is attempting to persuade the contemnor to obey a previous order. *Id.*; *see also Ex parte Harrison*, 741 S.W.2d 607, 609 (Tex. App.—Dallas 1991, orig. proceeding) (explaining purpose of civil contempt order is to encourage obedience). A judgment providing that a contemnor is to be committed unless and until he performs the affirmative act required by the court's order is a civil contempt order. *In re Mott*, 137 S.W.3d 870, 875 (Tex. App.—Houston [1st Dist.] 2004, orig. proceeding); *Ex parte Johns*, 807 S.W.2d at 770. Where the contemnor can avoid incarceration by obeying the court's order, the contemnor is said to "'carr[y] the keys of [his] prison in [his] own pocket.'" *Ex parte Werblud*, 536 S.W.2d 542, 545 (Tex. 1976) (orig. proceeding) (quoting *Shillitani v. U.S.*, 384 U.S. 364, 368, 86 S. Ct. 1531, 16 L. Ed. 2d 622 (1966)).

The purpose of a criminal contempt order is to punish for disobedience. *Ex parte Harrison*, 741 S.W.2d at 609. A criminal contempt order is punitive and unconditional in nature and is an exertion of the court's inherent power to punish the contemnor for a completed act that affronted the court's dignity and authority. *Ex parte Werblud*, 536 S.W.2d at 545; *Gonzalez v. State*, 187 S.W.3d 166, 170 (Tex. App. — Waco 2006, no pet.). Generally, the punishment for criminal contempt is fixed and definite; no subsequent voluntary compliance on the part of the defendant can enable him to avoid punishment for his past acts. *Ex parte Werblud*, 536 S.W.2d at 546 (quoting *Ex parte Hosken*, 480 S.W.2d 18, 23 (Tex. Civ. App. — Beaumont 1972, orig. proceeding)). The key feature that distinguishes criminal contempt from civil contempt is that its penalty is unconditional. *Ex parte Johns*, 807 S.W.2d at 771.

With regard to "criminal contempt," the October 31, 2008 order states:

Criminal Contempt

IT IS ORDERED that punishment for each separate violation is assessed at confinement in the county jail of Galveston County, Texas, for a period of one hundred and seventy-nine (179) days.

IT IS THEREFORE ORDERED that Respondent is committed to the county jail of Galveston County, Texas, for a period of one hundred and seventy-nine (179) days for each separate violation enumerated above.

IT IS ORDERED that each period of confinement assessed in this order shall run and be satisfied concurrently.

The order further probated relator's commitment for one year on the conditions that relator pay: (1) the $124,000.00 in four equal installments of $31,000.00 on December 1, 2008, January 3, 2009, February 2, 2009, and March 2, 2009; (2) pay McMaster's attorney's fees and costs in the amount of $8, 694.15 by March 2, 2009; and (3) all spousal support as ordered on November 1, 2005.

The order also set four compliance hearings, at which relator is ordered to appear, to determine whether relator has made the $31,000.00 installment payments to McMaster. The fourth compliance hearing is also to determine whether relator has made the $20,000 for support payments awarded on April 20, 2006 (the first contempt order), the $25,000.00 in attorney's fees awarded on November 1, 2005, and the $8,694.15 in attorney's fees awarded on October 29, 2008.

Even though the order states relator is being sentenced to a jail term for "criminal contempt," it also provides relator may avoid jail time by making the four installment payments to McMaster. Therefore, we conclude the order is actually a civil contempt order. *See Ex parte Werblud*, 536 S.W.2d at 545 (quoting *Shillitani*, 384 U.S. at 368) (explaining, where contemnor can avoid incarceration by obeying court's order, contemnor is said to "'carr[y] the keys of [his] prison in [his] own pocket'").

Bankruptcy courts take two approaches to determining whether a civil contempt proceeding is subject to the automatic bankruptcy stay. Some courts hold, because civil contempt is not among the exceptions found in section 362(b), such actions are considered private collection devices and come within the scope of the automatic stay. *In re Wiley*, 315 B.R. 682, 687 (E.D. La. 2004) (quoting *In re Newman*, 196 B.R. 700, 704 (S.D. N.Y.

1996)); *In re Lincoln*, 264 B.R. 370, 373–74 (E.D. Pa. 2001).[1] Other courts do not look to the civil or criminal nature of the state court proceedings, but look at the circumstances surrounding the issuance of the order of contempt to determine whether the intent of the court was (1) to enforce compliance with a court order, i.e., satisfy a judgment, or (2) to uphold the dignity of the court or simply to punish. *In re Wiley*, 315 B.R. at 687; *In re Lincoln*, 264 B.R. at 373–74. Where the contempt citation is designed to uphold an order of the court and not calculated to enforce a money judgment, i.e., pursue a "collection motive," enforcement of that order does not violate the bankruptcy stay. *In re Rook*, 102 B.R. 490, 493 (E.D. Va. 1989).

We need not decide which approach to follow because, under either, the October 31, 2008 contempt order violates the bankruptcy stay. Under the first approach, the civil contempt order is subject to the bankruptcy stay because civil contempt is not one of the enumerated exceptions found in the bankruptcy code. The contempt order also violates the bankruptcy stay under the second approach because it is designed to coerce relator's compliance with the November 1, 2005 order awarding the temporary spousal support.

Moreover, we further conclude the bankruptcy court's February 15, 2008 order for partial relief from the bankruptcy stay does not allow the trial court to enter a civil contempt order. Although McMaster may have a "monetary damages claim" against relator with regard to her claim for temporary support, the February 15, 2008 order only permits the trial court to determine the amount of such claim. The February 15, 2008 order also only allows the trial court to determine the amount of any future support owed by relator to McMaster so long as support is paid from relator's future earnings and not from property of the bankruptcy estate. McMaster sought payment for past support.

CONCLUSION

We conclude the trial court's October 31, 2008 order granting McMaster's fifth motion to enforce, and holding relator in civil contempt is void in violation of the bankruptcy stay. Accordingly, we conditionally grant relator's petition for writ of mandamus and direct the trial court to vacate its October 31, 2008 order. The writ will issue only if the trial court fails to act in accordance with this opinion.

Jenkins v. Jenkins
Texas Court of Appeals — Ft. Worth, 1999
991 S.W.2d 440, no writ

Statute of Limitations

Although Michael stopped making alimony payments on June 1, 1993, the Trustee did not move to enforce the AID until July 19, 1995. In points 14 and 15, Michael complains that the trial court erred by concluding that the Trustee was not barred by limitations from collecting any alimony payments owed before July 19, 1993.

---

1. This was the approach taken by the Corpus Christi Court of Appeals in *In re Wiese*, 1 S.W.3d at 249. In that case, the court of appeals held the civil contempt portion of an order violated the bankruptcy stay and was void, but held the criminal contempt portion of the order was not subject to the bankruptcy stay and considered the merits of the criminal contempt. *Id.*

The family code provides that a motion to enforce the division of future property not in existence at the time of the original decree must be filed within two years after the right to the property matures or accrues or after the decree becomes final, whichever is later, or the suit is barred. *See* TEX FAM.CODE ANN. §9.003(b) (Vernon 1998); *Ex parte Goad,* 690 S.W.2d 894, 896 (Tex.1985). However, the family code also allows a party who does not receive payments of money awarded in a divorce decree to sue the defaulting party for a money judgment in the amount of the unpaid payments. This remedy of reduction to a money judgment is in addition to the other remedies provided by law. *See Bowden v. Knowlton,* 734 S.W.2d 206, 207–08 (Tex. App.—Houston [1st Dist.] 1987, no writ).

The parties' AID was approved by the court and incorporated into their divorce decree; thus, the AID was enforceable as part of the decree. *See* TEX. FAM. CODE ANN. §7.006(b) (Vernon 1998) (providing that terms of AID approved by trial court are binding on court and may be incorporated into divorce decree); *McCray v. McCray,* 584 S.W.2d 279, 280–81 (Tex.1979) (holding that contractual alimony agreement approved by trial court in divorce decree was enforceable as part of decree); *Chess v. Chess,* 627 S.W.2d 513, 515 (Tex. App.—Corpus Christi 1982, no writ) (holding that property settlement agreement incorporated into divorce decree is binding as final judgment). But section 9.003(b)'s two-year statute of limitations does not apply to this case because the Trustee did not seek to compel a *division* of property via his motion to enforce. A division of property was unnecessary, because the divorce decree awarded Bee a specific amount of alimony. The Trustee merely sought a money judgment for alimony awarded but not paid, plus additional money damages for Michael's alleged repudiation of the AID. Because the Trustee sought a reduction of the specific monetary award in the AID to judgment, rather than a division of property, the Trustee's claim is not governed by section 9.003(b).

This case is analogous to *Bowden,* in which the appellant was awarded a specific amount of money in the divorce decree and later sued to enforce it. The First Court of Appeals held that the two-year statute of limitations did not apply to the appellant's claim because she sought to reduce a monetary award to judgment, not the division of property. 734 S.W.2d at 207–08.

Michael's reliance on *Goad* is misplaced. The divorce decree in *Goad* did not award the appellee a specific money amount that she later sought to reduce to judgment. Instead, the decree awarded the appellee 12/27 of the appellant's future retirement benefits. 690 S.W.2d at 895. When the appellant retired but refused to divide his retirement benefits as ordered in the divorce decree, the appellee filed a contempt proceeding. Because the appellee sought to enforce a division of future property, the Texas Supreme Court held that the two-year statute of limitations applied. *Id.* at 896. We overrule points 14 and 15.

DISCUSSION

Morales v. Morales, 195 S.W.3d 188 (Tex. App—San Antonio 2006, pet. denied) disagrees with *Jenkins.*

Williamson v. Williamson

Texas Court of Appeals—El Paso, 1999
986 S.W.2d 379, no pet.

OPINION

Charlotte Lynn Ward Williamson contends that the trial court improperly granted Ralph Ervin Williamson's motion for summary judgment.

FACTS

Charlotte and Ralph Williamson were divorced on November 7, 1995 by a final decree of divorce entered by the 318th Judicial District Court of Midland County, Texas. On appeal, Charlotte Williamson urges that the property settlement should be set aside by virtue of a bill of review. She maintains that division of the community estate was improper by reason of extrinsic fraud and fraudulent inducement. According to Charlotte Williamson's petition for bill of review, her husband threatened that if she did not sign the divorce judgment approving the settlement, he would turn all of the community property over to her because he knew she could not handle the management responsibilities. These threats occurred prior to the signing of the divorce decree. Mr. Williamson also misrepresented the health of the community estate. Throughout the entire process leading up to the divorce settlement, Charlotte Williamson was represented by counsel, and employed two accountants to assist in the divorce.

Ralph Williamson moved for summary judgment based on two theories: first, that Charlotte Williamson failed to exhaust her available remedies without sufficient excuse and therefore, had no right to an equitable action seeking a bill of review; second, that Charlotte Williamson made no prima facie showing of a meritorious defense and is barred from proceeding as a matter of law. Upon reviewing the motion for summary judgment, the trial court agreed with Ralph Williamson and granted his motion for summary judgment without specifying the theory upon which the court relied. This appeal follows.

DISCUSSION

When a trial court's order does not specify the grounds relied on for its ruling, the reviewing court will affirm the order if any theory advanced is meritorious.[1] The reviewing court considers only the evidence before the trial court at the time of the summary judgment motion hearing.[2]

Courts do not look on bills of review with favor.[3] The burden on the bill of review petitioner is heavy, as judgments must be accorded some finality.[4] A bill of review is an independent action of an equitable nature brought by a party to the former action seeking to set aside a judgment that is no longer appealable or subject to a motion for new trial.[5] A bill of review is designed to prevent manifest injustice,[6] but the fact that an injustice oc-

---

1. *Lawrence v. Lawrence*, 911 S.W.2d 443, 446 (Tex. App.—Texarkana 1995, writ denied).

2. *Id.*

3. *Law v. Law*, 792 S.W.2d 150, 153 (Tex. App.—Houston [1st Dist.] 1990, writ denied).

4. *Bakali v. Bakali*, 830 S.W.2d 251, 255 (Tex. App.—Dallas 1992, no writ).

5. *Tice v. City of Pasadena*, 767 S.W.2d 700, 702 (Tex. 1989).

6. *French v. Brown*, 424 S.W.2d 893, 895 (Tex. 1967); *Hesser v. Hesser*, 842 S.W.2d 759, 765 (Tex. App.—Houston [1st Dist.] 1992, writ denied).

curred is not sufficient cause to justify relief by bill of review.[7] Relief by bill of review is available only if a party has exercised due diligence to pursue all adequate legal remedies against a former judgment, and through no fault of its own, no adequate legal remedy was available.[8] Thus, to be entitled to a bill of review, Charlotte Williamson must show a good excuse for failure to exhaust adequate legal remedies.[9] If legal remedies were available but ignored, the equitable remedy of a bill of review will not later intervene.[10]

In this case, Ms. Williamson's failure to file a motion for new trial or regular appeal is fatal to her bill of review. Clearly, she knew of the threats by her husband because they occurred before the signing of the divorce decree. She had sufficient time to file a motion for new trial or regular appeal; however, she did not pursue those options.

Moreover, misrepresenting the value of known community assets does not alone constitute extrinsic fraud.[11] Divorce litigants commonly assert differing valuations and differing versions of facts.[12] If each party has access to the evidence that will prove or disprove an assertion, the party making the assertion has concealed nothing.[13] One purpose of divorce proceedings is to resolve the differences in the parties' perceptions or assertions of fact.[14] Charlotte Williamson, aided by her lawyer and accountants, should have known about any misrepresentations concerning the financial condition of the community estate because Ralph Williamson gave them access to the underlying financial information. Nevertheless, she did not pursue a timely appeal or new trial on that issue. The purpose of a bill of review is not to reopen litigation every time a party, upon further reflection, decides that she is dissatisfied with the result in a case.[15] The trial court correctly granted Ralph Williamson's motion for summary judgment. Appellant's sole issue before this court is overruled.

CONCLUSION

We affirm.

Phillips v. Phillips
Texas Court of Appeals—Waco, 1997
951 S.W.2d 955, no writ

OPINION

JOHN A. JAMES, JR. Justice (Retired)

Plaintiff-Appellant Royce Lourene Phillips is the former wife of Defendant-Appellee Clarence Ervin Phillips, Jr. She brought this suit against her former husband seeking partition of the proceeds from the 1990 wheat and grain-sorghum crops, asserting that since the court did not divide these crops in the divorce judgment, that she and Mr. Phillips owned the proceeds from these crops as tenants-in-common.

---

7. *Alexander v. Hagedorn*, 148 Tex. 565, 226 S.W.2d 996, 998 (1950); *Hesser*, 842 S.W.2d at 765.
8. *Tice*, 767 S.W.2d at 702; *Lawrence*, 911 S.W.2d at 447.
9. *Hesser*, 842 S.W.2d at 765.
10. *Id.*
11. *Kennell v. Kennell*, 743 S.W.2d 299, 301 (Tex. App.—Houston [14th Dist.] 1987, no writ).
12. *Id.*
13. *Id.*
14. *Id.*
15. *Id.*

Defendant Mr. Phillips moved for summary judgment, whereupon the trial court granted a summary judgment in favor of Defendant to the effect that Mrs. Phillips take nothing. The trial court's judgment did not state the basis upon which said judgment was rendered.

Mrs. Phillips appealed upon three points of error, and after she had perfected her appeal, she died intestate on November 13, 1996, and this appeal continues pursuant to Rule 9 of the Texas Rules of Appellate Procedure.

Appellant Mrs. Phillips comes to this court on three points of error, all of which assert the trial court erred in granting Appellee's Motion for Summary Judgment for the following reasons:

(1) Because the evidence shows genuine fact issues exist as to whether or not the cause was barred by the two-year statute of limitations pursuant to Sec. 3.90 of the Texas Family Code.

(2) Because under Texas law, Appellant pled and was entitled to maintain her cause of action pursuant to Sec. 23.001 of the Texas Property Code.

(3) The trial court erred if the basis for such judgment was that the wheat and grain-sorghum corps were not community property in existence at the time the divorce was granted.

We sustain Appellant's points of error one and two and accordingly reverse the trial court's judgment and remand the cause to the trial court for trial on the merits.

We revert to Appellant's first point of error wherein she contends the evidence shows genuine fact issues exist as to whether or not this case was barred by the two-year statute of limitations pursuant to Sec. 3.90 of the Texas Family Code.

Section 3.90 in its pertinent parts provides as follows:

Procedure for Division of Certain Property not divided on Divorce or Annulment.

(a) Property not divided or awarded to a spouse in a final decree of divorce or annulment may be divided in a suit under this subchapter....

(b) The suit may be brought by either former spouse.

(c) The suit must be filed before two years after the date on which a former spouse unequivocally repudiates the existence of the ownership interest of and communicates that repudiation to the other spouse....

The parties were divorced by judgment of the District Court of Navarro County, Texas, effective May 8, 1990, in which judgment the court purported to make a division of the community property belonging to the parties; however, the judgment did not mention nor divide community rights in the 1989–1990 wheat crop or the 1990 grain-sorghum crop.

Mr. Phillips states in his affidavit attached to his Motion for Summary Judgment that the 1989–1990 wheat crop was planted with community funds in the fall of 1989 (prior to the divorce judgment).

In the same affidavit Mr. Phillips stated that he did not begin seed-bed preparation for the 1990 grain-sorghum crop until May 15, 1990, and that the grain-sorghum crop was not planted until May 21 through May 27, 1990. However, he certified in his Application for Disaster Credit to the United States Department of Agriculture that he disked the land twice and planted the grain crop in April 1990 (prior to the divorce judgment).

Accordingly, on May 8, 1990, the date the divorce decree was effective, both the wheat and grain-sorghum crops were in existence and were community assets which were not divided in the divorce judgment.

Mrs. Phillips filed her original petition to partition the net proceeds from the 1989–1990 wheat crop and the 1990 grain-sorghum crop on April 14, 1994, pursuant to Sec. 3.90 of the Texas Family Code and Sec. 23.001 of the Texas Property Code.

Appellee Mr. Phillips, in his Motion for Summary Judgment, contended that the suit was barred by the two-year statute of limitations provided for in Sec. 3.90 of the Texas Family Code by reason of the fact (he asserts) that he had unequivocally repudiated Mrs. Phillips's claim for partition of the wheat and grain-sorghum crops more than two years prior to the date Appellant Mrs. Phillips filed suit. Mr. Phillips made summary judgment proof claiming the repudiation occurred on September 24, 1990. Mrs. Phillips originally filed suit on April 14, 1994.

There is a lot of summary judgment proof in the record presented by Mrs. Phillips to the effect that the unequivocal repudiation in question was not made by Mr. Phillips until January 26, 1993. In essence, her proof in this regard is as follows:

She said she learned of certain payments Mr. Phillips had received on the wheat and grain-sorghum crops and confronted him about the payments on September 25, 1990, and that he stated he was not going to pay her anything until his lawyer, Rob Dunn, said he had to; that they tried several times unsuccessfully to reach Rob Dunn by telephone; that Mr. Phillips suggested that they call James E. Cummins (another attorney); that Mr. Cummins told Mr. Phillips that Mrs. Phillips was entitled to one-half of the payments; that shortly afterward they reached Rob Dunn who also told Mr. Phillips that Mrs. Phillips was entitled to one-half of the payments; that Mr. Phillips claimed that he had received only $5,000 in payments; whereupon, after talking to Rob Dunn, Mr. Phillips wrote a check for $2,500 to Mrs. Phillips to pay her for her one-half interest of the payments which he said he had received.

In further response to Mr. Phillips's Motion for Summary Judgment, Mrs. Phillips made a second controverting affidavit in which she outlines how she later learned that Mr. Phillips had received a much greater amount of crop insurance and Federal Disaster Funds for the 1990 wheat and grain-sorghum crops than the $5,000 that Appellee Mr. Phillips claimed he had received.

In this second controverting affidavit, she sets forth five additional dates in which she confronted Mr. Phillips about the additional money that he had received on the crops, and how each time, except one, Mr. Phillips promised her he would "get back to her" about the matter. The one exception occurred on October 29, 1992, on which day she says he came to her and offered her $2,000 in final settlement of all her claims for the crop insurance and disaster payments, which sum she refused to accept.

She further swears that it was not until January 26, 1993, that Mr. Phillips told her he was not going to pay her and there was nothing she could do about it.

The controverting affidavits in the record with regard to the date on which Mr. Phillips unequivocally revoked the claims of Mrs. Phillips with reference to the crop insurance and disaster payments on the crops in question, clearly creates a genuine fact issue of a material fact, precluding summary judgment.

The duty of the court hearing the motion for summary judgment is to determine if there are any issues of fact to be tried, and not to weigh the evidence or determine its credibility, and thus try the case on the affidavits. Tex. R. Civil Proc. 166-A; *Wylie v. Reed*, 579 S.W.2d 329 (Tex. Civ. App.—Waco 1979), *affirmed* 597 S.W.2d 743.

In the case at bar, not only is a fact issue raised regarding whether or not Mr. Phillips repudiated Mrs. Phillips's claims on September 25, 1990, but also whether such a repudiation, if made on that date, was unequivocal in view of the later negotiations and settlement offer. Appellant's first point of error is sustained.

Appellant's second point of error asserts the trial court erred in granting Appellee's Motion for Summary Judgment because, under Texas law, Appellant pled and was entitled to maintain her cause of action pursuant to Sec. 23.001 of the Texas Property Code. We agree.

When Appellant and Appellee were divorced, the division of property set out in the divorce decree did not make any reference to a division of the 1990 wheat and grain-sorghum crops. Appellant Mrs. Phillips filed the instant suit for partition on April 14, 1994, seeking partition under both Sec. 3.90 of the Texas Family Code and Sec. 23.001 of the Texas Property Code.

Section 23.001 provides as follows:

Partition.

A joint owner or claimant of real property or an interest in real property or a joint owner of personal property may compel a partition of the interest or the property among the joint owners or claimants under this chapter and the Texas Rules of Civil Procedure.

It is well settled that where, as in the case at bar, a divorce decree fails to provide for a division of community property, the husband and wife become tenants-in-common or joint owners thereof. *Busby v. Busby,* 457 S.W.2d 551, 554 (Tex.1970); *Taylor v. Catalon,* 140 Tex. 38, 166 S.W.2d 102 (Tex.1942). Since this property was not partitioned at the time of the divorce, the judgment entered in the divorce suit did not preclude Mrs. Phillips from seeking a partition of the undivided community property sought to be now partitioned. *Busby v. Busby, supra.*

Even if Sec. 3.90 of the Family Code applied to bar an enforcement action under the Family Code, that section would not operate to bar an otherwise valid partition under the Property Code. *See Carter v. Charles,* 853 S.W.2d 667, 671 (Tex. App.—Houston [14th Dist.] 1993, no writ). The *right to partition is absolute.* Tex. Prop. Code § 23.001; *Ware v. Ware,* 809 S.W.2d 569, 571 (Tex. App.—San Antonio 1991, no writ).

Summary judgment proof offered by Mrs. Phillips shows that the following payments were made to Mr. Phillips relative to the 1990 wheat crop and the 1990 grain-sorghum crop:

1. From the Agricultural Stabilization and Conservation Service:
   A. Disaster Funds—1990 Wheat Crop $11,983.81
   B. Disaster Funds—1990 Grain-sorghum Crop   469.33

   TOTAL $12,453.14
2. From the Federal Crop Insurance Corporation
   A. Crop Insurance—1990 Wheat Crop $21,746.00
   B. Crop Insurance—1990 Grain-sorghum Crop   11,329.10

   TOTAL $33,075.10
3. Total of Disaster and Crop Insurance Payments $45,528.24

We sustain Appellant's second point of error.

The judgment of the trial court is reversed and remanded to the trial court for trial on the merits.

VANCE, Justice, concurring.

Although I agree with the majority's conclusion, I differ in the analysis. I agree with the disposition of point one, disagree about point two, and believe point of error three should also be sustained.

Section 3.90 of the Texas Family Code governs the division of property which was not divided on divorce. I agree that the evidence shows genuine fact issues exist as to whether this case is barred by the two-year statute of limitations under Sec. 3.90. The controverting affidavits in the record with regard to the date on which Mr. Phillips unequivocally revoked Mrs. Phillips' claim with reference to the crop insurance and disaster payments creates a fact issue, precluding summary judgment. I would sustain point one.

When an order granting a summary judgment does not specify the ground or grounds relied on, the summary judgment will be affirmed if any of the theories advanced are meritorious. *Carr v. Brasher,* 776 S.W.2d 567, 569 (Tex. 1989). The nonmoving party on appeal must negate any grounds on which the trial court could have granted the order. *State Farm Fire & Casualty Co. v. S.S.,* 858 S.W.2d 374, 381 (Tex. 1993); *Malooly Brothers, Inc. v. Napier,* 461 S.W.2d 119, 121 (Tex. 1970). As such, it is necessary that Mrs. Phillips negate all possible grounds for summary judgment. In point three, she urges that if the trial court granted summary judgment on the basis that the assets were not in existence at the time of divorce, it was error. As the majority agrees, the evidence conclusively shows that both the wheat and grain-sorghum crops were in existence and were community assets that were not divided at the time of divorce. I would sustain point three.

After sustaining points one and three, we need not address point of error two. However, if I were to consider whether Mrs. Phillips could maintain her cause of action under the Property Code, I would reject the assertion. In holding that a suit for partition can be brought alternatively under either the Family Code or the Property Code, the majority relies on *Carter v. Charles,* 853 S.W.2d 667 (Tex. App.—Houston [14th Dist.] 1993, no writ). To the extent *Carter* approves of alternative actions under the Family Code and the Property Code, I disagree. The divorce decree in *Carter* awarded each party fractional interests in parcels of real property, creating a tenancy-in-common. Section 3.90 of the Family Code applies only to property that is not divided or awarded in a final decree of divorce, so it was clearly inapplicable. Although, as in *Carter,* section 23.001 of the Property Code is applicable to most tenancies-in-common, it does not apply in this case. I say this because I believe that the legislature intended that the Family Code provide the exclusive remedy in situations where community property was not divided on divorce. Section 23.001 should not be held to be an alternative method of bringing such a cause of action. Thus, I disagree with the disposition of point two.

Chapter Seventeen

Dividing the Community Estate at Death

A. Intestacy

If a spouse does not have a will, the decedent's property passes by the intestacy rules of Texas. These rules are set forth below.

Married Man or Woman With No Child or Children
[Father and Mother Surviving]

1. SEPARATE PROPERTY

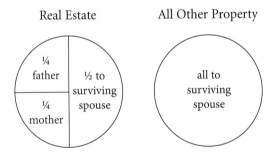

If only one parent survives, he or she takes 1/4 of the separate property real estate and 1/4 is equally divided between brothers and sisters of the deceased, and their descendants. If there are no surviving brothers and sisters, then the surviving parent takes 1/2 of the real estate. If neither parent survives, the 1/2 of the real estate is equally taken by brothers and sisters of the deceased and their descendants. If no parents and no brothers or sisters or their descendants survive the deceased, then all the real estate is taken by the surviving husband or wife. Tex. Prob. Code § 38.

2. COMMUNITY PROPERTY

All community property, real or personal, is taken by the surviving husband or wife. Tex. Prob. Code § 45.

Married Man or Woman with Child or Children

1. SEPARATE PROPERTY

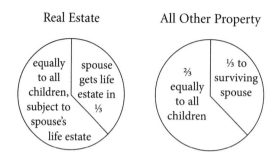

The surviving husband or wife only inherits an estate for life in one-third of the land of the deceased. Tex. Prob. Code § 38. When such surviving husband or wife dies, all of the real estate is owned by the deceased's child or children.

2. COMMUNITY PROPERTY

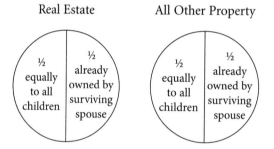

The inheritance rights of a surviving child to community property of the decedent via intestacy depend upon (I) whether the decedent and the surviving spouse executed a survivorship community property agreement and (ii) whether the surviving child is a child of both the decedent and the surviving spouse. If the spouses did not execute a survivorship community property agreement and the child is not the child of both spouses, the chart above is accurate. If the spouses signed a survivorship community property agreement, the property covered by that agreement descends to the surviving spouse. (Survivorship community property agreements are discussed in Chapter 20.) Similarly, if the surviving child is the child of both spouses, the surviving spouse inherits all the community estate of the decedent. The drafters apparently assume that the surviving spouse will at his or her death leave any remaining property to the children, as long as the surviving spouse is not a stepparent. *See* Texas Prob. Code § 45.

B. Testate Succession

A spouse has the right to devise a one-half interest in each item of community property, and all separate property owned by the decedent at death. Note that Texas is an item state. A spouse may not, without the consent of the other spouse, devise 100% of certain community property even if all community property devised has an aggregate value of less than one-half the value of the community estate.

If a spouse attempts to devise more than one-half of any item of community property, and the other spouse is devised something under the will, the spouse is put to an "election" whether to take the benefits under the will (and to permit the devise of more than 50% of the item of community property), or whether to reject the benefit under the will and take 50% of each item of community property.

Estate of Patton

Washington Court of Appeals, 1972
494 P. 2d 238

SWANSON, Justice.

Does Washington community property law prohibit a husband from devising the whole interest in any specific item of community property, notwithstanding that by the terms of his will his surviving spouse receives one-half or more of the community estate when it is considered in the aggregate? That is the primary question presented in this appeal. We answer it in the affirmative.

The respondent Mildred Patton and John George Patton were married January 6, 1937, in Vancouver, B.C. and remained husband and wife until the death of John George Patton on February 26, 1969. No children were born to this marriage. Appellants Ronald G. Patton and Eileen Patton Clark, children of the decedent by a previous marriage, appeal from the trial court's decision construing a disputed provision in their father's will and determining the validity of a gift of certain stock certificates adversely to them and in favor of respondent Mildred Patton. This appeal followed.

The dispute over the proper construction to be given the decedent's will centers upon the meaning of clauses 3 and 4 which provide as follows:

> I give, devise and bequeath all items of property which bear both my name and my wife's name, Mildred M. Patton, such as stock certificates, government bonds, bank accounts, savings certificates, insurance policies, retirement fund proceeds, real estate contracts, interest in the family home, to my wife, Mildred M. Patton.

> I give, devise and bequeath all other property to my children, Ronald G. Patton and Eileen Patton Clark, per stripes [sic] and not per capita, share and share alike.

[The court here analyzes H's intent in the foregoing provisions of his will.]

Having considered the terms of the will as a whole, as well as extrinsic evidence of the surrounding facts and circumstances, we hold that it was the intent of the testator to devise to his wife, the respondent, the whole interest in community property held jointly by him with her, and to devise to the children, the appellants, the whole interest in all other community property. In reaching this conclusion, we are mindful of the presumption that a testator must be presumed to have known the law and that he can dispose of only his half of the community property, so that such disposition must relate to his own property only. But such presumption is rebutted by our interpretation of the will and the undisputed evidence. Having so held as to the intent of the testator, such intent must be carried out if it is lawful.... In the instant case it is necessary to decide whether the testator's intent may be carried out under the community property law of this state.

It is well settled that neither spouse has testamentary power over more than his or her half of the community property. It is also clear that each spouse has an undivided one-half interest in the community property.

What has never been made explicit, however, is whether under our community property law the equal interests of husband and wife in the community property must always be manifested as a collection of undivided half interests in each specific item of community property, or whether it is sufficient to protect the equal interests of the spouses if each is guaranteed at least an undivided one-half interest in the community property when viewed in the aggregate.

Counsel for respondent Mildred Patton relies upon the well-established rule in the case of *inter vivos* gifts that a husband may not give away substantial community property without the consent or acquiescence of his wife. *Marston v. Rue*, 92 Wash. 129, 159 P. 111 (1916). The argument is essentially that inasmuch as Washington has an "item" theory for gifts during life, it must also have an "item" theory for gifts at death through testamentary disposition.

[I]t has been established that the husband must act for the benefit of the community, at least in an economic sense. *Jarrett v. Arnerich*, 44 Wash. 2d 55, 265 P. 2d 282 (1954). Consistent with this rule is the corollary rule that a husband cannot make enforceable gifts of community personal property without the consent of the wife. *Marston v. Rue, supra.* If one spouse could make *inter vivos* gifts of community property without the consent of the other, the whole of the community property would be lessened in violation of the rights of the non-giving spouse to one-half thereof.

We hold that one spouse may not designate whole interests in community property to pass by testamentary disposition to named beneficiaries, and therefore we must reject appellants' contention that such devises of whole interests in community property may be enforced so long as the other spouse's community interest is not impaired — that is, as long as it can be shown that the other spouse is guaranteed at least a one-half interest in the community estate when it is viewed in the aggregate.

Having determined that the testator purported to dispose of more than his share of community property by including the entire community estate in his plan of testamentary disposition, we are faced with the troublesome question of whether the widow must, in such circumstances, elect either to renounce her community property right in each item of property and assent to the will, or to insist upon her community interest and take independently of the will.

To create the necessity for a widow's election upon the husband's death, there must appear on the face of the husband's will a clear and unmistakable intention to dispose of property which is not in fact his own and which was not within his power of disposition. It has been determined that it is immaterial whether the testator knew the property he purported to dispose of in his will was not within his power of disposition, or whether he erroneously believed it to be, because, in either case, if the intention to dispose of it specifically appears, the necessity for an election exists.

We conclude that the respondent widow must elect to take either under the will, or independently of it.

Wright v. Wright

Supreme Court of Texas, 1955
274 S.W.2d 670

GARWOOD, Justice.

The questions in this case, arising from the will of the late David C. Wright (hereinafter called testator) involve the doctrine of election under the law of wills and the practice of summary judgment.

Generally speaking, the contending parties are, (a) the respondent here and defendant below, Mrs. May M. Wright, who was the testator's widow and an executrix and beneficiary of the will as well as community survivor with respect to virtually all property that stood in the name of the testator at his death; (b) the petitioners here and plaintiffs below, who are the other executors and beneficiaries of the will, these beneficiaries being the nephews, nieces and sisters of the testator and also James Oren Price, a ranch employee of the testator.

The will dated May 1, 1950, and set out in full in the footnote,[1] was duly probated following the death of the testator on April 30, 1952, and parties (b) above filed this suit

---

1. "WILL
"The State of Texas
"County of Hemphill
"I, DAVID C. WRIGHT, of the County of Lipscomb, and the State of Texas, being of sound mind and disposing mind and memory, and being desirous to settle my worldly affairs while I have strength to do so, do make this my last will and testament, hereby revoking all others by me heretofore made.
"1. I desire and direct that all of my just debts be paid out of my estate as soon after my death as is practical to do so having due regard to my estate and to my creditors. That all of my debts be paid out of my personal property before resorting to the sale of any of my real estate for the purpose of paying my just debts. The debts I have reference to in this paragraph are the debts I owe at the time of my death, and the last illness and funeral expenses of myself, and the expenses of probating this will, and settling up my estate. The State of Texas Inheritance Taxes, and the Federal Estate Taxes my estate may owe are to be paid by the beneficiaries named in this will in proportion to the appraised value of the share of my estate property received by each of them under this will for such State Inheritance and Federal Estate Taxes.
"2. I give devise and bequeath to my beloved sister Cecelia Hext, of Canadian, Texas, all of the following described real estate lying and being situated in Lipscomb County, Texas, to-wit: All of Section No. Seventy-seven (77) in Block No. Forty-three (43), H. & T.C. Ry. Co., Original Grantee.
"3. I give devise and bequeath to my beloved sister, Labena Beard, the wife of Ben Beard of Canadian, Texas, all of the following described real estate lying and being situated in Hemphill County, Texas, to-wit: All of Lot No. Four (4), and one-half (1/2) of Lot. No. Five (5), adjoining Lot No. Four (4), and running full length of said Lot Four (4), in Block No. Seventy (70), of the Original town of Canadian, Hemphill County, Texas. In fee simple to sell and dispose of as she may wish or see proper.
"4. I give, devise and bequeath to James Oren Price all of Section No. One Hundred (100) in Block No. Forty-three (43) H. & T.C. Ry. Co., Original Grantee, lying and being situated in Lipscomb, Texas, in fee simple, and to sell and dispose of as he may wish or see proper.
"5. All of the balance of my real estate which I now own and which I own at the time of my death I hereby declare to be the community property of myself and my wife, May M. Wright, and I hereby devise and bequeath to my beloved wife, May M. Wright, all of my community one-half of said community real estate for her natural life time, and at her death to vest in fee simple in my nephews and nieces, to-wit: Charles H. Wright, Nephew; W. R. Hext, Nephew; Wiley David Wright, Nephew; Mrs. Verdie Terrel, niece, and wife of Virgil R. Terrel, and Mrs. Marie Brown, niece, and wife of Marvin Brown, and share and share alike. In this connection my wife, May M. Wright, is hereby given the full power of sale to sell my community one-half of said community real estate along with her community one-half of said real estate for any price she may see fit and proper, and for all cash. However, should she sell my community one-half of said community real estate, then and in that event she is to invest the proceeds from my one-half of said community real estate in United States Government Bonds, and she is to have the interest from said United States Government Bonds until her death,

shortly thereafter. According to our view of their amended pleadings, they sought adjudications: (1) that the will disposes of the respondent's, as well as the testator's, interest in the community and thus confronts the respondent widow with an election between taking under it (to the exclusion of her rights as community half-owner) and repudiating the will along with whatever benefits it may afford her (thus taking only her community half under the statutes). *Smith v. Butler*, 85 Tex. 126, 19 S.W. 1083; *Dakan v. Dakan*, 125 Tex. 305, 83 S.W.2d 620; *Colden v. Alexander*, 141 Tex. 134, 171 S.W.2d 328; also *Graser v. Graser*, 147 Tex. 404, 215 S.W.2d 867; (2) that, assuming the election to be required, the respondent widow has in fact elected to reject the will; (3) that the rights of the parties under certain particular provisions of the will were as asserted by the plaintiffs; (4) that, contingent upon the respondent being bound by actual election to reject the will, certain property standing in the name of the testator at his death was either his separate property or subject to a substantial claim in favor of his separate estate for the value of improvements.

The petitioners in due course filed a motion for summary judgment seeking thereby (as we construe the motion) the abovementioned adjudications numbers (1), (2) and

---

and at her death said United States Government Bonds are to vest in fee simple in my three (3) nephews and two nieces named above herein, and share and share alike.

"6. I give, devise and bequeath unto my nephew, W. R. Hext my Diamond Finger Ring.

"7. I give, devise and bequeath to my beloved wife, May M. Wright, the following personal property, to-wit:

"(1) All of my life insurance. (2) All Government Bonds of every kind and character. (3) My automobile. (4) All household furniture and fixtures, and all chickens and poultry. All in fee simple to sell and dispose of as she may wish or see proper.

"8. It is my will and desire that all of the residue of my personal property not disposed of in paragraphs Nos. 6 and 7, of this will, after the payment of all of my just debts, including my funeral expenses, and the expenses incident to the probating of this will shall go to the following named persons, and in the following portions, to-wit:

"(1) To my beloved wife, May M. Wright, an undivided one-half interest therein. (2) To my nephew, Charles H. Wright, an undivided one-tenth interest therein. (3) To my nephew, W. R. Hext, an undivided one-tenth interest therein. (4) To my nephew, Wiley David Wright, an undivided one-tenth interest therein. (5) To my niece, Mrs. Verdi Terrell, wife of Virgil R. Terrell, an undivided one-tenth interest therein. (6) To my niece, Mrs. Marie Brown, wife of Marvin Brown, an undivided one-tenth interest therein. All in fee simple to sell and dispose of as they may wish or see proper.

"9. It is my further will and desire that should any of my nieces and nephews precede me in death, then and in that even their share of my estate herein devised and bequeathed to such niece or nieces, and nephew or nephews, who precede me in death, is to go to such deceased niece or nieces child or children, who survive them, share and share alike, but if any of my nieces or nephews who precede me in death, should die without issue of their body, then such niece or nephew who precede me in death without issue of his or her body, his or her share of my estate assets hereby devised and bequeathed to her or him in this will shall go to my surviving nieces and nephews, in fee simple, and share and share alike.

"10. I hereby constitute and appoint my wife, May M. Wright, Charles H. Wright and W. R. Hext, my nephews, joint executrix and executors of this, my last will and testament, and direct that no bond, or security be required of them as such executrix and executors.

"11. It is my will and desire that my said executors, Charles H. Wright and W. R. Hext, to be paid the sum of $ 500.00 each, out of my estate, for the performance of their duties as such executors of my estate, and this in lieu of any commissions and fees allowed by law for such services, and that they are not to be paid any other compensation for such services.

"12. It is my will that no other action shall be had in the county court in the administration of my estate than to prove and record this will and to return an inventory and appraisement of my estate and list of claims.

"In Testimony Whereof I have hereto set my hand this the 1st day of May, A.D. 1950.

"S/David C. Wright."

(3). The trial court granted the motion as to numbers (1) and (3), but refused it as to number (2). Both sides appeal, the respondent widow thereby attacking all of the court's rulings except its refusal to hold that she had actually made an election, while the plaintiffs-petitioners complained only of the latter. The Court of Civil Appeals held that genuine fact issues were involved and remanded the entire cause for a full trial. 274 S.W. 2d 414. In this court, the respondent widow defends the full remand, while the petitioners seek to restore their summary judgment and to add to it an adjudication of actual election which even the trial court refused. The issue as to whether a particular item or items of the property was separate or community (pleaded point No. 4 above-mentioned) appears to have been settled against the petitioners by their judicial admission that all of the property standing in the name of the testator at his death, except his diamond ring, was community property of himself and the respondent.

We now pass to the remaining issues, to wit, the necessity of an election and the related matters of construction of the will. As to both, we conclude that summary procedure was proper, since only law questions were involved. We further conclude the terms of the summary judgment to be correct to the extent that the will, generally speaking, requires an election, the detailed effect of such election, if made, and the effect of particular provisions of the will being as hereinafter specifically determined.

On the first question, the sole matter for determination is one of law, to wit, whether the will is "open to no other construction" than that the testator intended to dispose of property (community interests) of the respondent, as well as his own community half. If the will does not dispose of property of the beneficiary, the latter is not put to an election, but may simply take what the will gives and also take his or her own community half interest. On the other hand, if the will disposes of property of the beneficiary and at the same time gives the latter some "benefit," however small, the beneficiary cannot take the benefit under the will without accepting also the disposition it makes of his or her own property. In the latter case, where a community interest is involved, the beneficiary must accordingly elect between taking under the will, with consequent loss as well as benefit, and, on the other hand, repudiating the will and taking only his or her community half interest independently of the will. In determining whether the will disposes of property of the beneficiary, the rule is, of course, that it does not so dispose unless it is "open to no other construction." If the will is open to a different construction, that is, if it is ambiguous to this or a greater degree on the point, then, as a matter of law, the beneficiary is not required to elect, since as a matter of law his or her property is not disposed of by the will. This is the rule of all the decisions hereinabove cited.

Accordingly, in cases like the present, no fact question arises as to the actual (as distinguished from constructive) intent of the testator, since such an issue cannot exist unless the will is uncertain on the point, and that very uncertainty determines as a matter of law that no election is required. We therefore disagree with the reasoning of the Court of Civil Appeals that a fact issue was involved because parol evidence was needed to resolve ambiguity in the will. The case in this connection is therefore a proper one for summary proceedings since only the law question mentioned in the preceding paragraph is involved.

As to the merits of that question, the will, at least as to certain items of property, is open to no other construction than that it disposes of the interest of the respondent. It need not, of course, dispose of the respondent's interest in every item of the community estate in order that a case of election be presented; and, by the same token, the fact that we construe dispositions of particular items of property to include the community half of the respondent, so as to require an election, does not necessarily mean that every other disposition (concerning other property) is meant to include it. And as to particular provisions that dispose merely of the testator's interest, the respondent's interest in the same item of property is not affected by her election to accept the will.

The question of whether the benefits which the will purports to give are benefits within the doctrine of election is likewise one of law and, as before indicated, does not depend upon the value of the benefits. Nor is it to be determined by comparing them with what the statutes of descent and distribution would afford the beneficiary in the absence of a will. If such were the test, the result in a case like the present, wherein there were no children of the testator, would be to regard the will as giving the respondent merely a part of what she was already entitled to, that is, the whole community estate. This is unsound, since her right to the whole is clearly subject to the testator's right to will his half to another. The proper test, therefore, is whether the alleged benefits granted her by the will are or are not something of which she could legally be deprived without her consent. If they are, there is a benefit, which she can accept only by accepting also the burdens; if they are not there is no benefit and thus no case of election. Accordingly, a bequest to the respondent of the testator's half of all or any part of the community estate is a benefit to her, although, absent a will, she would have inherited it and everything else.

Paragraphs 2, 3 and 4 of the instant will by their terms dispose respectively of specific tracts of land "in fee simple to dispose of as she" (or he) "may wish or see proper" to each of the testator's two sisters and his ranch employee, James Oren Price. Such a disposition we have held to be open to no other construction than that the testator intended to include in the devise the community interest of the surviving spouse in the property as well as his own interest.

No less clearly did the will confer benefits on the respondent. For example, paragraph 5 gives her a life estate in "all of my community one-half" of "all of the balance of my real estate which I now own and which I own at the time of my death," and paragraph 7 either gives her the testator's half interest in government bonds and other particular items of property or it is meaningless.

The will thus requires an election. But the effect of the election, should the respondent make it or be determined upon a trial to have already made it, will not necessarily be the same as it would be under the summary judgment of the trial court. The theory of the court was evidently that, all the estate in question being community as it was, and the terms of the will generally being what they are, every disposition of property in the will was intended to include the respondent's half interest therein. The respondent's attack on the judgment seems accordingly to have been on a similar basis—that either the will forced an election by disposing of the respondent's interest in the entire estate or else it disposed of none of her interest. However, the respondent's points in the Court of Civil Appeals undoubtedly present also separate attacks on the trial court's construction of particular provisions of the will, which we must review in order that the extent and effect of the election under our view of the will may be understood and applied. The questions thus presented being of construction and therefore of law, the result of our rulings will be to reform the summary judgment where we deem it to be erroneous and sustain it otherwise.

The next point involves paragraph 5, which follows the before mentioned devises of specific tracts to the testator's sisters and ranch employee in paragraphs 2, 3 and 4, respectively, and thus clearly refers to all other lands standing in the testator's name. The judgment treated paragraph 5 as disposing of both community halves of the property in question, one of the halves thus going to the respondent in fee simple and the other to her for life with the additional privileges and responsibilities specified. The respondent's assertion that her half is not incorporated in this devise was in rebuttal of the petitioners' argument that the will required an election and is now largely immaterial, since we have held an election to be required by reason of other provisions. However, her construction of paragraph 5 is, in our opinion, clearly correct, with the result that her half interest, not being dealt with at all, is not affected by either her acceptance or rejection of the will, although rejection will mean foregoing the life estate in the testator's half.

Paragraph 6 gives the testator's diamond ring to a nephew; paragraph 7 gives to respondent the life insurance, government bonds, and other specific property; and paragraph 8 relates to "the residue of my personal property."

The trial court appears to construe paragraph 7 as disposing of both community halves of the specific property mentioned, although the effect of such construction is that the provision bequeaths in fee to respondent her own half as well as the testator's. The respondent's contrary view, like her argument concerning paragraph 5, is now immaterial as regards the requirement of an election; and it can have no significance otherwise, since the respondent's half will go to her whether she accepts or rejects the will, although rejection will, of course, entail her abandonment of the bequest of the testator's half.

Paragraph 8 was construed to dispose of both halves of the personalty residue, with the result that, by accepting the will, the respondent would receive only the same amount (one-half) which she already owned as community partner, whereas, if she is correct in her contention that the bequest deals only with the testator's half, she would be entitled to half of the testator's half (one-fourth) under the will, and could accept this one fourth and keep her own community half, thus having a total of three-fourths, without "disappointing" the will.

To uphold the court's construction is to sustain the thesis of the petitioners that the will taken as a whole disposes of both halves of the entire community estate, including the contention that the word "my" and similar possessive language, used throughout in connection with property, debts and so on, means "our" or "the interest of myself and my wife in." As previously suggested, we cannot accept this view. Although it may well be even the more probable construction, it is not the only one to which the will is open and, therefore, we must hold that it refers only to the interest of the testator except in the particular instances where we have concluded that it refers to both. Decisions reaching a contrary result relied upon other provisions in the wills there involved which required the construction there given to the possessive pronoun or its equivalent.

It also follows that the summary judgment should be affirmed to the extent that it requires the respondent widow to make an election.

DISCUSSION

In order to create an election, the court must determine that the spouse intended to devise more than 50% of an item of community property. The court will not make such a determination unless the intention of the testator is clear. So, if the will states that a third party will get "all" of a certain item of property, a court will normally interpret this as meaning all of *the decedent's interest* in the property.

If the surviving spouse is put to an election, the only properties at issue are those items of community property that the decedent devised more than a 50% interest in, as well as the items the decedent willed to the spouse. If the surviving spouse accepts the will, the devise to third parties of more than 50% of the community property items is effective, and the spouse acquires all property that was to pass to the spouse under the will. In addition, the surviving spouse retains a 50% interest in all items of community property of which the decedent did not attempt to devise more than 50%.

If the surviving spouse does not accept the will, the surviving spouse retains a 50% interest in each item of community property. All bequests to the survivor under the will are thereby renounced and pass under the residuary clause of the will. (If there is no residuary clause, or if the surviving spouse is the residuary legatee, the property passes by intestacy.) The bequest to a third party of more than 50% of any item of community property is construed as being a bequest of a 50% interest.

C. Reimbursement and Debts

The death of one spouse obviously dissolves the marriage. At dissolution, it is appropriate to consider whether any estate of the parties is entitled to reimbursement from another estate. So, before the extent of the separate and community estates is calculated, reimbursement issues should be considered.

The decedent's estate is liable for all separate debts, and one-half of all community debts. *See* Tex. Prob. Code § 156.

In *Bailey-Mason v. Mason*, 2008 WL 5158912 (Tex. App.—Dallas 2008, pet. denied) after the parties separated, the husband died. The husband's estate used separate property to improve the parties' community property home. The court treated the spouses as cotenants, and applied the rule that a cotenant must contribute toward expenses for the *preservation* of the property, but not (without consent) for expenses for *improvements*.

D. Life Insurance

Under Texas law, a life insurance beneficiary designation pursuant to a community property policy is considered an *inter vivos* gift made at the time of the designation. However, the reasonableness of the gift is determined at the time of death. If the gift is deemed reasonable, based on the need of the beneficiary, the relationship between the decedent and the beneficiary, and the amount of the policy, as compared to the total value of the community estate, the beneficiary is allowed to keep all of the policy proceeds. If the gift is deemed unreasonable, the beneficiary keeps 50% of the proceeds and the surviving spouse receives the other 50%. *See Redfearn v. Ford*, 579 S.W.2d 295 (Tex. Civ. App.—Dallas 1979, writ ref'd n.r.e.).

E. Joint Tenancy Designation

If a spouse acquires something during marriage with community funds and takes title with a third party as joint tenants, if the designation is challenged after the death of the spouse, the designation will be treated as an *inter vivos* gift. *See Krueger v. Williams*, 359 S.W.2d 48 (Tex. 1962).

F. Homestead Rights

The surviving spouse has continuing homestead rights in the parties' homestead, unless and until the homestead is abandoned. *See* Oldham, Texas Homestead Law (1991).

Chapter Eighteen

Conflicts of Law

A. Ownership of Property Outside the Marital Domicile

Under traditional conflicts principles, the spouses' property rights in personalty are determined by the law of the marital domicile. So, if a spouse earns wages while temporarily residing in another state, under the majority rule the property would be characterized under the law of the marital domicile. Courts have not devised a rule regarding how to determine the location of the marital domicile if both spouses maintain permanent residences in two different states. If children reside at one location, or if both parties spend a majority of their time at one residence, that would be the marital domicile.

Rights in realty are normally determined according to the law of the *situs* of the realty.

Tirado v. Tirado
Texas Court of Appeals—Texarkana,
1962 357 S.W.2d 468, writ dism'd

DAVIS, Justice.

Plaintiff-appellee, Merle Lewis Tirado, sued the appellant-defendant, Tom Vick Tirado, for a divorce, for partition of their community property, and asked that their separate properties be set aside to each of them. The appellant filed a cross-action but later decided not to contest the divorce. The trial court referred the issues as to the extent and nature of their separate property as well as the community property to a Master in Chancery, F. T. Baldwin, hereinafter referred to as Master. The Master heard evidence as to the identities of the properties of the parties prior to their marriage on April 5, 1956, and after the marriage to and including December 31, 1959. Later, the Master heard evidence to bring the status of the properties forward to August, 1960. Prior to her marriage to the appellant, the appellee had been the wife of Dale W. Moore who died on November 1, 1954. Under the last Will and Testament of Dale W. Moore, the appellee was named independent executrix, without bond, and she was the principal and residuary beneficiary of the large estate.

As above stated the appellee married the appellant on April 5, 1956. They separated on July 21, 1959.

A final judgment was entered on February 14, 1961, granting appellee a divorce and awarding certain properties to each of them as their separate property, and dividing the other property of the parties as community property. Both the appellant and appellee excepted to the judgment of the trial court as to the division of the property and each perfected an appeal.

The appellee brings forward six counterpoints of error and three points of error and one proposition. The six counterpoints of error challenge the seven points of error brought forward by the appellant. By her points of error and proposition, she challenges the judgment of the trial court as to awarding the appellant one-half (1/2) interest in and to the 660 shares of stock in the 885 Park Avenue Corporation, the lease, improvements and the furnishings contained in the apartment in New York.

Appellant takes the position that the sale of the oil and gas from the separate estate of the appellee that is situated in Louisiana became community property. Appellant admits that at the date of the marriage that the appellee owned extensive oil and gas interests lying wholly within the State of Louisiana. The property is actually a working interest in and to certain oil and gas leases situated in Louisiana. It was the separate property of the appellee on the date of marriage, and which she owned and held at the date of the judgment. During the marriage, the production of the oil and gas was sold to various companies and the proceeds from the sale thereof were deposited in the First City National Bank at Houston, Texas, in the name of Dale W. Moore, Production Account. From the date of the marriage to the date of divorce, there was produced and sold from the Louisiana leases large quantities of oil and gas. During said marriage, there was produced oil and gas from lands in Texas. During the marriage relation, monies were withdrawn from the production account for living expenses, and to pay a salary to the appellant of $1,750.00 per month. There was also withdrawn from the production account expenses to pay for appellee's portion of the production cost of the oil and gas, insurance, etc. On the date of the judgment, there was a small amount of money in the production account. The balance was accounted for.

The appellant takes the position that he is entitled to one half (1/2) of all the production on the oil and gas in both Louisiana and Texas because of the commingling of the funds from the sale of the oil and gas in Louisiana with that which was produced in Texas. Appellee takes the position that the property was her separate property on the date of the marriage, that the sale of the oil and gas was actually a sale of movable personal property and the cash received by a married woman domiciled in Texas and deposited in a Texas bank from oil and gas leases situated in Louisiana was and is her separate property. Oil and gas in place in Louisiana is a part of the realty and is so classified by Title 9, Section 1105 of the Louisiana Statutes. But, oil and gas, both by the law of Louisiana and Texas, becomes personal property upon its production and severance.

Oil and gas that has been produced from the realty becomes movable property and in this case, the separate property of the appellee, under the laws of Texas. The appellant and the appellee were married in Texas, lived and resided in Texas during their entire married life, the contract to marry was entered into in Texas, and there were no agreements, anti or postnuptial, shown by the record, as to what was to become of the separate property of the appellee. The income from the appellee's properties for the sale of the oil and gas produced and severed, constituting her personal property, a part of her separate estate, was sold and the purchaser became indebted to her and paid their debts to her in Houston, Harris County, Texas; not in Louisiana.

Under the evidence in the case, the oil and gas, after it was produced from the realty, was movable personal property. That being true, the Conflict of Law rules apply and determination of its status as separate property, or community property, is made by the law of the state of the domicile of the parties. The Statutes and Codes of Louisiana which appellant seeks to have enforced have no extra-territorial effect. The Statutes and the Codes are contrary to the laws of Texas, and the Texas courts will refuse to go against or contrary to such statutes or codes and will enforce its own law as a matter of public policy.

The statutes and codes and judicial decisions of Louisiana upon which the appellant relies are contrary to the law and public policy of Texas. Therefore, the personal movable property and all income, profits, fruits and benefits arising from the Louisiana property of appellee, together with all Louisiana property which the law constitutes movable, will fall as separate or community as the laws of Texas dictate.

Speer's Third Edition on *Law of Marital Rights in Texas* on Conflict of Laws, agrees with the above holdings. *See* Sections 29, 58, 75 and 83. From the beginning of the history of our Texas courts down to the present time, there are cases that show how deeply imbedded is the public policy of this State as to the rule of a wife's separate property from which the Texas courts have never deviated.

Most courts and writers agree that the law of the domicile should control. Stumberg 2d Edition, *On Conflict of Laws*, 312; Restatement Sec. 289; 11 Tex. L. Rev. 53. There is eminent authority for the proposition that the law of the domicile controls as to property rights in movables owned at the time of the marriage, during the marriage and at the time of the judgment of divorce. Stumberg 2d Edition, *On Conflict of Laws*, 313. As hereinabove stated, the contract of marriage was created in Texas. The rights, or better, the legal relation arising out of its creation, depend upon the laws of Texas and as vested rights should be given effect. Stumberg 2d Edition, *On Conflict of Laws*, 226.

One of the various articles of the Louisiana Civil Code upon which the appellant relies has to do with property of people who contract a marriage in the State of Louisiana. The cases bearing on the subject will show that the Louisiana courts have consistently treated Article 2400 of the LSA-Civil Code as being the premise for the existence or nonexistence of a community of equates and gains, and have treated Article 2402 LSA-Civil Code as setting out the basis by which property comes into the community. Article 2399 of the LSA-Civil Code begins with this phrase: "Every marriage contracted in this State." For decisions of the Courts of Louisiana *see The Succession of Watkins*, 156 La. 1000, 101 So. 395; *Kittredge v. Grau*, 103 So. 723; *Smith v. Gloyd*, 182 La. 770, 162 So. 617, and *Succession of Robinson*, 23 La.Ann. 174.

Appellant's contention that the operation of the oil and gas interest in Texas and Louisiana was the operation of a business is not only contrary to the evidence, the findings of the Master, and the trial court; but, also, is immaterial to the determination of the status as separate or community for monies received for oil and gas from appellee's separate property. Actually, the appellee did not own the oil and gas lease from which the oil and gas was produced. She owned a working interest therein. Other properties in Texas produced oil and gas and she received a portion thereof. Dale W. Moore, during his lifetime had acquired the property. By his Will, it was transferred to the appellee. The Master found from the evidence that the appellant and the appellee were non-operators of the working interest and that no labor, effort or talent was required of them other than to deposit the receipts from the oil and gas and pay the expenses in connection with their production. The findings were adopted by the trial court. The evidence is sufficient to support the actions of the Master and of the trial court. Article 4614 Tex. Rev. Civ. Stat. Appellee had the right of the sole management, control and disposition, both real and personal.

The finding of the Master, adopted by the trial court, that the production account did not at any time become so commingled with community funds as to make applicable the presumption contained in art. 4619, T.R.C.S., that the funds on deposit were not community funds, is supported by the evidence. The appellee sustained the burden of establishing, by satisfactory evidence, that the assets acquired after marriage with funds from the production account were the separate property of the appellee. This having been done, it then became the duty of the appellant to produce some evidence to show otherwise. This the appellant failed to do.

The Master made findings of fact pertaining to the stock in the 885 Park Avenue Corporation and improvements and furnishings contained in the New York apartment. The Master found that appellee purchased 660 shares of stock of 885 Park Avenue Corporation; that the appellant requested that in payment therefor checks be drawn on the production account; that the improvements and furnishings were all paid for out of the production account, the separate property of the appellee. The Master further found that after the purchase of the property and the status of the property had become fixed as appellee's separate property, then a contribution of $10,000.00 from the community estate for improvements or furnishings was made. The Master further found, from the evidence introduced, that it was the intention and understanding of both the appellant and the appellee that the stocks purchased, the lease, the improvements and furnishings, were the separate property of the appellee.

By the testimony by Miss Lewellen, and by appellee's checks, it was established beyond all doubt that all of the money that was paid for the stock was paid by checks drawn on the production account of the appellee and was her separate property. The stock was purchased by appellee's separate funds, and she intended it to be her separate property at the time of purchase. Its status as appellee's separate property was established.

Concerning the improvements and furnishings located in the New York penthouse apartment, appellee carefully traced by the testimony of Miss Lewellen, the testimony of Mr. Greer, the admissions of appellant, and appellee's exhibits before the Master, and showed them to be appellee's separate property.

Appellant made no effort to refute or dispute the amount of money used to acquire the shares of stock in the New York apartment, improvements and furniture. His sole claim that these properties were community is based upon his contention that the production account funds were community funds. We cannot agree with this contention.

The appellee owned an excessively large estate at the time of her marriage. The appellant owned a considerable amount of separate property. At the time of the divorce, he had some four bank accounts and quite a few shares of stock. We are not impressed with his attitude and contention in the trial of the case. The appellee had spent large sums of money during their marriage for the support of the community estate, and had paid the appellant a salary of $1,750.00 per month for doing nothing. There was nothing said about what he used the $1,750.00 per month for, nor where it went. From the evidence in the case, the appellant received by far more than his just and fair share of the property of the parties. The judgment of the trial court was in error in awarding to the appellant one-half interest in the shares of stock and the furniture and fixtures in the New York apartment.

The judgment of the trial court insofar as any contention of any error is made by the appellant, is affirmed.

We hold, from the evidence and admissions in the case, that the 660 shares of stock in the 885 Park Avenue Corporation in New York, and the furniture and fixtures in the apartment should be the separate property of the appellee; and, that the appellant should be entitled to a judgment for 1/2 of the $10,000.00 that was invested out of the community funds in the furniture and fixtures that were placed in the New York apartment. That part of the judgment is hereby reversed and remanded to the trial court for further proceedings.

DISCUSSION

Tirado is an example of traditional "vested rights" conflict of laws analysis. Under this approach, it can be quite important whether the court considers the issue one involving "personalty" or "realty."

Why did the husband's lawyer argue that the wife's oil and gas interests constituted a business?

In *Commissioner v. Skaggs*, 122 F.2d 721 (5th Cir. 1941) the court attempted to characterize the nature of rents received during marriage by a married Texas resident from separate property realty located in California. Under California law, rents and profits from separate property are separate property. The court concluded that this was an issue pertaining to realty and applied California law, so the rents were the husband's separate property.

To date, when a resident of a common law state has used wages earned during marriage to buy Texas realty, Texas courts have traditionally concluded that the realty is the spouse's separate property, and the other spouse has no rights in it. *See Huston v. Colonial Trust*, 266 S.W.2d 231 (Tex. Civ. App.—El Paso 1954, writ ref'd n.r.e).

Texas has recently adopted the "most significant relationship" approach to choice of law issues. *See Duncan v. Cessna Aircraft Co.*, 665 S.W.2d 413 (Tex. 1984). It is unclear whether this will change the rules set forth above.

Ossorio v. Leon

Texas Court of Appeals—San Antonio, 1985
705 S.W.2d 219, no writ

REEVES, Justice.

This is an appeal from a summary judgment wherein it was held that the disbursal of funds deposited in a Texas bank by a citizen of Mexico was governed by the law of Texas.

Appellant, Edna Probert Ossorio (Ossorio) and her husband, General Adolfo Leon Ossorio, citizens of the Federal District of Mexico, deposited funds in the International Bank of Commerce of Laredo. The account provided that all deposits would be owned by the depositors as joint tenants with the right of survivorship. After the death of General Ossorio, appellant's attempt to withdraw the funds was challenged by appellees, two children of the General by prior marriages, who contended they were entitled to a portion of the funds under the descent and distribution laws of the State of Texas. After the Bank interpled the funds, appellant and appellees moved for summary judgment and the court granted appellees' motion.

Appellant's pivotal ground of error is that the trial court erred when it applied Texas law instead of the law of Mexico to determine the ownership of the certificates of deposit.

. . . .

The procedural and evidentiary issues aside, the remaining issue is the ownership of the certificates of deposit. Ownership depends on the validity of the interspousal gift. The validity of the gift depends on whether Texas law or Mexico law is applicable. If Texas law is applicable, the gift is invalid, regardless of intent of the donor, and the estate of General Ossorio owns half of the funds deposited in the Texas bank. *See Hilley v. Hilley*, 161 Tex. 569, 342 S.W.2d 565 (1961). If the law of Mexico is applicable, the gift is valid and complete upon the death of the donor spouse, and the appellant owns the entire sum as her separate property. Appellee asserts that the law of the state in which the contract was made should govern the contract. Appellant argues that the law of the domicile of the parties should be applied.

Based on the following uncontroverted facts, we conclude that Mexico's law governs the ownership of this property:

(1) The Ossorios were citizens of the Federal District of Mexico, and had resided in Mexico during their forty-two year marriage.

(2) The property in controversy consists of proceeds of the liquidation of properties held by the Ossorios during their marriage. None of the certificates of deposit was purchased with funds earned in Texas.

(3) The funds were deposited in the name of Adolfo Leon Ossorio or Edna Probert Ossorio, and the signature card read "Joint Account — Payable to Either or Survivor."

(4) General Ossorio's Will provided that on his death, his wife would own all his property if she survived him. The Will made no provision for the appellees.

(5) No party to this suit (after the bank's interpleader was severed and settled) is a Texas citizen or domiciliary.

In choice of law questions dealing with ownership of personal property, as between spouses, the *rule of domicile* predominates. *King v. Bruce*, 145 Tex. 647, 201 S.W.2d 803, 809 (1947).

In *King v. Bruce*, spouses who were Texas citizens and domiciliaries took property characterized in Texas as community property to New York for the declared purpose of avoiding the effects of Texas law, and there entered an agreement in an attempt to partition certain personal property so that the wife could hold her share of the property as her sole property for her benefit and enjoyment in Texas. The court held that notwithstanding the rule regarding the place of the contract, the rule of domicile predominated.

There is uncontroverted evidence that the Ossorios were citizens and domiciliaries of Mexico. They took property that was characterized in both Mexico and Texas as community property and deposited it in a Texas bank, each contracting at that time to make a gift to the other in the event of one's death. Her use and enjoyment of the funds would be in Mexico, not Texas. The Ossorios' motive could not have been to avoid the effects of Mexico's community property laws, because the contract they attempted to make was quite permissible in Mexico. Thus, the summary judgment proof established that all of the contacts considered significant in *King v. Bruce* were contacts between the Ossorios and Mexico, not between the Ossorios and Texas.

Finally, appellees contend that where there is a conflict of laws issue, the place where the contract was made determines which law will be controlling. Their contention ignores the recent case of *Duncan v. Cessna*, 665 S.W.2d 414 (Tex. 1984). The *Duncan* court establishes that the rule that the validity of a contract is governed by the laws of the place where the contract was made has been abandoned in favor of the "most significant relationship" rule as set forth in Section 6 of the *Restatement (Second) of Conflict of Laws* (1971).[1] "[I]n all choice of law cases, except those contract cases in which the parties have

---

1. (1) A court, subject to constitutional restrictions, will follow a statutory directive of its own state on choice of law.

(2) When there is no such directive, the factors relevant to the choice of the applicable rule of law include

(a) the needs of the interstate and international systems,

agreed to a valid choice of law clause, the law of the state with the most significant relationship to the particular substantive issues will be applied to resolve that issue." *Duncan v. Cessna*, at 421.

Here, the parties agreed to no valid choice of law clause. The resolution of this matter will have no effect whatsoever on the State of Texas or any of its citizens. The bank no longer has an interest in the lawsuit. Whether the bank pays the money to the appellant or the appellees is of no consequence to the bank or to the State. Also, the Ossorios' justified expectations deserve to be protected. Thus, the Ossorios have established the State of Mexico has a more significant relationship to the issue of ownership than the State of Texas. We consequently hold, based on *King v. Bruce* and *Duncan v. Cessna*, that the gift made to appellant was valid under the laws of Mexico, and that the laws of Mexico should apply.

G. W. Equipment Leasing, Inc. v. Mt. McKinley Fence Co., Inc.

Washington Court of Appeals, 1999
982 P.2d 114

This appeal presents the question whether an Arizona husband may enter into a contract in Washington which obligates his community property when, under Arizona law, he could not bind the community because his wife had not signed the contract as a party. We conclude that Arizona law applies in this situation and reverse the trial court's entry of summary judgment in favor of G.W. Equipment Leasing, Inc.

FACTS

In August 1995, Washington corporations Mt. McKinley Fence Co. and G.W. Equipment entered into a leasing agreement which provided that it would be "governed by and construed at all times by the laws of the state of Washington." As security for this lease, Edward Lindstrom, Mt. McKinley's sole shareholder, signed a guaranty agreement which personally bound him to "each and every covenant and obligation" under the lease. The guaranty agreement itself reflects that Lindstrom signed and his wife Georgia witnessed the agreement in Scottsdale, Arizona, where they live.

Mt. McKinley eventually defaulted on the leasing contract, and G.W. Equipment brought suit in Washington against Mt. McKinley, Lindstrom, and "his marital community." In response to G.W. Equipment's second summary judgment motion, Lindstrom admitted liability to G.W. Equipment for the claimed amounts, but contended that neither the Lindstrom[1] marital community nor Georgia Lindstrom was liable for this debt. The trial court granted G.W. Equipment's motion for summary judgment and entered judgments against McKinley, Lindstrom and the marital community, ruling that "Washington law applies to the interpretation and governance of defendant Lindstrom's guaranty

---

(b) the relevant policies of the forum,
(c) the relevant policies of other interested states and the relative interests of those states in the determination of the particular issue,
(d) the protection of justified expectations,
(e) the basic policies underlying the particular field of law,
(f) certainty, predictability and uniformity of result, and
(g) ease in the determination and application of the law to be applied.
1. "Lindstrom" refers collectively to Mt. McKinley and Lindstrom.

contract with plaintiff, and there is jurisdiction in Washington over the marital community." This appeal followed.

DISCUSSION

In his "jurisdictional challenge," Lindstrom contends that the trial court had no authority to enter a judgment binding his marital community because (1) a marital community cannot be a "party" against whom judgment may be entered under CR 54, (2) the trial court did not have personal jurisdiction over Georgia Lindstrom, and (3) "jurisdiction over one nonresident spouse is not sufficient to confer jurisdiction in Washington over either the other spouse or the 'marital community,' where the law of the domicile of that community bars community liability on the type of debt at issue." Later in his brief, Lindstrom clarifies that the crux of his argument is that he "does not have the power unilaterally to bind the community under Arizona statute." Washington law supports this contention.

Washington and Arizona community property statutes similarly provide that a debt incurred by one spouse while acting for the benefit of the marital community is a community obligation, regardless of whether or not the other spouse approves it.[2] Arizona, however, restricts this power with respect to guaranty agreements, the transaction at issue in this case, by requiring that both spouses sign these agreements in order to bind their marital community.[3] The Arizona statute was enacted to ensure that the marital community will be bound "only by consent of the community." Lindstrom analogizes his Arizona marital community to a principal/agency relationship and contends that, because Arizona law would not allow him to enter into a guaranty agreement without Georgia's express consent and because Georgia signed the contract "as a witness, not as a binding party," she is not legally bound by her husband's "unauthorized act."[4]

G.W. Equipment responds that "traditional choice of law principles dictate that Washington law will apply the [g]uaranty." G.W. Equipment is correct that in the absence of an effective choice of law by the parties, the validity and effect of a contract will be governed by the law of the state having the most significant relationship with the contract. But in *Potlatch No. 1 Fed. Credit Union v. Kennedy*,[5] the Washington Supreme Court recognized that, depending on the ultimate issue being considered, some contacts are more significant than others:

"Application of [the significant relationship] principle does not involve merely counting the contacts. Rather these contacts are guidelines indicating where the interests of particular states may touch the transaction in question. For instance, the state of contracting (the place where the last act necessary to create a binding contract was performed)

---

2. *See* RCW 26.16.030; A.R.S. §§ 25-214 and 215. Both parties agree that the leasing agreement benefited the Lindstrom marital community.

3. A.R.S. sec. 25-214 provides that "[e]ither spouse separately may acquire, manage, control, or dispose of community property, or bind the community, except that joinder of both spouses is required in any of the following cases ... Any transaction of guaranty, indemnity, or suretyship."

4. As an initial matter, G.W. Equipment argues that the choice of law provision in the leasing agreement is dispositive because "parties may legally contract to be bound by the law of either jurisdiction...." *Escrow Serv. Co., v. Cressler*, 59 Wash.2d 38, 42, 365 P.2d 760 (1961). But as Lindstrom points out, Georgia was not a party to the original leasing agreement. Although Washington courts have not addressed this issue, Arizona courts hold that choice of law provisions in leases are not controlling on related guaranty agreements which describe duties and obligations of different people. *Phoenix Arbor Plaza, Ltd. v. Dauderman*, 163 Ariz. 27, 785 P.2d 1215 (1989). This is a logical approach.

5. 76 Wash.2d 806, 459 P.2d 32 (1969).

may be relatively insignificant unless it is also the state of the domicile of the parties ... in which case that state may have some real interest in protecting its residents or policing acts occurring within its borders...."[6]

In *Potlatch,* the court analyzed the community liability of a Washington couple on an Idaho debt incurred by the husband alone. It identified significant contacts and considered "the interests and policies" of Washington and Idaho along with the expectations of the parties. After noting that Washington's community property system "constitutes the most important element of married women's property rights," the *Potlatch* court concluded that "[t]he wife's rights to her share of the community property, and the concurrent restrictions on the husband's power to manage that property, are basic to Washington law."[7] Implicit in the *Potlatch* court's comments and holding is that when management of community property is at issue, the state with the most significant interests is typically the state where the spouses reside.[8]

In *Colorado National Bank v. Merlino,*[9] this court reached a similar conclusion in a case involving a Washington man who executed a Colorado real estate agreement without his wife's knowledge or consent, contrary to RCW 26.16.030(4) requiring joinder for real estate transactions. After pointing out that RCW 26.16.030(4) is "designed to restrict the legal authority of a Washington spouse to contract to purchase real property without the joinder of the other spouse, and its protections are appropriately the concern of the law of the domicile[,]" the court held that "[s]ince Gary Merlino was acting outside his authority under RCW 26.16.030(4), his attempt to act for the community benefit and bind the community had no effect."[10] This reasoning applies directly here because RCW 26.16.030(4) is the Washington analogue to Arizona's A.R.S. sec. 25-214. The Legislatures of both states decided to enact statutory joinder requirements to protect community property within their borders. In *Merlino,* the court determined that these restrictions do not evaporate when a spouse crosses the border into another state. Although this case deals with an Arizona marital community instead of a community domiciled in Washington, its underlying reasoning applies with equal force to this case.

As evidenced by *Potlatch* and *Merlino,* Washington courts apply Washington law to determine the rights and authority of Washington spouses to enter into contracts affecting their community property. For Washington courts to conclude that residents of other community property states are bound by Washington community property law as well,

6. *Id.* at 810, 85 P. 102.

7. *Id.* at 813, 88 P. 433. The court also endorsed the California Supreme Court's observation that: "disabilities to sue and immunities from suit because of a family relationship are more properly determined by reference to the law of the state of the family domicile. That state has the primary responsibility for establishing and regulating the incidents of the family relationship and it is the only state in which the parties can, by participation in the legislative processes, effect a change in those incidents. Moreover, it is undesirable that the rights, duties, disabilities, and immunities conferred or imposed by the family relationship should constantly change as members of the family cross state boundaries during temporary absences from their home." *Id.* (quoting *Emery v. Emery,* 45 Cal.2d 421, 428, 289 P.2d 218, 223 (1995)).

8. *See also Pacific Gamble,* 95 Wash.2d 341, 622 P.2d 850, where the Washington Supreme Court determined that Colorado law should apply where a Colorado couple signed a promissory note in Colorado which related to a Colorado business, but then moved to Washington after defaulting on the note. Under those facts, it was more reasonable to conclude that, although the couple resided in Washington at the time of the action, Colorado had a more significant relationship with the contract, and the couple's rights were governed by Colorado law at the time they signed the note.

9. 35 Wash.App. 610, 668 P.2d 1304, review denied, 100 Wash.2d 1032 (1983).

10. *Id.* at 620, 621, 99 P. 101.

rather than the law of their own state, would be illogical and unjust. The Arizona Legislature has enacted a statute which prohibits one spouse from entering into guaranty contracts without the other spouse's consent. Arizona spouses, therefore, may not alter the rights and liabilities of their marital communities, irrespective of the protective policies of their domiciliary states, by choosing to contract in another forum and contractually consenting to the application of that forum's laws.

Although not controlling here, Arizona courts have adopted this approach. In *Lorenz-Auxier Financial Group, Inc. v. Bidewell*,[11] the Arizona Court of Appeals considered the question of whether an Oregon husband's separate debt in Arizona could be charged to his marital community when Oregon law does not permit community obligation on separate debt. After observing that "the property rights of a husband and wife are governed by the law of the couple's matrimonial domicile at the time of the acquisition of the property [,]" the court held that Oregon law should apply. It found "no authority in Arizona or Oregon that permits one spouse, acting extraterritorially without the other spouse's consent, to enlarge his dispositional power over the other spouse's property beyond the limits imposed by the law of the domiciliary state." It added that the noncontracting spouse "obtained a measure of protection through these statutes that her husband could not unilaterally sign away." Although "[h]er husband may have agreed that he would be bound by Arizona law, [ ]he did not thereby bind his wife." The court went on to speculate about the issue presented in this case, noting that if the reverse conclusion were true, one spouse "could defeat Arizona's protective requirement that both spouses must consent when binding community property to guarantee a third party's obligation, A.R.S. sec. 25-214(C)(2)."

Having determined that Arizona law should govern the question of whether Lindstrom's marital community was bound by his execution of the guaranty agreement, the next question is whether, under Arizona law, Georgia ratified the agreement by signing it as a witness.[12] G.W. Equipment contends that even if Arizona law applies, Georgia's signature is evidence of her ratification of the agreement. In *All-Way Leasing, Inc. v. Kelly*, the Arizona Court of Appeals addressed a creditor's argument that a wife ratified her husband's lease agreement by having a general knowledge of its terms and accepting its benefits. The court stressed that although Arizona law permits joinder by ratification, courts "must … be cautious when applying the general law of ratification to cases arising under A.R.S. sec.25214(C), which is intended to protect the marital community."[13] The court explained that the statute "draws a bright and readily understandable line: one who wishes to bind a marital community in a statutorily designated transaction must get both spouses to sign.… This clear policy would be circumvented, and the bright line of required joinder blurred, if the courts too readily permitted ratification to be inferred." G.W. Equipment, as the party moving for summary judgment, had the burden of producing evidence sufficient to support its inference that Georgia signed with full knowledge of the contract's contents. Because it did not provide such evidence, we cannot accept its argument that Georgia acquiesced to the guaranty's terms. Although there are two reasonable inferences which could be drawn from Georgia's signing the agreement, we must view these inferences in the light most favorable to Lindstrom, the non-moving party.

---

11. 160 Ariz. 218, 772 P.2d 41 (1989).

12. G.W. Equipment's estoppel argument fails because there is no evidence that G.W. Leasing relied on an understanding that the Lindstrom marital community would be obligated by the lease. *See All-Way Leasing, Inc. v. Kelly*, 182 Ariz. 213, 217, 895 P.2d 125, 129–30 (1994).

13. *Id.* at 216, 125 P. 816.

Because Arizona law applies to this contract, and because G.W. Equipment has failed to meet its burden of proving that Georgia ratified the guaranty agreement, we reverse and remand for further proceedings consistent with this opinion.

B. Migrant Spouses

Spouses increasingly do not remain in one state throughout the marriage. Family lawyers must have some familiarity with how courts characterize property the couple acquired while domiciled in another state.

1. Change of Domicile From Community Property to Common Law State

Quintana v. Ordono
Florida Court of Appeals, 1967
195 So. 2d 577

HENDRY, Chief Justice.

Plaintiffs, children of the deceased by a prior marriage, sought a declaratory decree to determine the rights of the defendant widow, and the estate of the deceased in certain property. The chancellor granted the plaintiff's motion for summary decree and found that the property was solely owned by the deceased at the time of his death. He therefore decreed that the estate of the deceased is now the owner of the property and the widow Carmen Campos de Quintana has no right, title or interest in the property except such interest as may be set off to her by the County Judge's Court of Dade County, Florida under the probate laws of Florida.

There is no substantial conflict as to the material facts. The defendant and the deceased were married on September 10, 1936, in Oriente Province in Cuba. Both parties were Cuban Nationals. Under the then existing laws of Cuba the marriage was under the regime of "Sociedad de Gananciales," a form of community property marriage. The deceased had no assets at the time of his marriage. The husband and wife were domiciled in Cuba until 1960. A Florida domicile was established when the couple moved here in 1960. They remained in Florida up to the time of the husband's death on September 1, 1962. The husband died intestate.

On or about June 12, 1952, the husband purchased for $50,000.00, five thousand shares of Okeelanta Sugar Refinery, Inc. stock, a Florida corporation. An additional five thousand shares was acquired for $50,000.00 on October 30, 1958. On December 29, 1961, as a result of a ten-for-one stock split, these shares were exchanged for one hundred thousand shares.

On October 1, 1963 [sic], the husband received the promissory note of Stewart Macfarlane, then President of Okeelanta Sugar Refinery, Inc., payable to the husband in the amount of $810,000.00 and a contract for additional monies from Macfarlane for the alleged sale of the one hundred thousand shares.

The interest of the estate of the deceased and the widow in the promissory note and contract are the subject of this action.

Paragraph 1401, Civil Code of Cuba provides:

1401. To the Society of gains belong:

1. Property acquired by onerous title, during the marriage, at the expense of community property, whether the acquisition is made for the community or for only one of the consorts....

2. That obtained by the industry, salaries or work of the consorts or of either of them.

3. The fruits, rents, interests collected or accrued during the marriage, and which came from the community property, or from that which belongs to either one of the consorts.

Initially, it must be determined what interest, if any, the widow had in the one hundred thousand shares of Okeelanta Sugar Refinery, Inc. stock.

The plaintiffs submitted an affidavit that the husband came to Florida in 1951 to act as plant manager and supervise the operation of the Okeelanta Sugar Refinery, Inc. Further, that from 1951 until the time of his death in 1963, almost all of the husband's income and assets were acquired in Florida. It is also alleged that as an inducement to continue working in Florida, the husband was given an opportunity to buy stock in Okeelanta Sugar Refinery, Inc., and, that while he was employed in Florida, the husband returned to Cuba for weekends and other occasional visits.

The defendant submitted an affidavit which indicated that the source of the purchase price of the stock was from profits and salaries of enterprises within Cuba, and a loan on an estate in Cuba.

Whether the source of the purchase price of the stock was from enterprises within Cuba or Florida is not material. What is material and not in conflict is that the husband and wife were domiciled in Cuba at the time of the acquisition of the stock.

As plaintiffs contend, the law of the *situs* has primary control over property within its borders. However, by the almost unanimous authority in America, the "interests of one spouse in movables acquired by the other during the marriage are determined by the law of the domicile of the parties when the movables are acquired." This rule is applicable where the money used to purchase the movables is earned from services performed in a place other than the place of the domicile. We accept this rule, founded on convenience, as the only logical method of determining marital interest in movables.

Therefore, under the laws of Cuba the stock did not vest in the husband but in the "Sociedad de Gananciales." Thus, the wife had a vested interest in the stock equal to that of her husband.

The interest which vested in the wife was not affected by the subsequent change of domicile from Cuba to Florida in 1960.

While domiciled in Florida, the husband allegedly sold the stock and received in exchange therefor the promissory note and contract with which we are concerned.

Since the promissory note and contract were acquired while the husband and wife were domiciled in Florida, this transaction is controlled by our law.

Under Florida law, if a portion of the consideration belongs to the wife and title is taken in the husband's name alone, a resulting trust arises in her favor by implication of law to the extent that consideration furnished by her is used. A resulting trust is generally found to exist in transactions affecting community property in noncommunity property estates where a husband buys property in his own name. Therefore, while the husband held legal title to the note and contract, he held a one-half interest in trust for his wife.

[T]he decree appealed is reversed and the cause remanded with directions to enter a decree in accordance with this opinion.

———————

DISCUSSION

Cuba was a community property jurisdiction when the spouses lived there. During this period did it make any difference whether the husband received his wages in Florida (not a community property state) or Cuba?

Quintana is an example of how common law courts have not had great difficulty reaching reasonable results when a couple moves from a community property jurisdiction to a common law state. Community property states have had a great deal more difficulty when attempting to characterize property accumulated by a couple in a common law state before the couple moved to a community property state.

2. Change of Domicile from a Common Law to a Community Property State

Pacific States Cut Stone Co. v. Goble
Supreme Court of Washington, 1967
425 P.2d 631

FINLEY, Chief Justice.

The transaction with which we are here concerned involved the sale of some quarry machinery located near Madras, Oregon. The machinery was owned by the Pacific States Cut Stone Company, a Washington corporation and the plaintiff in this action. The purchasers were Roy E. Goble and J. F. Wallace, who with their respective wives were Washington residents. The Gobles and the Wallaces are the defendants in this action. A conditional sale contract was prepared in Oregon by the Oregon attorney for the plaintiff and executed in Oregon by Roy E. Goble and J. F. Wallace as purchasers and by the plaintiff as seller. The purchasers made a down payment of $6,000 when the contract was signed and immediately removed the equipment to Washington, where it was used for some time. Total payments made under the contract were $20,000, and a balance of $20,000 remains unpaid.

The defendant-purchasers being in default in their payments, the stone company brought an action for the unpaid balance against Goble and Wallace, their wives, and the respective marital communities. [In determining rights and obligations under the contract the trial court applied Oregon law.] Following this court's decision in *Escrow Service Co. v. Cressler,* 59 Wash. 2d 38, 365 P.2d 760 (1961), the most recent in a line dating back to the second *La Selle* case, *La Selle v. Woolery,* 14 Wash. 70, 44 P. 115, 32 L.R.A. 73 (1896), the trial court held that under Oregon law neither the defendant wives nor the defendant communities incurred any obligation by the execution of the contract by Goble and Wallace. The stone company thus recovered a judgment for the unpaid balance of $20,000 with interest and attorney's fees only against Goble and Wallace individually. From the portion of the judgment dismissing the action against the wives and marital communities of the defendants Goble and Wallace, plaintiff has taken this appeal.

In our view of the matter the instant appeal does not present a true conflict choice of law problem. *See* Marsh, *Marital Property in Conflict of Laws* 148 (1952). For the reasons which will be discussed below, it is our decision that the result of this case is no different under applicable Oregon law than it would be if Washington law were applied.

It is necessary for us to examine the line of decisions, beginning with the second *La Selle* case, relied on by the trial court for the proposition that the obligation incurred by the husbands of the Goble and Wallace families is not chargeable on the community property of the families in Washington. The result in *La Selle* was based on the reasoning that the obligation the husband incurred in Wisconsin was "separate" under Wisconsin law, since that state had no community property system, and therefore only his separate property in Washington could be subjected to the satisfaction of the debt. This reasoning, which this court has preserved, has been subject to much criticism.

The rule of the second *La Selle* case produces results which are very nearly absurd. For example, assume the case of a married man domiciled in Vancouver, Washington, who begins a business across the Columbia River in Portland, Oregon. The income the husband earns by his exertions would be community property, since the character of marital personal property is determined by the law of the matrimonial domicile at the time of acquisition. Under the rule of the second *La Selle* decision and similar cases, however, the obligations incurred in operating the business would be "separate" obligations of the husband and could be satisfied only out of his separate property, which might well be nonexistent. Thus it follows that upon termination of the business an Oregon business creditor of the husband could not even reach the income from the business once it had been withdrawn into Washington.

The reasoning which produced the rule of the second *La Selle* case was palpably fallacious. A much quoted passage from Marsh, *op. cit. supra* at 150, demonstrates the fallacy in the reasoning:

> Nevertheless, the court [in the second *La Selle* case] purported to find that by the law of Wisconsin this debt was a "separate" or "noncommunity" debt of H, and gave judgment for the defendants. How was it possible to find such a rule in the law of Wisconsin? The reasoning is very simple. The court found assertions in the Wisconsin decisions that debts incurred by the husband in that state were his "separate" debts, meaning thereby that the "separate" property of the wife was not liable for them. Of course, every debt contracted by the husband in Wisconsin would be a "separate" debt in this sense. The Washington court then reasoned as follows: This debt of the husband is a "separate" debt by the law of Wisconsin (meaning, "not chargeable upon the wife's 'separate' property"). The law of the place of making of the contract (Wisconsin) governs the "character" of the debt. Therefore, this is a "separate" debt of the husband (meaning, "not chargeable upon the community property of husband and wife"). The verbal fallacy in this argument is about as obvious as that in the old syllogism: All batteries are torts. An automobile has a battery. Therefore, an automobile is a tort.

A most significant point is that the court, in the line of cases beginning with the second *La Selle* case, has not been, although it has claimed to have been, applying the law of the foreign state involved. As was said in Marsh, *op. cit. supra* at 153, in regard to *Mountain v. Price*, 20 Wash. 2d 129, 146 P.2d 327 (1944), a tort case of the second *La Selle* decision ilk:

By the rationale of this case, if a married man domiciled in Washington should drive down the highway on "community business" and negligently strike Plaintiff A ten feet on the Washington side of the state line, and then negligently strike Plaintiff B ten feet on the Oregon side of the line, and both sued in the Washington court, Plaintiff A could levy on community property to satisfy his obligation but Plaintiff B could not. This is not the result of applying Oregon law to the second case (although the court thought so), butane arbitrary discrimination by the Washington court.

We note also that this fact was at least implicitly recognized in the first *La Selle* decision, where Hoyt, Chief Justice, stated for the court, 11 Wash. at 340–341, 39 P. at 664:

It appears from the statutes set out in the answer that in that state [Wisconsin] there is no such thing as community property, as understood here, nor is there any such thing as separate property of the husband, as defined by our laws. The wife alone could own separate property. It will be seen from these provisions that a debt incurred by the husband could there be enforced against all of the property acquired by the husband and wife either before or after marriage, excepting such as under the laws of that state, would be the separate property of the wife. This is substantially the result of the laws of this state as interpreted by former decisions of this court.

In our opinion the comity which one state owes to another goes to the substance rather than the form of things. If a certain right is given in on estate as to property of a certain nature, comity would require that those rights should be enforced in another state as to property of the same nature though it might be called by a different name.

We have reviewed the Oregon law pleaded by the defendants in this case and which we must take judicial notice of under RCW 5.24.010. We have particularly scrutinized the two statutes emphasized by the defendants on this appeal, *viz.*, Oregon Revised Statutes 108.020 and 108.050. These two statutes provide that generally neither husband nor wife is liable for debts incurred by the other and that a married woman's property shall not be subject to the debts of her husband. These statutes have only the limited relevance here of supporting the unquestioned conclusion that, under Oregon law, the separate property of Mrs. Goble and Mrs. Wallace is not subject to the liability involved.

Since there is no community property law in Oregon, no solution to the instant problem of the liability of community property can be found in Oregon statutes or decisions. As far as we can proceed in applying Oregon law is to say that, if the contract before us had been executed by Oregon husbands who thereafter remained in Oregon, the plaintiff-creditor would have been able to reach all property of the couple in satisfaction of the debt, except that separately owned by the wives. This logical view of Oregon law as applied to this Washington problem produces more just results as it accords with the expectations of creditors, husbands, and wives, under either Washington or Oregon law. This view is also more in accord with the dictates of comity, as expressed by Chief Justice Hoyt in the first *La Selle* case, in that it gives effect to the substance, not just the form, of the foreign law involved.

We conclude, therefore, that the second *La Selle* case and its progeny, which *Baffin, supra,* determined is no longer applicable as to the contract choice of law question, should no longer be adhered to on the question of community liability involved here. Rather we conclude that, since the obligation of a husband in Oregon subjects all the property of the married couple to the debt except the separate property of the wife, the effect of applying Oregon law to the situation before us is that all property, including community property, held by the Gobles and the Wallaces, with the exception of the wives' separate property, is subject to the obligation involved.

That portion of the judgment below which dismissed the action as to the defendant communities is reversed, and the case is remanded for proceedings consistent with this opinion.

DISCUSSION

Pacific States is a wonderful example of the confusion of community property courts in this area. What is a "separate" debt under Oregon law? Is it the same thing as a "separate" debt under Washington law? If not, why did the court determine there was no conflict?

The Texas Supreme Court in *Cameron* (*see* Chapter 13) discusses the different meanings of "separate."

Community property courts consistently have characterized wages earned during marriage by a couple while domiciled in a common law state as the "separate" property of the wage earner after the couple moved to Texas. This proved to be a public policy disaster. If the spouse divorced in Texas soon after the move, the court could not "divest" the wage earner of the wages saved from the prior domicile, and little other property remained. Dependent spouses were left in a terrible situation.

The Texas legislature attempted to solve this problem with Tex. Fam. Code § 7.002. After a couple moves to Texas, what is the character of wages earned in the prior domicile and brought to Texas?

Section 7.002 clearly permits Texas divorce courts to divide property earned in the prior domicile. The new statute applied to all actions in which there had not been a hearing prior to September 1, 1981. The statute probably governs all property acquired before the effective date, if the action is filed after the effective date of the statute. This certainly was the construction of the law by the court in *Cameron v. Cameron*, 641 S.W.2d 210 (Tex. 1982). Property acquired while domiciled in another state is sometimes referred to as quasi-community property.

In *Cameron*, the court was faced with a dispute that was not governed by the new law. The court "judicially adopted" Section 7.002. Quasi-community property was deemed divisible, even though the statute did not govern the action. What does this mean? Does this decision change the character of quasi-community property before the divorce is filed? Does the *Hanau* case, *infra*, help answer this question?

Texas has no statute regarding the rights of the surviving spouse to quasi-community property. What happens if a person dies and attempts to devise to a third party all the quasi-community property earned by him in another state?

In re Estate of Hanau
Supreme Court of Texas, 1987
730 S.W.2d 663

ROBERTSON, Justice.

This case involves the question of whether the rule announced in *Cameron v. Cameron*, 641 S.W.2d 210 (Tex. 1982) applies to probate as well as divorce matters. Robert and Dorris Hanau were married in Illinois in 1974 and five years later moved to Texas. After moving here, Robert prepared a will leaving his separate property to his children by a prior marriage, and his community to Dorris. Robert and Dorris each had substantial amounts of separate property before the marriage, and at all times kept such property under their own names. While married in Illinois, Robert accumulated numerous shares of stock through the use of his separate property. Under Illinois common law, this would have remained his separate property. Robert died in Texas in 1982 and Dorris was granted letters testamentary on May 10, 1982. In February 1983, Dorris transferred large amounts of the estate's stock to the son, Steven, and the daughter, Leslie Ann. In May 1983, however, Steven brought an original petition seeking to have Dorris removed as executrix, claiming that she was intentionally mismanaging and embezzling from the estate. Dorris soon thereafter filed an inventory and appraisal listing all of the property owned by Robert, claiming that all stocks obtained by Robert during their marriage were community property, even though they were originally acquired in a common law state. Thus, Dorris sought the return of some of the stock she had already delivered to the children. The parties stipulated that the stocks acquired before marriage were Robert's separate property and that stocks acquired while married in Texas were community property. The only question presented to the trial court was the status of those stocks bought during the marriage in Illinois using Robert's separate property.

The trial court severed the question of proper distribution of the assets and granted a partial summary judgment to Dorris on the characterization issue. The trial judge ruled that all the amounts that accrued during the marriage would be considered as community property in Texas, despite their characterization as separate property outside the state. He concluded that "the Texas Supreme Court in *Cameron v. Cameron* could not have intended to limit its new characterization of common law marital property to divorce proceedings, but rather intended that said characterization to be applied to any situation where the issue arose, including probate proceedings."

The court of appeals affirmed in part and reversed in part. 721 S.W.2d 515. The court determined that *Cameron* was not applicable to probate situations, rather it should be limited only to divorce matters. Therefore, the court held that most of the stocks should have been classified as separate property, and rendered judgment that they go to the son and daughter. The court did, however, affirm as to one specific stock (TransWorld) where it held that a proper tracing could not be shown so as to classify it as separate property. Both parties appeal here; Dorris as to the former holding, Steven as to the latter. We affirm in part and reverse and render in part.

In her application, Dorris relies exclusively on Section 3.63 of the Family Code and *Cameron v. Cameron*, 641 S.W.2d 210 (Tex. 1982). Dorris admits that *Cameron* dealt with divorce rather than probate, but argues that this court intended to make "a fundamental change in its characterization of common law marital property." She argues that a broad interpretation of the result in *Cameron* should be applied because no distinction can be made between dissolution of the marriage by death or divorce. We disagree.

The long-standing general rule is that property which is separate property in the state of the matrimonial domicile at the time of its acquisition will not be treated for probate purposes as though acquired in Texas. *Oliver v. Robertson*, 41 Tex. 422, 425 (1874); *McClain v. Holder*, 279 S.W.2d 105, 107 (Tex. Civ. App.—Galveston 1955, writ ref'd n.r.e.). In *Cameron*, we held, however, that separate property acquired in common law jurisdictions merits different treatment in the limited context of divorce or annulment. While there were solid reasons for creating the *Cameron* rule in those situations, the same rationales are not applicable to probate procedures.

In *Cameron*, this court used three bases for its holding. First, the court examined the laws of some of the other community property states, and agreed that a difference exists between common law marital property and the separate property of community property jurisdictions. This court cited to several cases, including *Rau v. Rau*, 6 Ariz. App. 362, 432 P.2d 910 (Ct. App. 1967), in support of its holding. In examining *Rau*, however, it is clear that the court there refused to apply the rule to probate cases because "the statutory regulation of rights of succession has been regarded as something apart from the determination of property rights between living persons." *Id.* at 914. Furthermore, nothing in the other cases used for support in *Cameron* reveals an intent to extend the rule to probate cases in those jurisdictions. See *Hughes v. Hughes*, 91 N.M. 339, 573 P.2d 1194 (1987); *Berle v. Berle*, 97 Idaho 452, 546 P.2d 407 (1976). In fact, it appears that the only community property states which have extended the rule reach such a result based completely upon statutory authority. *See* California Prob. Code Section 66 (West 1985); Idaho Code Section 15-2-201 (1971). Thus, there is no case law or trend which supports change of the rule here.

The second basis used in *Cameron* was the Texas legislature's action in adopting Section 3.63 of the Family Code. Section 3.63 provides that a trial judge shall make a "just and right" division of property, which may include: "Property that was acquired by either spouse while domiciled elsewhere and that would have been community property if the spouse who acquired the property had been domiciled in the state at the time of the acquisition." Therefore, this court merely judicially adopted Section 3.63 into the substantive law of this State. Dorris suggests that we apply Section 3.63 to the probate situation, but by its own terms the Family Code provision applies only "in a decree of divorce or annulment." In addition, there is no provision similar to Section 3.63 in the Probate Code, nor in any other statute of this state, which would logically require us to follow her suggestion. Therefore, there is also a lack of statutory authority which mitigates against extending *Cameron*.

The final foundation in *Cameron* dealt with the necessity of giving the trial court the power to effect an equitable distribution of property. Without such power, unfair results could occur because one spouse's equitable share of the other spouse's separate property under common law might not be considered under our community property definition of separate property. The *Cameron* holding merely made such an interest in common law separate property one which is susceptible to a Texas trial court's equitable division. The key is that there is no similar right in a probate proceeding, nor is there any need for any. If there is a valid will, the will should usually be enforced regardless of the equity of the devises or bequests within. *Huffman v. Huffman*, 161 Tex. 267, 339 S.W.2d 885, 889 (1960) (while a court can relax rules of construction, it may not redraft a will). Similarly, if the property is to pass through intestacy, a specified statutory formula is invoked which operates without the need to make equitable determinations. *See* Tex. Prob. Code Ann. Section 38 (Vernon 1980).

In sum, to extend *Cameron* would make a shambles of 150 years of Texas probate law, thus, without a clear showing of supporting case law, statutory authority or a clear need for such broad power in the trial court, we refuse to do so. Because the court of appeals refused to enlarge *Cameron*, its judgment on this point is affirmed.

SPEARS, J., filed a concurring opinion.

SPEARS, Justice, concurring.

I concur in the result reached by the court. *Cameron v. Cameron*, 641 S.W.2d 210, 221–23 (Tex. 1982) was based in large part upon Section 3.63 of the Family Code which provided statutory authorization for the characterization of property acquired outside of Texas as quasi-community property. No such provision is present in the Probate Code; therefore, I concur.

The court's opinion creates two rules for the characterization of the same property. A husband and wife from a common law state could retire to Texas with the majority of their property characterized as the husband's separate marital property. If the wife brought divorce proceedings, the "separate" marital property would be characterized as quasi-community property under *Cameron* and Section 3.63 of the Family Code. The trial court would then be authorized to divide the marital property between the spouses in a manner that it deemed just and right. Under the majority's decision in this case, the same husband could execute a will devising all the "separate" marital property to a third party leaving the wife without any means of support after he dies.

More jurisdictions have some method to protect the interest and insure the support of surviving spouses. This court's holding leaves surviving spouses without the protection afforded by either common law or community property statutory schemes in certain situations. Accordingly, I urge the Legislature to eliminate this illogical and potentially inequitable difference in the characterization of marital property by adopting a Probate Code section similar to Section 3.63 of the Family Code and the probate codes of other jurisdictions. *See* California Prob. Code Section 66 (West 1985); Idaho Code Section 15-2201 (1971).

DISCUSSION

Professor Weintraub has suggested a way for Texas courts to reach a fairer result than that dictated by the *Hanau* analysis. *See* Weintraub, *Obstacles to Sensible Choice of Law for Determining Marital Property Rights on Divorce or in Probate: Hanau and the Situs Rule*, 25 Hous. L. Rev. 1113 (1988).

Ismail v. Ismail

Texas Court of Appeals—Houston [1st Dist.], 1985
702 S.W.2d 216, writ ref'd n.r.e.

WARREN, Justice.

This is a divorce case between two Egyptian citizens. The trial court granted the parties a divorce and divided certain property, including real property located in Egypt.

In six points of error, appellant contends that the trial court erred or abused its discretion: (1) in applying the Texas "quasi-community property statute" to this case, (2) in failing to decide this case under Egyptian law, (3) in failing to dismiss *for forum non conveniens*, (4) in dividing the alleged "quasi-community estate," (5) in awarding excessive attorney's fees to the appellee, and (6) in entering sanctions against the appellant.

Appellant and appellee, both Egyptian citizens, were married in July 1966. Shortly thereafter, they moved to Houston and lived there until 1972. During their stay in Houston, they both obtained permanent resident status (green cards), two children were born to them, and both received Ph.D degrees.

In 1972, the family returned to Egypt, but moved to England the following year. By the end of 1977, both were back in Egypt, and appellee was teaching at Al-Azhar University in Cairo. During that period, appellant bought Houston real estate, which is a subject of this appeal. The family lived together in Cairo until 1981, when appellee came back to Houston on a research fellowship. The fellowship was conditioned on appellee returning to Cairo and completing her research. Appellant accompanied appellee to Houston but only stayed long enough to rent an apartment, buy a car, and generally see that appellee was properly situated.

In December 1981, appellant began proceedings in Egypt to obtain permanent custody of the two children, who were living in Egypt. In January 1982, appellee filed for divorce in a Houston district court, seeking a division of the marital estate and custody of the two children. In May 1982, appellee returned to Egypt and resumed her position at Al-Azhar University. While there, she contested the custody suit and returned to Houston in July 1982, where she remained until the divorce trial.

In February 1982, appellant filed a general denial to appellee's divorce suit. From then until the decree was entered on August 9, 1984, both sides made extensive discovery, here and in Egypt. The trial court granted appellee a divorce, divided the property by giving appellee title to all Texas real property, her personal automobile, funds deposited in Texas bank accounts, and the personal property in her possession. Appellant was awarded all Egyptian real and personal property, all interest in certain business ventures, and all interest in pending lawsuits. Finally, the court awarded appellee $15,000 "as sanctions against appellant for his acts and omissions" as alleged by the wife, and $82,881.72 in attorney's fees. The court declined to decide child custody.

On August 21, 1984, the appellant requested that the court file findings of fact and conclusions of law. The same day, he filed his motion for extension of time in which to file findings of fact and conclusions of law. On September 10, 1984, he filed a motion for new trial. Neither the request for findings of fact and conclusions of law, nor the motion for new trial, was ever acted upon by the trial court.

I. QUASI-COMMUNITY PROPERTY

In his first point of error, the appellant contends that the trial court erred in characterizing the Texas real estate as "quasi-community property" under Section 3.63(b) of the Texas Family Code. In his fourth point of error, he contends that even if Section 3.63(b) was properly applied in this case, the trial court abused its discretion in awarding all of the Texas realty to the appellee. That section, adopted in 1981, states:

> (b) In a decree of divorce or annulment the court shall also order a division of the following real and personal property, wherever situated, in a manner that the court deems just and right, having due regard for the rights of each party and any children of the marriage:
>
> > (1) property that was acquired by either spouse while domiciled elsewhere and that would have been community property if the spouse who acquired the property had been domiciled in this state at the time of the acquisition; or
> >
> > (2) property that was acquired by either spouse in exchange for real or personal property, and that would have been community property if the spouse who acquired the property so exchanged had been domiciled in this state at the time of its acquisition.

Tex. Fam. Code Ann. Sec. 3.63(b) (Vernon Supp. 1985). The appellant's arguments are essentially twofold: First, as a matter of statutory construction, Section 3.63(b) does not apply to this case, since the appellee unilaterally moved to Texas; second, application of the statute in this case renders the statute unconstitutional.

The quasi-community property statute does not expressly limit its reach to situations where both spouses have migrated from a common law jurisdiction to Texas. Nonetheless, the appellant contends that the purpose of the statute is to remedy the inequities of prior decisions awarding all "common law separate property" acquired during the marriage to the acquiring spouse. He argues that where only one spouse migrates to Texas, the quasi-community property statute does not apply because the migrating spouse may enforce his or her rights to marital property by filing for divorce in the previous domicile. He further contends that because the appellee did not migrate from a common law jurisdiction (Egypt is neither a "community property" nor a "common law" jurisdiction), the statute does not apply.

We conclude that Section 3.63(b) applies in the division of migratory spouses' property regardless of the nature of the previous domicile's legal system. This conclusion is supported by the plain meaning of the statute; it applies to property "wherever situated," acquired by either spouse while domiciled "elsewhere." Admittedly, the usual application of the statute will likely be in situations where the spouses were previously domiciled in a common law state. The legislative history of the provision indicates that this scenario was the primary focus of the legislation. See House Comm. on the Judiciary, Bill Analysis, Tex. H.B. 753, 67th Leg. (1981). No logic is given, however, to support the appellant's request that we limit the application of the statute to migrations from common law jurisdictions. The same potential problems exist in other migrations. The problems may even be exacerbated when the spouses migrate from a foreign country that has neither a common law nor a community property system. Moreover, applying the quasi-community property statute to migrations to Texas from all jurisdictions is the better rule in terms of uniformity and ease of application.

The appellant also argues that the statute should not be applied where only one spouse migrates to Texas. He contends that application of the statute in this context is unconstitutional. In support, he first cites California precedent for the proposition that the quasi-community property statute[1] only applies where both spouses have migrated to the community property state. *See In re Marriage of Roesch*, 83 Cal. App. 3d 96, 147 Cal. Rptr. 586 (Cal. Ct. App. l978), cert. denied, 440 U.S. 915, 99 S.Ct. 1232, 59 L.Ed.2d 465 (1979). *See also* Oldham, *Property Division in a Texas Divorce of a Migrant Spouse: Heads He Wins, Tails She Loses?* 19 Hous. L. Rev. 1, 25 n. 134 (1981).

In *Roesch*, the California Court of Appeals held that its quasi-community property statute could be constitutionally applied only when two conditions were met: "(1) both parties have changed their domicile to California; and (2) subsequent to the change of domicile, the spouses sought in a California court legal alteration of their marital status." 83 Cal. App. 3d at 107, 147 Cal. Rptr. at 593; *see also Addison v. Addison*, 62 Cal. 2d 558, 399 P.2d 897, 43 Cal. Rptr. 97, (1965) (upholding the constitutionality of California's quasi-community property statute against constitutional attack based on (1) the due process clause's prohibition against legislation impinging upon "vested rights" via retroactive legislation and (2) the privileges and immunities clause of article IV of the United States Constitution). The *Roesch* court acknowledged that vested property rights may constitutionally be diminished by retroactive marital property legislation when demanded by a sufficiently important state interest. 83 Cal. App. 3d at 106, 147 Cal. Rptr. at 593. The court concluded, however, that the interest of California in the marital property was minimal and that the interest of Pennsylvania, the migrant spouse's previous domicile, was sub-

---

1. *See* Cal. Civ. Code Sec. 4803 (West 1970). The California statute is virtually identical to the Texas statute.

stantial. Finally, the *Roesch* court concluded that the non-migrant spouse (appellee) was sufficiently protected under the laws of Pennsylvania. *Id.* at 107, 147 Cal. Rptr. at 593. The *Roesch* court failed, however, to enunciate the precise rationale for its conclusion that application of the quasi-community property statute to a unilateral migration violated due process. *See* Oldham, *supra*, at 28 n. 134. Professor Oldham noted:

> Unfortunately, the [*Roesch*] court did not state whether it believed that the application of the California law violated due process because California had no interest in the application of its law, or because California had insufficient contacts with the parties, or because California's contacts with the parties were so late in the chronology of the matter that the application of its law would constitute unfair surprise. The court also asserted that the wife was "entitled to the protection of the laws of [Pennsylvania]." This is, at best, a strange statement, since Pennsylvania law did not permit the equitable distribution of the spouses' property at divorce and gave the wife no protection.

Id.

The appellant also argues that the Texas Constitution[2] as interpreted by the Texas Supreme Court, prohibits the divestment of a spouse's "separate" property. In *Eggemeyer v. Eggemeyer*, 554 S.W.2d 137 (Tex. 1977), the court held that a trial court may not divest one spouse of his separate realty and transfer title to the other spouse. In *Cameron v. Cameron*, 641 S.W.2d 210 (Tex. 1982), the court adhered to the principle enunciated in *Eggemeyer* and concluded that art. 3.63(b) does not order division of what is considered "separate" property under community property law:

> [W]e hold that the property spouses acquire during marriage, except by gift, devise or descent should be divided upon divorce in Texas in the same manner as community property, irrespective of the domicile of the spouses when they acquire the property.

Id. at 220.

The appellant notes, however, that the *Cameron* court expressly held that its decision did not run afoul of the *Eggemeyer* prohibition against divestment because the Texas division of property in the case before it approximated a common law equitable distribution:

> A Texas court that makes a distribution on divorce of the common law marital estate equivalent to what would occur in the common law jurisdiction where the couple was domiciled when they acquired the property, does not impair the rights of spouses in the common law marital property. No divestment transpires because the acquiring spouse loses no more in a Texas divorce than he loses in a judgment rendered in an equitable distribution common law state. Our judicial adoption of the quasi-community property amendment of Tex. Fam. Code Ann. Sec. 3.63 does not violate article I, Section 19 of the Texas Constitution.

Id. at 222–23.

We conclude that the *Eggemeyer, Cameron,* and *Roesch* decisions do not prohibit application of the quasi-community property statute to this case. The real property that is

---

2. "No citizen of this State shall be deprived of life, liberty, property, privileges or immunities, or in any manner disfranchised, except by the due course of the law of the land." Tex. Const. art. I, Sec. 19. The appellant is entitled to due process even though he is not a domiciliary of Texas. *See Pintor v. Martinez*, 202 S.W.2d 333, 335 (Tex. Civ. App.—Austin 1947, writ ref'd n.r.e.).

the subject of this appeal is located in Texas. Texas obviously has a significant interest in controlling the disposition of property located within its boundaries, and indeed, Texas follows the general rule that marital rights of spouses in real property are determined by the law of the place where the land is situated. See *Commissioner v. Skaggs*, 122 F.2d 721, 723 (5th Cir. 1941), cert denied, 315 U.S. 811, 62 S.Ct. 796, 86 L.Ed. 1210 (1942). Additionally, the appellant, unlike the non-migrant spouse in *Roesch*, has had other significant continuous business and personal contacts with Texas: the Ismails lived in Houston for six years, maintained bank accounts here, and traveled to Texas on various other occasions. Thus, from a due process perspective, appellant's contacts with Texas, when coupled with Texas' interest in protecting the migrant spouse in this case, warrant application of Texas law to the division of the Texas property.[3]

Also, we should not interpret the language of *Cameron* to hold that in every case where a party receives less in the Texas community property division than he or she would have received under the system of the previous domicile, the party has been deprived of due process. Clearly, where the Texas division of property approximates what another domicile's law requires, the non-migrant spouse may not complain of divestment of "separate" property. But neither can the appellant in this case complain of an unconstitutional divestment of "separate" property under our state's constitution when, through his extensive contacts with this state, and through his personal appearance in this litigation, he has implicitly consented to Texas courts exercising their jurisdiction in equitably dividing the marital property.

Finally, the appellant contends that the application of the quasi-community property statute is unconstitutional, since it constitutes a retroactive application of the statute. We reject this argument. First, the statute itself appears to have been enacted with the intent that it would apply retroactively. See *Sampson, supra*, at 1354. Second, an overriding public interest justifies application of Section 3.63(b) of the Family Code to property acquired before the enactment of this statute. See *Cameron*, 641 S.W.2d at 219. If this court were to limit the effect of the statute to property acquired after the effective date of the statute, its remedial benefits would be lost for a generation of ill-fated marriages.

Lastly, the Texas Supreme Court, in *Cameron*, judicially adopted Section 3.63(b). That court's decision to adopt the statute retroactively is binding on this court.

We conclude that Section 3.63(b) of the Texas Family Code applies to the facts presented in this case and that application of the statute in our case violates neither the United States nor the Texas Constitutions. Finally, we overrule the appellant's fourth point of error, complaining of an abuse of discretion in the division of the marital property. The court awarded substantial property, both real and personal, located in Egypt to the appellant.

In considering whether or not the court abused its discretion in the division of property, it is the duty of the court to indulge every reasonable presumption in favor of a

---

3. See Sampson, *Interstate Spouses, Interstate Property, and Divorce*, 13 Tex. Tech. L. Rev. 1285 (1982). It is arguable that a different outcome from that in *Roesch* is warranted in unilateral migratory divorces in Texas. Professor Sampson hypothesized:

When the spouses reside in different states, the Texas outcome could well be exactly opposite from the *Roesch* decision under California law. After all, the California approach to dividing property is very different from the Texas formulation—a 50/50 split plus possible alimony versus equitable division and no alimony. Further, California law characterizes property earned or acquired after the spouses actually begin living separate and apart as separate. Texas law is exactly opposite. It is reasonable for a Texas court to equitably divide all the property before it, and in fact, this long has been the accepted procedure.

Id. at 1347–48. We should, however, heed the professor's admonition that "[p]redicting future applications of the quasi-community statute may be hazardous to one's health." *Id.* at 1346.

proper exercise of discretion by the trial court in dividing the property of the parties. *Thompson v. Thompson*, 380 S.W.2d 632, 636 (Tex. Civ. App.—Ft. Worth 1964, no writ). Further, the court may consider the value of real property lying outside of Texas in an equitable division of property. Texas courts do not assert jurisdiction to determine title to such land but may consider the foreign investment when dividing property. *See In re Read*, 634 S.W.2d 343, 348–349 (Tex. App.—Amarillo 1982, writ dism'd); *In re Glaze*, 605 S.W.2d 721, 724 (Tex. Civ. App.—Amarillo 1980, no writ). After reviewing the evidence, we note that the court considered in its award a substantial amount of property that was valued at over $2,000,000. Approximately one fourth of this amount, consisting of the property located in Houston, Texas, was awarded to the wife. The balance of the property was awarded to the husband. We find that the court did not abuse its discretion in its division of the property.

Appellant's first and fourth points of error are overruled.

II. CHOICE OF LAW

In his second point of error, the appellant argues that the trial court erred in deciding this case under Texas law because applicable choice of law principles, both traditional and those contained in the *Restatement (Second) of Conflicts*, dictate that this case be determined under Egyptian law. He cites *Orr v. Pope*, 400 S.W.2d 614 (Tex. Civ. App.—Amarillo 1966, no writ), and *Joiner v. Joiner*, 131 Tex. 27, 112 S.W.2d 1049 (1938). Both cases, decided long before the enactment of Section 3.63(b), merely restate the rule of law that was the impetus for the enactment of the quasi-community property statute: Property acquired by a spouse when domiciled in another jurisdiction was, under pre-*Cameron* common law, characterized according to the previous domicile's laws.

The enactment of Section 3.63(b), however, obviates the need to apply this anachronistic conflict-of-laws principle. *See Cameron*, 641 S.W.2d at 222. As Professor Sampson recently wrote:

> [Section 3.63(b)] constitutes a rejection of, or rather, a substitution for, the standard conflict-of-laws solution. This remedy has become unworkable in modern mobile America. In short, a legislative solution has been provided to cut through the tangled jungle that has necessarily grown from the inherent limitations of the judge-created answer supplied by traditional conflict-of-laws theory.

Sampson, *supra* note 3, at 1344. Since the court properly applied Section 3.63(b) to this case, there was no error in refusing to apply Egyptian law.

Appellant's second point of error is overruled.

DISCUSSION

Should *forum non conveniens* ever be applicable to a divorce? *See Jagger v. Superior Court*, 158 Cal. Rptr. 163 (Cal. App. 1979).

In *Ismail*, the Texas court applies Texas community property when only one spouse moved to Texas and filed for divorce. The Louisiana Supreme Court has determined that Louisiana courts should not apply their law unless both spouses were domiciled in Louisiana. *Hand v. Hand*, 802 So.2d 560 (La. 2001). Which is the better approach?

Should Texas courts always apply Texas law to govern the rights of parties divorcing in Texas? Does it matter if Texas was ever the marital domicile? What if one spouse moved here after the couple separated?

Dawson-Austin v. Austin, 968 S.W.2d 319 (Tex. 1998) involved a number of interesting points. The husband and wife were domiciled in Minnesota; when the couple separated, the wife moved to California and the husband to Texas. The wife filed for divorce first in California before the husband filed in Texas; should Texas courts stay a divorce proceeding when one is already pending in another state? Here the Texas court did not stay the proceeding. The parties' most valuable asset was a corporation formed by the husband before marriage which had greatly increased in value during marriage, largely due to the husband's efforts in Minnesota. Minnesota law was similar to *Pereira, supra,* and was favorable to the wife; Texas law, *Jensen,* is favorable to the husband. If the Texas court has personal jurisdiction over both spouses, what law should the court apply?

In *Smith v. Lanier*, 998 S.W.2d 324 (Tex. App.—Austin 1999), a married couple lived in Texas for decades. The wife died in Texas and devised all of her estate to charity. Her will was admitted to probate in Texas. The husband's child from a prior marriage came to Texas and moved him and all property controlled by him (which apparently included most of their community estate) to South Carolina where she lived. He died in South Carolina after the move. The husband devised all his estate to his daughter. The husband's will was admitted into probate in South Carolina. What law should govern the disposition of the assets now in South Carolina?

3. People Moving to Texas from Another Country

At times it is quite important whether parties will be deemed married. Should Texas courts honor marriages and divorces procured in other countries? Does it matter if the parties were domiciliaries of that country at the time?

Seth v. Seth

Texas Court of Appeals—Ft. Worth, 1985
694 S.W.2d 459, no writ

FENDER, Chief Justice.

This is a choice of law conflicts case arising out of divorce proceedings. Three main parties are involved: Mohan Seth, (appellee and hereinafter "Husband"); Saroj Seth, (appellee and hereinafter "Wife One"); and Anuradha Mohan Seth, (appellant and hereinafter "Wife Two").

We affirm.

In 1982 Wife Two filed a petition for divorce in Dallas County and named Husband as respondent. Wife One then filed a plea in intervention, alleging that she was the lawful wife of Husband and that Wife Two was never lawfully married to Husband. After the filing of this plea in intervention by Wife One, Wife Two filed an amended petition for divorce. In pertinent part that petition stated:

III.

The parties were married as Moslems under the Law of Islam in Bombay, India, on or about June 17, 1975, and ceased to live together as husband and wife on or about September 27, 1981. In the alternative, the parties were married as Moslems under the Law of Islam in Kuwait, Kuwait, on or about November 26, 1976, and ceased to live together as husband and wife on or about September

27, 1981. In the further alternative Petitioner alleges that the parties are informally married as common law husband and wife in that they agreed to be married and thereafter lived together in Texas as husband and wife and there represented to others that they were married.

The marriage has become insupportable because of discord or conflict of personalities between Petitioner and Respondent that destroys the legitimate ends of the marriage relationship and prevents any reasonable expectation of reconciliation. There is no child born or adopted of this marriage, and none is expected.

IV.

Petitioner specially pleads the Moslem law known as the Law of Islam and the Laws of the Nation of India as each relates to the validity of the parties' marriage and same will be offered by Petitioner to support the marriage between the parties. The Court will be asked to take judicial notice of the foreign decrees showing the marriages of the parties and the divorce of Respondent from Intervenor as revealed during depositions and discovery in this case. Copies of these foreign decrees will be offered at trial under article 3731a of the Revised Texas Civil Statutes and the common law recognized therein. Respondent and Intervenor have been previously furnished copies.

Husband then filed an amended answer and a cross action in which he, more or less, joined the position taken by Wife One in her plea in intervention. In their pleadings, neither Wife One nor Husband actually denied that the key events alleged by Wife Two in her amended petition occurred.

After a pre-trial conference the trial court ordered that the trial would proceed in three stages. The first stage would address the question of which law—foreign, domestic, religious, civil or otherwise—to apply to the issues in the case. This determination would be made by the trial court. In the second stage the substantive issues raised by the pleadings—the validity of Husband and Wife One's divorce and the validity of Husband and Wife Two's marriages—would be determined, based upon the law selected in stage one. Finally, the trial court allowed for a third stage if necessary to litigate any questions of property division arising out of the stage two proceedings.

At the first stage of the trial, three experts—two called by Wife Two and one called by Wife One—testified about Islamic law and "talak," an ex parte Islamic divorce procedure alleged by Wife Two to have occurred in this case. No evidence was submitted at this hearing about the underlying events. After this hearing and the submission of trial briefs by the parties, the trial court held that the law of the State of Texas would apply to all issues raised by the pleadings. It is this decision of the trial court, to apply the law of the State of Texas to the stage two issues, which Wife Two complains about on appeal. Wife Two does not complain about the stage two proceedings themselves.

At the conclusion of the stage two proceedings the trial court granted Wife One's motion for an instructed verdict. Pursuant to this motion, the trial court ruled as a matter of law that the marriage between Husband and Wife One was a valid marriage which had never been dissolved in any manner (this is a reference to talak) subject to recognition by the trial court; that the alleged marriage of Husband and Wife Two in Bombay, India, on or about June 17, 1975, was void as a matter of law; and further that the alleged marriage of Husband and Wife Two in the Republic of Kuwait on or about November 22, 1976, was void as a matter of law. Although the trial court, at the conclusion of the evidence, ruled as a matter of law that Wife Two was never validly married to Husband, the trial court did allow the following two special issues to be submitted to the jury: (1) did Wife Two believe, in good faith, that Husband validly divorced Wife One on November 21, 1976?; and (2) did Wife Two participate in good faith in a marriage ceremony with Husband in Kuwait on November 22, 1976? The jury answered both these issues no.

After receiving the unfavorable verdict, Wife Two filed a supplemental petition in which she asserted various non-marriage relationship theories to support her claim for certain real and personal property held or acquired by Husband.

In its final judgment rendered several months after the stage two proceedings, the trial court apparently rejected Wife Two's supplemental petition and held, based on the jury's answers to the above two special issues, that the relationship between Wife Two and Husband was meretricious and that as a result, no valuation or division of property was warranted.

Wife Two then filed an appeal. On May 23, 1984, the statement of facts and the exhibits from the first stage of trial were filed with this court. No statement of facts or exhibits from the second stage were ever introduced.

Wife Two's appellate brief was filed on July 9, 1984. In her brief, Wife Two made various factual assertions which can be summarized as follows:

On June 6, 1957, Husband and Wife One were married in Udaipur, India. In 1966, Husband began cohabiting with Wife Two. In 1967, Husband was granted permanent resident alien status in the United States. Approximately eight years later, on June 17, 1975, the Husband and Wife Two converted to Islam and were married in Bombay, India, in an Islamic ceremony. Over a year later, on November 21, 1976, Husband divorced Wife One in Kuwait according to Islamic law. This divorce was rendered through a summary, *ex parte* procedure known as talak. Under this procedure, the divorce was rendered when husband pronounced three times: "I divorce you." Wife One was not notified of this procedure. The day after this talak procedure, Husband and Wife Two were married again in another Muslim ceremony. On March 8, 1977, Wife Two was granted permanent resident alien status in the U.S. as wife of Husband, who had already been granted resident alien status. Husband is a petroleum engineer with his own consulting business serving customers in the Near East. He has lived in Dallas for several years with Wife Two.

We now turn to the merits of the case. In two points of error, Wife Two contends the trial court erred in applying Texas law to resolve the issues raised by the marriage and divorce ceremonies which occurred in Kuwait and India.

Traditionally, courts have chosen and used the law of the place a divorce or marriage purportedly occurs to determine the validity of the ceremony. *Braddock v. Taylor*, 592 S.W.2d 40, 42 (Tex. Civ. App.—Beaumont 1979, writ ref'd n.r.e.) (court applies California law, which does not recognize common law marriages, to hold that a relationship carried on in California does not rise to the level of marriage); *Nevarez v. Bailon*, 287 S.W.2d 521, 522 (Tex. Civ. App.—El Paso 1956, writ ref'd) (court applies Mexican law to hold that a concubinage relationship carried on in Mexico does not rise to the level of marriage). Two recent decisions by the Supreme Court of Texas, however, indicate that choice-of-law decisions should not be made on the basis of the mechanical test of where the act occurred (lex loci) but should instead be made on the basis of the most significant relationship approach, using the factors set forth in the *Restatement (Second) of Conflict of Laws*, Sec. 6 (1971). *See Duncan v. Cessna Aircraft Co.*, 665 S.W.2d 414, 420–21 (Tex. 1984); *Gutierrez v. Collins*, 583 S.W.2d 312, 318 (Tex. 1979). Thus, based on *Duncan* and *Gutierrez*, we hold that Sec. 6 criteria, and not the place of celebration test, should be applied to determine choice of law in a marriage or divorce context.

Before making such a determination, we note that appellant failed to request findings of fact or conclusions of law. In a trial to the court where no findings of fact or conclusions of law are filed or requested, the judgment of the trial court implies all necessary findings of fact in support thereof. Where the implied findings of fact are supported by the evidence, it is the duty of the appellate court to uphold the judgment on any theory of law applicable to the case. This is so regardless of whether the trial court articulates the correct legal reason for the judgment.

The expert testimony and voluminous exhibits presented at the first stage of the trial present a somewhat conflicting view of Islamic law as it applies to conversion to Islam and to the talak. On the one hand, Wife Two's experts testified to the effect that a purported conversion by a man to Islam for the sole purpose of divorcing his wife through talak, and the talak itself, are not subject to any attack whatsoever on the grounds that they were simply sham ceremonies. According to this view, Islamic law recognizes and validates any conversion and subsequent talak so long as certain formalities are complied with, regardless of the man's underlying intentions and motives. Wife One's expert, on the other hand, stated that under Islamic law, conversion accomplished for the purpose of circumventing the law will not be enforced. The expert went on to say that, in his opinion, the alleged divorce between Husband and Wife One, procured through talak, would be invalid.

We now list the Sec. 6 choice of law principles:

Sec. 6. Choice-of-Law Principles

(1) A court, subject to constitutional restrictions, will follow a statutory directive of its own state on choice of law.

(2) When there is no such directive, the factors relevant to the choice of the applicable rule of law include:

(a) the needs of the interstate and international systems,

(b) the relevant policies of the forum,

(c) the relevant policies of other interested states and the relative interests of those states in the determination of the particular issue,

(d) the protection of justified expectations,

(e) the basic policies underlying the particular field of law,

(f) certainty, predictability and uniformity of result, and

(g) ease in the determination and application of the law to be applied.

Restatement (Second) of Conflict of Laws, Sec. 6 (1971)

Our review of the record convinces us that the most critical consideration is (b), the relevant policies of the forum. Before examining factor (b), we note that while it is true that the critical events in the case did not occur in Texas, that at the time of the events, the parties themselves had no apparent connection with Texas, and that even today, Husband and Wife Two are citizens of India and not the U.S. Texas' interest in this suit does not arise simply from the fact that it is the place of the trial. Texas' nexus to this lawsuit lies in the fact that Husband and Wife Two have lived here since 1977, during which time they acquired real property within the State. That connection would enhance the prerogative of the trial court to consider the relevant policies of Texas in deciding the present conflicts of law question.

With that connection in mind, we now turn to the policy question itself. Based on the testimony of Wife Two's experts, the trial court could have found that Islamic law simply allows a non-Muslim man to convert to Islam by pronouncing a short phrase, and then divorce his wife through the *ex parte* procedure of talak. The harshness of such a result to the non-Muslim divorced wife runs so counter to our notions of good morals and natural justice that we hold that Islamic law in this situation need not be applied. *See Robertson v. Estate of McKnight*, 609 S.W.2d 534, 537 (Tex. 1980); *Gutierrez*, 583 S.W.2d at 321.

Nor do we see how any of the other Sec. 6 factors might outweigh factor (b). Because the facts of this case are so unusual, it hardly seems likely that the needs of the international systems will be implicated by it. Furthermore, there was no factual showing that any official state body in either India or Kuwait had actually executed or confirmed the divorce and marriage, and thus factor (c) is not overly critical. *Cf. Chaudry v. Chaudry*, 159 N.J. Super. 566, 388 A.2d 1000, 1005 (New Jersey 1978) (talak was confirmed by a Pakistani court after it had been contested). We also note that, in regards to factor (d), the jury found that Wife Two did not in good faith believe that Husband had divorced Wife One, or that she was married to Husband. While these jury findings were made after the court's decision to apply Texas law, so that the trial court could not have relied on them, they nonetheless support our decision to affirm the judgment. As for factors (e), (f), and (g), none of them cut strongly in favor of Wife Two's position. Wife Two's points of error one and two are overruled.

The judgment is affirmed.

DISCUSSION

What is the court concerned about in *Seth*? Would it have mattered to the court if the divorce clearly was valid under the law of the prior domicile? Should it have mattered?

Is the result in *Seth* consistent with Texas public policy concerns?

C. Foreign Realty

In re Marriage of Glaze

Texas Court of Appeals—Amarillo, 1980
605 S.W.2d 721, no writ

COUNTISS, Justice.

[Mr. and Mrs. Glaze owned realty in New Mexico. In connection with a Texas divorce, a court ordered her to convey the realty to her husband. Mrs. Glaze appealed, arguing that the Texas court did not have the power to affect title to New Mexico realty.]

Mrs. Glaze is correct in stating that jurisdiction cannot be conferred on a court by agreement of the parties. *See Marriage of Johnson*, 595 S.W.2d 900, 902 (Tex. Civ. App. —Amarillo 1980, writ ref'd n.r.e.). Likewise, a Texas court does not have, and cannot acquire, in rem jurisdiction over real estate lying outside the state of Texas. *See Kaherl v. Kaherl*, 357 S.W.2d 622 (Tex. Civ. App.—Dallas 1962, no writ). When a party is properly before a Texas court, however, the court has in personam jurisdiction over the person and can sometimes do indirectly what it cannot do directly. In a divorce case, where the parties own out-of-state real property, the trial court can consider the existence and value of that realty in dividing the community property of the parties[4] and can in the ex-

---

4. Neither party contends the New Mexico ranch was separate property.

ercise of its equitable powers, order one party to execute a conveyance of the out-of-state property to the other party. *Brock v. Brock*, 586 S.W.2d 927, 930 (Tex. Civ. App.—El Paso 1979, no writ).

In this case, the trial court did not exceed its jurisdiction. It is apparent from the findings of fact that the trial judge considered the value of the New Mexico ranch in dividing the property, in accordance with the parties' agreement. By ordering Mrs. Glaze to convey the New Mexico property to Mr. Glaze, the court exercised its equitable power to compel action by a party over whom it had in personam jurisdiction. The second point of error is overruled.

Chapter Nineteen

Marital Agreements

A. The Traditional Approach

1. Restatement

This is an excerpt from the *Restatement (Second) of Contracts:*

Sec. 189. Promise in Restraint of Marriage. A promise is unenforceable on grounds of public policy if it is unreasonably in restraint of marriage.

Comment:

a. *Rule of reason.* Marriage is regarded by the common law as of concern to the state as well as to the individual, and the freedom of individuals to marry should not be impaired except for good reason. A promise in restraint of marriage is not necessarily unenforceable, but is subject to a rule of reason, analogous to that applicable to promises in restraint of trade. See Sec. 186. Here, as there, the duration of the restraint and its extent, in terms of the narrowing of the likely area of choice, are important. In order for the restraint to be reasonable, it must serve some purpose other than that of merely discouraging marriage. The most common acceptable purpose is that of providing support until marriage. Courts are, therefore, relatively tolerant of restraints on marriages that condition a promise of support on the promisee's not marrying and thereby acquiring another provider. Particularly is this so when the restraint is imposed by one spouse on remarriage by the other spouse, since both the close family relationship and the limitation of the restraint to a subsequent marriage argue in favor of enforceability.

Illustrations:

1. A pays B, his twenty-one-year-old child, $100,000 in return for B's promise not to marry for ten years. B's promise is unreasonably in restraint of marriage and is unenforceable on grounds of public policy.

2. A, a man of seventy years, promises B, his fifty-year old unmarried niece, that if she will remain in his home as housekeeper and will not marry, he will leave her $50,000 in his will. B does so until A's death. A's promise is not unreasonably in restraint of marriage and its enforcement is not precluded on grounds of public policy.

3. A and B, who are about to marry, make an antenuptial agreement in which A promises B that in case of A's death B shall receive a specified income from A's estate as long as B remains unmarried. A's promise is not unreasonably in re-

straint of marriage and its enforcement is not precluded on grounds of public policy.

Sec. 190. Promise Detrimental to Marital Relationship.

(1) A promise by a person contemplating marriage or by a married person, other than as part of an enforceable separation agreement, is unenforceable on grounds of public policy if it would change some essential incident of the marital relationship in a way detrimental to the public interest in the marriage relationship. A separation agreement is unenforceable on grounds of public policy unless it is made after separation or in contemplation of an immediate separation and is fair in the circumstances.

(2) A promise that tends unreasonably to encourage divorce or separation is unenforceable on grounds of public policy.

Comment:

a. *Change in essential incident of marital relationship.* Although marriage is sometimes loosely referred to as a "contract," the marital relationship has not been regarded by the common law as contractual in the usual sense. Many terms of the relationship are seen as largely fixed by the state and beyond the power of the parties to modify. Two reasons support this view. One is that there is a public interest in the relationship, and particularly in such matters as support and child custody, that makes it inappropriate to subject it to modification by the parties. Another is that the courts lack workable standards and are not an appropriate forum for the types of contract disputes that would arise if such promises were enforceable. The rule stated in Subsection (1) reflects this view by making a promise unenforceable if it changes an essential incident of marriage in a way detrimental to the public interest in the relationship. The rule, however, does not prevent persons contemplating marriage or married persons from making contracts between themselves for the disposition of property, since this is not ordinarily regarded as an essential incident of the marital relationship. Nor does it prevent their making contracts for services that are not an essential incident of the marital relationship within the rule stated here. But it does, for example, preclude them from changing in a way detrimental to the public interest in the relationship the duty imposed by law on one spouse to support the other. Whether a change in the duty of support is detrimental in this way will depend on the circumstances of each case. The presence of an unenforceable promise in an otherwise enforceable antenuptial or separation agreement does not, of course, necessarily entail the unenforceability of the entire agreement. *See* Secs. 183, 184. The principles underlying this Section also apply to an agreement under which a third person as trustee is to hold sums in trust for the other spouse on separation. The rules stated in this Section apply only to the relations between the parties and do not govern the enforceability of promises relating to the duty of support owed to children. Even though enforcement of a promise is not precluded under the rule stated in Subsection (1), it may be precluded under the rule stated in Subsection (2).

Illustration:

1. A and B, who are about to marry, make an antenuptial agreement in which A promises to leave their home at any time on notice by B and to make no further claims against B and B promises thereupon to pay A $100,000. The promises of A and B alter an essential incident of the marital relationship in a way detrimental to the public interest in that relationship and are unenforceable on grounds of public policy.

b. *Separation agreements.* The policy that limits the parties in modifying the marital relationship does not apply if that relationship has ended. The rule stated in Subsection

(1) thus does not apply to a promise that is part of an enforceable separation agreement. A separation agreement, to be enforceable, must be made after the parties have separated or when they contemplate immediate separation, so that the marriage has, in effect, already disintegrated. It must also be fair in the circumstances, a matter as to which the court may exercise its continuing discretionary powers. Separation agreements commonly deal with such matters as support and are generally enforceable because the parties could usually accomplish the same result through a judicial separation. They are still subject to the rule stated in Subsection (2) if they tend unreasonably to encourage divorce.

Illustration:

2. A and B, who are married but have decided to separate, make a separation agreement that is fair in the circumstances, in which A promises to pay B a stated sum each month in return for B's promise to relinquish all other claims to support. Although the promises of A and B change an essential incident of the marital relationship, their enforcement is not for that reason precluded on grounds of public policy because they are part of a separation agreement. But see Subsection (2) and Comment (c).

c. *Tending to encourage divorce or separation.* When persons contemplating marriage or married persons seek to determine by agreement their rights in the event of a divorce or separation, the rule stated in Subsection (2) comes into play, along with that stated in Subsection (1). See Illustration 2. Because of the public interest in the marriage relationship (see Comment a), a promise that undermines that relationship by tending unreasonably to encourage divorce or separation is unenforceable. Although the parties are free, if they choose, to terminate their relationship under the law providing for divorce or separation, a commitment that tends unreasonably in this direction will not be enforced. Whether a promise tends unreasonably to encourage divorce or separation in a particular case is a question of fact that depends on all the circumstances, including the state of disintegration of the marriage at the time the promise is made. A promise that merely disposes of property rights in the event of divorce or separation does not of itself tend unreasonably to encourage either.

Illustrations:

3. A, who is married to B, promises to pay B $50,000 in return for B's promise to obtain a divorce. The promises of A and B tend unreasonably to encourage divorce and are unenforceable on grounds of public policy. The result does not depend on whether or not there are grounds for divorce or on whether or not B has performed.

4. A, who was married to B but has obtained a divorce that can possibly be set aside for fraud, promises to pay B $50,000 in return for B's promise not to attempt to have the divorce set aside. The promises of both A and B tend unreasonably to encourage divorce and are unenforceable on grounds of public policy. The result does not depend on whether or not B has performed.

5. A and B, who are about to be married, make an antenuptial agreement in which A promises that in case of divorce, he will settle $1,000,000 on B. A court may decide that, in view of the large sum promised, A's promise tends unreasonably to encourage divorce and is unenforceable on grounds of public policy.

6. A, who has begun divorce proceedings against B, promises B that if divorce is granted, alimony shall be fixed at a stated sum, in return for B's agreement to relinquish all other claims to alimony. A court may decide that in view of the disintegration of the marriage relationship, the promises of A and B do not tend unreasonably to encourage divorce and their enforcement is not precluded on grounds of public policy.

2. Pre-1980 Texas Cases

Williams v. Williams
Supreme Court of Texas, 1978
569 S.W.2d 867

McGEE, Justice.

The question presented by this cause is whether a premarital agreement to waive the constitutional and statutory rights of a surviving spouse to a homestead and other exempt property is valid. The trial court held such an agreement to be valid. The court of civil appeals reversed the judgment. 548 S.W.2d 492. We reverse the judgment of the court of civil appeals and affirm that of the trial court.

William Wesley Williams, Sr., and Mildred Disch Lawrence were married on September 9, 1973. Both parties had children by previous marriages and both brought substantial property into this marriage. Four days before their marriage, the parties executed a premarital agreement. The basic agreement containing the provisions relative to the waiver of the homestead right and right to have exempt property set aside to the survivor provided:

> Whereas the parties desire that all property now owned or hereafter acquired by each of them shall, for testamentary disposition, be free from any claim of the other that may arise by reason of their contemplated marriage,
>
> It is therefore agreed:
>
> 1. *Property to be separately owned.* After the solemnization of the marriage between the parties, each of them shall separately retain all rights in his or her own property, whether now owned or hereafter acquired, and each of them shall have the absolute and unrestricted right to dispose of such separate property, free from any claim that may be made by the other by reason of their marriage, and with the same effect as if no marriage had been consummated between them.

A supplemental agreement was simultaneously executed and incorporated into the basic agreement. It disclosed the properties that each spouse would bring into the marriage, set forth certain guidelines concerning living and other incidental expenses to be incurred during the marriage, and further provided:

> 5. All income from the separate estate of each party, including dividends, interest, rents and salaries, and any increases, sales proceeds, reinvestments or changes in said separate estate, shall remain under control of the party receiving the same and shall be deposited in such party's separate account. It is the intent of the parties that such income, except for the personal living expenses hereinabove set forth, shall remain the separate property of each party.

The marriage lasted but 141 days. Shortly after the parties were married, Mr. Williams became ill and died on January 29, 1974. He died testate and his sole devisees were his children, William Wesley Williams, Jr. and Geneva W. Canion, who are the petitioners in this cause. Approximately one year after the death of their father, and relying on the executed premarital agreement, they requested possession of the residence, the household furnishings therein, and a 1971 Chrysler automobile. It is undisputed that the property sought had been the separate property of the deceased and had been devised to the petitioners. Mildred Williams refused to abide by the premarital agreement, choosing instead to claim her rights as a surviving spouse. Tex. Const. art. XVI, Sec. 52; Tex. Prob. Code Ann. Secs. 271, 272, 284 (1956).

As a result of Mrs. Williams' refusal to vacate the property, the children filed this suit for declaratory judgment. The case was withdrawn from the jury and the trial court rendered judgment in favor of the children. The trial court held that the portion of the premarital agreement by which Mrs. Williams relinquished her constitutional and statutory rights to the homestead was valid and binding on her. The court then ruled that the agreement was void to the extent that it provided that income or other property acquired during marriage should be the separate property of the party who earned or whose property produced such income or acquisition. But the trial court held that the valid and void provisions of the agreement were severable and ordered that the children recover possession of the residence, all personal property belonging to their father at the time of his death, and the Chrysler automobile.

Article XVI, Section 52 of the Texas Constitution provides that the homestead shall not be partitioned among the heirs of the deceased during the lifetime of the surviving husband or wife, or so long as the survivor may elect to use or occupy the same as a homestead. This is sometimes referred to as the probate homestead. O. Speer, *Texas Family Law*, Sec. 36:62, at 208 (5th ed. 1977). This homestead right of the survivor has been held to be one in the nature of a legal life estate or life estate created by operation of law. The Probate Code requires that the probate homestead and certain exempt personal property be set aside to the surviving spouse. Tex. Prob. Code Ann. Secs. 271, 272, 283, 284 (1956). These rights are provided by law for the protection of the family and to secure a home for the surviving spouse. Therefore, we must decide whether these rights may be waived by a premarital agreement.

The statutory authorization for premarital agreements in Texas is Section 5.41 of the Family Code. This statute should be construed as broadly as possible in order to allow the parties as much flexibility to contract with respect to property or other rights incident to the marriage, provided the constitutional and statutory definitions of separate and community property or the requirements of public policy are not violated. *See* generally, O. Speer, *Texas Family Law* sec. 16:5, at 192 (5th ed. 1976); McKnight, *Commentary to the Texas Family Code*, Title 1, 5 Tex. Tech. L. Rev. 281, 374–76 (1974).

Mrs. Williams argues that the policy of the law favoring the security of the widow by preventing an improvident relinquishment of the homestead, or other similar rights, is paramount to the policy of the law favoring flexibility in premarital agreements. Decisions from Kansas and North Dakota support this view. *In re Neis' Estate*, 170 Kan. 254, 225 P.2d 110 (1950); *Swingle v. Swingle*, 36 N.D. 611, 162 N.W. 912 (1917). The weight of authority and the better rule, however, allows the premarital waiver of these rights. See *e.g., Smith v. Tang*, 100 Ariz. 196, 412 P.2d 697 (1966); *In re Howe's Estate*, 81 Cal. App. 2d 95, 183 P.2d 329 (Dist. Ct. App. 1947); *In re Estate of Taylor v. United States National Bank*, 248 Or. 538, 436 P.2d 256 (1968); *In re Schwarzwalter's Estate*, 47 Wash. 2d 119, 286 P.2d 699 (1955); Annot., 65 A.L.R.2d 727 (1956) and other cases cited therein.

Furthermore, the premarital agreement in question does not violate the public policy of this state. The parties to the agreement were mature individuals. There was no suggestion of fraud, overreaching, or a lack of understanding. Full disclosure was made of the nature and extent of the property interests involved. Both parties had substantial separate property which they desired to preserve for themselves. There were no interests of any minor children to protect. Viewing this agreement in light of these facts and circumstances, as well as the underlying purpose of the transaction, we are of the opinion that neither party would be adversely affected by the premarital agreement.

Mrs. Williams also contends that article XVI, Section 52 of the Texas Constitution, in effect, prohibits the premarital agreement now before us. This contention, however, is based on an incorrect interpretation of Section 52. While a "surviving" spouse is granted the right to occupy the homestead by Section 52, such language is not to be construed as a constitutional prohibition to a waiver of that right by prospective spouses. Therefore, we hold that Mrs. Williams waived her rights to the probate homestead and exempt property by the premarital agreement in question.

The trial court correctly concluded that the agreement was void to the extent that income or other property acquired during marriage should be the separate property of the party who earned or whose property produced such income or acquisition. Such provisions were no more than a mere agreement between the parties to establish the character of the property prior to its acquisition during marriage in violation of both the Texas Constitution and the Family Code, Tex. Const. art. XVI, Sec. 15; Tex. Family Code Ann. Sec. 5.01 (1975); *see Gorman v. Gause*, 56 S.W.2d 855 (Tex. Comm'n. App. 1933, judgmt adopted); *Arnold v. Leonard*, 114 Tex. 535, 273 S.W. 799 (1925); *Hilley v. Hilley*, 161 Tex. 569, 342 S.W.2d 565 (1961). Mrs. Williams contends that the entire agreement is vitiated by these void provisions. On the assumption that the provisions in question constituted part of the consideration for the agreement, she asserts that when a contract is based upon several considerations, one or more of which is illegal, then the entire contract is void. We disagree.

We are of the opinion that the agreement here is controlled instead by the rule that where the consideration for the agreement is valid, an agreement containing more than one promise is not necessarily rendered invalid by the illegality of one of the promises. In such a case, the invalid provisions may be severed and the valid portions of the agreement upheld provided the invalid provision does not constitute the main or essential purpose of the agreement. Mutual promises to marry, subsequently performed, provide valid consideration for the premarital agreement in question. The invalid provisions of the agreement are only a part of the many reciprocal promises in the agreement concerning the rights of the parties to the marriage. Moreover, they did not constitute the main or essential purpose of the agreement. Therefore, we hold that the trial court was correct in severing the invalid provisions from the premarital agreement and enforcing the valid provisions regarding Mrs. Williams' waiver of her rights as a surviving spouse to the homestead and other exempt property.

Accordingly, we reverse the judgment of the court of civil appeals and affirm that of the trial court.

DISCUSSION

This case reflects the traditional (that is, until the 1980 constitutional amendment) Texas view that property is characterized according to the Texas Constitution; the understanding of the parties regarding the character of future acquisitions was irrelevant. According to traditional doctrine, community property, *after* it was acquired, could be transmuted into separate property by partition, exchange or gift. Partition connotes a division of an item of community property into separate property interests. In contrast, an exchange connotes a swap of one spouse's community interest in certain property for the other spouse's community interest in other items of community property. Finally, if one spouse makes a completed gift of his or her interest in an item of community property to the other spouse, the property becomes the donee's separate property. *See Pankhurst v. Weitinger & Tucker*, 850 S.W.2d 726 (Tex. App.—Corpus Christi 1993, writ denied). The traditional doctrine did not allow spouses to transmute separate property into community property (except by commingling).

Williams shows that, before 1980, it was impossible to try to recharacterize community property before it was received. It was therefore impossible for parties to alter their marital property rights in a premarital agreement. This rule was consistent with the traditional rule that spouses could not specify in a premarital agreement what their rights and responsibilities would be if the marriage ended in divorce. What might have been the policy justification for this rule?

B. The Modern Approach

The 1980 amendment to article XVI, Section 15 of the Texas Constitution significantly expands the rights of spouses to alter their marital property rights. However, are all types of contracts now permitted? Can separate property be transformed into community property? What if both spouses want their wages earned during marriage to be the recipient's separate property? How would you draft such an agreement?

During the last 30 years, many states have abandoned the rule that spousal agreements regarding the economic consequences of divorce will not be enforced. Why are marriage contracts now more accepted?

Recent amendments to the Texas Constitution and Tex. Fam. Code § 4.001-4.205 allow spouses significant freedom of contract in establishing the character of future acquisitions. The cases set forth below may shed some light on how Texas courts might apply this new system regarding marriage contracts.

1. Cases from Other States

Ranney v. Ranney
Supreme Court of Kansas, 1976
548 P.2d 734

MILLER, Justice.

The defendant wife appeals from the judgment of the trial court divorcing the parties and upholding and enforcing an antenuptial agreement. She does not challenge that portion of the order granting a divorce. The principal issue before us is whether the antenuptial agreement is valid and enforceable.

The parties were first married on June 21, 1947. Two children, Virginia and Joseph, were born of that marriage. The Cowley County District Court, Honorable Jerome Harman presiding, entered a decree divorcing the parties on July 7, 1958. The wife was awarded the home and furnishings, an automobile, the sum of $25,000 as alimony, and child support. The alimony and support were payable in monthly installments.

The parties discussed remarriage and set January 22, 1961 as the date for the ceremony. Prior to the remarriage, John Ranney consulted an attorney and the antenuptial agreement which is at the heart of this conflict was prepared. On January 21, 1961, the day before the proposed remarriage, the plaintiff presented to the defendant, in the presence of the minor children, the following agreement which he announced was a prerequisite to the marriage:

> This is an agreement between Helen R. Ranney a single person and John M. Ranney a single person. This agreement made prior to marriage.
>
> It is our intention to be married. Both of us intend the marriage to be successful, but fully realize in view of past difficulties, it may not.
>
> In the event for any reason the marriage is dissolved or separated [sic], then Helen shall have the property she owned at the time of this last marriage and John shall have the property he owned at the time of this last marriage. John shall complete the payment of the alimony awarded Helen in her divorce decree and Helen will make no further claim for alimony, support or division of property.
>
> In other words both Helen Ranney and John Ranney shall be in the same financial position as they were before the marriage.
>
> /s/ Helen R. Ranney /s/ John M. Ranney

While some of the evidence is conflicting, it is clear that Helen signed the agreement, returned it to John, and he placed it in his safety deposit box. Helen did not have the advice of counsel and she denies that she read the agreement prior to signing it.

The second marriage lasted for over eleven years. Then on February 22, 1972, the plaintiff instituted this action for divorce and sought to enforce the antenuptial agreement. Following trial, the court found that both parties knew the extent and value of the property of the other at the time the agreement was entered into; that there was no undue influence, overreaching, duress, threat, deception or fraud; that Helen examined the document, knew it was a property settlement agreement, and signed it voluntarily and of her own free will. The court held that the agreement was enforceable, effective and binding upon the parties.

Helen was awarded the home and furnishings (which had been awarded to her in the first divorce), a "replacement" automobile, and a one-third interest in a business property she had acquired by gift from John during the remarriage. The court made no division of property and did not award Helen alimony or support.

She raises five points on appeal, asserting that the court erred (1) in its construction of the agreement; (2) in failing to award alimony and to divide the property; (3) in failing to find the agreement void as against public policy; (4) in finding that the agreement was fairly and understandingly made; and (5) in limiting discovery as to plaintiff's financial condition and refusing to admit evidence thereof.

She contends that the phrase "no *further* claim for alimony, support or division of property" (emphasis supplied) should have been construed to apply only to any request for an additional share of the property owned by the parties at the time of the first divorce and not as a limitation on any *future* division of property. This is a strained construction of the phrase and one not in harmony with the explanatory paragraph which follows it. Even in the absence of this agreement, Helen could not have secured additional alimony through the original action, in which the judgment had become final. The trial court correctly construed the language of the agreement.

The trial court found that the agreement was fairly and understandingly made. Defendant points to evidence to the contrary. Suffice it to say that we have carefully reviewed the record and find substantial competent evidence to support this finding of the trial court. Such a finding will not be disturbed on appeal though there is evidence in the record which tends to support a contrary conclusion. The trial court heard and weighed the conflicting evidence. This court will not reweigh the testimony and substitute its judgment for that of the trier of fact.

Of the remaining three points, two are dependent upon the other. If the antenuptial agreement is valid, then the trial court properly restricted discovery and evidence as to plaintiff's financial worth, and properly refused the alimony and division of property sought by defendant. We turn to the seminal issue, the validity or invalidity of the agreement.

The terms of the agreement are significant. They provide that in the event the marriage fails, each party should have the property each owned at the time of the marriage; that John would continue to pay alimony during the marriage; and that Helen would make no further claim for alimony, support or division of property.

We note that John continued to make the alimony and child support payments through the clerk of the court, and that he paid the alimony judgment in full long before this case was commenced. The evidence is undisputed that Helen used the money so paid for family living expenses, though the trial court found that the family would not have gone without if she had not done so. There is no evidence that she accumulated any savings out of the "alimony" payments, or that she had any funds in her own right at the time of the present divorce other than the proceeds from the sale of the home which was sold pendente lite.

The agreement contains no provision relating to assets acquired during the marriage, unless because of the language prohibiting Helen from seeking further alimony or division of property it tacitly assigns all of such after-acquired property to John. This is the precise result of the trial court's application of the contract. As we have noted, discovery into the area of John's holdings was limited and evidence thereon was sparse. However, there are suggestions in the record that his net worth was in excess of one million dollars.

We discussed antenuptial contracts at length in *Fincham v. Fincham*, 160 Kan. 683, 165 P.2d 209. Mr. Justice Wedell, speaking for the court, said:

> The general rule in this state is that contracts, made either before or after marriage, the purpose of which is to fix property rights between a husband and wife, are to be liberally interpreted to carry out the intentions of the makers, and to uphold such contracts where they are fairly and understandingly made, are just and equitable in their provisions and are not obtained by fraud or overreaching. Generally speaking, such contracts are not against public policy, although a different rule obtains where the terms of the contract encourage a separation of the parties.

> Public policy relating to marriage is to foster and protect it, to make it a permanent and public institution, to encourage the parties to live together and to prevent separation.

> A separation provision in an antenuptial contract which permits the parties to separate at any time and for any cause whatsoever, whether legal or otherwise, and in which the wife relinquishes all rights she may have against the husband personally and in and to his property, on terms that are unreasonable and inequitable, tends to encourage separation and to defeat the marriage relation, is contrary to public policy and unenforceable by either party.

In *Fincham*, the husband brought suit for divorce and sought to enforce an antenuptial agreement which provided that in the event of a separation, then the husband upon demand would pay the wife the sum of $2,000 as a complete settlement of every claim the wife might have against the husband. His financial worth was shown to be $160,000. The court held that portion of the contract providing for a payment of $2,000 in full settlement of all rights and obligations arising out of the marriage to be against public policy, tending to invite and encourage a separation, unreasonable, inequitable and void.

Is the contract before us void for the same reason? We think it is. It did not invite and encourage Helen to take steps to dissolve the marriage, for though she would retain her home and automobile she would lose all right to support and maintenance for the rest of her life and she would lose all right to share in the assets acquired through the joint efforts of the parties during the marriage. John, however, tended to gain by bringing about a separation. He would lose nothing except his inchoate right in the home, furnishings and car; he would be relieved of all obligation to support Helen; he would retain all property acquired during the marriage; and Helen could make no claim against him. John was not even required to make a token cash payment such as the *Fincham* agreement provided.

These parties were not once married to others; they had no children by prior marriages to others; and their property is that acquired by their joint efforts during their marriage to each other. The agreement did not contemplate future accumulation of property, and made no provision for the disposition of such property. The provision for the continued payment of "alimony" during the marriage in fulfillment of the husband's duty of support, both during and after dissolution of the marriage, is clearly a sham and a subterfuge and against public policy. The inadequacy of this provision for support of the wife and the absence of any provision for disposition of after-acquired property, as well as the circumstances of the parties and all provisions of the contract must be considered together in determining whether the contract is fair, just and equitable. As noted above, the provision for payment of "alimony" during the marriage is void, and should not be taken into consideration in construing the overall effect of the agreement. As we held in *Bremer v. Bremer*, 187 Kan. 225, 356 P.2d 672, and *Fincham v. Fincham, supra*, an antenuptial agreement which tends to promote separation or divorce and which is unfair is unenforceable and may be set aside. This agreement would leave Helen with a house and car, and no part of the assets acquired through their joint efforts during the eleven year span of the marriage.

Under all of the facts and circumstances here before us we conclude that the agreement entered into on January 21, 1961 is unfair, inequitable, contrary to public policy and unenforceable.

The judgment of the trial court is therefore reversed with directions to determine the value of the holdings of the parties and to enter such order for alimony, division of property and support as justice may require.

SCHROEDER, Justice (concurring): I cannot agree that the antenuptial contract challenged herein is unenforceable and void.

The parties in this case were previously married and lived together for a period of approximately eleven years, during which time they had two children born of the marriage. The first divorce resulting in a decree on July 7, 1958, was bitterly fought and protracted with both parties adequately represented by counsel.

The court was informed in argument the remarriage of the parties was in part due to efforts of the minor children of the marriage who wanted their parents together.

The second marriage lasted over eleven years when divorce proceedings were instituted. After hearing the divorce action the trial court found both parties knew the extent and value of the property of the other at the time the antenuptial contract was entered into; that there was no undue influence, overreaching, duress, threat, deception or fraud; that Helen examined the document, knew it was a property settlement agreement, and signed it voluntarily and of her own free will. The court in its opinion recognizes the record discloses substantial competent evidence to support the finding of the trial court that the agreement was fairly and understandingly made.

Under these circumstances I cannot agree that the antenuptial contract is void.

First, the provision for continued payment of alimony is innocuous. Continued payment of alimony pursuant to the divorce decree dissolving the first marriage after remarriage could not be required, but John M. Ranney paid the full amount in accordance with the agreement, and for present purposes any argument based upon this provision is moot.

Second, the last two paragraphs of the agreement regarding the parties' property in the event the marriage is "dissolved or separated," when read together, are ambiguous in the sense that nothing is said concerning the accumulation of property by the joint efforts of the parties after the second marriage.

In *Frontiero v. Richardson*, 411 U.S. 677, 93 S.Ct. 1764, 36 L.Ed.2d 583, four members of the U.S. Supreme Court said statutory classifications based upon sex were inherently suspect and must be subjected to close judicial scrutiny, and under such standard of judicial scrutiny, the challenged statutes were unconstitutional as constituting invidious discrimination against servicewomen in violation of the due process clause of the Fifth Amendment. A fifth member of the court concurred in the judgment, agreeing that the statutes worked an invidious discrimination in violation of the constitution.

The Kansas Act Against Discrimination (K.S.A. 1975 Supp. 44-1001, *et seq.*) prohibits discrimination against individuals in employment relations, public accommodations or in housing by reason of sex, among others.

If under modern constitutional doctrine women are constitutionally recognized as free agents on an equal footing with men, certainly a corresponding equal obligation attaches to the free and voluntary acts of a woman when she enters into a legitimate contract with a man.

Such change in modern constitutional doctrine regarding the rights of women, in my opinion, foreshadows a requirement that courts shed their overzealous supervisory protecting mantle concerning women's acts when women exercise their constitutional freedom.

In my opinion the antenuptial contract should be upheld and the trial court's decision should be affirmed on this point. However, the judgment should be reversed and the case remanded to the trial court for a determination of the property accumulated by the joint efforts of the parties after the second marriage, with directions to make an equitable division of the property accumulated after the second marriage.

KAUL, Justice, joins in the foregoing concurring opinion.

DISCUSSION

The court concluded that the agreement was unenforceable because, among other things, the terms were unfair. How did the court determine this? What are the advantages and disadvantages of the *Ranney* rule?

Can an agreement be invalidated under the current Texas scheme if it is "unfair"? Why do you think Texas has decided to enforce an agreement, even if it could be shown to be "unfair"?

The *Ranney* court argued that the terms of the agreement encouraged divorce, so the agreement should not be enforced. What does this mean? Don't all marital agreements in some sense facilitate divorce?

Most courts (and the Texas statute) agree that marriage contracts need to be voluntarily signed to be enforceable. Note, though, that courts have not agreed how this should be determined.

Lutgert v. Lutgert
Florida Court of Appeals, 1976
338 So. 2d 1111

McNULTY, Chief Judge.

We void this day an antenuptial agreement because of involuntariness on the part of the wife.

The ten-year marriage of the parties hereto was dissolved upon the petition of the husband. An antenuptial agreement which, among other things, provided for the matter of support or alimony and a waiver by the wife of attorneys fees in the event of separation or divorce was sustained by the trial court and the questions relating to alimony and attorneys fees were adjudicated accordingly. The relevant portions of the agreement are as follows:

> FIRST: The said RAYMOND L. LUTGERT represents that his present estate consists of approximately Three Million Dollars ($3,000,000.00) in value. The nature of his assets are such that precise valuation is impossible, but this is believed to be a reasonable and conservative figure at this time.
>
> ....
>
> THIRD: All the personal and real estate now owned by the said RAYMOND L. LUTGERT shall be his own personal estate to be dealt with by him during his lifetime or by will as freely as though this agreement had not been executed in all respects except as indicated immediately hereinafter, namely:
>
> ....
>
> C. The foregoing provisions hereof are in contemplation of the parties remaining married to and living with each other until the death of one of them. However, it is the desire of the parties to recognize the possibility of presently unanticipated separation or divorce.
>
> Each of the parties has been previously married and is aware of the expense and possible publicity with resultant personal embarrassment, which may result from court controversy in a divorce or separate maintenance action over financial matters, in addition to great emotional strain.
>
> The parties therefore further agree as follows:
>
> In the event of the separation of the parties with or without divorce the said RAYMOND L. LUTGERT will pay to the said MURIEL STEVENSON the sum of One Thousand Dollars ($1,000.00) per month so long as she shall live, and not remarry. Such payments shall be in full of any support money or alimony from the said RAYMOND L. LUTGERT to the said MURIEL STEVENSON, and each party shall pay his or her own attorneys fees and other expenses in any separation or divorce proceeding.

In sustaining the agreement the trial court found in pertinent part as follows:

1. The parties entered into a valid prenuptial agreement according to the standards set forth in *Del Vecchio*, 143 So. 2d 17. In reaching this conclusion the Court weighed the testimony of all witnesses concerning the circumstances of the signing of the agreement, the fact that the time element from the first discussion of the agreement by the parties and, actually, from her reading of the first draft, would have allowed her to consult any attorney of her own choosing for advice on the agreement but that she did consult with the law firm of Cummings and Wyman ... and also, the Court considered that both parties were mature and this was not a first venture onto the sea of matrimony for either party.

As to the full and frank disclosure to wife, before signing of agreement of husband's worth, or, absent such disclosure, a general and approximate knowledge, by the wife of the prospective husband's property as set forth in *Del Vecchio, supra*, the Court has the benefit of statements of the financial condition of husband on July 1, 1963 ($53,163.00) and again on September 30, 1974, ($3,915,929.00), together with a statement as to the financial condition of the prospective husband as set forth in the agreement itself.... In addition, testimony showed that the parties lived in close proximity to each other, moved in the same social circles, and had ample opportunity to observe the others standard of living for a considerable period of time prior to their marriage to each other.

The Court specifically finds that the agreement was signed freely and voluntarily by the parties, that when the wife signed same she had or reasonably should have had a general and approximate knowledge of the character and extent of the husband's property, and, as to the variation in the husband's financial status at the time of the signing of the agreement and the hearing of this cause "the vicissitudes of his fortune in the interval were only that which can be said to have been reasonably contemplated from the nature of his assets," *Singer v. Singer*, 4th DCA, (1975), 318 So. 2d 438. The testimony also shows that the personal financial standing of the wife also changed considerably for the better during the period of the marriage of the parties.

There is sufficient evidence in the record to support the foregoing findings of the trial court except, in our view, the findings of validity as respects the free and voluntary execution by the wife; and as indicated this is the basis of our determination that the wife can avoid the agreement.

While the testimony relating to the execution of the agreement is conflicting in several particulars, we accept the husband's version except as to the undenied portions of the wife's version. A narrative of significant events follows:

The parties, and their then spouses, were acquainted socially for a considerable period of time before their marriage in Chicago, where they previously resided. Their relationship ripened into a love affair after their respective former spouses became illicitly involved with each other and two divorces ensued. They kept company for approximately a year and became engaged some four weeks prior to their marriage herein at 12:30 in the early morning hours of Friday, April 30, 1965.

An understanding of the odd hour of the marriage can be had from the events which began on Monday evening of that fateful week, April 26, when appellee husband called and suggested that they be married shortly after midnight on Thursday, April 29, provided they could book passage for an extended honeymoon cruise on the SS Constitution, scheduled to sail from New York later on that same day. She ecstatically agreed.

On Tuesday morning, April 27, the husband advised appellant by telephone that he had succeeded in getting passage on the Constitution and that the wedding plans could go ahead. The parties met shortly thereafter and spent the rest of that day purchasing a sable stole for her and a wedding outfit for him; getting their passports straightened out; getting blood tests; arranging for a state Court of Appeals judge to marry them; acquiring the use of V.I.P. facilities, called the "Topflight Room" of Northwest Airlines, at the O'Hare Airport in Chicago; and inviting family and friends to the wedding.

On Wednesday, April 28, the wife purchased her trousseau, after which the parties met at their jewelers to select and fit wedding rings. Thereafter, a marriage license was procured.

The following day, Thursday, April 29, is the critical date concerning the execution of the antenuptial agreement. That afternoon the parties met again at the jewelers to finalize the sizing of the wedding rings. While they were being readied the husband took the antenuptial agreement out of his pocket and for the first time presented it to appellant and asked her to sign it. She objected, saying that it indicated lack of trust on his part and that she didn't want the marriage to start out on such a weak footing. He made light of that suggestion, proclaiming that the agreement was of no consequence anyway since they wouldn't be getting a divorce. He joked about being married for some 80 years, getting married at their age. The wife still objected; so the husband called his Chicago lawyers, Cummings and Wyman, while still at the jewelers and apparently some conversation ensued between the lawyers and the wife after the husband put her on the telephone. While the evidence is conflicting as to whether this phone conversation resulted in any change in the wording of the agreement (the husband contends it did), the documentary evidence itself irrefutably demonstrates that the document was in fact drawn up and finally drafted the preceding Monday, April 26, and was not changed in any respect thereafter.

As a further insight into the events leading up to the agreement herein, it is agreed that the subject of an antenuptial agreement had been brought up on more than one occasion for perhaps up to a year before the marriage herein. The husband testified that he wanted such an agreement because his father had advised it and because he had had extreme difficulty during his first divorce. No specific agreement nor draft thereof was made, however, until the instant agreement was prepared on April 26 of that eventful week in 1965 as aforesaid. The wife insists that she consistently objected to such an agreement, whatever its terms, and the sole testimony in rebuttal of this is the husband's statement that "there was no refutation of any willingness to sign such an agreement."

In any case, following the aforementioned phone call, the wife finally agreed reluctantly to sign the agreement after the husband insisted that the wedding would otherwise be called off. She contends that she signed the agreement then and there at the jewelers; but we can accept the husband's version that it wasn't signed until just before the wedding that night (*i.e.*, about 12:30 a.m. on Friday) when the minute hand of the clock was on the rise "for luck," as several of the witnesses testified. Two witnesses corroborated the husband's version that the agreement was indeed signed at the airport shortly before the wedding, one Williams, the husband's nephew, who also was a notary public and who appears to have taken the acknowledgment of the parties, and one of the husband's attorneys who was a member of the aforementioned Cummings and Wyman firm. Each additionally testified that he did not hear the wife voice any objections to the agreement as she executed it.

After the marriage, as may be gleaned from the admitted wealth of the husband the parties enjoyed a lifestyle reserved only to the fabulously rich. While the trial court found that during the times material herein the husband was worth from approximately $3,100,000 at the beginning to $3,900,000 at the present time, the wife points to much of the record tending to the conclusion that he is really presently worth nearer to $25,000,000. Indeed the admitted opulent lifestyle would appear to be supportable only if the latter figure were found to be the fact. For example, the present homeplace in Naples, Florida, is a palatial mansion directly on the Gulf of Mexico. It has eight bedrooms, twelve baths, a five-car garage, a guest house and servants' quarters and is surrounded by some four and a half acres of formal gardens with a gate house at its entrance. The parties owned at least three luxury motor yachts, one of them a 50-footer custom built in North Carolina, and one a 63-footer custom built in Japan. They at one time owned a private turbojet airplane. They drove only luxury cars, including Rolls Royces and Lincoln Continentals. They took at least one round-the-world cruise and several extended cruises to Europe and other parts of the world. They had staffs of servants and gardeners. He gave expensive gifts of valuable jewelry. The husband has a hobby of collecting classic automobiles, his present collection having a value in excess of $900,000; and on one occasion he bid for and purchased an original Duesenberg automobile for some $207,000.

The wife was fully aware before the marriage, of course, that the husband was a man of great wealth—and lived it. But all this, it seems to us, should only point up the expectancy of security on the part of the wife at the time of her acceptance of the marriage proposal, as well as the disproportionate relative positions of the parties, when it is emphasized that she had only a relatively small amount of cash in her own right at that time, together with some interest in the marital home of her prior marriage, and approximately $600 a month alimony (for only 10 years) as a result of a prior divorce. Clearly, since the agreement herein limits her simply to $1,000 a month alimony in the event of separation or divorce, and no attorneys fees, a grossly disproportionate benefit to the husband as a result of the agreement is startlingly patent.

Now, it is black letter law that the parties to an antenuptial agreement do not deal at arms length with each other. Their relationship is one of mutual trust and confidence. While such agreements are not per se suspect in the law, the courts nevertheless scrutinize them with care; and the parties must exercise the highest degree of good faith, candor and sincerity in all matters bearing on the terms and execution of the proposed agreement, with fairness being the ultimate measure. Moreover, a presumption of undue influence or overreaching arises in transactions or contracts between persons in such a confidential relationship when it is clear that the dominant party thereto is the grossly disproportionate beneficiary of the transaction.[1] It is well settled, for example, that with respect to the issue of full disclosure of the prospective husband's wealth, a disproportionate benefit to the husband in an antenuptial agreement casts upon him the burden of showing that the wife in fact did have full or sufficient knowledge of the husband's wealth.[2]

The presumption which arises in these cases operates against the party receiving such benefit and imposes upon him the burden of coming forth with evidence sufficient to rebut it to the extent necessary to avoid its preponderating on the issue to which it relates. We see no reason why the burden on the part of the husband ought be any less with respect to the issue of voluntariness on the part of the wife in entering into such an agreement, than it is with respect to the issue of full disclosure, when there is a grossly disproportionate benefit to him together with sufficient coercive circumstances sur-

1. See e.g., 25 Am.Jur.2d, *Duress and Undue Influence,* Sec. 44, at p. 404, and 41 Am.Jur.2d, *Husband and Wife,* Sec. 314, at p. 225.
2. See *Posner v. Posner,* 257 So. 2d 530, 534 (Fla. 1972).

rounding the execution of the agreement as to give rise to a presumption of undue influence or overreaching.

Here, it appears that the wife was in her middle or late thirties at the time of the agreement. The instant marriage was her third, following one of approximately seventeen years during which she bore three children. Her first marriage was of very short duration having been entered into when she was seventeen years old. Concededly, therefore, it can hardly be said that she was mesmerized by prehymeneal ardor when she entered into the agreement. But that doesn't mean that her volition could not still have been overcome by circumstances sufficiently coercive in nature.

There is ample conclusive evidence of such circumstances in this case. To begin with, the husband sprang the agreement upon her and demanded its execution within twenty four hours of the wedding; and it has been said that a woman ought not be "too much hurried" into such an agreement. Passage had been booked for a honeymoon cruise to Europe; rings had been bought; a trousseau had been bought; all invitations to family and friends had been given; all arrangements otherwise had been made; an ultimatum had been delivered by the husband: "No agreement, no wedding;" and, obviously, there arose a sudden stark awareness of the potential immediate loss of a future life of enormous grandeur.

Surely, particularly at the last moment, a prospective wife ought not be forced into a position of being "bought" at the price of losing all if she does not agree to a grossly disproportionate benefit to the husband should she leave him under any and all circumstances, any more than she should be permitted to "sell" herself at zero hour for an agreement resulting in a grossly disproportionate gain to her upon the same eventuality. Along with public policy considerations this is the very reason why "fairness" is the polestar in these agreements; and fairness would certainly include an opportunity to seek independent advice and a reasonable time to reflect on the proposed terms.

Clearly, in our view, all the circumstances surrounding the execution of the agreement in this case, including its disproportionate terms, militate against fairness and are sufficient to support a presumption, as a matter of law, of undue influence and overreaching which bore adversely on the free exercise of the wife's will. We certainly couldn't indulge a contrary presumption; the wife could hardly say more in rebuttal. Nor need we go so far as to say that the wife proved involuntariness as a matter of law. The device of a presumption such as that we employ here is the prevalent judicial tool commonly used in the determination *vel non* of undue influence or overreaching in transactions arising out of confidential relationships.

The burden thus shifted to the husband to rebut this presumption by coming forth with some competent evidence to the contrary. We have searched the record in vain to find it — it simply isn't there. The mere statement by the husband that "there was no refutation of any willingness [on the part of the wife] to sign such an agreement," which alluded to prior discussions of an antenuptial agreement generally and not to the specific one involved here which was objected to, will not alone suffice.

The question here is not whether the wife knew what she was signing or what she was or was not getting. The agreement is clear on its face and she can't be heard to deny its contents. The question is whether she, in the free exercise of her will, voluntarily signed it. Evidence that she may have gotten some legal advice has no great impact on this issue either. For one thing, the only evidence of legal advice is that within twenty four hours before the wedding, when the husband first presented the antenuptial agreement and she rebelled, she spoke on the telephone to his lawyers; and we have already indicated that the documentary evidence conclusively demonstrates that this conversation could not and did not result in any change in the agreement enuring to the benefit of the wife. Additionally, in the face of the grossly disproportionate benefit to the husband, whatever legal advice she may have gotten at that time certainly wouldn't tend to neutralize the other coercive factors bearing on her volition. In short, the presumption of undue influence and overreaching which we perceive to have been established as a matter of law is not rebutted at all and thus, remaining in the case, it must prevail as though the conclusion to which it points is admitted. The wife is entitled to avoid the agreement.

In view of our disposition hereof, it is unnecessary at this time to consider the other points raised on appeal. It is also unnecessary to consider the improved financial condition of the wife. This factor will undoubtedly bear on the equities existing between the parties as may be appropriate in the determination of alimony and/or the settlement of property rights generally.

DISCUSSION

Why was the agreement not enforced here? If one person says to the other, "I will marry you only if you sign this," is this duress? Does it matter if this is said three months before the wedding or the day of the wedding? Would this agreement in *Lutgert* be enforced in Texas?

Why are courts concerned about enforcing contracts negotiated and signed shortly before the wedding? How is the bargaining process less than optimal? What forces might be affecting the prospective spouses immediately before the wedding? Do any pressures of the moment discourage a person from calling off the wedding? If parties are considered unable to make reasoned decisions shortly before the wedding, when do these pressures begin? Should marital contracts be enforced if they are negotiated and signed one week before the wedding?

Some argue that prenuptial agreements should not be enforced unless each party is represented by independent counsel in connection with the execution of a marital agreement. What are the advantages and disadvantages of such a rule?

DeLorean v. DeLorean

New Jersey Superior Court, Chancery Division, 1986
511 A.2d 1257

IMBRIANI, J.S.C.

This matrimonial case examines the circumstances under which an antenuptial agreement may be enforced and whether that issue may be resolved by arbitration. The intent of most marriage is to create an "indivisible union of one" in which both spouses generally contribute whatever they own prior to the marriage or acquire thereafter into a common marital fund. Upon death the survivor usually receives whatever has been accumulated but, if a divorce ensues, in the usual case they share all marital assets equally.

However, when parties enter into an antenuptial agreement their purpose is to alter that usual arrangement and enter into an economic partnership whereby many or all of the assets owned prior to the marriage or acquired thereafter are not contributed into a common marital fund but are kept segregated and, when the marriage ceases, whether by death or divorce, they are not shared equally but pursuant to a plan conceived and agreed upon before the marriage was consummated. It is important that we understand that normally the intent of most antenuptial agreements is to deny a spouse an interest in assets held in the sole name of the other which the former would ordinarily receive by operation of law when the marriage ceased.

These parties entered into an antenuptial agreement on May 8, 1973 (only a few hours before they married) which provided that:

> any and all property, income and earnings acquired by each before and after the marriage shall be the separate property of the person acquiring same, without any rights, title or control vesting in the other person.

The potential assets could exceed $20 million and practically all of them are in the sole name of the husband. Absent this agreement and considering that this is a thirteen-year marriage in which there are two minor children, under New Jersey law this wife could reasonably have anticipated receiving approximately 50% of the marital assets at the time of divorce. But if this agreement is upheld she will receive relatively little. She asserts that this agreement should not be enforced because (1) she was not provided with a full and complete disclosure of her husband's financial affairs before she signed it and (2) undue influence was exerted upon her by her husband who possessed far greater financial knowledge and experience than she.

Initially, it is clear that "antenuptial agreements fixing post-divorce rights and obligations [are] ... valid and enforceable" and courts should "welcome and encourage such agreements at least 'to the extent that the parties have developed comprehensive and particularized agreements responsive to their peculiar circumstances.'" In determining whether to enforce an antenuptial agreement there are at least three requirements that have to be met.

First, that there was no fraud or duress in the execution of the agreement or, to put it another way, that both parties signed voluntarily. The wife alleges she did not sign voluntarily because her husband presented the agreement to her only a few hours before the marriage ceremony was performed and threatened to cancel the marriage if she did not sign. In essence she asserts that she had no choice but to sign. While she did not have independent counsel of her own choosing, she did acknowledge that before she signed she did privately consult with an attorney selected by her husband who advised her not to sign the agreement. Yet for whatever reasons she rejected the attorney's advice and signed.

While her decision may not have been wise, it appears that she had sufficient time to consider the consequences of signing the agreement and, indeed, although she initially refused to sign it, after conferring with her intended spouse and an attorney, she reconsidered and decided to sign it. Concededly, the husband was 25-years older and a high powered senior executive with General Motors Corporation, but she was not a "babe in the woods." She was 23-years old with some business experience in the modeling and entertainment industry; she had experienced an earlier marriage and the problems wrought by a divorce; and she had advice from an attorney who, although not of her own choosing, did apparently give her competent advice and recommended that she not sign. While it may have been embarrassing to cancel the wedding only a few hours before it was to take place, she certainly was not compelled to go through with the ceremony. There was no fraud or misrepresentation committed by the husband. He made it perfectly clear that he did not want her to receive any portion of the marital assets that were in his name. At no time did she ever make an effort to void the agreement and, of course, it was never voided. Under these circumstances the court is satisfied that the wife entered into the agreement voluntarily and without any fraud or duress being exerted upon her.

Second, the agreement must not be "unconscionable." This is not to say that the agreement should be what a court would determine to be "fair and equitable." The fact that what a spouse receives under an antenuptial agreement is small, inadequate or disproportionate does not in itself render the agreement voidable if the spouse was not overreached and entered into the agreement voluntarily with full knowledge of the financial worth of the other person. So long as a spouse is not left destitute or as a public charge the parties can agree to divide marital assets in any manner they wish. Mrs. DeLorean presently enjoys substantial income from her employment as a talk show television hostess and was given a life interest in a trust of unknown amount created by Mr. DeLorean, which he testified had assets of between $2 and $5 million dollars. She will not be left destitute. The court is unaware of any public policy which requires that the division of marital assets be made in what the court believes to be fair and equitable if the parties freely and voluntarily agree otherwise. In the final analysis it is for the parties to decide for themselves what is fair and equitable, not the court. So long as a spouse had sufficient opportunity to reflect on her actions, was competent, informed, and had access to legal advice and that of any relevant experts, a court should not, except in the most unusual case, interject its own opinion of what is fair and equitable and reject the wishes of the parties. Since the wife voluntarily agreed to this division of the marital assets and she will not become destitute or a public charge, the agreement is not unconscionable.

Third, the spouse seeking to enforce the agreement made a full and complete disclosure of his or her financial wealth before the agreement was signed. Obviously, one cannot make a knowing and intelligent waiver of legal and financial rights unless fully informed of all of the facts; otherwise one cannot know what is being waived. The husband asserts that the wife acknowledged that she received a full and complete disclosure of his financial wealth because the agreement states:

Husband is the owner of substantial real and personal property and he has reasonable prospects of earning large sums of monies; these facts have been fully disclosed to Wife.

However, that statement is not very meaningful and is insufficient to satisfy his obligation to make a full and complete disclosure of his financial wealth. While several states hold that a full and complete disclosure is not synonymous with a detailed disclosure, those cases can be distinguished because they impose upon each spouse a duty to inquire and investigate into the financial condition of the other. However, as far as this court can ascertain, New Jersey imposes no such duty.

A conflict arose as to precisely what financial information was disclosed by Mr. DeLorean. However, the court is satisfied that even if it accepted as true the testimony of Mr. DeLorean he did not satisfy his legal obligation to make a full and complete disclosure. But we should address the question of how to avoid disputes of this nature in the future. It is clear that we can ascertain with complete certainty whether there was a full and complete disclosure only by requiring a written list of assets and income be attached to the antenuptial agreement. Anything less will encourage a plethora of plenary hearings which would frequently be complicated by contradictory and conflicting testimony, often tainted by memory lapses.

While the wife was aware that Mr. DeLorean was a person of substantial wealth, there was no way that she could have known with any substantial degree of certainty the extent of his wealth. This is important because one can appreciate that while a wife might waive her legal rights to share in marital assets of $1 million, she might not be willing to do so if she knew the marital assets were worth $20 million. And the suggestion that Mrs. DeLorean had a duty to investigate to ascertain the full nature and extent of his financial wealth is both unfair and unrealistic. How many people when about to marry would consider investigating the financial affairs of their intended spouse? How many people would appreciate or tolerate being investigated by an intended spouse? And how many marriage would be cancelled when one of the parties is informed of an investigation being conducted by the other? Such a requirement would cause embarrassment and impose a difficult burden. The better rule is that the burden is not on either party to inquire, but on each to inform, for it is only by requiring full disclosure of the amount, character, and value of the parties' respective assets that courts can ensure intelligent waiver of the statutory [and other] rights involved. When a spouse has a duty to fully and completely disclose his financial wealth we would eviscerate and render meaningless that duty if we imposed upon the other spouse a duty to investigate.

The only way that Mrs. DeLorean could knowingly and intelligently waive her legal rights in Mr. DeLorean's assets was if she was fully and completely informed what they were. And for Mr. DeLorean to merely state that he had an interest in a farm in California, a large tract of land in Montana, and a share in a major league baseball club fell far short of a full and complete disclosure. If this issue were decided under New Jersey law the court would conclude that Mr. DeLorean did not make a full and complete disclosure of his financial wealth before his spouse signed the antenuptial agreement and, therefore, it would not be valid and enforceable.

However, it is argued that California, not New Jersey, law should be applied. The parties married and executed the agreement in California. It is hornbook law that when an agreement is silent as to which law should be applied, the validity and construction of a contract shall be determined by the law of the place of contracting. But this agreement is not silent and expressly provides that it:

> shall be construed under the laws of the State of California and enforceable in the proper courts of jurisdiction of the State of California.

When the agreement was executed the parties had substantial contacts with California and reasonably expected to retain many of them which, indeed, has been the case. For these reasons the law of California must be applied in this case.

That being so, what duty does California law impose upon a party to an antenuptial agreement with regard to the disclosure of one's financial wealth? In both California and New Jersey fiduciaries are required to exercise a high degree of trust, good faith and candor in their dealings with each other. Where California and New Jersey law part is in their determination of what constitutes a fiduciary because, unlike New Jersey, California does not treat a party to an antenuptial agreement as a fiduciary on the theory that "parties who are not yet married are not presumed to share a confidential relationship." So long as the spouse seeking to set aside such an agreement has a general idea of the character and extent of the financial assets and income of the other, that apparently is sufficient in California. Indeed, absent fraud or misrepresentation, there appears to be a duty to make some inquiry to ascertain the full nature and extent of the financial resources of the other. As this court reads California law, the disclosures made by John DeLorean appear to be sufficient for purposes of enforcing this agreement.

And this court does not have to rely solely upon its review of California law because here we have the benefit of a decision by a retired California judge (see infra) who also was of the opinion that the disclosures made by John DeLorean were sufficient. Accordingly, the court is satisfied that under California law there was a sufficient disclosure by the husband and the antenuptial agreement of May 8, 1973, is valid and enforceable.

DISCUSSION

Do you agree with the result here? Is it consistent with *Lutgert*? Would a Texas court have enforced this agreement?

California has attempted to clarify by statute when a premarital agreement is voluntarily signed. In its version of the Uniform Premarital Agreement Act, California has added this subsection (c) to its version of Tex. Fam. Code § 4.006, California Family Code § 1615:

(c) For the purpose of subdivision (a), it shall be deemed that a premarital agreement was not executed voluntarily unless the court finds in writing or on the record all of the following:

(1) The party against whom enforcement is sought was represented by independent legal counsel at the time of signing the agreement or, after being advised to seek independent legal counsel, expressly waived, in a separate writing, representation by independent legal counsel.

(2) The party against whom enforcement is sought had not less than seven calendar days between the time that party was first presented with the agreement and advised to seek independent legal counsel and the time the agreement was signed.

(3) The party against whom enforcement is sought, if unrepresented by legal counsel, was fully informed of the terms and basic effect of the agreement as well as the rights and obligations he or she was giving up by signing the agreement, and was proficient in the language in which the explanation of the party's right was conducted and in which the agreement was written. The explanation of the rights and obligations relinquished shall be memorialized in writing and delivered to the party prior to signing the agreement. The unrepresented party shall, on or before the signing of the premarital agreement, execute a document declaring that he or she received the information required by this paragraph and indicating who provided that information.

(4) The agreement and the writings executed pursuant to paragraphs (1) and (3) were not executed under duress fraud, or undue influence, and the parties did not lack capacity to enter into the agreement.

Burtoff v. Burtoff

District of Columbia Court of Appeals, 1980
481 A.2d 1085

GALLAGHER, Associate Judge.

This appeal concerns the validity of an antenuptial contract setting the spouses' rights to support upon dissolution of the marriage, an issue of first impression in the District of Columbia. We agree with the trial court that such contracts are not void per se on public policy grounds. After a careful examination of this antenuptial agreement according to the criteria set out below, we uphold the contract.

Dr. and Mrs. Burtoff were married on October 14, 1975, after a courtship of several years. Both parties were of mature years, with adult children from previous marriages. Dr.

Burtoff insisted on an antenuptial contract to avoid a possible repetition of the property battle attendant to his first divorce, and to ensure that the bulk of his estate would pass to his children upon his death. Mrs. Burtoff resisted the idea, feeling the contract indicated a lack of trust on his part. Nevertheless, she signed, after it became apparent that Dr. Burtoff otherwise would not agree to the marriage. She was represented by counsel of her choice, who examined the agreement drawn up by Dr. Burtoff's attorney. Dr. Burtoff fully disclosed his considerable wealth, an estate of over a million dollars, by attaching an income tax return and a list of assets to the document. Mrs. Burtoff, an operating room nurse, also disclosed her $10,000 in assets and her salary for the preceding year, something under $8,000.

The contract called for a lump sum payment to Mrs. Burtoff on dissolution of the marriage, in full settlement of all obligations for support and maintenance, pendente lite or otherwise. The amount of the payment was keyed to the length of the marriage: $10,000 if the marriage lasted less than a year; $25,000 if the marriage lasted one to three years, and $35,000 if the marriage lasted longer than three years. If Dr. Burtoff were to die while the parties were still married, Mrs. Burtoff would receive $50,000.

After a few months of marriage, the couple began to experience difficulties, attributable in part to Mrs. Burtoff's resentment of the contract. Eight days before their first anniversary, while Mrs. Burtoff was attending a spiritualism class, Dr. Burtoff changed the locks on the couple's apartment and moved Mrs. Burtoff's belongings to another apartment he rented on her behalf. A private investigator hired by Dr. Burtoff handed her a letter as she left the class, explaining that he had effected a separation.

Mrs. Burtoff sued for pendente lite relief on March 15, 1977. The court held her motion in abeyance on the condition that Dr. Burtoff immediately tender $10,000 as provided for in the antenuptial agreement. A separate trial was held to determine the validity of the agreement. At this trial, the trial judge upheld the agreement in large part, but stated that the agreement would not control a spouse's support obligation before the marriage terminated; therefore, Mrs. Burtoff might be entitled to additional pendente lite support to prevent her from becoming a public charge. Mrs. Burtoff did not take further action to secure pendente lite relief until approximately ten months later, when Dr. Burtoff sued for absolute divorce. The court later granted the divorce but denied as moot the request for pendente lite support.

I.

The validity of an antenuptial contract setting property rights at the death of a spouse has long been accepted in the District of Columbia. *Pollock v. Jameson*, 63 App. D.C. 152, 70 F.2d 756 (1934). Prospective spouses may contractually define their rights in property and waive rights that otherwise would arise as a matter of law. *See Snow v. Snow*, 50 App.D.C. 242, 270 F. 364 (1921). As it implied in the language of the following District of Columbia Code Section, antenuptial contracts contemplating divorce are acceptable to arrange property rights. "Upon the entry of a final decree of annulment or absolute divorce, in the absence of a valid antenuptial or postnuptial agreement in relation thereto, all property rights of the parties in joint tenancy or tenancy by the entirety shall stand dissolved...." [D.C. Code 1973, Sec. 16-910 (amended 1977).]

Although antenuptial contracts relating to a spouse's rights in the other's estate at death or to property rights at dissolution of marriage are clearly acceptable in the District of Columbia, appellant contends that antenuptial contracts setting alimony are void because they encourage divorce and thus should be held to violate public policy. Support for this argument is found in cases of a number of jurisdictions. The reasoning behind this view is well expressed in *Crouch v. Crouch*, 53 Tenn. App. 594, 604, 385 S.W.2d 288, 293 (1964):

> Such contract could induce a mercenary husband to inflict on his wife any wrong he might desire with the knowledge his pecuniary liability would be limited. In other words, a husband could through abuse and ill treatment of his wife force her to bring an action for divorce and thereby buy a divorce for a sum far less than he would otherwise have to pay.

In particular, appellant relies on *Cohn v. Cohn*, 209 Md. 470, 121 A.2d 704 (1956), which involved an antenuptial contract similar to the one at issue here, with a lump sum payment in lieu of alimony, increasing with the duration of the marriage. The husband left the wife just prior to the time when the stipulated amount would have advanced from one level to the next, a circumstance which led the court to believe that the agreement induced the husband's desertion.

The reasoning in *Cohn* is no longer determinative today. Public policy considerations change along with societal conditions.

In the last ten years, courts in a number of jurisdictions have concluded that antenuptial agreements establishing rights to support upon divorce are no longer void *ab initio* as contrary to public policy. *E.g., Parniawski v. Parniawski*, 33 Conn. Sup. 44, 359 A.2d 719 (1976); *Posner v. Posner*, 233 So. 2d 381 (Fla. 1970); *Volid v. Volid*, 6 Ill. App. 3d 386, 286 N.E.2d 42 (1972); *Buettner v. Buettner*, 89 Nev. 39, 505 P.2d 600 (1973); *Unander v. Unander*, 265 Or. 102, 506 P.2d 719 (1973).

In *Posner v. Posner, supra*, the Florida Supreme Court upheld the agreement because of the right of married couples to control their property.

> With divorce such a commonplace fact of life, it is fair to assume that many prospective marriage partners whose property and familial situation is such as to generate a valid antenuptial agreement settling their property rights upon the death of either, might want to consider … — and agree upon, if possible — the disposition of their property and the alimony rights of the wife in the event their marriage, despite their best efforts, should fail.

[233 So. 2d at 384.] Accord, *Parniawski v. Parniawski*, 359 A.2d at 721.

We believe that an antenuptial agreement taking into consideration a future divorce is not necessarily void as against public policy. However, the court will scrutinize such an agreement more carefully than an ordinary contract, because of the likelihood that the contracting parties have not been dealing at arm's length. As the Florida Supreme Court said in *Del Vecchio v. Del Vecchio*, 142 So. 2d 17 (Fla. 1962), "[t]he relationship between the parties to an antenuptial agreement is one of mutual trust and confidence. Since they do not deal at arm's length they must exercise a high degree of good faith and candor in all matters bearing upon the contract." *Id.* at 21. We retain an interest in the marital relationship greater than our interest in other contractual subjects, and therefore will examine the facts in each case to decide if the agreement is valid.

The starting point of our examination is the contract's fairness. *Id.* at 20. If the contract is fair to both parties, then the party challenging the contract has the burden of proof on two further issues, namely, (1) whether the contract was voluntarily entered, and (2) after full disclosure of assets. If, on the other hand, the contract greatly disadvantages one spouse, then the other spouse will have the burden of showing that the disadvantaged spouse signed freely and voluntarily, with full knowledge of the other's assets. *Id.* at 20. To decide whether an antenuptial contract is fair, we will look at many of the traditional factors which have been taken into consideration in granting alimony awards, such as the duration of the marriage, the age and health of the spouses, their respective economic condition and earning capacity, their contributions to the accumulation of property, and society's interest in preventing a person from becoming a public charge. *See Quarles v. Quarles*, 86 U.S. App. D.C. 41, 179 F.2d 57 (1949). In marriages of short duration, such as the Burtoffs', an agreement will be considered fair if it allows each spouse to live as well as before the marriage. *See Del Vecchio v. Del Vecchio, supra* at 20. There was testimony to the effect that Mrs. Burtoff's award was calculated with reference to the amount she would have earned if she had continued to work during the marriage. By marrying, Mrs. Burtoff did not forgo any source of income, nor did she lose her ability to support herself through her profession.

Since we find the agreement to be fair and reasonable, if she is to invalidate the agreement, Mrs. Burtoff must sustain the burden of proving either (1) that she signed under duress, or (2) that she did not have knowledge of Dr. Burtoff's wealth when she signed. She cannot prevail on either issue. It is clear that Mrs. Burtoff signed the contract freely and voluntarily. The parties began to discuss the matter several months before the contract was executed. There was testimony to the effect that Dr. and Mrs. Burtoff negotiated terms and that the amount of the award to be granted after one year was raised in response to Mrs. Burtoff's suggestion. Mrs. Burtoff consulted her own attorney, and thus can be said to have understood any legal rights she might have waived.

Nor can there be any question that Mrs. Burtoff understood the extent of her husband's income and property. Dr. Burtoff fully disclosed his assets in documents attached to the antenuptial contract. Thus, after consideration of the circumstances involved, we uphold the agreement.

DISCUSSION

Note that the contract is enforced in *Burtoff* and not enforced in *Lutgert* or *Ranney*. Does the *Burtoff* court apply a different test than that applied in *Ranney* and *Lutgert*? Are the facts of this case distinguishable from the prior two cases?

Based on these cases, how should negotiations for a marital agreement be structured in order to increase the probability that the agreement will be enforced?

Does the *Burtoff* court suggest that the contract would have been enforceable regardless of the length of the marriage?

Does the contract in *Burtoff* encourage separation? If so, should it be enforced?

2. The Current Texas Rules

Texas adopted the Uniform Premarital Agreement Act in 1987. The Texas statute permits premarital or postnuptial agreements. They are to be enforced unless: (1) they were not signed "voluntarily," or (2) they were "unconscionable" at the time of signing, the party losing rights did not have adequate knowledge relating to the financial condition of the other spouse, and the spouse losing rights did not waive the right to obtain such knowledge. Tex. Fam. Code § 4.006. A jury finding that the agreement was "unfair" at the time of execution is not sufficient to invalidate a premarital agreement. *See Chiles v. Chiles*, 779 S.W.2d 127 (Tex. App. — Houston [14th Dist.] 1989, writ denied).

Williams v. Williams

Texas Court of Appeals—Houston [14th Dist.], 1986
720 S.W.2d 246, no writ

CANNON, Justice.

This is an appeal from a divorce proceeding tried before the court. Appellant complains of the trial court's finding that the agreement in contemplation of marriage was valid.

Appellant (Linda Henderson Williams) and appellee (Louis Edward Williams) were ceremonially married just before noon on Saturday, April 17, 1982 in Boerne, Texas. The record reveals that the parties had spent much time together and had traveled together extensively before this marriage ceremony. Both parties had a child or children from former marriages. Appellee, age 60 at the time of this marriage, was paying child support for a minor son. Appellant was 40 years of age at the time of the marriage. Late in the afternoon, on the day before the marriage, appellee presented appellant with a typed agreement in contemplation of marriage. The parties were on the parking lot of the Boerne State Bank. Appellee reminded appellant that he had discussed this agreement with her before and was sure she would have no objection to signing it. Appellant indicated she did not like the agreement. However, because approximately twenty guests had been invited to the wedding and were to arrive the next day, she agreed. The parties entered the bank, secured a notary and executed the agreement. Appellant is now complaining of this agreement.

In points of error one through four, appellant argues that the trial court erred in finding that the agreement in contemplation of marriage was a valid agreement because appellee failed to sustain his burden of proof by clear and convincing evidence that the appellant entered into the agreement (1) knowingly, (2) after giving informed consent, and (3) without being subjected to duress. [Ed. note—this is the statute that was in effect before 1987.]

Agreements in contemplation of marriage are controlled by Tex. Fam. Code Ann. Secs. 5.41, 5.45.

The agreement presented on appeal defines the separate estate of the parties and provides that income and increases from the respective separate estates of each party remains the separate property of each and further, that all rights in the separate estates then owned or thereafter acquired by each party remain free from any claim by the other party by reason of the marriage.

The testimony surrounding discussions of the agreement prior to its execution conflicts. At trial, appellant denied that she and appellee ever discussed the agreement prior to the day of its execution. Appellee, however, stated that the parties discussed and consented to the agreement's terms about six months prior to the wedding. This discussion took place, according to his testimony, while sitting on the couch at appellant's house on Olympic Street in Houston. Appellee also stated that during the discussion, he promised to execute a codicil to his will and leave everything to appellant if the parties remained married until his death. Four days after the marriage, appellee did, in fact, execute a codicil to his will, leaving all his property to appellant. Moreover, he gave appellant a copy of this codicil.

We also note that, at the time of the marriage, appellant was an educated person who had substantial business experience. She had attended business seminars and training seminars sponsored by the American Institute of Banking. Significant also is the fact that appellant's job exposed her to contracts which dealt with banking financial records. Further, appellant worked as a Move Coordinator for the relocation of the American Bank in Houston. This assignment included soliciting and reviewing the bids submitted for the furnishings and safety boxes of a large bank and for moving the furniture from one location to another. The fact that the president of the bank acted on her recommendation is an indication of her business acumen.

Additionally, we note that appellant was also familiar with the contents of the premarital agreement. She was of the opinion that the items designated in the agreement as the respective separate property of herself and of appellee were in fact their respective separate property at the time the agreement was executed. Appellant conceded that, at the time she executed the agreement, she had no objection to the division of the property as set forth therein. She did think, however, that the agreement put a romantic relationship on a crudely businesslike basis. Appellee's testimony disclosed that the agreement was a condition of his pending marriage and further, that he was motivated to protect his children by prior marriages.

We have considered the public policy in favor of such agreements in the September 1, 1981 amendments to the Texas Family Code. Our courts have construed the Family Code provisions as broadly as possible to allow the parties flexibility to contract with respect to property incident to a marriage. *Williams v. Williams*, 569 S.W.2d 867, 870 (Tex. 1978). Considering the maturity of the individuals, their business backgrounds, their educational levels, their experiences in prior marriages, their experiences with the sale of properties, their respective ages and further, their motivations to protect their respective children, we do not find that the agreement in contemplation of marriage was obtained by fraud, duress or overreaching.

DISCUSSION

Are you surprised by the result? If you were the judge, what would be the crucial issue? Note that this case involved a statute that was somewhat different from the 1987 statute.

Bradley v. Bradley

Texas Court of Appeals — Corpus Christi, 1987
725 S.W.2d 503, no writ

UTTER, Justice.

This is an appeal from a decree of divorce in which the trial court held that "no community property other than personal effects has been accumulated by the parties." We reverse the judgment of the trial court and remand for a new trial.

The parties were married on July 31, 1982, and were divorced on July 9, 1986. On July 26, 1982, prior to their marriage, appellant and appellee entered into a prenuptial agreement. During the marriage, appellant was not gainfully employed outside the home, and appellee's income was derived from his medical practice.

In interpreting the prenuptial agreement, the trial court found that "the separate property of each of the parties as well as the revenues, increases, and income from such separate property, and from the respective personal efforts of each party belongs to that party." The trial court obviously considered appellee's income as being derived from appellee's personal efforts and concluded that such income was appellee's separate property.

By her second point of error, appellant contends that the trial court erred in determining that the prenuptial agreement operated to convert appellee's income from personal earnings into his separate property.

Paragraph 2, entitled "Stipulations of Parties," provides that "the general purpose and intent of the parties" is:

> (a) that VICTOR and MARGARET will each continue to own and to manage his or her separate property,
>
> (b) that all revenues, increases, and income from such separate property, and from their respective personal efforts will be subject to the sole management and control of the party whose separate property or personal efforts generated such revenues or income,
>
> (c) that the parties will do any and all things necessary in order to establish or preserve the separate character of all revenues, increases, and income from such separate property, and from their respective personal efforts....

Section (b) merely restates Tex. Fam. Code Ann. Sec. 5.22 (Vernon 1975). Section (c) sets out the parties' intent to preserve the "separate property character" of "their respective personal efforts." However, the "respective personal efforts" do not acquire separate property character until they have partitioned and exchanged their respective community property interests in the income from each other's personal efforts.

Paragraph 7 of the agreement, entitled "Annual Partition and/or Exchange of the Community Estate, Pursuant to Section 5.42 of the Texas Family Code," provides:

> that on or before the 15th day of April of each year during the existence of this marriage, VICTOR and MARGARET will fairly and reasonably partition (and/or exchange) in writing all of the community estate of the parties on hand that will have accumulated since January 1 of the preceding year whether it be in the form of cash, realty, or other assets.

Upon acquisition, appellee's earnings from his personal efforts became community property. They remain community property until partitioned and exchanged pursuant to Tex. Const. art. XVI, Sec. 15, and Tex. Fam. Code Ann. Sec. 5.42 (Vernon Supp. 1987). The prenuptial agreement does not itself effect a partition and exchange of the parties' respective community interests in each other's personal earnings. It merely evinces an intent to do so in the future. Appellee testified and admitted that they have never done so.

Section 7 also provides that "[t]he failure of the parties to partition in writing the community estate, if any, ... shall not constitute a waiver of the parties' obligations and rights hereunder." Appellee contends that this provision should be interpreted to mean "that any *failure* by them to conduct their annual partitions would *not* constitute a waiver of their rights to claim the separate character of their property." [Emphasis appellee's.] Appellee's interpretation of this provision is contrary to the express provisions of Tex. Const. art. XVI, Sec. 15, which requires a "written instrument" in order to partition and exchange community property interests.

We hold that the prenuptial agreement itself does not operate to partition and exchange the community property interests in each other's income from personal efforts. To the contrary, it merely contemplates a partition and exchange of community property interests in the future. Therefore, the trial court erred in its interpretation of the prenuptial agreement and in holding that appellee's income from his personal earnings was his separate property. Appellant's second point of error is sustained.

Appellant's third point of error, which contends that the trial court erred in determining that there was no community property of the estate, is also sustained.

The trial court has broad discretion in dividing the property in a divorce action and its division will not be disturbed absent an abuse of discretion. The trial court's mischaracterization of property will require a reversal only if we determine that the division of the property made was, because of the legal error upon which it was based, so unfair as to constitute an abuse of discretion. In other words, appellant must show that, due to the trial court's legal error, the division of the property was so disproportionate so as to be manifestly unfair. Furthermore, appellant must show that the trial court would have probably made a different division of the property if it had been properly characterized.

In this case, the trial court made no division of the property of the marital estate because it determined that there was no community property to divide. The trial court decided that the marital estate consisted entirely of separate property and awarded it accordingly. Had the trial court properly characterized appellee's personal earnings, it would probably have made a different division of it. Therefore, the trial court's error in characterizing appellee's personal earnings resulted in a division which was so disproportionate as to be manifestly unfair.

That portion of the trial court's judgment which dissolves the marriage of the parties is left undisturbed. The portion of the judgment dividing the marital estate is REVERSED and REMANDED to the trial court for further proceedings consistent with this opinion.

DISCUSSION

The Texas Constitution now enables "prospective spouses" to partition and exchange interests that would otherwise be community property into separate property interests. A "partition" is a division of one item into two separate parts. An "exchange" normally would involve at least two items. So, for example, if a prospective husband and wife wanted to make their respective wages the separate property of the salary recipient, the husband would "exchange" the interest he otherwise would have in the wife's wages in exchange for the wife relinquishing her interest in his wages. Note that neither a partition nor an exchange needs to be equal.

Bradley highlights that care must be taken when drafting the premarital agreement to partition or exchange property to be accumulated during marriage. Any suggestion that the parties are merely agreeing to partition property at some point in the future could well be disastrous. Courts will be reluctant to enforce marital agreements, and drafting must be done carefully.

The 1980 constitutional amendment and the new statutes regarding marriage contracts presented interesting retroactivity questions. The Texas Supreme Court announced in *Sadler v. Sadler*, 769 S.W.2d 886 (Tex. 1989) that the enforceability of a marriage contract would be governed by the law in effect when the divorce decree is rendered. In *Beck v. Beck*, 814 S.W.2d 745 (Tex. 1991), the court clarified that this was true even if the agreement was signed before the 1980 constitutional amendment.

It was unclear whether, in addition to the grounds set forth in the Family Code, additional common-law grounds exist for challenging a marital contract. 1993 amendments to Sections 4.006 (c) and 4.105 (c) state that the grounds set forth in Family Code are "exclusive," at least as to contracts signed after the effective date of the amendment. Does this mean, for example, that "encouraging divorce" is not a ground for invalidating a contract?

McClary v. Thompson

Texas Court of Appeals — Fort Worth, 2002
65 S.W.3d 829, affirmed and severed in part, reversed and remanded in part.

INTRODUCTION

This is an appeal from a judgment granting a divorce and dividing the parties' community estate, following a trial to the court. In four issues, Appellant, Jennifer Lynne McClary, f/k/a Jennifer Lynne Thompson (McClary), complains of the trial court's characterization of funds contained in her ex-husband's retirement plan account at the time of the divorce and acquired during the marriage as his separate property.

ISSUES

Conceding that the initial contributions to the retirement plan made before the marriage are the separate property of her ex-husband, Appellee Darrell Ray Thompson (Thompson), McClary contends by her first issue that the trial court erred in failing to characterize the contributions made to the plan during the marriage and the interest earned on those contributions as community property. By her second issue, McClary asserts that the parties' premarital agreement did not address contributions to be made during the marriage and, therefore, did not convert community contributions to the plan to separate property.

We hold that the contributions and interest earned during the marriage were community property and that the premarital agreement did not convert the character of those contributions into separate property. We affirm that portion of the trial court's judgment granting a divorce to the parties and dividing the parties' estate in accordance with their agreement. We reverse that portion of the judgment holding the entirety of the retirement plan to be Thompson's separate property and remand to the trial court as to the division of the Texas District and County Retirement System Plan.

FACTUAL AND PROCEDURAL HISTORY

The relevant facts are undisputed. McClary and Thompson were married on October 11, 1985. At the time of their marriage, Thompson had been employed for approximately five and one-half years by Tarrant County as a medical investigator in the Medical Examiner's Office. As an employee of Tarrant County, Thompson participated in the Texas County and District Retirement System Plan during his employment. At the time of the marriage, the balance in Thompson's account in the retirement plan was $11,962.28. The retirement plan was a "defined contribution plan" to which both Tarrant County and Thompson regularly made contributions.

Before their marriage, McClary and Thompson entered into an "Agreement in Contemplation of Marriage" (the premarital agreement) with the stated desire "to partition and divide their separate property so that, as [therein] provided, each party shall become the separate owner of such properties in the event of dissolution of the contemplated marriage." The agreement, drafted by the husband's attorney, provided that four assets owned by McClary and Thompson at the time of the marriage would remain the separate property of each as long as that property was not sold or liquidated prior to the dissolution of the marriage; however, if the property was sold during marriage the proceeds would become community property.

Specifically, the agreement addressed Thompson's equity in real property in Benbrook, Texas, a 1977 Marquis boat owned by Thompson, a certificate of deposit (CD) owned by McClary, and Thompson's proceeds in the retirement plan. During the marriage the parties disposed of the real property, the boat and the certificate of deposit. When Thompson filed for divorce in 1999, the only remaining asset addressed in the premarital agreement was Thompson's account in the retirement plan.

At the time of divorce, the balance in the retirement plan account was $ 116,754.39. Before trial, the parties agreed upon the division of all assets and liabilities of the marital estate except that portion of the retirement plan account acquired during the marriage, which totaled $ 104,771.72. As to that portion of the account, the parties stipulated that each was to be awarded 50% of that portion of the retirement plan found by the trial court to be community property. Pursuant to the parties' agreement, trial was limited to the issue of what portion of the retirement plan account was Thompson's separate property and what portion was community property, including construction of the premarital agreement as to its effect, if any, on the nature of that interest. The trial court awarded the [entirety of the retirement account, including that portion acquired during the marriage, to Thompson as his separate property.

DISCUSSION

In McClary's first issue, she contends that the portion of the retirement plan acquired during the marriage was community property. Specifically, McClary argues that Thompson's retirement plan was a defined contribution plan and, as a matter of law, all contributions made and interest earned in the account during the fifteen-year marriage were community property.

We agree with McClary that the contributions to and interest earned in the retirement plan during the marriage were community property.

The Texas Family Code requires the trial court to order a "just and right" division of the parties' estates in a divorce proceeding. TEX. FAM. CODE ANN. §7.001 (Vernon 1998); *Lipsey v. Lipsey*, 983 S.W.2d 345, 350 (Tex. App.—Fort Worth 1998, no pet.). The trial court has wide discretion in the division of marital property, and we will not disturb its decision unless the trial court has clearly abused its discretion. *Jacobs v. Jacobs*, 687 S.W.2d 731, 733 (Tex. 1985); *Lipsey*, 983 S.W.2d at 350. However, the mischaracterization of a major asset of the estate of the parties is reversible error affecting the just and right division of the community estate. *Jacobs*, 687 S.W.2d at 733; *In re Marriage of Joiner*, 755 S.W.2d 496, 499 (Tex. App.—Amarillo 1988, no writ).

I. The Defined Contribution Retirement Plan

Because benefits in a retirement or pension plan are regarded as earned over a period of time, Texas courts have fashioned apportionment formulas to allocate to the community estate benefits earned during the marriage. The formula used depends upon whether the plan is a "defined contribution plan" or a "defined benefit plan." *See* Steven R. Brown, Comment, An Interdisciplinary Analysis of the *Division of Pension Benefits in Divorce and Post-Judgment Partition Actions*, 37 BAYLOR L. REV. 107, 136–37 (1985).

The plan at issue here is a defined contribution plan whereby the employee has an individual account. *Baw*, 949 S.W.2d at 768 n.2. The employee makes periodic contributions to the account, which may be matched by the employer. *Id.* (Brown, *An Interdisciplinary Analysis*, 37 BAYLOR L. REV. at 112–13). An employee participating in a defined contribution plan has a separate account, analogous to a savings account, the value of which is easily ascertained at any given time by simply looking at the account. *Smith*, 22 S.W.3d at 148–49; *Hatteberg v. Hatteberg*, 933 S.W.2d 522, 531 (Tex. App.—

Houston [1st Dist.] 1995, no writ); Brown, An Interdisciplinary Analysis, 37 BAYLOR L. REV. at 112–13.

To determine the portion as well as the value of a defined contribution plan that is community property, courts subtract the amount contained in the plan at the time of the marriage from the total contained in the account at divorce.[1] *See, e.g., Smith*, 22 S.W.3d at 149; *Baw*, 949 S.W.2d at 767–68; *Pelzig v. Berkebile*, 931 S.W.2d 398, 402 (Tex. App.—Corpus Christi 1996, no writ); *Hatteberg*, 933 S.W.2d at 531; *Iglinsky v. Iglinsky*, 735 S.W.2d 536, 538 (Tex. App.—Tyler 1987, no writ).

2. The Premarital Agreement

Having held that the contributions made during marriage were property of the community estate, we are now left to determine if, as argued by Thompson, the trial court correctly construed the premarital agreement in such a manner that all contributions and interest accruing during the marriage would nevertheless constitute Thompson's separate property upon dissolution of the marriage.

In her second issue, McClary asserts that the plain language of the premarital agreement does not specifically classify Thompson's contributions during the marriage to the retirement plan as separate property. McClary thus argues that the agreement cannot be interpreted to convert the community property portion of the plan to Thompson's separate property and thereby divest McClary of any interest in that community asset. Alternatively, she contends that the premarital agreement is void in its entirety by virtue of language in the agreement attempting to convert other property from separate to community, in violation of the Texas Constitution. TEX. CONST. art. XVI § 15 (1987, amended 1999).

Thompson argues that the effect of the premarital agreement is clear or, alternatively, that its effect in converting all contributions to the plan to his separate property was established by testimony regarding the parties' intent, and that it may only be attacked as involuntarily made or unconscionable and that those defenses were not supported by any evidence offered by McClary.

The only provision of the premarital agreement expressly addressing the retirement account reads:

DARRELL THOMPSON has as his separate property all benefits, dividends and earned and unearned proceeds in a retirement program established with Tarrant County, Texas. It is the desire of DARRELL THOMPSON that should such retirement benefits be cashed in or redeemed during the marriage of the parties hereby contemplated, that such proceeds shall become the community property of the parties and shall be considered as such in the event of dissolution of the marriage; provided however, if such retirement bene-

---

1. A defined benefit plan, as contrasted with a defined contribution plan, provides a benefit based on years of service along with other factors such as age and salary history. *Smith*, 22 S.W.3d at 148. Accrued benefits in such a plan, earned during the marriage but not vested and matured during the marriage, have been held to be a contingent property interest that is an asset of the community estate. *Cearley*, 544 S.W.2d at 665–67; *Burchfield v. Finch*, 968 S.W.2d 422, 423 (Tex. App.—Texarkana 1998, pet. denied); *May v. May*, 716 S.W.2d 705, 707 (Tex. App.—Corpus Christi 1986, no writ). Apportionment and valuation of portions of a defined benefit plan as community or separate are based on three factors: the community share, the community extent, and the value of the retirement benefit. *Berry v. Berry*, 647 S.W.2d 945, 947 (Tex. 1983) (adopting formula for calculating value of share of non-employee spouse); *Taggart v. Taggart*, 552 S.W.2d 422, 424 (Tex. 1977) (adopting formula for determining extent of community share); *Cearley*, 544 S.W.2d at 665–67) (applying formula); *see also* Brown, *An Interdisciplinary Analysis*, 37 BAYLOR L. REV. at 136–37.

fits remain intact and the marriage is dissolved, such retirement benefits shall remain the separate property of DARRELL THOMPSON.

The Texas Family Code provides that spouses may agree to partition or exchange any part of their community property as they desire. TEX. FAM. CODE ANN. § 4.102 (Vernon 1998); *Winger*, 831 S.W.2d at 859. In order to exchange such property the parties must do so by written agreement. TEX. FAM. CODE ANN. § 4.104 (Vernon 1998); *Winger*, 831 S.W.2d at 859. Here, Thompson and McClary had a written agreement establishing the disposition of certain real and personal property.

A premarital agreement should be interpreted in accordance with the true intentions of the parties as expressed in the instrument. *Coker v. Coker*, 650 S.W.2d 391, 393 (Tex. 1983); *Pearce v. Pearce*, 824 S.W.2d 195, 200 (Tex. App.—El Paso 1992, writ denied). If a written instrument is so worded that it can be given a certain or definite legal meaning or interpretation, then it is unambiguous. *Coker*, 650 S.W.2d at 393.

When construing marital property agreements, courts construe agreements narrowly in favor of the community estate. *See, e.g., Byrnes v. Byrnes*, 19 S.W.3d 556, 558 (Tex. App.—Fort Worth 2000, no pet.) (holding that a purported agreement to partition community property was unenforceable for lack of specific partition language). In *Scott v. Scott*, the Waco court of appeals held that income from separate property that had been set aside and saved by a spouse was community and had not been transformed into separate property under a premarital agreement because there was no compliance with the agreement, which required that the funds be deposited into the corpus of the spouse's separate property. 805 S.W.2d 835, 837 (Tex. App.—Waco 1991, writ denied). If there are no provisions in an agreement that specifically address the issue of future wages, time, toil, or talent, then the agreement does not convert income constituting community property to separate property. *Winger*, 831 S.W.2d at 859; *Pearce*, 824 S.W.2d at 200; *Scott*, 805 S.W.2d at 837; *Dewey*, 745 S.W.2d at 517; *Maben*, 574 S.W.2d at 232.

Thompson maintains that the trial court's determination that the retirement account was converted to separate property is supported by the language of the agreement. He contends that the phrase "all benefits, dividends and earned and unearned proceeds in a retirement program" is sufficient reference to protect his contributions and interest as separate property.

McClary counters with the argument that the present tense nature of the statement refers solely to the contributions he made prior to marriage and does not specifically reference future contributions or income. If a written instrument is worded such that it can be given a certain or definite legal meaning or interpretation, then it is unambiguous and the courts must, as a matter of law, construe the meaning of the contract. *Coker*, 650 S.W.2d at 393.

The agreement is written in the present tense. It begins "DARRELL THOMPSON *has* as his separate property." (Emphasis added.) It references "such benefits" previously referred to in the present tense, i.e., at the time of execution of the agreement prior to marriage, and concludes that those benefits "*shall remain* the separate property of DARRELL THOMPSON." (Emphasis added.) The use of the term "remain," in reference to the benefits, clearly refers only to those benefits that were separate property at the time of execution of the agreement. The funds contained in Thompson's retirement account at that time amounted to $11,962.28. The clear intent of the agreement is that "such retirement benefits" (not benefits to be obtained in the future) would remain Thompson's separate property unless he removed them prior to any dissolution of the marriage, in which event they would convert to community property. No portion of the agreement provides that future contributions or benefits will become separate property. Indeed, the plain language of the premarital agreement makes no mention of salary, earnings, income, or employment benefits earned or acquired during the marriage. A similar argument was rejected by the court in *Dewey*. 745 S.W.2d at 514. In that case, the husband contended that income received from his professional corporation during marriage was intended by a premarital agreement to be his separate property. *Id.* The agreement listed certain separate property of each party and provided that all profits, dividends, interest, and proceeds that accumulated after marriage from each of the parties' separate property would remain their separate property. *Id.* at 517. However, because the agreement did not expressly mention the appellant's salary received from his professional corporation during the marriage, the court held that there was no ambiguity and that the salary utilized to fund the appellant's retirement plan was clearly community property. *Id.*

Thompson argues that Texas law has permitted premarital agreements to convert income from community to separate property, waive rights regarding claims to community property, and determine the character of increases in the value of property from separate to community. Thompson insists that the premarital agreement at bar fits in the line of cases allowing for the conversion of income from community into separate property.[2] The cases upon which Thompson relies are distinguishable because in those cases, changing income from community to separate property, the premarital agreement explicitly excluded either the creation of community property[3] or specifically stated that future income would be separate rather than community property.[4] Thompson and McClary's premarital agreement has no such explicit provision.

We hold that the contributions and interest accrued in the retirement account during the marriage of McClary and Thompson are community property, that there is no ambiguity present on the face of the premarital agreement and that the plain and unambiguous language of the agreement does not address and, thus, does not affect the character of the contributions, interest, or benefits accrued in the retirement account of the parties during the marriage as community property. Consequently, we sustain McClary's second issue.

Because we hold that the trial court abused its discretion by characterizing the retirement plan contributions and interest accrued during marriage as separate property, we need not address McClary's third and fourth issues that the agreement is void and that the trial court abused its discretion in admitting parol evidence. Applying the formula espoused in *Baw*, and pursuant to the stipulations of the parties in open court, the trial court should have awarded each party 50% of the value of the community portion of the retirement account at divorce. 949 S.W.2d at 767.

Having determined that the trial court abused its discretion in mischaracterizing the retirement account, we are authorized to affirm and sever the judgment of divorce and to remand the division of property to the trial court. *See Herschberg v. Herschberg*, 994 S.W.2d 273, 277 (Tex. App.—Corpus Christi 1999, no pet.) (holding that appellate court has authority to sever the issue of divorce and remand for redivision of property alone). Having further determined that the trial court's judgment should be reversed to the extent that it mischaracterized the portion of the retirement account acquired during the marriage as separate property, we would ordinarily be required to remand the entire com-

---

2. *See, e.g., Dokmanovic v. Schwarz*, 880 S.W.2d 272, 275 (Tex. App.—Houston [14th Dist.] 1994, no writ); *Winger*, 831 S.W.2d at 856.

3. *Dokmanovic*, 880 S.W.2d at 275.

4. *Winger*, 831 S.W.2d at 856.

munity estate for redivision by the trial court as "just and right." *Jacobs v. Jacobs*, 687 S.W.2d 731, 733 (Tex. 1985) (holding that remand of entire community estate is necessary when mischaracterization of property materially affects just and right division of community estate); *see also McElwee v. McElwee*, 911 S.W.2d 182, 189 (Tex. App.—Houston [1st Dist.] 1995, writ denied).

In this instance, there is no need to redivide the entirety of the community estate because, as previously stated, the parties agreed before trial and the judgment reflects their agreement as to the division of all assets and liabilities of the marital estate, with the exception of expressly submitting to the trial court the issue of the characterization of that portion of the retirement plan acquired during the marriage. We will reverse only as to that portion of the retirement plan.

CONCLUSION

Accordingly, we affirm and sever the trial court's decree granting the divorce and the property division except as to the Texas District and County Retirement System Plan. We reverse and remand the division of the Texas District and County Retirement System Plan to the trial court for further proceedings in accordance with this opinion.

Fanning v. Fanning

Texas Court of Appeals—Waco, 1992
828 S.W.2d 135, affirmed in part, 847 S.W.2d 225

CUMMINGS, Justice.

Whitney Fanning appeals the final decree of divorce in which the trial court awarded the vast majority of the Fannings' assets and the custody of their three children to Nita Fanning. Because the court failed to enforce a premarital agreement and an enforceable partition agreement, we reverse that part of the judgment divesting Whitney Fanning of title to his separate property and dividing the community property contrary to the agreement of the parties. However, we affirm that part of the judgment awarding custody of the children to Nita Fanning and ordering Whitney Fanning to pay $3,000 per month for the support of the children.

The Premarital Agreement

Whitney Fanning and Nita Kissel entered into a premarital agreement on August 15, 1980, pursuant to section 5.41(a) of the Texas Family Code, which purported to authorize premarital agreements. Both parties were practicing attorneys when the premarital agreement was executed. They were married on September 27, 1980.

In point two, Whitney Fanning contends that the trial court erred in setting aside the premarital agreement because (1) the court erroneously concluded that the agreement was unconstitutional and void, (2) the court erroneously concluded that the agreement did not operate to partition or exchange the future income from separate property or the community interest in income from personal efforts, (3) Nita Fanning failed to satisfy the burden of proof required by section 5.46 of the Texas Family Code, and (4) the evidence was legally or factually insufficient to support the court's failure to enforce the premarital agreement.

Paragraph six of the agreement provides:

6.01) During their marriage, all income and revenue (other than that which is part of the property itself) from the separate property of each party hereto is the community property of the parties if so defined by Texas law. However, the parties understand that the 66th Texas legislature approved H.J.R. 54, to be submitted to the voters on November 1980, by the terms of which spouses may, by agreement between themselves, provide that the income from separate property owned by either of them, or thereafter acquired, shall be the separate property of the spouse owning such separate property. If such amendment to Article XVI, Section 15, of the Texas Constitution is approved by the voters, the parties agree that as soon as legally possible all income from their respective estates shall be the separate property of the spouse from whose separate estate such income is derived.

6.02) The parties agree that each may, from time to time, designate certain banks as his or her agent to assist in carrying out this Agreement by administering accounts in the name of the respective party, by the name of the party adding "as separate property," or otherwise, to the end that all funds which are deposited to the separate accounts of the parties hereto and income there from will be identified as the separate property of the party in whose name such funds are held. As received, the respective parties shall deposit funds received that are the income or revenue from their respective separate property into one of their respective several or separate property accounts created in their respective and on deposit (if not before) such funds shall be the separate property of the spouse whose separate property produced such income or revenue, if so provided by this Agreement. The parties hereto hereby instruct any bank holding such funds on deposit as provided in this paragraph that such funds are the separate property of the party in whose name such deposit was made as provided in this paragraph.

Validity of the Premarital Agreement

When this premarital agreement was executed in August 1980, it was void to the extent that it attempted to recharacterize income or other property acquired during the marriage as separate property. *See Williams v. Williams*, 569 S.W.2d 867, 870 (Tex. 1978).[1] Furthermore, income and revenue from separate property was community property because it was not acquired by "gift, devise or descent." *See* Tex.Const. art. XVI, § 15. However, article XVI, section 15, of the Texas Constitution was amended in November 1980 to allow "persons about to marry and spouses" to partition or exchange community property "then existing or to be acquired" in the future. *Id.* The 1980 amendment also provided that "the spouses may from time to time, by written instrument, agree between themselves that the income or property from all or part of the separate property then owned by one of them, or which thereafter might be acquired, shall be the separate property of that spouse...." Tex.Const. art. XVI, § 15 (1980, amended 1987).[2]

---

1. *But see Beck v. Beck*, 814 S.W.2d 745, 749 (Tex. 1991) (agreement entered under the 1948 amendment to article XVI, section 15, of the Texas Constitution was "voidable" rather than "void").

2. Non-substantive changes were made to this clause by constitutional amendment in 1987. Article XVI, section15, of the Texas Constitution now provides, "spouses also may from time to time, by written instrument, agree between themselves that the income or property from all or part of the separate property then owned or which thereafter might be acquired by only one of them, shall be the separate property of that spouse...." Tex. Const. art. XVI, § 15.

The Texas Supreme Court held in *Beck* that the 1980 constitutional amendment impliedly validated section 5.41 of the Texas Family Code and all agreements entered into before November 4, 1980, pursuant to that statute. *Beck*, 814 S.W.2d at 749. in *Beck*, the parties agreed that "all the properties ... held or standing in the name of only one of them shall be considered as a separate property of the one of them in whose name such property is held or stands." *Id.* at 746. Apparently, the supreme court found that the agreement was validated by the clause authorizing the "partition ... or exchange ... of community property ... to be acquired." *See id.* at 747.

Because paragraph 6.02 of the Fannings' premarital agreement was substantially similar to the agreement upheld in *Beck*, that portion of the agreement was enforceable. Therefore, the court erred in setting aside paragraph 6.02 of the premarital agreement.

Unlike the agreement upheld in *Beck*, however, paragraph 6.01 of the Fannings' premarital agreement deals with income from separate property, regardless of whether it was deposited into an account designated as the separate property of one of the spouses. *See id.* at 746. Although the portion of the constitutional amendment validating the partition and exchange of property "then existing or to be acquired" applies to "persons about to marry and spouses," the portion of the amendment validating written agreements concerning income or property derived from separate property applies only to spouses. *See* Tex.Const. art. XVI, § 15.[3]

Section 5.41 of the Texas Family Code, as it existed at the time the Fannings entered into the premarital agreement, appeared to allow persons intending to marry to enter into enforceable agreements concerning their property as they saw fit.

Because the Texas Constitution remains the ultimate authority on the character of marital property, a premarital agreement entered into pursuant to section 5.41 may not violate the constitutional definitions of separate and community property. *See Arnold v. Leonard*, 273 S.W. 799, 802 (Tex. 1925). We note that the Texas Supreme Court in *Beck* addressed only the retroactive application of the 1980 amendment, rather than the scope of premarital agreements authorized by that amendment. *See Beck*, 814 S.W.2d at 748.

The 1980 amendment did not authorize persons intending to marry to enter into agreements that the income from one spouse's separate property would thereafter be the owner's separate property.[4] Therefore, we hold that the trial court correctly concluded that paragraph 6.01 of the premarital agreement was unenforceable to the extent the parties merely agreed that "as soon as legally possible all income from their respective separate estates shall be the separate property of the spouse from whose estate such income is derived."

According to section 5.44 of the Texas Family Code, "A premarital agreement becomes effective on marriage." Tex. Fam. Code Ann. § 5.44 (Vernon Supp. 1992). As a result, some commentators have suggested that, by statutory definition, a premarital agreement is between spouses who are authorized to enter into agreements concerning income or prop-

---

3. This constitutional distinction between partition and exchange agreements and agreements concerning income from separate property was reflected by the 1981 and 1987 amendments to the Texas Family Code, enacted by the legislature to implement the 1980 amendment to article XVI, section 15, of the Texas Constitution. Although section 5.53 of the Texas Family Code authorized agreements between spouses concerning income or property derived from separate property, the Texas Uniform Premarital Agreement Act does not expressly authorize such an agreement between "prospective spouses." *See* Tex. Fam. Code Ann. §§ 5.41–.50, 5.53 (Vernon Supp. 1992).

4. *See* Featherston & Springer, *Marital Property Law in Texas: The Past, Present and Future*, 39 Baylor L. Rev. 861, 884 (1987).

erty derived from separate property.[5] However, the constitutional distinction between partition and exchange agreements and agreements concerning income from separate property cannot be redefined by the legislature. *See Arnold*, 273 S.W. at 802. Therefore, section 5.44 provides no basis for validating paragraph 6.01 of the premarital agreement.

Arguably, a premarital agreement could partition or exchange income from separate property as property to be acquired in the future.[6] However, the language of paragraph 6.01 indicates that the parties were not contemplating a partition or exchange of property to be acquired during the marriage. Instead, paragraph 6.01 expressly refers to the portion of the 1980 amendment that authorized agreements concerning income or property derived from separate property. Because they were clearly attempting to implement the portion of the 1980 amendment that applied only to spouses, we hold that paragraph 6.01 was not validated by the constitutional amendment authorizing the partition and exchange of property to be acquired in the future. Therefore, the income from separate property remained community property unless otherwise recharacterized by a valid provision of the premarital agreement or an enforceable partition agreement executed during the marriage. As in *Williams*, the invalid provision is severable from the valid portions of the agreement because the invalid provision does not constitute the agreement's main or essential purpose. *See Williams*, 569 S.W.2d at 871.

Paragraph two of the premarital agreement provided that the property described in Schedule A "is and shall remain the separate property of Future Husband," and that the property described in Schedule B "is and shall remain the separate property of Future Wife." The "incomes and revenues from Witney E. Fanning practice of law" were designated as his separate property. Likewise, "all incomes derived from future Wife's law practice" were designated as her separate property. In *Huff v. Huff*, 554 S.W.2d 841, 84244 (Tex.Civ.App.—Waco, 1977, writ dism'd), this court held that section 5.41 of the Texas Family Code authorized such an agreement. Furthermore, as a partition or exchange of property to be acquired in the future, this agreement was impliedly validated by the 1980 constitutional amendment. *See* Tex. Const. art. XVI, §15. Therefore, the court erred in finding that during the marriage all income earned by Whitney Fanning in the practice of law was community property. The court also erred in concluding that the provision of the premarital agreement providing for the exchange of future earnings from the practice of law was "unconstitutional and therefore void at the time of its execution." However, to the extent that either spouse earned income from personal efforts other than the practice of law, the court correctly concluded that the premarital agreement, "did not operate to partition and/or exchange the community property interest in the parties' income from personal efforts."

In point five, Whitney Fanning argues that the court erred in refusing to make an equal division of the community property. Paragraph ten of the premarital agreement provides:

> In the event the parties marriage is dissolved by divorce or annulment by any court, wherever located, each party is to retain his or her separate estate as his or her separate property following the dissolution. *All community property is to be divided equally between the parties according to its value.* To effectuate this provision, Future Husband and Future Wife relinquish and disclaim any right they

5. *See* Mercing, *The Uniform Premarital Agreement Act: Survey of its Impact in Texas and Across the Nation*, 42 Baylor L. Rev. 825, 844 (1990).

6. Section 5.41 of the Texas Family Code, as amended in 1987, defines property as "an interest, present or future, legal or equitable, vested or contingent, in real or personal property, *including income and earnings.*" Tex. Fam. Code Ann. §5.42(2) (Vernon Supp. 1992) (emphasis added).

may have to seek a division of their property other than in accordance with this paragraph, and agree to indemnify the other for the value of any property that may be awarded by a court in excess of the value that would result if division were in accordance with this paragraph.

(Emphasis added).

In determining the validity of paragraph ten, we again construe the former section 5.41 of the Texas Family Code[7] as broadly as possible in order to allow the parties as much flexibility to contract..., provided the constitutional and statutory definition of separate and community property or the requirements of public policy are not violated." *See Williams*, 569 S.W.2d at 870.

Article XVI, section 15, of the Texas Constitution provides that "the portion of interest set aside to each spouse shall be and constitute a part of the separate property and estate of such spouse or future spouse." Tex. Const. art. XVI, § 15. By definition, a partition or exchange of community property results in the recharacterization of community property. Because an agreement to equally divide the community property involves the disposition of community property upon dissolution rather than the recharacterization of community property as separate property, the 1980 amendment to the constitution does not appear to authorize such an agreement. However, article XVI, section 15, also authorizes the legislature to more clearly define "the rights of the spouses, in relation to separate and community property...." *Id*. This is exactly what the legislature was attempting to do in the former section 5.41 of the Texas Family Code, as well as in the Uniform Premarital Agreement Act, which replaced section 5.41 in 1987. Therefore, paragraph ten of the premarital agreement was constitutionally authorized by section 5.41.

An agreement to equally divide community property also appears to encroach upon the trial court's statutory duty to "order a division of the estate of the parties in a manner that the court deems just and right, having due regard for the rights of each party...." *See* Tex. Fam. Code Ann. § 3.63(a) (Vernon Supp. 1992). However, because section 5.41 had more clearly defined "the rights of the parties," the trial court, according to section 3.63(a), must give "due regard" to the terms of a premarital agreement authorized by the constitutional. *See* Tex. Const. art. XVI, § 15; Tex. Fam. Code Ann. § 3.63(a) (Vernon Supp. 1992). Therefore, the court erred to the extent that it failed to equally divide any community property of the parties.

Enforceability of the Premarital Agreement

The court expressly found that "[o]n or about August 15, 1980, the parties executed an Agreement in Contemplation of Marriage." However, the court did not find that the agreement was executed involuntarily or that it was unconscionable. *See* Tex. Fam. Code Ann. § 5.46 (Vernon Supp. 1992). Because Whitney Fanning requestioned additional findings of fact related to the court's failure to enforce the premarital agreement, the judgment may not be supported upon appeal by a presumed finding that the agreement was unenforceable under section 5.46. *See* Tex.R.Civ.P. 299.

---

7. Section 5.43(a)(3) of the Texas Family Code now authorizes parties to a premarital agreement to contract with respect to "the disposition of property on separation [or] marital dissolution...." Tex. Fam. Code Ann. § 5.43(a)(3) (Vernon Supp. 1992). However, as in *Beck*, 814 S.W.2d at 746, we apply the law in effect at the time the agreement was executed. The retroactive application of sections 5.46 and 5.55 of the Texas Family Code is distinguishable because the enforcement provisions of the statute are procedural in nature. *See* Tex. Fam. Code Ann §§ 5.46, 55 (Vernon Supp. 1992).

The premarital agreement, with the exception of paragraph 6.01, was both valid and enforceable. Because, the trial court erred n setting the premarital agreement aside, points two and five are sustained.

The Partition Agreements

Whitney and Nita Fanning executed partition agreements on August 14, 1981, and May 14, 1986, pursuant to section 5.42 of the Texas Family Code,[8] which purported to authorize the partition or exchange of community property. Each partition agreement recharacterized property listed on attached exhibits as the separate property of the designated spouse. In points one and three, Whitney Fanning contends that the court erred in setting aside the 1986 partition agreement and in refusing to enforce the 1981 partition agreement.

Validity of the Partition Agreements

The court concluded that neither partition agreement operated "to partition and/or exchange the community property interest in future income from the separate estates of the parties." In fact, neither partition agreement provides "that the income or property from all or part of the separate property then owned or which thereafter might be acquired by only one of them, shall be the separate property of that spouse." *See* Tex. Const. art. XVI, § 15.

However, both of the partition agreements provide that:

> There shall be from this day no community property interest in the above described real and personal property and we shall each hold the above described real and personal property as our sole and separate property in the manner indicated to the exclusion of the other spouse.

This provision extended the partition and exchange of the property listed on the attached exhibits to property "to be acquired" in the future, as authorized by the 1980 constitutional amendment. *See* Tex. Const. art. XVI, § 15. Therefore, as in *Beck*, the future income from the separate property assets listed on the attached exhibits remained the separate property of the designated spouse. *See Beck*, 814 S.W.2d at 746.

The court also concluded that neither partition agreement operated "to partition and/or exchange the community property interest in the parties' income from personal efforts." Although such an agreement was authorized by the 1980 constitutional amendment, as the partition or exchange of community property "to be acquired" in the future, neither partition agreement attempted to recharacterize the parties' income from personal efforts as separate property. *See* Tex. Const. art. XVI, § 15.

---

8. When the 1981 partition was executed, section 5.42(a) of the Texas Family Code provided: "At any time, the spouses may partition between themselves, in severalty or in equal undivided interests, all or any part of their community property. They may exchange between themselves the interest of one spouse in any community property for the interest of the other spouses in other community property. A partition or exchange must be in writing and subscribed by both parties." Act of June 2, 1969, 61st Leg., R.S. ch. 888, § 1, 1969 Tex.Gen.Laws 2707, 2729, *amended by* Act of May 22, 1981, 67th Leg., R.S., ch 782, § 2, 1981 Tex.Gen.Laws 2964, 2965.When the 1986 partition was executed, section 5.42 of the Texas Family Code provided: "At any time, the spouses may partition or exchange between themselves any part of their community property, then existing or tobe acquired, as they may desire. Property or a property interest transferred to a spouse by a partition or exchange agreement becomes his or her separate property." Act of May 22, 1981. 67th Leg., R.S. ch. 782, § 2,1981 Tex.Gen.Laws 2964, 2965, *amended by* Act of June 1, 1987, 70th Leg., R.S. ch. 678, § 1, 1987 Tex.Gen.Laws 2530, 2531–32 (current version at Tex.Fam.Code Ann. § 5.52 (Vernon Supp. 1992)).

The 1986 partition agreement designated Whitney Fanning's law practice as his separate property. However, because the 1986 partition agreement did not expressly designate the income from his law practice as his separate property, the court correctly concluded that neither partition agreement operated to partition or exchange the community-property interest in the parties' income from personal efforts. *See Dewey v. Dewey*, 745 S.W.2d 514, 517 (Tex. App.—Corpus Christi 1988, writ denied). This is of little consequence, however, because the premarital agreement had previously effected a partition or exchange of the community-property interest in the primary source of the parties' income from personal efforts — "all incomes and revenues from [the] Whitney E. Fanning practice of law."

Enforceability of the Partition Agreements

The court concluded as a matter of law that the 1986 partition agreement was unconscionable. The court also found that:

> Prior to the execution of the Partition Agreement dated May 12, 1986, Nita Kissel Fanning was not provided a fair and reasonable disclosure of the property or financial obligations of the other party; and Nita Kissel Fanning did not voluntarily and expressly waive, in writing, the right to disclosure of the property or financial obligations of the other party beyond the disclosure provided; and Nita Kissel Fanning did not have, or reasonably could not have had, an adequate knowledge of the property or financial obligations of the other party.

Whitney Fanning argues that the evidence was legally or factually insufficient to support the court's conclusion of law that the agreement was unconscionable or the court's findings of fact related to the disclosure of property or financial obligations. Concisely stated, Witney Fanning contends that Nita Fanning failed to carry her burden of proof under section 5.55 of the Texas Family Code. Section 5.55 provides that:

> (a) A partition or exchange agreement is not enforceable if the party against whom enforcement is sought proves that:

> > (1) that party did not execute the agreement voluntarily; or

> > (2) the agreement was unconscionable when it was executed and, before execution of the agreement, that party:

> > > (A) was not provided a fair and reasonable disclosure of the property or financial obligations of the other party;

> > > (B) did not voluntarily and expressly waive, in writing, any right to disclosure of the property or financial obligations of the party beyond the disclosure provided; and

> > > (C) did not have, or reasonably could not have had, an adequate knowledge of the property or financial obligations of the other party.

> (b) An issue of unconscionability of a partition or exchange agreement shall be decided by the court as a matter of law.

Tex. Fam. Code Ann. § 5.55 (Vernon Supp. 1992).

In response, Nita Fanning argues that section 5.55 does not apply to the 1986 partition agreement. Prior to September 1, 1987, the enforcement of marital agreements was governed by section 5.45. When the legislature amended the Texas Family Code in 1987, it did not expressly provide that the amendatory provisions should be given retrospective application. However, the general rule is that, in the absence of an express intention to the contrary, legislation dealing with a procedural matter applies to pending litigation to the extent that subsequent steps in the case are to be taken under the new rule. Section 5.55 simply sets forth the revised procedural scheme for challenging the enforceability of a partition or exchange agreement. Therefore, Nita Fanning had the burden of proof under section 5.55 because the provisions of former section 5.45 no longer applies. *See Daniel v. Daniel*, 779 S.W.2d 110, 113 (Tex. App.—Houston [1st Dist.] 1989, no writ).

Although section 5.55(b) provides that the issue of unconscionability shall be decided by the court as a matter of law, the legislature and the courts have not defined "unconscionable" in the context of marital-property agreements. instead, the issue of unconscionability must be addressed on a case-by-case basis, looking to the entire atmosphere in which the agreement was made. *See Pearce v. Pearce*, 824 S.W.2d 195, at ___ (Tex. App.—El Paso, 1991, no writ). In *Chiles v. Chiles*, 779 S.W.2d 127, 129 (Tex. App.—Houston [14th Dist.] 1989, writ denied), the court held that a factual finding that an agreement was unfair to one spouse did not satisfy the burden of proof required by the statute.

In *Wade v. Austin*, 524 S.W.2d 79, 86 (Tex. Civ. App.—Texarkana 1975, no writ), the court addressed unconscionability of a contract under section 2.302 of the Texas Business and Commerce Code:

> In determining whether a contract is unconscionable or not, the court must look to the entire atmosphere in which the agreement was made, the alternatives, if any, which were available to the parties at the time of the making of the contract; the non-bargaining ability of one party; whether the contract is illegal or against public policy, and whether the contract is oppressive or unreasonable. At the same time, a party who knowingly enters a lawful but improvident contract is not entitled to protection by the courts ... A contract is not unenforceable on the ground that it yields a return disproportionate to the expenditures in time and money, where there has been no mistake or unfairness and the party against whom it is sought to be enforced has received and enjoyed the benefits.

As in *Wade*, we will focus upon the circumstances at the time the agreement was executed rather than the disproportionate effect of the agreement. *See id.* Mr. Fanning testified that severe marital problems developed in April and May 1986. On the night before the agreement was signed, Mrs. Fanning had played tennis as a substitute in a mixed-doubles tennis league. When she returned home, Mr. Fanning would not talk to her, and he was "pouting." She testified that, when she asked him what was wrong, he expressed his concern about going to prison in connection with a criminal investigation against the district attorney of McLennan County. According to Mrs. Fanning, her husband wanted to make sure that she did not take all the money he had accumulated and "run off with someone else" while he was in prison—a possibility that he envisioned because she had played tennis with another man that night.

Mrs. Fanning testified that Mr. Fanning assured her that he would never use the agreement against her, and that he threatened to divorce her and take the children if she did not sign the partition agreement. At that time, Mr. Fanning had won ten consecutive custody cases for fathers. Because Mrs. Fanning considered his threats to be valid, she believed that her only alternative was to sign the agreement. *See Matthews v. Matthews*, 725 S.W.2d 275, 279 (Tex. App.—Houston [1st Dist.] 1987, writ ref'd n.r.e.) (threatening to permanently deprive spouse of custody of the children constituted duress in the execution of a partition agreement).

That night, Mr. Fanning got out of bed and went to his law office to prepare the partition agreement. He called her the next day and told her to come to the office to sign the agreement. Although she remembered signing the partition agreement, she did not remember signing the accompanying deeds. She testified, however, that she would have signed whatever he put in front of her that day. A witness called by Mrs. Fanning testified that Mr. Fanning "just doesn't take no for an answer." According to the witness, when Mr. Fanning "wants to do something, he wants to do it and he wants to do it his way." Even the psychologist who testified on Mr. Fanning's behalf characterized him as manipulative and that, given his competitiveness, his manipulative tendencies, and his aggression, "he could get very angry and be retaliatory."

Considering the circumstances, the alternatives, and Nita Fanning's bargaining ability, we hold that the court did not err in concluding that the 1986 partition agreement was unconscionable when it was executed. Next, we must determine if the evidence is legally or factually sufficient to support the court's findings related to the disclosure of Mr. Fanning's property or financial obligations.

On direct examination, Mrs. Fanning testified that "[a]t no time did [she] have a disclosure nor did [she] waive in writing any disclosure, which she [she] since learned was a requirement." She believed that her husband wanted to keep her "ignorant of everything for [her] own protection" during the criminal investigation against the district attorney. She also testified that, because the district attorney's house had been searched, her husband was afraid that their house would be searched and that there was no safe place in Waco to keep anything.

Mrs. Fanning also testified that she did not have any knowledge of how much money was in an account, how much money her husband was making, or how much property he actually owned. Furthermore, Mr. Fanning's own psychologist described him as secretive. We find the evidence legally and factually sufficient to support the court's findings related to Mr. Fanning's failure to disclose his property or financial obligations. Therefore, we overrule point of error one.

The court expressly found that "[o]n or about August 14, 1981, the parties executed a Partition Agreement." However, the court did not find that the 1981 partition agreement was executed involuntarily or that it was unconscionable. Because Whitney Fanning requested additional findings of fact related to the court's failure to enforce the 1981 partition agreement, the judgment may not be supported upon appeal by a presumed finding that the agreement was unenforceable under section 5.55

The 1981 partition agreement was both valid and enforceable. Because the trial court erred in refusing to enforce the 1981 partition agreement, point three is sustained.

Divestiture of Separate Property

In point four, Whitney Fanning contends that the trial court's failure to enforce the premarital agreement and the partition agreements resulted in the divestiture of his separate property. Because the court correctly concluded that the 1986 partition agreement was unenforceable, we will limit our discussion to any divestiture resulting from the court's failure to enforce the premarital agreement and the 1981 partition agreement. Although trial courts have a broad latitude in the division of the marital community property, that discretion does not extend to a taking of the fee title to the separate property of one spouse and its donation to the other spouse. *Eggemeyer v. Eggemeyer*, 554 S.W.2d 137, 142 (Tex. 1977). Separate property may, however, be set aside to assure compliance with an order for child support. *Id.*; Tex. Fam. Code Ann. § 14.05(a) (Vernon Supp. 1992).

In amended findings of fact, the court found that "[a]ll property not specifically listed as separate property in these Findings of Fact is community property of the parties." Although assets valued at approximately $50,000 were listed as Nita Fanning's separate property, nothing was listed as Witney Fanning's separate property. In an amended conclusion of law, the trial court concluded that a divestiture of Witney Fanning's interest in the assets awarded to Nita Fanning was "a just and fair division of the assets of the parties." The court awarded Nita Fanning at least a fifty-percent interest in a number of assets that appear to have been recharacterized as Whitney Fanning's separate property by the premarital agreement and the 1981 partition agreement. Some of the assets recharacterized by agreement as his separate property, such as "all retirement and pension accounts in his name," were expressly awarded to Nita Fanning by the trial court. However, it is unclear from the divorce decree whether certain other assets awarded to Nita Fanning are the same as or traceable to similar assets recharacterized by agreement as Witney Fanning's separate property. Because the court's failure to enforce the premarital agreement and the 1981 partition agreement resulted in the divestiture of his separate property, we sustain point of error four with regard to the property recharacterized by those two agreements. On remand, the court must determine the character of the assets according to the valid and enforceable agreements of the parties. As in *Eggemeyer*, however, the trial court is also instructed to determine whether any further arrangements for the support of the children should be made pursuant to section 14.05 of the Texas Family Code. *See Eggemeyer*, 554 S.W.2d at 142; Tex. Fam. Code Ann. § 14.05 (Vernon Supp. 1992).

Because our disposition of points two through five requires a reversal and remand regarding the property division, we do not reach points six and seven, which are related to the court's just and right division of community property.

DISCUSSION

Fanning holds that, as the Constitution and the TFC now imply, spouses may transmute personal earnings received during marriage into separate property via a prenuptial agreement. *See also, Winger v. Pianka*, 831 S.W.2d 853 (Tex. App.—Austin 1992, writ denied). *Fanning* also shows how technical language can be important in drafting marital agreements. Here the appellate court did not enforce the provision in the premarital agreement regarding income from separate property because the court concluded that the parties were referring to the language in the Constitution that permits spouses, but not others, to "agree" that income from separate property will be separate. The *Fanning* opinion does suggest that the same result could be achieved in a prenuptial agreement by stating that each intended spouse "exchanges" his or her interest in the separate property income of the other in exchange for the other spouse's waiver of any claim to that spouse's separate property income. Other cases have accepted this argument. *See Dokmanovic v. Schwarz*, 880 S.W.2d 272 (Tex. App.—Houston [14th Dist.] 1994, no writ).

Fanning is also representative of the way a duress (voluntariness) issue could be presented in connection with a postnuptial partition. This question was dealt with in a similar manner in *Matthews, infra* chapter 20.

Fanning is the first case to accept that courts should enforce the parties' agreement regarding how the community estate should be divided at divorce. Notice that the parties in *Fanning* agreed that community property should be divided equally. No case has decided whether to enforce an agreement to divide the community estate unequally.

Wedding plans sometimes change. For example, in *Dokmanovic, supra*, the parties signed a premarital agreement a week before their planned wedding date. They postponed the wedding and actually married three months later. Should this affect the enforceability of the marriage contract?

Provisions in a marital contract regarding child custody or waiving an obligation to pay child support are not enforceable. Tex. Fam. Code § 4.003(b).

Most marriage contracts set forth the parties' property rights that will accrue during marriage. In most instances, these rights are not affected by the parties' behavior during marriage. In *Laudig v Laudig*, 624 A.2d 651 (Pa. Super. 1993) the court upheld a marriage contract where the wife agreed to waive any right to accumulated marital property if she was unfaithful during marriage. Is this a good result? Would such a waiver be enforceable under Texas law?

Marital agreements generally must be written to be enforceable. Remember that general exceptions to the statute of frauds apparently could apply. *See Hall v. Hall*, 271 Cal. Rptr. 773 (Cal.App.1990) (applying the doctrine of partial performance).

Other spouses sometimes try to address other concerns in a marriage contract. For example, in *Coggins v. Coggins*, 601 So.2d 109 (Ala. Civ. App. 1992) the court considered the enforceability of the parties' agreement that they would never divorce. The agreement provided that, if a party filed for divorce, that party owed the other spouse (apparently as liquidated damages) $1,000 per week for 20 years. A similar, but less burdensome, provision was considered in *Diosdado v. Diosdado*, 118 Cal. Rptr. 2d 494 (Cal. App. 2002). Should the court enforce such a provision? What about an agreement not to file for divorce for three years after the wedding, or without first trying marriage counseling for six months?

Marsh v. Marsh

Texas Court of Appeals — Houston [14th Dist.], 1997
949 S.W.2d 734, no writ

ANDERSON, Justice.

In this appeal, we must determine whether the parties' premarital agreement is unconscionable as a matter of law. The trial court found that it was not, enforced the agreement, and ordered that appellant, William T. Marsh ("Bill"), is indebted to appellee, Juanita Jacobs Marsh ("Juanita") in the amount of $867,778, plus pre- and post-judgment interest and attorney's fees. In seventeen points of error Bill argues that the agreement is unenforceable because it is unconscionable.

Bill and Juanita were married on March 19, 1991. At the time of the marriage, Bill was 78 and Juanita was 58. Both had been married previously. Juanita was reluctant to agree to marry because of the financial losses she incurred from the long illness and decline of her deceased husband. She agreed to marry Bill on the condition that he would provide for her financially.

On the morning before their evening marriage, Bill and Juanita executed an "Agreement in Consideration of Marriage" ("the premarital agreement"), a Trust Agreement, and a Release. The documents were prepared by Juanita's attorney, Robert Jarrard, and Bill was not represented by counsel. According to the premarital agreement, as consideration for Juanita's agreement to marry him, Bill agreed to pay to Juanita, as her separate property, one-half of his assets, which included several accounts in his name at Legg Mason Wood Walker, Inc. ("Legg Mason"). The assets were to be transferred to the Juanita Jacobs Trust ("the Trust") within thirty days of the marriage. The Trust Agreement provides that Juanita is the trustee and sole beneficiary of the corpus of the Trust. Bill and Juanita are equal income beneficiaries of the Trust, as long as both are living. The Trust terminates at Bill's death and the corpus is to be distributed to Juanita. The Release recites that Bill was "strongly requested to obtain counsel," but he elected not to do so. The

Release further states that each party fully understood the terms of the premarital agreement, each entered it freely and with informed consent, and it was not procured by fraud, duress or overreaching.

After their marriage, Bill paid approximately $189,000 into the Trust, but thereafter refused to make further payments. Juanita filed suit to enforce the agreement.[1] Bill answered, claiming the agreement is unconscionable, he did not receive adequate disclosure of Juanita's assets, he had no way to acquire adequate knowledge of the property or financial obligations of Juanita, and did not waive this right. Alternatively, he claimed the agreement was achieved through fraud, duress, or overreaching, or that his performance was excused because of a failure of a predicate to his performance. He also counterclaimed, seeking return of the funds paid to the Trust. The trial court entered temporary orders which required Bill to maintain a minimum balance of $1,200,000 in his Legg Mason account through final hearing. The case was tried to the court, which ruled in favor of Juanita and incorporated its ruling in a written judgment dated August 15, 1995. The trial court entered a Supersedeas Order requiring Legg Mason to hold $1,282,249 in escrow to secure the judgment. On September 14, 1995, Bill filed a motion for new trial, which was overruled by operation of law.

I. Enforceability

Effective September 1, 1987, Texas adopted the Uniform Premarital Agreement Act, which is codified in Chapter 5 of the Texas Family Code. Section 5.46 of the Family Code, which governs the enforcement of premarital agreements, provides as follows:

(a) A premarital agreement is not enforceable if the party against whom enforcement is sought proves that:

(1) that party did not execute the agreement voluntarily; or

(2) the agreement was unconscionable when it was executed and, before execution of the agreement, that party:

(A) was not provided a fair and reasonable disclosure of the property or financial obligations of the other party;

(B) did not voluntarily and expressly waive, in writing, any right to disclosure of the property or financial obligations of the other party beyond the disclosure provided; and

(C) did not have, or reasonably could not have had, an adequate knowledge of the property or financial obligations of the other party.

(b) An issue of unconscionability of a premarital agreement shall be decided by the court as a matter of law.

(c) The remedies and defenses in this section are the exclusive remedies or defenses, including common law remedies or defenses.

Tex. Fam. Code Ann. §5.46 (Vernon 1993 & Supp.1997). Juanita agrees that subsection (c), which was added by 1993 amendment, applies only to an agreement executed on or after September 1, 1993. An agreement executed before that date is governed by the law in effect at the time the agreement was executed. Therefore, Juanita concedes the premarital agreement is subject to common law defenses, in addition to those provided in section 5.46.

---

1. At the time of trial, the parties were still married although they were separated. When the cause was submitted to this court, neither party had filed for divorce.

Bill has not raised the issue of voluntariness on appeal. Instead, he contends the agreement is unconscionable as a matter of law. In his points of error one, two, five, six and seven, Bill attacks the trial court's findings and conclusions which impliedly determined the agreement was not unconscionable. Specifically, the trial court determined in conclusion of law no. 2 that the premarital agreement is a valid and enforceable agreement pursuant to the Texas Family Code.

A. Standard of Review

We review the trial court's findings of fact by the same standards we use to review a jury's findings. It was Bill's burden to establish that the premarital agreement was unenforceable. Tex. Fam. Code Ann. § 5.46(a) (Vernon 1993). When an appellant attacks the legal sufficiency of an adverse finding on an issue on which he had the burden of proof, he must demonstrate on appeal that the evidence conclusively established all vital facts in support of the issue. When reviewing a "matter of law" point, we apply a two-prong test: (1) we examine the record for any evidence that supports the finding, ignoring all evidence to the contrary; (2) if there is no evidence to support the finding, we then examine the entire record to determine if the contrary proposition is established as a matter of law. If the contrary proposition is established conclusively, we sustain the point.

When reviewing a challenge to the factual sufficiency of the evidence, we must examine all of the evidence in the record, both supporting and contrary to the judgment. After considering and weighing all the evidence, we will sustain the challenge only if the finding is so contrary to the overwhelming weight and preponderance of the evidence as to be clearly wrong and manifestly unjust.

Our standard of review of the trial court's legal conclusions is to determine their correctness. Conclusions of law are always reviewable on appeal. The issue of unconscionability is a question of law for the court. Tex. Fam. Code Ann. § 5.46(b) (Vernon 1993). We review questions of law *de novo*, without deference to the lower court's conclusions. *State v. Heal*, 917 S.W.2d 6, 9 (Tex.1996); *Hull & Co., Inc. v. Chandler*, 889 S.W.2d 513, 517 (Tex. App.—Houston [14th Dist.] 1994, writ denied). As an appellate court, we have a duty to independently evaluate the trial court's findings on matters of law. *Daniel v. Daniel*, 779 S.W.2d 110, 114 (Tex. App.—Houston [1st Dist.] 1989, no writ). We will uphold conclusions of law on appeal if the judgment can be sustained on any legal theory supported by the evidence. *Kotis v. Nowlin Jewelry, Inc.*, 844 S.W.2d 920, 922 (Tex. App.—Houston [14th Dist.] 1992, no writ).

B. Unconscionability

The legislature and people of Texas have made a public policy determination that premarital agreements should be enforced. *Beck v. Beck*, 814 S.W.2d 745, 749 (Tex. 1991). Therefore, premarital agreements are presumptively enforceable. *Grossman v. Grossman*, 799 S.W.2d 511, 513 (Tex. App.—Corpus Christi 1990, no writ). According to the statute, Bill, as the party opposing enforcement, bore the burden of proof to rebut the presumption of validity and establish the premarital agreement is not enforceable. *Id.*; Tex. Fam. Code Ann. § 5.46(a) (Vernon 1993).

However, neither the legislature nor Texas courts have defined "unconscionable" in the context of marital or premarital property agreements. Instead, Texas courts have addressed the issue of unconscionability on a case-by-case basis, looking to the entire atmosphere in which the agreement was made. *Pearce v. Pearce*, 824 S.W.2d 195, 199 (Tex. App.—El

Paso 1991, writ denied).[2] In the absence of clear guidance as to the definition of "unconscionability" in marital property cases, courts have turned to the commercial context. For example, the following general discussion of unconscionability, taken from a case involving a suit on a real estate listing agreement, is sometimes cited:

"In determining whether a contract is unconscionable or not, the court must look to the entire atmosphere in which the agreement was made, the alternatives, if any, which were available to the parties at the time of the making of the contract; the non-bargaining ability of one party; whether the contract is illegal or against public policy, and, whether the contract is oppressive or unreasonable. At the same time, a party who knowingly enters a lawful but improvident contract is not entitled to protection by the courts. In the absence of any mistake, fraud, or oppression, the courts, as such, are not interested in the wisdom or impolicy of contracts and agreements voluntarily entered into between parties compos mentis and sui juris. Such parties to contracts have the right to insert any stipulations that may be agreed to, provided they are neither unconscionable nor otherwise illegal or contrary to public policy. It has accordingly been said that, almost without limitation, what the parties agree upon is valid, the parties are bound by the agreement they have made, and the fact that a bargain is a hard one does not entitle a party to be relieved therefrom if he assumed it fairly and voluntarily. A contract is not unenforceable on the ground that it yields a return disproportionate to the expenditures in time and money, where there has been no mistake or unfairness and the party against whom it is sought to be enforced has received and enjoyed the benefits."

Wade v. Austin, 524 S.W.2d 79, 86 (Tex. Civ. App.—Texarkana 1975, no writ) (citation omitted).

Both the premarital agreement and the Release expressly state that each party entered the agreement freely and knowingly. Bill testified that there were no threats, fraud, overreaching, duress, or misrepresentations made to him to induce him to execute the agreement. He also acknowledged that he was free to consult an attorney and accountant before its execution. There was no evidence presented that Juanita took advantage of Bill. There was no evidence that Bill was senile, and he denied that he was. He was active in trading stocks. A letter Bill wrote to Legg Mason requesting specific transfers to the Trust from one of his accounts showed Bill appeared to be well aware of what he owned.

Juanita testified that Bill agreed to the transfer of one-half of his Legg Mason accounts to the Trust. She denied ever seeing the Legg Mason documents before they were attached to the agreements. She also stated she "thinks" Bill read the agreement before signing it. Juanita testified she never threatened or dominated Bill, and that the agreement was not procured through fraud or duress.

Jarrard, the attorney who prepared the agreement, testified that Bill provided all the financial documents needed to draft the premarital agreement, and that he dictated portions of the agreement. Specifically, Bill requested that he be a lifetime beneficiary of one-half of the income from the Trust. This provision was incorporated in the Trust. Jarrard

2. Most reported Texas cases discussing enforcement of marital property agreements deal with those entered during marriage, rather than before. *See, e.g., Blonstein v. Blonstein,* 831 S.W.2d 468 (Tex.App.—Houston [14th Dist.]), *writ denied per curiam,* 848 S.W.2d 82 (Tex.1992). The statutory defenses for premarital and postmarital agreements are identical, making these cases instructive as to the issues before us. However, in post-marital agreements a fiduciary duty exists that is not present in premarital agreements between prospective spouses. *See Daniel,* 779 S.W.2d at 115 (recognizing the confidential relationship between a husband and wife imposes the same duties of good faith and fair dealing on spouses as required of partners and other fiduciaries).

also testified that he met with both parties over several hours in discussing the proposed agreement, including three visits with Bill alone. Jarrard stated he discussed the gift tax consequences with Bill, and Bill offered to have his accountant prepare any required tax return. Jarrard further testified he believed the parties were provided a copy of the documents to review before they were executed and he was sure that Bill understood the documents. Jarrard testified he "strongly" recommended Bill obtain counsel. Bill[3] admitted Jarrard encouraged him to see a lawyer, but contends that he was not emphatic.

Clearly, there is some evidence supporting the factual basis for the trial court's conclusion that the agreement is not unconscionable. Therefore, we now consider all the remaining evidence in the record to evaluate whether the trial court's determination is against the great weight and preponderance of the evidence.

In reviewing the validity of a marital property agreement, this court has considered such factors as the maturity of the individuals, their business backgrounds, their educational levels, their experiences in prior marriages, their respective ages and their motivations to protect their respective children. *See Williams v. Williams*, 720 S.W.2d 246, 249 (Tex. App.—Houston [14th Dist.] 1986, no writ). Bill argues, however, that he established the following factors which make the agreement in this case unconscionable:

(1) the onerous circumstances of its execution, including:

(a) the parties' disparate bargaining power;

(b) the agreement's proximity in time to the marriage;

(c) the absence of counsel representing Bill's interests;

(2) the oppressive, one-sided nature of the agreement; and

(3) the failure of the agreement to effect the parties' intent.

Our review of the entire record does not reveal that the evidence overwhelmingly established these factors. We disagree that the parties had disparate bargaining power. Both were mature, educated, and had business experience. Juanita had grown children to consider, and Bill was childless. Both Bill and Juanita had been married before, and Juanita had seen her assets diminished through the lengthy illness of her late husband. Only Juanita had previously executed a premarital agreement, however.

The fact that the premarital agreement was signed shortly before the wedding does not make the agreement unconscionable. *See Williams*, 720 S.W.2d at 248–49 (holding that an agreement signed on the day of marriage was not procured through fraud, duress or overreaching because the wife had substantial business experience and the husband testified they had discussed the agreement's terms six months before the wedding). Likewise, the fact that Bill was not represented by independent counsel is not dispositive. *See Pearce*, 824 S.W.2d at 199 (enforcing a postmarital agreement where the wife testified she was not represented by counsel and did not read or understand the agreement, yet she encouraged her daughter-in-law to sign a similar agreement against the daughter-in-law's attorney's advice). Moreover, Bill consulted his long-time attorney, James Baker, shortly after his marriage and admitted that Baker pointed out several problems with the agreement. Juanita testified Bill told her the agreement was worthless. Contrary to his attor-

---

3. The Agreement provides: It has been strongly recommended, by the counsel of [Juanita], that [Bill] obtain counsel for representation in the negotiations of this "agreement," however, [Bill] has elected not to retain independent counsel. [Bill] represents that he enters into this "Agreement" with informed consent and that this "Agreement" was not procured by fraud duress or overreaching. The Release contains similar language.

ney's advice, Bill requested transfers of approximately $189,000 from his Legg Mason account to the Trust.[4]

We also do not accept Bill's assertion that the one-sided nature of the agreement strongly preponderates toward a finding of unconscionability. This court has found that even though a premarital agreement may be disproportionate, unfairness is not material to the enforceability of the agreement. *Chiles v. Chiles*, 779 S.W.2d 127, 129 (Tex. App.—Houston [14th Dist.] 1989, writ denied). A factual finding that a premarital agreement is unfair does not satisfy the burden of proof required to establish unconscionability. *Id.*

Bill argues that when he wrote the check to pay for Jarrard's services, he made a mistake in writing the amount, demonstrating that he was "not thinking straight" when he executed the agreement. While Bill testified that he remembered very little about the events leading to the execution of the premarital agreement, that he did not know the contents of envelopes he delivered to Jarrard to draft the agreement, and that he did not read the agreement, he was quite clear as to the value of the assets he transferred to the Trust and corrected Juanita's counsel as to the total amount. Bill acknowledged that before the marriage, he and Juanita did not live together and had no access to each other's financial information. He denied seeing the documents before their execution and testified he only spent about twenty minutes in Jarrard's office that day. The fact that Bill denied reading the premarital agreement is not grounds for avoiding the contract. Absent fraud, one is presumed to know the contents of a document he has signed and has an obligation to protect himself by reading a document before signing it. *Nautical Landings Marina, Inc. v. First Nat'l Bank in Port Lavaca*, 791 S.W.2d 293, 298 (Tex. App.—Corpus Christi 1990, writ denied).

The trial court, as the trier of fact, was the sole judge of the credibility of the witnesses and the weight to be given to their testimony. The court may not have believed Bill's denial that he knowingly provided his financial documents and helped draft the premarital agreement because the testimony showed that only Bill had access to his personal financial documents and that Juanita had never seen the documents until they were attached to the premarital agreement. We cannot retry the case or otherwise substitute our judgment for that of the trier of fact.

Over objection to testimony on matters of law, the trial court permitted Bill to present expert testimony from Donn Fullenweider, a board certified family law practitioner, who concluded that the premarital agreement is unconscionable per se. He testified the agreement was suspect because it was executed the day of the marriage and that Juanita's lawyer should have insisted that Bill have independent counsel. He also faulted the agreement for failing to contemplate the divorce of the parties. He conceded, however, that the Trust did not terminate upon divorce, and the Trustee had a duty to care for Bill during his lifetime with the Trust income. However, only Juanita has the power to withdraw the corpus of the trust and may do so at any time. In rebuttal, Juanita's expert, Warren Cole, also board certified in family law, testified that in his opinion, the premarital agreement is an enforceable contract. He opined that the agreement was definitely not unconscionable. For an agreement to be unconscionable, it must be "so far one-sided that no reasonable person could consider it to be an arm's length transaction." He testified fairness is not determinative of unconscionability.

In the absence of any evidence that the premarital agreement was obtained through an unfair advantage taken by Juanita, we must conclude Bill has not sustained his burden to

---

4. Based on these transfers, Juanita argues that even if the agreement is unconscionable, Bill nevertheless ratified the contract by his partial performance.

defeat the presumption of enforceability. *Cf. Fanning v. Fanning*, 828 S.W.2d 135 (Tex. App. —Waco 1992), *rev'd in part on other grounds*, 847 S.W.2d 225 (Tex. 1993) (holding a postmarital partition agreement was unconscionable based on the husband's threats to divorce the wife and deprive her of custody of the children and a psychologist's testimony that the husband was manipulative and aggressive). "[T]he fact that a bargain is a hard one does not entitle a party to be relieved therefrom if he assumed it fairly and voluntarily." *Wade*, 524 S.W.2d at 86. Having reviewed all the evidence in our record, we conclude the evidence is both legally and factually sufficient to support the trial court's implied finding that the agreement is not unconscionable. Therefore, the trial court's conclusion of law that the agreement is enforceable is correct. We hold that the premarital agreement is not unconscionable as a matter of law.[5] Therefore, we overrule appellant's points of error one, two, five, six and seven.

C. Lack of Disclosure

In his points of error three and four, Bill asserts that the trial court erred in its implied finding that he had been properly informed of Juanita's property and financial obligations. He contends he established as a matter of law that he received no such information before executing the premarital agreement. Alternatively, he asserts this finding is against the great weight and preponderance of the evidence.

Having determined that the agreement is not unconscionable, we need not reach the issue of lack of disclosure. Because disclosure forms the second prong of the test to rebut the presumption of enforceability, lack of disclosure is material only if the premarital agreement is unconscionable. *See* Tex. Fam. Code Ann. §5.46(a)(2)(A), (C) (Vernon 1993).

In conclusion, we affirm the judgment of the trial court.

Deanda Osorno v. Osorno

Texas Court of Appeals—Houston [14th Dist.], 2002
76 S.W.3d 509, no pet. h.

SCOTT BRISTER, Chief Justice.

Gloria was forty years old when she met Henry in February 1992. In August, Gloria discovered she was pregnant. According to her, Henry wanted her to have an abortion, which she refused for religious reasons. In September, Henry agreed to marry her if she signed a premarital agreement. Both Henry and Gloria signed an Agreement in Contemplation of Marriage on October 9, 1992, and were married the following day.

Henry filed for divorce on December 22, 1998. Gloria contested the enforceability of the premarital agreement. A hearing was held before a master at which both Henry and Gloria testified. The master found the agreement enforceable.

Enforceability of the Premarital Agreement

As the party attacking a premarital agreement, Gloria had the burden to show (1) she did not sign the agreement voluntarily or (2) it was unconscionable and she did not re-

----

5. Because we hold the agreement is valid, we do not reach Juanita's argument that Bill ratified the contract by making payments to the Trust.

ceive proper disclosure of Henry's property. Tex. Fam. Code Ann. §4.006(a) (Vernon 1998). Gloria relies on the first ground, arguing she signed the premarital agreement involuntarily because she was forty, unmarried, and pregnant. The Family Code provides no definition of "voluntarily." In construing section 4.006(a), this Court has previously referred to commercial law governing enforcement of contracts for guidance. *See Marsh v. Marsh*, 949 S.W.2d 734, 739–40 (Tex. App.—Houston [14th Dist.] 1997, no writ) (looking to contract cases for definition of "unconscionable").

For duress to be a contract defense, it must consist of a threat to do something the threatening party has no legal right to do. *See Brown v. Aztec Rig Equip., Inc.*, 921 S.W.2d 835, 845 (Tex. App.—Houston [14th Dist.] 1996, writ denied). In this case, aside from his moral duties, Henry had no legal duty to marry Gloria. His threat to do something he had the legal right to do is insufficient to invalidate the premarital agreement. Gloria was faced with difficult choices, but we cannot find her decision to sign the agreement was involuntary. *See In re Marriage of Dawley*, 17 Cal.3d 342, 131 Cal.Rptr. 3, 551 P.2d 323, 331 (Cal.1976) (refusing to set aside premarital agreement signed under pressure of unplanned pregnancy). We overrule Gloria's first point of error.

DISCUSSION

Another case that discusses voluntariness is *Nesmith v. Berger*, 64 S.W.3d 110 (Tex. App.—Austin 2001, pet. denied).

C. The Distinction Between Postnuptial and Prenuptial Agreements

Texas has adopted similar rules to govern marital agreements signed before marriage and those signed during marriage. Is this sensible? Do agreements signed during marriage present different issues? For example, is it the same thing to say "I'll divorce you unless you sign this," as it is to say "I won't marry you unless you sign this"? The *Matthews* case, Chapter 20 *infra*, considers a related problem.

Note that based on the differences between 4.003 and 4.102, the scope of matters that can be addressed in a postnuptial agreement may be more limited than that for premarital agreements. *See Ahmed v. Ahmed*, 261 S.W.3d 190 (Tex. App.—Houston [14th Dist.] 2008, no pet.) (limiting postnuptial agreements to partition and exchanges).

If a spouse is sick when an agreement is signed, this could present additional issues, as shown by the case below.

Borelli v. Brusseau
California Court of Appeal, 1993
16 Cal. Rptr. 2d 16

PERLEY, Associate Justice.

Plaintiff and appellant Hildegard L. Borelli (appellant) appeals from a judgment of dismissal after a demurrer was sustained without leave to amend to her complaint against defendant and respondent Grace G. Brusseau, as executor of the estate of Michael J.

Borelli (respondent). The complaint sought specific performance of a promise by appellant's deceased husband Michael J. Borelli (decedent) to transfer certain property to her in return for her promise to care for him at home after he had suffered a stroke.

Appellant contends that the trial court erred by sustaining the demurrer on the grounds that the "alleged agreement [appellant] seeks to enforce is without consideration and the alleged contract is void as against public policy." We conclude that the contention lacks merit.

On April 24, 1980, appellant and decedent entered into an antenuptial contract. On April 25, 1980, they were married. Appellant remained married to decedent until the death of the latter on January 25, 1989.

In March 1983, February 1984, and January 1987, decedent was admitted to a hospital due to heart problems. As a result, "decedent became concerned and frightened about his health and longevity." He discussed these fears and concerns with appellant and told her that he intended to "leave" the following property to her.

1. "An interest" in a lot in Sacramento, California.

2. A life estate for the use of a condominium in Hawaii.

3. A 25 percent interest in Borelli Meat Co.

4. All cash remaining in all existing bank accounts at the time of his death.

5. The costs of educating decedent's step-daughter, Monique Lee.

6. Decedent's entire interest in a residence in Kensington, California.

7. All furniture located in the residence.

8. Decedent's interest in a partnership.

9. Health insurance for appellant and Monique Lee.

In August 1988, decedent suffered a stroke while in the hospital. "Throughout the decedent's August, 1988 hospital stay and subsequent treatment at a rehabilitation center, he repeatedly told [appellant] that he was uncomfortable in the hospital and that he disliked being away from home. The decedent repeatedly told [appellant] that he did not want to be admitted to a nursing home, even though it meant he would need round-the-clock care, and rehabilitative modifications to the house, in order for him to live at home."

"In or about October, 1988, [appellant] and the decedent entered an oral agreement whereby the decedent promised to leave to [appellant] the property listed [above], including a one hundred percent interest in the Sacramento property.... In exchange for the decedent's promise to leave her the property ... [appellant] agreed to care for the decedent in his home, for the duration of his illness, thereby avoiding the need for him to move to a rest home or convalescent hospital as his doctors recommended. The agreement was based on the confidential relationship that existed between [appellant] and the decedent."

Appellant performed her promise but the decedent did not perform his. Instead his will bequeathed her the sum of $100,000 and his interest in the residence they owned as joint tenants. The bulk of decedent's estate passed to respondent, who is decedent's daughter.

DISCUSSION

"Marriage is a matter of public concern. The public, through the state, has interest in both its formation and dissolution.... The regulation of marriage and divorce is solely within the province of the Legislature except as the same might be restricted by the Constitution." (*Haas v. Haas* (1964) 227 Cal.App.2d 615, 617, 38 Cal.Rptr. 811.)

In accordance with these concerns the following pertinent legislation has been enacted: Civil Code section 242 — "Every individual shall support his or her spouse...." Civil Code section 4802 — "[A] husband and wife cannot, by any contract with each other, alter their legal relations, except as to property...." Civil Code section 5100 — "Husband and wife contract toward each other obligations of mutual respect, fidelity, and support." Civil Code section 5103 — "[E]ither husband or wife may enter into any transaction with the other ... respecting property, which either might if unmarried." Civil Code section 5132 — "[A] married person shall support the person's spouse while they are living together...."

The courts have stringently enforced and explained the statutory language.

"Indeed, husband and wife assume mutual obligations of support upon marriage. These obligations are not conditioned on the existence of community property or income." (*See v. See* (1966) 64 Cal.2d 778, 784, 51 Cal.Rptr. 888, 415 P.2d 776.) "In entering the marital state, by which a contract is created, it must be assumed that the parties voluntarily entered therein with knowledge that they have the moral and legal obligation to support the other." (*Department of Mental Hygiene v. Kolts* (1966) 247 Cal.App.2d 154, 165, 55 Cal.Rptr. 437.)

Moreover, inter-spousal mutual obligations have been broadly defined. "[Husband's] duties and obligations to [wife] included more than mere cohabitation with her. It was his duty to offer [wife] his sympathy, confidence [citation], and fidelity." (*In re Marriage of Rabi* (1974) 40 Cal.App.3d 917, 922, 115 Cal.Rptr. 594.) When necessary, spouses must "provide uncompensated protective supervision services for" each other. (*Miller v. Woods* (1983) 148 Cal.App.3d 862, 877, 196 Cal.Rptr. 69.)

Estate of Sonnicksen (1937) 23 Cal.App.2d 475, 479, 73 P.2d 643, and *Brooks v. Brooks* (1941) 48 Cal.App.2d 347, 349–350, 119 P.2d 970, each hold that under the above statutes and in accordance with the above policy a wife is obligated by the marriage contract to provide nursing type care to an ill husband. Therefore, contracts whereby the wife is to receive compensation for providing such services are void as against public policy and there is no consideration for the husband's promise.

Appellant argues that *Sonnicksen* and *Brooks* are no longer valid precedents because they are based on outdated views of the role of women and marriage. She further argues that the rule of those cases denies her equal protection because husbands only have a financial obligation toward their wives, while wives have to provide actual nursing services for free. We disagree. The rule and policy of *Sonnicksen* and *Brooks* have been applied to both spouses in several recent cases arising in different areas of the law.

Webster's New Collegiate Dictionary (1981) p. 240, defines consortium as "The legal right of one spouse to the company, affection, and service of the other." Only married persons are allowed to recover damages for loss of consortium. (*Elden v. Sheldon* (1988) 46 Cal.3d 267, 277, 250 Cal.Rptr. 254, 758 P.2d 582.)

Rodriguez v. Bethlehem Steel Corp. (1974) 12 Cal.3d 382, 115 Cal.Rptr. 765, 525 P.2d 669, held that a wife could recover consortium damages. The Supreme Court's reasoning was as follows. "But there is far more to the marriage relationship than financial support. The concept of consortium includes not only loss of support or services, it also embraces such elements as love, companionship, affection, society, sexual relations, solace and more.' [Citation.] As to each, 'the interest sought to be protected is personal to the wife' (*ibid*)...." (*Rodriguez v. Bethlehem Steel Corp., supra*, at pp. 404–405, 115 Cal.Rptr. 765, 525 P.2d 669.) "The deprivation of a husband's physical assistance in operating and maintaining the family home is a compensable item of loss of consortium." (*Id.* at p. 409, fn. 31, 115 Cal.Rptr. 765, 525 P.2d 669.)

In *Krouse v. Graham* (1977) 19 Cal.3d 59, 66–67, 137 Cal.Rptr. 863, 562 P.2d 1022, an action for the wrongful death of the wife, the husband was allowed to recover consortium damages "for the loss of his wife's 'love, companionship, comfort, affection, society, solace or moral support, any loss of enjoyment of sexual relations, or any loss of her physical assistance in the operation or maintenance of the home.'" The wife "had recently retired as a legal secretary in order to care for her husband, Benjamin, whose condition of emphysema, in turn, caused him to retire and necessitated considerable nursing services."

The principal holding of *Watkins v. Watkins* (1983) 143 Cal.App.3d 651, 192 Cal.Rptr. 54, was that a marriage did not extinguish a woman's right to recover the value of her homemaker services rendered prior to the marriage. Much of the opinion is devoted to a discussion of *Sonnicksen* and *Brooks*. Those cases are approved by the court but not expanded to cover the period before marriage. (*Id.* at pp. 654–655, 192 Cal.Rptr. 54.)

Vincent v. State of California (1971) 22 Cal.Ap.3d 56, 99 Cal.Rptr. 410, held that for purposes of benefit payments spouses caring for each other must be treated identically under similar assistance programs. In reaching such conclusion the court held: "Appellants suggest that one reason justifying denial of payment for services rendered by ATD attendants who reside with their recipient spouses is that, by virtue of the marriage contract, one spouse is obligated to care for the other without remuneration. (Civ.Code, § 5100; *Estate of Sonnicksen* (1937) 23 Cal.App.2d 475, 479, 73 P.2d 643.) Such pre-existing duty provides a constitutionally sound basis for a classification which denies compensation for care rendered by a husband or wife to his spouse who is receiving welfare assistance. [Citations.] ... [¶] ... But insofar as one spouse has a duty created by the marriage contract to care for the other without compensation when they are living together, recipients of aid to the aged, aid to the blind and aid to the disabled are similarly situated." (*Vincent v. State of California, supra,* 22, Cal.App.3d at p. 572, 99 Cal.Rptr. 410.)

These cases indicate that the marital duty of support under Civil Code sections 242, 5100, and 5132 includes caring for a spouse who is ill. They also establish that support in a marriage means more than the physical care someone could be hired to provide. Such support also encompasses sympathy, love, companionship and affection. Thus, the duty of support can no more be "delegated" to a third party than the statutory duties of fidelity and mutual respect (Civ.Code, § 5100). Marital duties are owed by the spouses personally. This is implicit in the definition of marriage as "a personal relation arising out of a civil contract between a man and a woman." (Civ.Code, § 4100.)

We therefore adhere to the longstanding rule that a spouse is not entitled to compensation for support, apart from rights to community property and the like that arise from the marital relation itself. Personal performance of a personal duty created by the contract of marriage does not constitute a new consideration supporting the indebtedness alleged in this case.

We agree with the dissent that no rule of law becomes sacrosanct by virtue of its duration, but we are not persuaded that the well-established rule that governs this case deserves to be discarded. If the rule denying compensation for support originated from considerations peculiar to women, this has no bearing on the rule's gender-neutral application today. There is as much potential for fraud today as ever, and allegations like appellant's could be made every time any personal care is rendered. This concern may not entirely justify the rule, but it cannot be said that all rationales for the rule are outdated.

Speculating that appellant might have left her husband but for the agreement she alleges, the dissent suggests that marriages will break up if such agreements are not enforced. While we do not believe that marriages would be fostered by a rule that encouraged sickbed bargaining, the question is not whether such negotiations may be more useful than unseemly. The issue is whether such negotiations are antithetical to the institution of marriage as the Legislature has defined it. We believe that they are.

The dissent maintains that mores have changed to the point that spouses can be treated just like any other parties haggling at arm's length. Whether or not the modern marriage has become like a business, and regardless of whatever else it may have become, it continues to be defined by statute as a personal relationship of mutual support. Thus, even if few things are left that cannot command a price, marital support remains one of them.

The judgment is affirmed.

ANDERSON, P.J. concurs.

POCHE, Associate Justice, dissenting.

A very ill person wishes to be cared for at home personally by his spouse rather than by nurses at a health care facility. The ill person offers to pay his spouse for such personal care by transferring property to her. The offer is accepted, the services are rendered and the ill spouse dies. Affirming a judgment of dismissal rendered after a general demurer was sustained, this court holds that the contract was not enforceable because—as a matter of law—the spouse who rendered services gave no consideration. Apparently, in the majority's view she had a pre-existing or pre-contract nondelegable duty to clean the bed pans herself. Because I do not believe she did, I respectfully dissent.

The majority correctly read *Estate of Sonnicksen* (1937) 23 Cal.App.2d 475, 73 P.2d 643 and *Brooks v. Brooks* (1941) 48 Cal.App.2d 347, 119 P.2d 970 as holding that a wife cannot enter into a binding contract with her husband to provide "nursing type care" for compensation. (Majority opn., *ante*, p. 19.) It reasons that the wife, by reason of the marital relationship, already has a duty to provide such care, thus she offers no new consideration to support an independent contract to the same effect. (*See* Civ.Code, §§ 1550, 1605.) The logic of these decisions is ripe for re-examination.

Not only has this doctrinal base for the authority underpinning the majority opinion been discarded long ago, but modern attitudes toward marriage have changed almost as rapidly as the economic realities of modern society. The assumption that only the rare wife can make a financial contribution to her family has become badly outdated in this age in which many married women have paying employment outside the home. A two-income family can no longer be dismissed as a statistically insignificant aberration. Moreover today husbands are increasingly involved in the domestic chores that make a house a home. Insofar as marital duties and property rights are not governed by positive law, they may be the result of informal accommodation or formal agreement. (*See* Civ. Code, § 5200 et seq.) If spouses cannot work things out, there is always the no longer infrequently used option of divorce. For better or worse, we have to a great extent left behind the comfortable and familiar gender-based roles evoked by Norman Rockwell paintings. No longer can the marital relationship be regarded as "uniform and unchangeable." (*In re Callister's Estate, supra*, 47 N.E. 268 at p. 270.)

Restraints on interspousal litigation are almost extinct. With the walls supposedly protecting the domestic haven from litigation already reduced to rubble, it hardly seems revolutionary to topple one more brick. Furthermore, in situations such as this, where one spouse has died, preserving "'domestic life [from] discord and mischief'" (*Brooks v. Brooks, supra*, 48 Cal.App.2d 347 at p. 350, 119 P.2d 970) seems an academic concern that no modern academic seems concerned with.

Fear that a contract struck between spouses "degrades" the spouse providing service, making him or her no better than a "hired servant" justifies the result in several cases. (E.g., *Brooks v. Brooks, supra,* 48 Cal.App.2d 347 at p. 350, 119 P.2d 970; *In re Callister's Estate, supra,* 47 N.E. 268 at p. 270.) such fears did not prevent California from enacting a statute specifying that "either husband or wife may enter into any transaction with the other, or with any other person, respecting property, which either might if unmarried." (Civ.Code, §§ 5103, subd. (a), 4802.) This is but one instance of "the utmost freedom of contract [that] exists in California between husband and wife…." (*Perkins v. Sunset Tel. and Tel. Co.* (1909) 155 Cal. 712, 720, 103 P. 190.)

No one doubts that spouses owe each other a duty of support or that this encompasses "the obligation to provide medical care." (*Hawkins v. Superior Court* (1979) 89 Cal.App.3d 413, 418–419, 152 Cal.Rptr. 491.) There is nothing found in *Sonnicksen* and *Brooks,* or cited by the majority, which requires that this obligation be *personally* discharged by a spouse except the decisions themselves. However, at the time *Sonnicksen* and *Brooks* were decided — before World War II — it made sense for those courts to say that a wife could perform her duty of care only by doing so personally. That was an accurate reflection of the real world for women years before the exigency of war produced substantial employment opportunities for them. For most women at that time there was no other way to take care of a sick husband except personally. So to the extent those decisions hold that a contract to pay a wife for caring personally for her husband is without consideration they are correct only because at the time they were decided there were no other ways she could meet her obligation of care. Since that was the universal reality, she was giving up nothing of value by agreeing to perform a duty that had one and only one way of being performed.

However the real world has changed in the fifty-six years since *Sonnicksen* was decided. Just a few years later with the advent of World War II *Rosie the Riveter* became not only a war jingle but a salute to hundreds of thousands of women working on the war effort outside the home. We know what happened thereafter. Presumably in the present day husbands and wives who work outside the home have alternative methods of meeting this duty of care to an ill spouse. Among the choices would be: (1) paying for professional help; (2) paying for non professional assistance; (3) seeking help from relatives or friends; and (4) quitting one's job and doing the work personally.

A fair reading of the complaint indicates that Mrs. Borelli initially chose the first of these options, and that this was not acceptable to Mr. Borelli, who then offered compensation if Mrs. Borelli would agree to personally care for him at home. To contend in 1993 that such a contract is without consideration means that if Mrs. Clinton becomes ill President Clinton must drop everything and personally care for her.

According to the majority, Mrs. Borelli had nothing to bargain with so long as she remained in the marriage. This assumes that an intrinsic component of the marital relationship is the *personal* services of the spouse, an obligation that cannot be delegated or performed by others. The preceding discussion has attempted to demonstrate many ways in which what the majority terms "nursing-type care" can be provided without either husband or wife being required to empty a single bedpan. It follows that, because Mrs. Borelli agreed to supply this personal involvement, she was providing something over and above what would fully satisfy her duty of support. That personal something — precisely because it was something she was not required to do — qualifies as valid consideration sufficient to make enforceable Mr. Borelli's reciprocal promise to convey certain of his separate property.

DISCUSSION

When prospective spouses sign a contract before marriage that deals with the economic ramifications of marriage, consideration is not a problem because it has been accepted that the participation in the marriage ceremony by both spouses constitutes consideration. When spouses sign an agreement after the wedding, however, consideration can become an issue. Is this true in Texas?

Are you persuaded by the majority opinion in *Borelli*? Could other arguments be made in support of the result that might be more convincing?

The Employees Retirement Income Security Act (ERISA) contains specific procedures to be followed if a spouse wishes to waive benefits accruing under private pension plans. Courts have reached conflicting conclusions regarding whether prospective spouses may waive such rights in a prenuptial agreement. Compare *Hurwitz v. Sher*, 982 F.2d 778 (2d. Cir. 1992) with *Estate of Hopkins*, 574 N.E.2d 230 (Ill. App. 1991).

In re Marriage of Mehren & Dargan

California Court of Appeals, 2004
118 Cal. App. 4th 1167 (Cal. App. 4th Dist. 2004)

RYLAARSDAM, J.

After obtaining permission from this court pursuant to California Rules of Court, rule 5.180, Christopher Dargan (husband) appealed from an order after a bifurcated trial upholding the validity of a postmarital agreement. In the agreement he promised to grant respondent Monica Mehren (wife) all of his interest in certain of the parties' community property should he use illicit drugs. We conclude that such an agreement is unenforceable because it violates the public policy favoring no-fault divorce. We therefore order the trial court to vacate its order and enter a new order providing that the agreement is unenforceable.

FACTS

Husband has suffered an off-and-on addiction to cocaine for many years. It is not necessary for us to relate his unsuccessful attempts to free himself from his addiction other than to note that several years after their marriage, the parties separated after another episode resulting from husband's use of cocaine. Months later, the parties agreed that husband would return to the family home. Subsequently, the parties entered into an "Agreement re Transfer of Property." The agreement recited that wife "consented to the resumption of marital relations on the condition that [husband] abstain from the deliberate, intentional use or ingestion of any mind altering chemical or substance excluding such use that may be prescribed or approved by a medical doctor. In the event of such deliberate, intentional use or ingestion of mind altering chemicals or substances by [husband], [husband] agrees that he will forfeit all of his right, title and interest in [described property]." Husband and wife signed the document before a notary public.

Unfortunately, husband did not keep his promise. Thereafter wife filed for divorce, asking that the property described in the agreement be confirmed to her as her separate property. The trial court concluded in a pretrial proceeding that the agreement did not violate public policy. During the subsequent trial, a number of issues concerning the circumstances under which the agreement was prepared and executed were resolved against husband. Some of these issues are also raised in this appeal. But because none of them form the basis for our decision, we will not relate them here or state the disputed facts surrounding the execution of the agreement.

DISCUSSION

The Contract Violates Public Policy

As far as we and the parties were able to determine, the specific issue before us is a novel one. Although reported cases have dealt with contracts between spouses, many of these deal with premarital agreements. But we can look to these cases for guidance. In *In re Marriage of Bonds* (2000) 24 Cal.4th 1 [99 Cal. Rptr. 2d 252, 5 P.3d 815], our Supreme Court noted the difference between commercial contracts and contracts regulating the marital relationship (in that case, a premarital agreement). Commercial contracts have a specific object, and parties to such contracts generally enter into them intending that the objects be achieved. Marital contracts, on the other hand, are generally entered into in the expectation that they will never be invoked. (*Id.* at pp. 24–25.) "Furthermore, marriage itself is a highly regulated institution of undisputed social value, and there are many limitations on the ability of persons to contract with respect to it, or to vary its statutory terms, that have nothing to do with maximizing the satisfaction of the parties or carrying out their intent." (*Id.* at p. 25.)

The *Bonds* opinion rejects a freedom-of-contract analysis of marital contracts (*In re Marriage of Bonds, supra,* 24 Cal.4th at p. 25) and recites a number of examples of marital contracts that will not be enforced as violating public policy. (*Ibid.*) Citing Family Code section 721, subdivision (b), *Bonds* also draws a distinction between premarital and postmarital contracts when it notes a difference in the fiduciary relationship between the parties; no such relationship exists preceding the marriage. It does following marriage and therefore affects spouses' ability to enter into contracts between themselves. (*Id.* at p. 27.)

Starting with *Bonds's* conclusion that marriage "is a highly regulated institution of undisputed social value" (*In re Marriage of Bonds, supra,* 24 Cal.4th at p. 25), we must decide whether the statutory regulations pertaining to marriage would be frustrated were we to enforce the agreement. We answer this query in the affirmative. Because the conduct of one spouse would affect the division of community property, the agreement frustrates the statutory policy favoring no-fault divorce.

The case most analogous to the one confronting us here is *Diosdado v. Diosdado* (2002) 97 Cal.App.4th 470 [118 Cal. Rptr. 2d 494]. There husband and wife entered into a written agreement wherein each promised to remain faithful to the other; the agreement also provided for $ 50,000 liquidated damages, to be paid upon dissolution of the marriage, should either spouse breach the agreement. The court adopted the reasoning of the trial court that the agreement was not enforceable "because it was contrary to the public policy underlying California's no-fault divorce laws." (*Id.* at p. 473.) The court noted that since the 1969 enactment of Civil Code section 4506 (now Fam. Code, § 2310), "[f]ault is simply not a relevant consideration in the legal process by which a marriage is dissolved. Recovery in no-fault dissolution proceedings 'is basically limited to half the community property and appropriate support and attorney fee orders—no hefty premiums for emotional angst.' [Citation]" (*Diosdado v. Diosdado, supra,* 97 Cal.App.4th at p. 474.) The *Diosdado* court concluded the liquidated damage clause "attempt[ed] to impose just such a premium for the 'emotional angst' caused by [husband's] breach of his promise of sexual fidelity." (Ibid., fn. omitted.) As such, the contract had an unlawful object and was invalid under Civil Code section 1667. (Diosdado, at p. 474.)

We see little analytical difference between the angst experienced by the wife in *Diosdado* and the angst undoubtedly suffered by wife here. In this case too, the agreement purports to award a community property premium because of the behavior of husband.

Thus, as in *Diosdado*, the agreement attempts to avoid the no-fault provisions of Family Code section 2310. As such, its objective is illegal under Civil Code section 1667, which renders a contract unlawful if it is "[¶] 1. [c]ontrary to an express provision of law; [¶] 2. [c]ontrary to the policy of express law, … or, [¶] 3. [o]therwise contrary to good morals."

Wife seeks to distinguish *Diosdado* by arguing that the present "agreement was a contract independent of the court, and required no court action," while the agreement in *Diosdado* "could only be implemented in the context of a divorce suit." True, the *Diosdado* agreement would only be effective upon a dissolution. Thus the policy considerations are slightly different. It is also correct that in theory, and assuming the agreement was valid, once husband started again using illicit drugs, wife could have invoked her rights under the agreement and acquired the community property assets without obtaining a divorce. But such a scenario would not affect the relationship of the parties in the same manner as a transfer of these property interests following a divorce. And, significantly, wife did not seek to obtain the transfer of husband's share of the community property when he again relapsed into his addiction; she sought it as part of the dissolution proceedings. Further, the very issue determining whether she was entitled to the property would necessarily involve a judicial determination concerning husband's drug use, a factual adjudication of fault that the no-fault statute seeks to avoid.

Was the "Agreement" a Contract?

For the first time during oral argument, wife's lawyer argued that the "agreement" did not constitute a contract but rather was a gift subject to a condition precedent. Although case law uses the terms "contract" and "agreement" interchangeably, a leading treatise on contract law recognizes that the latter term is broader. "In some respects, the term agreement is a broader term than contract, and even broader than the term bargain or promise. It also covers executed sales, gifts and other transfers of property." (1 Williston on Contracts (4th ed. 2003) § 1.3, fn. omitted.)

But, assuming the distinction makes a difference, wife waived such an argument by failing to raise it in the trial court. (366–386 Geary St., *L.P. v. Superior Court* (1990) 219 Cal. App. 3d 1186, 1199 [268 Cal. Rptr. 678].) And even here, in her respondent's brief, wife acknowledges that the "agreement" constitutes a contract. For example, as we noted earlier, in attempting to distinguish *Diosdado v. Diosdado*, *supra*, 97 Cal.App.4th 470, she argued "[t]he … agreement was a *contract* independent of the court, and required no court action." (Italics added.) And later in the brief, arguing that husband did not lack capacity to consent to the agreement she states, "at the time [husband] drew up and entered into this *contract* he was a lawyer…." (Italics added.) Furthermore, the agreement has all the elements of a contract. It recites that wife "consented to the resumption of marital relations on condition that [husband] abstain from [illegal drug use]." In addition, the agreement contains a formal consideration clause. It is basic that what distinguishes a contract from a gift is that the latter only takes place in the absence of consideration. (Civ. Code, § 1146; *Jaffe v. Carroll* (1973) 35 Cal. App. 3d 53, 59 [110 Cal. Rptr. 435].)

But, even were we to determine that the agreement was not a contract but rather a gift subject to a condition precedent, as wife belatedly argues, it would be unenforceable. Where a condition precedent to a gift has the effect of preserving the purported donor's dominion and control over the property, the transaction " 'becomes merely an unexecuted gift and unenforceable promise to make a future gift. (*Rollinson v. Rollinson* (1955) 132 Cal. App. 2d 387, 390 [282 P.2d 98]; see *In re Marriage of Pashley* (1974) 40 Cal. App.

3d 1079, 1083 [115 Cal. Rptr. 537] ["[a] gift to be made in the future is no gift at all"]; *see also Kelly v. Bank of America* (1952) 112 Cal. App. 2d 388, 395–397 [246 P.2d 92].) In addition, the gift would fail under Civil Code section 709 which voids an agreement subject to a condition precedent that "requires the performance of an act wrong of itself...."

The Contract Fails for Lack of Legal Consideration

The Restatement of Contracts provides: "A bargain, the sole consideration of which is refraining or promising to refrain from committing a crime or tort, or from deceiving or wrongfully injuring the promisee or a third person, is illegal." (Rest., Contracts, § 578; *see also Schaefer v. Williams* (1993) 15 Cal.App.4th 1243, 1246–1247 [19 Cal. Rptr. 2d 212] [a promise to follow the Code of Fair Campaign Practices is not valid consideration].) Here the sole consideration offered by husband was his promise to refrain from using illegal drugs, a crime. Hence the contract fails.

DISPOSITION

The trial court is ordered to vacate its order regarding judgment after bifurcated trial and to enter a new order providing that the postmarital agreement between the parties is unenforceable. Appellant shall recover his costs on appeal. The trial court shall determine whether appellant should be awarded attorney fees on appeal and, if so, the amount thereof.

———

DISCUSSION

In *Penhallow v. Penhallow*, 649 A2d 1016 (R.I. 1994) the husband and wife agreed in a prenuptial agreement that the wife would get 50% of the husband's property (including his premarital acquisitions) if he filed for divorce. If she filed for divorce, she would get none of his property. She retained all of her property regardless which one filed for divorce. Should this agreement be enforced? *McBride v. McBride*, 797 S.W.2d 689 (Tex. App. — Houston [14th Dist.] 1990, writ denied) considered such an agreement, and concluded it was an agreement of forfeiture based on the occurrence of a future event, not a partition, and shouldn't be enforced when the wife filed for divorce.

D. Changing Separate Property
Into Community Property

As of 2000, Texas law was changed to permit spouses to change separate property into community property. *See* Tex. Fam. Code § 4.202. Rules regarding the enforcement of such agreement are set forth in TFC §§ 4.203 and 4.205. Notice that the disclosure requirements of § 4.205 are broader than § 4.006 or § 4.105.

Chapter Twenty

Spousal Gifts and Partitions

A. Interspousal Gifts

Community property may be changed into separate property by partition. In addition, if one spouse makes a gift of his interest in certain community property or separate property to his spouse, the property becomes the recipient's separate property. *See Marriage of Morrison*, 913 S.W.2d 689 (Tex.App. — Texarkana 1995, writ denied).

Grimsley v. Grimsley
Texas Court of Appeals — Corpus Christi, 1982
632 S.W.2d 174, no writ

GONZALEZ, Justice.

This is a divorce case. After trial before the court, judgment was entered granting a divorce and awarding to wife appellee title to a house that was purchased after the marriage with proceeds of the sale of property that wife claimed was given to her by her husband-appellant prior to the marriage. We reverse and render.

In August 1978, appellant and appellee met. On October 2, 1978, appellant proposed marriage which proposal was accepted by appellee on October 10, 1978. Thereafter on October 18, 1978, appellant wrote the following letter to appellee:

Dear Pat and intended wife,

In appreciation of your past love and affection, your present love and affection, and your future love and affection I would be extremely happy to have you accept all of the items I have listed on my schedule of personal property enclosed with this letter which consists of all of my personal possessions prior to our marriage so that in the event of my death all of this will belong to you for you to do with as you wish.

Thank you Pat for being my friend and future wife.

I love you,

John

SCHEDULE OF PERSONAL PROPERTY

Stereo System:
    Panasonic AM-FM stereo
    Realistic turn table
    Pioneer reel to reel tape deck
    Akai 65-D cassette tape deck

Craig 8-track tape deck
Approximately 140 cassettes (recorded)
Approximately 10 Magell reel to reel tapes recorded
Approximately 50 Magell (90 minutes each side) blank tapes
Approximately 50 blank 8-track tapes
One stereo cabinet
Numerous albums—approximately 100 (one hundred)
Two Sterling speakers
Two smaller speakers
One Mediterranean sofa & chair
Two end tables w/two ginger-jar lamps
One Motorola color T.V.
One etagere
One recliner
One breakfast nook w/chair
One pair of binoculars
One coffee table
2000 shares of Energy Surveys stock consisting of the following:
    1000 shares of S.I.I. stock
    Savings account in Hub City Bank in the name of Energy Survey
    First mortgage on property on Breaux Bridge Highway, Lafayette, Louisiana
    payable $438x to Energy Surveys for 15 years
    Energy Survey Funds in Hub City Bank and Trust Co. checking account no.
    02-3637-3
    1976 Chevrolet Caprice—Energy Survey is owed $2,025 as of the date of
    this schedule
One two (2) bedroom residence on Odile St., Lafayette, La., valued at
$25,000.—owe $10,000x
All monies in E.M.C.D. savings plan
All monies owing from Helmer Directional Drlg. profit sharing
All contents of safety deposit box including $250 worth of silver coins.

No deed or formal transfers of the real estate or stock were ever effected.

The parties were married on November 18, 1978. This was a second marriage for both of them. At the time of the marriage, appellant was 50 years old and besides being the sole owner of Energy Surveys Co., he was an employee of a drilling company. Appellee was a 39-year-old school teacher with a Master's Degree who also was a part-time real estate salesperson. After the marriage, appellant moved into the rent house appellee was living in with her two little boys from the prior marriage.

Approximately three or four months after the marriage, the parties purchased a home in Corpus Christi Country Club Estates for Ninety Thousand Dollars ($90,000.00). They made a down payment of Sixty Two Thousand One Hundred Forty Seven and 94/100 Dollars ($62,147.94) and assumed a loan for the balance. The money for the down payment was traced, and it was undisputed that this consideration came from the sale of the property appellant owned before the marriage to wit:

(1) Twenty Thousand Dollars ($20,000.00) cash from Energy Surveys Inc. savings account.

(2) Thirty Thousand Dollars ($30,000.00) cash transferred from Energy Surveys Inc. to appellant following a loan to Energy Surveys Inc. of Thirty Thousand

Dollars ($30,000.00) by Citizens State Bank in Corpus Christi. The collateral for the Thirty Thousand Dollars ($30,000.00) loan was One Thousand (1,000) shares of Smith International Industries stock which appellant owned.

(3) Thirteen Thousand Five Hundred and 08/100 Dollars ($13,500.08) cash which is the net proceeds from the sale of appellant's house in Louisiana.

All of these sums were deposited by appellant into a joint checking account at the Citizens State Bank in Corpus Christi during the month of February 1979. All of these transfers were made by appellant. At the time of the transfers, appellee had no authority or ability to transfer or encumber these funds nor to sell or convey appellant's property in Louisiana. Appellee wrote the check on the parties' joint checking account which made the down payment for the Country Club Estates house. However, both appellant and appellee were named grantees to the deed on said house.

After the purchase of the house, the parties started having marital problems. Appellant moved out. There was a brief reconciliation but again appellant moved out and the case was tried within twenty four months from the wedding date. During the marriage, the parties actually lived together not more than ten months and only seven months in the Country Club Estates home. The court divided the property as follows: appellee was awarded as her sole and separate property the home on Country Club Estates, all escrow funds held by the mortgage company for payment of insurance, taxes and maintenance charges on the home and her community interest in the house; a property located at 717 Ponder Street, all oil and gas mineral interest owned by her or in her name and the following items of personal property; all household furnishings, appliances, fixtures, wearing apparel, jewelry and other personal property in her possession or subject to her control, all sums of cash in her possession or in her control including Nine Thousand Dollars ($9,000.00) in the Teacher's Credit Union, all life insurance policies and retirement benefits arising out of her employment, a 1978 Cadillac automobile and a 1977 Oldsmobile Cutlass.

Appellant was awarded all household furnishings, appliances, fixtures, wearing apparel, jewelry and other personal property in his possession or subject to his control including but not limited to Two Thousand Four Hundred (2,400) shares of Energy Surveys stock, a 1978 Chevrolet automobile, two individual retirement accounts, all policies of life insurance insuring his life and all pensions, retirement benefits and other benefits arising out of his employment, a power table saw, a Bulova quartz watch, a crystal candy dish and one Jefferson and buffalo nickel coin collection and a lawnmower. Appellant was also ordered to pay a Fifty Thousand Dollar ($50,000.00) promissory note signed individually to Energy Surveys Inc. and a One Thousand Five Hundred Dollar ($1,500.00) note to Citizens State Bank.

The trial court filed findings of fact[1] and conclusions of law[2] and we also have a complete statement of facts containing all oral and written testimony introduced in the trial.

---

1. We summarize the findings: (1) That appellee received into her possession the listed property as a "gift" on October 11 through October 31, 1978. (2) That the property listed was placed into her possession except a 1976 Caprice and some items of furniture. (3) That no children were born to the marriage.
2. Summary of conclusions of law: (1) That appellant made a gift of the property listed in the schedule prior to the marriage. (2) That the intent for a present gift is found in the letter. (3) That appellee accepted the gift. (4) That delivery was actual "for some property, and constructive and symbolic for other property." (5) That property on the schedule was a completed gift prior to the marriage and was therefore her separate property when the parties were married. (6) That the proceeds of the gift were used by appellee to purchase the home after the marriage. (7) That any community interest which may have inured to appellant's benefit in the home was offset by the division of other property that was awarded to appellant.

Appellant, in twelve points of error, contends that the trial court committed error in finding a gift of all of his personal property prior to the marriage because there was no evidence of a gift and there was also insufficient evidence or such finding is against the great weight and preponderance of the evidence.

Since the findings of fact regarding delivery filed by the trial court are without support in the evidence, we will pass upon appellant's points of error without regard thereto.

The character of title to property as to whether it is separate or community property is generally determined as of the date it is vested. Spears, *Marital Rights in Texas*, Sec. 392 (4th Ed. 1961). The question then is whether appellant made a gift of all of his assets to appellee before the marriage, thus making the down payment come from her separate property and giving her a separate interest in the home at the time it was purchased.

The well-established rule of law regarding gifts is that three elements are necessary to establish the existence of a gift: They are: (1) intent to make a gift; (2) delivery of the property, and (3) acceptance of the property. One who is claiming the gift has the burden of proof.

Delivery of the property should be such that all dominion and control over the property is released by the owner. The rule has been stated as follows:

> Among the indispensable conditions of the valid gift and the intention of the donor to absolutely and irrevocably divest himself of the title, dominion and control of the subject of the gift at the very time he undertakes to make the gift.
>
> The irrevocable transfer of the present title, dominion, and control of the thing given to the donee, so that the donor can exercise no further act of the dominion or control over it.
>
> A mere intention to make a gift, however clearly expressed, which has not been carried into effect, amounts to nothing, and enforces no rights in the subject matter of the proposed gift upon the intended donee. The intention must be effected by complete and unconditional delivery. *Harmon v. Schmitz*, 39 S.W.2d 587, 589 (Tex. Com. App.— 1931).

Since there were no documents to indicate a formal transfer, endorsement or assignment of the property listed on the schedule, the only evidence of a gift prior to the marriage is the letter and the conduct of the parties as shown in the evidence. Appellee tried the case on the theory that all of the items listed on the schedule attached to the letter were given to her by appellant prior to the marriage. Appellant, on the other hand, denied the making of the gift and contended that the letter was a will. The court found for appellee, finding that the letter expressed an intent to make the gift, that appellee accepted the gift and that the delivery was constructive or symbolic. We disagree that there was delivery of the house in Louisiana, the Energy Surveys Inc. assets and the S.I.I. stock.

HOUSE IN LOUISIANA

There are two ways to make a gift of real estate. One is by deed, and the other is a parol gift of realty when certain conditions are met.

> A parol gift of realty is enforceable in equity if there is established, (1) a gift *in praesenti*, (2) possession under the gift by the donee with the donor's consent and (3) permanent invaluable improvement made on the property by donee with

donor's knowledge or consent or without improvements, the existence of such facts as would make it a fraud upon the donee not to enforce the gift.

Moody v. Ireland, 456 S.W. 494, 496 (Tex. Civ. App.—Waco 1970, writ ref'd n.r.e.).

In the case at bar, appellee did not receive a deed for the house. The evidence shows that she saw the house one time. There is no evidence that she made valuable improvements thereon or spent any time at the house. The evidence is conclusive that appellant did not relinquish dominion and control over the house. To the contrary, when the house was sold after the marriage, it was appellant who signed the deed as grantor. Approximately Fourteen Thousand Two Hundred Sixty Eight Dollars ($14,268.00) was obtained from the sale of this house and eventually used to make a down payment on the Country Club Estates house. This represents a separate interest in the house to appellant, and the trial court was in error in finding to the contrary.

ENERGY SURVEYS, INC.

At the time appellant wrote the letter to appellee, he was the sole owner and stockholder of Energy Surveys, Inc. The assets of said corporation consisted primarily of:

(1) Twenty Thousand Dollars ($20,000.00) in cash in deposit in the Energy Surveys, Inc., savings account in a bank in Louisiana.

(2) One Thousand (1,000) shares of stock in Smith International Industries. (The stock was issued to Energy Surveys, Inc., and had a value of approximately Forty Thousand Dollars [$40,000.00]).

(3) A Thirty Eight Thousand Dollar ($38,000.00) promissory note held by Energy Surveys Inc. from the sale of the building to a Mr. Rice.

It was appellee's contention that appellant made a gift of all of these assets to her as per the letter of October 18, 1978. We will review each of these assets with the regards to the element of delivery.

(1) $20,000 ENERGY SURVEYS, INC., SAVINGS ACCOUNT

The evidence shows that appellee never saw or had possession of the original Energy Surveys, Inc., stock certificates. Appellant testified that he had them in his possession at the time of the trial. The Twenty Thousand Dollar ($20,000.00) cash that Energy Surveys, Inc., had in a savings account was withdrawn by appellant in February 1979, almost three months after the alleged gift. This money was deposited in a joint checking account of the parties and eventually made part of the consideration for the Country Club Estates house.

Appellant also had possession of the savings account passbook. Prior to the money being withdrawn by appellant, he did not change or transfer the account into appellee's name. The evidence is conclusive that there was no total relinquishment of control over the Twenty Thousand Dollars ($20,000.00) prior to the marriage. Therefore, there was no gift and these funds represent appellant's separate property interest in the Country Club Estates house, and it was error for the trial court to hold to the contrary.

(2) S.I.I. STOCK

Appellee claimed that appellant, via the letter, made a gift to her of One Thousand (1,000) shares of a Smith International Industry stock that was owned by appellant's company. She claims that this gift was also made before the marriage.

The law on the gift of stock is clearly stated in the case of *Carrington v. Commissioner of Internal Revenue,* 476 F.2d 704, 709 (1973). In that case, the Fifth Circuit said "a gift of stock between competent parties requires donative intent, actual delivery, and relinquishment of dominion and control by the donor."

A review of the evidence shows that this stock was never endorsed over to appellee nor did appellant ever relinquish total dominion and control over such stock to appellee. In February 1979, appellant used this stock as collateral for a Thirty Thousand Dollar ($30,000.00) loan to Energy Surveys, Inc., which is evidenced by a promissory note to the bank which appellant signed as president of the corporation. The Thirty Thousand Dollars ($30,000.00) was then transferred by appellant into the joint checking account of the parties and used as part of the down payment on the house. Since appellant never relinquished total dominion and control of stock to appellee prior to the marriage, the stock was and is appellant's separate property.[3] Therefore, appellant's use of the Thirty Thousand Dollars ($30,000.00) to help make the down payment on the Country Club Estates house represents a separate property interest in said house, and it was error for the court to find to the contrary.

In summary, appellant's no-evidence points are sustained. There is no evidence to support a gift of any of the assets that were liquidated after the marriage and used to make the down payment on the Country Club Estates house. Appellant is therefore entitled to a separate property interest in that house to the extent he used his separate property funds for the down payment. *Gleich v. Bongio* 128 Tex. 606, 99 S.W.2d 881 (Tex. Com. App. 1973); *Bell v. Bell,* 593 S.W.2d 424 (Tex. Civ. App. — Houston [14th Dist.] 1980, no writ). Since appellant provided 69% of the purchase price of said house with separate property funds, he is hereby awarded a 69% separate property interest in said house. The balance (31%) is owned by appellant and appellee as tenants in common.

The judgment of the trial court is reversed and rendered in accordance with this opinion.

O'Neill v. O'Neill

Kentucky Court of Appeals, 1980
600 S.W.2d 493

HOGGE, Justice.

The marriage of Richard and Susan O'Neill has been dissolved. Dr. O'Neill appeals from a portion of the decree of the Fayette circuit court dividing the marital property which he and his former wife acquired during their marriage. Dr. O'Neill contends that the trial court erred by excluding from the marital property certain items which Mrs. O'Neill describes as gifts from Dr. O'Neill.

The issue in this case is whether the trial court erred by failing to consider as marital property certain jewelry and other items of personal property which Dr. O'Neill pre-

---

3. Some time later the S.I.I. stock was sold by a stockbroker, the loan to Citizens Bank was paid off, and the net proceeds were deposited in the joint checking account of the parties.

sented to Mrs. O'Neill on her birthday, at Christmas and other occasions. [Ed. note: Kentucky law is similar to Texas law—accumulations during marriage, other than gifts or inheritances, may be divided at divorce.] The items were purchased out of Dr. O'Neill's salary, and included a ring with an appraised value of $35,000.00 and other jewelry with an appraised value of $15,900.00. The circuit court held that these items were gifts to Mrs. O'Neill and should not be included in the marital property.

This issue involves the interpretation of KRS 403.190, which excludes from marital property items acquired by gift.

Under the statute, we start with the premise that all property acquired by either spouse subsequent to marriage is marital property. Without reading the statute further, there is no doubt that the property transferred to Mrs. O'Neill was marital property as it was acquired by her subsequent to marriage. Then the statute excepts from marital property that which is acquired by "gift." The issue, at this point, is whether this property given to Mrs. O'Neill by Dr. O'Neill were "gifts" within the meaning of the statute as intended by the legislature.

In determining this issue, the court's decision would necessarily have to be based on the pertinent facts of each case. In each case, consideration should be given to the source of the money with which the "gift" was purchased, the intent of the donor at that time as to intended use of the property, status of the marriage relationship at the time of the transfer, and whether there was any valid agreement that the transferred property was to be excluded from the marital property.

Further, we note that Dr. O'Neill testified that the jewelry and certain other items were purchased as an investment. He hoped that the purchases would appreciate in value, and that they could be converted into cash in the event money was needed for the children's education. This is evidence of probative value that he intended that the transfer of possession of this property would not divest him of this marital property and that, if necessary, the property could be reconverted into cash, at a future time, at an appreciated price, for a purpose of mutual benefit to the parties, the education of their children. Further, we find no evidence at all that there was any agreement that the property so transferred herein was to be excluded or be treated as the separate property of Mrs. O'Neill. Under these circumstances, we hold that these transfers were not a gift within the meaning of the statute and that the trial court erred in so determining.

As to the "gifts" the judgment of the circuit court is reversed and remanded for further proceedings consistent with this opinion.

DISCUSSION

Grimsley shows that normally there must simultaneous be an intention to make a gift and delivery to complete the gift. *O'Neill* presents the issue of the understanding of the spouses regarding property exchanged as presents at occasions such as anniversaries, birthdays, etc. There normally is delivery of the present, but is there truly an intention to make a gift, in the sense that the donor spouse is relinquishing any interest in it? If community property is used for such gifts, should courts treat such exchanges as true "gifts," thereby making the item the separate property of the recipient? Should the value of the gift, compared to the value of the community estate, affect this rule? Texas generally treats such presents as "gifts" which can change the character of the property. Compare Cal. Fam. Code § 852.

B. Joint Tenancy and Community Property with Right of Survivorship

Jameson v. Bain
Texas Court of Appeals—San Antonio, 1985
693 S.W.2d 676, no writ

TIJERINA, Justice.

This is an appeal from a declaratory judgment that determined the character of the parties' funds, on deposit in savings accounts and trust accounts at San Antonio Savings Association, to be community property. Under the trial court's order, one-half of the balances in the accounts passed to the estate of Paul E. Jameson, Sr., deceased. Appellant, Bessie A. Jameson, the surviving wife, claims the funds as her separate property and appeals the ruling of the court.

Appellant and her husband used community property funds to open the joint tenancy accounts with rights of survivorship between husband and wife. On the first four accounts, the parties signed a partition agreement on the reverse side of the account card after they signed the joint tenancy account with rights of survivorship. These accounts are identified as follows:

1. Account number 21-052204, opened May 5, 1971 with community funds.
2. Account number 21-901748, opened August 1, 1973 with community funds.
3. Account number 21-903485, opened January 3, 1977 with community funds.
4. Account number 21-903979, opened April 6, 1978 with community funds.

There were two other joint tenancy accounts with rights of survivorship also containing partition agreements on the reverse side of the account cards. These accounts are distinguished by their individual effective dates and the fact that appellant and her husband did not sign the partition agreement. The accounts are identified as follows:

5. Account number 17-902785, opened April 20, 1981 with community funds.
6. Account number 17-903177, opened December 16, 1981 with community funds.

Additionally, appellant and her decedent husband opened three savings accounts as revocable trust accounts with San Antonio Savings Association identified as follows:

7. Account number 17-901573, opened January 14, 1980 with community funds. The account was under the name of Paul E. Jameson, Sr., trustee, for Bessie A. Jameson.
8. Account number 21-904933, opened February 20, 1980 with community funds. The account was under the name of Paul E. Jameson, Sr., trustee, for Bessie A. Jameson.
9. Account number 21-904956, opened with community funds by appellant on March 11, 1980. This account was under the name of Bessie A. Jameson, as trustee for Paul E. Jameson.

Mr. Jameson died April 3, 1982, and appellant withdrew all the balances in the nine accounts, claiming all funds as her property. Appellees, the Independent Executor of the Estate of Paul E. Jameson, Sr., deceased, and the charitable beneficiaries under the will of decedent, claimed that one half of the balances of the accounts belonged to the estate.

The first assignment of error challenges the trial court's ruling which disregarded the partition agreements on the reverse side of the six (6) joint tenancy accounts with rights of survivorship. Article XVI, Section 15 of the Texas Constitution specifically provides that husband and wife may by an instrument in writing partition their existing community property. Tex. Fam. Code Ann. Sec. 5.42 (Vernon Supp. 1985) authorizes the spouses to partition all or part of their community property, and Sec. 5.44 requires that the partition be in writing and subscribed by both parties. Thus the Texas Constitution and the Family Code require the partition agreement between spouses to be in writing. Community property must be rendered separate by statutory partition before survivorship rights arise from a joint tenancy agreement between husband and wife. *Williams v. McKnight*, 402 S.W.2d 505, 508 (Tex. 1966). Section 5.42 of the Family Code, *supra*, has been interpreted as requiring a two-step procedure. First, the partition of the community property must be effected in accordance with Section 5.42 of the Texas Family Code. Then, the joint tenancy agreement with right of survivorship may be entered into. *Bowman v. Simpson*, 546 S.W.2d 99, 102 (Tex. Civ. App.—Beaumont 1977, writ ref'd). In *Maples v. Nimitz*, 615 S.W.2d 690, 695 (Tex. 1981), the supreme court addressed a question concerning an intended partition under Tex. Rev. Civ. Stat. Ann. art. 852a, Sec. 6.09 (Vernon 1964) (Joint Accounts by Husband and Wife—Under the Texas Savings and Loan Act), and stated:

> We conclude that mere execution of the signature agreement providing for a joint tenancy with right of survivorship as authorized by Section 6.09 does not accomplish a one-step partition of community funds. Rather, a partition of community funds must be accomplished by the spouses before creation of the joint tenancy with right of survivorship.

Maples v. Nimitz, 615 S.W.2d at 695; *see also McCarver v. Trumble*, 660 S.W.2d 595, 597 (Tex. App.—Corpus Christi 1983, no writ).

It is undisputed that appellant and decedent signed the joint tenancy agreement with rights of survivorship first in account 1–4. Thus, the purported partition was not valid; the funds on deposit in those accounts remained community property. It is further uncontradicted that in the other two saving accounts, accounts 5 and 6, appellant and decedent signed the card creating the joint tenancy account with right of survivorship but did not sign the partition agreement. These two accounts were opened on April 20, 1981, and December 16, 1981, respectively. Article XVI, Section 15 of the Texas Constitution was amended November 4, 1980; article 46(b) of the Texas Probate Code became effective September 1, 1981. Article 46(b) provides in pertinent part, *viz.*:

> (b) A written agreement between spouses and a bank, savings and loan, credit union, or other financial institution may provide that existing funds or securities on deposit and funds and securities to be deposited in the future and interest and income thereon shall by that agreement be partitioned into separate property and may further provide that the property partitioned by that agreement be held in joint tenancies and pass by right of survivorship.

We do not accept the contention that the constitutional amendment and article 46(b) abrogated the requirement that a valid partition of community property must be executed and subscribed separately and prior in time to the execution of the joint tenancy with rights of survivorship. In any event, the question appears to be moot since all parties acknowledged that appellant and decedent did not sign the partition agreement. Tex. Fam. Code arts. 5.42 and 5.44 which became effective September 1, 1981, both require that the partition agreement be in writing and subscribed by all parties. Accordingly, the funds on deposit on these two accounts remained community property. Point of error one is overruled.

DISCUSSION

Article XVI, Section 15 of the Texas Constitution was amended in 1987 to permit spouses to agree that some or all of their community property would become the property of the survivor when the first spouse died. This amendment now apparently creates a system whereby spouses have two different ways to create a survivorship interest in property. A joint tenancy can be created with separate property (or previously partitioned community property), or the spouses can sign a written agreement creating survivorship community property. The formalities governing such survivorship agreements are set forth in Tex. Prob. Code Sections. 451 and 452, as are examples of language that establish the survivorship right. For example, phrases that create survivorship community property rights include "with right of survivorship" and "will become the property of the survivor." *See* §452. The survivorship agreement may be revoked by either party (*see* §455). Survivorship community property remains community property until one spouse dies, and is subject to the same management and creditors' rights rules (*see* §§453, 461). *See generally,* "Community Property with Right of Survivorship," Chapter H, 1989 Advanced Estate Planning and Probate Course, Texas State Bar.

Haynes v. Stripling, 812 S.W.2d 397 (Tex. App.—Eastland 1991, no writ) involved a few interesting issues. In 1984 and 1985 the spouses opened "joint tenancy with right of survivorship" accounts with community funds, without signing a partition agreement first. After *Jameson,* this clearly doesn't establish a joint tenancy with right of survivorship. The wife died in 1988. The husband argued that, after the 1987 constitutional amendment, this created a community property survivorship account. The appellate court determined that the 1987 amendment should be applied retroactively, and that the account was a community property survivorship account.

A survivorship account cannot be created with community property if the account owners are a father and son. *Haas v. Voight,* 940 S.W.2d 198 (Tex. App.—San Antonio 1996, writ denied).

Holmes v. Beatty
Supreme Court of Texas, 2009
290 S.W.3d 852

After decades of debate in the bench, bar, and the Legislature about the ability of spouses to obtain rights of survivorship in community property, Texas citizens changed the constitution to confirm that right. The 1987 amendment provides that "spouses may agree in writing that all or part of their community property becomes the property of the surviving spouse on the death of a spouse." TEX. CONST. art. XVI, §15. Two years later, the Legislature enacted Probate Code sections 451 through 462 to address the formalities necessary to the create a survivorship arrangement. *See* TEX. PROB. CODE §§451–62. Today we are asked to determine how these sections operate with respect to rights of survivorship in certain brokerage accounts and securities certificates issued from those accounts. We conclude that the account agreements and certificates at issue here created rights of survivorship. Accordingly, we reverse and render in part and affirm in part the court of appeals' judgment.

I

Factual and Procedural Background

Thomas and Kathryn Holmes married in 1972. During their marriage, Thomas and Kathryn amassed over ten million dollars in brokerage accounts and acquired securities certificates issued from those accounts. Kathryn died in 1999. Her will appointed Douglas Beatty, her son from a previous marriage, as the independent executor of her estate. Thomas died approximately nine months later. His son, Harry Holmes II ("Holmes"), also from a previous marriage, was appointed independent executor of his estate. The accounts and certificates were variously listed as "JT TEN"; "JT TEN defined as 'joint tenants with right of survivorship and not as tenants in common'"; "JTWROS"; and "Joint (WROS)." If those acronyms and definitions establish a right of survivorship, then Thomas acquired 100% upon Kathryn's death, and upon his death, the holdings would have passed under his will, which left nothing to Kathryn's children. If those designations were insufficient to create survivorship interests then, as community property, only 50% would have passed to Thomas, with the remaining 50% of the accounts and certificates passing under Kathryn's will, which left nothing to Thomas's children.

Beatty sought a declaration that all of the assets were community property; Holmes countered that the assets passed to Thomas through survivorship, and then to Thomas's beneficiaries following his death. On competing motions for summary judgment, the trial court concluded that some of the assets were held jointly with survivorship rights and others were community property. In two opinions, the court of appeals affirmed in part, reversed and rendered in part, and remanded for further proceedings. 233 S.W.3d 475, 494; 233 S.W.3d 494, 522–23. Holmes and Beatty petitioned this Court for review, which we granted. 52 Tex. Sup. Ct. J. 149 (Dec. 4, 2008). Because these two appeals involve "substantially similar facts, arguments, and briefing," we have consolidated them into a single opinion and judgment. *Hubenak v. San Jacinto Gas Transmission Co.*, 141 S.W.3d 172, 179 (Tex. 2004).

II

Development of Rights of Survivorship in Community Property in Texas

A

The Hilley Era

Texas has not always allowed spouses to create rights of survivorship in community property. In *Hilley v. Hilley*, 161 Tex. 569, 342 S.W.2d 565, 568 (Tex. 1961), we held that it was unconstitutional for spouses to hold community property with rights of survivorship. The dispute in *Hilley* concerned whether stock purchased with community funds and "issued in the names of the husband and wife 'as joint tenants with rights of survivorship and not as tenants in common'" actually conferred rights of survivorship. *Id.* at 566. We reasoned that because this property was acquired during marriage with community funds and thus "by definition became community property," it was required to pass either under the decedent's will or under the intestacy statutes, absent a written agreement signed by the spouses partitioning the stock from their community property, thereby making it separate property. *Id.* at 568. We noted that to hold otherwise would directly contravene the constitution's community property provision. *Id.* (citing TEX. CONST. art. XVI, § 15; Act of May 12, 1949, 51st Leg., R.S., ch. 242, § 1, 1949 Tex. Gen. Laws 450, 450, repealed by, Act of June 2, 1969, 61st Leg., R.S., ch. 888, § 6, 1969 Tex. Gen. Laws 2707, 2733 (former TEX. REV. CIV. STAT. art. 4610)).

After *Hilley*, the Legislature amended the Probate Code in an attempt to recognize survivorship rights in community property. Act of April 27, 1961, 57th Leg., R.S., ch. 120, § 1, 1961 Tex. Gen. Laws 233, amended by Act of May 22, 1969, 61st Leg., R.S., ch. 641, § 3, 1969 Tex. Gen. Laws 1922, 1922 ("It is specifically provided that any husband and his wife may, by written agreement, create a joint estate out of their community property, with rights of survivorship."). In *Williams v. McKnight*, 402 S.W.2d 505, 508 (Tex. 1966), we considered the amendment's constitutionality. Citing *Hilley*, we held that any statutory attempt to grant survivorship rights in community property would be unconstitutional. *Id.* ("Constitutional limitations are as binding upon the Legislature as they are upon the Judiciary."). We reaffirmed that the only way for a couple to create survivorship rights was to partition their community property into separate property, then execute survivorship agreements for that separate property. *Id.* at 508. This process came to be known among practitioners as the "Texas Two-Step." *See*, e.g., Robert N. Virden, Joint Tenancy with Right of Survivorship & Community Property with Right of Survivorship, 53 TEX. B.J. 1179, 1179 (1990). Subsequent decisions echoed this result. *See*, e.g., *Allard v. French*, 754 S.W.2d 111, 115 (Tex. 1988) ("This holding is based on a firmly rooted principle of community property law which requires the actual partition of community property before a valid joint tenancy with the right of survivorship can be created."); *Maples v. Nimitz*, 615 S.W.2d 690, 695 (Tex. 1981) (same).

B

The 1987 Constitutional Amendment and Subsequent Legislation

In 1987, the Legislature passed, and the Texas voters approved, a constitutional amendment authorizing rights of survivorship in community property. Tex. S.J. Res. 35, 70th Leg., R.S., 1987 Tex. Gen. Laws 4114, 4114–15. The amendment provided that "spouses may agree in writing that all or part of their community property becomes the property of the surviving spouse on the death of a spouse." TEX. CONST. art. XVI, § 15. Two years later, the Legislature passed Senate Bill 1643, which added Part 3 to Chapter XI of the Probate Code concerning non-testamentary transfers. Act of May 26, 1989, 71st Leg., R.S., Ch. 655, § 2, 1989 Tex. Gen. Laws 2159, 2159–63. This new section governs "[a]greements between spouses regarding rights of survivorship in community property." TEX. PROB. CODE § 46(b).

Probate Code sections 451 and 452 are at issue in this case. Section 451 states: "At any time, spouses may agree between themselves that all or part of their community property, then existing or to be acquired, becomes the property of the surviving spouse on the death of a spouse." *Id.* § 451. Section 452 lays out these requirements:

> An agreement between spouses creating a right of survivorship in community property must be in writing and signed by both spouses. If an agreement in writing is signed by both spouses, the agreement shall be sufficient to create a right of survivorship in the community property described in the agreement if it includes any of the following phrases:
>
> (1) "with right of survivorship";
>
> (2) "will become the property of the survivor";
>
> (3) "will vest in and belong to the surviving spouse"; or
>
> (4) "shall pass to the surviving spouse."
>
> An agreement that otherwise meets the requirements of this part, however, shall be effective without including any of those phrases.

Id. § 452. The Legislature stated that these agreements do not change the nature of community property: "Property subject to an agreement between spouses creating a right of survivorship in community property remains community property during the marriage of the spouses." *Id.* § 453.

With this constitutional amendment and legislation, the Legislature hoped to finally resolve the battle over survivorship rights in community property. The proponents urged that these sorts of agreements were common in other states and simplified the transfer of certain assets to surviving spouses. *See* GERRY W. BEYER, 10 TEXAS PRACTICE SERIES: TEXAS LAW OF WILLS § 60.1 (3d ed. 2002). As Professor Beyer noted, a community property survivorship agreement "is a simple, convenient and inexpensive method for many married people to achieve an at-death distribution of their community property that is in accord with their intent." *Id.* § 60.9.

As the amendment's drafters noted at the time, "[m]any Texas spouses hold a substantial amount of assets in a form that is ineffective to achieve their desired purpose." Senate Judiciary Comm., Resolution Analysis, Tex. S.J. Res. 35, 70th Leg., R.S. (1987). Supporters argued that the proposed constitutional amendment would "eliminate a trap for the unwary married couple who would execute a signature card provided by a financial institution and believe, mistakenly, that they have created an effective joint tenancy with right of survivorship in relation to their community property." TEXAS LEGISLATIVE COUNCIL, ANALYSES OF PROPOSED CONSTITUTIONAL AMENDMENTS AND REFERENDA, INFO. REPORT, NO. 87-2 at 36 (Sept. 1987).

The purpose of the amendment and accompanying legislation, then, was to provide "[a] simple means … by which both spouses by a written instrument can provide that the survivor of them may be entitled to all or any designated portion of their community property without the necessity of making a will for that purpose." Senate Judiciary Comm., Resolution Analysis, Tex. S.J. Res. 35, 70th Leg., R.S. (1987). As the committee observed, "many banks and savings and loans associations have often failed to provide forms by which their customers can create effective joint tenancies out of community property." *Id.* The amendment addressed these concerns by removing the constitutional hurdles to creating rights of survivorship in community property.

III
Application

The assets at issue in this case fall into two categories: (1) securities accounts and (2) securities certificates issued from those accounts. These two categories of assets are affected by distinct legal analyses, so we address each in turn.

A
The Securities Accounts

Thomas and Kathryn Holmes maintained investment accounts with multiple financial institutions. Each of them was governed by an account agreement that dictated terms, such as who could manage the accounts and whether the accounts were held with rights of survivorship.

1
Accounts Agreements With a "JT TEN" Designation

At the time of Kathryn's death, the Holmeses held two investment accounts whose agreements included the designation "JT TEN": one with Dain Rauscher, Inc. and another with First Southwest Company. Thomas and Kathryn opened the Dain Rauscher account in 1994. The account agreement, titled "JOINT ACCOUNT AGREEMENT" was styled "THOMAS J. HOLMES AND KATHRYN V. HOLMES, JT TEN." The agreement gave the account holders an option to strike through "paragraph (a) or (b) whichever is inapplicable." Paragraph (a) stated "it is the express intention of the undersigned to create an estate or account as joint tenants with rights of survivorship and not as tenants in common." Paragraph (b) gave the account holders the option to designate who would receive the interest in the account upon their death and the percentages each recipient would receive. The Holmeses struck neither provision. They both signed the agreement, and "Jt. Ten" appeared next to Kathryn's name on the signature line.

The Holmeses opened the First Southwest Account in 1997. The account agreement listed their names as "THOMAS J. HOLMES, KATHRYN V. HOLMES JT TEN." The agreement did not define "JT TEN" and did not include any further discussion of survivorship rights. Both Thomas and Kathryn signed the First Southwest account, as well.

The court of appeals held that neither of these agreements "clearly reflect[ed] intent to own the account with a right of survivorship." 233 S.W.3d 475, 481; *see also* 233 S.W.3d 494, 505. As to the Dain Rauscher account, the court noted that because the couple did not strike through paragraph (a) or (b), the agreement "did not affirmatively reflect any intent to effect a non-testamentary transfer—through a right of survivorship or otherwise." 233 S.W.3d 475, 481. The court also rejected Holmes's argument that the "JT TEN" designation on the agreements satisfied section 452's requirements: the "mere inclusion of 'JT TEN' next to Kathryn's and Thomas's names in the account title did not sufficiently convey intent to create a right of survivorship." *Id.* at 483. The court agreed with Beatty's argument that "parties may own property as joint tenants without being subject to a right of survivorship." *Id.*; 233 S.W.3d 494, 505.

We disagree with the court of appeals on each point. A joint tenancy carries rights of survivorship. *See*, e.g., *United States v. Craft*, 535 U.S. 274, 280, 122 S. Ct. 1414, 152 L. Ed. 2d 437 (2002) ("The main difference between a joint tenancy and a tenancy in common is that a joint tenant also has a right of automatic inheritance known as 'survivorship.' Upon the death of one joint tenant, that tenant's share in the property does not pass through will or the rules of intestate succession; rather, the remaining tenant or tenants automatically inherit it."); 2 William Blackstone, COMMENTARIES ON THE LAWS OF ENGLAND 183 (3rd ed. 1768) ("[The] remaining grand incident of joint estates [is] the doctrine of survivorship...."); LITTLETON'S TENURES, Book III, ch. III, § 280 (Eugene W. Wambaugh ed., 1903) ("And it is to be understood, that the nature of joint-tenancy is, that he which surviveth shall have only the entire tenancy according to such estate as he hath...."); 7 RICHARD R. POWELL, POWELL ON REAL PROPERTY § 51.03[3] (Michael Allan Wolf ed., 2000) ("Survivorship is central to a joint tenancy."). Contrary to Beatty's and the court of appeals' assertion then, a joint tenancy cannot be held without rights of survivorship; such a joint agreement would be a tenancy in common. See Craft, 535 U.S. at 280; 7 POWELL ON REAL PROPERTY § 51.01[1] ("[A joint tenancy] is distinguished from a tenancy in common principally by the right of survivorship."). The financial industry's use of "joint tenancy" is also consistent with this view. *See*, e.g., SEC. TRANSFER ASSOC., Guidelines of the Securities Transfer Association AV-1 (Oct. 2005) (defining "Joint Tenancy" as a "[f]orm of ownership where two or more individuals hold shares as joint tenants with right of survivorship. When one tenant dies, the entire tenancy remains to the surviving tenants. JOHN BROWN & MARY BROWN JT TEN.").

Citing *Stauffer v. Henderson*, 801 S.W.2d 858, 865 (Tex. 1990), the court of appeals held that it could not consider information that is not explicitly referenced in the agreement itself. 233 S.W.3d 494, 507. It therefore evaluated the designations "JT TEN" and "Jt. Ten" without reference to guidelines, codes, or custom. *Id.* at 509–13. In *Stauffer*, we held that under Probate Code section 439(a), concerning survivorship rights between non-spouses, parties could only establish survivorship using the statute's language (or language "substantially" similar to it), and a court could not consider other evidence to ascertain the parties' intent. *Stauffer*, 801 S.W.2d at 863–65 (citing TEX. PROB. CODE § 439(a)). Applying this holding to the current case, the court of appeals stated:

> [W]e are addressing a situation in which Texas law dictates parties do not even have a certain type of agreement — a survivorship agreement — unless they have executed a written instrument complying with statutory formalities, including expression of their intent to create a right of survivorship. Therefore, if we must look outside the written instrument to determine that a term used therein means "right of survivorship," the parties have not expressed their intent within the written instrument.

233 S.W.3d 494, 511.

The court of appeals' reliance on *Stauffer*, however, was misplaced. Section 439(a) requires that a survivorship agreement between non-spouses use either the statute's language or a substitute that is "in substantially the [same] form." TEX. PROB. CODE § 439(a). Section 452 is less restrictive, presumably because agreements between spouses are less vulnerable to fraud. The constitutional amendment permitting survivorship agreements in community property was intended to facilitate the creation of such agreements, *see*, e.g., Senate Judiciary Comm., Resolution Analysis, Tex. S.J. Res. 35, 70th Leg., R.S. (1987), and the Legislature's use of less confining language comports with that goal. Moreover, *Stauffer* precludes outside evidence, not reference to the common law or trade usage. Cf. RESTATEMENT (SECOND) OF CONTRACTS § 222 cmt. b ("There is no requirement that an agreement be ambiguous before evidence of a usage of trade can be shown....").

Precedent, trade usage, and seminal treatises make clear that joint tenancies carry rights of survivorship, and the Holmeses' agreement included this designation. This does not fully answer, however, the inherent tension in owning community property as "joint tenants." Professor Reed Quilliam noted in an article published shortly after the constitutional amendment and statutes were adopted that "[j]oint tenancy is a form of separate property ownership and is wholly incompatible with community property concepts." *See* W. Reed Quilliam, Jr., *A Requiem for* Hilley: *Is Survivorship Community Property a Solution Worse than the Problem?*, 21 TEX. TECH L. REV. 1153, 1167 (1990). In the same discussion, though, Professor Quilliam predicted that situations like this case were likely to arise:

> It is likely that misconceptions about the new form of property ownership will result in instances of spouses agreeing to hold community property "as joint tenants with right of survivorship" rather than merely "with right of survivorship." What will be the effect of such designation?

> Manifestly the property will remain community, although the spouses' agreement to hold with right of survivorship should be given effect to impress *this* characteristic on it. The property *cannot* be joint tenancy property, a form of separate property ownership, unless it has first been rendered separate by partition. The agreement of the spouse violates the constitution insofar as it seeks to establish a joint tenancy in community property. But the agreement to hold such property with right of survivorship is now constitutionally sanctioned.

Id. at 1168–69 (emphasis in original). We agree with Professor Quilliam. A "joint tenancy" or "JT TEN" designation on an account is sufficient to create rights of survivorship in community property under section 452. The Dain Rauscher and First Southwest accounts included this designation, and we "give effect to the written expression of the parties' intent." *Balandran v. Safeco Ins. Co. of Am.*, 972 S.W.2d 738, 741 (Tex. 1998). Because the "JT TEN" designation was sufficient to indicate the Holmeses' intent to hold those accounts with rights of survivorship, we reverse the court of appeals' judgment on the Dain Rauscher and First Southwest accounts.

2
The Raymond James Account

The Holmeses opened an investment account with Raymond James & Associates in 1995. The "New Account Form" gave Thomas and Kathryn the option to check a box for the "Account Classification." They chose "Joint (WROS)." The form also listed their names as "THOMAS J. HOLMES & KATHRYN V. HOLMES JTWROS." The trial court held that this account did not carry rights of survivorship, but the court of appeals reversed, holding "the Raymond James account agreement sufficiently conveyed Kathryn's and Thomas's intent to create a right of survivorship." 233 S.W.3d 494, 515.

The court of appeals reached this decision primarily based on the Holmeses' affirmative act of checking the "Joint (WROS)" box:

> Kathryn and Thomas affirmatively selected an "Account Classification." They were presented with fourteen options for the account classification and selected "Joint (WROS)" to the exclusion of all other options. Significantly, Kathryn and Thomas rejected "tenancy in common"—the very designation that Beatty attempts to assign to this account. We can conceive of no other meaning Kathryn and Thomas could have contemplated for "Joint (WROS)," considering that none of the other options can possibly be construed as meaning joint tenancy with rights of survivorship.

Id. at 515.

We agree with the court of appeals that "Joint (WROS)" means "joint tenancy with rights of survivorship." As such, this indicated the Holmeses' intent to obtain rights of survivorship in this account. This designation, along with Thomas's and Kathryn's signatures on the form, satisfy section 452's requirements. We therefore affirm the court of appeals' judgment on the Raymond James account.

Conclusion

The 1987 constitutional amendment and accompanying legislation sought to facilitate the creation of rights of survivorship in community property and eliminate the constitutional hurdles spouses faced when attempting to establish such rights. The Holmeses' account agreements clearly indicated their intent to create rights of survivorship in those accounts. The rights were not lost when the Holmeses later obtained some of their investments in certificate form. Pursuant to these survivorship agreements, each of the accounts and certificates at issue in this case passed to Thomas upon his wife's death, and then by will to Thomas's beneficiaries when he died. If the Holmeses had wished an alternate devise, they could have made appropriate provisions in their respective wills. As they did not, we reverse and render in part and affirm in part the court of appeals' judgment. TEX. R. APP. P. 60.2(a), (c).

C. Partitions

Patino v. Patino

Texas Court of Appeals – San Antonio, 1985
687 S.W.2d 799, no writ

DIAL, Justice.

This is an appeal from the property division in a divorce decree.

Isaac and Trong Patino were married while Isaac was a member of the service. He has since retired from the military. On February 22, 1980, the parties entered into a "SEPA-RATION AGREEMENT (PROPERTY SETTLEMENT AND SUPPORT AGREEMENT." The agreement recited that the parties were presently married but that differences had arisen, and they intend to live separate and apart from each other for the rest of their natural lives. Under the section entitled "Division of Assets" the husband declared himself to be a trustee for his wife's child's benefit of all his military retirement pay. He further agreed to execute an allotment of his retirement pay to his wife. In a separate and attached schedule the homestead of the parties was set aside to the wife along with other personal property. Another schedule set aside various personal property to the husband. The agreement also contained the language:

> If venue of any suit arising from or relating to this agreement cannot be fixed under the preceding sentence, it shall lie in the county in which the judgment of divorce is granted.... The parties respectfully request the court having jurisdiction of their divorce to approve this agreement and to incorporate it into any divorce decree that may be entered in this case.

The agreement was signed by the parties and acknowledged by each of them before a notary public.

Contemporaneous with the separation agreement, Isaac executed a special warranty deed of the homestead to Trong. The deed was executed with all necessary formalities and was filed of record. No action was taken by either of the parties with respect to the military retirement pay except to permit the existing allotment to continue in the joint bank account of which each party had full access. Isaac moved out of the house two days later. There was a brief reconciliation followed by an extended separation and the filing of a divorce suit by Isaac on January 15, 1982.

A non-jury trial was held following which the trial judge announced that he found the separation agreement entered into by the parties was not just, fair, and equitable, and therefore, the agreement was set aside. Trong was awarded the homestead and the other personal property she had received in the agreement. Isaac was awarded all military retirement pay that accrued after the date of the divorce, which was April 28, 1982. The written decree was not signed by the judge until January 28, 1983.

After the decree of divorce was signed by the court, a request for findings of fact and conclusions of law was filed. When the court did not file additional findings, a reminder to file findings of fact was timely presented to the trial court. No additional findings were filed.

Trong complains on this appeal of the action of the trial court in setting aside the separation agreement and awarding the military retirement to Isaac. Trong contends that though it is labeled, "SEPARATION AGREEMENT," the document was in fact a partition agreement executed in writing and subscribed by all the parties as required by Tex. Const. art. XVI, Section 15 and Tex. Fam. Code Ann. Section 5.44 (Vernon Supp. 1984).

Article 16, Section 15 of the Texas Constitution and Section 5.42 of the Texas Family Code do provide a way for spouses who contemplate continual conjugal relations to partition or exchange community property and change its character to separate property. There is no requirement for judicial approval of such a partition or exchange agreement. *Morgan v. Morgan*, 622 S.W.2d 447, 450 (Tex. Civ. App.—Beaumont 1981, no writ).

There is extensive common-law precedent empowering a husband and wife to effect a division of their property on permanent separation. The only prerequisite to such agreement is that it be fair and equal. *Harding v. Harding*, 461 S.W.2d 235 (Tex. Civ. App.—San Antonio 1970, no writ) (and cases cited therein at Footnote No. 1).

Section 3.631 of the Texas Family Code authorizes the parties to enter into a written agreement concerning the division of all their property and liabilities. Tex. Fam. Code Ann. Sec. 3.631 (Vernon Supp. 1984). In a subsequent proceeding for divorce, the terms of such agreement are binding on the court unless it finds that the agreement was not just and right.

Since the trial court ruled on the fairness of the agreement, he obviously was treating it as a property settlement made in contemplation of divorce and not a partition agreement that did not require his approval. We hold that the action of the trial court in setting aside the "SEPARATION AGREEMENT" was a proper exercise of his duty and power under Section 3.631 of the Texas Family Code.

The wife does not challenge the sufficiency of the evidence to support the finding of the court that the separation agreement was not just, fair and equitable. She does, however, contend that the trial court should have made a specific finding as to whether the agreement was incident to divorce or a partition of community property.

The trial court is only required to make findings of fact on the ultimate or controlling issues. *Harding v. Harding, supra*, at 236; *Friedman v. Cohen*, 429 S.W.2d 510, 512 (Tex. Civ. App.—Houston [14th Dist.] 1968, writ ref'd n.r.e.); Tex. R. Civ. P. Sec. 298. The court made the finding that the agreement was not just, fair and equitable. This issue was the controlling and ultimate issue, and no other findings were necessary.

Also, although no formal conclusions of law appear in the record other than the decree, we are authorized to recognize findings which are necessary legal implications of the judgment entered below. *Donahoe v. Allen*, 608 S.W.2d 745, 747 (Tex. Civ. App.—Beaumont 1980, no writ); *Sentry Development Corp. v. Norman*, 553 S.W.2d 664, 665 (Tex. Civ. App.—Tyler 1977, writ ref'd n.r.e.). Accordingly, we find that the trial judge's specific finding carried with it the implication that the agreement in question was not a partition agreement but, instead, an agreement incident to divorce which required a "just and right" finding by the judge in order for it to be enforced. Tex. Fam. Code Ann. Sec. 3.631 (Vernon Supp. 1984).

Matthews v. Matthews

Texas Court of Appeals—Houston [1st Dist.], 1986
725 S.W.2d 275, writ ref. n.r.e.

SAM BASS, Justice.

Our opinion issued September 18, 1986, is withdrawn, and the following is substituted. Appellant's motion for rehearing is overruled.

This was a divorce suit and a suit affecting the parent-child relationship. The primary issue surrounds an Indenture for the Partition of Community Property ("the indenture").

The appellee alleged that the indenture was void based on fraud, undue influence, duress, invalid partition and exchange, public policy, and breach of fiduciary duties. After a non-jury trial, the court set aside the indenture and found that it was procured by duress.

Appellee signed the indenture on June 20, 1980, and appellant signed it on June 21, 1980. The appellee's attorney, Williams, testified that he first consulted with appellee in July 1979, regarding a proposed divorce from appellant. Williams had no further contact with appellee until May 29, 1980, when she retained him to represent her in a divorce action against appellant. On this same day, all the necessary paperwork was prepared to initiate the divorce action. Appellee's contact with, and retention of, Williams was unknown appellant. On May 28, 1980, one day before appellee retained Williams, she and the two children had left the house and were staying in a motel.

On June 1, 1980, appellee and the children returned home, and she instructed Williams not to file suit. On June 16, 1980, appellee consulted Williams regarding the partition. He testified that he made no recommendation to her. On June 25, 1980, appellee informed Williams that the family had reunited and that his services were no longer required.

Mrs. Gross, a psychotherapist, testified that in June 1980, she had been counseling appellee. Prior to a meeting with appellant and appellee, Gross received a call from appellant stating that his wife was abusing medication, that she had left with the children, that she had stolen money from the company's safe, and that he was having detectives go after her. In June 1980, before the signing, Gross learned that the couple was separated, that appellant had taken the couple's son and moved in with his parents, and that the couple was in the process of making a separation agreement. She testified that appellee seemed confused, and that appellee confessed the alleged theft. Gross had no contact with appellee after June 9, 1980.

Another attorney, Ogier, testified that he met with appellant and appellee in June 1980 regarding the partition agreement. He said that his primary function was in preparing the agreement and not rendering advice on its benefits. He testified that appellee seemed calm and normal, that she never indicated to him that she believed the agreement to be fraudulent, and that, in his opinion, both parties were fully aware of what they were doing.

Appellee testified that during the time period before the signing, appellant threatened that if she did not sign the indenture she would never see her son again. She testified that she had possession of their daughter and that appellant had possession of their son.

Appellee testified to the following:

Q. Did you fear anything, if you didn't sign the document as he said and have it on his desk by Friday?

A. I feared the worst.

Q. Being what?

A. Loss of my child.

Q. Was there ever any discussion between you and Mr. Matthews relative to custody litigation?

A. Yes.

Q. Were you in fear of that?

A. Yes.

Q. Why?

A. I was just afraid that he would do it.

On cross-examination, appellee testified that her attorney, Williams, had advised her to not sign the agreement and that she signed the agreement four days later. Appellee testified that during the four day period, she was not, physically or otherwise, abused by appellant. She testified that their son had gone voluntarily with appellant and that she was able to talk to her son on the telephone. She knew that he was all right; however, she testified that the only reason she signed the agreement was to prevent appellant from getting custody of her son. During May and June of 1980, the couple was using cocaine and alcohol, and there were disputes over company business and assets.

A third attorney, Lindsay, testified that appellee consulted him in October 1982, concerning a divorce. Although appellee told him about the 1980 partition agreement, the extent of her reference to it was that she wished she had not signed it.

The trial court made findings of fact and conclusions of law, the relevant portions of which are as follows:

> (8) The parties signed a document entitled Indenture for the Partition of Community Property ("Indenture") on or about June 20–21, 1980, after approximately 2 months of extreme marital stress, during which period parties attending [sic] mental health counseling.

> (9) During said period Petitioner and the children separated from Respondent. Sometimes [sic] after the initial separation Respondent took possession of the son, just turned 12 years of age, against the will of Petitioner and refused to let her see him, talk with him, or know of his whereabouts and threatened to continue to do so.

> (10) During said period Respondent made continual threats against Respondent [sic] relating to her drug use, stealing of company money and assets, criminal prosecution, pursuing her with the use of detectives, issuance of a warrant for her arrest, and matters relating to the son.

> (11) Petitioner believed and feared the threats and conduct of Respondent. Respondent made said threats and engaged in said conduct for the purpose of coercing Petitioner into signing said Indenture for his personal gain.

> (12) Petitioner's free will was destroyed by the acts and threats of Respondent and she signed said Indenture because of them. Said Indenture was procured by duress.

> (13) Respondent's testimony relating the facts and circumstances surrounding the period of April through June 1980 inclusive was not credible.

Conclusions of Law

> (6) The indenture for the partition of community party should be and is set aside, vacated, and held for naught for all purposes.

Appellant's second through sixth points of error contend that the trial court's fact findings eight through twelve are supported by no evidence and are against the great weight and preponderance of the evidence.

We hold that there is sufficient evidence to support fact findings, eight through twelve, as they relate to appellant's threat to institute custody litigation. Therefore, it is not necessary to decide whether other acts and threats by appellant are also supported by the record. Points of error two through six are overruled.

Appellant's first point of error contends that the trial court erred as a matter of law in concluding that the indenture should be set aside, and that such finding is against the great weight and preponderance of the evidence. Appellant's seventh point of error contends that the trial court erred in finding that the partition was procured by duress, because any evidence on which the trial court relied does not conform to the legally accepted definition of duress. We evaluate appellant's claim in light of the threat to initiate custody litigation.

What constitutes duress is a question of law for the court. However, whether duress exists in a particular situation is a question of fact dependent on all the circumstances, including the mental effect on the party claiming duress. *Lewkowicz v. El Paso Apparel Corp.*, 614 S.W.2d 198, 200 (Tex. Civ. App.—El Paso), rev'd on other grounds, 625 S.W.2d 301 (Tex. 1981); *Sanders v. Republic National Bank*, 389 S.W.2d 551, 554 (Tex. Civ. App.— Tyler 1965, no writ). Texas courts have uniformly held that:

> There can be no duress unless there is a threat to do some act which the party threatening has no legal right to do. Such threat must be of such character as to destroy the free agency of the party to whom it is directed. It must overcome his will and cause him to do that which he would not otherwise do, and which he was not legally bound to do. The restraint caused by such threat must be imminent. It must be such that the person to whom it is directed has no present means of protection. [Citation omitted.] Where a demand made is wrongful or unlawful, and it is necessary for the party making such demand to resort to the courts to enforce same, there is no duress, for the one upon whom demand is made has adequate means of protection, and there is no imminent restraint. [Citation omitted.] But where the party making such demands has, or is supposed to have the power to injure the business or property interest of the one upon whom such demand is made, without resort to the courts to enforce the demand, and threatens to do an act which would cause such injury and which he has no right to do, and thereby induces a compliance with his demand against the will of such party through fear of injury to his business, property interest, such threats amount to duress, if it appears that the party making such demand and threat ought not in good conscience to retain the benefit received by reason thereof. [Citation omitted.]

Dale v. Simon, 267 S.W. 467, 470 (Tex. Comm'n. App. 1924, judgmt. adopted); *State National Bank of El Paso v. Farah Manufacturing Co.*, 678 S.W.2d 661 (Tex. App.—El Paso 1984, writ dism'd by agr.).

It is never duress to threaten to do that which one has a legal right to do. *Ulmar v. Ulmar*, 139 Tex. 326, 162 S.W.2d 944 (1942); *Fischer v. Richard Gill Co.*, 253 S.W.2d 915 (Tex. Civ. App.—San Antonio 1952, writ ref'd). However, a vice arises when one employs extortive measures or, lacking good faith, makes improper demands. *Sanders*, 389 S.W.2d at 554, 555.

The record reflects that the couple was having severe marital problems. Although appellee could have resorted to the courts to prevent appellant from permanently depriving her of custody, the record establishes that appellant was successful in preventing her from having any contact with their son, other than by telephone, without appellant having to resort to the courts to accomplish his objective. It is significant that when appellee agreed to appellant's demands on June 20, 1980, appellee terminated Williams' representation because the family had reunited.

The indenture partitioned title to a significant portion of the community assets to appellant, in exchange for relieving appellee of responsibility for the debts relative to the assets. Appellee received no assets from the partition. Although the equality of the division is not necessarily fatal to the agreement, *Morgan v. Morgan*, 622 S.W.2d 447 (Tex. App.—Beaumont 1981, no writ); *Dalton v. Pruett*, 438 S.W.2d 926 (Tex. Civ. App.—Texarkana 1972, no writ), it is a factor to be considered in evaluating appellee's claim of duress.

Appellant and appellee, as husband and wife, owed each other special fiduciary duties. *Carnes v. Meador*, 533 S.W.2d 365 (Tex. Civ. App.—Dallas 1975, writ ref'd n.r.e.). The fiduciary relationship requires that appellant demonstrate the basic fairness of the transaction. *Texas Bank & Trust Co. v. Moore*, 595 S.W.2d 502, 508 (Tex. 1980).

Indeed, Texas Family Code section 5.45 (Vernon 1981) requires that:

> In any proceeding in which the validity of a provision of an agreement, partition, or exchange agreement made under this subchapter is in issue as against a spouse or a person claiming from a spouse, the burden of showing the validity of the provision is on the party who asserts it. The proponent of the agreement, partition, or exchange agreement or any person claiming under the proponent has the burden to prove by clear and convincing evidence that the party against whom enforcement of the agreement is sought gave informed consent and that the agreement was not procured by fraud, duress, or overreaching.

Whether the proponent, appellant, met the burden of section 5.45, was a question of fact.

Appellant's demands and threats to initiate custody litigation, if appellee did not execute the agreement, may have been lawful. However, under the circumstances of this case, the trial court, as the trier of fact, did not have to believe appellant's testimony and could have reasonably concluded that appellant failed to prove, by clear and convincing evidence, that appellee's consent was not procured by duress or overreaching.

Considering the fiduciary relationship, the contents of the indenture, the circumstances surrounding the couple's relationship, and the nature of the demands by appellant, we hold that the trial court did not err in finding the indenture void based on duress, and that its finding was not against the great weight and preponderance of the evidence. Points of error one and seven are overruled.

DISCUSSION

Is it a surprise to learn that a threat to initiate a custody dispute can be duress, which could invalidate a postnuptial agreement due to involuntariness? Does this suggest a different standard for voluntariness for premarital and postnuptial agreements? *See also Martin v. Martin*, 287 S.W.3d 260 (Tex. App.—Dallas 2009, pet. denied); *Izzo v. Izzo*, 2010 WL 1930179 (Tex. App.—Austin). Cf. *Sheshunoff v. Sheshunoff*, 172 S.W.3d 686 (Tex. App.—Austin 2005, pet. denied). *Matthews* and *Fanning* certainly suggest that involuntariness might become a significant limit to the enforcement of postnuptial agreements, particularly if the agreement was signed during a turbulent period of the marriage.

Byrnes v. Byrnes

Texas Court of Appeals—Ft. Worth, 2000
19 S.W. 3d 556, no writ

OPINION

SAM J. DAY, Justice.

In this appeal, Appellant Kathleen Byrnes challenges the trial court's refusal to enforce a document entitled "Agreement Incident to Divorce" signed by Kathleen and her ex-husband, Appellee William Thomas Byrnes.

We affirm.

BACKGROUND

Kathleen and William Byrnes were married May 2, 1978. On October 31, 1997, William told Kathleen that he wanted a divorce and moved out of the couple's home. On November 2, 1997, Kathleen and William met at a restaurant, where Kathleen presented William with a document entitled "Agreement Incident to Divorce." Kathleen had drafted the document with the assistance of her attorney. William had not reviewed the document prior to the meeting and was not represented by counsel at that time. After reading the document, he signed it. The document was signed by two witnesses and notarized. The meeting lasted approximately 40 minutes to one hour.

On November 12, 1997, Kathleen filed a petition for divorce asking the trial court to enforce the parties' agreement, which she attached to her petition. William filed a general denial and formally repudiated the agreement, alleging it was not a just and right division of the parties' community property, it was unconscionable, it was procured by fraud and duress, it was not supported by consideration, and it was not voluntary.

On October 19, 1998, a bench trial was held solely on the issue of division of the parties' marital estate. Kathleen argued that the trial court should uphold the parties' Agreement Incident to Divorce as a contract and incorporate the agreement into the final divorce decree. Alternatively, Kathleen argued it should be enforced as a partition agreement.

During the trial, the court ruled that the agreement was not enforceable as a mediated settlement agreement, but withheld its ruling as to whether the document was enforceable as an agreement incident to divorce or as a partition of the couple's community property. Without issuing a final ruling, the trial court asked both parties to submit a proposed division of their assets. Both parties did so and the trial court signed the proposal submitted by William.

On appeal, Kathleen raises sixteen issues challenging the trial court's failure to enforce the parties' agreement. Specifically, she argues that the trial court erred in failing to award William's interest in his military retirement to her as provided in the parties' agreement.

Section 7.006 of the family code provides that to promote the amicable settlement of disputes in divorce cases, spouses may enter written agreements concerning the division of their marital property, the liabilities of the spouses, and the maintenance of either spouse. Tex. Fam. Code Ann. § 7.006(a) (Vernon 1998). The spouses' agreement may be revised or repudiated before rendition of the divorce unless the agreement is binding under another rule of law. *See id.* In this case, William repudiated the agreement immediately after Kathleen filed her divorce petition. However, Kathleen contends William's repudiation was ineffective because the agreement was binding "under another rule of law." *Id.* First, Kathleen argues that the agreement constituted a valid partition that vested William's interest in his military retirement in her at the moment the agreement was signed. Alternatively, Kathleen argues that the agreement, when signed, was a valid, enforceable contract that the trial court was required to accept. Finally, she argues the trial court should have approved of the document as an agreement incident to divorce that was not properly repudiated.

WAS THE PARTIES' AGREEMENT A VALID PARTITION?

Section 4.102 of the family code provides that spouses may at any time partition between themselves any part of their existing community property. *Id.* § 4.102. The partition agreement must be in writing and signed by both parties. *See id.* § 4.104. The term "partition" as used in this section contemplates a division of property among the parties, not a complete forfeiture or assignment. *See McBride v. McBride,* 797 S.W.2d 689, 692 (Tex. App.—Houston [14th Dist.] 1990, writ denied). Absent a specific reference to a partition or language indicating that such a division was intended, Texas courts have refused to uphold transactions between spouses as partitions. *See Maples v. Nimitz,* 615 S.W.2d 690, 695 (Tex.1981); *Collins v. Collins,* 752 S.W.2d 636, 637 (Tex. App.—Fort Worth 1988, writ ref'd).

In this case, the specific provision that Kathleen argues constitutes a valid partition is entitled "PAYMENTS TO SPOUSE" and provides, "In order to fully discharge all obligations arising from the marriage, other than division of property, *Husband agrees to assign to Wife all total current and future financial benefits* that Husband is entitled to from retirement pay from the United States Air Force." [Emphasis added.] Nowhere in this paragraph or in the remainder of the couple's agreement is there any reference to a partition of interest. Indeed, the pertinent provision appears on its face to contemplate a complete forfeiture of William's interest. Because the parties' agreement makes no specific reference to a partition, contains no language indicating that the parties intended a partition, and provides for a forfeiture of William's interest, the document is not a valid partition under section 4.102 of the family code. [1] *See Maples,* 615 S.W.2d at 695; *Collins,* 752 S.W.2d at 637. Issue two is overruled.

WAS THE PARTIES' AGREEMENT ENFORCEABLE AS A CONTRACT?

We turn next to Kathleen's contention that William's repudiation was ineffective because the agreement constituted a binding, enforceable contract at the moment it was signed. First, Kathleen argues that "[a]greements incident to divorce are contracts and may be enforced as such," citing *Traylor v. Traylor,* 789 S.W.2d 701 (Tex. App.—Texarkana 1990, no writ.). However, *Traylor* actually held that, "Agreements incident to divorce *which are incorporated into a final divorce decree* are correctly considered as contracts." *Id.* at 703 (emphasis added). *Traylor* involved the enforcement of an agreement that had been incorporated into the parties' final divorce decree without contest and thus does not support Kathleen's contention. *Id.* at 702.

Next, Kathleen points us to language in the couple's agreement stating that it is binding on the parties' heirs and assigns as evidence that the parties intended for the agreement to take immediate effect. She also directs us to language in the final paragraph of

---

1. The parties' agreement also specifically provides that it is subject to judicial approval. A partition agreement does not require judicial approval, while an agreement incident to divorce does. *See* Tex. Fam. Code Ann. § 7.006; *Patino v. Patino,* 687 S.W.2d 799, 801 (Tex. App.—San Antonio 1985, no writ).

the agreement, which provides that it is immediately enforceable. However, the "immediately enforceable" language appears to refer only to the parties' agreement for temporary support. Moreover, Kathleen overlooks the unambiguous language in paragraph VIII, entitled "*Approval by Court.*" This paragraph provides, "This agreement will be submitted to the court for approval. This agreement is made in accordance with [section 7.006] of the Texas Family Code."[2]

Nothing in the parties' agreement indicates that the parties intended to effect an immediate transfer of interest upon the signing of this agreement, or that the parties intended this document to constitute a binding contract. Rather, it is evident from the agreement's unambiguous language and the parties' specific reference to the provision in the family code governing agreements incident to divorce that the parties contemplated their agreement would not be binding unless approved by the court. Tex. Fam. Code Ann. §7.006(b), (c); *Myers v. Myers,* 503 S.W.2d 404, 405 (Tex. Civ. App.—Houston [14th Dist.] 1973, no writ) (holding that an agreement between parties that was conditioned on trial court's approval was not binding at the time it was signed). Because Kathleen has not established that the document was "binding under another rule of law," the trial court did not err in impliedly finding that William's repudiation before rendition of the parties' divorce was valid. *See* Tex. Fam. Code Ann. §7.006(a). Issues three and four are overruled.

---

2. Section 7.006 (formerly section 3.631) provides in relevant part:

(b) If the court finds that the terms of the written agreement in a divorce or annulment are just and right, those terms are binding on the court. If the court approves the agreement, the court may set forth the agreement in full or incorporate the agreement by reference in the final decree.

(c) If the court finds that the terms of the written agreement in a divorce or annulment are not just and right, the court may request the spouses to submit a revised agreement or may set the case for a contested hearing.

Tex. Fam. Code Ann. §7.006(b), (c). Thus, the parties' agreement cannot be included in the trial court's final decree of divorce or incorporated by reference unless the court approves the agreement as being just and right. *See id.*

Index